CYCLES OF DISADVANTAGE

MICHAEL RUTTER
NICOLA MADGE

Cycles of Disadvantage

A REVIEW OF RESEARCH

H·E·B
HEINEMANN · LONDON

Heinemann Educational Books Ltd
LONDON EDINBURGH MELBOURNE AUCKLAND TORONTO
HONG KONG SINGAPORE KUALA LUMPUR
IBADAN NAIROBI JOHANNESBURG
LUSAKA NEW DELHI
KINGSTON

ISBN 0 435 82851 7
Paperback ISBN 0 435 82852 5

First published 1976

Published by Heinemann Educational Books Ltd.,
48 Charles Street London WIX 8AH
Typeset in IBM Century by Preface Ltd., Salisbury, Wilts.
Printed in Great Britain by Richard Clay (The Chaucer Press),
Bungay, Suffolk

Preface

The first suggestion for a survey of literature on cycles of disadvantage came from the DHSS/SSRC Joint Working Party on Transmitted Deprivation at its second meeting in October 1972. This Working Party had been convened on the initiative of the then Secretary of State for the Social Services, Sir Keith Joseph, in June 1972. He had called attention to the persistence of deprivation, despite general economic advance, and to the evidence that the same families tended to be deprived generation after generation. He suggested that this latter phenomenon might be a useful area for research. If ways could be found of breaking this cycle or this recurrence of deprivation in successive generations, it would be valuable for policy. The Secretary of State and his Department recognized that there were many unclear and controversial features about the concept. The task of the Working Party was to consider whether research on it was feasible and if so by what means.

It was agreed that before any major programme of research could be started, a survey of literature was required, to draw together the result of existing research on deprivation, both British and American. Such a survey clearly would require a great deal of expertise and hard work from the author and would be time consuming. We were very pleased when Professor Michael Rutter and Nicola Madge agreed to accept a consultancy for the work. The task turned out to be a much bigger one than the authors originally envisaged, since it soon became clear that references to the continuity of deprivation could not be isolated from the literature on deprivation generally.

The Working Party submitted a report to the Secretary of State in October 1973 which recommended that the DHSS, through the SSRC, should make available a sum of money for research into the transmission or recurrence of deprivation. A seven year contract was signed between the Department and the Council, effective from January 1974. A small Organizing Group, under the Chairmanship of Professor Peter Willmott, was set up to administer the programme.

An earlier version of the literature review has been available to this Group since July 1974. So far eleven research sub-contracts have been awarded and most of them concentrate on the psychological or individual aspects of continuity. This may partly be because, as is clear from the literature survey, research in this area is more substantial and therefore new research has a more authoratative base on which to build. The intention, however, is not to limit research to these areas and readers will see from the survey that there is scope for further work in a wide number of different areas.

The survey is, of course, much more than an input into the planning of a research programme. It is a major contribution in its own right and should prove of interest to a wide readership, both among academics and in the social services.

R. C. O. Matthews
Chairman, SSRC

Acknowledgements

This review had its origins in the preliminary discussions in 1972 between SSRC members of the DHSS/SSRC Joint Working Party on Transmitted Deprivation. We are most indebted to Robin Matthews, Tony Atkinson, Maurice Freedman, Jeremy Mitchell, Roy Parker and Peter Willmott, who were members of the original group. Our thinking about the issues was much influenced by their views and suggestions. Particular thanks are due to Tony Atkinson, Alan Clarke, Joan Court, Alan Little, Roy Parker, Michael Rodda, James Shields, Jack Tizard and Donald West. They made most valuable critical appraisals of what we had written and drew attention to important ideas and findings which had escaped our notice. We would also like to thank John Creedy, Philip Graham and Della Nevitt, who provided very helpful detailed comments on individual chapters. Keith Hope kindly allowed us access to unpublished material from the Oxford Mobility Studies and Cedric Carter clarified our thinking on the phenomenon of 'regression to the mean'. Catherine Cunningham, Ann Edmond and Margaret Edwards were most helpful throughout the preparation of this review. Many thanks are also due to Joy Maxwell and Janet Shand who patiently and efficiently typed repeated drafts of the manuscript and also helped in the checking of references. This book owes much to the generous help and guidance we have received from all these people. However, this book is not a Working Party report and we alone must be held responsible for any errors of fact or judgement which remain.

Contents

1 Introduction

'When *I* use a word', Humpty Dumpty said in rather a scornful tone, 'it means just what I choose it to mean — neither more nor less.'

'The question is', said Alice, 'whether you *can* make words mean different things.'

'The question is,' said Humpty Dumpty, 'which is to be master — that's all.'

(*Through the Looking Glass*: Lewis Carroll, 1872)

THE CYCLE OF TRANSMITTED DEPRIVATION

The term 'deprivation' must be one of the most overworked words in the English language. The literature is full of countless articles and books on the nature, causes and consequences of 'deprivation', and the research reports are outnumbered only by the emotional and polemical monologues and interchanges on a variety of theoretical, practical and political aspects of the topic. Much of the controversy is a consequence of the very diffuseness of the concept which is used by different writers (usually with force and conviction) to cover quite different issues and problems. In the first place, 'deprivation' may refer to very varied aspects of a person's environment. Thus Bowlby (1951) and Ainsworth (1962) in their discussion of 'maternal deprivation' were primarily concerned with the consequences of lack of mother love; Casler (1961), on the other hand, saw the issue as a lack of sensory stimulation; Runciman (1972), by contrast, discussed deprivation in terms of financial and material resources; and Jessor and Richardson (1968) considered the matter more broadly in terms of psychosocial disadvantage. All these writers were concerned with lacks of one kind or another. But, that is not the only way the word has been employed. Eckland and Kent (1968) defined deprivation in terms of deviation from what is considered normal or appropriate, and suggested that it could only be understood in terms of society's responses and society's values. Following the same theme, Ginsberg (1972) and others have dismissed the whole notion of deprivation as a myth based on middle-class misconceptions about poor children.

Not only has 'deprivation' been used to refer to quite diverse aspects of a person's environment, but it has also included circumstances which have nothing to do with deprivation in the dictionary sense of 'dispossession' or 'loss' (Ainsworth, 1962; Jessor and Richardson, 1968; Rutter, 1972a). With respect to 'maternal deprivation' Ainsworth wrote '(it) has been used also to cover nearly every undesirable kind of interaction between mother and child — rejection, hostility, cruelty, over-indulgence, repressive control, lack of affection and the like.' Jessor and Richardson pointed out that the term was both restricting and logically misleading in that the conditions of disadvantage included under 'deprivation' were often characterized as much by excess (of stigma, of deviant role models, of stressful experiences, etc.) as by lack, and that the problems often lay in what was present as much as in what was lacking. Rutter (1972a) ended his review of the evidence on 'maternal deprivation' by concluding that the experiences covered by the term were too heterogeneous and the effects too varied for it to continue to have any usefulness. The concept had been valuable in focussing attention on the sometimes grave consequences of deficient or disturbed care in early life, but it had served its purpose and should now be abandoned.

Our review of writings on the topic of deprivation has strongly reinforced that view. The word almost functions as a projective test in which each person reads into the concept his own biases and prejudices, regardless of how the word has been used in the article or book in question. The result has been an inordinate amount of fruitless friction and heat concerning words and their usage. This might be dismissed as mere academic disputation not worthy of further consideration were it not for the fact that behind the words lie people who continue to suffer from various forms of personal and social disadvantage. The term may generate semantic confusion but the human predicament is real enough.

There are many facets of that predicament which warrant serious attention and require political action. Thus, Wedge and Prosser (1973) emphasized the extent of social disadvantage in present day Britain — one in six children live in an overcrowded home where the density exceeds 1½ persons per room; one in eleven children live in a family without the exclusive use of a hot water supply; one in sixteen in a one parent household; and one in six is part of a family where there are five or more children. Field (1974) on the other hand, stressed the inequalities in our society: infantile mortality is much higher in social classes IV and V than in I and II and the gap between the classes is not narrowing; the gap in financial resources between the rich and the poor remains as wide as ever; the unemployment rate for unskilled men is over ten times that for professional men; and manual workers have more dental decay than the middle class but receive dental care less often. Daniel (1968) and Smith (1974) have shown that black people in this country continue to be subjected to extensive discrimination in the fields of housing and employment. To a considerable extent their disadvantage lies in what society does to them to restrict their opportunities. Others have suggested that stigma socializes people to disabling roles and that this process may explain the disadvantage of many groups other than ethnic minorities (Eckland and Kent, 1968). Within the field of 'maternal deprivation', by contrast, most attention has been paid to the nature of psychological processes which lead children to be damaged by adverse early experiences within the family

(Ainsworth, 1962; Bronfenbrenner, 1968; Rutter, 1972). However, research into causal processes has by no means been restricted to psychological variables. For example, various writers have been concerned to identify the social and political forces which lead to disadvantage within the school system (e.g. Hargreaves, 1967; Ginsberg, 1972), or which underlie the particularly high rates of personal problems among families living within inner city areas (e.g. Rutter, 1975).

Of course, these different perspectives do not constitute alternatives. Each has some validity and concerns itself with an important aspect of the problem. There is not, and cannot be, any one 'right' way of considering the predicament of disadvantaged persons. Nevertheless, the choice of perspective has crucial implications for both research and policy. Raising national housing standards would do much to remedy the disadvantages highlighted by Wedge and Prosser, but unless differentials between the best and worst housing were reduced it would do nothing to right the inequalities noted by Field. Even a levelling (upwards) of housing facilities would not be sufficient if it left some people subject to discrimination. The improved material conditions might make parenting easier but they would not eliminate the adverse family experiences which Bowlby outlined and which are found in all levels of society. Furthermore, betterment of family circumstances and of household facilities might make little difference to the problems associated with school disadvantage or to the stresses associated with inner city life. In short, the topic of 'deprivation' and of disadvantage constitutes not one, but many problems. The search for a 'best' research approach or a single political solution would be as futile as it would be silly.

In 1972, Sir Keith Joseph, then Secretary of State for Social Services, drew attention to another aspect of 'deprivation' in a speech made to the Pre-School Playgroups Association. He asked 'Why is it that, in spite of long periods of full employment and relative prosperity and the improvement in community services since the Second World War, deprivation and problems of maladjustment so conspicuously persist?' By deprivation he was referring to 'circumstances which prevent people developing to nearer their potential — physically, emotionally and intellectually — than many do now', which often showed itself in 'poverty, in emotional impoverishment, in personality disorder, in poor educational attainment, in depression and despair'. He suggested the operation of a cyclical process whereby, in a number of cases, problems reproduced themselves from generation to generation.

The purpose of this book is to review the evidence on the extent to which the 'cycle of transmitted deprivation' mentioned by Sir Keith Joseph in fact exists, and in so far as it does exist, to consider the possible mechanisms which may underlie the intergenerational continuities. For reasons which are implicit in all that has been said so far, we have made three variations from the then Secretary of State's terminology in choosing a title for this book. Firstly, we have preferred the broader term of 'disadvantage' to the more narrow and restricting concept of 'deprivation'. According to the Oxford English dictionary, disadvantage refers to unfavourable conditions or circumstances, detriment, loss, injury or prejudice. We will be discussing all of these in our examination of the extent to which troubles persist across generations. Secondly, we have emphasized the many processes involved by putting cycles in the plural. Even in the terms of Sir Keith Joseph's question several different phenomena are suggested. The first quotation above raises the issue of why various problems remain in spite of rising prosperity. This leaves open the question of whether the problems are still with us because they keep recurring (possibly in different groups of the population) or because they are being passed on within defined subgroups. If they are being passed on, the question next arises as to whether the continuities are most evident in families, in geographical areas, in social groups, or in minorities subjected to discrimination. These considerations led us to drop the adjective 'transmitted' from the title, in that the term might be thought to prejudge the nature of the processes involved.

Not surprisingly, in view of the background of controversy and conflict over the whole area of 'deprivation', Sir Keith Joseph's speech has been subjected to many (often contradictory) interpretations. Although others have felt more confident in their analysis of the motives and meanings behind the 1972 speech, we have not considered it either appropriate or fruitful to engage in these speculations. We have simply attempted to review research findings and concepts as objectively as we could, and in so doing to avoid taking any one theoretical position. This book does not present 'a view', nor does it provide a prescription for policy. Naturally, we have our own concepts and views on what is most important in the field we have reviewed. But, although our reading of the evidence has inevitably been coloured by our own training, experience and personalities, we have tried to avoid the excessive intrusion of our own theoretical constructions. Also, we strongly believe that social research should lead to appropriate political action and in our other writings we have not shirked our responsibilities in that direction. However, our role here is different and it must be left to others to draw policy implications from our conclusions. What we have tried to do is to summarize the current state of knowledge on this rather broad and diffuse question and to make a few comments about the most pressing research needs.

Whether what we have done fits in with the assumptions of Sir Keith Joseph's speech is not our concern. Nevertheless, in view of the controversy surrounding both the concepts of the speech it is necessary to clarify a few points. Firstly, Jordan (1974) and others have criticized the 'cycle of transmitted deprivation' because it links poverty with maladjustment and seems to assume that parental inadequacy and neglect are features of low income families. Such a view might be read into a later statement of Sir Keith Joseph's (1974), although the original speech did stress that deprivation occurred at all levels of society. Be that as it may, we wish to make quite clear that in no sense do we equate poverty with maladjustment. The extent to which poverty is associated with personal difficulties of various kinds is an empirical question and the evidence (discussed in later chapters) indicates that the associations are never of more than moderate strength and in any case apply only to certain forms of difficulty.

Secondly, in his 1972 speech, Sir Keith Joseph explicitly linked his suggestion of a cycle of transmitted deprivation with parenting and with the need for 'preparation for parenthood'. Thus, he said: 'It seems perhaps that much deprivation and maladjustment persist from generation to generation through what I have called a "cycle of deprivation". People who were themselves deprived in one or more ways in childhood become in turn the parents of another generation of deprived children'. In our view this apparent focus on the family is too narrow. In the first place, as already mentioned, continuities over time regarding high rates of various forms of disadvantage can be seen in terms of schools, inner city areas, social classes, ethnic groups and other social and cultural situations which lie outside the family. These are also highly important. In the second place, even with respect to familial continuities, the reason for the intergenerational continuity may not be familial at all but rather may reflect the influence of a common social environment or a common political structure on successive generations. Our review of cycles of disadvantage is not family-based. Possible family influences and family continuities are considered in turn alongside many others — personal, social, cultural and political.

Thirdly, the very use of the term 'deprivation' is often taken to imply environmental causation. Undoubtedly, many of the disadvantages considered in this volume do stem in considerable measure from environmental forces. However, in most cases, genetic and biological factors play some part in the process of disadvantage and this review aims critically to discuss the role of both environmental and constitutional factors without preconception as to which constitute the more important influence in any particular situation. As will become apparent in later chapters, no great meaning can be attached to numerical estimates of the proportion of human variation attributable to a particular factor because the proportion necessarily changes with changing environmental circumstances and for different population groups. Nevertheless, there is value in an attempt to determine some measure of the importance of different variables and in particular to assess how variables might operate and how they interact. Unfortunately, evidence on these last points is limited.

Fourthly, as discussed later in the book, even with the variables showing the strongest continuities across successive generations, discontinuities are prominent and frequent. Among children reared under conditions of severe multiple disadvantage, many develop normally and go on in adult life to produce happy, non-disadvantaged families of their own. Although intergenerational cycles of disadvantage exist, the exceptions are many and a surprisingly large proportion of people reared in conditions of privation and suffering do *not* reproduce that pattern in the next generation. Regrettably little research attention has been paid to the elucidation of the less identifiable processes which enable people to break out of cycles of disadvantage. However, we will discuss what little evidence there is during the course of the review.

Fifthly, intergenerational continuities in disadvantage are, of course, only one aspect of the more general problem of disadvantage and they must be examined in that broader context. In focussing on continuities in this review, we have necessarily had to consider these in relation to data on the extent and patterns of disadvantage, on trends concerning increases or decreases in disadvantages and on factors leading to disadvantage within as well as across generations. Where possible we have tried to determine the proportion of different kinds of disadvantage which persists from previous generations together with the proportion that arises anew each generation.

Types of Disadvantages

Various issues had to be considered in deciding how to tackle this review. The first problem stemmed from the fact that the disadvantages suffered by mankind are legion and some selection had to be made if the review was not to achieve infinite length. We were guided in the first instance by the various items noted in Sir Keith Joseph's 1972 speech — namely poverty, unemployment, poor housing, poor educational attainment, crime, psychiatric disorder, inadequate parenting and problem families. He also made mention of alcoholism and drug addiction but we decided that these problems were too specific for inclusion as topics in their own right. In addition, it was decided not to discuss intergenerational continuities with respect to chronic physical handicap and psychosis as such, although both would receive some attention in so far as they were responsible for continuities in other forms of disadvantage.

However, we thought that special attention should be paid to the situation of ethnic minority groups in this country in order to focus on the possible importance of discrimination in creating disadvantage. The American literature clearly shows the persisting disadvantages suffered by black people in that country. The social and political circumstances in Britain are different and, unlike the American situation, many black people are fairly recent immigrants. We thought it essential to determine how disadvantage occurred in ethnic minority groups in order that appropriate action may be taken to prevent the country repeating the errors made elsewhere and also that light might be shed more generally on the processes involved in the creation of disadvantage. It would have been appropriate to consider the same issues with respect to the disadvantage and discrimination suffered by women in our society but this seemed a major topic in its own right and it was regarded as outside our remit.

We are aware that this selection of topics is somewhat arbitrary and other choices could be equally justified. However, our aim has not been to provide a comprehensive survey of all that is known on disadvantage — an impossible task in any event — nor even a total coverage on all that has been written on intergenerational continuities in disadvantage. Rather, our purpose has been to take a quite limited set of examples of different kinds of disadvantage in order to examine patterns and processes which might apply both to these particular disadvantages and others.

Throughout the book we have culled world-wide literature but in doing so we have been particularly concerned to review it in terms of its implications for present-day Britain. This was necessary as it was apparent from the outset that the pattern of continuities and the causal processes differed substantially according to socio-cultural context. No universal answer is possible and in the circumstances it seemed best to focus on the British situation. Nevertheless a great deal of what we have to say is applicable much more generally.

SOME METHODOLOGICAL CONSIDERATIONS

Inevitably, our discussion of cycles of disadvantage has been constrained by the strategies and methods employed in published studies. Nevertheless, it was essential to approach the task with some notion of the main methodological pitfalls, particularly as many of the investigations reviewed were planned for purposes other than the assessment of intergenerational continuities. The first point concerns the range of variables. Although the main purpose of the review was to examine disadvantage, it would be unduly restricting to confine attention to the disadvantaged end of the continuum regarding any variable. The persistence or non-persistence of disadvantage might well be explicable in terms of continuities in the middle of the range or in terms of the transmission of advantage. Thus, it could be that poverty was in part a consequence of the social structures which underpin the passing on of wealth and privilege. On the other hand, it is necessary to appreciate that continuities may differ at differing points on a continuum. Thus, the causes of severe mental retardation, which shows very little intergenerational continuity, are quite different from the causes of mild retardation, where continuity is much greater, and somewhat different again from the factors determining individual differences in the middle range of intelligence.

The second issue was how to measure disadvantage. Several dimensions of measurement suggested themselves. Disadvantage might be defined in *statistical* terms according to its frequency in the general population. In this way, a concept like 'poverty' might be defined in terms of an income in the bottom decile. Alternatively, an *administrative* category might be used, so that poverty could be defined in terms of the receipt of supplementary benefits from the State. Neither of these definitions bears a necessary or constant relationship to whether or not a person is impeded in his day to day life. For this purpose, a definition based on *impairment* may be used. This might define poverty in terms of a specified degree of deterioration in life circumstances, or by a person's inability to purchase certain life essentials. A fourth dimension is provided by a person's *self-perception*. Thus, social status may be defined in terms of a classification of occupations (or statistical definition) or by whether people rate themselves as 'middle class' or 'working class'. The two definitions overlap but they lead to many people's status being classified quite differently (Runciman, 1972). Similarly, poverty could be assessed according to whether people regard themselves as poor. Yet again, disadvantage may be measured in terms of individual *values*. In this sense, poverty could be seen as a state of affairs in which people are dissatisfied with their income. Interestingly, this bears very little relation to actual income level (Runciman, 1972), just as dissatisfaction with housing is only weakly linked with quality of housing (Wedge and Prosser, 1973; Rutter, 1976; Rutter, Quinton and Yule, 1976). These dimensions are not interchangeable and the one used will to some extent determine the findings on intergenerational continuities.

Each dimension of disadvantage has its own particular problem. At first sight, a statistical definition seems the most precise approach as it allows of ready quantification. However, very few variables can be measured in absolute terms so that the choice of reference group becomes a critical issue. Measures will change if population norms change. Thus, when educational standards in the general population are low, an individual in the bottom 10 per cent will have a much lower level of attainment than will an individual in the same percentile grouping in a population with high standards. Similarly, a reading age of 10 years in 1945 may not mean the same thing as a reading age of 10 years in 1975. This is a real problem as standards in Britain with respect to almost all the disadvantages considered here have changed considerably over the last few generations (but not always in the same direction). For example, crime and divorce have increased but illiteracy and poor housing have decreased. The nature of unemployment will differ according to whether 1 in 1000 men or 1 in 10 men is out of work. When comparing across generations some techniques must be found to equate the reference groups used to provide a norm for each generation. As will be seen, this has rarely been done.

Administrative definitions of disadvantage are often the most convenient because of the availability of official statistics. While they are of value for some purposes they have marked limitations. Thus, once a family is 'known' to the authorities, the offspring are more likely to come to official notice for difficulties which might not otherwise have led to administrative action. Not only is this a matter of selective administrative surveillance but also a person's attitudes and behaviour may change as the result of derogatory labelling. In this way, stigma may cause quite artifactual continuities. Moreover, even when this does not occur, it is important to recognize that an administrative category involves two factors; firstly disadvantage and secondly the disadvantage coming to official notice. With data on administratively defined continuities, it is quite difficult to determine how far the continuities refer to the disadvantage and how far to the process of coming to notice. It is also noteworthy that an administrative category in one generation may not be equivalent to the same category in another generation. For example, police practices as well as the law are subject to change, and the regulations on the provision of welfare benefits vary over time.

The dimension of impairment usefully provides an assessment of how far an individual is impeded in his various life activities. In this connection, of course, impairment strictly refers to level of functioning and carries no implications about the individual as a person. Because of this it necessarily follows that impairment applies to specific functions. A person may be impaired in his capacity to work but not in his interpersonal relationships. Also it should be emphasized that impairment can only be seen as relative to a person's life circumstances and must depend ultimately on value judgements. Loss of a leg in a road accident would cause little work impairment to a university teacher or a writer but would be catastrophic to a manual labourer or a professional sportsman. This may be one of the reasons why absences from work through sickness are so much higher among unskilled workers than among professional workers.

Similar questions arise when considering disadvantage in terms of self-perception or values. It should be added that a variety of other conceptual frameworks may also be employed. Thus, disadvantage may be considered in terms of disease states or illness which are qualitatively different from normality. This medical frame of reference involves additional methodological problems. However, as the transmission of disease falls outside our terms of reference these will not be considered here. Almost none of the research considered in this review is entirely free from these various methodological problems and the findings must therefore be viewed with appropriate caution. Where the research strategy makes serious biases possible these are pointed out in the text, but in order to avoid unduly tedious repetition and excessive qualification, the methodological points made in this chapter will not be discussed with every study mentioned.

Intragenerational Continuities

In order to study intergenerational continuities adequately it is necessary to study two or more generations at the same stage in the life cycle. Furthermore, to understand the practical implications of disadvantage, it is essential to know something about its persistence or non-persistence within a single life span, and to appreciate its associations with other forms of disadvantage. For all these reasons, attention is paid in this review to *intra*generational as well as *inter*generational continuities. It is important, for example, to appreciate the frequency with which juvenile delinquency is purely a transitory phenomenon which does not persist into adult life. To the extent that it is transitory, comparisons between parental crime in adult life and delinquency in the offspring during childhood are not a comparison of like with like and so provide an invalid estimate of continuities. Similarly, if occupational status fluctuates over the life cycle it would be misleading to measure social mobility by the disparity in status between parents and children at one point in time (and hence at different points in their respective life cycles).

It is not enough, however, to study the extent to which the *same* phenomena persist throughout life. There are some features which by their nature can only be manifest at certain points in the life cycle. Thus, parenting skills can only be studied in adult life during the period of child rearing. However, it may well be that there are attitudes or behaviour shown in childhood which provide the basis for later parenting. Similarly, occupational status can only be measured meaningfully after school leaving and up to the point of retirement. Nevertheless, it is of value to know how far school attainment is associated with later occupational level. In short, a study of life cycle continuities must include consideration of patterns of associations as well as mere persistence of the same features.

Intergenerational Continuities

Much of the literature on intergenerational continuities simply reports the proportion of disadvantaged adults who had disadvantaged parents or who have disadvantaged children. On their own, however, these data mean very little. Changes over time in the base rates of disadvantage within the population can readily create a quite misleading picture of continuities or discontinuities. For example, during this century crime rates have steadily risen (see Chapter 6). As a result, many more criminal adults will have criminal children than have criminal parents. The impression of an increasing intergenerational continuity may be largely an artefact resulting from secular trends in crime. Accordingly, the study of intergenerational continuities requires systematic comparisons between disadvantaged and non-disadvantaged individuals or groups as well as information on general population base rates. For these reasons, most reliance in this review is usually placed on the data from epidemiological studies of the general population.

Some of the other issues involved in the assessment of continuities will emerge during the course of later chapters but two matters require mention here. First, when continuities are being examined within non-familial groups, it is important to know whether the continuities are a function of differential movement in and out of the group or whether they apply to those who remain. For example, it will be shown that certain forms of disadvantage are especially common in inner city areas. However, the meaning of this finding very much depends on whether the high rate of disadvantage is a function of disadvantaged individuals moving into the city or whether the high rate also applies to people born and bred in the city.

The second matter concerns familial continuities. Since any one individual has two parents, four grandparents and may have several children, the question of continuity, even within a single family, is not susceptible to a simple 'yes' or 'no' answer. Comparisons between generations need to take into account differences in family size. It should also be appreciated that over several generations the continuity for any one person involves many families. Each parent comes from a different family and so does each grandparent. The extent to which there is intergenerational continuity will depend to a certain extent on the nature of the marriage network. The wider the network the less continuity there will be.

Causal Processes

Simple estimates of the extent of intergenerational continuities provide no guide to social policy or political action. Knowledge on the causal processes is also required. The use of the word 'processes' deliberately emphasizes that it is an understanding of a chain of circumstances which is required rather than the identification of any supposed 'basic' cause. Furthermore, the use of the plural notes that with almost all forms of disadvantage several different mechanisms are likely to be operating and interacting one with another. In order to determine the relative importance of different mechanisms (genetic, biological familial, extra-familial, institutional, political and societal), these are considered in turn in individual chapters. However, this should not be taken to imply any concern to find 'the' cause. As the results clearly show, multifactorial and interactive causation is the rule, although the relative importance of different factors varies with different sorts of disadvantage.

The futility of a search for a basic cause is well illustrated by the medical syndrome often called 'deprivation dwarfism' (see Rutter, 1972a). This is a condition found in young children who come from grossly disturbed families and who are of extremely short stature. The dwarfism is not associated with any disease or illness and at first it was thought that lack of love or emotional privation impaired growth even when the intake of food remained adequate. This now seems not to be so, at least in most cases. The answer is more humdrum — the children have not received enough to eat. To that extent the dwarfism is 'caused' by starvation. However,. that leaves open the question of why the children had been inadequately fed and the answer to that question often lies in parental neglect or in the child's depression following chronic stress. Therefore it could be said that parental neglect or lack of love is really the cause. But that only puts the matter back one stage further. Why did the parents neglect the child? The answer may lie in current social disadvantage (e.g. loss of job and housing) or in adverse childhood experiences which failed to provide the proper basis for parenting. Are these then the causes? Of course, in a sense all of them are and appropriate action requires an understanding of the process as a whole.

It should be added, too, that different aspects of disadvantage may involve different causal processes. For example, the 'causes' of poverty involve at least three distinct questions. First, what are the factors which underlie the extent of *inequalities* in our society (i.e. the difference between the highest and lowest incomes)? Second, what are the factors which underlie the *level* of poverty (i.e. how many poor people there are)? Third, what are the factors which determine *who* is poor (i.e. whether Mr Brown or Mr Smith is in poverty)? The answers to each of these questions may involve quite disparate mechanisms, as will be discussed in later chapters.

PLAN OF BOOK

The book starts with a discussion of economic status and then housing. Although these are forms of disadvantage about which there is very little evidence on intergenerational continuities, they constitute two of the most important aspects of a person's material environment. They differ from most of the other forms of disadvantage considered in the book in one important respect. It would be possible by one stroke of the pen to give someone adequate financial resources and a good house. The particular disadvantage could be removed in an instant (although associated personal disadvantages might remain). This is in sharp contrast to the situation with poor educational attainments or psychiatric disorder or inadequate parenting where remedial action takes time to be effective and also involves changes in personal functioning. However, the distinction is more apparent than real in that, in practice, poverty and poor housing tend to be very persistent disadvantages, and in that the other difficulties are to some extent dependent on immediate social circumstances which are also potentially subject to instant improvement.

Nevertheless, these differences have meant that the various forms of disadvantage have been tackled in somewhat different ways in this book. Thus, social and political influences receive more consideration with respect to economic status and housing than they do in other chapters. To some extent this is appropriate in terms of the relative weight of different influences with different forms of disadvantage. But we have inevitably been constrained by what is available in the literature. There are several important topics which deserve a fuller treatment but a lack of evidence has made this impossible. Because of these constraints, the length of individual chapters provides no indication of their relative importance. The length is simply a reflection of what is available in the literature.

Although obviously we are deeply concerned with the alleviation of disadvantage this was not part of our remit. Intervention programmes are discussed in individual chapters where they are thought to be of possible relevance to factors influencing intergenerational continuities, but there has been no attempt to provide a systematic coverage of preventive or therapeutic actions.

Finally, the concluding chapter brings together some of the conceptual issues which emerged from our review of the literature but it does not attempt to summarize all the findings. The book as a whole is a summary of research and to summarize the summary seemed a pointless exercise. Unfortunately, the subject is too complex to be dealt with by a few succinct conclusions and we request the reader's indulgence and patience in asking that the book be read as a whole.

2 Economic Status

How much money people have determines their access to goods and services and hence shapes their standard of living and influences their social status. Poverty shows important associations with poor physical development (Birch and Gussow, 1970) and, as described in other chapters, with many other indices of disadvantage such as inadequate housing, low educational attainments, problems in parenting and crime. For this reason, poverty has often been seen as the critical factor in cycles of disadvantage which recur in successive generations of the same family (Birch and Gussow, 1970). The extent to which poverty may underlie various personal troubles and social problems is considered elsewhere in this book, but first it is appropriate to discuss the main findings on the causes and transmission of both economic advantage and low economic status. As noted below, very little is known on the extent to which economic status shows intergenerational continuities. Nevertheless, regardless of whether continuities in income are strong or weak, and regardless of whether poverty stems from social, political or family influences, low economic status may influence cycles of disadvantage through its effect on other aspects of life. Hence, it is considered first.

MEASUREMENT OF ECONOMIC STATUS

Three main measures of economic status are employed in this chapter: income level, poverty and wealth. None of these is straightforward to define and they have not been interpreted consistently in the literature.

Net income is the sum of occupational earnings, welfare state benefits and income from wealth and/or savings assets less tax deductions. Indirect benefits such as housing subsidies, use of National Health Service facilities and free legal aid may be taken into account. Estimates of income will depend on the method of measurement used and the number of income components, as listed, that are considered. They will also depend upon the unit for which income is calculated, i.e., whether for individuals, families or households. For example, a low-income individual or family will not necessarily live in a low-income household but may settle with other, possibly related, low-wage earners to maximize possible standards of living.

Many different poverty measures have been used by writers, researchers and politicians, but two basic approaches are discernible. According to the first, 'the poor' are all those with incomes below a certain specified poverty line — varying with family circumstances and the national economic situation. This was the approach of Rowntree

(1901; 1941; Rowntree and Lavers, 1951) in his historic surveys of poverty in York; he calculated minimum levels of income necessary for food and other basic expenses and then estimated the numbers of families not reaching these levels. More recently the 'poverty line' has been drawn to correspond with the income level theoretically maintained by social welfare services. For example, Abel-Smith and Townsend (1965) drew a line at an income of 140 per cent of the supplementary benefit level plus an allowance for rent. The second definition of poverty is not concerned with standards so much as with relativity; the poor are those who suffer most from inequalities in the distribution of income. Thus families in the lowest decile for income, those with income less than half the national average or those with below median value incomes may be viewed as poor. Both these types of poverty definition have their advantages and disadvantages, and both need to be specified precisely before numbers of the poor can be estimated.

Whatever approach to poverty measurement is adopted, it is important to note that assessments represent personal situations at just one point in time. Abel-Smith and Townsend (1965) noted the frequency with which people moved into and out of poverty, and in the USA the same has been found with welfare dependency (Schiller, 1973). With regard to wage distributions, a Department of Employment survey (1973) showed how, of a sample of men continuing in employment over a two-year period, only about half of those in the lowest decile of earnings at a date in the first year were again in it in the next. These findings underline the fact that poverty is a dynamic, not a static, state.

Wealth, like income and poverty, presents problems of definition. It is usually taken to include physical assets (e.g. house, land and car), financial assets (e.g. cash, savings and investments) and financial liabilities (e.g. hire purchase and mortgage commitments). However there is less consensus as to how far pension and other rights should be included. The proportion of the population with wealth will depend to some extent upon whether or not these universal benefits are taken into account.

TRENDS IN INCOME LEVELS AND DISTRIBUTIONS

Before examining the factors influencing both overall and individual patterns of economic status it is important to consider how far income levels and distributions have changed over time. There are two relevant issues; whether there has been a shift in real income levels over time, and whether there have been changes in the spread of income. The first is more difficult to quantify than the second because of varying links between income and prices, and of changing judgements concerning minimally adequate standards of living.

There is evidence of marked improvements in average income

standards over this century. Early descriptions of the London poor by Mayhew (1851–61) and Booth (1902–3) indicated large-scale and severe poverty. Quantitative estimates of the poor are not given by Mayhew (1851–61) but Booth (1902–3) discussed the size of the problem. He classified 29 per cent of the working-class population as either 'the lowest class — occasional labourers, loafers and semi-criminals' or 'the very poor — casual labour, hand-to-mouth existence, chronic want' and 44 per cent as 'the poor — including alike those whose earnings are small, because of irregularity of employment, and those whose work, though regular, is ill-paid'. By 1953–4 Abel-Smith and Townsend (1965) indicated that 1.2 per cent of people in a sample of households had expenditure levels, excluding rent, below 100 per cent of the national assistance scale rate — a minimum subsistence level — and that 7.8 per cent were spending not more than 140 per cent of this rate. In 1960, 3.8 per cent and 14.2 per cent of the sample had income, net of rent, at or below 100 per cent and 140 per cent respectively of national assistance levels. These figures suggested a reversal in the trend towards higher standards during the late 1950s although this was exaggerated by sampling and income measurement biases. The real increase in the proportion of 'the poor' appeared to result from larger numbers of old people, large families and the chronic sick within the population, and possibly from disproportionate wage increases for the lowest paid (Abel-Smith and Townsend, 1965).

The best data on changing standards of living over time are from Rowntree's studies of poverty in York (1901; 1941; Rowntree and Lavers, 1951). The numbers of families in 'primary poverty', 'whose total earnings were insufficient to obtain the minimum necessaries for the maintenance of merely physical efficiency', calculated according to the prices of nutritional, clothing and other requirements were examined in 1899, 1936 and 1950. In 1899 about 10 per cent of the total population and over 15 per cent of the working class population were living in 'primary poverty'. On the same criteria the numbers of the very poor had been halved by 1936 and it was estimated that standards of living available to the working classes were about 30 per cent higher than in 1899. However, Rowntree (1941) changed his definition of 'primary poverty' for the 1936 survey and allowed for extra items of expenditure and higher nutritional standards that seemed appropriate to the new context, while maintaining the relationship between the poverty line and average wages. Eighteen per cent of the total and 31 per cent of the working class population then fell into the 'primary poverty' category. This combination of approaches showed that although there had been an increase in objective income and living standards between 1899 and 1933, there had still been a rise in the numbers in poverty relative to current minimum acceptable standards. This seemed largely attributable to the massive increases in unemployment due to the economic recession. In the third study of poverty in York in 1950, however, and in spite of the further rise in level of the 'primary poverty' line, only 1.7 per cent of the total and 2.8 per cent of the working class populations of York were judged to be poor. This dramatic improvement in standards of living for large numbers of people was attributed to rising employment and the role of the welfare state (Rowntree and Lavers, 1951).

Levels of economic status have undoubtedly changed over this century. However whether distributions have also changed is less clear. The remainder of this section will examine the evidence for trends towards either greater equality or inequality in occupational earnings, pre-tax and post-tax income measures and wealth.

There have been several empirical demonstrations of time factors affecting the distribution of earnings. Knowles and Robertson (1951) looked at wage levels within the building industry. They compared the earnings of craftsmen and labourers and found that there was a skill differential in pay at all dates examined. However, there were changes in its magnitude. Between 1880 and World War I there was relative stability in the differential although the gap then narrowed until the early 1920s, when it widened again. 1922–37 once again saw greater stability in comparative levels although the differential narrowed somewhat between 1937 and 1941. In the following years relative incomes for the craftsmen and labourers remained fairly even until 1948. These patterns of change in the UK ran almost exactly parallel to those in the USA, although the differential was consistently lower in Britain.

Thatcher (1971) studied the weekly earnings of full-time manual workers in Britain for 1886, 1906, 1938, 1960, 1968 and 1970. He concluded that there had been little change in the distribution of earnings over this period. However, this finding may be restricted to the situation of manual workers. Routh (1965) analysed distributions of pay between 1906 and 1960 and found, as did Thatcher (1971), few changes in the distribution of manual workers' earnings but more marked changes in the relative earnings of professional and clerical workers. Overall this had meant a substantial narrowing of the distribution of earnings over these years.

The distribution of income has been considered for both pre-tax and post-tax values. Seers (1951) examined pre-tax incomes and concluded that they were more equal in 1947 than in 1938 although the trend towards equality halted in 1944. By contrast, Lydall (1959) reported a constant trend towards greater equality of pre-tax income between 1938 and 1957. Webb and Sieve (1971) reviewed research findings on the distribution of post-tax income (including studies by Barna, 1945; Cartter, 1955, and regular reports in various issues of *Economic Trends*) and concluded that inequality in net income remained almost constant between 1937 and 1959 despite the contemporary growth of the welfare state. There was some evidence of small reductions in the inequality between — but not necessarily within — income groups between 1961 and 1969. The lack of change seemed to result from the balance between greater benefits for the poorly paid on the one hand and the increased extent to which the poorly paid were affected by taxation on the other. Nicholson (1967c) reached broadly the same conclusion. He reported no trend towards greater equality in post-tax incomes from 1947 to 1963. Atkinson (1973) maintained that there was no subsequent trend in the following four years.

Analyses of changing income distributions are not straightforward. Titmuss (1962) claimed that less is known than believed. He outlined how 'the unit of time, the unit of income, and the definition of income itself' were three issues rarely dealt with satisfactorily by investigators. Thus failure to consider sufficiently long time spans, failure to allow for changes in the size and structure of the income-owning population and failure to make appropriate allowances for income components, such as social service benefits, were shortcomings of many studies.

Wealth also influences economic status although it is relevant for only a minority of the population and has minimal impact upon patterns of poverty. There is some debate concerning changes in inequality on this measure. Atkinson (1972) has argued that inequality persists now to much the same degree as in the past. He claimed that the main redistribution between 1911 and 1960 was between the very rich (the top 1 per cent) and the rich (the next 4 per cent). Any apparent redistribution was believed to be due to reallocation of resources and assets within, but not between, families. These conclusions, however, have been challenged by Polanyi and Wood (1974). They presented data from Lydall and Tipping (1961) for 1911–13, 1924–30, 1936, 1951–6 and new estimates based on Inland Revenue statistics for 1960, 1965 and 1970. Analyses indicated a trend towards equality, although their sources of data may not have been entirely comparable. Over the period there was a gradual decrease in the wealth of the top 1 per cent and an almost even increase in the fortunes of the lowest income groups. The proportion of wealth held by the next 4 per cent remained fairly constant over the whole period whereas that of the remaining top two deciles increased.

A recent Royal Commission (1975) has reviewed the evidence on charges over time in the distribution of income and wealth in Britain. They pointed out the considerable problems of definition and measurement but concluded that, while there had been some decline since 1954 in the share of the income distribution held by the top 5 per cent, there had been little change in the rest of the distribution. The tax system had little effect as the progressive effect of direct taxation was largely offset by the regressive effect of indirect taxation. The evidence on the distribution of wealth was less satisfactory but it was clear that there had been a substantial fall in the share of wealth owned by the richest 1 per cent of the population (from an estimated 69 per cent in 1911–13 to 42 per cent in 1960 and 28 per cent in 1973). However, most of the redistribution occurred within the top 10 per cent so that the increase in share of wealth by the bottom 80 per cent was relatively small. On the other hand, inequalities (although still very substantial) were less marked if State pension entitlements were taken into account.

It can be concluded that the rises in real standards of living over this century have been more dramatic than the reductions of inequality. While there has probably been some contraction at the top end of the distribution of earnings the effects on the overall spread of net income have been quite small. At all times the majority of people have occupied the middle ranges and the minority the extremes. When wealth distributions are considered, however, somewhat different conclusions are necessary. Firstly, patterns of advantage do not parallel those for income, as most wealth is owned by a very small minority of the total population. Unfortunately we have very little information on small wealth holdings and the number of persons who own them. Secondly, although inequalities in wealth have decreased, it is not clear whether there have been noteworthy changes in the distribution of the larger wealth holdings over the last generations. There are contrasting opinions and the issue is not easily resolved. Wealth estimates are based on estate duty or Inland Revenue data and both methods of assessment have their source of error. Finally, the judgement as to whether *much* or *little* change in inequality has occurred is somewhat subjective.

INTRAGENERATIONAL CONTINUITIES

Life-cycle Poverty

Seebohm Rowntree (1901) coined the phrase 'life-cycle poverty' to describe an individual's changes in earning power in conjunction with his varying levels of expenditure at various points in time. He indicated that childhood, the early years of marriage and childbearing and old age were the three main periods of relative poverty. His analysis applied to those in full-time employment but the effects may be exaggerated in atypical family situations. The situation is the same today (Young and Willmott, 1973). In all social classes the periods of lowest income per head are firstly after age 65 and secondly (to a lesser extent) during the childbearing years. The most affluent period is in early adult life except in the professional and managerial group when it is at age 50—64.

Abel-Smith and Townsend (1965) showed that large numbers of children and young people lived in households with an expenditure or income less than 140 per cent of the national assistance scale rate plus housing allowances. In 1953—4 29 per cent of all persons living in such households were less than 15 years old. This meant that 8.2 per cent of all the children in their sample were poor and implied that there were 1,150,000 children in poverty in Britain. In 1960 the same proportion of the poor were less than 15 years of age although this accounted for 17 per cent of all children sampled. By this date it appeared that 2¼ million young persons were living under poverty conditions within the country as a whole. These figures suggested that although the problem of poverty had increased over these years, partly because operational definitions had altered, the relative proportion of children in poverty was unchanged.

The large number of children in poverty reflects the conditions of many families during the childbearing period, particularly those with the largest families (Land, 1969; Bottomley, 1971). Abel-Smith and Townsend (1965) demonstrated that although less than one in five of all low expenditure households in 1953–4 comprised a man, a woman and dependent children, the chances of being poor increased with family size: whereas only about 1 in 40 two-parent families with one child had household expenditures below 140 per cent of statutory requirements, one in 13 with three children and almost 1 in 4 with four or more children were similarly poor. Comparable data were not available for 1960, but it was shown that an increase in household size (which did not necessarily reflect family size) above three meant a greater likelihood of minimal resources. Single person households still had the greatest incidence of low income (over 50 per cent), but with four, five and six or more householders, low income prevalence rates rose from 6.4 per cent through 10 per cent to 25.2 per cent.

The Abel-Smith and Townsend (1965) data did not distinguish between families with or without a father in full-time employment. The Ministry of Social Security (1967) survey of families with two or more children recorded that, of those with fathers in full-time work, 2 per cent had total resources below statutory requirements on a national assistance base and 4 per cent on a supplementary benefit base. Again, a larger family size substantially increased the chances of low household income. A more recent government study of the resources and needs of two parent families (DHSS, 1971) indicated that in December 1971 about three-quarters of the 100,000 families living below supplementary benefit level had a father in full-time work. This meant that 1 per cent of two parent families with an employed head of household were in poverty. As found by the other studies, the larger the family size the greater the risk of a low income.

At the parenthood stage, one-parent family households face particular economic difficulties. Both the fatherless (Marris, 1958; Wynn, 1964; Marsden, 1969) and the motherless (George and Wilding, 1972) suffer in this respect but much more attention has been paid in the literature to the plight of the former. Abel-Smith and Townsend (1965) showed that in 1953–4, 11 per cent of single mothers with one and 36 per cent with two or more children had expenditure below 140 per cent of the national assistance scale. Of all the households with children, one-third of those living at this level were fatherless. No comparable data were presented for 1960. A 1966 survey of families with two or more children (Ministry of Social Security, 1967) showed that 48 per cent of fatherless families had initial resources below national assistance levels and that 6 per cent received no financial benefits and remained below requirement levels. However, less than

10 per cent of all families living below requirement levels during the previous year were fatherless. The apparent improvement in the situation of single-parent families is likely to be an artefact of sampling families with at least two children. It is probable that an over-representation of widows and divorcees — with a greater likelihood of private sources of income — and an under-representation of unmarried mothers were included within the study group.

Hunt *et al.* (1973) examined the incomes of different family types in five British areas. One-parent families were considerably worse off than two-parent families. The fatherless were the most deprived, especially if the mother was under 25 years, single and not working. The motherless were also disadvantaged, often because the father did not work or tended to have low earnings. The relative situation of different types of family was illustrated by the proportions falling into a defined lower income group. Over three-quarters of the fatherless from all areas fell into this category, between about a quarter and a half of the motherless did so, but less than a quarter of two-parent families were in the low income group. The report recognized that their sampling procedure may have led to a slight over-representation of lower income one-parent families. However, appropriate adjustments did not alter the pattern.

The most recent and comprehensive source of information on the circumstances of one-parent families is the Finer Report (DHSS, 1974). The number of one-parent families in November 1971 was estimated to be 620,000, of which 520,000 were fatherless and 100,000 motherless. One-third of all one-parent families relied on supplementary benefit for their main source of income although this third was mainly composed of unmarried, separated or divorced mothers. Only 7.2 per cent of motherless families drew supplementary benefit in November 1972 but, as reported by George and Wilding (1972), they were much more likely to do so if they had larger families to support, if they had pre-school children or if their employment would have required them to be away from home at inconvenient times. The smaller proportions of motherless (compared with fatherless) families relying on state support is largely due to the wage differentials that exist between men and women in industrial earnings. The Finer Report stressed that unless mothers could work full-time to earn an income above supplementary benefit level there was little incentive to work at all. They gained little from part-time employment as all earnings above £2 (at current rates) meant an equivalent reduction in benefits.

Of one-parent families the fatherless (excluding widows' families) are in the most financially disadvantageous position (DHSS, 1974). At the end of 1970 45 per cent of this group had net weekly resources of less than £5 and 27 per cent had less than £2. By contrast, the comparable proportions for two-parent families were 11 per cent and 3 per cent. It was concluded that single, separated and divorced mothers, and to a lesser extent widows and lone fathers, need extra help. Low incomes, long-term dependence on supplementary benefit and large numbers living below the supplementary benefit level (about 43,000 fatherless families in 1971) put them in a very disadvantaged position relative to the standard two-parent family. Widows' families were much less often on supplementary benefit and in poverty. This is largely because widows are awarded a contingency, rather than a means-tested, benefit and are not penalized if they earn. Moreover, many have additional income from life assurance policies or occupational pensions deriving from their deceased husbands.

The elderly are the third group to be particularly affected by income depression during the life cycle. Abel-Smith and Townsend (1965) found that at least two-thirds of the low-income households surveyed in 1953–4 were headed by persons above retirement age. Data did not allow a precise estimate of the proportions of those over 65 years who were 'poor' in 1960, although it seemed that the figure might have been 3 million out of 7½ million. Townsend and Wedderburn (1965) examined the regular income and assets of 3,146 single people or married couples over 65 years. One-quarter of the same, representing 1¼ million income units in Britain, had very low levels of income, combined with minimal assets. In general the aged had incomes at about half the average level for the total population. Single and widowed women were in a particularly poor position as were those without a job. Age was also important: a regular income tended to be at lower levels for older age groups as income was often set at retirement and was not adjusted for rising costs of living. The low incomes of many retirement pensioners were also shown by a large-scale government survey (Ministry of Pensions and National Insurance, 1967). A quarter (27 per cent) of married couples, a third (35 per cent) of single men and over half (55 per cent) of single women were eligible for income supplements. The proportions with incomes below minimal requirements increased sharply with age so that the majority of married couples over 80 years of age required financial assistance. It was striking that a third of those eligible for benefits did not apply for them — sometimes through lack of knowledge about entitlements and sometimes through pride.

In recent years there have been large and increasing numbers of the aged among the poor (Atkinson, 1969). This is partly due to the reduction in poverty among other groups but also because of increased longevity and earlier retirement. Old people who do not collect their benefits and those without occupational pensions from their previous employment are the worst off.

Age and family circumstances influence spending and saving although personal life-cycle patterns depend on factors such as household composition and the time intervals between starting work, getting married, having children and retiring. General trends, however, are discernible. Lydall (1955) wrote: 'Perhaps we may hazard an impressionistic picture of the typical life cycle. Young men and women, before marriage, do not normally earn very large incomes. They spend what they earn very freely, with little thought for the future. Immediately before and after marriage, however, they begin to set aside what surplus they can for building up a home. In the next twenty years or so they are usually preoccupied with supporting their children, and their savings are not, on balance, very great. After middle age, the number of dependents declines more rapidly than income, expenditure on durables also falls away, and people begin to put aside larger sums for their old age. After retirement they usually draw down their capital to supplement their shrunken incomes.'

Life-cycle Earnings

Wage and salary levels are not constant over the life cycle although the association between earnings and age varies with occupation. Dublin and Lotka (1947) showed that this was the case in America and Woytinsky (1943) noted how those in higher-paid work tended to reach their income peak later than those earning less. In Britain similar effects of age and type of employment upon age-earnings profiles are evident (Lydall, 1955). The New Earnings Survey for 1973, shows that age and skill level still show important associations with earnings. Besides skill level, specific occupation is also an important determinant of age increments in income. Creedy (1974) showed that there are changing patterns of inequalities in income over time for workers within occupations but that the features of changing spreads are occupation-specific. Inequalities increased with age to varying degrees according to type of employment. For example, the distribution of earnings for surveyors showed the greatest increase in spread over successive age cohorts, whereas that for university teachers showed the least.

Age-earnings profiles are derived from cross-sectional analyses which show general trends but give no insight into individual life-cycle earnings. Very little information has been gathered of a longitudinal nature although several preliminary investigations have been made. Thatcher (1971) reported an analysis of the annual earnings of a random sample of male employees who paid at least 48 national insurance contributions in each of two consecutive years, 1963—4 and 1964—5. There were percentage increases across the board which were marginally greater for the lower paid workers. The Department of Employment (1973) examined data from the New Earnings Survey on the weekly earnings of a constant sample of male manual workers who had paid national insurance contributions in at least 48 weeks of each year for 1970, 1971 and 1972 and for male non-manual and female manual and non-manual workers for 1970 and 1971. These data supported the earlier findings of larger percentage increases, and hence regression to the mean, for manual workers but found that non-manual workers, on average, increased their income by the same percentage at all levels of earnings. Both manual and non-manual female workers increased their earnings levels over 1970—1971 although this was more marked for the non-manual group. A particularly interesting and relevant finding to emerge from this study concerned the stability of the lowest paid. The 10 per cent of the sample of manual men with the least earnings in 1970, 1971 and 1972 were considered to see to what extent this decile included the same individuals in all three years. It was found that the composition of the group changed markedly. Five per cent of the sample were among the lowest paid in all three years and 17 per cent were in the lowest decile of earnings in at least one of the three years.

The main drawback to this Department of Employment (1973) survey, other than the fact that data cover a span of only three years, is that calculations are based on one week's earnings in each year. The shorter the period of income measurement the more marked will be the effects of transitory components (Friedman, 1957). The initial findings of a somewhat similar study, but employing annual rather than weekly earnings data, were reported by Hart (1974). The incomes of 800 men aged 30 in 1963 were examined for the years 1963, 1966 and 1970. The spread of income within the sample increased by 4 per cent between 1963 and 1966 and by 18 per cent between 1966 and 1970. Over the first period there was a slight redistribution to the poorer sections whereas over the second there was no further change in this direction. For individuals a larger than average increase in income between 1963 and 1966 meant a smaller than average increase over the subsequent years and vice versa, although the effect was small. Findings relating to the lowest paid groups were very similar to those of the Department of Employment (1973) survey: five per cent of the total sample remained in the lowest decile of earnings for each of the three years studied.

INTERGENERATIONAL CONTINUITIES

Family Cycles

It is largely unknown whether or not there are family similarities in economic status. We have some evidence that the wealthy in one generation are frequently related to the wealthy in the next (see below). Also it is often believed that poverty recurs in families. Thus some writers have postulated poverty cycle syndromes (Cravioto *et al.*, 1966; Birch and Gussow, 1970) and the 1964 US legislative programme for the War on Poverty was based on the belief that a cyclical process was in operation: 'The vicious cycle, in which poverty breeds poverty, occurs through time, and transmits its effects from one generation to another' (quoted in Moynihan, 1968). However, as Atkinson (1973b) wrote: 'There is inadequate evidence to measure the continuity of poverty throughout lifetimes, and we know little about its persistence across generations. At the same time all the indirect evidence suggests that this is a marked feature of our society.' But with regard to continuities within normal income ranges our knowledge is even less.

Economic status and poverty are family attributes. This implies parent-child similarities over a number of years, provided that there is a reasonably equal distribution of income within the family. Allocation is probably equitable in most families although instances have been reported both where children are treated better than their parents (e.g. Pilgrim Trust, 1938) and worse than them (e.g. Harrison, 1973). In general, all household members will be subject to similar environmental factors although there may be individual differences in the food, clothing and pocket money received. Young (1952) reported that reliable data on income distribution within families were hard to obtain but nevertheless found suggestions of considerable family differences in allocation. This underlines the fact that individual economic status is *not necessarily* reflected by family economic status.

Beyond childhood we have no clear knowledge of the relative economic status of fathers and sons. The only evidence on this issue relates to a Norwegian sample. Soltow (1965) analysed the correspondence in net income for 115 father-son pairs living in a specified city in 1960 and found that the association was not strong. It appeared that there was some regression to the mean for sons' earnings. Soltow stated that: 'Father A, with 10 per cent more income than Father B, will have a son A^1 earning 1.4 per cent more than son B^1'.

The conclusions to be drawn from this study are limited. Firstly, the sample studied is a special one: fathers and sons had to be of certain ages, they had both to live in a specified city and the father had to have lived there in 1930. These restrictions reduced the possible number of men in the correct age bracket living in the city from 771 to 115, and meant that the sample represented a particularly static population. Also the analysis took no account of the respective ages of fathers and their sons. However, further calculations were presented for 52 father-son dyads in which sons had been 14 years old in 1930. Income levels were dichotomized into high and low and the correspondence between paternal income in 1930 and filial income in 1960 examined. The relationship was statistically insignificant and again suggested little intergenerational continuity in income level.

Other evidence is less direct. For example, Bowles (1972) indicated that socio-economic background, including a measure of parental income, has a strong influence upon filial income and that this background factor has more importance than schooling. Nevertheless, the independent effects of income were not demonstrated so that this study provides inconclusive support for intergenerational continuities. Jencks *et al.* (1973) presented data and a hypothetical model indicating that family background is not highly predictive of personal income and that it does not even guarantee similar economic status for brothers. Again the model did not incorporate the factor of paternal income. Jencks *et al.* (1973) believed that inclusion of this measure could not raise the implied correlation for fraternal income above 0.2 but this has not been demonstrated. However, if this estimate were correct it would lead to the prediction that the difference in economic status between brothers would be 90 per cent of the difference between random individuals. This would imply very low intergenerational continuities, but there are no empirical data to show whether or not Jencks' estimate is correct.

It remains an open question as to how great the association is between income levels in successive familial generations. Continuities are the norm during the childhood stage and opportunities for discontinuities only arise at the time of leaving school and either taking a job or getting married. At these points the second generation member may well become dependent on either his own or his spouse's income. The sooner that a poor child adopts his own status and gains an income distinct from that of his parents, the greater the likelihood that he will become caught in a cycle of poverty. This follows because early employment or early marriage are likely to be associated with low social status and hence low wages. Minimal schooling will discourage upward social mobility (Hall and Glass, 1954) and assortative mating generally occurs with respect to educational level and/or social background (Berent, 1954). Accordingly, marriage at a young age is likely to be with a partner from a similar background who has a low earning potential and who has also completed schooling. The longer the period of schooling and the later the age of marriage, the greater will be a child's likelihood of breaking out of a poverty cycle as a result of enlarging occupational and marriage markets.

More is known about family continuities in wealth than in income. Wedgwood (1939) wrote: 'The evidence . . . supports the opinion that, in the great majority of cases, the large fortunes of one generation belong to the children of those who possessed the large fortunes of the preceding generation. . . . The rich men who have sprung from parents with insignificant resources are almost certainly a minority of their class. The attention which that minority attracts seems to be due to the fact that those who compose it are exceptional phenomena rather than numerous.' Similar conclusions were drawn by Harbury (1962) one generation later in a study modelled on the earlier work of Wedgwood (1939). In both investigations it was found that about two-thirds of sons leaving very large fortunes had fathers in the top 0.25 per cent of wealth-holders. There was not complete correspondence between paternal and filial wealth but the relationship was statistically highly significant. A further study (Harbury and McMahon, 1973) found that the situation remained virtually unaltered over the next decade; there was no marked change in the role of inheritance in familial wealth continuities between the mid 1950s and the mid 1960s. Over both the time periods inheritance had differential importance for different paternal and filial occupations. For example, in agriculture, forestry and fishing inheritance was important, whereas in metal goods, construction, clothing and engineering industries there was more chance that a wealth-holder was self-made. Marriage apparently played a small role in determining wealth although this issue was not systematically examined.

These studies suggest that, amongst the top wealth-holders, paternal fortunes are inherited by sons in about 60 per cent of families. These findings are based on very small proportions of the population (0.1 per cent of total adult deaths in the study of Harbury and McMahon, 1973) and have few implications for the transfer of wealth where physical and financial assets are much less. Even within this special group it is possible that the degree of transfer has been exaggerated as not all the wealthy in both generations were considered. However, the effects of this sample bias might be counteracted by underestimates of wealth due to the increasing practice of distributing fortunes before death (Atkinson, 1974).

Certain factors will affect patterns of intergenerational inheritance of wealth. Meade (1973) outlined how the degree of assortative mating with respect to property ownership, the growth rate of the population and the laws and customs affecting the inheritance of property were each important.

The Culture of Poverty

A somewhat different approach to intergenerational poverty is provided by views on the 'culture of poverty'. This theory suggests that a distinct culture exists amongst certain of the poor. Poverty is defined not merely in economic terms but also by behaviour. The issue has caused heavy debate and is paralleled at the opposite end of the income scale by the interchange: F. Scott Fitzgerald: 'The rich are different from you and me'. Ernest Hemingway: 'Yes, they have more money'.

The chief proponent of the culture of poverty has been Oscar Lewis, who made extensive studies of poor communities in countries such as Mexico and Puerto Rica (Lewis, 1959, 1961, 1966). His thesis was that the culture of poverty develops to provide a structure and rationale for the lives of poor people who would otherwise have greater difficulty in coping with their problems. It is presumed to be an adaptation to alienation from the wider society arising from economic and social factors. The subculture becomes self-perpetuating as it develops its own local solutions to problems and reduces its dependence upon outside institutions. A poverty culture has distinct characteristics which transcend regional, national and generational differences. The subculture is best described by its seventy or so characteristic social, economic and psychological traits, the combination of which is said to be culture-specific (Lewis, 1968).

The cycle of poverty is said to be self-perpetuating within families and within subcultures and the mechanism of transmission is thought to be the family with its characteristic patterns of child rearing and socialization. Lewis (1968) listed the major traits of the culture of poverty at the family level as 'the absence of childhood as a specially prolonged and protected stage in the life cycle; early initiation into sex; free unions or consensual marriages; a relatively high incidence of the abandonment of wives and children; a trend towards female-or-mother-centred families and consequently a much greater knowledge of maternal relatives; a strong predisposition to authoritarianism; lack of privacy; verbal emphasis upon family solidarity, which is only rarely achieved because of sibling rivalry; and competition for limited goods and maternal affection'. Such childhood experiences are assumed to influence values and behaviour which in turn determine future responses to situations. Lewis (1968) claimed that the process of transmission is set by 6 or 7 years; by this time children have generally adopted the characteristic values and attitudes of the culture to such an extent that they become unable to respond to changing opportunities and conditions.

Despite elaborate formulation, the culture of poverty argument has been severely criticized on both empirical and theoretical grounds. Empirical support comes mainly from the anthropological studies of Lewis and others. However, the deductions drawn from these are not free from criticism. Valentine (1971) made a thorough appraisal of some of Lewis' writings and concluded that the poverty culture thesis is, as yet, little more than a hypothesis. He gave illustrations of the many inconsistencies and contradictions that are to be found between the biographical and descriptive accounts of daily life and Lewis' interpretations. Evidence for subcultures of poverty stemmed more from the absence of certain characteristics than from the presence of others. It seemed to Valentine (1971) that the scientific validity of the culture of poverty thesis, as revealed by Lewis, was slight. This conclusion is in keeping with other surveys. Rossi and Blum (1968) reviewed post World War II empirical social science literature to find support for the poverty culture hypothesis, but they found little; data indicated that the poor were different only in degree. Moreover, they discovered no convincing evidence to suggest that intergenerational transmission of a poverty culture existed. Many of the studies purporting to show this were based on samples of families on relief. Rossi and Blum (1968) concluded that, in general, investigators had not collected enough information — for instance data on *all* descendants in families and data relating to the general population — to throw light on the issue.

The thesis has certainly gained wide currency on the basis of vivid reporting of a small number of families. Impressionistic reportage, however, suffers from the general limitations that beset attempts to examine different cultures. Leacock (1971) specified these difficulties in relation to poverty culture literature. She claimed that population behaviour might be inaccurately assessed if generalizations were made from a small sample of behaviour or from a non-representative subject group. Moreover, attributes may become classified from a middle-class, white, academic viewpoint, so that quantitative and qualitative differences are confused. Unwarrantable extrapolations are sometimes made from trends to universal differences. Furthermore, differences have often been described on the basis of assumptions regarding middle-class patterns rather than from systematic comparisons between social groups. As a result, conclusions based on the observation of a particular subculture require careful examination.

A lack of firm empirical support for the culture of poverty thesis may, in some measure, reflect the inadequacies of the basic theoretical concept. The failure to consider alternative hypotheses and the acceptance of unwarranted assumptions have been the main criticisms. Leacock (1971) outlined some of the ways in which individual behaviour was discounted by the culture of poverty proponents. For example, the theory made no allowance for human variability in responses to a particular environment, both between and within individuals. She also questioned the assumption, made by Lewis (e.g. 1968), that values and motivations are irreversibly determined by the age of 6 or 7 years. At the group level, Leacock (1971) stressed the way in which roles are developed and maintained throughout life; children are not robots who respond automatically throughout their lives without the constant reinforcement of their status and position. Discrimination, and other forms of differential treatment, perpetuate behaviour.

Probably the most widespread criticism of a subcultural interpretation of poverty is that it ignores the effects of societal structure. A situational interpretation is favoured by those who believe that certain distinct behaviour patterns do exist among the poor, but who maintain that it is the structural features of society and not family factors which encourage their intergenerational transmission. The precise variables considered important vary between writers. Leeds (1971) stressed the role of economic factors: 'In briefest summary, the behavioural characteristics, residential conditions, etc., that stimulated Oscar Lewis to posit a culture of poverty are largely interpretable as direct consequences of the operation of some specific aspect of capitalist societal systems . . . especially the labour market and its control by capitalist elites, the capital flow and control system, and the structure of profit management . . .'. Leacock (1971) emphasized the important impact of 'socio-economic organization, technological developments, and unresolved conflicts within and among institutional structures with which the individual must cope'. These and other societal features and constraints are believed to limit the opportunities and fortunes of the poor and to *cause* the development of specific behaviour patterns. Apparent values, psychological characteristics and family organization may thus arise as the most appropriate responses to adverse circumstances (Valentine, 1971).

The situational interpretation does not accord with the subcultural view in which primary emphasis is placed upon the family as the perpetuator of poverty. Lewis (1968), as the chief proponent of this latter view, nevertheless did claim that poverty cultures were most likely to arise in specific contexts. They tended to develop in societies with characteristics such as a cash economy, high unemployment and underemployment for unskilled workers, little social, political or economic provision for the low income groups, a bilateral kinship system, and an attitude of derision towards those of low economic status. 'Most frequently, the culture of poverty develops when a social and economic system is breaking down or is being replaced by another, as in the case of the transition from feudalism to capitalism or during periods of rapid technological change. . . . The most likely candidates for the culture of poverty are the people who come from the lower strata of a rapidly changing society and are already partially alienated from it' (Lewis, 1968). The sub-cultural thesis recognizes the importance of societal features, but does not believe them to be directly causal; the removal of socio-structural constraints would not lead to behaviour modification.

It would seem that neither a wholly sub-cultural nor a wholly situational interpretation of the behaviour and attributes of poor communities is tenable. Each has its own limitations and both fail to explain or take account of individual differences. Some attempts have been made to reconcile the two viewpoints. For example, Gurin and Gurin (1970) suggested an 'expectancy theory' model according to which behaviour is influenced, among other things, by expectations of achieving a desired goal. Expectancy is determined both by subcultural attitudes and values and also by experience of reality and success in the wider society. Nevertheless it is still important to be able to assess the relative weight of the two spheres of influence. Recent opinion has tended to stress the role of situational factors and even Lewis (1969) has reached the position that 'in the long run the self-perpetuating factors are relatively minor and unimportant as compared to the basic structure of the larger society'.

It may be concluded that the culture of poverty debate is largely academic. In its stated form it is not presumed to apply to all 'poor' people: Lewis (1968) estimated that only about 20 per cent of the United States population below the poverty line are members of the culture of poverty. It is unlikely that the thesis is relevant to the situation in Britain. Lewis (1968) maintained that the culture was most likely to develop in 'rapidly changing societies', which Britain is not. Moreover there is little documentation of any communities in this country which might correspond with the descriptions of a culture of poverty given by Lewis. The culture of poverty concept is inadequate for an analysis of British society.

Regional Cycles

National indices of economic status and poverty obscure regional variations. Great Britain is frequently divided into ten standard regions for analytical purposes: North, Yorkshire and Humberside, South East, South West, East Anglia, West Midlands, East Midlands and North West regions and Wales and Scotland. Extensive comparative data suggest that regional inequalities are persistent.

Prosperity of a country is frequently assessed in terms of its Gross Domestic Product (GDP) which, in very simple terms, is a measure of industrial out-put. Recently, similar analyses have been applied to United Kingdom regions and data are available over a ten-year span. Woodward (1970) estimated regional GDP for 1961 and 1966, and the Central Statistical Office (1973) made similar calculations for 1966 until 1971 inclusive. This latter source showed how regional inbalance of GDP per head was consistent over the six years. At each date the South East region appeared most prosperous and the West Midlands was in second place. The poorest region was the North, although Wales and Scotland also fared relatively badly.

Trends in public and private investment are another index of regional growth. Glasson (1974) discussed national data on this issue. In terms of public spending between 1965 and 1970 and industrial building since 1960 there was an apparent relative advantage obtained by the poorest regions. However, further examination showed that the growth in industry was largely accounted for by new branch firms, which are generally more vulnerable to economic stress. Also the increase in industry in these disadvantaged areas was not paralleled by a comparable growth in employment rates.

Woodward (1974) stressed the importance of unemployment levels as indicators of regional prosperity and there is good information on comparative rates over time. Despite the marked increases in overall numbers of the unemployed in recent years, e.g. from 1.3 per cent of the UK population in 1951 to 3.7 per cent in 1971 (Glasson, 1974), the distribution across regions has remained fairly constant. Thus Department of Employment figures show that the North, Scotland and Wales have been the three areas with greatest unemployment and the South East the area with the least. In 1971, for example, the unemployment rates in the North and in Wales were about 6.5 per cent and in Scotland about 5 per cent, but in the South East only 2.2 per cent were unemployed. Moreover, a survey of the unemployed on one day in 1973 showed that the duration of unemployment tended to be greatest in Scotland and the North and least in the South East 1973). Generally speaking, regional variations in unemployment rates have been maintained for more than 20 years; nevertheless there have been some changes, such as the recent increase in unemployment in the West Midlands.

The numbers of people in work have also remained stable between regions over the last years (Central Statistical Office, 1973). The West Midlands has consistently had the highest regional rates of people in work, and the South West and Wales the lowest. Regional rates do not completely parallel local unemployment as official unemployment figures have generally underestimated the real numbers of people out of work (Bosanquet and Standing, 1972).

Wages and salary levels of the employed are a further index of regional prosperity. One good source of data on this issue is the New Earnings Survey conducted by the Department of Employment. Unfortunately, this was only begun in 1968 so that information is limited to the last six years. Over this period, however, there has been little change in the relative positions of regions in the proportions of full-time workers gaining low pay. This is illustrated by the percentages of all full-time male workers with gross weekly earnings of less than £15 in 1968 and less than £25 in 1973. These wage levels are not equivalent (7.9 per cent of all workers in Great Britain earned less than £15 in 1968 and 9.5 per cent earned less than £25 in 1973) but they are similar. In both years the highest proportions of low paid workers were recorded for East Anglia and the lowest for the South East and West Midland regions. Bearing in mind that the figures are not directly comparable, 12 per cent of workers from East Anglia, and 6 per cent from the South East and West Midlands earned less than £15 in 1968, whereas 13 per cent and 7 to 8 per cent respectively earned less than £25 in 1973. Regional differences were largely maintained over this period although relative wage levels in Wales showed a marked improvement.

These data show that the pattern of regional inequalities has remained fairly stable over time. Some of the interrelations between poverty and prosperity indices, and some possible mechanisms of association and causation, are discussed in the following sections.

STRUCTURAL FACTORS INFLUENCING POVERTY

Regional Variation

Despite changing levels of national prosperity, employment and income levels, there are strong and persistent patterns of regional inequalities. These suggest that local structural factors may be important influences upon both regional and individual poverty.

Glasson (1974) discussed theoretical approaches to area growth and decline, and distinguished between short-run and long-run change. In the short term, prosperity changes depend upon local resources and their ability to satisfy demand for goods and services. Contraction and expansion of individual firms have negative and positive 'multiplier' effects respectively. For example, the decline of a firm may mean not only that it is unable to offer so many jobs itself but also that there are further redundancies in linked firms or industries where ability to produce is restricted by the downfall of the first. By contrast the expansion of a firm might create more jobs both in its own factories and in others that are encouraged to expand as a result. However, the type of industry and its particular organization will influence its impact upon the regional economy.

There seems to be no straightforward association between industrial structure and regional growth. External factors, including demand for goods, appear to be as important as local factors such as labour and capital supplies.

At a more empirical level, area-specific patterns are identifiable. For example the South East region has the highest Gross Domestic Product of any of the standard regions, the lowest unemployment rates and the highest average household expenditure. By contrast northern regions of the country, Wales and Scotland fare relatively badly.

Such patterns probably reflect varying relationships between activity rates and earnings within regions. Certainly the South East had the lowest proportion of workers with low earnings in 1968, although by 1973 it had been overtaken by the West Midlands (New Earnings Surveys, 1968 and 1973). However, the apparent relationships between factors are further complicated as, at both dates, it was East Anglia that had the highest proportion of low-paid workers.

Low pay in employment and a shortage of jobs do not necessarily coincide regionally although higher pay and more jobs tend to. Local structure of employment is probably important. In prosperous areas there tend to be high activity rates and relatively high wage levels. However, in less prosperous areas it seems that there may either be few jobs, a large proportion of which are well-paid, or alternatively a larger number of jobs but with lower pay.

Regional disparities in earnings can arise in two ways. Firstly there may be local differences in the jobs available and the wages offered. Secondly, there may be similarities in employment opportunities but dissimilarities in wage levels. Woodward (1970) stressed the importance of the former pattern. Many areas have concentrations of particular types of industry and there is clear evidence from the New Earnings Survey of different rates of pay between industrial sectors. Moreover, differentials between many industries have remained fairly constant over the last quarter of a century (Central Statistical Office, 1973) which can help to explain the persistence of regional inequalities. Nevertheless it is also important that there are area differences in the pay offered for comparable work. From the New Earnings Survey (1973) it can be seen that average gross weekly earnings within the main categories of industry differ considerably between regions. The South East (particularly for non-manual workers) and the West Midlands offered the highest wages and East Anglia the lowest. As an illustration, the average gross weekly wage for manual workers in all industries and services was £35.50 in East Anglia, £39.30 in the South East and £40.30 in the West Midlands. This must largely explain East Anglia's position with regard to area proportions of low-paid workers. These figures give some indication of regional differences important for aggregate and individual poverty.

Labour Market Characteristics

Within any area, and even for comparable occupations, employers may offer unequal conditions of work and pay and may attract different categories of employees. This argument has attracted much recent discussion, particularly in the United States. Doeringer and Piore (1970) summarized this labour market thesis as follows: '. . . the labour market is divided into a *primary* and a *secondary* market. Jobs in the primary market possess several of the following characteristics: high wages, good working conditions, employment stability, chances of advancement, equity and due process in the administration of work rules. Jobs in the secondary market, in contrast, tend to have low wages and fringe benefits, poor working conditions, high labour turnover, little chance of advancement, and often arbitrary and capricious supervision. There are distinctions between workers in the two sectors which parallel those between jobs: workers in the secondary sector, relative to those in the primary sector, exhibit greater turnover, higher rates of lateness and absenteeism, more insubordination, and engage more freely in petty theft and pilferage . . . Disadvantaged workers . . . are confined to the secondary market by residence, inadequate skills, poor work histories, and discrimination'. It is believed that industrial decisions on wage levels set off a chain of events. Low pay without opportunities for on-the-job training and promotion means the recruitment of workers with few skills and those who have suffered from discrimination elsewhere. As capital investment in such labour forces is minimal, and so long as there is a free supply of labour, employers are not worried by high turnover. Hence no effort is made to offer incentives and conditions to encourage stability of employment.

There is not enough evidence to claim the existence of a dual labour market in Britain. Bosanquet and Doeringer (1973) presented some indirect support for its validity although their analyses ignored certain categories of workers and were based on average wage levels rather than distributions. They suggested that certain groups of workers, e.g. young people, unskilled workers and women, were more likely than others to have low pay and to change jobs frequently and that unskilled workers were more likely than skilled or non-manual workers to suffer unemployment. However the labour market thesis did not seem as applicable to black people in England as in America. In both countries workers were concentrated within 'secondary market employments' but it was only in the USA that they exhibited secondary market characteristics such as unemployment and job instability.

The dual labour market hypothesis is interesting but there is insufficient information available to judge its applicability to the British employment scene. In particular there is no adequate documentation on the nature and operation of internal labour markets in this country, especially in relation to characteristics of the employed. Furthermore it is not known whether individuals are mobile between the two market sectors. Nor is it known to what extent industry determines the nature of the labour force and to what extent employee characteristics determine proffered wages and conditions.

The Role of Trade Unions

Can trade unions influence wages? This is again an area where there are more American than British empirical investigations. It would seem that as unions vary in strength by region, industry, membership, degree of demarcation and extent of organization (Hunter and Robertson, 1969) and as their effects are not independent of prevailing economic conditions (Lewis, 1963), only very tentative generalizations can be made. Nevertheless some unions will be comparatively powerful. Organization is important, and this may have implications for 'secondary labour market' sectors. Presumably it is difficult to establish and maintain trade unions in industries with transient labour forces. Such low skill employments would suffer further in union strength for other reasons. The more specialized a trade or occupation, the more control trade unions may gain over labour supply and wage levels (Hunter and Robertson, 1969). Workers may stipulate conditions of entry into the occupation, they may demand certain levels of skills or periods of apprenticeship and they may restrict entrants if they fail to comply with 'rules' or if a quota has been reached. Additionally, they may stipulate conditions of work and methods of working.

There are many potential ways in which unions can alter the wages of their members relative to non-members in comparable occupations. Collective bargaining within industries can lead to wage increases, particularly if there is a strong threat of strike. Effects, however, may not be restricted to the industry in question. Rees (1973) discussed the 'threat effect' which sets off a chain of wage increases within different employments. Non-union employers may increase wages to match union rates in order to keep workers and to discourage them from forming their own unions. On the other hand, union increases may have less advantageous repercussions on other workers. This can result if union rises are sufficient to reduce demand for union employment so that labour supply is increased and wages lowered elsewhere.

Some empirical examinations of union/non-union wage differentials have been made. Lewis (1963) estimated that the effective difference in the USA in the late 1950s was in the range of 10 to 15 per cent. However smaller effects of unionism have been found in later studies that have taken account of the personal characteristics of workers (Weiss, 1966; Boskin, 1972). Similarly-controlled studies have not been conducted in Britain. Nevertheless some interesting data are reported by Pencavel (1974). He concluded that, during the early 1960s, the difference in hourly earnings between union and non-union manual workers was between zero and ten per cent. This average figure, however, concealed a very important factor. It was not industry-wide bargaining that had had an effect, but workshop bargaining by shop stewards in industries with sufficient organization. Thus trade unions had an important influence on wages if they could raise the earnings of their members above the levels negotiated by senior trade union officials.

POLICIES AND ACTION INFLUENCING POVERTY

The net income of the majority of the population is the sum of occupational earnings and welfare benefits minus taxation. Government policies can have strong effects on all three components. This section does not present a comprehensive account of real and potential policies regulating net income but gives a few examples with some indication, where possible, of their actual or probable repercussions upon the poorest sections of the community.

Occupational Earnings

Three main types of policy directed at the problem of low pay may be identified. First, there are policies designed to guarantee a minimum wage or to encourage greater equality of earnings. Second, there are attempts to effect structural changes in employment opportunities so that access to well-paid jobs is facilitated. And third, there are programmes designed to raise the skill levels of workers and to increase their employment aptitude.

The relative advantages of different types of income policies have been hotly disputed. The effectiveness of strategies generally depends upon the broad economic context in which they are set. For example, this would apply to the impact of a national minimum wage (Hughes, 1971). If increased earnings for the lowest paid lead to increases across the board, redistribution will be minimal. Similarly, incomes policies effecting obligatory standstills and restricting rises will not benefit the low paid if permitted increases are based on a percentage of original earnings. In this instance hierarchies in pay are unchanged (Trinder, 1974) and any small actual gains achieved by the lower paid are likely to be eroded by inflation.

A structural strategy to increase the equality of wage levels is to reduce the regional imbalance of labour supply and demand. A thorough account of the relevant issues, policies and practices is given by Glasson (1974). The two basic approaches have been either to encourage workers to move to work or for work to move to the location of the available labour force. Thus the practicalities of relocating industry and labour migration become important. In general the development of industry in new areas is favoured and there is some evidence of employment multiplier effects — new industries within an area lead to the development of further 'linked' industries, and hence more jobs — for some sizes and types of industry (Lever, 1974). But this must be weighed against the observation that where industries have moved from older industrial areas, the people left behind find that their jobs are in jeopardy (Moor, 1974).

Alternatively the gap between employment opportunities and employee characteristics might be narrowed by providing opportunities for on-the-job training and retraining. Empirical data on the effectiveness of this practice are largely lacking. Moor (1974) reported that, at least within the four old industrial areas studied, the Department of Employment schemes did not attract sufficient workers nor did they seem to increase employability of those that did enrol.

The Welfare State

National welfare benefits supplement low occupational wages or, in some situations, substitute for an earned income. The welfare state has expanded considerably since the last world war and its general aim has been to help those without alternative support. However, its effectiveness has been questioned (Kincaid, 1973). Abel-Smith (1958) observed that the social services since the war had apparently most benefitted the middle classes and Webb and Sieve (1971) noted that this was still the case over a decade later.

Direct monetary benefits may be either contingent upon circumstance (such as family allowances) or economic status (such as supplementary benefit). There has been much discussion of the relative merits of universal and selective benefits (Lynes, 1971; Collard, 1971). The theoretical value of progressive benefits for low income families is reduced by their low take-up (Land, 1969; Ministry of Social Security, 1967; Bottomley, 1971; Field, 1971). The cause of non-take-up is sometimes ignorance of availability or eligibility and sometimes fear of stigma. On the other hand, flat rate benefits will not reduce income inequalities unless they are subject to taxation or clawback.

One criticism that has sometimes been levelled against welfare benefits is that they may have adverse effects upon incentives. The general cry raised is that unemployment benefits will discourage men from work. However, on the whole the evidence is against a major effect of this kind (Atkinson, 1969; Hill *et al.*, 1973) and, as discussed above, the majority of the unemployed appear keen to work. Men who are judged 'workshy' do, in any case, forfeit most of their benefits.

Taxation

Incentives may however be affected by combined effects of benefits and taxation. There is the example of the 'poverty trap' whereby large changes in income status are not reflected in large changes in net take-home pay. This catches the low wage earner hoping to improve his financial position. If he has an income below the statutory requirement level, but is working full-time, he is not entitled to supplementary benefit. His alternative is to gain a larger occupational income. However, if he is able to achieve permanent increases in earnings he may become caught in the trap and make only very slight gains in net income, or possibly even a loss (Piachaud, 1971; Field and Piachaud, 1971; Bradshaw and Wakeman, 1972). The trap is that higher wages are accompanied by greater tax demands and the loss of certain means-tested benefits. Piachaud (1971) indicated that a married man with four children could become subject to what amounted to a 130 per cent tax rate on extra earnings below the poverty line. Field and Piachaud (1971) showed that a family man earning an extra £1 gross per week could in fact benefit by only 15p. Income rises might thus have no effect greater than that of combatting inflation. Bradshaw and Wakeman (1972) examined the situation following certain policy changes — including tax threshold moves and the introduction of Family Income Supplements and rent rebates — to assess the hypothetical effects. It appeared that full take-up of benefits would mean a reduction of severe poverty but not an eradication of the poverty trap phenomenon. The low-paid worker would be caught on a plateau at the supplementary benefit level: a four-child family man would, by doubling his wage from £14 to £28 only raise his net disposable income by £1.42. Those with the largest families would have the highest marginal rates of taxation. Bradshaw and Wakeman (1972) wrote: 'the families that are having to bolster their standard of living by taking up means-tested benefits are trapped in or around poverty. Their situation is hopeless. If they increase their income they may suffer from a deterioration in their living standards. Whether they know the real reason or confuse it with the general effects of rising prices is really immaterial. The important point is that they start in poverty and end in poverty.'

Fatherless families are trapped in a similar way. As described earlier, mothers with dependent children receive supplementary benefit and are not obliged to work. However, if they do wish to have a job they are unable to increase their net income unless they can earn above the supplementary benefit level.

Lower paid workers have increasingly suffered from taxation. More and more people have been drawn into the tax net since the last world war and recently the lower paid have been at a further disadvantage as the tax threshold has not increased at the same rate as earnings. Moore (1973) has argued that the situation of the low paid has become worse even over the last decade. The abolition of reduced rates of taxation at lower income levels in 1969 and 1970 helped the low paid but this was counterbalanced or more than counterbalanced by the increasing number of low paid workers coming above the tax threshold because of inflation.

The possibility of extending the existing system of taxation to incorporate negative income tax awards has been much discussed. This scheme is seen as an alternative to family allowances. The relative merits of the two approaches are debatable. Barker (1971) discussed the issues involved and indicated that some groups would benefit more from one scheme and others more from the other. Two problems of negative income tax strategies seemed to be firstly, the difficulties of being generous and at the same time maintaining worker incentives and secondly, ensuring that employers did not see the scheme as providing a subsidy for low wages. However, the main criticism of the negative income tax approach was that such a policy would probably not do much to redistribute incomes and would make families with incomes just above the tax threshold a particularly disadvantaged group.

Action-research

Apart from direct policies, there are government intervention experiments which seek both to define problems and to provide remedies at a Community Level*. The Community Development Project (CDP) is important in this context. It is an action-research experiment launched by the Home Office in 1969 as 'a modest attempt at action research into the better understanding and more comprehensive tackling of social needs, especially in local communities within the older urban areas, through closer coordination of central and local official and unofficial effort, informed and stimulated by citizen initiative and involvement' (Home Office, 1969a). This experiment constituted part of the Government's attack on poverty and multiple deprivation through the urban programme.† It has involved twelve areas — Liverpool, Southwark, Coventry, Glamorgan, Newham, Newcastle-upon-Tyne, Paisley, Cumberland, the West Riding, Oldham, Tynemouth and Birmingham — and has concentrated in each upon a population of between five and fifteen thousand inhabitants. There has been a particular concern with future generations, and the development of long-term solutions to local problems. However, a major problem concerns the high mobility of many of the deprived living in the target areas. There is likely to be less success in altering environment and attitudes where the population is rapidly changing.

At its conception the emphasis of CDP was upon the social services. It was assumed that 'families suffering from chronic poverty or dependence on the social services tend to be found in large numbers in particular areas, such as those suffering from urban or industrial decay' (Home Office, 1969b). Further assumptions of the project were that it was not enough merely to provide 'more of the same' services but that what was necessary was to mobilize untapped local resources and lead the community to a position of self support. Research and action were accordingly located in each locality to assess need, intervene accordingly and evaluate the outcome.

The CDP, however, has not developed exactly as was envisaged. The focus of intervention has broadened considerably over the years of the

*As in most of this chapter, discussion is restricted to British projects — see Holman (1974a) for an account of the American poverty programme.

†This was initiated in 1968 as a broad based project involving a variety of local projects. See Holman and Hamilton (1973) and Batley and Edwards (1974) for critiques of its aims and achievements.

experiment, far more attention having been paid to environmental issues and less to personal pathology than was originally intended. In several areas, aspects such as town planning, housing and public transport have claimed major emphasis. More in line with the early emphasis, many localities have placed energies into developing information and opinion centres and in organizing programmes to provide services such as employment advice for teenagers or preschool play and educational facilities. A major objective that has remained throughout is to help the community to stand on its own feet by briefing people on their rights, encouraging them to decide what provisions the locality most needs and involving them in programmes to deal with such requirements.

There are several reasons why an evaluation of CDP is difficult. One is that consensus between action and research teams within areas has been imperfect. This is partly because in many areas the two teams have not entered the project at the same time and in others because the team members have changed frequently. Such lack of coordination between action and research groups in the CDP* has serious repercussions for evaluation: often there is no knowledge of the situation before the inception of the project and where the action has not developed in a predictable way there is no obvious basis on which an assessment can be made. These points may account for the fact that evaluation has largely been ignored by CDP. Research teams have tended to concentrate upon identifying the problems within a particular area and constructing a social and economic profile. The workers have usually collected data from the local inhabitants concerning neighbourhood problems and it has been their job to decide what type of strategy might be needed and to advise the action group on how to proceed in the light of various evidence. The extent to which these goals have been realized is not clear.

The Centre for Environmental Studies (CES) is now responsible for co-ordinating the experiment and has presented its initial inter-project report (CES, 1974) which compares and contrasts the characteristics and action strategies of the 12 localities. All areas had distinct features but most included similar symptoms of disadvantage comprising: 'lower than average incomes: disproportionately high rates of unemployment; high dependence on state benefits; poor health records — particularly high infant mortality rates in certain areas; and poor housing — lack of amenities, overcrowding, dilapidation or stigma'. No data on the outcome of action are yet available although the CES (1974) identified the main implications that CDP might have for national policy. These included experience and practical solutions relating to industrial incentives, unification of local organizations, job creating, housing policy, alternative tenure arrangements, modifications

*See Lees (1973) for an account of the difficulties of action-research and the ways these were met in one CDP.

to systems of means tests, use of educational resources and communication.

Little more can yet be said about the evaluation of CDP. It remains to be seen what further material emerges and whether the guides to policy, suggested by the CES (1974), come to fruition. What is unfortunate is that there are no plans for any long-term follow-up studies of the areas once the experiment ceases. Without this type of evaluation it will be impossible to know whether or not the project has been successful and whether the communities have become self-supportive, not only *while* the action teams are still present but also *after* they have left. This is particularly critical, bearing in mind the relatively high population mobility in many of the project areas. Another crucial point that does not appear to be answerable is whether or not this type of strategy has managed to reach not merely the deprived but the *most* deprived within an area.

INDIVIDUAL FACTORS INFLUENCING POVERTY

Ability and Education

There have been frequent assertions (e.g., Burt, 1943; Eysenck, 1973b) that intellectual ability strongly influences income level, although these claims lack adequate empirical support. This issue has not been systematically examined in Britain. Jencks *et al.* (1973) reported on an American population group and concluded that cognitive skills had only a small impact upon income distribution. Hereditary components of intelligence were of minor significance in determining income: it was estimated that there would be only about 3 per cent less income inequality in genetically homogeneous sub-populations than in the entire American population. Somewhat larger differences obtained when measured intelligence (taking account of environmental effects on test scores) was considered. In no case, however, was there a large direct effect of cognitive skill upon earnings.

In contrast to the uncertainty of the relationship betweeen intelligence and income there is clear documentation of an association between level of schooling attained and earnings. Blaug (1970) demonstrated how remarkably similar age-earnings profiles by level of education are found in both rich and poor countries. Data for USA, UK, India and Mexico revealed three typical characteristics. First, for all profiles, and regardless of schooling, earnings reached a peak and then levelled off or declined. Second, the more education received the steeper the increase in income over time and possibly the higher initial wage or salary level. And third, the higher the educational attainment, the later the peak in earnings and the higher the level of retirement earnings. These profiles are based on cross-sectional analyses of population groups. They are free from the complicating influences of the trade cycle and inflationary processes, but they cannot reveal the idiosyncracies of individual life-cycle patterns.

There is a large volume of other evidence pertaining to the relationship between education and economic status. Many economists have taken a 'human capital' approach to describe education-related earnings increments. They view prolonged education as a form of investment which pays off in increased earnings once employment begins. Henderson—Stewart (1965) demonstrated returns to additional education for a British sample. It was shown that the earnings foregone by investment in three years' secondary school education beyond the minimum leaving age in 1963 repaid through subsequent wages or salary at an interest rate of about 13 per cent. For three years of higher education the comparable rate of return was about 14 per cent.

There is, additionally, a large volume of regression or correlation studies pertaining to the relationship between education and economic status. These are not totally consistent. Many have indicated a positive association. Wolfle (1960) found that increased education remained associated with higher earnings even when position in high-school class, measured intelligence and paternal occupation were controlled. Similarly Becker (1964) deduced from five data sets that, after adjustments had been made for ability and social class, further education was the major determinant of high earnings. Blau and Duncan (1967) reported that schooling level had a strong impact upon earnings, independent of social class background, and Morgan *et al.* (1962) found that education appeared to be the single most critical factor for wage or salary level out of age, schooling, on-the-job training, sex, race, IQ, motivation, parental education, family size, paternal occupation, religion, area of residence, city size, occupational choice, social mobility, unemployment and hours worked.

Other investigations have suggested a smaller relationship between education and economic status. Bowles (1972) showed that years of schooling had only a small impact on earnings once social class background was taken into account and that socioeconomic status was the critical factor for income. Both social and educational level determined occupational opportunity but it was hypothesized that social class, more than years of schooling, influenced occupational choice. Jencks *et al.* (1973) also found that controlling for family background — which included a wide range of variables — and ability test scores reduced the apparent effect of schooling on income to an almost negligible level. Nevertheless none of the variables examined seemed critical and it was found that when men identical on family background, cognitive skill, educational attainment and occupational status indices were compared with regard to income level, there was only 12—15 per cent less intra-group inequality than among men selected randomly. However, this finding is not really comparable to those reported by other studies as it relates to total income and not earnings and is based on a sample which includes self-employed men and does not control for age or transitory income components.

Yet other studies have indicated that schooling has an effect on income, although not independently of ability (Griliches and Mason, 1972; Hause, 1972; Wolfle and Smith, 1956). There are suggestions both that schooling has more impact on the earnings of those with higher ability and that ability level is more strongly related to income among the most educated.

Findings are inconsistent. However, in any case, statistical associations between years of education and subsequent average earnings reveal nothing about the mechanisms involved (Vaizey, 1962; Balogh and Streeten, 1963). The interdependence of a large number of personal, family and social factors means that it is virtually impossible to isolate the pure effects of education on economic status. Cognitive ability, parental social status, motivation, informal education at home, family composition and household income are but a few of the factors that are likely to be associated with length of education and at the same time to influence earning capacity.

It may be concluded that education is related to earnings — although it is not known whether or not the association is directly causal. It is also unclear whether the relationship would persist if there were vast increases in the numbers of people undertaking prolonged education. Evidence is not easy to evaluate, but there are indications that the association may be stable. As demonstrated by Blaug (1970), comparable earnings profiles are found in countries with large increases in the average length of schooling. These have not altered the typical association between education, wage and salary levels (Miller, 1960; Becker, 1964).

Most of the evidence and discussions on education and earnings relate to the situation in America, and cannot necessarily be applied to the situation to Britain. As Blaug (1965) discussed, certain differences exist in this country. He suggested that there is a greater premium on schooling in Britain, because higher education is restricted to smaller numbers. Other important differences may be the relative structure of occupations, contrasting emphasis on paper qualifications and comparative educational systems. In Britain at least, type (as distinct from level) of education can be related to earnings. For example, Stanworth and Giddens (1974) illustrated the vast over-representation of British ex-public school and ex-Oxbridge students among company chairmen: nevertheless family background is probably largely influential here. All these, and many other, considerations must be taken into account in extrapolating the largely American literature on human capital theory to the British situation.

Occupational Income

Abel-Smith and Townsend (1965) showed that in 1960 about 41 per cent of persons living below the national assistance statutory level were in households where income came primarily from earnings. The Ministry of Social Security (1967) study demonstrated that, of the 3 million families with at least two children and a fully-employed father,

125,000 had total resources less than supplementary benefit requirements. The DHSS survey (1971) of the two-parent families maintained that 74,000 families were below the supplementary benefit level despite full-time work.

The direct disadvantage of a low occupational income is increased by the effect of economic policies and context. For example the operation of the 'poverty trap', current rates or taxation and the means-tested nature of many benefits (and consequent low take-up) hit the poorest families and households hardest. There is also evidence that inflation usually affects the lower paid groups most severely. Muellbauer (1974) examined the increases in costs of 'luxuries' and 'necessities' in Britain between 1964 and 1970. Over this period price rises had been greater for necessities than for luxuries and durables and between 1970 and 1972 price increases for food had been particularly marked. Muellbauer constructed cost of living indices for different expenditure levels on the basis of information from the Family Expenditure surveys for 1964 and 1970. He concluded that price increases between 1964 and 1972, and particularly over 1971–1972, had been less unfavourable to the better-off. The strength of this conclusion was probably underestimated as no account was taken of factors such as the greater increase in cost of public over private transport and the probable increase in value for money of many durables relative to more necessary expenditure such as public transport. Since 1972, however, the situation has probably changed. The introduction of new food subsidies and rent controls should, on the whole, reduce the relative disadvantage of those with the lowest incomes, although there is some evidence that this is not happening (Pond, 1975).

A low income allows little flexibility in patterns of expenditure. It means limited saving and investment opportunities — any small amount of money that can be put aside will generally raise only low rates of interest which, over time, may become eroded by inflation: high interest rates are awarded only for guaranteed long-term deposits of large sums. The limited benefit from savings facing the low paid worker upon retirement will be exacerbated by the likelihood of low pension provisions. It is the higher paid workers who are more likely to receive industry- or company-awarded pensions. A low income places restrictions upon bulk purchasing, access to competitively priced shops and availability of credit and mortgage facilities (Harrison, 1973; Piachaud, 1974). The poor make greater use of hire purchase facilities which means that, in the long run, they pay more for goods than do the better off. There are also the additional advantages that attend higher wages (Wedderburn and Craig, 1974): the occupational pensions already mentioned, expense-account meals, use of a telephone, opportunities for petty pilfering and other perks that are infrequently offered to the lower paid employee.

In short, low earnings have both direct and indirect effects. As Atkinson (1973a) wrote: 'Low pay must be seen more generally as a disadvantage in the labour market, and as associated with high incidence of job instability and ill-health and with the absence of fringe benefits. The low paid worker is more vulnerable to the interruption or loss of earning power, and lacks the resources to meet such needs. Low earnings mean that people cannot save for emergencies or for old age. They cannot get a mortgage and the only way in which they can borrow is through HP or not paying the electricity bill. In these and other ways, low pay plays an important role in the cycle of poverty'.

Mental Disorder and other Personal Attributes

Mental illness and personality disorders may influence income either by leading to downward occupational mobility (which is discussed in Chapter 5) or through unemployment which is considered more fully below.

Any of the personal attributes which influence occupational status will have a consequent impact upon income. The limited findings on this issue are also discussed in Chapter 5.

Sex Differences

Prior to the recent legislation which outlawed pay differentials for men and women in comparable employment, widespread sex differences existed. Thus, in 1973 (New Earnings Survey), the average wage of all full-time male employees over 21 years was £40.90, nearly twice that for women over 18 years (for whom it was £22.60). In manual occupations men earned on average £37.00 and women earned £19.10. For non-manual workers the relative earnings were £47.80 and £24.50 respectively (New Earnings Survey, 1973). Discrimination is indicated by the contrasting associations in men and women between income and years of education (Blaug, 1970).

The economic disadvantages experienced by women are important in their own right. However the most critical concern with respect to cycles of disadvantage is for women bringing up families on their own. Earlier discussion (see pages 20–22) has indicated how fatherless families are financially worse off than motherless families, especially if they are headed by unmarried or separated mothers (DHSS, 1974). This is largely due to the lower wages offered to women and to the disadvantages in systems of benefits as they apply to men and women with children.

UNEMPLOYMENT

Unemployment whether long-term, short-term or intermittent means loss of earnings and a likely low income. Because of this it deserves separate discussion. Many of the unemployed rely on minimal maintenance incomes (Hill *et al.*, 1973; Sinfield, 1970; Daniel, 1974) although evidence suggests that they do not necessarily live under poor housing conditions (Hill *et al.*, 1973). Low incomes are often due to the low level of wages earned whilst in earlier employment (Hill *et al.*, 1973; Sinfield, 1970), and operation of the 'wage stop', whereby supplementary benefit payments are paid at a level not exceeding 'potential earning capacity', means that poor wages in work are replaced by reduced benefits out of work (Lister, 1972). Moreover, the unemployed worker may well be financially worse off out of work than he was in work, as wage stop calculations rarely allow for the perks and overtime payments gained while employed. The Ministry of Social Security (1967) estimated that about 15,000 families with at least 2 children were living on the wage stop. Twenty five per cent of the sick or unemployed had total resources below the statutory level and a further 15 per cent had a surplus of less than £3. The situation was worst in large families and where the mother was not at work.

Poor families will be particularly hit by unemployment if they are disqualified from receiving full benefits. Reductions are made if insufficient national insurance contributions have been paid, if unemployment follows 'misconduct' or voluntary resignation 'without just cause', or if 'suitable' employment or training is offered but refused. Workers involved in trade disputes may also be subject to forfeitures. They will also suffer more than necessary if they do not claim the benefits to which they are entitled.

The number of unemployed persons at any one point in time, together with regional variations and changes over time in rates of unemployment, are largely determined by social and political factors. These have been discussed already. However, the question of why one person rather than another becomes unemployed involves a further set of personal variables. Information on this issue has largely come from studies comparing employed and unemployed persons.

The three most important variables determining which individuals are unemployed have usually been found to be old age, lack of skills and poor mental or physical health (Sinfield, 1968; Wedderburn, 1965; Department of Employment, 1974b; Hill *et al.*, 1973; Daniel, 1974; Bosanquet and Standing, 1972). Unskilled workers generally have much higher rates of unemployment than skilled manual or non-manual workers. Typically, the unskilled suffer intermittent unemployment when young but more prolonged unemployment when older. Old age is probably the single factor most influencing the likelihood of unemployment, but physical disability is also a frequent characteristic of those out of work. The association of old age and failing health is particularly likely to lead to unemployment. Psychiatric disorder is a common cause of short-term absence from work due to ill-health (Fraser, 1947) but chronic neurosis is not a particularly important factor in relation to a poor work record (Harrington, 1962) and it is of only slight importance in relation to persistent unemployment. Among psychiatric patients it is those with personality disorder who are most likely to remain unemployed (Markowe *et al.*, 1955). In a representative sample of men who had been psychiatric patients four years earlier, Rutter *et al.* (1976) found that 30 per cent had experienced unemployment during the last year, a rate three times that experienced by a comparable general population sample. However, the high rate of unemployment among patients was entirely due to men with personality disorders. Those with neurotic conditions or depressions had a work record similar to non-patients. Alcoholics and people with various forms of personality defect or mental illness are particularly common in the hard core of men on skid-row or attending a reception centre (Edwards *et al.*, 1966 & 1968).

There is controversy concerning the importance of a lack of motivation to work as a cause of unemployment. The Department of Employment (1974b), using personal judgements of unemployed office staff, estimated that 70 per cent of unemployed persons were keen to work. Daniel (1974) reported that twenty-three per cent of a sample of unemployed men stated quite definitely that they had no intention of working, an additional 19 per cent claimed that it was 'not important' for them to have a job and a further 17 per cent said that they found it only 'quite important' for them to work. These data do not indicate, however, how far lack of interest in work stemmed from the lack of morale consequent upon long unemployment or how far lack of motivation led to loss of job. Even strongly expressed motivation to find a job may not mean willingness to move to an area with greater opportunities. Sinfield (1970) reported that many of a sample of unemployed in a high unemployment area were reluctant to be geographically mobile. Hill *et al.* (1973) found that reluctance to move, but not versatility concerning acceptable types of occupation and methods of job hunting, distinguished between men unemployed for differing periods of time.

Motivation to work may be related to the chances of employment. Sinfield (1970) indicated that men unemployed for long periods of time were likely to have given up hope of finding a job. Daniel (1974) found that the elderly were over-represented among those least keen to work; he also found that large numbers of managerial and professional workers did not want to work. Thus, 63 per cent of non-manual registered unemployed, as compared with 37 per cent of manual, had either no intention of working or considered it unimportant to have a job. It would seem that there are a variety of factors affecting attitudes to work. No evidence was presented by any of these studies that state benefits served as an incentive to unemployment in more than a small minority of cases. Often, and especially in high unemployment areas, unemployment is involuntary. Sinfield (1970) reported that two-thirds of a sample of unemployed in Shields had been paid off because there was no work and only one quarter had left their last job for more personal reasons. Recent evidence suggests that young people from ethnic minority groups are experiencing particular difficulties in employment (see Chapter 10).

Personal characteristics are associated with unemployment to varying degrees in areas with contrasting industrial structure, prosperity and demand for labour. There is more discrimination against older workers in areas of high unemployment (Department of Employment, 1973) and mental illness assessed by interview schedule is associated with different patterns of unemployment in regions with differing employment levels (Hill *et al.*, 1973). It also appears that unskilled workers suffer less unemployment in more prosperous areas (Bosanquet and Standing, 1972). Hill *et al.* (1973) concluded that low skill is not a handicap in regions with strong demand for labour and varied employment opportunities. This would account for the lack of association between level of skill and unemployment reported by Gittus (1970) in a survey of Merseyside. Motivation and morale, by contrast, may be constant between areas. Daniel (1974) reported that, despite the differing composition of unemployed men between areas, much the same proportion expressed little interest in working. He concluded that expectations of employment are a function of the local demand for labour and not only a reflection of personal attributes.

The evidence suggests that, within a particular context, the elderly, the disabled and the unskilled are more likely than other groups to be unemployed. These personal characteristics influence *who* becomes unemployed in a specific labour market, and are in contrast to the structural factors predictive of temporal and regional *levels* of employment.

CONCLUSIONS

Over recent generations there have been marked improvements in standards of living in Britain, possibly accompanied by some marginal reduction in the spread of income within the population. At the same time, regional variations in patterns of disadvantage have continued with little change. Within this context very little is known about family continuities in economic status. There is evidence that large fortunes of wealth have been transmitted between successive generations of the same family, but this applies to only a very small population group. Also there is some indication of cycles of poverty, although empirical evidence on this point is weak. Within the middle range of income, however, very little is known on intergenerational continuities. Parental and filial patterns of economic status have not been examined in Britain. Life-cycle factors and a variety of political, social, and personal variables are associated with marked differences in income level.

3 Housing

A person's life circumstances are shaped to a considerable extent by the type of house in which he lives, and poor housing, like low income is associated with a wide range of personal troubles as well as social disadvantage. This chapter outlines the general supply and adequacy of housing in Britain and examines both the situation in which disadvantage is most often to be found and also the kind of people most likely to suffer. The scanty evidence on intergenerational continuities in housing patterns is examined and is followed by a review of the much larger literature on ways in which housing factors might be involved in the transmission of disadvantage.

HOUSING DISADVANTAGE, PAST AND PRESENT

The Housing Stock

The size and suitability of the housing stock in relation to demand is an important index of housing advantage and disadvantage. However, whereas the stock can be easily estimated, demand is not readily measurable. In spite of considerable fluctuations in the amount of new building, there has been a steady increase in housing stock throughout this century. Recently, however, there has been a slight recession. By 1973 both new constructions and to a lesser extent, slum clearance rates, had decreased (Housing and Construction Statistics, 1974), so that during 1973 the net gain in dwellings was one of the lowest since the early fifties.

Changes in the housing stock depend on the relationship between house building, house improvement and conversion programmes on the one hand and slum clearance and obsolescence on the other. New construction and demolition are the most important factors.

Despite the considerable programmes of slum clearance and house building over recent years, and the average increase in the British housing stock of about 2 per cent per annum, much sub-standard housing still remains. The House Condition Survey for 1971 (Housing and Construction Statistics, 1973) indicated that 1¼ million dwellings in England and Wales were statutorily unfit. This represented 7.3 per cent of the entire housing stock.

Viewed in the long-term, the growth of the housing stock has roughly kept pace with the growth of population over the last century (Department of the Environment, 1971). However, changes in demography and life-cycle patterns have altered the number and composition of households. More marriages and earlier marriage have led people to form their own households at a younger age; increased longevity has meant an increase in the proportion of old people living in single-person households. The limited available data suggest that these factors, rather than a marked decrease in the extended family, accounted for the increase in households between 1861 and 1961 (Hole and Pountney, 1971). As a result of these trends, average household size had become smaller over the period 1911–1961.

There have been steady increases in the numbers of dwellings over the century although there are some signs of a recent decline in rates of growth. The extent and duration of this trend will have critical implications for future patterns of housing disadvantage. This is particularly true as 1 in 14 dwellings are currently statutorily unfit and as further increases in the numbers of households are forecast over the next decade (Holmans, 1970).

Housing Standards

Housing standards are assessed on a number of criteria such as structural soundness, availability of basic facilities and degree of crowding. Some official and recommended standards are outlined in the 1957 and 1969 Housing Acts, and in the Parker Morris (1961) and Denington (1966) reports.

The structural status of a dwelling depends on state of repair, stability, dampness, lighting, ventilation, water supply, drainage and sanitation. Many houses are substandard in basic cooking facilities and toilet amenities. The 1971 Survey found that 12 per cent of dwellings had no private W.C., 10 per cent had no fixed bath in a separate room, and 12 per cent lacked a wash basin. In all, one sixth of dwellings lacked at least one of the basic facilities. This represented about four-fifths of unfit houses and over one-eighth of those not unfit.

Over the years there has been a continuous trend towards higher standards. Improvements were noticeable even during the four years separating the 1967 and 1971 House Condition Surveys. For example, the total proportion of dwellings lacking an internal W.C. dropped from about 19 per cent to 12 per cent over this period and the proportion lacking fixed bath from approximately 13 per cent to 8 per cent. Census data indicate that steady improvements had been made prior to 1967 in the provision of most basic household facilities.

Various assessments of overcrowding have been made but in recent years most have used a simple ratio of persons per room. A measure of 1½ persons per room is generally taken to indicate overcrowding, although, as the Milner–Holland report (1965) indicated, this falls far short of what is generally regarded as acceptable. Thus, a family of two parents and four children living in a 'two up, two down' house would *not* be overcrowded.

Marked decreases in the numbers of households with high person to room densities have occured over the last half century (Hole and Pountney, 1971). In 1911 about one-third of households had more than one person per room and about half this number had more than

1½ persons per room. By 1961 the comparative proportions had dropped to 11 per cent and 3 per cent.

However, to a considerable extent, these figures give a misleading impression of the number of individuals who suffer from overcrowding at some time in their life. Childless couples and people living alone less often live in overcrowded conditions, whereas young children are particularly likely to do so. The National Child Development Study (Davie *et al.*, 1972; Wedge and Prosser, 1973) showed that one in seven children age 7 were living in a home with a density of more than 1½ persons per room, and one in six did so at either 7 or 11 years of age.

Housing conditions have improved very considerably since the beginning of this century, but it still remains true that many children are brought up in deplorably overcrowded circumstances. Furthermore, this proportion varies greatly by region — from 39 per cent in Scotland to 7 per cent in East Anglia (Davie *et al.*, 1972).

Patterns of Tenure

The housing market consists of two main sectors, the private (with either owner-occupied or rented occupation) and the public, in which the majority of dwellings are occupied by local authority tenants. Different types of housing tenure have unequal advantages and disadvantages. A higher proportion of private tenants than of owner-occupiers or council tenants live in unfit dwellings. The 1971 House Condition Survey (Housing and Construction Statistics, 1973) revealed that whereas 1 in 25 of owner-occupied and 1 in 80 of local authority housing units were unfit, almost one quarter of dwellings in other tenure groups were similarly substandard. The General Household Survey for 1972 showed that more than nine in ten owner-occupied or council homes had an inside W.C., compared with only about six in ten privately rented homes. Within the private rented sector, poor housing is particularly found in furnished accommodation. A 1970 tenants' survey (see Francis Committee Report, 1971) showed that furnished rented housing was less likely to be self-contained, more likely to have inferior amenities and more likely to be overcrowded than unfurnished housing. This was confirmed by the 1972 General Household Survey for Great Britain: 1 in 25 of owner-occupied dwellings, twice this proportion of local authority and private unfurnished tenancies, but four and a half times as many privately-rented furnished housing units were overcrowded.

Private tenants are more likely than council tenants or owner-occupiers to live in poor housing conditions; nevertheless the majority have satisfactory accommodation. Disadvantage in the private-rented sector is restricted to a minority and in some respects may be exaggerated by the statistics. For example, bedsit and single room accommodation, where shared facilities are the norm, is almost always privately rented. Also there may be discrepancies between objectively- and subjectively-defined disadvantage. Many persons, especially the elderly, who live in statutorily unfit properties which have been their homes for many years, possibly for a very low rent, may not view themselves as disadvantaged.

Traditionally, security of tenure has differed according to type of occupation. Owner-occupiers and council tenants have been in the most advantageous position and private tenants in the least. The main threat to the security of homeowners has been slum clearance programmes, although in such situations the local authority has been obliged to offer financial compensation and/or alternative accommodation. Council tenants are officially subject to four weeks' notice to quit; however, in practice, households are usually evicted only for reasons such as severe rent arrears. Again, if a household is moved as a result of redevelopment it is rehoused by the local authority. The situation of tenants in private property is less clear. Those renting unfurnished accommodation have had security of tenure for many years, and this guarantee was extended to tenants in furnished housing by the 1974 Housing Act. The latter group had previously suffered considerably through the continual threat of eviction (Francis Committee Report, 1971), through abuse by private landlords (Ministry of Housing and Local Government, 1965) and, as they had no right to rehousing, by the local authority if displaced through redevelopment. Now, in a legally more secure position, the situation of furnished tenants may be better. However, it remains to be seen to what extent benefits follow.

Housing costs also tend to differ between tenure categories. For example, in England and Wales (but excluding Greater London), the average weekly rent for local authority housing in 1972 was £2.87 and for privately rented unfurnished accommodation, £3.65 (Economic Trends, 1973). Costs in furnished privately-rented dwellings were not given but these are generally higher than for unfurnished housing (Francis Report, 1971). These can be contrasted with the net monthly mortgage repayment on an average priced new house in 1972 which was £38.57 (Economic Trends, 1973). All these prices, however, are averages, and refer to comparative costs at one point in time. Both the national economic situation and government legislation will affect costs within and between housing tenure groups.

At the present time the most advantageous housing is generally provided by owner-occupation and local authority tenancies. It is noteworthy that in recent years there has been a marked increase in the proportion of the population in both these types of housing, and a corresponding decline in the numbers renting from private landlords. During the last century most people lived in privately-rented housing and by 1947 61 per cent of households were still doing so (Gray, 1949). By December 1973, however, only 17 per cent of households were in the private tenure group (Housing and Construction Statistics, 1974), whereas 52 per cent of households were owner-occupiers and 31 per cent were in council or new town corporation tenancies. In 1947 the comparable figures for the last two groups were 26 per cent and 13 per cent respectively (Gray, 1949).

Changing tenure distribution reflects household formation, movement and loss. New households are formed when children leave home and set up house either alone or with friends, when married couples first move into their own home and when larger households dissolve into smaller units. It is likely that the composition of a new household will influence the tenancy obtained. Thus, young single persons are less likely than married couples to become owner-occupiers or council tenants. Overall, a survey of households studied in 1960–62 showed that two-fifths of new householders bought their own homes, three-tenths became tenants in private unfurnished accommodation and approximately equal proportions of the remainder obtained council tenancies or private unfurnished housing (Cullingworth, 1965). Holmans (1970) estimated the tenure distributions of new households formed by married persons in 1967. He suggested that equal proportions (about 46%) had become owner-occupiers and tenants of private landlords and only very few had entered public housing.

Once formed, considerable numbers of households move between tenure categories. Cullingworth (1965) reported that each year about 7 per cent of a sample of households changed tenure group. Both these findings and also estimates by Holmans (1970) suggested that movement was generally to a more advantageous situation. Private tenants in furnished private accommodation tended to move to unfurnished property and tenants in unfurnished private housing were most likely to become council tenants or owner-occupiers. There was some shift between council housing and owner-occupation, particularly from the former to the latter, but this was comparatively small.

Households are lost when smaller households amalgamate, such as when single persons marry or when old persons join friends or relatives, and when people die. There is very little evidence as to which types of tenure lose the most households in this way. Donnison (1967) estimated that, between 1960 and 1962, households dissolved at an annual rate of just over 1 per cent. Of these almost three-quarters were presumed to have been private tenants. However, there are no available data to confirm these figures.

Future trends in household formation, movement and loss depend to a large extent on government policies of development, redevelopment and finance and also upon changing demands. Holmans (1970) made projective estimates of tenure distributions for 1976 and 1981. His forecasts indicated an overall decrease in movement between tenure groups; less mobility of tenants in privately rented accommodation to either owner-occupation or local authority tenancies, but slight increases in the movement between owner-occupied and council housing. Of the new households formed by married couples, continuing increases in the proportions of owner-occupiers and council tenants and a continuing decrease in private tenants were predicted.

Changing patterns of tenure reflect the changing distribution of the housing stock between public and private sectors. In keeping with previous trends in England and Wales during 1972, there were *net* increases of 269,000 dwellings in the owner-occupied and 27,000 in council rented categories together with a loss of 93,000 dwellings from the private rented sector (Housing and Construction Statistics, 1973).

Since the early 1950s there has been a fairly steady increase in new buildings for private owners, but a more fluctuating pattern of development in the public sector. In very recent years, however, there has been an overall decline in the number of houses completed, especially in local authority housing. During 1972 there was a substantial difference in the building rates of the two main sectors: over 90,000 houses and flats were completed in England and Wales for local authorities but about twice this number for the private market (Housing and Construction Statistics, 1973). Slum clearance rates are also relevant, although there are no published statistics by housing sector. Rates not only have direct consequences for the housing stock but they also influence the movement of households between tenure types. Holmans (1970) outlined how the larger the clearance programme the greater the subsequent demand for local authority housing. This followed because large supplies of privately-owned property would be likely to be demolished.

Net increases in owner-occupied and local authority rented dwellings are also affected by the transfer of housing between council and non-council ownership. Recently there has been a marked increase in the sale of local authority properties. Over the two-year period between 1971 and 1973 the stock of rentable council housing decreased in this way by almost one hundred thousand dwellings (Housing and Construction Statistics, 1974).

Relationships between finance variables (such as house prices, mortgage rates, levels of rents, earnings and capital) influence housing patterns. For example Amos (1974) showed how the man with average earnings became far less able to buy a house between 1971 and 1973. This happened because average earnings in 1971 were able to secure a mortgage for a much higher proportion of the average house price than they could in 1973. For these reasons Amos predicted that households would turn increasingly from home ownership to local authority tenancies. At the same time, however, there are policies which may encourage movement in the opposite direction. For example the Housing Finance Act of 1972 has allowed higher rents in council houses, although means tested rebates are available. This move could result in more families coming to view owner-occupation as preferable to renting from the council. Other ways in which income levels and finance policies affect housing are considered in later sections.

Homelessness

Officially, homelessness refers to those who apply for, or who are admitted to, temporary accommodation provided by local authorities under the 1948 National Assistance Act. Other definitions stress that anyone living in a situation where a normal home life is impossible is, in effect, homeless (Shelter, 1969). Thus, families in decaying and poorly equipped properties, those in multi-occupation and those who have had to separate would fall into this category.

Prevalence rates of homelessness will depend upon the definition used. Official statistics (Social Trends, 1973) recorded that 25,854 persons and 5,448 families were in temporary accommodation for the homeless throughout England and Wales in March 1972. During 1972, over 16,000 families applied for temporary accommodation and nearly 4,000 had been admitted. These figures do not include all those with severe housing difficulties. Shelter (1969) estimated that the 'real' prevalence of homelessness according to criteria such as those listed above would be nearer three million persons.

The number of the officially homeless is increasing. This does not necessarily imply a deteriorating situation as the number of families admitted to temporary accommodation will depend upon local authority provision. The more provided for, the fewer will be the persons and families left without aid. In 1966 there were 13,000 persons and 2,500 families recorded as officially homeless, but about twice this number by 1972. It is likely that increases will continue following 1974 legislation which makes local authorities responsible for the provision of temporary accommodation for all homeless persons, and not only those made homeless by the actions of councils. People living in unsatisfactory conditions are more likely to apply for assistance when the chances of provision are high, and households are more likely to turn out members if it then becomes encumbent on the local authorities to provide alternative accommodation.

Many of the comprehensive surveys of the homeless have focussed upon the London area where official homelessness is most prevalent (e.g. LCC, 1962; Greve, 1964; Greve *et al.*, 1971). Rates of homelessness in the inner London boroughs, in September 1968, were almost twice the rates in Greater London as a whole and over eleven times those in the rest of England and Wales (Greve *et al.*, 1971). Gross regional differences in homelessness suggest that factors are area-specific. Some evidence for this comes from a comparison of Greve *et al.*'s (1971) findings for the London area with Glastonbury's (1971) for South Wales and the West of England.

As in the earlier London studies (LCC, 1962; Greve, 1964), Greve *et al.* (1971) found that the chief cause of homelessness was the very severe housing shortage. Families evicted from furnished tenancies by private landlords were at particular risk, as were those living with relations, those with low incomes and those with small children. Personal shortcomings were not the major factor in the majority of cases. Greve *et al.* (1971) suggested that 'socially inadequate' families were only a small minority of the total, although some such families were kept moving in the 'welfare cycle': 'When rehoused from temporary accommodation they fail to meet required standards to such an extent that they are eventually evicted and returned once more to homeless family accommodation.'

Glastonbury (1971) found different patterns of homelessness in

South Wales and the West of England. On the surface, housing problems, such as rent arrears, illegal tenancies, overcrowding and poor conditions seemed to be the most frequent precipitating causes of homelessness. But further examination suggested that the underlying causes involved behavioural and relationship problems within families. The homeless frequently displayed elements of personal inadequacy and incompetence which were independent of the prevailing housing situation. These families probably correspond to the small core of 'socially inadequate' families found by the Greve *et al.* (1971) survey. In regions not suffering from severe housing problems they constituted a much larger and more noticeable proportion of the total homeless.

Glastonbury (1971) discussed the history of provision for the homeless. The turning point came with the 1948 National Assistance Act when local authorities were first made officially responsible for providing temporary accommodation for those in need. The shelter initially provided was often in old workhouses or wartime structures and conditions were frequently poor. Substandard housing and family separations were common. Today's provision is better and authorities are responsible for *all* homeless persons. But husbands and wives may still be separated (Shelter, 1972), particularly in some of the accommodation provided by voluntary bodies, and children are still taken into care because of homelessness (DHSS, 1972). Some of the possible consequences of these aspects of homelessness are discussed in a later section.

There is great regional variation in the length of time that families remain in temporary accommodation. Data on the duration of homelessness of persons discharged from temporary accommodation in 1972 showed how periods of stay were longer in Greater London than in the rest of England and Wales (Social Trends, 1973). In Greater London half of the families discharged had been in residence for more than 6 months and a quarter for more than 18 months. For the rest of the country half left after more than 1 month and a quarter after at least 6 months. In Greater London over 80 per cent of people leaving temporary accommodation became council tenants. Within the rest of England and Wales, however, only 40 per cent did so. The homeless in London were disadvantaged relative to those in the rest of the country in that they remained in temporary accommodation for longer but were better off in so far as they were more likely to gain council housing upon discharge.

Minns (1972) studied a group of homeless families in one London borough, and concluded that things did not go well after discharge. Personal problems, the structure of local authority priorities and the inadequate organization of follow-up support meant that many families fulfilled gloomy expectations. Many continued to be in arrears with rent and several were evicted from their new housing.

Regional Variations

The ratio of dwellings to population is remarkably similar in all ten standard regions in Britain. Within each, including Wales and Scotland, there was an average of just over one-third of a dwelling per person in 1971 (Housing and Construction Statistics, 1974; 1971 Census Housing Tables, 1974). In each case the proportion of houses to persons had risen very slightly since 1966. These figures, however, do not take account of empty houses and second homes within a region, nor do they reflect disparities within regions.

Despite similarities in regional housing supplies, there are some differences in housing standards. In 1971 (Census Housing Tables, 1974) 6.4 per cent of households in England and Wales had no hot water supply, 8.7 per cent had no fixed bath or shower, 10.9 per cent had only an outside flush toilet and 1.1 per cent had no flush toilet at all. Overall, Wales had the lowest rate of adequate housing. 78 per cent of households had exclusive use of hot water, a fixed bath and an inside W.C., whereas the average for England and Wales was 82 per cent and the highest rate (in the South West) was 86 per cent. If these figures are compared with the situation five years earlier (1966 Census data) it is found that the proportion of the population with these basic amenities increased by about 10 per cent over the period. The improved standards have been to the advantage of all regions.

Even though dwellings per person do not differ regionally, rooms per person do. This implies great variability in either the size or the use of dwellings between regions. The 1971 Census data showed that almost 1 in 25 persons in England and Wales was living in households with more than 1½ persons per room, and a further 1 in 10 had between 1 and 1½ persons per room. The most overcrowding was in Scotland where one-third of persons were in households with over 1 person per room. The North and the West Midlands had the next highest rates, but the proportion was less than half that in Scotland. East Anglia was the least overcrowded, and well below the national average.

Patterns of tenure also show regional variation. It was estimated that, in December 1972, half the dwellings in Britain were owner-occupied and almost a third were in local authority or new town tenancies (Social Trends, 1973). The largest proportions of owner-occupiers were in the South East (excluding Greater London) and the South West where almost 60 per cent of households owned their own homes; the smallest were in Scotland and the North where only 31 per cent and 43 per cent did so. In general, low proportions of owner-occupiers meant large numbers of council tenants and vice versa. The situation was somewhat unusual in Greater London where there was a much higher than average stock of privately-rented properties —almost a quarter of all dwellings.

House purchase and rental costs vary markedly by region. Thus, in 1972 average house prices varied from £4,826 in Yorkshire and Humberside to £11,113 in Greater London (Social Trends, 1973). Moreover, these prices represented unequal percentage increases on 1971 prices. The lowest inflation rate of 15 per cent was found in Scotland and the highest of 42 per cent in East Anglia. In 1972 rent charges were also higher in Greater London than in the rest of England

and Wales but lowest in Scotland. Weekly rents for local authority housing were £4.01, £2.87 and £1.84 respectively and for privately rented unfurnished accommodation £6.63, £3.65 and £1.85.

In summary, there are many respects in which housing conditions vary by region. However, two important qualifications should be made. Firstly, it is not always the same regions which receive all the advantages or disadvantages. For example the housing standards in the Northern regions are lower than some of the Southern regions, but so are costs. Secondly, overall assessment can obscure local patterns. Thus the South East region includes some of the best and some of the poorest housing in the country. Much smaller-scale regional analyses are necessary to get a true picture of the geographical distribution of housing deprivation. Nevertheless, if severe overcrowding, lack of basic amenities and male unemployment are taken as indicators of poor life circumstances, disadvantage is clearly heavily concentrated in Scotland, and especially in Clydeside (Department of the Environment, 1975).

POLICY INFLUENCES UPON HOUSING PROVISION

Housing Finance

Government housing finance policies play a critical role in the supply and distribution of different types of housing. Housing finance programmes have had a large hand in the growth of owner occupation, the increase of local authority provision and the decline of the private landlord.

The redistribution of housing within the private sector reflects the ways in which taxation systems have increasingly favoured the house owner as occupier but disfavoured him as landlord. In effect the latter is becoming priced out of the housing market. Unless he owns his property outright he is likely to be borrowing capital at high rates of interest. This is not an economic proposition (Nevitt, 1966). To cover his costs the landlord must gain a rent sufficient to cover his interest payments, a return on his capital investment and an allowance for overheads such as rates and repairs. Any profit obtained once these items have been allowed for is subject to unearned income tax. Thus, unless the landlord can ask, and obtain, high rents it is not to his advantage to remain in the housing market. In a free market situation he might be able to do this, particularly if supply of housing is low relative to demand. However, during the years since rent controls were introduced, the landlord's position has been unfavourable. Many tenants in unfurnished accommodation remained for long periods paying very low fixed rents. The 1972 Housing Finance Act gave landlords the opportunity to raise these levels as 'fair rent' schemes were introduced. Nevertheless, many other landlords have not profited from this legislation and are forced to accept less than economic rents from tenants granted security of tenure. Contrary to the practices in most countries, whereby rent controls are complemented by government subsidies to landlords, in Britain the person renting property must foot his own losses (Donnison, 1967).

Other aspects of policy have further weakened the private landlord's position. The security of tenure granted to all tenants has meant that he has little control over his property, once occupied. He cannot put the housing to alternative use and if he wishes to sell, its value is likely to be drastically reduced. If, on the other hand, he has vacant possession of his property and can sell it for an increased price he will, unlike the owner-occupier, be subject to taxation on any capital gains that have been made. There is little financial incentive to keep the private landlord in business.

For those who have the choice, buying a house can be a considerably more attractive proposition than renting one from a private landlord. Not only does the house purchaser gain a disposable asset, but he is treated more favourably than the tenant by the taxman. The income tax concession on mortgage interest repayments gives the owner-occupier a 'hidden subsidy'. Nevitt (1966) calculated the comparative tax payments of families with the same earned income renting and buying their homes in 1963—64. At income levels of £800, £1,000 and £1,250 effective subsidies of over £10, £23 and £30 per annum were gained by owner-occupiers over tenants.

Public sector housing is subsidized more directly than the private sector out of central government funds and local rates. Prior to the 1972 Housing Finance Act there had been little uniformity in the policies of finance by local authorities (Parker, 1967). Rents were often influenced by current interest rates and by the age and structure of the local housing stock. The 1972 Act attempted to rationalize administration and to reduce the disparity in rents between areas. The more recent Housing Rents and Subsidies legislation, however, returns much of the incentive for pricing decisions to the local authorities: it is not yet clear what will be the impact of this move.

Housing finance policies can mean unequal subsidies and advantages for households in different types of occupancy. Currently, the owner-occupier obtains the greatest advantages and, in general (see below) those with the largest incomes gain the greatest benefits. This contrasts with the position of tenants in private or local authority housing, where rent allowances and rebates are granted only to households with the lowest incomes. The owner-occupier is also favoured administratively. His income tax allowances are automatic, provided details of mortgage interest repayments are given on his income tax form. For the tenant, however, rebates or allowances depend on knowledge of availability, and a successful application.

The finance system as a whole is complicated: whereas it is relatively easy to give a qualitative account of the benefits associated with different forms of tenure it is difficult to quantify the differences. The whole issue of finance, including who benefits most from policies, is currently being examined by the Department of Environment.

Local Authority Housing Policies
Council houses in Britain are now more numerous than ever. For persons and families with low per capita income who cannot afford to become owner-occupiers, and who otherwise face the prospect of obtaining poor value for money in the fast shrinking privately-rented housing market, they represent an important alternative. Nevertheless council accommodation is not available for all those with the greatest housing problems.

Prior to the 1949 Housing Act council housing was available only to the 'working classes'. Following this date, however, entry has not been restricted to particular occupation and income groups. Since the 1935 Housing Act, and indeed since the beginning of the century, local authorities have given priority to those in insanitary and overcrowded houses, to those with large families and to those living under unsatisfactory housing conditions. Persons displaced through slum clearance have been included in these categories. Points schemes based on these criteria are in operation. The Cullingworth Report (Ministry of Housing and Local Government, 1969) outlined the main problems arising from such organization and allocation policies. It criticized the strong emphasis placed by local authorities upon 'housing lists' as indicators of housing need and the consequent disadvantage to the uninformed, the geographically mobile and recent immigrants to the country.

Economic circumstances and family characteristics influence housing needs. The Cullingworth Report recognized the special requirements of large families, the elderly, the single, students, the homeless and black people. Groups such as fatherless families, families with a mentally ill parent and 'problem families' were in particular need of help. Nevertheless there is a growing body of evidence to suggest discrimination against some of these groups by some local authorities (Burney, 1967; DHSS, 1974; Runnymede Trust, 1975).

Councils are now obliged to provide the homeless with accommodation. In the past they have sometimes been given a special priority over and above families who have waited in the housing queue for long periods (SHAC Annual Report, 1973) although they have not always received favoured treatment. Minns (1972) concluded that local authority political and professional interests have meant that homelessness was afforded a low priority. This in turn had led to a low availability of temporary accommodation, strict entry criteria and a high control over persons rehoused. Families with histories of rent arrears, or otherwise seen as 'problem families', were housed away from others. They were often offered poor quality accommodation at rents higher than they could afford. In such ways families fulfilled people's expectations of them and continued to default in rent and behaviour.

Planning Policies
Land use policies provide another example of ways in which housing availability can be restricted by administrative decisions (Hall *et al.*, 1973). For example, green belt legislation can create scarcities of land for housing and thus raise costs of dwellings. In this way poorer families can be priced out of the housing market. Similarly, industrial location within areas with existing housing shortages can exacerbate the problem (Amos, 1974). The lower income groups suffer from reduced bargaining power in comparison with migrant workers in the new industries.

Harvey (1973) discussed how changes in the spatial form of a city can lead to a redistribution of income and hence other advantages. It is the geographical relationship between housing and employment that is critical. If the poor reside in the city centres, but many jobs are located in the suburbs, the opportunities for low skilled workers are vastly reduced, because of the costs of travel to the city outskirts. If the numbers of jobs in the city centres are very low, unemployment among the poor and unskilled can become a large-scale problem. In these ways planning policies can create and perpetuate cycles of disadvantage.

PERSONAL FACTORS INFLUENCING ACCESS TO HOUSING

Income Level
Housing is a major item of expenditure for the vast majority of persons and families. Gross housing costs may be regarded as 'high' if they exceed 30 per cent of total income, but 'low' if they account for 15 per cent or less (Nevitt, 1966). What is a reasonable proportion will vary according to such factors as life-cycle stage, the extent to which a transaction is long-term, the importance of a specific house or location and, most importantly, income level. The Family Expenditure Survey Data for 1973 showed that as income rises so the proportion spent on housing decreases. This is largely because there is greater variability between personal incomes within the normal range than between mortgage repayments and rents. For example, households with an average weekly income of less than £15 spent about 22 per cent of this on housing whereas when average weekly income was between £60 and £100 only 12 per cent was utilized in this way.

As a group, households with lowest incomes allocate the highest proportion of their resources to housing but still pay, in absolute terms, the least. They are also less likely to have any capital or savings to meet additional or unexpected expenses. In this way the poorest are virtually excluded from owner-occupation. Only in rare cases do they own their own houses outright (e.g. if inherited or if bought at an earlier stage in the life-cycle when relative income level was higher). Moreover, income is important not only to buy a house, but to keep it in adequate repair. Older houses may deteriorate badly if necessary improvements are not carried out (Donnison, 1967) and so reduce their asset value.

The greater the income and wealth the easier it is to own a house. Property purchase usually requires some capital deposit although a few 100 per cent mortgages are available. These will enable some low income households without savings to become owner-occupiers but they tend not to benefit those with either very low or very variable incomes. Mortgages are seldom awarded for more than three times the annual salary or wage level of the potential house buyer. This may not be sufficient for an adequate house if income is very low. The mortgagee must also be able to guarantee regular interest repayments; thus anybody with a fluctuating income probably would not be a successful applicant for a full mortgage. The best opportunities for low income households to buy their own homes may arise for tenants of local authorities willing to sell properties. House buyers in these circumstances usually get good value for their money and frequently obtain favourable mortgage arrangements.

Whatever the possibilities of house purchase at lower income levels, greater advantages undoubtedly accrue to those with greater assets. Firstly, the higher the income the greater the chances of gaining a mortgage from a building society or insurance company — because of the larger deposit that can be paid and the greater securities against which a loan may be made. The uneven distribution of house ownership by income level was shown by Nevitt (1966). The percentage of individuals borrowing money from either building societies or insurance companies in 1959–60 increased steadily with income level. For example whereas 1 in 20 of those with incomes between £200 and £250 and 1 in 4 with incomes between £600 and £700 held loans, almost all persons with £10,000 or more did so. Moreover, in general, the larger the income the larger the amount borrowed from the building societies and insurance companies, at least for income levels above about £700. On average, almost fifteen times as much capital was borrowed by a person with an income of at least £10,000 as by someone with £200–£250 income. The implication is that the more money people have, the greater likelihood they have of getting a loan, the more they can borrow, and the better housing they can obtain.

A higher income also provides greater security against the effects of increased interest rates. This reduces the chances of becoming priced out of the housing market. The recent trend for mortgage interest repayments to rise more rapidly than average earnings means that fewer and fewer people can compete for owner-occupation (Amos, 1974).

Persons with the lowest incomes are frequently tenants in furnished housing. The tenants' survey for the Francis Committee in 1970 (Francis Report, 1971) indicated that the cheapest accommodation available to poor persons and families was in furnished rooms in rundown areas. In most other situations, however, rents were higher for furnished than unfurnished housing. A typical rent for a furnished tenancy in the Greater London conurbation as a whole and in the stress areas was about 33 per cent and 24 per cent of the relatively low take-home pay of tenants. This compared with proportions of 19 per cent and 17 per cent for tenants in unfurnished housing.

Recent legislation has had an effect on housing prices. Prior to 'fair rents' many rents in unfurnished housing were kept artificially low by rent control so that many persons were paying a nominal sum for housing contracted many years earlier. In these cases rents will have been increased. But in others, where housing is in very poor condition, rents may have been reduced. Changes depend on the levels of 'fair rents' and the criteria used to assess them. The simultaneous introduction of rent allowances on a means-tested basis implies that, theoretically, rents paid will depend upon income level. However, as there is not full take-up of rent allowances (Lister, 1974), it becomes impossible to estimate the relationship between net rent paid and quality of housing obtained.

Whatever the law, persons with higher incomes fare better than those with lower incomes in privately-rented housing. Even rent allowances do not eliminate the stronger bargaining power of the better-off. This is especially true as allowances may not be granted to lower income groups if the housing selected is considered too large or too expensive, and as gross rental costs must be borne by tenants until claims for allowances are both accepted and paid. The Francis Report tenants' survey indicated the existence of a group of furnished tenants with considerable incomes who selected their occupancy for reasons of mobility and independence. In this housing sector, as in others, the richest lead the field. A filtering process operates whereby as the most advantaged move into newer and better houses, those lower in the income hierarchy move up a place.

Income level is a less important determinant of housing availability within the public sector. Regulations regarding eligibility are more critical. Nevertheless, there has been enormous variation between local authorities in the rents charged (Parker, 1967) and this will probably continue as councils determine the 'fair rents' in their own localities. There has always been a conflict as to whether levels should be set according to the costs borne by the council or whether they should be geared towards the amounts that tenants can afford. Both considerations were taken into account under the 1972 Housing Finance Act. Local authorities no longer provide subsidized housing for families with middle income levels but continue to provide cheap accommodation for those most in need.

Age and Family Circumstances

Donnison (1967) outlined the five 'housing stages' typically passed through during the life cycle. The first stage covers childhood spent in the parental home and the second is the period of living alone, with friends or with a spouse before children are born. The third stage begins with parenthood and extends to the fourth, in middle age, when children begin to leave home and household size decreases. The final stage is in old age.

It is often not possible to distinguish between young and old single householders from census and survey data. Overall, this group live under the least crowded conditions but they are most likely to share or to be without facilities. This is shown clearly by the 1971 Census data. Four in five of these households (as compared with an average of 1 in 3 for the country as a whole) had at least three rooms for their personal use. But, on the other hand, only 2 in 3, relative to an overall figure of 4 in 5, had exclusive use of hot water, a fixed bath and an inside W.C.

The majority of households are families and family size, paternal presence and occupation are all related to housing indices (Ministry of Social Security, 1967). The report indicated that only 18 per cent of families with a father in full-time work ('standard' families) lived in defective housing compared with 40 per cent with a sick or unemployed father and 32 per cent of the fatherless. For 'standard' families, family size was related to differential standards of housing structure only when the number of children exceeded five. Availability of basic household amenities was not particularly associated with type or size of family. Overcrowding was associated with both paternal status and family size. One in ten families with a fully-employed father, but three in ten of the other groups, were overcrowded. Within the group of 'standard' families only 8 per cent with two or three children were overcrowded whereas one-third with four or more were. Among families with a sick or unemployed father 18 per cent of families with less than four children were overcrowded as compared with half of those with more children. The 1971 Census also showed that household size (which is not quite synonymous with family size) was associated with overcrowding but not with the availability of basic amenities. The vast majority of households with 7 or more members had less than one room per person. However, even when there were 10 or more members, 80 per cent of households had exclusive use of basic facilities.

The relatively satisfactory situation of large families in terms of household facilities reflects the large proportion in public sector housing. The 1971 Census data showed that less than a quarter of single-person households, but over half of households with 8 or more persons, were in council housing. The over-representation of large families as council tenants and slight under-representation as owner-occupiers was also shown by the Ministry of Social Security (1967) study of families with at least two children. Whereas over half of two parent 'standard' families with only two children owned their homes and a further quarter were council tenants, the proportions were approximately reversed in families with six or more children. Overall, almost 60 per cent of families with a sick or unemployed father were council tenants and only 20 per cent were owner-occupiers.

One-parent families are a group deprived in many ways and housing is no exception. The Finer Committee Report (DHSS, 1974) using a wide variety of data sources, concluded that the biggest contrast between one and two parent families was in the proportion living in shared households. Hunt *et al.* (1973) had found that whereas very few two-parent families shared a home, about a quarter of the fatherless did so. Family Expenditure Survey data and DHSS supplementary benefit statistics showed much the same pattern. Within the group of single parent families unmarried mothers were most likely, and widows least likely, to be sharing their accommodation.

Hunt *et al.* (1973) found that single-parent families lived under worse conditions than others and that they had relatively high housing costs. This was largely because they were over-represented within the most disadvantaged tenure groups. The fatherless in particular were unlikely to be owner occupiers. Evidence from the National Child Development Study to the Finer Committee showed that 25 per cent of fatherless and 50 per cent of two parent families owned their own home. Within the private rented sector fatherless families were particularly likely to be in a furnished dwelling. The 1970 tenants' survey of Greater London for the Francis Committee (1971) found that fatherless families constituted 12 per cent of all families with children living in furnished and 8 per cent of those in unfurnished accommodation, but in stress areas the proportions rose to 31 per cent and 11 per cent respectively.

Family variables associated with homelessness are shown by two complementary studies of Greater London (Greve *et al.*, 1971) and of South Wales and the West of England (Glastonbury, 1971). The majority of persons admitted to housing for the homeless are parents and children and many are families without a father. Single or married adults without children under 16 years are rarely admitted. Greve *et al.* (1971) reported that 41 per cent of families admitted to London temporary accommodation between 1966 and 1969 were headed by lone mothers and Glastonbury (1971) indicated a figure of 30 per cent for South Wales and the West of England. Homeless families tended to be young. About half of the mothers in the study by Greve *et al.* (1971) and almost two-thirds in Glastonbury's (1971) sample were aged 30 years or less. More than three-quarters of all the families in temporary accommodation in Greater London between 1966 and 1969 had pre-school children and over half of the children entered before 5 years (Greve *et al.*, 1971). A similar picture for South Wales and the West of England was shown by Glastonbury (1971): half the children in temporary accommodation were pre-schoolers and one-fifth were less than two years old.

The relationship between family size and homelessness is also important. In the London survey (Greve *et al.*, 1971), large families were over-represented in temporary accommodation in 1966–9 although they had not been to such a degree ten years previously. Twenty-five per cent of homeless families had four or more children as compared with the 1966 sample Census figure of 8 per cent for Greater

London. This difference was attributed to the increasing numbers of Commonwealth families becoming homeless. However, this could not have been the explanation for the large size of homeless families in the west country (Glastonbury, 1971). The average number of children per family in this sample was 2.8 and, of all the families with children, 38.6 per cent had at least four children.

CYCLES OF HOUSING DISADVANTAGE

The Extent of Intergenerational Similarities

Marked increases in the housing stock and improvements in housing conditions over the last generations imply that although 'disadvantage' still exists, it does not mean the same now as it did even half a century ago. To what extent housing disadvantage involves the same families in each generation is largely unknown although there is some suggestion of continuities in some small segments of the population. For example, accounts of stable communities nurturing successive generations (Young and Willmott, 1957; Vereker *et al.*, 1961) indicate group continuities. Also the apparent continuities in family wealth (see page 26) have implications for transmitted cycles of advantage. But even in these cases there are intervening considerations. Policy changes (for example in housing development, improvement, allocation or in taxation) can alter the situation. Redevelopment or natural deterioration may mean that even when parents and children live in the same area, they may do so under contrasting conditions. Changing economic policies can also mean that generations differ in their resources.

Evidence suggests that income level and family circumstances are the most important personal features influencing housing conditions and that area of residence is a further crucial variable. Family continuities in these respects are most likely to perpetuate relative disadvantage in housing.

Shared households will sometimes involve continuities between generations. Married children may live in the parental home, as may the aged grandparent. The extended family household occasionally includes four generations but more frequently it involves two or three. Larger households will usually mean more crowding, less privacy and greater sharing of facilities within the family, but the general standards of living will depend on the ratio of earners to dependents within a dwelling.

Throughout this chapter, occupancy patterns have been stressed as good indicators of housing standards, security and value. With the rapidly rising proportions of owner-occupied dwellings in the housing market, it is likely that many children of house owners will also become house owners in their turn. This tendency will be increased if a house is transferred directly from one generation to the next. Owner-occupation is a means of saving which can be passed to the next generation. Alternatively, house owners may borrow capital on the security of their own dwelling to raise the deposit on a home for their children. For council and private tenants housing is not an asset which can be passed from parents to children or used to realize capital. Nevertheless, there may well be a tendency for children in these types of occupancy to follow the housing pattern of their parents. In particular, the children of council tenants may be more likely than others to put their names on the housing list and, if their parents before them have been reliable tenants, they may have a good chance of being awarded a house. Their chances may be higher if their continued residence in the parental home would lead to overcrowding. Similarly, there could be a family pattern of private renting, particularly in the less mobile and more cohesive neighbourhoods.

However, these are theoretical considerations and very little is known about the actual similarities or differences in the housing histories of successive family generations. The total housing context is critical, but so are experiences, traditions and expectations on the one hand and comparability in real earnings and family composition on the other.

Breaking Cycles

Cycles of housing disadvantage exist, even if they are not transmitted by the family. Slum clearance and policies of finance are two important ways in which attempts have been made to break such cycles. Large-scale redevelopment programmes have been launched to improve deteriorating areas. However, these may have repercussions upon social interaction and behaviour, particularly in previously stable and close-knit communities. Hartman (1963) showed the relation between satisfaction with housing and identification with an area. Of residents in an American neighbourhood who liked the area very much, 98 per cent with 'good' housing and 86 per cent with 'poor' housing were pleased with their apartments. But, as feelings towards the area became more negative, respondents were correspondingly less satisfied with their own accommodation. Other investigators have shown how ties to a residential area can influence the satisfaction that people feel for their housing, whatever its condition. Vereker *et al.* (1961) reported that in Liverpool 62 per cent of the occupants of blocks of flats, considered by others to be the least desirable local accommodation, did not want to move. Also, a report on life in a decaying area of Oldham (Ministry of Housing and Local Government, 1963) noted that slum dwellers often said that they did not mind leaving their home but did not want to quit the district.

Under any conditions, but particularly where housing and area satisfaction go hand in hand, uprooting may be disruptive. Fried (1963) claimed that the response could be severe long-term grief. He interviewed subjects rehoused from slum areas two years previously. Of the 250 women questioned, 26 per cent were still sad following their move and 20 per cent had suffered from grief for up to two years.

Thirty-eight per cent of the men had shown long-term grief reactions related to feelings of loss concerning both the original area of residence and old neighbours and friends. These findings are extreme and in the absence of controls the link with moving house is tenuous, particularly as depression in women is common (Richman, 1974b; Brown *et al.*, 1975; Rutter, 1976). The more common pattern following a move is adaptation to the new environment, after an initial period of dislocation. Broady (1968) quoted a study which found that although 54 per cent of residents in a new estate had been reluctant to move there, only 17 per cent wished to return to their old area a few years later. Wilner *et al.* (1962) reported some improvement in adjustment and mental health over a three-year period by mothers who had been rehoused from an American slum area, although the change was not as dramatic as had been anticipated.

Rehousing frequently means the break up of neighbourhood friendships and altered patterns of social interaction. Jennings (1962) described how other factors also contributed to the isolation of housewives on a new housing estate. High rents meant that husbands worked longer hours and so were out of the house more. Ties between family members were often weakened as many two-generation family households were split as a result of rehousing. However, the precise impact of mobility will depend upon the housing situation left and the new conditions gained. Social interaction patterns in a new housing area will be influenced by physical design and layout characteristics (see pp. 76—78) and by the social composition of the district. Rehousing policies may have an effect. Sometimes allocation of persons to dwellings is random but at other times attempts are made to move social groups en masse. A study of attitudes on five council estates in Hammersmith (1974) concluded that friendships within estates are encouraged when group rehousing takes place. This is also the impression that has been gained from a London experiment in preserving a community despite redevelopment (Campbell, 1974).

Some incidental, although important, side-effects of rehousing have been discussed. These should be taken into account in formulating redevelopment programmes, although changes in patterns of housing must inevitably effect some degree of change in life style. Holman (1970) indicated how poor housing areas frequently suffer from multiple disadvantages. New housing estates may mean better schools and services, and Glass (1948) demonstrated that a change in area could mean increased educational opportunities for children. Nevertheless, in a few cases the social problems may be due in part to personal inadequacies rather than environmental factors, so that improved conditions change the character of problems but do not necessarily remove them (Amos, 1974). It has been suggested that there is a small core of multiple-problem families living under substandard conditions whose prognosis would not improve greatly if rehoused. But this applies to only a minority of homeless families and the number of people who are poorly housed is largely determined by the quality of the existing housing stock. Greve *et al.* (1971) concluded that the majority of the homeless in Greater London did not have any special problems other than those due to poor housing. Follow-up studies of groups of rehoused families would be informative. Certainly people who have spent long years under slum conditions cannot be expected to alter standards and ways of life overnight and although in some cases rehoused slum dwellers may make slums of new housing estates this is not the usual pattern.

Government finance policies have also gone some way towards reducing cycles of disadvantage. Rent controls and systems of taxation have done much to change tenure patterns over the generations by encouraging the owner-occupier and discouraging the private landlord. The increased allocation of funds for council housing of an approved standard has been to the advantage of large numbers of persons and families.

At the same time policies have had negative effects. The private landlord has lacked financial incentives to improve the standards of his property (Nevitt, 1966). This has often meant poor conditions for some groups of private tenants. More recent legislation has not halted this process. Improvement grants are now given to house owners, with the highest rates offered in the General Improvement Areas, which coincide to some degree with areas of poor housing. The negative aspect of this policy concerns the practice of 'gentrification' by which low-income housing areas are transformed into middle-class districts. The poor are certain to lose out if the renovated houses are sold and are likely to do so if the improved houses are rented at a higher cost. The Notting Hill Peoples Association Housing Group (1972) illustrated how this process had occurred in Colville and Tavistock. They found that, since 1967, 40 per cent of all the privately rented houses in their survey area had become 'high rent' from 'low rent' accommodation. The average gross rent of converted houses had become £14.50, from £4.80 before conversion in 1967, and average gross rents in adapted houses had increased from £4.75 to £9.50. This inevitably meant that the poorest households had been priced out of the market.

There are two ways in which legislation may effectively discourage gentrification. The first is through the introduction of 'fair rents' for all rented dwellings and means-tested rent allowances for all tenants. It has not yet been shown what effects these policies have. However, discrimination by landlords, local authority decisions that accommodation is unsuitable, and the necessity for tenants to pay gross rent until a rent allowance is granted undoubtedly will keep the majority of the poor from benefitting from privately-owned redeveloped housing. The second is the proposed legislation to urge councils to declare 'special control areas' in which landlords wishing to sell property must first offer it for sale to the local council. It remains to be seen whether this will improve the housing opportunities of the poorer sections of such communities.

THE ROLE OF HOUSING IN CYCLES OF DISADVANTAGE

Housing conditions may not themselves be transmitted intergenerationally but they may yet have long-term effects upon health, attitudes and behaviour. A number of possibilities have been considered in the literature and this section will discuss observations and findings concerning the impact of housing fitness, homelessness and housing design.

Housing Fitness

Wilner *et al.* (1956) outlined some of the ways in which physical health could be affected by inadequate housing conditions. They attributed increased rates of infection and of minor digestive troubles to the multiple use of washing and toilet facilities, to problems of food storage, to overcrowded conditions and to poor heating and ventilation systems. Home accidents were made more likely by structural defects, overcrowding, poor electrical fittings and inadequate lighting.

While undoubtedly health can be affected by *highly* insanitary conditions and dangerous structural defects it is less clear how far illness in Britain today is influenced by housing circumstances. In the past, high rates of tuberculosis amongst those in substandard housing have often been found (Pond, 1957; Stein, 1954; Benjamin, 1953). Martin (1967) reviewed a large body of evidence on these questions which suggested a positive, although decreasing, relationship between health and housing. Changes in overall housing standards and advances in preventive medicine appeared responsible. Others have challenged the assumption that crowding can ever encourage the spread of infections. Cassel (1972) maintained that increased contact is an inappropriate interpretation for the transmission of non-infectious diseases and an insufficient explanation for infections.

Besides physical health, poor housing may affect attitudes and behaviour. Research is not necessary to indicate that the most disadvantaged would prefer to live under better conditions. Despair, apathy and shame are examples of the terms which have often been used to describe their feelings. Children may be affected. Shelter (1973) claimed that 'As a result of our research and interviews we are now convinced that the country's inadequate housing is directly responsible for health, educational, social and mental problems of many children; that these problems occur at an age when the children are most vulnerable and have effects which last well into adulthood'. They stressed the influence of ill-health and of stresses and strains within families due to poor conditions. However, the available evidence does not support such a strong claim.

Poor housing, as assessed by lack of basic household amenities, has been shown to be associated with educational backwardness (Davie *et al.*, 1972) and with delinquency (West and Farrington, 1973). However, the associations do not necessarily reflect direct causal influences.

Ferguson (1952) found a positive association between poor housing and delinquency, but also demonstrated a significant relationship between family factors and antisocial conduct independently of housing conditions. West and Farrington (1973) showed that boys living in poor or neglected housing were more likely to become delinquent than were those in better housing. Poor housing and low income were strongly associated and it was not possible to determine which aspect of social disadvantage was most important with respect to delinquency. However, delinquency was linked more directly with personal characteristics than with living conditions. Thus, for example, family income was *not* related to delinquency after controlling for the boys' level of intelligence, but intelligence was still independently associated with delinquency, even after income had been taken into account.

Poor housing may well have an effect on educational progress as a result of the increased difficulties of studying at home as well as through the strains and tensions of living under disadvantageous conditions. Poor housing may also be indirectly linked with educational failure because of the concentration of poor houses in areas with the poorest schools (DES, 1967). Glass (1948) noted the interactive effects of home and school conditions. She compared the examination results of children in different schools and different areas of Middlesborough. Poor school attendance and low examination success rates were much more prevalent in the poorer areas of town and in the schools with the lowest ratings for school environment. It was the mutual reinforcement of home and school environment that seemed critical.

Glass (1948) found that rehousing was associated with improved educational performance but this has not always been the case. Wilner *et al.* (1962) conducted a longitudinal study of Negro families living in Baltimore. They followed 402 test families (who were successful applicants to move from a slum area to a new housing development) and 654 control families, who were unsuccessful applicants for rehousing. No beneficial effect of rehousing upon the educational attainment of the test children was found. The mean scores on intelligence, arithmetic and reading tests were very similar for all children in both the 'before' and two-year 'after' periods. However, rehoused children were more likely than controls to have received regular promotions at school and were less likely to have been held back one or more terms in the two year 'after' period. These findings suggest that sudden improvements in housing do not have dramatic repercussions upon educational attainment. However, higher scores in academic tests for the rehoused children might have been found if a longer 'after' period had been selected. Also the *age* of the children at transfer could be relevant; rehousing of families at different stages of development may have different effects. Lastly, as indicated by Glass (1948), the broader context of relative deprivation is important. There is no evidence to demonstrate that higher school attainment follows from a change in housing conditions alone although improved housing may help.

Homelessness

The problems associated with homelessness are likely to be a consequence both of the adverse prior living conditions and also the effects which follow being without a home.

Prior to the recent legislation, only a minority of people who applied for temporary accommodation were successful. During 1972, 19,056 families in England and Wales applied for assistance but only 4,555 were accepted (DHSS, 1973). As a result many families were, in the most literal sense, homeless. Very little is known about their fate although a number of case histories have been documented in Shelter reports. It remains to be seen how far the new legislation provides remedies for this situation.

More is known of the families provided with local authority temporary accommodation. Conditions within hostels vary enormously and in some both basic facilities and privacy are lacking (Shelter, 1972). The Seebohm Report (1968) emphasized the need for privacy if families are to regain their independence following rehousing. The hitherto frequent practice of breaking up families has now become much less common although some break-ups still occur (Shelter, 1972). Apparently, in some cases husbands have not been allowed into hostels except for brief visits (Solidarity and Socialist Action, 1967). This practice is likely to strain family relationships (Seebohm, 1968) and, in time, enforced family separation might become voluntary. Families may also be split up as a result of children being taken into care. As discussed in other chapters (see p. 207) this may be associated with disturbance in the children. Yet, many children continue to be taken into care because of family homelessness. During 1971, 4 per cent of all homeless young persons under 19 years spent time in care.

On 31 December 1971, there were 5,459 families, but 25,969 children, in temporary accommodation. One implication of homelessness for young persons is that it may involve frequent moves of both 'homes' and schools which might impair educational progress (see below). Cox (1971) suggested that children in temporary accommodation also sometimes suffered from lack of adequate play facilities in the hostels and from the poor quality of schools in their neighbourhood.

Homelessness may sometimes bring about social stigma. Cox (1971) reported her impression that the overriding feeling expressed by homeless families was shame which often resulted in withdrawal from contacts with family and friends. She noted that children in local authority hostels sometimes suffered hostility from others. In one school, mothers refused to let their children attend if they had to mix with youngsters from the local hostel for homeless families. This boycott followed the outbreak of a head infection, although whether this was due to a homeless child was not known. In one London borough it was found that the truancy rate among homeless children was particularly high, apparently because of the unsettled conditions of life in temporary accommodation and the concern about apparent discrimination against the homeless (Cox, 1971).

How far homelessness is associated with disadvantage which continues across succeeding generations in unknown. However, several writers have suggested that few children brought up in conditions of homelessness receive any help for their difficulties and the experience of apathy, distress, shame and social withdrawal may later impair their skills as parents (Greve *et al.*, 1971; Cox, 1971).

Moves of Home and School

The evidence concerning the educational consequences of frequent moves of home and school is somewhat contradictory (Kantor, 1965). Douglas (1964) found that school progress was not affected by frequent moves during the primary school period, but that children did less well at school if they had a history of frequent moves during the first five years of life. However, the children had caught up educationally to some extent by 11 years of age. The London literacy survey (ILEA, 1972) showed that children who had attended at least three schools by 8 or 9 years of age had lower reading scores than those who had been at only one or two schools. Justman (1965) found the same pattern in New York. Disadvantaged children who had moved schools several times had lower test scores than those who remained at the same school throughout. On the other hand, from the limited available evidence, it seems that children from Naval families may not suffer educationally from their repeated moves of home and school (Matthews, 1974). Collins and Coulter (1975) found an association between number of schools attended and school achievement, but pupils who moved often and who moved across State boundaries tended to have lower attainments. Obviously any changes of school carry the risk of disrupting teaching and impairing scholastic progress. But whether or not educational retardation actually occurs probably depends in large part on the extent to which the moves of school and home are associated with other forms of social or personal disadvantage.

Kantor (1965) found that families who moved house within the same city had children with somewhat more behavioural disturbance than those who did not move house. On the other hand, moving house was not associated with any change in the children's behaviour. The finding is in keeping with other research and suggests that it is not moving house *as such* which matters most with respect to behavioural or emotional disturbance, but families who move house frequently within the same city may include a higher than average proportion who are disadvantaged in other ways. However, families who move to another part of the country do not appear disadvantaged compared with those who remain living in the same area (Rutter, 1976).

Overcrowding

Numerous studies have shown that children living in overcrowded homes tend to have less good educational attainments than other children (e.g. Douglas, 1964; Petzing and Wedge, 1970; Rutter *et al.*, 1970; Davie *et al.*, 1972). Overcrowding may influence school performance through lack of play space, the unavailability of a quiet room to study, and perhaps through disturbance of sleep by other family members. However, families living in overcrowded circumstances tend to be disadvantaged in many other ways as well and, in part, the association between overcrowding and poor attainments may reflect these other disadvantages. Certainly the connection between overcrowding and large family size is important as the number of children in the household is more strongly associated with educational attainment than is overcrowding as such (see chapter 4 for a discussion of family size and educational attainment).

Overcrowding has also been shown to be associated with delinquency (West and Farrington, 1973) with psychiatric disorder in children (Rutter, 1976) and adults (Schorr, 1964; Galle *et al.*, 1972), and with family disorganization, including problems between parents and their children, marital difficulties, personality problems and family dissolution through divorce or separation (Loring, 1956).

However, the mere fact of overcrowding is not the whole story. Rehousing, even when it leads to an improvement in objective housing conditions, can cause initial dislocation and disturbance (Martin *et al.*, 1957; Fried, 1967). It would seem that overcrowding does not influence mental health independently of housing history, household composition and family characteristics. The nature and degree of overcrowding are also important. The effects of two people living in one room are likely to be different from the effects of six. The diversity of roles among members of an overcrowded household (Ministry of Housing and Local Government, 1961; Loring, 1956) may be related to the duration of overcrowding. Some households are continuously crowded, whereas others congregate only for small portions of the day, such as to eat and sleep. The quality of previous personal relationships and social behaviour within a group may also be relevant. Crowding will test personal and social relationships and the breaking point may come sooner if the initial tensions are great. The relative importance of these variables has not been tested empirically.

A variety of animal studies have shown that overcrowding can lead to extreme social disorganization (Calhoun, 1962) and heightened aggression (Hamburg, 1971). However, there is also some preliminary evidence that the process of becoming overcrowded may be more important than a stable state of high density. Kessler (reported by Cassel, 1972) noted that extreme crowding was only associated with asocial behaviour in mice while population growth was occurring. Second generation mice, growing up under steady conditions of overcrowding, showed no higher incidence of pathology than did a control group living under crowded conditions.

It has often been supposed that population density will have similar effects in humans as in animals. It has been hypothesized that the higher rates of crime and mental disorder in cities than in rural areas (see chapter 6) may be a result of overcrowding (e.g. Carlestam, 1971). However, the parallel between animal studies and the human situation is not particularly close and population density per se may not be the crucial factor (Gillis, 1974). In the first place, most of the animal studies have involved a competition for limited resources and this factor may be at least as important as the crowding together of people. City slums may or may not be overcrowded but they usually involve a lack of community facilities as well as household amenities and financial resources. Secondly, there is a good deal of confusion in the literature between population density in terms of persons per square mile and overcrowding in the sense of number of persons per room in the home. High densities in some cities are not always associated with high rates of disorder (Jacobs, 1961; Schmitt, 1963) and the study by Galle *et al.* (1972) indicated that crime and mental disorder were more strongly associated with overcrowded households than with population density. Furthermore, Gillis (1974) found that delinquency was more strongly correlated with multiple occupancy dwellings than with either type of overcrowding. A Ministry of Housing and Local Government report (1970) on families living at high densities also failed to find adverse effects upon family life of high density housing (130 housing units per acre). Although a point may be reached where population density has serious consequences it seems that personal overcrowding in the home is usually more important than the number of people living in a particular geographical area.

People need both privacy (Westin, 1967) and social contacts (Alexander, 1972) and stress may arise when the right balance between the two is not attained. Mitchell (1971) in a study in Hong Kong found that high density housing in Hong Kong was mainly associated with emotional disturbance when the crowding meant enforced contact with non-family members, as with household units involving several families living in the upper stories of tower blocks where it was difficult to get away from the home. He suggested that many of the strains arose from lack of control over living space. This is in keeping with Proshansky *et al.*'s (1970a and b) hypothesis that the important adverse effects of a lack of privacy stem from low control over personal territory and the restrictions imposed upon free choice of movement and behaviour.

The need for both privacy and social contact is also illustrated by the findings from Hole's (1959) study of families moved from a slum to a new housing estate. The increase in available space led to a decrease in family tensions, particularly between fathers and daughters, but did not prevent the continuation of many social activities under crowded conditions.

Another factor which may be important in relation to the higher rates of social disorder in inner city areas is the anonymity and lack of mutual obligation compared with small town life (Hamburg, 1971). Several studies have shown that big city dwellers are less likely than small town inhabitants to give aid to strangers and are less likely to respect other people's property (Zimbardo, 1969; Milgrim, 1970).

Housing Design

Quite apart from the quality of household amenities and the amount of space provided, the design of housing may influence behaviour and attitudes. Churchill once remarked: 'We shape our buildings and they shape us'. Most residential areas and most buildings are designed and built to span the lifetimes of several generations. If aspects of housing estate and building design are influential, it is important to identify the crucial factors. Unfortunately, in practice, it has proved difficult to do this as the effects of design are closely interwoven with the social conditions of the area and the people living in the buildings.

There is now a considerable literature on the the importance of personal space in various settings (Sommer, 1969; Canter, 1974). This is shown by the marked tendency even in institutional settings, for people to identify and defend their own territory in the form of 'their chair' or 'their part of the room', and by the social consequences of different interpersonal distances. Various naturalistic and experimental studies have shown that personal contacts are influenced by the layout of buildings and of furniture within them. It seems likely that the same may apply to the design of homes and of housing estates, although there is little systematic evidence on the matter. A study by the London Borough of Hammersmith (1974) indicated that people living in smaller estates, which were less isolated from the neighbourhood than the larger estates, tended to have more friends. Satisfaction, in turn, was related to high social interaction. The Department of the Environment (1972) studies in London and Sheffield, however, found that housewives' reactions to housing were largely independent of physical design. In their review, Darke and Darke (1969) concluded that physical factors were important in establishing contacts with other people but that personal characteristics determined their quality.

Much attention has been paid in recent years to the effects of living in apartments and especially of living in multi-storey tower blocks (Stewart, 1970; Jephcott, 1971; Richman, 1974a). The concern over the possible adverse effects of high rise dwellings is reflected in the marked drop in the number built between 1965 and 1971 both in

London (GLC, 1973) and in the country as a whole (Housing and Construction Statistics, 1974). However, systematic evidence concerning life in tower blocks is largely lacking.

Family satisfaction with high rise living has been found to depend most strongly on the age of the children in the family (Ministry of Housing and Local Government, 1970; Department of the Environment, 1972). In the Department of the Environment study, only 16 per cent of the 984 householders who lived off the ground disliked doing so. However, about one-third of those with a child under 5 years expressed some dissatisfaction in contrast to only one in seven of the mothers with older children and one in nine of those without children. Thus, young families with young children seem least suited to life in high rise apartments; this was also indicated by Jephcott (1971).

The problems of mothers with young children may be related to the difficulties in supervising play, and many writers have emphasized the restrictions upon play imposed by flat life. Nevertheless, the differences are not as strong as sometimes claimed. Maizels (1961) found that somewhat more mothers living above the fifth floor were anxious about their children's safety and a third (compared with a quarter of those living on a lower storey) spontaneously mentioned play difficulties. Stewart (1970) reported that a majority of mothers with small children living above the third floor were dissatisfied and thought their children were restricted. However, no controls were used and the study does not warrant the claims by the NSPCC (Annual Report, 1972) that the children's personalities might be permanently damaged.

Fanning (1967) reported a greater incidence of psychoneurotic disorders among Army wives living in low rise blocks of flats than among those in houses, and Richman (1974a) found the same in a London study of mothers of pre-school children. Maternal depression was particularly common in mothers living in high rise apartments (Richman, 1974a). However, Moore (1974) found that psychiatric illness in adults was not related to either building height or design. The findings with respect to children are contradictory (Richman, 1974a and b).

In short, there is some evidence that the mothers of pre-school children face particular difficulties if they live in high rise flats. They are probably more likely to express dissatisfaction and more likely to become depressed than women living in ground floor flats or houses. But, it is uncertain how far the children themselves suffer, or to what extent the problems also apply to the mothers of older children. In some degree the difficulties stem from living in an upper storey but it may well be that many problems arise from the overall design of the housing estate. This is implicit in Newman's views (1973) on the way in which the physical design of building and housing estates can influence crime. He has hypothesized that a lack of 'defensible space' (meaning personal territory with clearly identifiable status and a layout which enables people to know their neighbours and easily spot strangers) encourages vandalism and delinquency. Such a lack of defensible space is found in many large high density multi-storey apartment blocks. Newman suggested that building design lays the seeds of future behaviour and wrote: 'In our newly-created dense and anonymous residential environments, we may be raising generations of young people who are totally lacking in any experience of personal or communal space and by extension, of the personal rights and property of others. In many ways, therefore, defensible space design also attempts to attack the root causes of crime. In the area of crime prevention, physical design has been traditionally relegated the role of *mechanical prevention*, leaving intact the structure of motivation and attitudes which eventually lead to the criminal event. Defensible space design, while it uses mechanical prevention, aims at formulating an architectural model of *corrective prevention*. Our present urban environments, created with such speed and determination, may be little more than the spawning grounds of criminal behaviour.'

The main quantitative evidence presented by Newman (1973) to support his thesis is a comparison of vandalism and crime rates on two housing projects of similar size and overall density situated on opposite sides of the same street and an analysis of types and locations of crimes within a large number of New York housing projects. The findings are interesting although not conclusive. For example, the finding of considerable differences in felony rates between the two adjacent housing projects might be because of physical design features but it might also be due in part to the contrasting characteristics of new tenants entering the projects (Hillier, 1973). Also the strong associations found between felonies and building height may be attributable to a household density factor. Newman discounted this possibility as he claimed that densities had been very similar in the two adjacent projects showing differing crime levels. However, examination of the data reveals that the majority of the tenants on the higher crime rate estate lived under denser conditions than most on the lower rate estate.

It was not clear from Newman (1973) whether he supposed that architecture of a building actively influenced the amount of crime committed by its inhabitants, or whether architecture merely provided *opportunities* for crime by residents and outsiders alike. More recently Newman (1974) has taken a clearer stand. Further data analyses indicated that the characteristics of residents were better predictors of crime and vandalism than were physical design features. However, the best predictions were made when both sets of factors were combined. In the New York housing projects studied the most important social variables associated with crime were the proportion of single-parent 'welfare' families, the numbers of teenage children and the percentage of black residents. The crucial physical variables were the size of the housing project, the number of housing units sharing an entrance to the dwelling and the building height.

CONCLUSIONS

During this century there has been a very considerable improvement in housing conditions. Even so a substantial minority of children are still reared in overcrowded homes which often lack basic amenities and there continues to be a problem of homelessness. There is a marked regional variation in housing conditions with overcrowding particularly severe in Scotland and homelessness a special concern in London. The provision of good quality housing is influenced by both Government finance and planning policies, and by local authority housing policies. Housing disadvantage applies most of all to the poor, to fatherless families, to families in which the father is sick or unemployed and to a lesser extent to large families. Very little is known concerning intergenerational continuities in housing. There is only a limited association between the quality of housing and people's satisfaction with it. Rehousing may mean the break-up of neighbouring friendships and altered patterns of social interaction; it may also mean access to better schools. Accordingly, the benefits of rehousing are not entirely dependent on the changed housing conditions as such. Poor housing is associated with various other forms of disadvantage including low educational attainment and delinquency but for the most part the associations are indirect and the mechanisms ill-understood. Homelessness carries with it the problem of stigma but the extent of this is poorly documented. Personal overcrowding can be a considerable psycho-social stress but whether or not it actually constitutes a stress in an individual case depends very much on the circumstances. The design of housing and of housing estates is known to be psychologically and socially important but the ways in which design features have an impact on a person's life and behaviour remain to be established.

4 Intellectual Performance and Scholastic Attainment

Educational failure may well be one important link in a life cycle of social disability which shows some degree of intergenerational continuity. It has commonly been claimed that parental poverty and low social status lead children to fail at school, which in turn limits their own adult occupation and income (Birch and Gussow, 1970: Cravioto *et al.*, 1966; US Legislative Program, 1964). The potential effectiveness of attempts to interrupt the cycle through improved education depends on the strength of the links in the hypothesized cycle and on the mechanisms involved in the determination of scholastic success.

Educational failure is a frequent, but not universal concomitant of low intelligence, so that the transmission of poor scholastic attainments and low social status may to some extent reflect intergenerational continuities in intelligence. However, a high proportion of children who cannot read or who otherwise fail at school are of normal intelligence, so that this could not be a sufficient explanation. Accordingly, the chapter begins with a consideration of intelligence and its measurement, and of the social implications of intellectual retardation before going on to discuss the evidence on intergenerational continuities in both intellectual level and specific educational disabilities. This is followed by an appraisal of the relative contributions of nature and nurture in accounting for differences in measured intelligence, and then by a more detailed discussion of the effect of a variety of possible non-genetic factors on the development of intelligence and the acquisition of scholastic skills. Most of the published studies do not make a clear distinction between general intellectual retardation and specific educational disabilities, but the available evidence with respect to the latter is discussed as a particular issue. Lastly, the findings with respect to compensatory education are briefly reviewed in order to throw light on both the processes involved in low attainment and the extent of change possible.

INTELLIGENCE AND ITS MEASUREMENT

The concept of general intelligence has given rise to much controversy (see Butcher, 1970) and there has been even more dispute over the meaning of an IQ score. It would not be appropriate to review all the issues here but it is necessary to clarify some of the main points of dispute before proceeding further.

Tests of intelligence were first developed by Binet to enable the Paris education authorities to identify 'dull' children who would not benefit from the education then offered and who therefore needed special education (Ryan, 1972; Clarke and Clarke, 1974). Since then, IQ tests have continued to be employed to assess how children are likely to respond to particular types of schooling and to predict their scholastic achievement. Many studies have confirmed that well established IQ tests do indeed do this with reasonable accuracy both within the normal range and with respect to mentally retarded persons (Rutter, 1971a). Thus, for school age children in this country there is a product-moment correlation* of about +0.6 between IQ and reading (Yule *et al.*, 1974). IQ scores have also been found to correlate substantially with occupational achievement both within and between occupations (Jensen, 1969). Furthermore, when comparisons have been made, the IQ has been shown to be a better general predictor of achievement than is any other measure.

IQ scores have proved to be useful because (by means of a series of subtests or tasks) they sample on a wide basis general conceptual or reasoning skills which a person has built up over his life time. In selecting test items, care is taken to choose those that depend as little as possible upon specialized knowledge (such as literacy or computational ability) and to check that each of the items does indeed discriminate between dull and bright individuals, as judged by other criteria. The skills which are assessed on the test are mostly not acquired as a result of direct teaching but they are available for the child to apply in the acquisition of more specialized skills at school (Vernon, 1970). It is this which makes the IQ such a valuable predictor across a wide range of educational achievements. Even so, there are considerable limitations to intelligence tests (Tarjan *et al.*, 1972), and it is necessary to appreciate the substantial range of error in any IQ score. It must also be emphasized that the tests are devised to predict achievement in industrialized countries and they are of dubious value in other cultures.

The facts on these aspects of IQ testing are well established and not in dispute. However, other more controversial notions have become attached to the concept of intelligence and to the measurement of IQ. The most important of these is the view that the IQ (albeit imperfectly) measures 'innate potential' and that an IQ score reflects the maximum level of intellectual performance of which an individual is capable (Burt, 1955, 1970). Proponents of this view have argued that a well constructed intelligence test assesses ability in a way that is virtually free of cultural influences (Burt, 1955b). This view has been shown to be logically and practically fallacious (Anastasi, 1968; Vernon, 1970). An IQ test measures a sample of behaviour and insofar as culture affects

*This is a statistical measure which indicates the level of association between two items. A correlation of +1.0 means that there is perfect concordance such that if one score goes up the other goes up to the same extent. A correlation of 0.0 means that a score on the one bears no consistent relation to a score on the other.

behaviour the influence will and should be reflected in the test. Because the test assesses the person's performance on a variety of tasks it is assessing achievement just as much as are reading or arithmetic scores. The IQ is a more generally useful predictor than is a reading score, because it samples a wider range of behaviours which are less directly attributable to schooling and not because the IQ test is different in kind. Furthermore, the notion that mental age (derived from IQ scores) sets an upper limit on achievement is quite invalid. As shown by several studies, individuals *do* achieve at a level well above their mental age (Crane, 1959; Yule *et al.*, 1974). The question of how far intelligence is innate is considered in a later section of this chapter, but it may be stated at this point that the evidence clearly indicates the influence of both genetic and non-genetic factors. These conclusions apply to intelligence as measured by IQ tests. The *concept* of innate intelligence, as an abstraction concerning hypothetical genetic potentialities, is quite another matter, but one not relevant to the present discussion.

A further issue of controversy is the extent to which it is reasonable to consider intelligence as a single general ability (rather than a group of specific factors). This is a complex question upon which the evidence is to some extent contradictory (see Butcher, 1970 and Eysenck, 1973a). What is clear is that intellectual performance involves a variety of different specific skills but that, in general, an individual's score on one type of task shows a positive correlation with his score on another sort of task. For practical purposes, we can assume that there is some kind of general factor of intelligence but that in addition there are a number of distinct special abilities. The relative importance of these general and specific skills has been shown to vary with the type of population studied (e.g. Maxwell, 1972) and may also vary with the environmental circumstances encountered, as indicated by animal experiments (Searle, 1949).

In summary, the concept of intelligence is an abstraction, but one which has proved to have considerable practical utility. In spite of its limitations the IQ test continues to be the most reliable and valid indicator of *current intellectual performance*. However, it does not and cannot measure innate intelligence.

SOCIAL IMPLICATIONS OF INTELLECTUAL RETARDATION

It is important to recognize that intellectual retardation is not synonymous with the need for care by specialists in mental subnormality. Many children with an IQ* in the retarded range (i.e. below 70) cope adequately in ordinary schools (Rutter, Tizard and Whitmore,

*IQ scores are scaled so that 100 is the average. About 95 per cent of people have scores between 70 and 130.

1970). Conversely, many children in special schools for the subnormal have a normal IQ (but very poor educational attainments) and even some children in mental subnormality hospitals have normal intelligence. This is still commoner amongst adults who are often admitted to subnormality hospitals, not because they are intellectually retarded, but rather because of social or work difficulties or behavioural disturbance (Rutter, 1971a). It is necessary, therefore, to consider how far a low IQ is associated with other disabilities.

On the whole, a person with mild intellectual retardation is most handicapped during his school days when his intellectual incapacity is likely to lead to school failure in the face of the demands for new learning. Numerous studies have shown that identification of the mildly retarded almost always occurs during the years of compulsory schooling (Gruenberg, 1964). However, as shown by a variety of follow-up studies, well reviewed and abstracted by Goldstein (1964), Cobb (1969) and Tizard (1974b), social adjustment tends to be much better in adult life. In early life, mildly retarded persons show a higher incidence of marital, civic and occupational failure than do no-retarded controls but the differences tend to diminish over time. Thus, in the follow-up study by Baller *et al.* (1966) of 206 children in special classes and with an IQ of less than 70, 80 per cent of the men and 77 per cent of the women were 'usually employed' when aged 40 years or so, compared with 96 per cent of the control group. Most were in unskilled jobs but 13 per cent had their own business or were engaged in non-manual commercial employment. In early adult life, minor breaches of the law were several times more frequent in the retarded group, but again by middle life the difference between the retarded and the control subjects was much less. Closely similar findings have been obtained from other long-term follow-ups of mildly retarded individuals. Not surprisingly, mentally retarded people who marry one another experience many social problems but, even so, most remain together and half continue to have a supportive and affectionate partnership (Mattinson, 1970).

The same studies indicated that there tends to be a rise in IQ in late adolescence and early adult life among the mildly retarded. This rise is often slight but occasionally considerable. It seems not to occur in those with overt brain damage and is most marked among individuals from a very deprived home background, particularly if they leave home (Stein and Susser, 1969, 1970; Clarke and Clarke, 1953, 1954; Clarke *et al.*, 1958). The rise in IQ is associated with improvement in social adjustment and occurs in any reasonable environment, apparently largely as a result of removal from an environment which impedes intellectual development.

The outlook for persons with an IQ of below 50 is much worse. The vast majority suffer from gross structural damage to the brain, very few are capable of working in open employment (although many with an IQ between 35 and 50 can work in a sheltered environment), most remain dependent upon others throughout life, only a minority are fertile and they have a greatly reduced expectation of life. Although, with improved medical care, severely retarded persons are now living longer, those in hospital still die at a much younger age than do the general population (Richards, 1969; Richards and Sylvester, 1969). The death rate is particularly high among those with the severest degree of retardation, the main cause being a greatly increased rate of respiratory infection.

Rutter (1971a) has reviewed the extensive literature on associations between intellectual retardation and psychiatric disorder in childhood. Epidemiological studies have clearly demonstrated that the rate of psychiatric disorder in the mentally retarded is considerably higher than in individuals of normal intelligence. This excess of psychiatric problems is most marked in the severly retarded. Even so, in the Isle of Wight study (Rutter, Tizard and Whitmore, 1970), half of the children with severe intellectual retardation did not have any psychiatric disorder and the proportion without psychiatric problems was even higher among the mildly retarded. The same study showed that the association was not just between intellectual retardation and psychiatric abnormality. Rather, psychiatric disorder was associated with differences in IQ even within the normal range. Thus, persons of low average IQ had a higher rate of disorder than those of superior intelligence. Although emotional disorder may occasionally impair intellectual performance, investigations showed that it was usually the factors associated with low IQ which led to psychiatric disorder rather than vice versa.

Many mechanisms play a part in this association (Rutter, 1971a). However, it seems that organic brain dysfunction and deviant temperamental attributes are the two most important factors in the severely retarded child. Both are also important in the mildly retarded, but the adverse social consequences of educational failure are probably of equal importance. Social rejection, cerebral immaturity, and language retardation are important contributory factors. Poor quality institutional care too may be a crucial influence on some children. As with youngsters of normal intelligence, family and social pathology are also important in the genesis of psychiatric disorder.

The rate of delinquency is appreciably higher among mildly retarded youths than among those of normal intelligence, but in spite of this increased rate, most retarded individuals are not delinquent and most delinquents are of normal intelligence (Woodward, 1955a and b; Tizard, 1974b).

In summary, mild intellectual retardation is associated with a substantial increase in a variety of social disabilities. This increase is most marked in childhood and early adult life and decreases thereafter so that by middle age most mildly retarded individuals are reasonably well adapted in the community and not readily distinguishable from the rest of the population other than by their lower occupational status. On the other hand, severe mental retardation is usually associated with continuing social dependency and a much shortened life span.

SOCIAL IMPLICATIONS OF READING FAILURE

There is good evidence that children of normal intelligence with serious reading difficulties in primary school usually remain severely backward in reading right up to the time of school leaving (Yule, 1973; Rutter and Yule, 1974). They also tend to do badly in other school subjects and have low educational and occupational aspirations (Yule *et al.*, in preparation). However, surprisingly little is known about what happens to them after they leave school (Herjanic and Penick, 1972). Undoubtedly, some (perhaps most) become competent and well-functioning adults. However, it is a common observation that socially disadvantaged adults have often failed at school. There are no reliable data from which to judge whether the association between educational backwardness at school and social impairment in adult life is weak or strong.

LABELLING

Because low intelligence and social incapacity are far from synonymous, attention needs to be paid to the way the label 'mentally retarded' is applied. A Californian study (Mercer, 1973) showed that it was used in rather different ways by different community agencies. There was general agreement on its use for persons with an IQ below 50, many of whom also had physical disabilities, and all of whom were socially incapacitated. There was also little problem in the case of white persons with an IQ above 50 but below 70, as a low IQ was strongly associated with social failure. However, the situation was different with ethnic minority groups. A substantial proportion with low IQ scores were coping adequately in their everyday life. Although, with a few important exceptions, IQ and educational attainments correlate to much the same degree in all ethnic groups in Western society (see Rutter, 1971a), apparently the relationship between IQ and social competence is not the same. As a consequence, individuals from social and ethnic minority groups run the risk of being labelled 'mentally retarded' on the basis of IQ tests, although they are functioning satisfactorily outside school and outside the test situation. How much this matters and the way in which it matters will depend on the social consequences of the labelling. One study (Jaffe, 1966) suggested that people did not express unfavourable attitudes to someone who had been in a special class for retarded children but that to some extent they did have negative expectations of someone labelled 'mentally retarded'. However, so far there has been little systematic research on labelling with respect to mental retardation (see Hobbs, 1975a and b).

INTRAGENERATIONAL CONTINUITIES IN INTELLECTUAL LEVEL

Before considering intergenerational continuities it is necessary to examine the findings on the extent to which an individual's intellectual level remains the same over his life span. There are now several competent reviews which have considered studies on the predictability of later IQ on the basis of tests in the pre-school years (Bayley, 1955, 1970; Hindley, 1965; Thomas, 1967; Rutter, 1970b; McCall *et al.*, 1972). As the results of all the main studies are broadly similar, only the main conclusions will be summarized here.

1. Within a normal group, the correlations between test scores at 18 months of age or earlier and IQ scores after age 8 years are very low (about +0.2) and of no predictive value.
2. By age 2 to 2½ years they are more substantial (about +0.4 to +0.5) but still too low to be regarded as valid indicators of intellectual level at maturity.
3. Infant tests are better predictors of mental retardation than of intellectual level within the normal range, but even so an appreciable number of infants with scores in the retarded range will prove to be of normal intelligence when adult (and vice versa).
4. By age 7 years, IQ scores correlate about +0.7 with adult intelligence and are fair (but still far from perfect) indicators of intelligence in adult life.
5. During the period of childhood from the time of starting school, considerable fluctuations in intellectual level occur so that the average child will show a change in IQ of 10 to 17 points (Bradway, 1944; Sontag *et al.*, 1958).
6. Although in general, intelligence shows increasing stability with age (Bloom, 1964) the course of development in individuals is both variable over time and somewhat idiosyncratic in pattern. As a result of these considerations, it may be concluded that intergenerational continuities can only be meaningfully examined if IQ scores for individuals in all generations are obtained after starting school and preferably after seven years of age. Accordingly, when discussing intergenerational continuities, findings on pre-school children will be omitted.

There are many reasons why IQ scores in the early years of life fail to predict adult scores (Rutter, 1970b; McCall *et al.*, 1972). Among the more important are: (a) infant tests have a substantially different content from adult tests. In particular, verbal skills play a much larger part in adult IQ tests; (b) children differ in their rates of maturation and hence vary in the ages at which there are plateaux and spurts in intellectual growth, and (c) the environments encountered by a child during his process of development will influence his intellectual capacities (see below).

After childhood IQ levels show less change. It is usually said that IQ scores progressively decline from late adolescence or early adulthood onwards. However, as Anastasi (1956) pointed out, conclusions concerning age changes which are based on cross-sectional studies are subject to serious bias because most older subjects have had less education than younger subjects. Longitudinal studies indicate that in many cases mental growth continues well past adolescence but that the degree and timing of intellectual decline depend to a considerable extent on a person's job and education (Bradway and Thompson, 1962; Kangas and Bradway, 1971; Owens, 1953; Nisbet, 1957). Although those in manual jobs and not receiving further education probably show a fall-off in intellectual skills after the late-teens (Jones and Conrad, 1933), this is not necessarily so (Bayley, 1955). Individuals receiving academic secondary education show intellectual gains which continue through the teens and bright university graduates continue to show intellectual growth well into adulthood and maintain their verbal skills even longer (see section below on schooling: page 123). Vernon (1960) concluded that . . . (intellectual) 'growth continues so long as education or other stimulating conditions continue, though probably never beyond 25—30 years, and that when such stimulation ceases decline sets in'.

TRENDS IN INTELLIGENCE AND READING

The Scottish Survey of Intelligence (Scottish Council for Research in Education, 1949) showed no change in children's intelligence between 1932 and 1947 in terms of IQ scores on individual tests, but there was a slight rise in group verbal test scores. A variety of studies (Jones, 1962; Belmont and Birch; 1966, Scottish Council for Research in Education, 1967; Berger *et al.*, 1975) have all shown that British children today tend to have IQ scores on the Wechsler Intelligence Scale for Children (WISC) a few points above the American norms a quarter of a century ago. However, whether this reflects British-American differences or changes over time remains uncertain. It is evident that there has been no drop in intelligence in Britain over the last 40 years and it is possible that there may have been a rise of a point or two. But, any change there may have been must be quite small and it may be concluded that there has been no substantial change in intelligence level in Britain since 1932.

On the other hand, there have been alterations in reading standards. Between 1938 and 1948 the average reading age for 11-year-olds in England and Wales dropped by nearly a year (Ministry of Education, 1950); between 1948 and 1964 there was a progressive improvement, totalling some 17 months overall; but since 1964 there has been no further rise and there may have been a slight drop once more (Start and Wells, 1972). Similar changes were found in illiteracy rates. The reasons for these changes are poorly understood.

INTERGENERATIONAL CONTINUITIES

Intellectual Level

There is extensive evidence for the existence of considerable intergenerational continuities in intellectual level, both within the normal range and at the extremes. Thus, Erlenmeyer-Kimling and Jarvik (1963), in their review of twelve studies which had examined the relationship between the IQ level in parents and their children, showed that the median parent-child correlation in IQ was +0.50. Most of these studies had IQ data on only one parent and only one child, and the correlation is substantially higher if the IQ scores of *both* parents and *all* children are taken into account. In a systematic study of 51 families with at least four children, Outhit (1933) found that the mid-parent to mid-child correlation with respect to IQ was about +0.80, in comparison with an average correlation between single parent and single child of +0.58.

Data are available regarding continuities at the top end of the IQ distribution from Terman's (1921) study of highly gifted children who were followed into middle life (Terman and Oden, 1959). All the subjects had an IQ of at least 140 when selected in childhood and the mean IQ of the group was 151. The mean IQ of their children was 133, only a fifth had an IQ below 120 and only 0.5 per cent had an IQ below 70 (Oden, 1968).

Several early studies showed that a substantial proportion of the offspring of adult parents classified as mentally subnormal were themselves mentally retarded. Thus, the Brock Committee (1934) found that about 40 per cent of 7 to 13 year old children of defectives were retarded or defective. Burt (1937) reported 14 per cent defective and another 32 per cent dull or backward. Penrose (1938) investigated the children of female defectives and concluded that 30 per cent were mentally retarded and a similar proportion were of dull intelligence. In Brandon's study (1957) of the children of mentally subnormal mothers, 31 per cent of those aged at least 6 years were dealt with as either mentally retarded or educationally subnormal (Clarke and Clarke, 1974). More recently, Scally (1968) similarly found that about 30 per cent of the children of mentally defectives were regarded as ineducable or educationally subnormal. Åkesson (1961), using rather broader definition, reported that 40 per cent of the children of a group of mentally defective patients were mentally retarded. In summary, the findings are in general agreement that roughly a quarter to a third of the offspring of certified mental defectives are sufficiently handicapped intellectually to require special schooling or training. Conversely, however, this also means that between two thirds and three quarters of the offspring are able to attend ordinary schools.

In order to put the result into perspective, two further findings must be added. The first is that the same studies showed that the number of children produced by mentally defective adults was quite low, and a high proportion of those with severe subnormality produced no children at all. To a considerable extent, this is due to their long-term institutional care. Nevertheless, there is also evidence that even in the general population individuals of low IQ tend to have few children (Bajema, 1963). The second finding is that all studies have shown a high death rate among the children of mentally retarded adults. For example, Brandon (1957) found that 16 per cent had died before the age of 2 years and in the Brock (1934) investigation 22 per cent of the children had died. As a result of both low fecundity and high mortality the absolute numbers of retarded children born to retarded adults are low, although among their offspring the *proportion* with retardation is fairly high.

Intergenerational continuities can also be judged by examining intellectual levels in the parents of mentally retarded individuals. Such studies indicate considerable continuity. Penrose (1938) found that 7½ per cent of the parents of mental defectives were themselves mentally defective and another 13½ per cent were 'intellectually dull'. Burt (1937) reported that among mildly retarded children attending a special school, 6 per cent had a parent known to be mentally deficient and in another 38 per cent one parent was 'definitely dull'. In the recent Isle of Wight study (Rutter, Tizard and Whitmore, 1970), there was a family history of general backwardness in 37 per cent of intellectually retarded children compared with 12 per cent among children in the general population.

Some caution is required in the interpretation of all these figures because the findings are based on a mixture of administrative procedures, interview reports and psychometric tests. Nevertheless, systematic psychometric studies have given rise to broadly comparable findings. The largest investigation was conducted by Reed and Reed (1965) who studied the families of 289 patients with an IQ below 70. Altogether, 16 per cent of their children and 33 per cent of their parents had an IQ below 70. However, among the grandchildren the proportion was much lower — 4 per cent. Among those with a strong family history of mental retardation the proportion of retarded offspring was considerably higher: 28 per cent of the children and 16 per cent of the grandchildren. Reed and Reed also showed, confirming earlier studies, that the risk of retardation in the offspring was very much greater if both parents were retarded than if only one parent was. In the Reed study and in others (Åkesson, 1962) it was found that the rate of mental retardation in relatives was very much higher among the mildly retarded than the severely retarded. Thus, Åkesson found that only 1 per cent of the parents of severely subnormal individuals were retarded, compared with 11 to 28 per cent of the parents of the mildly retarded.

It may be concluded that there is very little intergenerational transmission of severe mental retardation (IQ < 50). The great majority of the parents are of normal intelligence and come from the same social background as the general population (Kushlick, 1968; Frew and Peckham, 1972). Furthermore, the severely retarded individuals themselves have very few children. On the other hand, there is substantial intergenerational continuity with respect to mild mental retardation. Even so, most of the offspring have an IQ within the normal range and a few are of superior intelligence. Among the grandchildren, the rate of retardation is much lower and the proportion of good intelligence much higher.

Specific Educational Disabilities

Intergenerational continuities in scholastic attainment have largely been examined with respect to specific reading retardation. Many reports have emphasized the high frequency with which there is a family history of this condition (Critchley, 1970; Vernon, 1971). Thus, in Hallgren's classical study of individuals with 'dyslexia' (1950), two fifths of the parents had the same condition. Most investigations have not employed control groups, but those with control have produced similar findings. Doehring (1968) reported reading problems in the parents or siblings of 22 out of 37 cases of reading retardation but in only 8 of 36 control cases. Similarly, in the Isle of Wight study (Rutter, Tizard and Whitmore, 1970) 34 per cent of the children with specific reading retardation had parents or siblings with reading difficulties compared with 9 per cent of the controls. Put another way, 7½ per cent of the individual members of retarded readers' families reported reading difficulties compared with 2½ per cent among the family members of the controls (Rutter and Yule, 1973). It should be noted that although there is a three-fold increase in family members with reading difficulties among the cases compared with the controls, nevertheless only a small minority showed these problems. Because the family data in all these studies have been based on reports rather than the direct study of relatives, it is not possible to differentiate adequately between *specific* reading difficulties and *general* learning difficulties. Whereas it may safely be concluded that intergenerational continuities in reading difficulties are often present, it remains uncertain how far the continuities refer to specific reading retardation and how far to more general cognitive or institutional problems.

GENETIC FACTORS

Intelligence

The relative influence of heredity and of the environment in accounting for variations in measured intelligence is an issue which has been subject to vigorous and often emotional academic debate. Conclusions have ranged from that of Watson (1931) who stated 'There is no such thing as an inheritance of capacity talent, temperament, mental constitution and characteristics', and that of Floud, Halsey and Martin (1956) who argued 'it is well known that intelligence is largely an acquired characteristic', to that of Jensen (1969) and Eysenck (1973a) who have maintained that genetic factors are much more important than environmental influences in producing differences in intelligence. No current theorists suggest that variability in intelligence is *entirely* determined by innate factors.

There is considerable evidence that genetic factors are of great importance. The detailed results have been reviewed by several writers including Jensen (1969), Eysenck (1971), Mittler (1971), Shields (1973) and Clarke and Clarke (1974) and will not be repeated here. The main findings are:-

1. The differences in IQ within monozygotic (MZ) twin pairs are much less than those within dizygotic (DZ) twin pairs (the respective intra-pair correlations are +0.87 and 0.53). It is possible, although unlikely, that these could be entirely due to parents treating monozygotic twin pairs more similarly. However, this interpretation could not account for the finding that monozygotic twin pairs reared apart show a median inter-pair correlation of +0.75 which is still considerably greater than that for dizygotic twin pairs or siblings reared together (+0.49). This is important evidence in favour of a genetic basis because with monozygotic twins reared apart there is a similar genetic background but a different (although usually only slightly different) environment, whereas in the latter cases the converse applies. The finding is inexplicable in environmental terms.*

2. The median inter-correlation for IQ between biological parent and child (+0.50) is considerably greater than that between foster-parent and child (+0.20). This would not be expected if IQ were entirely determined by environmental influences.

3. Within families which include both biological and adoptive off-spring, the biological child—mid-parent correlation is greater than the adoptive child—mid-parent correlation. Thus, in the Freeman *et al.* (1928) study the former was 0.35 and the latter 0.18, and in the Leahy study (1935) the comparable figures were 0.36 and 0.18. The difference suggests a genetic effect.

4. Even when children are reared apart from their biological parents, their IQ at 13 years still correlates +0.38 to +0.44 with that of their true mother (Skodak and Skeels, 1949). This could be explained in environmental terms only if there was a very strong tendency to selective placement. However, the low correlation between the true

*Kamin (1974) has pointed out that twin correlations may well be artefactually inflated by an association between IQ and age. However, as this applies to both MZ and DZ pairs it is not relevant to this argument.

mother's IQ and the foster parents' educational level (+0.24) indicates that this did not occur in the study cited.

5. There were very sizeable differences in mean IQ at age 13 years between the group of children whose true mothers had an IQ of less than 70 and the group of children who true mothers had an IQ of at least 105 in the Skodak and Skeels study. Although in all cases the children had been placed in an adoptive home under the age of 6 months, the mean IQ of the former group was 104 compared with 129 in the latter group (Skodak and Skeels, 1949). Again, the finding demands a genetic explanation.

6. The risk of having a second mentally subnormal child is considerably greater when there is a subnormal uncle or aunt (12.9%) than when there is not (5.7%), even when both parents are of normal intelligence (Reed and Reed, 1965). While this is readily explicable in genetic terms there is no satisfactory environmental explanation for the finding.

7. Among children reared in the same family there are very wide variations in IQ (Maxwell, 1969). The same applies to children reared in the same institutions (Clarke and Clarke, 1974). While it is known that parents respond differently to each of their children, it seems unlikely that the amount of environmental variation could explain the large intrafamilial variations in IQ (the median difference between the most and least intelligent sibs in the Maxwell study was 26 points). However, some of the variation could be an artefact of the different ages at which siblings are tested.

8. The correlations between the IQs of individuals and their relatives depend upon the closeness of the familial relationships in a predictable way (Erlenmeyer-Kimling and Jarvik, 1963; Jensen, 1969). Thus, the median inter-correlation (from several studies) between parent and child is +0.50, between grandparent and grandchild is +0.27, and between unrelated persons reared apart is —0.01. This is suggestive, but not compelling, evidence in favour of genetic factors. Conceivably, the correlations could be explained in terms of environmental similarities although the data are better predicted from a genetic model.

9. The IQ of adoptive children shows a much lower correlation with characteristics of the home in which they are reared than does the IQ of children brought up by their own biological parents. Thus, in the Leahy study (1935) adoptive children's IQ correlated 0.23 with the 'environmental status' score of their home, whereas the correlation in the control group was 0.53. Similarly, in the Burks study (1928) the adoptive child's IQ correlated 0.21 with the Whittier index compared with the correlation of 0.42 in the control group. This suggests that part of the association between IQ and environmental variables is due to genetic factors. Parents of higher IQ tend to provide an intellectually more stimulating environment. Hence environmental superiority of the biological parents' home will also reflect their genetic endowment.

10. The very extensive evidence discussed so far all points to

polygenic influences. There is also one item of evidence pointing to single gene and non-genetic biological influences. That is that the parents of severely retarded children are of higher intelligence than the parents of mildly retarded children (see above). The finding is incompatible with mental retardation due to psychosocial influences. But it is exactly what would be expected if severe mental retardation were due to either single gene abnormalities or to organic brain damage. In fact there is evidence that both occur (Berg and Kirman, 1959; Crome, 1960; Rutter, Graham and Yule, 1970). About a third of severely retarded children show Down's syndrome which is due to a chromosomal anomaly and slightly fewer have cerebral palsy, which is due to brain damage arising during or preceding the birth process. In some cases the retardation is part of a disorder due to a recessive gene.

Heritability

It may be concluded that genetic factors play an important part in determining both variations in intelligence within one generation and also continuities in intelligence across several generations. What is much more difficult to determine is how much of the variation in IQ between people is due to polygenic influences.

Jensen (1969), following Burt (1958), has argued that approximately 80 per cent of the variance (i.e. the differences between individuals) is due to genetic factors. While this figure has been widely quoted other workers have put the estimate rather lower at 50 to 70 per cent (Jencks *et al.*, 1973; Huntley, 1965; Anderson, 1974). It should be appreciated that different methods give rise to different levels of heretability and that in any case such calculations are open to serious misinterpretation (Bronfenbrenner, 1972; Rutter, 1974b). In the first place, the figure cannot be regarded as independent of environmental variation. In populations where environmental variation is low, heritability will necessarily be greater than in those where such variation is large. As heritability estimates are calculated largely on the basis of IQ correlations between different family members, the estimates mainly apply to the amount of genetic variation *within* families. As the range of environments *between* families is much greater than that within families the heritability figure in that situation is likely to be appreciably lower. Secondly, the calculation of heritability is complicated by the fact that genetic and environmental factors both covary and interact. Covariance implies that children may inherit both a superior intelligence and a superior environment from their parents whereas others may receive a poor intellect and disadvantaged conditions. Interaction means that a particular genetic, or environmental, endowment may have different implications for behaviour dependent upon the nature of the other. This is well illustrated in an investigation by Cooper and Zubek (1958) who bred two strains of rats under normal laboratory conditions, one 'maze-bright' and one 'maze-dull'. However, when the rats were transferred to very deprived or very stimulating environments the differential performance of the two groups was greatly reduced. Both groups performed badly in the deprived environment but well in the enriched environment. This suggests that genetic inheritance does not influence behaviour independently of environmental stimuli, at least in the case of rats learning to run mazes. It is not known how far such interactions apply with respect to human intelligence. Thirdly, even if heritability is as high as 80 per cent this does not mean that quite marked changes in intellectual level will not follow major environmental improvements. Because heritability is a *population* statistic, it necessarily refers to the average situation in that population. Heritability of 80 per cent is quite compatible with a large effect on intellectual level as a result of extreme environmental conditions. Fourthly, even when the heritability coefficient is high, this in no way restricts what might occur in some new environment that might come about or be deliberately constructed (Eysenck, 1971). Fifthly, heritability refers to the amount of the *variation* between individuals which is explicable in genetic terms. It is quite possible to have high heritability and yet have a major increase in *level* of IQ as a result of environmental improvement (see below).

In view of the many conceptual and statistical difficulties in arriving at a meaningful figure for the heritability of intelligence in any particular environment, no firm conclusion is possible on the proportion of the intellectual variation between individuals which is explicable in genetic terms (Anderson, 1974). That the proportion is substantial is clearly evident, that it is not more than about 80 per cent at most is agreed, and that non-genetic factors are also influential to an important degree (see below) is apparent. More than that cannot be said with any certainty.

Regression to the Mean

The term 'regression to the mean', in this context, refers to the tendency for children to be nearer to the population mean on a characteristic than are their parents. As a consequence, the children of very dull individuals are likely to be *more* intelligent than their parents, whereas the offspring of highly intelligent persons are likely to be *less* intelligent than their procreators. The effect is potentially important with respect to intergenerational cycles in that it could provide a 'mixing' of the population which would lessen familial continuities. It has also been claimed (although wrongly, as noted below) that the existence of regression to the mean provides strong evidence for the biological inheritance of intelligence (Eysenck, 1973a). Unfortunately, it is a much misunderstood phenomenon in which both the facts and concepts are frequently misquoted and wrongly used.

The first point at issue is the size of the effect with regard to intelligence. In most reviews particular reliance has been placed on the results of Burt (1961), who claimed that the average regression is usually halfway between the parental IQ and the population mean of

100. Unfortunately, there are so many errors and inconsistencies in his data (Jensen, 1974; Kamin, 1974), that no reliance can be placed on them. Other studies have shown much smaller regressions to the mean. Thus, Waller (1971) in a study of fathers and sons found a regression to the mean of 4½ points at the top of the range and 10 points at the bottom. Brandon (Brandon, 1957; Clarke and Clarke, 1974) reported a regression of 8 points for the children of mothers with a mean IQ of 83. However, like most others, both these studies were based on the IQ of only one parent. In the absence of information on the IQ of the other the figures have little meaning. The child's IQ may differ from that of his father (or mother) simply because parents of unusual intellect tend to marry partners of less unusual intellect, rather than for any other reason. The findings with respect to the regression of IQ for a child on one parent will necessarily be quite different to those for child on mid-parent (Carter, 1970). The former will be much influenced by the degree of assortative mating whereas the latter will not. Furthermore, the correlation coefficient and the regression of mid-parent on mid-child will be influenced by the number of children in the family (through an effect on mid-child variance).

Accordingly, in order to provide an adequate assessment of the degree of regression to the mean, studies based on the IQ of *both* parents and *all* children are required. Only three such studies could be found. The first by Outhit (1933) showed an average regression of 5 points at the top of the distribution and 9 points at the bottom. The study was based on a sample of only 51 families so that further investigations of larger groups are needed before any reliable assessment of the size of the regression effect on the normal population is possible. At the top of the IQ range, with Terman's sample of highly gifted individuals (Terman, 1921), Oden (1968) found that the children had an average IQ of 133, 18 points below that of the highly gifted parent when a child. However, when the IQ of the other parent (125 on average as judged from scores on the concept mastery test) was taken into account (Terman and Oden, 1959), the regression was only 6 points.*

Reed and Reed (1965) also examined regression to the mean in their systematic study of the offspring of retarded parents. When both parents had an IQ of less than 70, the average being 60, the mean IQ of the children was 67. When only the father had an IQ below 70, so that the average mid-parent IQ was 77, the average IQ of the children was 94. When only the mother had an IQ of under 70, so that the average mid-parent IQ was 80, the average IQ of the children was 86. It may be concluded that there is some evidence of a small degree of regression to the mean but that regression may be greater at the bottom end of the

*This figure is based on the parents' initial IQ and if their late adolescent IQ is used instead the regression effect disappears (McAskie and Clarke, 1976).

distribution than at the top. However, in the absence of data on large representative samples, no reliable conclusions can be drawn regarding the size of the regression effect.

As a result, any arguments regarding heritability which rely on regression to the mean necessarily have a very weak base (see McAskie and Clarke, 1976, for a fuller discussion of this issue). The potential strength of the genetic argument lies in the possibility to make precise predictions regarding the size of the regression effect with different degrees of heritability. These have been shown to work well with respect to characteristics such as finger-print ridge counts (Carter, 1974), but adequate data do not exist to test the exactness of match with respect to intelligence. In any case, such testing is made more difficult by the way predictions are changed if there is any degree of genetic dominance or if the genes are not truly additive. On the face of it a greater degree of regression at the bottom of the IQ distribution than at the top (as seems to occur — see above) would appear to demand a non-genetic explanation, but in fact dominance will automatically lead to non-linearity* of regression. It should be added that the assumption that regression to the mean is incompatible with multi-causal environmental transmission is also demonstrably false. Indeed regression would be predicted on statistical grounds alone, the size of the effect being altered by the relative importance of between-family and within-family variables. On the other hand, an environmental model (unlike a genetic one) provides no clear prediction of the size of regression effect expected with first, second and third degree relatives.

Finally it should be noted that little is known about the effects of regression across several generations. In certain circumstances regression to the mean can cause organisms, selectively bred to develop extreme characteristics, to revert gradually to the average over some two dozen generations (Dobzhansky, 1972). This was found, for example, in experiments with the drosophila fly for characteristics having less than 10 per cent heritability. Nevertheless, although this effect was probably genetic, the mechanisms remain obscure and may well be quite different to those operating in the case of human intelligence. Moreover, it should be appreciated that in the case of complete simple additive polygenic inheritance there should be *no* regression from mid-parent mean to mid-child mean (Carter, 1970). The topic of regression is conceptually complex and, so far as intelligence is concerned, very short on factual evidence. It provides no unambiguous guidelines with respect to intergenerational continuities or discontinuities.

Scholastic Attainment

The evidence on the heritability of scholastic achievement has been reviewed by Jensen (1967, 1973) with conclusions that are not in

*i.e. regression which differs in extent at different levels of IQ.

dispute: (a) genetic factors play some part in determining individual variation with respect to scholastic achievement; (b) their importance is very much less than for intelligence (Jensen estimated heritability as about 40 per cent); (c) estimates of the heritability of achievement are much more variable than for intelligence, and depend greatly on the environmental circumstances of the populations studied; and (d) most of the environmental variance is due to the differences *between* families rather than within families.

Less evidence is available on the importance (or otherwise) of genetic factors in the intergenerational transmission of specific educational disabilities. There are two sizeable series of twins with specific reading retardation (Hermann, 1959; Bakwin, 1973), both of which show greater concordance within monozygotic pairs than within dizygotic pairs. The findings certainly point to the importance of genetic influences but the data are inconclusive in view of the defects in sampling and in the assessment of specific reading retardation (Rutter and Yule, 1973, 1975).

The fact that children who have specific reading difficulties often have a family history of similar problems has already been noted but it is unclear how far it represents a biological inheritance and how far a social transmission. That the latter plays some part is suggested by the finding from the Isle of Wight study (Rutter, Tizard and Whitmore, 1970) that a family history of reading difficulties was much more common in children from large families (having controlled for the number of individuals at risk). There is no straightforward genetic reason to account for the findings, whereas there are possible social explanations.

NON-GENETIC FACTORS

Intelligence

It is necessary next to consider the evidence that non-genetic factors lead to variations in measured intelligence. The first point is that it is universally recognized that severe experiential privations can lead to serious intellectual impairment. Both animal experiments and human studies attest to this conclusion, and the findings are not in dispute (Rutter, 1972a; Clarke and Clarke, 1974).

Jensen (1969), who more than most has argued for the relative unimportance of environmental determinants of intellectual variation, stated that: 'There can be no doubt that moving children from an extremely deprived environment to good average environmental circumstances can boost the IQ some 20 to 30 points and in certain extreme rare cases as much as 60 or 70 points'. The reports of individual children reared in and then removed from an extremely limited and isolated environment illustrate this point (Mason, 1942; Davis 1947; Koluchova, 1972; Clarke, 1972). Children who had IQ scores in the severely subnormal range on removal from the restricted environments at age 6 or 7 years were able to attain normal levels of intelligence over the course of several years in a normal environment.

However, there is greater controversy over the severity of the privation which is needed if retardation is to occur and over the question of whether environmental variation within the normal range can appreciably influence intellectual level. The main findings on these issues are as follows:-

1. Children born to parents of low IQ, if adopted and reared in homes somewhat above the average, attain normal levels of intelligence (Skodak and Skeels, 1949). On the basis of regression to the mean the children in the Skodak and Skeels study might have been expected to have an average IQ of about 90 to 95. In fact at age 13 years the average IQ of the children was 106. *Within* this group of children, individual differences were still explicable in genetic terms to a significant degree (see above). But, in spite of this, placement in a good environment had led to a major increase in the overall level of intelligence. Whereas the individual variation in IQ was partially due to genetic influences, the overall rise in level must be attributed to environmental factors. The study is important in that the children were adopted in infancy so there was no question of righting the effects of a severely depriving environment. Furthermore, as the environment they were brought up in was above average but by no means exceptional, the findings strongly suggest that environmental influences within the normal range can affect intellectual development to a quite marked degree.

2. The evidence from twin studies, already discussed, indicated that heritability, although strong, is by no means complete. The lower correlation in IQ between monozygotic twins reared apart (+0.75) than between monozygotic twins reared together (+0.87) indicates an environmental effect. The Burt (1966) study of identical twins reared apart suggested that the environmental effect was quite slight but, as already noted, there are a number of unsatisfactory features of his study. The other studies of twins reared apart suggest a somewhat greater, although still slight, environmental effect. However, the range of environment included has been relatively narrow and the presence of selective placement would reduce the chances of demonstrating an environmental effect. Nevertheless, it should be said that studies have been relatively unsuccessful in demonstrating *which* environmental factors lead to intellectual differences between twins.

3. Studies of adoptive children (Burks, 1928; Leahy, 1935) have shown that their IQ is correlated with measures of the home environment to the level of between 0.20 and 0.25. Using these data Burks calculated that environmental factors accounted for some 17 per cent of the variance in IQ. However, the same data indicate that this is enough to create a 12 to 36 IQ point difference between children reared in the top 2½ per cent of environmental conditions and those reared in the bottom 2½ per cent (i.e. a 4 standard deviations difference in environmental circumstances).

4. Studies of institutional children have shown that differences between institutions in patterns of child care are systematically related to differences in the children's understanding of language (Tizard *et al.*, 1972). The findings provide convincing evidence that variations within the normal range of environmental experiences are associated with sizeable differences in children's language level (some 15 points between the 'best' and 'worst' institutions). However the children studied were under 5 years of age, and the measures were of language rather than intelligence, so that it remains uncertain how far the environmental differences will lead to differences in IQ at maturity.

5. Several longitudinal studies (see below) have indicated that both high quality schooling and prolongation of education lead to gains in intellectual level measurable at maturity (Husen, 1951; Lorge, 1945; Vernon, 1957).

6. Numerous investigations have indicated that first born children, on average, have a higher level of scholastic and occupational achievement than do later born children (Schachter, 1963; Altus, 1966; Bradley, 1968; Douglas, 1964; Douglas *et al.*, 1968; Davie *et al.*, 1972; Belmont and Marolla, 1973). The findings clearly indicate an environmental effect on achievement, but it should be noted that the association with measured intelligence is less consistent.

7. The IQ scores of the offspring of Terman's highly gifted children were higher than expected on the basis of genetic predictions (Eysenck, 1973a). The effect amounted only to some 5 points, but the importance of the observation lies in the fact that it was due to the difference between a superior environment and an average environment, and *not* to removal from a depriving environment.

8. As shown in the Reed and Reed (1965) study, children reared by a mentally retarded mother (and normal father) have a lower IQ than those reared by a mentally retarded father (and normal mother), in spite of a comparable mid-parent IQ in the two instances. As there is no indication of a sex-linked genetic effect, this argues for an environmental influence, resulting in some 5 points IQ difference. However, there are two alternative explanations. First, the assumption that both the father and mother are biologically related to the child may be false in some instances. Philipp (1973) reported that, on the basis of blood testing, 30 per cent of the mothers' husbands in a town in south-east England could not have been the fathers of their children! Secondly, Ahern and Johnson (1973) suggested that an inherited uterine inadequacy might be the explanation. They showed that, even after excluding the mentally retarded individuals' own children, female relatives had more retarded offspring than did male relatives, and also more abortions, stillbirths, and neonatal deaths.

In summary, it may be concluded that there are definite and demonstrable environmental effects on intellectual development. While environmental influences are most obvious with intellectual impairment stemming from rearing in a grossly depriving environment, and with the improvement that follows removal from such an environment, sizeable effects are also evident with respect to variations within the normal range. The size of the effect is often fairly small but the differences are real enough. Although the evidence is incomplete and variable in quality, the weight of findings is against Jensen's (1969) concept that environmental influences only operate below a threshold, i.e., that environmental deprivation can depress intelligence but superior environment can do little to raise it. Rather, the findings are more in line with Clarke and Clarke's (1974) notion of a 'wedge' effect. They suggested that environmental influences are active over the whole range of variation. However, gains in IQ are less likely to follow improvements in a good environment than improvements in a bad one.

Scholastic Attainment

The genetic studies referred to above clearly show that non-genetic factors play a major role in determining individual differences in levels of scholastic attainment. As this conclusion is universally accepted the detailed evidence will not be reviewed here. However, the influence of environmental factors will be considered below when discussing specific family, school and other variables.

PERSONAL CHARACTERISTICS AND EDUCATIONAL ATTAINMENT

Personality and Temperament

There has been a wide interest in the association between general personality variables and various aspects of cognitive performance (Rutter, 1974c). Vernon (1965) suggested that mental abilities 'depend upon personality and motivational factors, organic and social drives, curiosity and interests'. Eysenck (1967) hypothesized that variations in introversion/extraversion and neuroticism have an important relationship to intellectual and scholastic performance. While extraverts do seem to differ somewhat from introverts in the way they tackle tasks, tending to prefer speed to accuracy (Farley, 1966; Jensen, 1966), the associations with levels of achievement seem to be more complex. Although the results of research have been rather contradictory, it appears that the variations in findings are associated in part with differences in ability level, in age and in sex (see references cited in Rutter, 1974c). The evidence so far shows that correlations tend to be low and it seems unlikely that these personality variables play an important role in the genesis of either low IQ or low educational attainment.

Much the same applies to the effect of anxiety on learning (see Rutter, 1974c). It is usually said that a little anxiety helps learning but that too much anxiety interferes with it. Also it has been thought that high anxiety is most beneficial for simple tasks but lower levels of anxiety are optimal for difficult tasks. There is something in this, but the research findings cannot be said to give unequivocal support to such a view of the relationship between anxiety and learning. Probably a lot depends on the person's attitude to the task, the setting in which the learning takes place, and the responses he has previously encountered following success and failure.

Attitudes may have some indirect effects on educational attainment. Achievement motivation (McClelland, 1958), curiosity motivation (Berlyne, 1960), ability to delay gratification (Ausubel, 1963), low levels of school anxiety (Sarason *et al.*, 1960; Hill and Sarason, 1966) and appropriate aspirations (Proshansky and Newton, 1968) are all characteristics for which associations with intellectual performance have been claimed. However, these concepts have often been ill-defined and measures of achievement motivation have so far proved unsatisfactory (Entwistle, 1972). No meaningful conclusion on their importance (or otherwise) is possible from the available evidence.

The temperamental attributes most strongly associated with very low levels of reading attainment are poor concentration, restlessness, and impulsivity (see Rutter and Yule, 1973). As these attributes, even when measured outside the reading situation, correlate with reading attainment and as a few studies have shown that these temperamental measures may predict later reading performance, it seems likely that they play a role in determining scholastic achievement. However, the origins of the attributes remain ill-understood and it is uncertain how far they are modifiable by experiences in the home or at school.

Psychiatric Disorder

Low intelligence and low scholastic attainment to some extent increase the risk of all forms of psychiatric disability but the effect is most marked with respect to anti-social disorders. The evidence on these associations is briefly reviewed in Chapter 6.

Physical Illness

Chronic physical disorder in childhood has been shown to be associated with an increased rate of reading difficulties (Rutter, Tizard and Whitmore, 1970). Thus, in the Isle of Wight survey, among children with chronic physical handicaps not involving brain disorder, 14 per cent were at least 28 months retarded in reading compared with 6 per cent in the general population control group. Within the physical handicap group, there was a strong association between reading difficulties and a high absence rate from school suggesting that the children had fallen behind in their reading in part because they were missing lessons. In most cases the children had had repeated short absences, rather than one long period off school, and the resulting discouragement and lowering of morale and confidence may well have been as influential as the missed education itself.

The National Survey results (Douglas, Ross and Simpson, 1968) indicated that scholastic attainments were somewhat depressed in children with a moderate or severe chronic physical disability but were entirely normal in those with only a mild disability. It may be concluded that chronic physical illness (not involving brain pathology) is not a major cause of educational backwardness but that severe and chronic handicaps may impede scholastic attainments to a significant degree in some cases.

However, severe bilateral deafness is an exception in that the educational deficits are usually marked. In general, deaf children perform as well as hearing children on non-verbal tests of intelligence but rather below normal on intellectual tests involving concepts or linguistic skills; and most youngsters with bilateral deafness show serious educational backwardness (Furth, 1966; Peckham *et al.*, 1972; Kowitz and Levy, 1965). The deaf child's inability to utilize spoken language cuts him off from many opportunities for learning.

Conditions involving brain pathology (such as cerebral palsy) have much greater effects on school peformance than other physical handicaps. Among children with these conditions mental retardation is much commoner than in the general population and of those with normal intelligence, a high proportion have marked reading difficulties (see Seidel *et al.*, 1975 and review in Rutter, Graham and Yule, 1970). About a third of children with cerebral palsy have an IQ below 50, about a fifth have mild intellectual retardation, and the remaining half have a level of intelligence within the normal range. Children with uncomplicated epilepsy do not differ from the general population in general intelligence but, in spite of this, they are still two or three times as likely to have severe reading difficulties.

Developmental Delay

There is extensive evidence linking specific reading retardation with various forms of developmental delay (Rutter and Yule, 1973, 1975). The neurodevelopmental anomalies do not constitute a specific pattern, but speech or language difficulties and problems in sequencing are those most strongly and consistently associated with reading retardation. Right-left confusion, motor impersistence and weak intersensory integration are also important to a lesser extent. The exact cause of these developmental impairments (which tend to be inter-related) remains uncertain but several factors appear to be involved. In some cases there may be a relative failure in the normal maturation of certain special functions of the cerebral cortex (perhaps genetically determined); in others there may be some neurological damage; and in yet others the developmental retardation may stem from a lack of suitable environmental stimulation. The relatively strong intergenerational continuity with respect to specific reading retardation (see above) is linked with the strong familial element in the developmental impairments — particularly speech and language delay — which seem to underlie the reading difficulties. In part, this familial element probably reflects genetic influences, in part intergenerational repetitions of perinatal difficulties and in part the social inheritance of adverse patterns of parent-child interaction. The relative importance of each of these mechanisms is not known.

PHYSICAL INFLUENCES ON COGNITIVE DEVELOPMENT

Perinatal Complications

Factors operating during the period of foetal development and during the birth process itself are the first environmental hazards to impinge on the child, and there is good evidence to indicate that under certain circumstances, adversities encountered at this stage may impair later intellectual development. As the literature on this topic is large and has been previously well reviewed (Drillien, 1964; McDonald, 1967; Birch and Gussow, 1970), only the main findings will be summarized here.

Although various complications of pregnancy and delivery may occasionally lead to intellectual impairment, the only one that is at all consistently associated with deficits in development is very low birth weight. Until recent years most workers used a concept of prematurity that did not differentiate between low birth weight and a short period of gestation. It is now known that these two features do not necessarily go together and it has become evident that babies who, while growing normally, have a shorter than normal period in the womb (premature delivery) need to be differentiated from babies who have experienced slower than normal intrauterine growth and who at birth are undersized and underweight for their gestation age (small for dates). Premature delivery is associated with cerebral palsy (and hence with mental retardation when it is part of that disorder) but in the absence of cerebral palsy there is very little association with intellectual impairment. In contrast, small for dates babies show less tendency to have cerebral palsy but have a considerably greater risk of mental retardation when there is no overt neurological disorder. Thus, in the Isle of Wight study 17 per cent of the intellectually retarded children had been small for dates babies compared with only 4 per cent of the control group (Rutter, Tizard and Whitmore, 1970). Or viewed the other way round, of the small for dates babies without cerebral palsy followed up by McDonald (1967) 6.8 per cent had an IQ below 70, a rate three times as high as among premature delivery babies or normal babies.

Once children with overt brain pathology (cerebral palsy and the like) or frank mental retardation are excluded, the association between low birth weight and cognitive impairment is quite low, and in some studies non-existent (Drillien, 1964; McDonald, 1967; Barker and Edwards, 1967). In short, if children with gross sensory and mental defects are excluded, the mean intelligence and attainments of the remainder of the low birth weight children are only minimally lower than those of the general population.

Biological hazards of childbirth and social disadvantage tend to accompany one another. Maternal characteristics influence reproductive success and the health of the children. It has been established that the height of the mother affects her child-bearing performance, and that short stature (together with low social class) is associated with an increased incidence of small for dates babies, reproductive complications and perinatal deaths (Baird, 1949; Baird and Illsley, 1953; Thomson and Billewicz, 1963; Dawkins, 1965). In these associations there may lie one of the links involved in intergenerational cycles of disadvantage. Birch and Gussow (1970) argued that socially disadvantaged mothers 'tend to be less well fed, less well grown, and less well cared for before they reach child-bearing age. When they reach it, they begin to bear children younger, more rapidly, and more often, and they continue to bear them until a later age. When such a mother is pregnant, both her nutrition and her health will tend to be poorer than that of a woman who is better off, but she will be far less likely to get prenatal care and far more likely to be delivered under sub-standard conditions'. Mothers of small for dates babies have often had other low weight babies and to an appreciable extent this is a general characteristic of their reproductive performance (Dawkins, 1965; McDonald, 1967). It is well documented that, even within Britain, there are huge discrepancies between different parts of the country not only in rates of reproductive complications (Butler and Bonham, 1963) but also in the delivery of medical care (Townsend, 1974). It is an unhappy fact that in the field of maternal and neonatal care (as in other branches of medicine) those parts of the country most in need of services are least likely to get them.

In general, the association between IQ or attainment and social variables such as occupational class or family size are considerably stronger than those between IQ or attainment and any variety of reproductive abnormality. Thus, in the National Child Development Study social class variation was associated with a 17 months' difference in reading attainment at age 7 years (after holding other factors constant) whereas low birth weight was associated with only a 4 month difference (Davie *et al.*, 1972).

To a considerable extent, there appears to be an interaction between biological disadvantage in childbirth and social disadvantage in child-rearing. Among children from a socially favoured background, except in cases of frank brain damage, there is no association between low birth weight and depressed IQ score, suggesting that a 'good' postnatal environment can do much to compensate for a biologically poor start to life. On the other hand, in the lowest social groups there is an association between low birth weight and low IQ (Drillien, 1964; Illsley, 1966). It seems that mild biological impairment may render a child more vulnerable to the hazards of poor upbringing.

The degree of later handicap shown by a very low birth weight baby is much influenced by the quality of care he receives during the weeks immediately following birth. Follow-up studies of very small babies who have received modern methods of high quality intensive care show lower rates of mental and physical handicap than was previously the case (Rawlings *et al.*, 1971; Francis-Williams and Davies, 1974). So far the studies have not extended into later childhood so that it is too early yet to assess the full handicap, but the findings to date certainly suggest that intensive care can reduce (although not eliminate) the handicaps shown by 'small for dates' babies. Low birth weight babies can probably be divided into three main groups (Drillien, 1972): (a) infants whose premature delivery or low birth weight is primarily due to foetal abnormality; (b) infants who have suffered from inadequate oxygenation and nutrition in the later stages of pregnancy; and (c) infants who are prematurely delivered for other reasons. Postnatal medical care cannot eliminate the handicaps in the first group (although it may aid better development) but it may be crucial to normal survival in the second and third categories.

Pasamanick and Knobloch (1960) argued for the existence of a 'continuum of reproductive casualty'. According to this concept, abnormalities of pregnancy cause a number of infants to die, but among the survivors there is a fraction who are injured but yet survive. Depending on the nature of the trauma, these injured infants may go on to develop disorders ranging in severity from cerebral palsy and mental deficiency to various behavioural and learning difficulties. The first part of the hypothesized continuum in which reproductive hazard is linked to infant death and also to cerebral palsy and mental deficiency is well established, but the second part extending to more minor impairment remains much less certain. The evidence, at least so far as children in Britain are concerned, suggests that the link with poor intellectual and scholastic attainments is quite weak once the children with gross handicaps are excluded. Furthermore, such links as there are tend to be confined to children from socially disadvantaged sections of the community. But, although its impact is fairly small compared with other factors, low birth weight probably plays some part in the intergenerational transmission of disadvantage within this group.

Malnutrition

It is well established from animal studies (see review by Dobbing and Smart, 1974) that severe malnutrition in the early post natal period may restrict brain cell growth (Cheek *et al.*, 1972) and retard growth and maturation (Mönckeberg, 1972) but its association with mental impairment in humans is less clear. Certainly, malnutrition is not a unitary phenomenon and its impact is likely to be related to its severity, duration, timing and type (Dobbing, 1972).

The potential importance of malnutrition in cycles of disadvantage is indicated by several findings. Mönckeberg (1972) found a significant relationship between maternal intelligence and the nutritional status of the offspring indicating that malnourished youngsters tended to have parents of below average intelligence. Numerous studies have shown that, even in countries with a generally low standard of living, malnutrition is most commonly found in the socially disadvantaged sections of the community. Moreover, as Cravioto and DeLicardie's studies (1972) show, the development of the children is influenced both by their poor nutrition and by their family circumstances. They found that severely malnourished children in Mexico showed more impaired cognitive development than their matched controls. But the malnourished children came from homes with poor stimulation (as measured by Caldwell's inventory, 1967), and the home stimulation score was significantly related to the children's cognitive performance. Analyses suggested that severe malnutrition and poor family environment both contributed to the cognitive impairment. The same was found in the larger Jamaican study by Hertzig, Birch, Richardson and Tizard (1972). Children admitted to hospital with severe malnutrition during the first two years of life were found at follow-up several years later to be shorter, of smaller head circumference and of lower intelligence than their sibs or classroom controls. However, within the malnourished, as well as in the control group, IQ was also related to home stimulation as measured on Caldwell's inventory (Tizard, 1974a).

Direct intergenerational effects have been demonstrated in an interesting series of studies using rats. Cowley and Griesel (1959, 1966) raised successive generations of rats on a diet lacking about a quarter of the normal protein requirement. The first generation were smaller in size than normally-fed controls but were not inferior in exploratory behaviour or intelligence as measured by the Hebb-Williams closed-field test. The second generation of the experimental group, however, were not only small in size but were also retarded on the Hebb-Williams test. Of this group, a number were put back onto a regular diet and a number were not. The offspring of both sub-groups were retarded but the pups of the well-fed mothers not as much so as those of the protein-deficient mothers.

Birch (1972) suggested three possible mechanisms to account for any association between diet and intellect: malnutrition causes central nervous system damage which influences mental capacity; dietary deficiency leads to ill-health and/or hospital admission which interferes with learning opportunities and impairs responsiveness; inadequate food intake at critical times causes abnormalities in the direction and sequencing of development. One, two or all of these may act in particular circumstances. In many cases, however, the chain of associations may have been set in motion at a time long before the infant's own malnutrition. In short, malnutrition usually acts as part of a train of adverse circumstances rather than as a stress event in isolation. These mechanisms indicate possible ways in which malnutrition may lead to poor intellectual performance.

A review of published studies (Scrimshaw and Gordon, 1968; Stein and Kassab, 1970; PAHO, 1972; Hertzig *et al.*, 1972; Ricciuti, 1973; Tizard, 1975a) of chronic malnutrition in children from developing countries suggests the following conclusions:

1. Children who have been subjected to severe and chronic malnutrition leading to hospital admission in the early years of childhood tend to have slightly lower IQ scores than do their sibs or children living in closely similar socio-familial circumstances. Thus, in the Hertzig *et al.* (1972) study of Jamaican children, the full scale WISC IQ of the severely malnourished children was 4 points below that of their sibs and 8 points below that of the classmate or neighbour control children. The finding suggests that malnourishment can lead to impairment in intellectual development.

2. In this respect, however, the difference between the malnourished children and their sibs has generally been found to be less than that between both of these groups and the average run of children living in the same country. Either the effects of social disadvantage outweigh the effects of undernourishment, or the difference between severe malnutrition and sub-optimal nutrition (as experienced by the sibs) is less than that between sub-optimal nutrition and good nutrition.

3. In remedying the intellectual ill-effects of severe malnutrition in children from poor circumstances, the provision of adequate experiences and intellectual 'stimulation' is equally as important as the provision of better nutrition. Both are needed.

4. Whereas severe untreated malnutrition may play a substantial role in modifying subsequent psychological development, mild or moderate malnutrition probably plays a relatively minor part in children's intellectual growth, as compared with the influence of other factors — social, environmental and genetic.

5. Although the evidence is so far weak and inconclusive it seems that, at least in part, malnutrition may exert its influence on psychological development through changes in attention, responsiveness and motivation rather than through a more direct impairment of cognitive competence.

There is only one study of the intellectual growth of children from a developed country who have experienced malnutrition. Stein *et al.* (1972a and b) studied males exposed during gestation to the war-time famine in the Netherlands. They found that at 19 years of age there was no difference in IQ between individuals who had and those who had not experienced gestation during the famine. Caution is required in interpreting the finding because (a) there was no direct assessment of whether any particular individual experienced malnutrition (the slightly lowered birth weight in the famine cities suggested that there was some degree of undernourishment of the babies, but as the mean birth weight was still above 3,000 gms it is likely that the babies suffered less than the rest of the population); (b) the study examined the effects of acute starvation rather than chronic malnutrition; and (c) the malnutrition occurred during the period of gestation rather than during childhood. Nevertheless, it may be tentatively concluded that acute starvation during the period of gestation probably has little effect on intellectual development provided it is preceded and followed by good nutrition and provided it occurs in an adequate social environment.

In contrast, the effects of chronic malnutrition in socially disadvantaged children are probably more marked. Even so, it seems that the adverse consequences arise more from the social disadvantage than from the malnutrition. Although there is evidence that nutrition in this country is by no means optimal (Lambert, 1964; Lynch and Oddy, 1967), the level is far above that in the developing countries. It seems probable that in this country subnutrition plays at most a very minor part in the genesis of intellectual impairment but it may well be more important as a cause of low stature and by this means be implicated in cycles of disadvantage (see above).

Height and Intelligence

Numerous studies in a variety of social settings have shown a consistent although small, association between children's height and intelligence, the correlation between the two being between 0.15 and 0.25 (Tanner, 1969). This correlation persists into adult life although it diminishes somewhat at maturity. In all countries, university students are the tallest members of the population and mentally retarded individuals the shortest. Among the latter, the degree of shortness and degree of mental retardation are correlated. In seeking an explanation for this link between height and intelligence it is relevant that the greater the number of children in a family, the lower the height and intelligence of the children. This effect is most pronounced in poor families and largely disappears by adulthood. There are also social class differences in height which persist into adult life. On the average, taller men and women tend to rise in the social scale both occupationally and at marriage, and shorter persons tend to go down. At the moment, the causes of the association between height and intelligence remain uncertain. However, it is likely that genetic factors, damage during development in the womb, and poor nutrition after birth may all play some part.

Toxic Substances

During their development children may be exposed to a variety of toxic substances which in high dosage can induce mental impairment. The commonest of these is lead which can cause brain damage associated with permanent mental and physical disability (Byers and Lord, 1943). Because lead is frequently found in the peeling paint of old slum houses, lead intoxication has been suspected as a contributory factor in the mild mental retardation which shows a high prevalence in these same slum areas. Severe lead intoxication undoubtedly can cause neurological disorder and it has often been supposed that milder degrees of toxicity might lead to some degree of mental retardation even in the absence of encephalopathy. The repeated finding of relatively high blood lead levels in retarded and hyperkinetic children has appeared to support this view (Moncrieff *et al.*, 1964; David *et al.*, 1972). In these cases the lead intoxication has usually come from the ingestion of paint and other lead-containing substances so that it is uncertain how far the retardation and behavioural disturbance were factors leading the child to ingest inedible substances (and hence get lead intoxication) and how far the lead ingestion caused mental and behavioural impairment.

This issue is better resolved by the study of individuals exposed to high levels of lead as a result of factory pollution of the atmosphere with lead products. Two recent controlled studies of this type have been published. In London, Lansdown *et al.* (1974) found no relationship between children's blood lead level and any measure of mental or behavioural functioning. A comparable study in El Paso, Texas (Whitworth *et al.*, 1974) also found no relationship between blood lead level and verbal intelligence, hyperactivity, other forms of behavioural disturbance, or scores on the Bender Motor Gestalt test. Only one item out of a large range of neuro-developmental items differentiated between the groups with high or low blood lead levels. However, there was a statistically significant 7 point difference on the Wechsler Performance IQ between the high and low blood lead level groups. Both studies, although well planned and carefully conducted, have limitations and it should be noted that recent animal experiments indicate that lead can produce behavioural disorders (see Bryce-Smith and Waldron, 1974), perhaps especially in the young (Allen *et al.*, 1974). Certainly, in humans, lead intoxication can cause mental retardation following encephalopathy. However, the limited available evidence suggests that in the absence of encephalopathy, lead poisoning is probably not an important cause of mental impairment in children. Possibly, in some cases, it may lead to more subtle minor disturbances in motor and perceptual skills but this remains to be established.

Smoking during Pregnancy

The National Child Development Study (Davie *et al.*, 1972) has shown that children born to mothers who smoked during their pregnancy are shorter and read less well at age 7 years than do children whose mothers did not smoke. Follow-up at age 11 years (Butler and Goldstein, 1973) showed that children whose mothers smoked during pregnancy were, on average, three months behind other children in general intelligence, four months behind in reading and one centimetre shorter in height, after making appropriate statistical allowances for other factors. The effects are quite minor, and considerably less than those associated with family size or social class, but if the association reflects a truly causal relationship the ill-effects should be preventable. Smoking during pregnancy has been shown to be associated with lowered birth weight and with an increased risk of perinatal death (Butler and Alberman, 1969). It seems likely that some of the association between smoking and impaired later development represents damage from smoking but this has yet to be proven.

EXPERIENTIAL INFLUENCES ON INTELLECTUAL DEVELOPMENT AND SCHOLASTIC ATTAINMENT

Social Class Differences

Numerous studies in both this country and in other parts of the world have shown quite substantial correlations between parental social class and both the IQ and scholastic attainments of their children (Deutsch *et al.*, 1968; Plowden, 1967). At all ages, middle class children in the National Survey had considerably higher intelligence and attainment scores than did their working class counterparts (Douglas, 1964; Douglas *et al.*, 1968) and in the National Child Development Study parental social class was the variable which showed the strongest association with children's reading attainment at age 7 years. Furthermore, several studies (Eells *et al.*, 1951; Stein and Susser, 1960, 1963; Birch *et al.*, 1970; Rutter, Tizard and Whitmore, 1970) have clearly shown that mild mental retardation mainly occurs in families in which the father has an unskilled or semi-skilled manual job. Mild retardation is particularly common when, in addition, there is poverty, family disorganization, overcrowding and a large number of offspring. In such circumstances it is common for several of the children to be mildly retarded or have an IQ score near the bottom of the normal range. When mental retardation occurs in a professional or middle-class family it is usually associated with organic brain disease; this is less often the case with retarded youngsters from a socially disadvantaged background. The evidence clearly points to the conclusion that there are quite marked social class differences in intellectual functioning and scholastic achievement. In part this association is a reflection of genetically determined differences in intelligence influencing social class distribution (see chapter on social mobility and section above on genetics), but also there is evidence that the association reflects social influences on intellectual development (Stein and Susser, 1970). The chief relevant findings will now be considered.

The one direct way in which social class influences could be demonstrated is by determining the associations between parental social class and the children's IQ or attainment scores within a sample of adopted children in which selective placement has not occurred. Data which approach these requirements are available from several early American studies (Leahy, 1935; Burks, 1928; Skodak and Skeels, 1949). A recent report from Belgium (Claeys, 1973) is also relevant although the findings are limited by the skewed distribution of social class in the adoptive parents. Unfortunately, the one recent British study (Seglow *et al.*, 1972) with appropriate data, on a sample with a reasonable social spread, failed to utilize the opportunity so provided and did not relate the children's attainments to the adoptive parents' social status (Rutter, 1974b). The earlier studies indicated a low association between adoptive father's occupational status and the children's IQ (in the Leahy study a social class spread of 5 points in contrast to one of 16 points in families in which the parents and children are biologically related). However, Burks (1928) found a corrected multiple correlation between various 'fine grain' environmental variables (time spent reading to the children, etc.) and children's IQ of 0.42 which indicates a moderate influence attributable to family variables.

An indirect assessment of the importance of social class influences is obtainable by determining the mean IQ of children born to parents of low social class and reared by parents of high social class. This is provided by Skodak and Skeels' (1949) study of 100 adopted children. Three-quarters of the true fathers held unskilled or semi-skilled jobs, compared with only 13 per cent of the adoptive parents. The mean IQ of the children at 13 years was 106, some 20 points above that of their true mothers which indicated a substantial rise attributable to environmental influences associated with the marked social class difference between the biological and adoptive parents. The rise is well above that expected on the basis of regression to the mean (see above). Some of the earlier findings from the Iowa studies (of which this constitutes one part) were rightly criticized on psychometric grounds (McNemar, 1940) but the follow-up findings in adolescence are not subject to the same objections as those in early childhood. Some bias may have resulted from the failure to follow-up all children in the study. However, the findings indicated that this was unlikely to lead to any substantial distortion and it may be concluded that the children's improved social circumstances were indeed responsible for their improved intellectual development. In short, betterment of the environment had a substantial effect in raising the children's mean level of intelligence, although it made less difference to individual differences in IQ within the adopted group.

A further assessment of possible social class influences on cognitive growth can be obtained by determining which aspects of parent-child interaction relate to children's intelligence (in groups unrelated genetically), and then finding out how far social groups differ in these aspects of family interaction. Some findings relevant to the first issue are provided by Tizard's studies of children in residential nurseries (Tizard *et al.*, 1972, Tizard and Rees, 1974). It was found that the children's language development at 30 months was significantly related to measures reflecting the frequency of informative staff talk, the frequency with which the staff played with and read to the children and the frequency with which the staff answered the children's remarks. At 4 years small but significant correlations (about 0.25) were found between the children's IQ on the Wechsler scale and various measures of the breadth of their experiences (visits to the zoo, the library, etc.). In short, both the quality of the children's verbal environment and the richness of their 'family' activities were significant determinants of early cognitive development. These findings are in keeping with Jack Tizard's earlier finding (1964) that improvements in institutional care could lead to a gain in the verbal-cognitive skills of severely retarded children in hospital, and with the variety of experimental findings indicating the importance of meaningful linguistic experiences for good language development (see review by Rutter and Mittler, 1972). Numerous animal experiments also attest to the importance of rich varied experiences for normal intellectual development (see Rutter, 1972a).

Many of these aspects of family interaction have been shown to differ by social class. Hess and Shipman (1965, 1967) found that, compared with working class mothers, more middle class mothers said that they would give their children specific instruction and preparation on starting school. In a laboratory task situation middle class mothers were more effective teachers of their children, using more explicit instructions. Several studies have indicated social class differences in language usage, particularly with respect to abstract function. When describing something, middle class children are more specific and elaborate in a way which is intelligible without knowing the immediate context. In contrast, what the working class child says is less explicit, makes more assumptions and is only fully understandable in context (Hawkins, 1969). In the same way, middle class mothers have been found to be more explicit and informative than working class mothers when answering questions. They engage in more dialogue with their children and, in particular, are involved in more discussions over play and ideas (Wootton, 1974). Middle class families more often use language to express thoughts and concepts and they do so in a way which is precise and takes less for granted (Robinson and Rackstraw, 1967; Brandis and Henderson, 1970). Middle class parents are more likely to see toys and play as things which are of educational importance (Bernstein and Young, 1967). It is clear from these studies that there are important social class differences in styles of family language usage. The data do not indicate whether this has any effect on the children's intellectual development but the institutional studies suggest that it probably does.

Bernstein (1965), whose theorizing gave rise to most of these studies and whose work has been most influential in this area, has described the differences in terms of what he calls an 'elaborated' and a 'restricted' code or style of speaking. An elaborated code is one in which the speaker selects from a relatively extensive range of syntactic alternatives to express ideas or concepts in such a fashion that the message could be understood in its own right without knowledge of the speaker or the social context. In contrast, a restricted code is one where the range of syntactic alternatives is severely limited and where the understanding of the message is largely dependent on a knowledge of the speaker, the circumstances in which he spoke, and the social setting of the conversation. Although each code has its uses, an elaborated code is much more effective for educational purposes and it is for this reason that working class children are thought to be disadvantaged in their psychological development. Bernstein has been quite explicit that he has been concerned with styles of linguistic usage rather than with linguistic competence (Gahagan and Gahagan, 1970), and Robinson (1965) has convincingly shown that working class children who were normally restricted code users could be induced to use some features of the elaborated code by giving them a formal task in which the elaborated code was more appropriate (writing a letter to someone in authority). In short, what is suggested is that social groups differ in the emphasis that they place on various styles of communication and that this has an effect on the children's intellectual development. Labov (1970) in studying American Negro children has also shown that the problem lies not in grammatical competence but how language is applied in a school learning situation.

Bernstein's theorizing has been criticized by a number of workers (Lawton, 1968; Coulthard, 1969; Ryan, 1972) on the grounds of loose structure and lack of internal consistency, and Bernstein himself has modified his views somewhat over the last decade. Nevertheless, his theoretical writings have stimulated considerable research which has lent support to some of his basic tenets. It seems highly likely that not only are there marked social class differences in styles of communication but also that this has important implications for the children's development.

Further pointers to the influence of social factors on intellectual development stem from studies of gypsy and canal boat children (Gaw, 1925; Gordon, 1923), of children from isolated communities in Kentucky (Asher, 1935) and in the Tennessee mountains (Wheeler, 1942), of children from severely disadvantaged homes (Skeels and Fillmore, 1937) and of children of mothers with low IQ living in poor socio-economic circumstances (Heber, Dever and Conry, 1968). The studies show that verbal abilities are more seriously impaired than visuo-spatial skills (in line with the findings on communication above) and that retardation is greater in older children than in younger ones, suggesting progressive impairment due to some kind of experiential restriction or privation. The finding that, in the USA, the longer that black immigrants from the South had had schooling in the (less depriving) North the higher was their IQ (Lee, 1951) is also in keeping with this view. There are important flaws in all these studies either because the data were cross-sectional or because of the large number of children lost during follow-up. These flaws demand caution in accepting the results as they stand. But the weight of evidence suggests that the longer the privation the more intellectual development is impeded.

Parent-child correlations in IQ gradually increase up to the age of 5 or 6, (Jones, 1954) which could mean that heritability increases with age (Jensen, 1969). While this might well explain the drop in IQ during the pre-school years it appears unlikely that it could explain the continuing fall during middle and later childhood.

The social circumstances of the children in many of these studies were fairly extreme and it is not possible to generalize the findings to social class variations in intellectual and scholastic achievement in modern day Britain. Nevertheless, a somewhat similar (although considerably smaller) effect was noted by Douglas (1964) in the National Survey. Between 8 and 11 years the intellectual performance of children from poor home conditions deteriorated so that the gap between the social classes widened during the middle years of childhood. The finding was thought to reflect environmentally transmitted family influences but could have been an artefact due to statistical regression. However, the findings at 15 years were somewhat different and more complicated (Douglas *et al.*, 1968). Between 11 and 15 years the social classes continued to diverge in scholastic attainments (reading and mathematics), but the social class variation in intelligence narrowed considerably so that the gap at 15 years was actually less than that at 8 years. In short, insofar as environmental influences were having a progressive impact over time, their effect was most marked with respect to academic attainments and least evident in terms of measured intelligence. Acland's (1973) reanalysis of the Plowden longitudinal data found that the gap between middle class and working class children did not continue to widen appreciably as they grew older.

It may be concluded from these (and other) studies that social circumstances can and do influence children's intellectual development, and even more so, their scholastic achievement. What is much less clear is which aspects of the social environment are most important in this connection. The studies referred to above indicate that the quality of parent-child interaction and the range of experiences available to the child are among those aspects of the environment which are most important in this connection. Sometimes this effect is considered in terms of 'stimulation'. While it is true that a certain minimum of stimulation is necessary for development within ordinary circumstances in all social groups, it is not the amount of stimulation which matters most for development but rather the quality, meaningfulness and range of experience available to the child. In this connection family styles or codes of communication may well be particularly important but non-verbal experiences are also relevant. In terms of the linguistic environment in working class homes it is not so much that it is deficient in comparison with the middle class home but rather that it is different in a way which puts the child at an educational disadvantage.

Parental attitudes to learning and to education are probably also an important part of social class related influences on development.

Hertzig *et al.* (1968) in a well planned American study found important class and ethnic differences in the manner in which pre-school children responded to cognitive demands in the test situation. It appeared that their styles of approach to school type work stemmed from differences in family attitudes and in styles of interaction. Several studies (Douglas, 1964; Plowden, 1967) have claimed to show that parental interest and encouragement and parental contact with the school are associated with the child's scholastic progress. However, Douglas' data were based on teachers' reports so that the measures were not truly independent and a reanalysis of the Plowden findings (Acland, 1973) showed that the amount of contact parents had with the school and the amount they helped with homework bore little relationship to the children's scholastic attainments. On the other hand, as Wiseman (1964) also found, the literacy of the home was more important. Whether this represented a causal influence could not be determined from the data.

It has also been argued (Ginsberg, 1972) that the educational difficulties of poor children are due to a disparity between the skills used at home and those needed at school; that they are not in fact disadvantaged at all, and that the problem lies in schools taking a wrong approach. Cole and Bruner (1971), too, have suggested that poor children have the necessary skills but that these are not tapped by their teachers. There is probably something in this view, although it appears an oversimplification, but the question remains as to why so many children from a socially disadvantaged background should experience such widespread and persistent difficulties in school-type learning.

Several studies (e.g. Douglas, 1964; Birch *et al.*, 1970; Rutter, Tizard and Whitmore, 1970; Davie *et al.*, 1972) have shown that poor material circumstances such as poverty, overcrowding and lack of basic household facilities are associated with intellectual retardation and poor scholastic attainments. Lack of material resources may make it more difficult for parents to provide the sort of environment needed by the children, and lack of space and facilities is likely to interfere with the child's attempts to do homework or read. While this is important, it should be said that the effect of overcrowding and lack of facilities is considerably less than that attributable to social class and family size (see below).

A number of studies have looked at the effects of housing upon educational performance by comparing otherwise similar groups of families who have and who have not been rehoused (see chapter 3). It has usually been found that rehousing has little effect upon educational attainment. However, follow-up periods have been fairly short and it may be that rehousing has more effect on a school performance in the long-term. Certainly, even if poor housing conditions have led to depressed school performance the effect would not necessarily be reversed simply by removing the housing disadvantage. The material environment may aid or retard school progress but the effects are mostly indirect.

A further consideration concerning the association between social class and attainment is the extent to which this persists over several generations. Where this has been examined, the link between the grandparents' social class and the child's IQ and scholastic attainments has been found to be low (Rutter, Tizard and Whitmore, 1970; Birch *et al.*, 1970; Davie *et al.*, 1972). In the Isle of Wight study the social class distribution of grandparents did not differ between the general population control group, the group of intellectually retarded children and the group of youngsters with specific reading retardation. In the National Child Development Study the grandparents' occupations were unassociated with variations on arithmetic scores and were associated with reading scores only to a trivial degree (other factors having been taken into account). Birch and his colleagues concluded that the evidence: 'does not support the view of an inbred and highly stable lowest social class with an inferior genetic endowment but rather suggests the possibility of downward social movement into the lowest social class of some men and women who may provide either a poor endowment or an inadequate environment for the development of their children'.

The evidence so far has been concerned with social correlates of attainment. It is also necessary to consider how far social class determines educational opportunities. The National Survey findings (Douglas, 1964; Douglas *et al.*, 1968) showed that for children of very high ability there were equal opportunities in all social groups for selective schooling. However, among children of good, but not superior, ability the middle class child was considerably more likely to be placed in a selective (academic) school. Moreover, at all levels of ability the working class child was more likely to leave school early and less likely to gain good certificates. Even after equating for intellectual grading at age 11 years, more middle class children than working class children gain qualifications for higher education (Robbins, 1963). In short, quite apart from any social influences on intellectual attainment, the middle class child has advantages over the working class child in terms of the educational opportunities open to him at all stages of schooling. This is true in the USA as well as Britain (Wolfle, 1961). The fact that medical students from a professional background are *more* likely to fail their exams than are students whose fathers held an unskilled or semi-skilled job is perhaps a consequence of this social bias in selection (Todd, 1968). However, with some exceptions, in most courses the degree class of University students is unrelated to paternal occupations (Wolfle, 1961; Newfield, 1963).

In part, the social differences in educational opportunity are a function of an inability (or sometimes, failure) to take advantage of what is available. Thus, leaving school early may reflect social differences in attitudes to education, as well as selection processes. Even between comprehensive schools serving the same geographical area, there are major differences in the intake from primary schools

(Yule and Rutter, 1975). Sometimes this has been seen as a fault of examinations and intelligence tests but it should be noted that the social biases have been found to be *greater* when intelligence tests have been replaced by teacher judgements (Floud and Halsey, 1957). In part, too, the wastage of talent may well stem from the social divisions which exist in so many secondary schools (Hargreaves, 1967) and which serve to discourage large numbers of children. Many writers have seen comprehensive schools as the answer to this serious wastage of ability. However, the available evidence indicates that the wastage is no less in comprehensive schools, that comprehensive education has little effect on occupational choice, and that class consciousness in comprehensive schools is much the same as that found in other types of schools (Ford, 1969). There is no room for complacency about the problem of wastage but equally it is premature to think that we have found the answers.

Regional Variations

American studies have shown that reading difficulties are considerably more prevalent in areas of low social status and especially in deteriorating inner city areas (Miller *et al.*, 1957; Eisenberg, 1966). This finding may reflect the low occupational status of the parents living in such areas but this explanation could not account for some of the regional variations in reading attainment found within Britain. Both the British National Survey (Douglas *et al.*, 1968) and the National Child Development Study (Davie *et al.*, 1972) showed that the reading attainments of Scottish children were superior to those of English children in spite of fewer middle class families in Scotland and the lower non-verbal intelligence scores of Scottish children. Whether this finding is due to the better school teaching of reading skills in Scotland, whether to the greater involvement of Scottish parents in helping their children learn to read, or to other factors remains uncertain.

Berger, Yule and Rutter (1975) found that the rate of specific reading retardation in London 10-year-olds was more than double that in Isle of Wight 10-year-olds. The difference was not explicable in terms of area differences in either social class or general intelligence and genetic factors seemed unlikely to account for the findings. Rather, the much higher rate of reading difficulties in London children seemed to be due to less adequate schooling, larger families and the adverse social circumstances which were more prevalent in the metropolis (Rutter *et al.*, 1975b).

Family Disruption

There is a large literature on possible parental influences on children's intellectual development (Freeberg and Payne, 1967). But despite many studies, there is little knowledge on which parental practices or family circumstances are important in this connection. Following Bowlby's review (1951) on maternal deprivation, there developed a concern that separation experiences or other forms of interruption of parent-child relationships might seriously interfere with intellectual growth. As a result, mothers going to work, fathers being away from home and 'broken homes' all came under suspicion. However, numerous studies have now shown that, in themselves, these factors show very little association with mental retardation or educational failure (Douglas, 1964; Rutter, Tizard and Whitmore, 1970; Davie *et al.*, 1972; Herzog and Sudia, 1973).

Douglas *et al.* (1968) found that paternal death had no apparent effect on educational attainment, but that children whose fathers were often ill or unemployed performed less well at school. Children brought up by mothers on their own had slightly better attainments than those whose mothers remarried after divorce or widowhood (see Murchison, 1974). However, this is the converse of the findings in Santrock's study (1972). Frequent absence of the father (through work) made no difference to children's scholastic test score at 8 years, but those whose fathers were consistently away from home did slightly less well at fifteen. Davie *et al.* (1972) found that middle class seven year olds from broken homes read less well than other children, but this did not apply to working class seven-year-olds. Illegitimate children read less well, on average, than do legitimate children (Crellin *et al.*, 1971) but illegitimacy is associated with numerous social disadvantages and these may be more important than the family disruption or incompleteness as such. This has been the conclusion of several other studies in this country (see Murchison, 1974) and in the United States (Herzog and Sudia, 1973). It seems that it is not the fact of family disruption or loss of father *per se* which is important, but rather the more long-term family adversities which these sometimes reflect.

Family Size and Birth Order

Numerous studies have shown that individuals from large families tend to have a lower level of intelligence and inferior reading attainment than those from small families (Anastasi, 1956; Nisbet, 1953; Douglas, 1964; Davie *et al.*, 1972; Rutter, Tizard and Whitmore, 1970; Douglas *et al.*, 1968; Nisbet and Entwistle, 1967; Belmont and Marolla, 1973). Although there has been the occasional exception (Kennett and Cropley, 1970), the finding is remarkably consistent across a wide variety of samples. The association between large family size and low attainment applies most strongly to verbal intelligence and reading and is scarcely evident at all with respect to non-verbal intelligence. However, mathematics attainment also shows a moderate association with family size (i.e. low attainment in large families), and youngsters from large families are less successful in national examinations and tend to leave school earlier than those from small families. The finding applies to both boys and girls, remains even after controlling for birth order and social class, and occurs in all social groups although it is least evident in individuals from middle class homes. Belmont and Marolla

(1973) also found the association inconsistent among the sons of farm workers. The association is strongly evident by 8 years and does not increase during the later years of childhood or adolescence. There is some evidence that the relationship between family size and school performance is more marked among Protestants than among Catholics (see Clausen, 1966).

Various hypotheses have been put forward to account for the fact that youngsters from large families show lower academic attainments and inferior verbal intelligence. A purely genetic explanation seems improbable (Rutter and Mittler, 1972). As family size is associated with verbal, but not with non-verbal, skills this could reflect a hereditary mechanism only if either (a) verbal skills have a high genetic component whereas non-verbal skills do not; or (b) if highly verbal parents restrict the size of their families whereas parents with high non-verbal skills do not. The first possibility can be ruled out by the evidence that perceptual and spatial abilities have at least as strong a genetic loading as verbal abilities. There is no direct evidence on the second possibility but it seems inherently unlikely.

On the other hand, the observation that the association is less marked in upper social groups and may be less strong among Catholic families does suggest that part of the explanation may lie in differences between the sort of people who have large families and those who do not. Oldman *et al.* (1971) argued that family size was important only through its association with parental characteristics. However, the evidence put forward was highly circumstantial and, unfortunately, their analysis was based on the association between family size and non-verbal IQ which, as already noted, is neither as strong nor so consistent as the associations with reading and verbal skills. Nevertheless, it seems probable that among those parents who produce very large families are a proportion who have not planned their families, who do not manage their affairs very well and who tend to live for the present (Davie *et al.*, 1972). How large this proportion is remains unknown and how far such a group accounts for the association between family size and attainment is quite uncertain. Data on the association within groups who do and who do not use birth control would be informative, and evidence is needed concerning the characteristics of people according to the number of children they produce.

It has been suggested that achievement motivation may be less in large families (Rosen, 1961) and there is some evidence that children from large families receive less adequate infant care and less encouragement in schooling than do other children (Douglas, 1964). However, it has to be said that very little evidence is available on the ways in which either attitudes or family interaction vary by family size. These are topics worth further study.

Financial and material resources are considerably less in large families. Land (1969), in a London Study, found that unemployment, poverty and overcrowding were all more common among families with five or more dependent children. Similar findings emerged from the larger scale Ministry of Social Security enquiry (1967). It is an unfortunate fact that different forms of social disadvantage all tend to affect the same group of families. Thus, among 7-year-old British children, 23 per cent come from a one-parent family or large family, 14 per cent are in families with a very low income and 23 per cent live in poor housing (Wedge and Prosser, 1973). Six per cent of children are disadvantaged in all three ways — a rate 8 times that which would occur if the various types of disadvantage did not cluster together. It seems reasonable to suppose that lack of resources and poor living conditions play a part in the poor attainment of children from large families. Poverty, shortage of space and of books, lack of sleep due to bed sharing, interruption by other children and inadequate facilities for homework are all factors detrimental to scholastic success (Floud *et al.*, 1956; Dale and Griffith, 1965; Davie *et al.*, 1972). Nevertheless, even when overcrowding and lack of household amenities have been taken into account statistically, the association between family size and attainment remains.

The fact that the association between family size and attainment is strongest with verbal skills and the fact that it is already maximal during the early years of schooling have led workers to suggest that at least part of the explanation lies in the child's linguistic environment at home during the pre-school years (Nisbet, 1953; Douglas *et al.*, 1968; Rutter and Mittler, 1972). It has been suggested that a child's growth of vocabulary is affected by the extent to which, when learning to talk, he comes into contact with other pre-school children whose small vocabularies and elementary grammar offer little verbal stimulation, rather than with adults whose language is richer and more varied. In keeping with this view is the finding that children's vocabulary scores fall as the number of pre-school children in the family increases (Douglas *et al.*, 1968). Also, parents have only a finite amount of time available to interact with their children and as family size increases this time must be shared between more children. Although not systematically measured, there is probably less intensive interaction and less communication between parents and children in large families. On the other hand, it may be the *clarity* of the language environment, rather than its complexity, which is the key variable. In a study of tape recordings of family conversations in the home, Friedlander (1971) found that the presence of sibs led to a tumultous clamour in which several people spoke at once at different levels. Perhaps this kind of linguistic chaos makes verbal intellectual development more difficult in large families.

There is good reason to suppose that some aspect of the child's linguistic environment is one element, perhaps a major element, in the association between large family size and low attainment. However, in the absence of systematic family studies which compare the patterns of interaction and communication according to size of sibship, the mechanisms involved remain matters for hypothesis and speculation.

Although the association between family size and attainment is probably largely environmentally determined it is not possible to rule out a genetic explanation entirely. However, this problem does not arise with respect to birth order as there is no known way in which polygenic characteristics can be associated with birth order. Accordingly, the findings with respect to birth order are particularly important when considering possible environmental influences on intellectual development. There have been a number of reviews on this topic which have pointed to the considerable methodological problems and somewhat inconsistent findings (Jones, 1933; Clausen, 1966; Altus, 1966; Schooler, 1972). Much of the inconsistency stems from the use of highly selected samples and a failure to control for family size and social class.

Nevertheless, it is clear from numerous studies that eminent persons are far more likely to have been eldest or only children than to have been born later in the order (Roe, 1952; Schachter, 1963; Bradley, 1968). There seems no doubt that first borns show higher achievement than later born children but, until recently, there has been some doubt as to whether they are also of higher intelligence. This matter was investigated in a well-controlled study by Belmont and Marolla (1973) using scores on Raven's Progressive Matrices as obtained for 400,000 19-year-old males registering for National Service in the Netherlands. They found that in all social groups there was a gradient in level of ability related to birth order, such that those early in the birth order had consistently higher scores than those later in the order. The effect was regular and systematic in smaller families (two to four children), present but less consistent in five to six child families and present but inconsistent in still larger families. The size of the difference can be gauged by the fact that the disparity within the non-manual social group between first born and eighth born was as great as that between first borns in non-manual and in manual social groups.

Belmont and Marolla (1973) had data only on males so that sex differences could not be examined. However, the National Survey included data on both boys and girls, and Douglas *et al.* (1968) showed that the superiority of first borns (at least in 2 and 3 child families) applied only to boys. Furthermore, the higher scores of eldest boys were restricted to verbal intelligence and to scholastic attainments; no difference with respect to birth order was found for non-verbal intelligence. Nevertheless, eldest boys did consistently better than younger boys in national examinations and more stayed on at school. There was some tendency for achievement to be greater when there was an interval of 2–4 years between the children's births (rather than either a shorter or longer period). In the Douglas study, eldest sons had attainments superior to only sons but this did not apply in the Belmont and Marolla study (1973). In most investigations only children share the academic superiority shown by eldest children.

The National Child Development Study (Davie *et al.*, 1972) showed that the difference between first born and fourth or later born children was equivalent to nearly 16 months in reading attainment at age 7 years, after controlling for social class and other relevant variables (apart from family size which was *not* taken into account). First born children were also taller.

A study of children's verbal reasoning scores in the eleven plus examination showed that, even within the same family, youngsters born earlier in the birth order scored more highly than those born later (Record *et al.*, 1969). However, the differences were quite small (about one IQ point between consecutive sibs), and considerably less than in the population in the whole. This indicates that much of the birth order effect may be an artefact of between-family differences. Nevertheless, within families there was still a 3½ point difference between first born and fifth born children.

It is clear, then, that boys early in the birth order have a somewhat superior verbal IQ and superior attainments to those later in the order; and that this difference must be due to non-genetic factors. Jensen (1969) argued that the phenomenon is probably biologically determined, but suggested no plausible mechanism. It is possible that the lower attainments of later born children are a function of diminishing reproductive efficiency. Certainly perinatal mortality is greater in later born than early born children in large families but it is considerably *lower* in second and third born children than in first born (Butler and Bonham, 1963) which is entirely out of keeping with the birth order findings with respect to achievement. The fact that the birth order effect seems to apply to boys but not to girls also argues for a social rather than a biological explanation.* If this conclusion is correct it is, of course, incompatible with Jensen's (1969) threshold theory of environmental influences on intellectual development.

How birth order influences IQ remains quite uncertain. Douglas *et al.* (1968) suggested that the stimulus of competition from younger sibs may be one factor. Davie *et al.* (1972) saw the findings as a result of sharing of family resources. Lees and Stewart (1957) emphasized the greater responsibilities given to first born children; Schachter (1959) maintained that the first born had greater affiliative needs; and Sampson (1962) stressed the greater social conformity of first borns and their greater need for achievement. Several studies have indicated differences in the way parents interact with first born and later born

*Obviously, there are important biological differences between boys and girls (Hutt, 1972) but none of these are of a kind to explain why a biological birth order effect should only apply to the one sex.

children (see chapter on parenting behaviour) and Hunt (1961) claimed that first children enjoy a 'richer' early environment, in the form of more intense parental stimulation, than do later children. At present, the data needed to decide between these (or other) alternatives are not available.

Multiple births

Many studies have shown that children of multiple births (twins, triplets, etc.) are delayed in their language development and have a lower verbal intelligence than singletons (see review by Rutter and Mittler, 1972). This difference is not due to genetic factors and biological factors probably play only a small part. Twins and triplets are frequently of low birth weight and short gestation and are subject to a greater than usual risk of perinatal damage. This may be a minor factor in the impaired intelligence of the really small babies as there is a slight tendency for the lighter twin to have a somewhat lower verbal reasoning score than his heavier partner (McKeown, 1970). However, the importance of post-natal influences was most strongly shown by the finding that where one twin had been still-born or had died in infancy the verbal intelligence of the survivors was only a mere half point below that of singletons (Record *et al.*, 1970). In contrast, when both twins survived their score was 4.5 points below other children. Quite what these postnatal influences are which impair the verbal intelligence of twins is not known, but it is likely that they are related to diminished parent-child interaction and communication when there is a multiple birth. Twins and triplets probably receive a higher proportion of their verbal interchange from those of their own age (i.e. from each other) than do singletons.

SCHOOLING

Quite apart from the home influences discussed above, what a child is taught at school will obviously make a difference to his scholastic attainments. It is not quite so obvious that schooling will influence intellectual development and level of adult IQ, nor is it self-evident how much the type or quality of school attended will affect attainments.

The first issue has been studied by examining the effects of both different durations of schooling and also missed schooling. (See page 73, Chapter 3, for a discussion of the effects of moving from school to school.) The findings on whether nursery school attendance causes significant long-term changes in IQ are contradictory and inconclusive (Swift, 1964; Jencks *et al.*, 1973). In this country (Davie *et al.*, 1972) and in the USA (Gruenberg and Birch, 1954) children who start school early tend to have higher attainments during the primary stage than do those who commence education at the usual time. However, it is probable that there is little permanent effect on IQ (Jencks *et al.*, 1973). Nevertheless, there is good evidence from Husen's (1951) careful study that the duration of schooling during adolescence does make a difference. Data were available on the IQ of 85 per cent of males in a Swedish city at age 10 years and again at age 20 years. The child's initial IQ was taken into account through the use of a regression equation, and the effects of schooling were calculated on the basis of departures from the calculated regression effects. It was found that attendance at secondary school was associated with a mean gain of some 5 to 7 points of IQ. Harnqvist's (1968) similar study on another Swedish sample produced comparable findings.

The effects of missed schooling in Holland during the second World War were studied by De Groot (1951). A drop of some 5 IQ points was found for the generation of youngsters who missed out on their education. Similar effects were found following the closure of some schools in the USA to avoid integration (Jencks *et al.*, 1973). Jencks *et al.* concluded that elementary schools are helpful for middle-class children but crucial for the intellectual development of lower class children. Secondary schools and colleges make less difference but, nonetheless, improve intelligence more than do most jobs or housework.

Numerous studies in Britain (Kemp, 1955; Wiseman, 1964; Little *et al.*, 1971; Davie *et al.*, 1972; Rutter *et al.*, 1976; Yule and Rutter, 1976) and in the USA (Coleman *et al.*, 1966; Mosteller and Moynihan, 1972; Jencks *et al.*, 1973) have studied the variation between schools in average levels of attainment and have sought to relate this variation to school characteristics. Thus, in the inner London study (Rutter *et al.*, 1975), specific reading retardation (i.e. reading difficulties measured after partialling out the effect of IQ) was twice as common in primary schools with high rates of teacher turnover, or with a high proportion of children receiving free school meals. Similarly, in another large scale London study, Barnes and Lucas (1974) showed that within each social class grouping, children attending disadvantaged primary schools had lower reading attainments than did children attending more privileged schools (disadvantage being measured by scores on criteria derived from the Plowden report). Yule and Rutter (1976) found that London secondary schools also differed in levels of average reading attainment, even after taking into account the reading skills of the children prior to admission. In the National Child Development Study (Davie *et al.*, 1972) children at independent schools showed slightly superior attainments at age 7 years, compared with those at State maintained schools, after controlling for paternal occupation and education. Douglas *et al.* (1968) found only small differences and the advantages of private schooling were largely confined to boys of high ability. On the whole, girls did not do well at independent schools. It has also been shown that the type of special schooling provided makes a substantial difference to the education progress of severely handicapped children (Bartak and Rutter, 1973; Rutter and Bartak, 1973).

While there is good evidence that these various school characteristics are associated with significant differences in children's scholastic performance, several important questions remain. The first is whether the associations represent causal mechanisms, that is whether differences in the type or quality of schooling actually influence attainments. This question is very difficult to resolve in the absence of controlled experiments. The studies quoted attempted to deal with this point by controlling for variables such as the children's social and family background, IQ and area of residence. Systematic school differences still remained and it seems highly likely that school characteristics are causally related to educational performance.

The second question concerns the amount of the variation in children's academic performance which is attributable to school influences. All studies which have compared home and school influences (Wiseman, 1964; Plowden, 1967; Coleman *et al.*, 1966; Barnes and Lucas, 1974) have clearly shown that differences between schools account for far less of the variance than do features of the family or home. Barnes and Lucas (1974) showed that school variables accounted for only 6 per cent of the variance in London youngsters from a non-manual social group and even less in those from a working class background. The average reading performance of children from poor homes in disadvantaged schools was about three months behind that of similar children in the most privileged schools.

In the inner London study there was a difference of some 4 to 5 points in the reading attainments of 10-year-old children between schools with high and with low rates of teacher turnover (Rutter, 1976). At secondary schools, after partialling out differences in school intake, the 'best' and 'worst' schools differed in average reading attainment by about half a standard deviation (equivalent to some 7 or 8 IQ points). Jencks *et al.* (1973) concluded that the scores of American children in the best fifth of schools differed from those in the worst fifth by 10 points at most. These findings are important in showing the limits of what would be achieved by bringing the worst schools up to the level of the best, but too much should not be read into them. In the first place, schools vary less than homes, which necessarily limits the variance attributable to school characteristics. The results do not necessarily mean that school influences are of little importance but only that the difference between the 'best' and 'worst' schools is far less than that between the 'best' and 'worst' homes. Also, the proportions of schools markedly better or worse than average are less than the proportions of really privileged and seriously disadvantaged homes. This is because characteristics of school adversity seem to cluster together less than do features of family disadvantage — the correlation between school variables in one study averaged only 0.2 to 0.3 (Rutter, 1976). Secondly, most measures of school characteristics have been rather crude so that, to some extent, the failure to identify major school influences may merely reflect a failure to measure the most relevant variables. What are needed are more direct assessments of the quality of teacher-child interaction, the quality of teaching, and the motivating forces which lie in the social structure of the school.

This naturally leads on to the next issue — namely what it is about schools which most influences educational progress. Findings in both Britain and the USA suggest that material features (e.g. situation, state of repair, age of building) and provision of resources as reflected in the amount spent per pupil are of negligible importance for educational attainments (Kemp, 1955; Plowden, 1967; Coleman *et al.*, 1966; Mosteller and Moynihan, 1972; Jencks *et al.*, 1973). At least within the current range class size is also not a crucial variable. Indeed, several studies have indicated that children in large classes, or in schools with a low ratio of teachers to children, make better than average progress (Little *et al.*, 1971; Davie *et al.*, 1972; Rutter *et al.*, 1975). The reason for this finding is not known and it may be that only really small classes make an educational difference, but it seems that reducing the number of very large classes would do little to improve educational attainments. The findings with respect to pupil mix are contradictory (Kelsall and Kelsall, 1971). Coleman *et al.*'s findings (1966) in the USA suggested that high proportions of children from socially disadvantaged homes impeded school progress, but the evidence from this country is that the social mix makes a difference only at the extremes (Mabey, 1974; Barnes and Lucas, 1974). The findings on single-sex versus co-educational schools are complicated (Douglas *et al.*, 1968); while some groups of children do better at one rather than the other, neither type of school has a marked overall advantage.

The distinction between so-called traditional and progressive methods of teaching seems of rather minor importance (Gardner, 1966; Gooch and Pringle, 1966). Each suits some children and not others. Children in streamed and unstreamed schools also appear to make much the same progress on average (Passow *et al.*, 1967; Lunn, 1970; Jencks *et al.*, 1973). However, within streamed schools there is some scholastic advantage associated with being placed in the higher stream even after initial differences of achievement and social background have been taken into account (Acland, 1973; Lunn, 1970). The net effect of which stream a child is in on attainment amounts to the equivalent of no more than 5 IQ points — a small difference but not a trivial one. Almost certainly the effect of streaming has little to do with children's appreciation of their attainments relative to other children. Even in unstreamed classes, children are quite good judges of their academic ranking (Nash, 1971). Rather, the effect probably lies in the attitudes attached to relative positions. In a case study of a secondary school, Hargreaves (1967) noted the way pupil sub-cultures and teacher attitudes became polarized along the lines of streaming arrangement.

There is a tendency for lower stream children to be labelled as failures and to perceive themselves as such. Abolition of streaming would probably have no effect in raising or lowering overall educational attainments but it might slightly decrease disparities in attainment and improve attitudes to schooling.

Unfortunately, knowledge on which school variables are important is less extensive than knowledge on which are not. Youngsters are influenced in their educational aspirations by their friends (Campbell and Alexander, 1965; Haller and Butterworth, 1960; Duncan *et al.*, 1968). The social structure of the school is of little importance in this respect but its social climate may be more influential. Newcomb (1963) showed that school mores helped to shape political attitudes and it is likely that they also influence attitudes to education. There is some preliminary evidence that the academic climate in schools is of some relevance to scholastic attainment (McDill *et al.*, 1974). Students were found to make better progress in schools rated by teachers and pupils as placing a high value on achievement. However, exactly what serves to create particular school atmosphere remains uncertain. The social structure and stability of the school is probably important, as indicated by the studies showing that children have poorer attainments in schools with a high level of staff and pupil turnover (Rutter, Yule, Quinton *et al.*, 1975). The experience and skill of teachers, the quality of teacher-pupil relationships, the responsibility given to pupils and the use of incentives have all been suggested as possibly important. Research is needed to determine what difference in fact they make.

A further point is whether children from privileged homes or from disadvantaged homes are most affected by school conditions. Coleman *et al.*'s (1966) findings in the USA suggested that poor children were most held back by bad schooling but the findings from a London study indicated that children from a middle class background were most affected (Barnes and Lucas, 1974).

The last issue is how far a policy of positive discrimination in favour of certain educational priority area (EPA) schools is worthwhile. In the light of the English EPA action-research projects, Halsey (1972) argued for the validity of the concept and the utility of the approach, although he recognized its limitations. However, the careful analysis of the inner London survey by Barnes and Lucas (1974) casts considerable doubts on this conclusion. They found that most disadvantaged children were not in EPA schools and that even within such schools most children were not disadvantaged. Furthermore, policies which served to equalize performance between schools would do little to equalize opportunities between individuals. As they explicitly recognized, their data were limited and inadequate in several respects; nevertheless the evidence in favour of an EPA approach is based on equally unsatisfactory data. It may be concluded that (i) school influences make a difference to children's educational progress; (ii) we know little about the school variables which matter most; (iii) there are rather low correlations between different adverse school characteristics; (iv) disadvantaged children are widely scattered through very many schools; (v) positive discrimination in the form of EPA schools is a very clumsy way of meeting the needs of children from disadvantaged homes; (vi) improvements in schooling should raise overall educational attainments although they do little to reduce differences between individuals.

Quite apart from the quality of schooling, teacher attitudes and expectations may be related to pupil attainments. Rosenthal and Jacobson (1968), in a widely-reported study, claimed to have shown that manipulated teacher expectancies could become self-fulfilling prophecies. They handed teachers lists of children, chosen at random, who they said would make either much or little school progress during the year. At the end of the time they found that IQ scores of the younger, but not the older, pupils matched their predictions. Nevertheless the study as a whole has come in for severe criticism (Farley, 1972; Thorndike, 1968; Snow, 1969) and, with the occasional exception (Beez, 1968; Meichenbaum *et al.*, 1969), most attempts at replication have failed (Claiborn, 1969; Jose and Cody, 1971; Fleming and Anttonen, 1971; Dusek and O'Connell, 1973 – see also the comprehensive review by Brophy and Good, 1974). Thus, its conclusions cannot be accepted as they stand. As differently designed studies have shown the probable influence of teachers' self-formed expectations, the likely explanation is that most teachers are not so gullible as to be swayed by test scores which run counter to the child's actual performance at school. Moreover, studies of the relationship between teacher expectations and teacher behaviour (see Brophy and Good, 1974) show marked individual differences between teachers. Some teachers respond positively to high achievers and some to low achievers; other show no tendency of either kind. The streaming studies (see above) imply effects of expectations (of teacher and child), and other investigations have indicated that attention from teachers influences children's behaviour (Flanders and Havumaki, 1963). However, a study by Seaver (1973) comes nearest to a direct demonstration of the effects of teacher expectancies on attainments. He showed that if the same teacher taught two children from the same family the younger child performed better if his older sib had been a good student and worse if he had been a bad student. This effect was not found if the two children were taught by different teachers, suggesting a teacher expectancy effect. However, it should be noted that the differences were quite small indicating that teacher expectancies are unlikely to be a major influence in scholastic attainments for most children.

GrosslyAbnormal Environments

The studies considered so far in this section on 'experiential influences' have all concerned environmental variations within the normal range. It remains to consider the intellectual development of children reared under very abnormal circumstances. There are several well documented case reports of children reared in extreme degrees of social isolation (such as a girl locked up with a deaf-mute mother in a darkened attic until the age of 6 years). These have shown that such extreme privation may lead to gross mental retardation but also that extensive recovery (to a normal level of intelligence) may occur if the child is removed to a high quality environment, even if removal does not take place until the age of 6 or 7 years (Mason, 1942; Davis, 1947; Koluchova, 1972).

In addition, there are many studies indicating that children reared in very poor quality institutions frequently show marked mental impairment (Ainsworth, 1962; Haywood, 1967; Tizard, 1970; Rutter, 1972). However, institutions vary greatly in the quality of care which they provide (King *et al.*, 1971); children in some institutions show *no* intellectual retardation (Rutter, 1972a); whether or not retardation occurs seems to depend on the kind of care provided (Tizard, 1974a; Tizard *et al.*, 1972).

The effects are most dramatically shown in the series of studies by Skeels and his colleagues of children reared in a very unstimulating impersonal orphanage (Skeels and Dye, 1939; Skeels, 1966). They found that young children transferred to a mental retardation institution where they received more personal care and a more varied range of experiences, increased their IQ over the course of a year to eighteen months from the retarded range to average. The children received nursery school education, most were adopted into normal homes at age 3 or 4 years, and when seen at follow-up in adult life most were functioning normally. There can be no doubt, from the account given, that in early childhood this 'experimental' group of 13 children were intellectually impaired and that they showed quite remarkable improvements when transferred to a more normal environment. Of course, IQ's obtained in the first three years of life have little predictive power so that caution is required in the interpretation of IQ changes, but there is no denying the considerable gains shown by the children and the fact that these were related in time to marked improvements in their environmental circumstances. However, it is necessary to make several points about the study. First, the IQ increments followed a total change of environment and not just an 'enrichment' experience. Second, the improvement to a normal intellectual level took place over a relatively short time (12—18 months). Third, the initial gains (to a normal level) occurred in an environment (an institution for retarded girls) which could scarcely be regarded as ideal. Fourth, the retention of the intellectual gains occurred in the context of adoption and hence transfer, probably, to a better environment.

In an attempt to relate these changes more systematically to patterns of upbringing, the 13 'experimental' children were compared with another 12 who had remained in the orphanage. Unfortunately, the two groups showed marked initial differences; the 12 control children had worse family histories, more neurological disorder (one died at 15 years of a degenerative brain disease, another had persistent syphilis, and another had had birth injury), more physical illness (6 had had bilateral mastoid operations compared with 3 in the experimental group) and more were male (8 as against 3 in the experimental group). The follow-up findings indicated that, quite unlike the 'experimental' group, their adult status was quite poor; four were still in institutions, only two were married and of those working all held unskilled manual jobs. Although the groups were ill-matched, it seems reasonable to suppose that the different outcomes were related in considerable part to the differences between the groups in patterns of rearing. Certainly the good care in the 'experimental' group compensated for their bad start in life. However, it seems likely that the worse outcome in the control group was due in part to their greater physical and familial handicaps as well as to their unfortunate and deprived upbringing. Nevertheless, the differences cannot be explained entirely by differences in selection as several experimental studies have shown that improvements in institutional care can lead to an increase in children's verbal intellectual skills (Kirk, 1958; Lyle, 1960; Skeels, 1942; Tizard, 1964). Also, there is good experimental evidence from animal studies that experiential influences affect cognitive performance in important ways (see Rutter, 1972).

'COMPENSATORY EDUCATION'

During the last decade or so there has been a tremendous upsurge in studies of various forms of educative experience during the pre-school years designed to remedy the intellectual and scholastic impairment present in many children from socially disadvantaged homes. The stimuli for these endeavours came from work which pointed to the importance of experience in stimulating intellectual growth (Hebb, 1949; Bronfenbrenner, 1968); from Hunt's application of this work to the field of education (Hunt, 1961); from a widespread belief that the first five years were 'critical' in development (Bowlby, 1951; Bloom, 1964) and by a general concern regarding the low attainments of so many slum children (Coleman *et al.*, 1966; Eisenberg, 1966). The literature on the results of attempts to provide 'compensatory education' is now very large and as it has been well reviewed before (Bereiter and Engelmann, 1966; Little and Smith, 1971; Starr, 1971; Ryan, 1972; Blackstone, 1973; Robinson *et al.*, 1973; Bronfenbrenner, 1974; Clarke and Clarke, 1974), only the main findings and a few key studies will be outlined.

As the most work has been carried out in the USA this will be considered first. Four main compensatory strategies have been followed. The first involves the redistribution of pupil populations to reduce the concentration of 'deprived' children within particular schools and city areas. The second has been to improve (or introduce new) educational programmes at pre-school and primary levels. The third approach is based on the assumption that 'deprivation' will not be counteracted unless the home situation is in some way altered; many programmes intervene in both the home and the school situations, although some concentrate entirely on the home. The final strategy involves an attempt to change all aspects of the environment.

'Bussing'

A variety of school integration programmes have sought to minimize external social and racial inequalities. In some cases this has been attempted by altering catchment areas or the sizes of schools. However, increasingly there have been experiments in which black ghetto children have been transported from racially-segregated inner-city schools to predominantly white schools in the suburbs. Occasionally some white children have been bussed in the reverse direction. There have been many problems in the evaluation of these experiments owing to non-random assignment to bussed and non-bussed groups and to differences between the schools in factors other than racial composition. However, there are a number of fairly adequate longitudinal studies which have utilized a control group and in which there are before and after measures (St. John, 1970; Armor, 1972). These have generally shown that bussing has no consistent effects on academic achievement, educational or occupational aspirations, academic self-concept and self-esteem, or on race relations. Nevertheless, the changes, although slight, have tended to be for the better rather than for the worse. There is some indication that able black students who have been bussed to the suburbs may be more likely to go to College, although one study showed that this was associated with greater drop-out later. Interestingly, there is some evidence that bussing *increases* racial identity and solidarity, as indicated by support for organizations such as the Black Panthers. Although bussing may well bring disadvantaged black children into contact with both better schooling and a more academically oriented group of youngsters, it also tends to mean a loss in peer status (as shown by sociometry) and a lowering of relative academic position. The gains in aspiration from the former may well be counterbalanced by a reduction of aspirations from the latter.

'Head Start'

A large number of programmes have been concerned with the provision of appropriate educational experience at the pre-school and primary school levels. Pre-school education in the United States began with Froebel during the nineteenth century, but the present movement is different in its explicit focus on the socially disadvantaged. Recent work can be sub-divided into the massive, broadly-based government

Head Start programme and the smaller, often more specifically focussed projects.

The American Head Start programme, which was initiated in 1965, was designed as a summer course to be attended voluntarily by low social status children at a number of centres around the country. The aim was to provide an enriched (but traditional) nursery school environment. In 1967, 456,000 children were enrolled in the eight-week summer programmes and in addition 218,000 children were involved in year-long programmes. Only children whose family's income was below a certain level were entitled to places. It is estimated that by the criterion used there are some five million children eligible but only one million obtained places (Blackstone, 1973). By 1973, the cost of the programme was 390 million dollars per annum.

This large-scale venture, which was launched after only three months planning, set off with very wide objectives in its attack on social disadvantage. It set out to improve children's educational performance, to provide a comprehensive system of medical and dental care, to eliminate undernourishment, to provide social help, to make available employment opportunities and to encourage community and parental participation.

Such broad objectives, in conjunction with the large scale of the project, led to enormous problems in evaluation. Unfortunately, the programme attempted both to determine what worked and also whether the appropriate action could be applied on a community-wide scale — objectives which require quite different research strategies. It must also be said that the ideas behind Head Start were naive, ill-conceived and poorly thought through. To suppose that brief exposure to pre-school education could remedy the ill-effects of continuing deprivation was foolish and ran counter to the available evidence (Clarke and Clarke, 1974). The notion of critical periods is unduly simplistic and for most types of development in humans it is wrong to suppose that the infancy period is decisive and critical (Rutter, 1972a; 1974). The early years are especially important because what happens then may start a chain of events persisting into later life, but if early experience is to cause permanent effects it must subsequently be reinforced and built upon (Clarke, 1968). Also, no attempt was made to analyse the needs of disadvantaged children, so that often what was provided was just free activity along the lines of the traditional nursery school. The basic fallacy in this enrichment strategy was that disadvantaged children needed and could make use of the same kinds of experience as children from privileged homes (Clarke and Clarke, 1974). Finally, in spite of the broad objectives of the programme, most of the evaluations have been simply in terms of IQ gains — a most limited criterion (e.g. Westinghouse Learning Corporation, 1969).

In view of these extensive deficiencies it is scarcely surprising that Project Head Start has had such limited benefits. Evaluations have shown that there are no widespread or lasting effects upon intelligence or attainment. As already indicated, this may largely be due to the lack of precise goals characterizing the venture and to the absence of any criteria on which to base an evaluation. It is also probable that the short duration of most of the programmes has severely limited the project's success. Although some children have been enrolled in year-long programmes, the majority have attended courses only over the summer vacation period. It is unlikely that large and sustained gains in intellectual abilities could be obtained during this time. It has been argued that most success has been achieved in health and nutrition and certainly many children have received innoculations and dental treatment which they might not otherwise have had. There is also some evidence that Head Start has helped to open up training and educational opportunities for men and women without academic qualifications. In short, it may be concluded that it has largely been a failure as a form of special educational treatment, but it has had success in creating a wave of enthusiasm and an awakening of conscience which have led to better thought-out and more useful programmes and social action.

Evidence from a Canadian project indicated that although pre-school centres were situated to attract low status families they often failed to do so. If compensatory education programmes cannot attract the truly disadvantaged they have fundamentally failed.

Focussed Pre-school Projects

There have been a large number of smaller-scale pre-school intervention projects, most of which have had a sharper focus than Head Start and the majority of which have followed some kind of planned strategy. As Bronfenbrenner (1974) has pointed out in his comprehensive review, projects differ in selection and procedure. As a result there are major methodological problems both in assessing results and in comparing studies. A particularly common and serious fault has been to compare a volunteer experimental group and a non-volunteer control group with the result that the experimental group parents are likely to be much more positively oriented to education than are the controls. Nevertheless, there are an adequate number of well-planned studies with follow-up data extending over at least 2 years for conclusions to be possible.

The first finding is that pre-school intervention can and does produce important IQ gains of the order of 10 to 15 points. Secondly, several comparative studies (Di Lorenzo, 1969; Karnes, 1969), as well as indirect comparisons between different investigations (Bronfenbrenner, 1974), have shown that the best results stem from structured programmes with a focussed emphasis on the development of language. Thirdly, even when school-based intervention persists, there is a marked tendency for the gains to be lost and the differences between experimental and control groups to diminish during the early school years. While this regression is less marked in the structured programmes it occurs to some extent in nearly all. Fourthly, there is a tendency for a gain in IQ, more marked in control than in experimental children, to be evident on starting school. This gain is least marked in the most structured programmes indicating that to some extent the pre-school intervention is doing what regular school would in any case do later (although possibly less well).

Because of this fall-off in achievements, efforts have been made to continue compensatory education into the school years. Results are now being reported from the first two years' experience of the nation-wide, federally-sponsored Follow-Through programme which extended the basic philosophy of Head Start into the primary grades, by aiming to provide health and social services as well as to meet educational needs. The preliminary findings are encouraging in showing gains in achievement over the first year. As with the pre-school programmes, the children who made the most gains came from programmes with more highly structured curricula. However, the results must be viewed with caution as the follow-up period has been too short to assess long-term effects.

In England, Gahagan and Gahagan (1970) have shown that a language programme during the first two years of primary school produces significant increments in children's use of language. The finding is encouraging in indicating how modifications can usefully be made to the ordinary school curriculum.

Many of the other school-focussed attempts to help the disadvantaged have been projects designed to ameliorate the school situation itself. Some of these have poured resources into creating smaller classes and providing more and better teachers. Others have also encouraged teaching staff to have positive expectations about the abilities of their pupils. None of these projects, however, has been shown to have much impact upon pupil performance.

Home-Based Interventions

Because of the extensive evidence that, throughout early and middle childhood, family influences continue to have a marked effect on scholastic attainment (see above), the third strategy of compensatory education has been to include parents as the main agents of intervention. Three basic approaches have been adopted: home contact may complement a school programme, liaison being maintained by a home visitor; the focus may be entirely on the familial context, with the aim of developing mother-child understanding, communication and activities (Schaefer and Aaronson, 1972; Levenstein, 1970); or attempts may be made to 'train' mothers without their children being present through discussion of training activities and general child-rearing problems at weekly meetings (Karnes, 1969; Karnes *et al.*, 1970).

The results of home-based interventions have been quite encouraging. In contrast to projects which focus on teaching the child skills, programmes which have had the parent-child dyad as the specific target have shown gains in IQ which have persisted three or four years. The experimental effects have diminished with time but the reduction has been less than in other projects. There is one other difference of importance: it seems that with parent intervention programmes the benefits often extend to younger siblings whereas in projects focussed primarily on children in group settings this does not occur to any appreciable extent. It is clear that, at best, mother-child intervention programmes have led to environmental improvements which act throughout the day on other members of the family rather than just on the specific child during the teaching session. Nevertheless, there are important drawbacks to this approach. It is demanding of parents so that not all disadvantaged families are able to co-operate, and although fall-off is less than with pre-school groups it still occurs. Also, it has been found that attempts to combine parental programmes with direct teaching of the child have sometimes undermined the responsibility and status of the parents, so making them less effective in helping their child. Bronfenbrenner (1974) argued that the best approach might be a phased sequence in which family-centred intervention is begun when the child is one or two years old, direct teaching of the child is then introduced only two or three years later, with gradual extension of this element as the child approaches school age. During the school years intervention should continue in a way which forges links between the home and the school.

The Heber Project

Finally, one intervention experiment conducted by Heber and his colleagues has sought to change all aspects of the child's environment from infancy up to the time of starting school at age six years (Heber, 1971; Heber *et al.*, 1972; Heber and Garber, 1974). Their sample consisted of 40 Negro children without organic damage, born to mothers with a Wechsler scale IQ of less than 75, and living in the lowest social tract in Milwaukee. The sample was divided by month of birth into 20 experimental and 20 control children, both groups being systematically assessed at intervals up to 7 years of age. Although not strictly a random allocation, there is no reason to suppose that the method of selection introduced any bias and the two groups proved to be well matched in terms of both physical status and socio-economic variables.* Heber's earlier epidemiological studies (Heber *et al.*, 1968) had shown that the census tract used in sampling was not only extreme in terms of overcrowding, poor living conditions, and low educational

*Critics have claimed, on the basis of a misleading early report, that the two groups were mismatched because the experimental children were said to be taller and heavier (Eysenck, 1973a). In fact, this criticism is not supported by the data. At age 5 years, as at birth, the two groups were very closely similar in height and weight (Heber *et al.*, 1972).

level, but also gave rise to a very high proportion of children with mild mental retardation. Furthermore, within the group of families living in this tract, maternal IQ had proved to be much the best predictor of the children's intellectual development. Accordingly, the study children were likely to be at very high risk for mental retardation.

The experimental programme included intensive work with both the mothers (and some fathers) and the children. The mothers were seen regularly (initially four times per week) in adult education classes focussing not only on scholastic skills (i.e. the '3 Rs') but also on home economics, child care, interpersonal relationships, and community oriented social studies. In the second phase, of vocational training, each mother was paired for a period of six months with an experienced employee in a Nursing Home and trained in four different areas of Health Service work (nursing assistant, dietary aide, housekeeping and laundry) as these seemed to offer the best employment prospects in the district. Each mother was allowed to progress through training at her own individual learning rate and a number went on to obtain jobs as a result of the training.

The infant intervention programme began when the children were three months of age. A teacher went to the home, watched the mother care for her child and then gradually took over much of the child care. When the mother was confident in the teacher (usually after 2–8 weeks) the child went to the learning centre where he attended five days per week, twelve months of the year. Each teacher was taught to be responsive to the child's emotional as well as educational needs. To minimize the disruption when a teacher had to leave, each child had two main adults who looked after him and to whom he might become attached. In the first two years the infants were individually looked after. They were given a widening range of perceptuo-motor, linguistic and cognitive experiences; and they were encouraged in a play context to make use of toys and other objects to expand their activities, to solve problems, and generally to take up opportunities for learning. From age 2 to 6 years the children were taught in small groups; at first in a relatively structured setting but moving to a free flowing environment in which each child decided for himself what he would do out of a range of possible activities.

Evaluation measures showed that the experimental and control groups increasingly diverged from about one year of age. At age 5 years the mean Binet IQ of the experimental children was 118 compared with 92 for the control group. The children's scores on the Wechsler scale were rather lower but the difference between the groups was equally great (at 57 months the respective mean IQs were 111 and 81). Not all the children have reached 7 years of age, but in those tested so far the mean score in the experimental group was 110 as against 80 in the control group (Heber and Garber, 1974). Language measures showed the experimental children to be markedly superior to their controls. Heber and his colleagues also used a Hess and Shipman style approach

(Hess and Shipman, 1967) to assess mother-child interaction. In a task situation, there was significantly more verbal interaction in the experimental mother-child dyads and less ignoring behaviour by the mothers. The findings generally indicated a developmentally more sophisticated interaction pattern in the experimental group. As far as could be judged, this difference was due more to alterations in the children's behaviour than to changes in the mothers'.

Although the study is not yet complete, the findings to date indicate that the intervention has been remarkably successful in terms of the infants' improved cognitive development. Some of the benefits in the pre-school years may have been due in part to greater test sophistication and specific practice, but this explanation cannot account for the Wechsler scale findings in the 5 to 7 year age period. Because the intervention was so extensive and comprehensive, it is not possible to determine which features were more influential, but there seems little doubt that, given adequate resources, even children from a grossly deprived environment can be helped to reach a normal intellectual level. Whether the benefits will persist after age 7 years in the absence of further help remains much more doubtful. Although the pre-school years are particularly important in children's development the evidence suggests that they are not critical in the sense once supposed (Rutter, 1972a and 1974). It appears that if intellectual development is to continue optimally, adequate environmental circumstances must also continue to be provided.

The British EPA Project

The Educational Priority Areas (EPA) Project was an action-research programme, like Head Start, in which wide scale pre-school interventions were to be initiated with the broad objectives of raising the educational performance of the children, improving the morale of the teachers, increasing the involvement of parents in their children's education, and increasing the 'sense of responsibility' for their communities of the people living in them (Halsey, 1972). Also as with Head Start, the evaluations were much more restricted than the objectives, the outcome measures being largely confined to intelligence and language. Furthermore, the quality of the intervention varied and the results were disappointingly inconclusive. Allocation to the experimental groups was not properly random in two of the three centres in the national pre-school experiment; there was loss of information on refusals; of the 27 comparisons between the experimental and control groups only four were statistically significant (three favoured the experimental and one the control); no account was taken of baseline differences; no statistical tests were used to compare rates of progress (which appeared somewhat greater in the experimental groups); and there was no systematic assessment of teacher behaviour. The results tended to support the view that the pre-school intervention had benefited the children's intellectual development but the gains were small and in view of the many limitations to the study even this general conclusion must be tentative. Halsey (1972) claimed that, unlike the American experience, gains following pre-school programmes can be maintained into the infant school. This may be so but the data do not warrant such a firm conclusion.

In terms of knowledge about the value of pre-school intervention as a means of aiding intellectual development, very little can be learned from the EPA studies. However, the Project was impressive, both in that it gave rise to educational innovation during a very short period of time, and in that some community involvement in schooling was achieved. Although not systematically evaluated, the EPA Project led to a number of new developments in pre-school education which seemed to increase teacher morale and parental involvement which might mean lasting benefits for children's educational performance. One of the interesting innovations was the West Riding Home Visiting programme in which the 'educational visitor' played the same role *vis à vis* education as the health visitor does with respect to health, helping parents over their child's cognitive growth and development.

There is now a substantial number of recently established and more focussed British studies into various aspects of pre-school education (see B. Tizard's review, 1974b). Many of these are concerned to determine what makes for effective schooling and effective adult-child interaction. This appears to be one important and potentially fruitful field of research although few results are yet available.

Conclusions on Compensatory Education

Many of the pre-school interventions have been inadequate because too little was done, it was done for too short a time, and sometimes the wrong thing was done. Nevertheless, in spite of Jensen's (1969) declaration to the contrary, compensatory education has not failed. The best planned programmes have had worthwhile effects on intellectual development and scholastic achievement, and have also given rise to findings which should enable better programmes to be developed in the future. Because of the importance of home influences, effective remedies for socially disadvantaged children probably must involve improvement in the quality of parent-child interaction, family life and living conditions. This is most readily (but least practically) achieved by removing the child in early life to a completely different family setting, such as by adoption. However, programmes specifically designed to aid the parents in their role as the responsible persons bringing up their children may also achieve a good deal. This approach needs to start early, not because the early years are critical, but simply because the earlier disadvantage can be remedied, the fewer the handicaps to be overcome and the shorter the period of catching-up required. If benefits are to persist into later childhood, it is clear that the remedial approaches must also continue into the school years. In this connection, the importance of teaching the child directly becomes more critical. It appears that highly structured, task-specific programmes with a focus on language provide the best means of teaching a child particular skills but, on its own, this approach is likely to be quite restricted in its effects as it does not encourage children to learn things for themselves. It may be the best means of starting a child off if he lacks certain essential skills, but if the child is to progress outside the immediate teaching sessions, the programme probably should proceed to a less structured approach involving discovery and innovation in order to encourage interest and develop motivation. These are the conclusions which stem from a large number of varied studies. However, few have been tested directly so they must be viewed as hypotheses, with some circumstantial support, but requiring rigorous testing.

CONCLUSIONS

Although many people differ markedly from their parents in intellectual performance and scholastic attainment, substantial intergenerational continuities exist. It has been well established that genetic factors play a considerable role in the determination of individual variations in intelligence. They are of much less importance with respect to scholastic attainment although here, too, they play some part. Nevertheless, there is also good evidence that experiential factors and non-genetic biological influences also have a large effect in raising or lowering intellectual performance. The effect of environmental influences is evident within the normal range as well as at extremes and can readily account for IQ differences of 10 to 20 points (in extreme cases several times that). Home influences are the most important in this respect but school variables also exert an appreciable effect. With respect to home factors, the most crucial variable seems to be the quality of parent-child interaction and communication but further evidence on this point is needed before anything other than very tentative conclusions are drawn. Unfortunately, knowledge on *how* the environment influences cognitive development remains rudimentary, although the fact that it does is well established.

5 Occupational Status

Occupation has been widely used as an indicator of social class (Susser and Watson, 1971). Although a person's social standing may well vary according to his education, material possessions and where he lives (Hollingshead and Redlich, 1958), his job is probably the best single indicator of social status. Several studies have shown that there is a fair measure of agreement in the general population on the social ranking given to different occupations (e.g., Reiss, 1961; Hodge *et al.*, 1964; Inkeles and Rossi, 1956), and that a person's job provides an indication of many other aspects of his life style and circumstances (Lockwood, 1958; Routh, 1965; Kohn, 1969; Banks, 1970; Runciman, 1972; Young and Willmott, 1973). Characteristically those in manual or working class jobs have less autonomy in their use of time at work, less job security, less chance of promotion, and are more likely to work shifts. Those in middle class or non-manual jobs tend to express more satisfaction with work, although their work is more likely to be brought home and to interfere with family activities. On the whole, the middle class earn more and have more material possessions, although there are many exceptions to this. They are also more likely to own their home. People's jobs are associated with some differences in leisure activities (Young and Willmott, 1973) and to a greater extent with differences in patterns of child rearing (Bronfenbrenner, 1958; Newson and Newson, 1963 and 1968) and family values and orientation (Kohn, 1969). Babies born to working class parents are more likely to die in infancy; rates of illness are greater and life expectancy is shorter for people with manual, especially unskilled manual, jobs (Susser and Watson, 1971; Townsend, 1974). Also, as discussed in other chapters, occupational status is associated with differences in educational attainments, psychiatric morbidity, and rates of crime. People with very low prestige jobs tend to be disadvantaged in many other ways. Because of its association with so many other aspects of life, occupational status requires particular consideration in any discussion of cycles of disadvantage.

However, it would be misleading to view occupation as the sole basis for a social class hierarchy. Apart from anything else, people's perception of what social class they belong to agrees only moderately with classifications based on the job they hold (Runciman, 1972). Furthermore, the social status of jobs will vary with changing conditions. Thus, during the last half century clerical work has to some extent lost its middle class status, although it has not acquired working class status (Lockwood, 1958). There are many important basic and deep rooted distinctions between manual and non-manual workers but it is an over simplification to view society as divided into discrete social groups (Susser and Watson, 1971). There is considerable heterogeneity within most occupations and appreciable overlap between social classes, however they are defined.

Social status is a relative rather than an absolute concept. In terms of the existing social structure, the supply and demand for labour, and the existence of hierarchies it is evident that some individuals will occupy the lower and some the higher prestige positions. There are various important political questions which arise in this connection, especially the desirability of a social and economic system which involves marked hierarchies and which accords prestige and status according to occupational position. The importance of occupational status to the individual is likely to depend on many factors, including the distribution of occupations, the difference in status between 'top' and 'bottom' jobs, the values attached to particular occupations, the associated material advantages and disadvantages, and the degree of movement between occupations of different status. Economic inequality and social inequality are not synonymous, nor is objective inequality the same as perceived inequality. An individual's satisfaction with his lot in life will depend in part on what he has been led to expect and with whom he compares himself (Runciman, 1972). This is illustrated by the well known finding in *The American Soldier* (Stouffer *et al.*, 1949) that job satisfaction was greater in the Military Police where opportunities for promotion were very poor than in the Air Corps where promotion opportunities were particularly good. To a large extent the meaning and relevance of social comparisons are a functioning of the existing political culture and social system. These are important matters and are crucial to the planning of policies to reduce social disadvantage, but to a large extent they fall outside the scope of this review. The main issues considered in this chapter are: the extent of intergenerational occupational mobility; the degree to which such mobility is increasing or decreasing; whether mobility is equally likely in all social groups; and the factors that determine its likelihood.

INTERGENERATIONAL OCCUPATIONAL MOBILITY

Intergenerational mobility refers to any change in occupational level between parents and their children (or grandchildren). Thus, individuals are considered upwardly, downwardly or horizontally mobile when they have a status above, below or equal (but different) to that of their parents. There are many methodological issues that have to be taken into account in considering mobility (Glass, 1954; Hope, 1972) but the most important of these are: the definition of occupational groups; the range and distribution of social classes; intergenerational changes in status; and the effects of family size.

The definition of occupational groups poses a constant problem in studies of social mobility because there is no absolute criterion by which to judge status, because the prestige attached to particular occupations may change, and because different studies have used varying classifications (Goldthorpe and Hope, 1974). For all these reasons, caution must be exercised in making comparisons between different studies.

The range and distribution of classes is important for two reasons. First, the likelihood of intergenerational change will be influenced by the size of any given class. Thus, a child of a skilled manual worker is more likely to be in the same class as his father than is a child of a professional man simply because the class of skilled manual workers is much larger than that of professionals. The second point is that any changes over time in class distribution will necessarily influence mobility. If, for example, the proportion of the population in professional occupations has increased since the last generation there will necessarily be an increase in upward social mobility. In fact there is good evidence that the relative size of social classes in both Britain and the USA has changed markedly during the last 50 years (Glass, 1954; Susser and Watson, 1971). The non-manual groups have increased in size and the unskilled and semi-skilled manual groups have markedly decreased. More people are now employed in large industrial organizations and fewer people are in agriculture, mining, and fishing.

Changes in occupational status occur quite frequently as people get older. In many professional jobs there is a tendency for promotion to go with age and seniority so that the highest level is not reached until middle life. Conversely, especially in manual jobs, illness and physical decline may sometimes lead to a reduced status towards the end of a person's working life. Since these effects vary greatly according to type of job, it is necessary for intergenerational comparisons to be confined to individuals of a similar age. Also, of course, there will be different implications with respect to the upbringing of the next generation if a man reaches high status early in life rather than at the end of his career. If a man remains in a low status job during the period in which his children are growing up, his high status later will have only a limited impact on their experiences.

Most studies of social mobility have considered only one family member from each generation and attention has usually been confined to men. Nevertheless, the overall pattern will be affected by any sex differences in mobility as well as by family size. Groups in which larger families predominate will necessarily have a greater effect on the overall picture than groups where families are smaller. The picture will also be altered by any changes over time in the way family size relates to social class.

The Extent of Social Mobility in Britain

An important large-scale study of social mobility was undertaken by Glass and hid co-workers in 1949 (Glass, 1954), using a seven-fold classification of occupational level. The findings showed a moderate association between the occupational status of father and sons (r = 0.47). Altogether over a third of the sample fell into the same status category as their fathers. This association was particularly marked at the top occupational level, where nearly half the men had fathers of the same status and only 3 per cent had fathers with a manual job. Even among skilled manual workers only one in five had fathers with non-manual jobs. No semi-skilled or unskilled workers had fathers in professional or managerial positions. Even so, there were considerable changes in status between successive generations. Of the men whose fathers were in category 1, (the highest category), over 60 per cent were found in lower categories than their fathers. Conversely, for men whose fathers were in category 7 (the lowest), over 70 per cent were in higher status categories than their fathers. Intergenerational mobility was even more marked over three generations. In only 18 per cent of cases was the same occupational level maintained from grandfather to grandson. In general, individuals were closer in occupational level to their fathers than to their grandfathers.

The 1947 Scottish survey and 16 years follow-up by Maxwell (1969) also provide relevant data on social mobility (although the findings are limited by the fact that the second generation were considerably younger than the first at the time occupational status was assessed). Intergenerational mobility was quite slight in category 1, the professional and large employer class, but social changes were more marked for other occupational groups. Out of the 16 sample members whose fathers were in occupational class 1, 14 were themselves in that class. In contrast, of the 207 with fathers who were skilled manual workers, only 78 were in the same class. Eighteen of the 207 were in class 1, and altogether 70 held non-manual jobs. Fifty-five showed downward social mobility in that they had unskilled or semi-skilled manual jobs. Of the 73 individuals whose fathers had unskilled jobs, 4 had risen to professional or managerial positions, another 9 held non-manual jobs, and 19 were skilled manual workers. It was noticeable that the proportion in the professional class was considerably larger in the second generation, a factor necessarily associated with an overall upward mobility.

Intergenerational mobility was also examined by Maxwell for daughters' husbands. The findings were much the same. Class 1 tended to perpetuate itself but it was expanded by recruitment, mainly from the non-manual and skilled manual groups.

Trends in Social Mobility

As intergenerational social mobility takes place over time it will be affected by historical changes in social structure and social class distribution. The expanding middle class, with the associated increase in upward mobility, has already been noted. In addition, however, the period since World War II has seen marked economic, political and educational changes in Britain. Educational provision has widened in a way which has benefited children of all social classes. To some extent education has been made relatively more accessible to children from the lowest social groups, but this has not been the case with University education, and class differentials in education remain large (Westergaard and Little, 1970). The slight reduction in social inequalities in education might have led to an increase in social mobility. But at the same time professional skills and technical complexity in work have increased so that access to higher level occupations has come to depend more on formal educational qualifications — a trend that might work against social mobility (Westergaard and Little, 1970).

Noble (1972) examined the findings of five British studies to assess the extent to which patterns of social mobility might be changing. The evidence suggested a general increase in upward occupational mobility but, after taking this into account, there was no indication of any greater flow between classes. However, there are serious methodological difficulties in any comparisons between studies using rather different data. More valid comparisons are provided by the large-scale Oxford mobility study which set out to replicate the Glass inquiry of 1949 (Hope, 1972 and 1975), using the Hall-Jones (1950) social grading of occupations. Comparisons between the two studies were complicated as the 1949 method of classifying occupations could not be reproduced with certainty and as the completed interview schedules of the 1949 inquiry were no longer available. Nevertheless, the study provides the best data there are on possible changes over time in social mobility.

The Oxford analysis abstracts estimates of the underlying openness of society (exchange mobility) from the total observed mobility by statistically removing the effects of changes in occupational structure. At first sight, exchange mobility in 1972 appeared greater than in 1949, in that the intergenerational correlation of 0.36 in the Oxford study was lower than the figure of 0.47 obtained from comparable data in the Glass inquiry. However, when comparable cohorts in the two studies (i.e., the youngest in the 1949 inquiry and the oldest in the 1972 inquiry) were compared, the intergenerational correlation was still greater in the 1949 study. As this comparison referred to groups of individuals born during the same time period, the correlations would be expected to be similar. Accordingly, it seemed highly probable that the apparent difference in occupational mobility between 1949 and 1972 was an artefact of differences in the coding of occupations. Examination of successive five year birth cohorts in both studies did not show any increase in exchange mobility. Taking all available evidence, it may be concluded that, so far as men are concerned, social mobility is probably no greater today than it was in 1949 or indeed than it was half a century ago. It seems likely that the Oxford study intergenerational correlation of 0.36 (which indicates considerable changes in occupation between father and son) gives a better indication of the extent of social mobility, but this may be assessed more satisfactorily when further analyses using an improved classification scheme (Goldthorpe and Hope, 1974) are completed.

Comparisons with Other Countries

There are major difficulties in making international comparisons of social mobility if only because of the varying social structure and occupational groupings in different countries. Moreover, national variations may stem in part from the considerable differences in the balance between rural/agricultural communities and urban/industrial areas (Lipset and Bendix, 1959). To the extent that comparisons with other countries are possible, intergenerational social mobility seems to occur to much the same degree in Britain, the USA, Scandinavia and the European mainland (Lipset and Bendix, 1959; Blau and Duncan, 1967). At the time of the Glass survey, intergenerational mobility in Britain may have been slightly greater than in Italy and France (Glass, 1954).

American mobility data are reported by Waller (1971). Using five categories of social class, he found a correlation of 0.48 between the fathers' and sons' occupational levels — a degree of association roughly the same as that found by Glass (1954). It should be noted that the occupational class correlation in Waller's study was greater than that (0.36) between the IQ scores of fathers and sons. However, the American and British situations differ and the forces operating may not be the same (Hope, 1972). It would be unjustifiable to place much reliance on international comparisons.

Patterns of Social Mobility

Measurement of social mobility by intergenerational correlations implies that movement between classes is equally likely at all social levels, but this is not necessarily the case. Some idea of what lies behind such figures may be gained by examining patterns of social mobility.

In calculating how far patterns of mobility depend on social origins one must take into account the proportion of individuals in each class and hence the likelihood that sons will remain in, or move into, that class. The fact that individuals in the top class cannot show upward mobility and that those in the lowest class cannot exhibit downward mobility must also enter the reckoning. When the appropriate statistical corrections for the size and position of different occupational groups were made in the 1949 survey (Glass, 1954), it was found that social mobility was much less in the professional and managerial group than in any other occupational group. The likelihood of sons having jobs of the same level was far higher than for any other social class. Furthermore, the sons of individuals in occupational level 2 were relatively more likely to rise in level than to fall. This is strong evidence that there are particular forces which allow professional and managerial families to maintain their social position through succeeding generations. Maxwell's Scottish survey (1969) produced broadly similar findings. The self-perpetuating classes were mainly the professionals and farmers.

Whether there are factors which impede upward mobility from the lowest occupational levels remains uncertain. Glass (1954) found that the tendency for fathers and sons to have the same job was somewhat greater for unskilled labourers than for semi-skilled or skilled manual workers, but much less than that in the professional and managerial class. Askham (1969) has pointed out that the unskilled manual class can be subdivided into those with regular jobs and those whose work record is characterized by long-term or frequent unemployment. The Sheffield study of problem families (see Chapter 9) suggests that social mobility may be quite limited in this lowest category (Wright and Lunn, 1971). Of the sons studied, about 70 per cent of those working were in unskilled or semi-skilled jobs, and nearly a quarter were not employed at all. While this unemployment rate was half that of their fathers it was still very high. Movement away from a pattern of unemployment and labouring jobs was greater for the daughters' families. Only 16 per cent of their husbands were out of work and 43 per cent held skilled jobs.

The relatively low upward social mobility in the Sheffield study may be due to personal disabilities rather than to low social status as such (see section below). A recent study on the Isle of Wight (Rutter, Tizard and Whitmore, 1970) showed that there was considerable social mobility in a random sample of the general population. Even where both grandparents of 10 year old children had non-manual jobs, half the fathers held manual jobs. Conversely, where both grandparents had manual jobs, just under a quarter of the fathers were in non-manual occupations. In contrast, among the families of children with either intellectual retardation or specific reading difficulties there was negligible upward mobility when both grandfathers were manual and an overall downward mobility when both grandfathers were non-manual. In short, the patterns of social mobility were different (and disadvantageous) in the families of children with cognitive or learning difficulties. Whether educational difficulties in the parents constituted one reason for downward mobility or whether the explanation lay in factors outside the family could not be determined from the data.

Social Mobility and Marriage

One of the tests of the 'openness' of the class structure is the extent of marriage between persons of different social origins (Berent and Glass, 1954). In the 1949 survey it was found that with 45 per cent of couples both partners came from the same social class (using a four-fold classification); this gave rise to a correlation between husband and wife on social class of 0.37. Comparisons according to the year of marriage indicated that more recent marriages showed decreasing marital concordance on social class. The same study showed that marital concordance with respect to education was greater than that for social class. Seventy-one per cent of couples had reached a similar educational level. As with social mobility, social concordance in marriage was relatively greater for those in the upper occupational groups and educational concordance was greatest for those who had received higher education. Altogether a third of couples were concordant on both occupational background and education and one in six were concordant on neither. Maxwell (1969) found a similar pattern in his Scottish survey but the degree of concordance was less.

Illsley (1955), in a study of Aberdeen women having their first baby, also found considerable interclass movement at marriage, especially between adjacent classes. Forty-six per cent of women brought up in professional or managerial homes married men who were skilled manual or clerical workers, and 61 per cent of women brought up in homes where the father had an unskilled or semi-skilled job married skilled workers. On the other hand, intermarriage between extreme classes was rare. Out of the 648 women brought up in classes I and II (professional/managerial) only 47 married into IV and V (semi-skilled and unskilled manual). Conversely, only 56 women out of 1,517 brought up in classes IV and V married into classes I and II.

In short, although to an important extent people tend to marry someone from a similar social background, marriage is associated with considerable social mobility. The occupational correlation between men and the fathers of the women they marry (i.e., about 0.4) is roughly the same as that between fathers and sons. However, in marriage, as in intergenerational comparisons, social movement tends to be less in the professional and managerial group than in other classes.

FACTORS INFLUENCING OCCUPATIONAL MOBILITY

In much of the literature on occupational mobility there seems to be an assumption that the same set of factors lead to both upward and downward mobility. While this may sometimes be the case it is not necessarily so and as far as possible the two will be differentiated in the discussion that follows. Moreover, the forces that facilitate social movement may not be the same as those which *impede* mobility and these two will be distinguished where possible. Of course, there is no clear distinction between them and some factors both facilitate and impede in different circumstances. However, it is convenient to consider separately those which mainly facilitate movement and those which mainly impede it.

FACILITATING FACTORS

IQ and Occupational Mobility

Burt (1961) first developed the hypothesis that differences in intelligence constituted the main influence affecting an individual's rise or fall in occupational status, although differences in home background and in education were also important. He produced data to show that within each social class the offspring of higher IQ tended to rise in status whereas those of lower IQ tended to fall. Unfortunately, Burt's data are not reported in a form which allows proper evaluation of the findings. However, similar results have been reported from several smaller studies and a number of large-scale systematic investigations. Thus, Boalt (1954), in a study of 2,286 Swedish children followed into adult life, found that the individuals from his middle occupational group (using a 3 category classification) who rose in comparison with their fathers' jobs had a mean IQ of 129 (when aged 24 years) compared with a mean of 116 for those who remained in the same group and a mean of 107 for those who fell. In an American study, Waller (1971) showed the same for sons of men of intermediate social status. Most of the sons who rose in social class had a higher IQ than their fathers (24 out of 46 had an IQ in childhood at least 7.6 points higher), and very few had a lower IQ (only 3 out of 46 had an IQ as much as 7.6 points lower). In contrast, of those sons who fell in social class most had a lower IQ than their father (19 out of 35 had an IQ at least 7.6 points lower) and not many had a higher IQ (8 out of 35 had an IQ as much as 7.6 points higher).

The correlation between an individual's own IQ and occupational status was 0.5, and the correlation between father-son *difference* in IQ and father-son *difference* in social class was 0.29 for the total sample and 0.37 when extreme social classes were omitted. It may be concluded that father-son differences in social position are attributable in part to father-son differences in IQ. In a British sample of scientists, their fathers and sibs, Gibson (1970) also found that intra-familial disparities in IQ were related to social mobility. Anderson *et al.* (1952) estimated that the proportion of actual social mobility associated with differences in intelligence is about 50 per cent, but the figures given above suggest that this is an overestimate.

Much the same applies to social mobility in daughters through marriage, as shown by Illsley in his Aberdeen study (Illsley, 1955; Scott *et al.*, 1956). Of the women from social class III who married men in social classes I and II, 73 per cent had an above average IQ in adult life, compared with 47 per cent among those who married into the same class and 20 per cent among those who married into classes IV and V. Women who married husbands in higher social classes were not only likely to be of more than average intelligence, to have spent longer at school, and to have been themselves in more highly skilled and better paid jobs but also they were taller. Interestingly, in these respects the class III women who married up were superior in intelligence to the class I and II women who married down.*

*It should be noted that strictly speaking these results do not concern social mobility as a *result* of marriage. Many of the women had already obtained higher status jobs themselves before marriage.

Direction of Association Between IQ and Social Class

The literature is full of disputes about whether IQ leads to social class position, or whether a person's social origins determine his IQ. To some extent the dichotomy is false in that both probably occur. However, it is necessary to obtain some measure of their relative importance. Perhaps the best way to do this is to determine whether IQ is related more closely to social class of origin (which would suggest social influences on intellectual development) or to a person's own social class (which would suggest intellectual influence on social class distribution). Several studies have shown that the latter is the case. Waller (1971) showed that the childhood IQ score of sons correlated 0.5 with their own occupational level when adult but only 0.3 with their fathers' occupational level. Similarly, Boalt (1954) found that the son's IQ was much more strongly associated with his own social class than with that of his father. The difference between the mean IQ of the top and bottom social class (in a 3 category classification) was 25 in the former case but only 15 in the latter. Anderson *et al.*'s (1952) findings were similar.

A second approach is to examine the relationship between IQ and social mobility, as already done. This shows that within any social class of origin the individual child's IQ is an important determinant of whether, when adult, he is in the same, or in a higher or a lower social class than his father (Waller, 1971). A third approach is to determine the spread of IQ within individual families and within particular social groups. If social class of origin determines IQ the spread should be small. In fact it is large. Maxwell (1969) showed very considerable spreads of IQ even within single families of the same generation. The median IQ difference between sibs with the highest and lowest IQ in the same family was 26 and in 14 per cent of families the maximum IQ difference between sibs was at least 40. All studies which have examined the association between IQ and class origin have shown that there is a very wide range of IQ within each social class.

It may be concluded that IQ is one important determinant of movement between social classes (both up and down). Even so it would be quite wrong to conclude that that is the end of the matter. There is also evidence that social factors can influence intellectual development (see Chapter 4). Furthermore, the correlation between IQ and social class is far too low for IQ to account for even the major part of the social movement. Bowles and Nelson (1974) have combined data and inferences from a variety of American studies to argue that IQ is a relatively minor mechanism for the intergenerational transmission of social status. The evidence, discussed above, suggests that they under-estimate the role of IQ but it does indicate that IQ is far from the only important determinant of occupational mobility.

Educational Influences on Occupational Mobility

In general, individuals of higher intelligence tend to proceed to more advanced levels of education. The question arises whether educational differences constitute a major cause of intergenerational social movement and whether the importance of IQ is largely through its association with educational attainments.

Glass' 1949 survey showed that a grammar school education markedly increased the likelihood of a child from a low social status family rising in occupational level, and somewhat reduced the likelihood of one from a high status family falling in social status. Further education intensified this effect. Thus, education played an important part in allowing upward social mobility in individuals from a working class background. Better educated sons from any social class tended to show upward mobility whereas those from the same class of origin with little schooling tended to move down in occupational status. Nevertheless, the upwardly mobile group still contained a substantial proportion of individuals with relatively poor education. The findings showed that educational differences played an important part in social mobility but that their effects were by no means decisive (Anderson, 1961). Furthermore, the type of education attained by people was itself much influenced by the social status of their fathers.

Waller's (1971) American study is helpful in sorting out the relative contributions of social origin, IQ and education to variations in occupational status. The respective correlations were 0.32, 0.50, and 0.72, suggesting that education accounted for most of the variation in occupational status, and social origins the least. However, before the independent contribution of each variable can be assessed it is necessary to take into account the inter-correlation between variables. When this was done, the first order partial correlation between education and occupation ('holding IQ constant') was 0.31 for the fathers and 0.63 for the sons. The son's IQ and father's occupation were less important and each accounted for about the same amount of the variance (12.5%) in the son's occupation. This suggests that education, IQ and social origins all provide an independent contribution to variations in occupational status, but that even together they leave much of the variation unaccounted for.

The importance of educational attainment in leading to occupational status involves a variety of mechanisms. Some jobs require academic credentials provided by education. The benefits of higher education are obvious.

In this connection it should be noted that there is a middle class over-representation among those following higher education which increases at each successive educational level (Robbins, 1963). While this exists (whether due to biases in selection or to economic or motivational barriers impeding applications from working class youngsters) extending education may serve to maintain, rather than to change, social structure.

At the other extreme, both in this country and in the United States, minimum education is associated with a high frequency of job-changing (Borow, 1966; Maxwell, 1969). Not only is the future level of employment mainly determined at age 15—16 years when the decision of whether or not to remain at school is made, but so also may be future attitudes to employment (Hill, 1969). Jessor and Richardson (1968) argue that the transition from school to work is particularly difficult for adolescents from a socially disadvantaged background but they did not provide supporting evidence for this conclusion.

In short, it appears that the level of educational attainments is associated with both upward and downward mobility. The limited available evidence suggests that educational factors are most important in aiding upward mobility among individuals from a low social status background, and in maintaining high status in those from more privileged backgrounds.

Genetic and Environmental Effects on IQ and Social Mobility

Hereditary influences play a substantial role in the development of intelligence (see Chapter 4). Accordingly, in so far as IQ does determine movements between social class (as already noted it does so only to a limited extent), it is reasonable to assume that the effect is partially explicable in terms of genetic factors. Heredity is usually seen as leading to parent-child resemblances in attributes such as intelligence (which it does), but it is less often appreciated that heredity also leads to parent-child differences in the same attributes (Eysenck, 1973a). As a consequence, genetic factors should predispose to appreciable social mobility. The correlation between parental and child IQ is only moderate (about 0.5) and in any family the children will show a considerable spread in their level of intellectual abilities. The degree of this spread was shown in the Scottish survey (Maxwell, 1969) — see above — although part of the spread may reflect different ages of testing (Clarke and McAskie, 1976). The result is that some offspring are considerably superior and some considerably inferior in intelligence relative to their parents. This in itself will predispose to intergenerational mobility.

While genetically determined differences in intelligence are undoubtedly important in influencing social mobility, it is abundantly clear that they are far from the only influence and in some circumstances not even the most important one. In the first place the correlation between IQ and social class is only moderate (about 0.5) and leaves much of the variance unexplained. Secondly, IQ is determined by environmental as well as genetic forces (see Chapter 4). Thirdly, the particularly high intergenerational stability of the professional/managerial classes (at least in the recent past) suggests an environmental effect, although it could be a result of greater assortative mating.

To recapitulate; paternal social class, the child's IQ and educational attainments all provide independent contributions to social mobility. But, even together, they do not account for all the findings. In particular, they fail to explain the relative lack of mobility in the highest (and possibly the lowest) social strata.

Attitudes and Personality Traits

In an American study of 69 men, Elder (1969) compared the attitudes and personality characteristics of the upwardly mobile and the non-mobile (downwardly mobile were not investigated). The subjects were intensively studied during their second decade and also participated in an adult follow-up. During adolescence the two groups were generally similar but the upwardly mobile rated themselves as brighter, more ambitious, and more competent in personal functioning. In adult life they scored more highly on responsibility, well-being and achievement. They tended to be more orderly in their work-life and to take on family roles at a later age. In contrast, defeatist tendencies and withdrawal stemming from frustration were more prevalent among the non-mobile adults. These differences were most marked in working class individuals. It was argued that it is the more directly work-oriented qualities which differentiate the mobile and non-mobile but the sample was small and, in examining attitudes, there was no control for intellectual ability. Striving and energy in non-work pursuits have also been noted in the upwardly mobile (Havighurst, 1957) but how far these qualities are important in their own right, and how far they are causes rather than correlates or consequences of mobility, remains uncertain.

Marked changes in social status may be accompanied by both anxiety and impaired community integration (Kessin, 1971). Similarly, marked dissonance between education and occupation may be associated with emotional distress (Jackson, 1962; Abramson, 1966), although the findings are contradictory (Kleiner and Parker, 1963 and 1965).

Temperamental features and attitudes to work may well play a part in occupational mobility, but the studies are sparse and often methodologically weak so that few conclusions are possible.

Family Attitudes and Values

Much work has been undertaken to identify 'achievement motives' and their origins. Projective tests have usually been used to assess achievement motivation (McClelland *et al.*, 1953) and scores on such tests have been related to various parental practices and family influences. There is some evidence that children with high achievement motives tend to have parents with high aspirations who have encouraged self-reliance and independence from an early age (Crandall, 1963; Winterbottom, 1958; Rosen and D'Andrade, 1959) but the measures are unreliable (Entwistle, 1972), the associations differ to some extent in boys and girls and the findings are rather inconsistent (Freeberg and Payne, 1967). Furstenberg (1971) in a study of mobility orientation within 466 working class parent-child pairs found low concordance between parent and child. Even when the children were aware of parental goals they did not necessarily share them. Whether concordance would be greater within a middle class sample, as suggested by Chilman (1966), is unclear.

In this country, Douglas *et al.* (1968) have shown considerable social class differences in parental aspirations for their children and in the interest taken in their education. However, the differences in ambitions for the children are more strongly associated with the parents' own education than with their occupational level. These differences hold even when the child's own abilities are taken into account. The importance of these differences in aspirations and interest is evident in the association with the children's educational progress (Douglas, 1964).

Family Size

Family size is also related to social mobility. As discussed in Chapter 4, there is quite a marked tendency for children from large families to have a lower verbal IQ and worse reading attainments than those from small families. In keeping with these findings, individuals from small families are also more likely to be upwardly socially mobile and those from large families downwardly mobile (Glass, 1954; Lipset and Bendix, 1959). As individuals in the lowest social groups or with frequent unemployment also tend to have large families (Askham, 1969; Wright and Lunn, 1971; Tonge *et al.*, 1975), and since large families are more likely to suffer from poverty, overcrowding and poor nutrition (Ministry of Social Security, 1967; Land, 1969; Lambert, 1964), it is evident that large family size is linked with cycles of disadvantage.

Physical Factors

As already noted, physical factors are related to social mobility at the time of marriage. Illsley (1955) found that women who rise in social status at marriage tended to be taller, in better health, and to have lower prematurity and obstetric death rates than those from the same social class who fell in status at marriage.

SOCIAL AND ORGANIZATIONAL FACTORS IMPEDING OCCUPATIONAL MOBILITY

Although there is considerable social mobility in Britain, it is evident that there is not free movement between social classes. Factors impeding social mobility may be of two kinds; those that operate on the population as a whole or on social groups as a whole, and those that operate with respect to individuals. These will be considered separately. A further distinction is required between factors that prevent downward mobility and those that impede upward mobility.

Social Structure

Protection against downward mobility and impediments to upward mobility may both arise as a result of the organization of education, industry, the economy and social policy.* Because educational attainments have such an important influence on occupational status, any privileges or disadvantages which affect scholastic attainment are likely also to affect occupational level. These are considered in Chapter 4. The criteria for entry into an occupation and the possibilities for promotion may both affect social mobility. Chinoy (1955) examined the career structure for American industrial workers and argued that there were two main channels of advancement. The first was open to workers and involved a small number of steps upward, but only as far as the position of foreman. The second was open to those with greater initial education and training and provided the opportunity to rise to the highest ranks of industry. There was little possibility of moving from the first ladder to the second. Doubtless similarly restricted pathways exist within British industry. In the same way the distinctions between the 'commissioned' and 'non-commissioned' in the Armed Forces and between the 'executive' and 'administrative' grades in the Civil Service have had a similar effect in restricting opportunities.

Three main steps may be taken (and to some extent are being taken) to reduce the social constraints arising from these promotional patterns. The first is to make it easier for people who have left school early to receive further education during adult life. The second is to facilitate transfer from one promotional channel to another in industry, the Civil Service, the Armed Forces and the professions. Transitional positions are very important in this connection. The third is to reduce the power of nepotism and the 'old boy' network.

Packard (1959) argued that the elimination of stepping-stone jobs in some offices and factories had been an important factor operating to maintain a rigid social structure and to increase the segregation of workers and management. The production line practice, whereby workers are given only certain restricted and specific jobs, also served to discourage initiative and to reduce flexibility in job mobility. Nevertheless, Packard also suggested that technological development had increased the job opportunities for people who had had the appropriate training or experience.

A further constraint exists in the growing tendency to require educational 'credentials' for jobs so that applicants without the appropriate qualifications may be rejected in spite of proven personal competence and suitability. Educational attainments and qualifications demanded for jobs are sometimes unnecessarily high (Berg, 1970).

*The importance of geographical, temporal, and social variations in job opportunities are discussed more fully in the chapter on economic status.

Usually this emphasis on credentials works to the detriment of those with the least education but sometimes it can work to the disadvantage of the well qualified. There are occasions when bureaucratic red tape or union pressure precludes 'over-qualified' persons from applying for, or holding, certain jobs.

Social and economic policy can have an important effect in either increasing or decreasing these constraints on social mobility, as Miller and Roby (1971) have argued. They suggested that benefits should follow from strategies of educational reform, income supplements and a reduction in the differentials between social groups. The first course of action included compensatory education, the promotion of equal educational opportunities and a de-emphasis on credentials. While worthwhile, it remains uncertain how far those policies would influence social mobility. Compensatory education is too recent for long-term effects to be assessed but even the short-term gains have been limited (see Chapter 4). Equal educational opportunities are only effective if the opportunities are taken up, so that motivation, attitudes and material resources are also important. Real equality of educational opportunity is a will-o'-the-wisp while inequality remains in the homes (Clarke and Clarke, 1972).

Miller and Roby's second category of policy, which involves increases in income, is based on Rainwater's (1970) thesis that income and educational progress are intimately related, which in turn bears on the view that social mobility is achieved through education. The third approach also relies on economic benefits but does so through reducing social and economic differences rather than through raising the individual level. By reducing social disparities, Miller and Roby hope to increase educational and occupational opportunities and to provide more evenly distributed fringe benefits.

Unfortunately, little is known about the actual long-term benefits and disadvantages of all these policies (see Chapter 2). There is the possibility that in relieving immediate hardship, action may be taken which reduces long-term social gains. For example, it has been suggested that unemployment benefits may sometimes have this effect. Various writers studying families known to social service agencies or attending psychiatric clinics have maintained that some unemployed subjects with low earning capacity have little or no financial incentive to work (Markowe *et al.*, 1955; Veit, Wilson and Wilson, 1973). However, these studies have involved highly selected groups, assessments of incentives pose many difficulties, and there are no data to indicate either the individual importance of the effect or the proportion of unemployed persons to whom it applies. Certainly, there is evidence that many other factors of a quite different kind are relevant (see Chapter 2). Social policies designed to eliminate poverty and poor living conditions are essential to provide effective short-term solutions for the individual, but it is also necessary to determine how far they are successful in increasing the quality of life in the long term.

Socio-cultural Factors
Evidence is lacking on the importance of socio-cultural factors in either preventing downward mobility or impeding upward movement. Nevertheless, they may be important through opening or closing occupational opportunities, through attitudes to work, through neighbourhood and interpersonal ties and through effects on employer/employee relationships.

For example, there are indications of class differences in attitudes to employment (Lockwood, 1958). Bell (1968) suggested that, on the whole, middle class individuals saw work as a career with the goals of advancement to greater prestige, responsibility and remuneration. In contrast, although work might still constitute an important source of self-fulfillment for them (Fuller and Bonjean, 1972), working class men less often saw their job as a means of change and social progression. Morse and Weiss (1955), in an interview study of the extent to which work served non-economic functions, also found class differences. Typically, for the middle class man, 'working means having a purpose, gaining a sense of accomplishment, expressing himself. He feels that not working would leave him aimless and without opportunities to contribute', whereas for the working class man, 'working means having something to do. He feels that not working would leave him no adequate outlet for physical activity; he would just be sitting or lying around'. Of course, these are stereotypes and it is not known how much intra-class variation there is in these attitudes, nor is it known how they relate to social mobility.

Ties to a particular locality or job may also have implications for job availability and hence for social mobility. Geographical mobility removes the regional restrictions on jobs and there is evidence of some degree of association between spatial and occupational mobility (Pahl, 1965; C. R. Bell, 1968). Mobility in work and in place of residence is characteristic of people in scientific, technical, and administrative professions where promotion and upward social mobility is dependent in part on a willingness to move house in order to obtain a more responsible job. For this reason they have been termed 'spiralists' as distinct from the shopkeepers, owners of small businesses and certain professionals who have an essential interest in the area within which they practise (Watson, 1964). In one study a willingness to move was most common among young couples with a large number of children (Rossi, 1955) and high mobility is characteristic of many socially disadvantaged families. However, professional people are more likely to move to a quite different part of the country (Illsley *et al.*, 1963). Donnison (1961) showed that those in more socially prestigious jobs were not only more likely to have moved house frequently and over considerable distances, but also to have seen geographical mobility as a factor in job opportunities. In certain circumstances unwillingness to move might constitute a constraint on social mobility. In this way strong cultural ties might be self-reinforcing and social groupings self-perpetuating. To what extent this actually occurs is not known.

Geographical mobility will also influence the choice of marriage partners (Coleman, 1973), and so indirectly affect the likelihood of social mobility through marriage. Middle class individuals are more likely to marry someone outside their immediate locality than are manual workers. Also, people today are more likely than were those of earlier generations to marry someone from another town or village. Both differences are likely to be due in considerable part to the greater availability of cars and other means of personal and public transport.

A reluctance to leave family and friends might have the same effect. It has been noted that either upward or downward social mobility may lead to interpersonal stress (Blau, 1956; Durkheim, 1952) and to less satisfactory contact with a person's family of origin (Bruce, 1970). Various writers have described the 'marginal man' who, as a result of social mobility, experiences conflict between his culture of origin and the culture into which he moves (Merton, 1957; Lipset and Bendix, 1959). Not fully accepted by either, he may have to sacrifice ties with the one in order to aid acceptance by the other. Lopreato and Hazelrigg (1970) suggested that problems of cultural acceptance may be less in circumstances where mobility is achieved through education rather than through later job advancement. Prolonged formal education could lead to a more gradual and more effective transition from one culture to another. Even so, Jackson and Marsden (1962) noted ambivalent attitudes in many working class boys in grammar schools. Whether such attitudes persist into later life is not known, but it has been found that among young adults living in poor areas contact with middle class individuals and participation in their activities are associated with values and attitudes oriented towards upward social mobility (Sneden, 1970).

Cultural factors may also influence acceptance by different social groupings. This applies particularly at a person's place of work where cultural barriers between employer and potential employee may provide disadvantageous constraints on job opportunities and hence on social mobility. Extensive job discrimination on the basis of race has been shown in this country (see Chapter 10), and discrimination on the basis of sex (see below) and physical handicap (McDaniel, 1969) also occurs. Doubtless it also takes place with respect to other social attributes. Area of residence, previous employment history, accent and behaviour could all lead to employment constraints, although evidence on the degree to which they do so is lacking.

Conditions of Work

Occupational performance, which is related to maintenance of social level, may be influenced by conditions at work. Gadourek (1965) suggested that the nature of the work process and the industrial structure were more strongly related to work attitudes than were the personality characteristics of individual workers or the specific features of working groups. This Dutch study of twenty-one large industrial plants compared workers with high and with low absence records. The two groups did not differ significantly in terms of personal characteristics but it appeared that absence rates were related to the organizational structure of the factories. A similar conclusion was reached by Kornhauser (1964) in a study of the mental health of factory workers. Individual differences were attributed more to the job situation and associated life conditions than to personal attributes. On the other hand, Plummer and Hinkle (Hinkle and Plummer, 1952; Plummer and Hinkle, 1953 and 1955) in a systematic study of women telephonists with high and low absence rates, found that personality characteristics were relevant. As Harrington's review (1962) shows, occupational efficiency and satisfaction are related to job features, staff relationships, management practices, the current state of employment and prosperity, and a variety of personal traits. The relative importance of each of these will vary with the job and situation.

Inheritance

Inherited wealth, property or business are protection against downward social mobility. An individual may inherit resources which give him a socially prestigious position which, on the basis of his own abilities and interests, he would not otherwise have attained. In so far as this occurs it will lead to a self-perpetuation of the property and business-owning classes. The available evidence on this issue is discussed in Chapter 2.

PERSONAL FACTORS IMPEDING OCCUPATIONAL MOBILITY

Sex

There is extensive evidence that women tend to have lower status jobs than men (Fogarty *et al.*, 1971; Oppenheimer, 1973; Suter and Miller, 1973). Women tend to be concentrated in traditional female occupations (most of which involve lower rates of pay), few women achieve any kind of 'top' job and even for comparable work women are less well paid on the whole. Work opportunities for women have been limited by the sex labelling of jobs and by overt sex discrimination in employment. Attitudinal barriers are also important although studies of these remain rather inadequate (O'Leary, 1974). Restrictions remain. Nevertheless, it may be that, in the long run, discrimination as such will not prove to be the central issue (Fogarty *et al.*, 1971). There is a need to adapt work opportunities to women's pattern of life, with time off for child-bearing and part-time work while children are dependent. Also, many of the occupational disadvantages are linked with sexual discrimination in educational provision and in attitudes transmitted during schooling. Many of these influences and patterns may be changed to some extent by the current sexual equality legislation, although how far this will be the case remains to be seen.

Physical Disability

Physical disabilities may often be important both in leading to unemployment and in restricting job opportunities (Lewis, 1935). Thus, Hall and Tonge (1963) found that accidents, illness and bereavement were the precipitating events of unemployment in half their sample of psychiatric patients. Sometimes physical incapacity itself may constitute unsurmountable barriers to work, but Hewitt (1949) has claimed that it is often the attitude of mind of the disabled rather than the disability as such which is the most important factor. Physical disabilities may have repercussions on a person's motivation and self-image and also on other people's attitudes toward him, as McDaniel's review (1969) of American studies showed. However, it is likely that a person's attitudes and self-image will be greatly influenced by the social climate and the responses from other people which he encounters. Employer discrimination against the disabled occurs in some circumstances. Its presence is dependent on the characteristics of the employing institution, the type and severity of physical handicap, and on the competence and social skills of the applicant. It is not clear how far the disadvantages are similar at all social levels, as the findings on social class differences in attitudes toward physical handicap are contradictory (McDaniel, 1969; Lukoff and Whiteman, 1964; Dow, 1965).

Mental Disorder

The effects of mental disorder on work performance and on occupational mobility vary greatly with the type of disorder. Acute neurosis and mental illness have little persisting effect on either, although emotional disturbance is a very common cause of absence from work (Harrington, 1962). In contrast, individuals with either a personality disorder or schizophrenia tend to show downward social mobility, with the result that there is a considerable excess of persons with these disorders in the lowest social groups. This has been convincingly shown by Birtchnell's systematic study (1971) of nearly 3,000 male psychiatric patients in North-Eastern Scotland who were compared with some 1,500 men chosen at random from the general population. In both cases, data on parental social class and current social class were available. The downward social mobility of schizophrenic individuals has also been well documented by Goldberg and Morrison (1963) and Hare *et al.* (1972).

In her long-term follow-up study of child psychiatric patients diagnosed as showing antisocial disorder, Robins showed how personality disturbance might impede social mobility (Robins *et al.*, 1962). Compared with non-patients, or with children showing emotional disorders, antisocial youngsters showed downward social mobility. As the study was prospective it was clear that the antisocial behaviour had preceded the subjects' occupational career. The findings suggested that there were two main mechanisms by which antisocial behaviour in childhood was associated with low occupational status in adult life. First, antisocial behaviour interfered with school achievement and was associated with school drop-out. The low educational attainments then limited later occupational opportunities. Secondly, antisocial behaviour often continued into adult life where it was expressed in terms of poor job performance, absenteeism, fights with employers and fellow workers, drinking on the job, frequent changes of employers and chronic unemployment.

Family Circumstances

Both early and contemporaneous family experiences have been found to be associated with poor adult employment records and consequent low social status. Markowe *et al.* (1955), in a study of psychiatric patients, found that those who were unemployed were more likely to have a history of a disturbed or unhappy home atmosphere in childhood, as well as a currently unhappy marriage and domestic friction. Hall and Tonge (1963) in another patient study showed that unemployment was associated with parental loss before 9 years of age, and that this association was due to homes broken by divorce or separation rather than parental death (Gay and Tonge, 1967). The evidence shows that disturbed family relationships are linked with adult unemployment in patient samples but the findings do not indicate the mechanisms involved. It could be that the association occurs largely as a result of personality disorder and that the links would not apply in a non-patient population. On the other hand, Stevenson (1975) in a qualitative interview study of unemployed men found that unemployment was often associated with family problems. The matter requires further study.

Overview of Impediments to Social Mobility

It is evident that there are a variety of socio-cultural, familial and personal factors which act to limit social mobility, although less is known about their relative importance. Himes (1964) has noted that the net effect of cultural deprivation is to generate a 'trained unreadiness for smooth transition from family, school and neighbourhood to the social world and technical roles of work'. The crucial elements in such deprivation remain ill-explored but probably include many of those listed by Borow (1966) — limited life experiences, circumscribed and socially limited inter-personal relations, absence of successful achievement-oriented role models, lack of bi-parental child-rearing experiences due to parental separation, attitudes of distrust toward the law, negative or indifferent attitudes to school and to education, lack of encouragement from parents with respect to socially valued skills, lack of recognition of the child's intellectual abilities, poor facilities and teachers in local schools, and a lack of opportunity for vicarious learning of the meanings and rewards associated with work.

CONCLUSIONS

Although there has been much emphasis in the literature on the self-perpetuation of social classes and on the barriers to social mobility, the findings clearly indicate that present-day Britain is characterized by considerable social movement and intergenerational change. Even over two generations there is a substantial movement between social classes and over three it is greater still. Of the known factors, individual intelligence and educational attainments are the two most strongly associated with occupational mobility, but even between them they account for only a minority of the variance. Attitudes and personality traits, family values and circumstances and physical health also play a part although little is known about the strength of their influence .

Nevertheless, social mobility is far from free and the movements are by no means random. There is particularly limited movement at the top (and possibly also at the bottom) of the occupational hierarchy. It is necessary to look for other forces which act to keep individuals in positions of high social prestige and impediments which serve to prevent other people rising to such positions. There are substantial indications that such constraints exist, both in terms of factors operating on society as a whole and in terms of individual characteristics. Unfortunately, most of the studies have considered very limited samples and a very restricted range of variables, and many have not produced quantitative findings. As a result, it is not possible to draw any firm conclusions about the extent to which the chief limits on social mobility are personal, social, structural or political. Still less is it possible from existing data to determine either the interactions between these variables or their mode of operation. The issues are important, but much further research is required before the processes can be properly understood.

6 Crime and Delinquency

Numerous self-report studies have shown that most boys admit to behaviours which involve breaking the law (e.g. Clark and Wenninger, 1962; Gold, 1966; Belson, 1968; Farrington, 1973). Furthermore, a substantial minority make at least one Court appearance — one in eight boys in the country as a whole and one in five in inner London (Power *et al.*, 1974). About half of these youngsters do not come before the Courts again. In adult life, too, a high proportion of men appear in Court at some time. Thus, among the fathers of 10-year-old children in London, 28 per cent had done so already (Rutter *et al.*, 1975b). McClintock and Avison (1968) calculated that one out of three males and one out of twelve females are convicted at some time during their life. Most offences are quite trivial, few men are convicted again and most are ordinary adults living ordinary lives. The large group of one-time offenders has little to do with cycles of disadvantage.

On the other hand, the minority of highly persistent delinquents with repeated convictions not only pose a social problem by their frequent offences but also often present a wide range of other troubles such as poor scholastic attainments, unemployment, marital disharmony and psychiatric disorder (see sections below). Many come from homes disadvantaged in several ways and some are members of multiple problem families (e.g. Wilson, 1962; Wright and Lunn, 1971; Tonge *et al.*, 1975). It is for these reasons that it is important to consider delinquency and crime* in terms of cycles of disadvantage. Wherever possible, the focus will be placed on recidivists, but as much of the literature fails to distinguish between different categories of offender, the review will necessarily extend more widely.

IDENTIFYING DELINQUENTS AND CRIMINALS

A serious limitation of most studies of delinquents and criminals is that they are based on official statistics. Unless interview or questionnaire techniques are used, as they are increasingly, even population studies ultimately rely on comparisons between individuals who have and those who have not appeared in Court.

Comparisons between areas or over time are complicated by the numerous factors which can influence administrative statistics even when delinquent or criminal behaviour remains unchanged:

*There is no clear distinction between delinquency and crime, but for the purposes of this chapter delinquency will be used to refer to offences by juveniles and crime to those by adults.

1. From time to time there are alterations in the law as to what is regarded as an offence (Walker, 1972). Also, countries vary considerably both in definitions of crime and in responses to it (Gibbens and Ahrenfeldt, 1966).

2. The extent and patterns of police activity will influence who and how many are convicted (Wootton, 1959; Cicourel, 1968). Notions of the 'typical offender' may guide the police in their searches for delinquents and criminals (West and Farrington, 1973). In this way, certain categories of person, such as those from low social status backgrounds, from large or multiple-problem families or with criminal relatives may attract disproportionate surveillance and thus be over-represented among convicted offenders.

3. Those people appearing before the Courts are not all treated similarly. For example, one study (Hood, 1962) showed that low social status offenders received more severe sentences if the crimes were committed in a middle class area rather than a working class area. Another (Gold, 1966) indicated that police (in the USA) were more likely to deal informally with middle class offenders without taking them to Court. It appears that in general (in the USA) black people and those of low social status are treated more harshly than whites and those of high social status (Thornberry, 1973).

4. For many crimes the offender is never found. In 1965, for example, only 39 per cent of all recorded indictable crimes were cleared up (McClintock and Avison, 1968). The clear-up rate varies both by type of offence (being lower for offences against property than for those against persons) and by region (being particularly low in London).

For all these reasons, crime statistics must be treated with considerable caution. At best they provide a very imperfect reflection of human behaviour and they are subject to serious biases. Nevertheless, it would be a mistake to reject them as useless. Self-reported delinquency shows substantial, but imperfect agreement with administrative figures (Farrington, 1973). Although many boys who admitted a few delinquent acts in the Cambridge study never appeared before the Courts, and some official delinquents denied such acts, the number of admitted acts proved to be significantly related to Court appearance. Of the 14–15 year old boys who never appeared in Court, only 17 per cent admitted more than 12 acts, in comparison with 47 per cent of those who first came to Court during the next three years and 66 per cent of those already convicted at the time they completed the questionnaire. Furthermore, the associations between self-reported deviancy and broken homes, criminal parents, poor parental supervision and low intelligence were similar to those found with official delinquency. On the other hand, low income and large family size showed no significant association with self-reported deviancy although it did with official delinquency. This difference could reflect biases in who is brought to Court.

Administrative statistics provide a guide to delinquent behaviour, but this guide is subject to systematic distortions as well as random error. This needs to be kept in mind when interpreting the findings on familial and geographical concentrations of delinquency and the views on intergenerational transmission.

OFFENCES AND OFFENDERS IN BRITAIN

Crime Patterns and Trends

Offences are divided into the indictable and non-indictable. The vast majority of indictable offences involve some form of stealing, but crimes of violence (some 2 per cent of the total) and sexual offences (also about 2 per cent) are also included. Three quarters of non-indictable offences involve motoring transgressions, but tax offences (5 per cent of total), drunkenness (7 per cent) and certain forms of stealing, assault and malicious damage are also in the same class. In the population as a whole, non-indictable offences far outnumber the indictable but the pattern differs markedly by age. In adults, non-indictable offences outnumber the indictable by 4 to 1 but in youngsters under the age of 14 years the reverse is true and during the middle teens the two are about equally common. There are much more complete records for indictable offences and most reports deal exclusively with this group.

Since about 1900 there has been a regular increase in reported indictable crimes, but a more variable pattern of change in non-indictable offences (McClintock and Avison, 1968). In 1901 there were 250 indictable crimes reported per 100,000 population, whereas by 1965 there were almost 2,400 per 100,000 population – nearly a ten-fold increase. Five main stages are discernible. From 1900 until the beginning of World War I the crime rate remained fairly stable; during the next 15 years it rose about 5 per cent per annum; between 1931 and 1948 the increase accelerated to some 7 per cent per annum; it then fluctuated but remained roughly stable until 1954; and during the next decade crime increased at the record rate of about 10 per cent per annum. Since World War II crimes involving violence against the person have shown a particularly marked increase resulting in a three-fold rise in the proportion of offences falling into this category. However, this rapid rise does not apply to homicides and attempted murder. During recent years female crime has increased at a faster rate than male crime. The trends for non-indictable offences are very much less regular but during the last 20 years or so rates have risen steadily.

Wilkins (1961) argued that the statistics indicated a particularly marked rise in delinquency among youngsters whose early childhood occurred during World War II. The findings were disputed at the time

(Walters, 1963) and subsequent figures have shown the rise to be just as marked among people born after the war.

There are many problems involved in making reliable comparisons between crime rates at different periods. Changes in administrative classifications of offences, in public reporting of crime and in police practices and efficiency are among the factors that must be taken into account when analysing trends. Nevertheless, the marked increase in reported offences over this century appears far too great to be wholly attributed to such factors.

Characteristics of Offenders

Throughout the whole of this century, two features of criminal statistics are particularly evident. The first is that male offenders very greatly outnumber female offenders and the second is that (proportional to the population at risk) offences are most likely to be committed by those under the age of 21 years.

More males than females are convicted of offences in all broad categories of crime and at all age levels. This is not an artefact of police action since self-report and interview studies also show that delinquent behaviour is much more common in boys than in girls (Gold, 1966; Rutter, Tizard and Whitmore, 1970; Rutter, 1975a; Graham *et al.*, 1976). In 1973 (Criminal Statistics, England and Wales) 1.5 per cent of the population were found guilty of an indictable crime, 5.6 per cent of a motoring offence, and 1.8 per cent of other non-indictable offences. Males outnumber females in these categories in ratios of 7:1, 14:1 and 8:1 respectively. Sex differences are most marked in juveniles and young adults and least evident in those over 50 years of age. The *pattern* of crime also differs by sex. Female crime less often involves violence, breaking and entering or sexual offences, and more often involves theft from shops (McClintock and Avison, 1968). There is also some indication that recidivist delinquent girls are more likely to show psychiatric disorder and to come from grossly disturbed homes compared with their male counterparts (Cowie *et al.*, 1968).

In 1973 (Criminal Statistics, England and Wales), the greatest risk of being found guilty of an indictable offence was at 17 years for both sexes. The chances of being cautioned for similar offences were greatest at 14 years for boys and 13 years for girls. If numbers found guilty and cautioned are combined, it is found that the peak age for police contact is 15 years for boys and 14 years for girls. In the past the peak age of offending has consistently coincided with the last year of compulsory schooling (Walker, 1972; McKissack, 1973). The school leaving age was raised from 15 to 16 in 1970 and these early findings suggest that, at least for boys, the age of maximum delinquency may have shifted as well.

There are also age differences in the type of offences most

frequently committed (McClintock and Avison, 1968). Burglary and robbery are committed primarily by adolescents and young adults, violence especially by young adults, fraud and forgery by older adults and shoplifting is particularly characteristic of middle-aged women.

About two-fifths of persons found guilty of indictable crimes are recividist offenders (McClintock and Avison, 1968). Of these, about one-third are reconvicted only once, a further third receive between two and four further convictions and the remainder have longer crime records. Recidivism is more frequent in males and for crimes involving robbery or breaking and entering. Furthermore, over this century the increase in recidivism has been greater than that for first offences. McClintock and Avison estimated that, after allowing for population changes, convictions have trebled whereas crime has increased nine-fold.

INTRAGENERATIONAL CONTINUITIES

Although by definition, delinquency cannot occur under the age of 10, children's behaviour in earlier years has been shown to be linked with delinquency in later childhood. Thus, West and Farrington (1973) found that teachers' assessments of 'troublesomeness' at 8 years were better predictors of future delinquency (as assessed by either self-rating or Court appearances) than any combination of other background factors. Nearly two-fifths of the 'most troublesome' boys became delinquent and more than three-quarters of recidivists fell into this category. The British National Survey (Mulligan *et al.*, 1963; Douglas *et al.*, 1968) showed that 13-year-old pupils rated by teachers as aggressive were more likely than other youngsters to become delinquent. Recidivists were nearly five times as likely to be rated as aggressive compared with the general population. The Aberdeen survey found that, compared with other children, those with deviant scores at 10 years of age on a questionnaire (Rutter, 1967), completed by teachers, were twice as likely to become delinquent (May, 1975). The items most predictive of delinquency were 'truants', 'lies', 'steals', 'bullies', 'miserable', 'frequent school absences' and 'wets himself'. A London study (Rutter, 1975c), using the same scale also showed that behavioural deviance at age 10 years was associated with delinquency at age 14 years. Of the boys with deviance shown in terms of antisocial behaviour, 27 per cent became delinquent compared with 14 per cent among those with emotional difficulties only and 11 per cent among those without any type of deviance as shown by the questionnaire. Expressed another way, of the boys who were delinquent at 14 years nearly half were behaviourally deviant at 10 years.

Similar associations between children's behaviour at school and delinquency in adolescence have been obtained in several American studies. The Cambridge-Somerville project noted that behavioural ratings by teachers correlated 0.48 with later delinquency (Powers and

Witmer, 1951). Havighurst *et al.* (1962), too showed that teachers' evaluations predicted delinquency, and Hathaway and Monachesi (1957) found that the MMPI (a questionnaire completed by the youngsters themselves which measures aspects of personality) also predicted delinquency. Conger and Miller (1966), from a study of school records, showed that at as early as 8 years of age, boys who later became delinquent differed from other boys in terms of poor adaptation, anti-authority attitudes, poor peer relationships, aggression and a lack of interest in school work. These differences still held after controlling for social class, IQ and schools attended. Roff *et al.* (1972) found that boys who were unpopular with their peers were the ones most likely to become delinquent.

Both in earlier childhood and at the time of delinquency (Stott, 1966; Glueck and Glueck, 1950), groups of delinquents differ from other children in terms of their behaviour. The majority of studies show that these differences are most marked in the case of recidivists and more serious offenders. However, although there are important continuities between behaviour in early or middle childhood and delinquency in adolescence, it should be noted that the same studies show that at least half of the delinquents do *not* show behavioural deviance when younger. Conversely, most children with deviant behaviour in early childhood do *not* become delinquent. The behavioural links are important but they are not strong enough to be of much value for prediction in the individual case (May, 1975).

In most youngsters, delinquency proves to be a passing phase (West and Farrington, 1973). About half do not appear in Court again, and of those that do, only some continue to commit crime as adults. However, West's study showed that the men who continue active crime into adult life differ significantly from those who give up delinquency on reaching adulthood (Knight and West, 1975). The men who continue crime include more from a socially deprived background, more with criminals in the family, more with serious juvenile records and more who have committed offences alone. Those who give up delinquency include more who report dropping the male peer groups of their adolescent delinquent phase and more who attribute their offences to motives of enjoyment.

On the other hand, the outlook appears less satisfactory when delinquency is persistent *and* associated with other problems. Robins *et al.* (1971) found that among black American schoolboys who showed serious problem behaviour at school (expulsion, suspension, very frequent absences, etc.) *and* juvenile delinquency (administratively defined), a third were diagnosed as showing an 'antisocial personality' in adult life and another quarter suffered from alcoholism or drug addiction. Among boys with either a delinquent record or serious problems at school (but *not* both) only 9 per cent were diagnosed as having an 'antisocial personality' when followed up in their thirties. Of those with neither delinquency nor serious school problems only 2 per cent were so diagnosed. Comparable findings emerged from Robins' (1966) earlier follow-up study of white youngsters referred for antisocial behaviour* to a child psychiatric clinic. Most of these children had a Juvenile Court record but they probably differed from other delinquents by having many other long-lasting problems. Three quarters were arrested as adults for a non-traffic offence and 44 per cent had committed major crimes — a rate nearly four times that in controls. Moreover, the antisocial children differed from controls on a wide range of other troubles in adult life. More suffered marital breakdowns, more were unemployed (23 per cent of the men at follow-up compared with 2 per cent of the controls), more were on relief or welfare assistance, more were socially isolated, more were alcoholic, and more had received psychiatric care. Similarly Tonge *et al.* (1975) found that, in English families known to social agencies for multiple problems, men with a juvenile record were likely both to commit crimes in adult life and to show a personality disorder. This association between juvenile delinquency and adult disorder was not found in the control group.

In summary, there are important continuities between behavioural difficulties in early childhood and juvenile delinquency. Children who get on badly with their peers, who are aggressive, who show troublesome behaviour at school, and who lack interest in schoolwork are the ones most likely to become delinquent. On the other hand at least half of delinquents (particularly one-time offenders) have not shown these problems when younger and most children with troublesome behaviour do not become delinquent. The continuity between early behavioural problems and later delinquency is strongest in the case of severe and persisting delinquency. In the great majority of cases juvenile delinquency does not persist and only a small minority continue to commit crimes after their mid-twenties. The tendency to persistence is very much greater when delinquency is associated with other problems in childhood and within the broader group of delinquents there is a small hard core who show severe, widespread and lasting problems which continue into middle life.

INTERGENERATIONAL CONTINUITIES

Intergenerational continuities have been shown with respect to families, geographical areas and schools and it is evident that rather different mechanisms apply in each case.

*This term was used by Robins to include 'theft, burglary, robbery, forgery, truancy, chronic tardiness at school, running away or sleeping out, sexual perversion, public masturbation, excess heterosexual interest or activity, vandalism, false fire alarms, carrying deadly weapons, incorrigibility, refusal to work, lying, keeping late hours, fighting or physical cruelty'.

Families

Many studies have examined the frequency with which delinquency and criminality are apparently transmitted between family members. Wootton (1959) reviewed a number of the older British surveys with evidence on this question. She reported that although most surveys had examined the question of familial crime, findings were generally presented in such a way as to make comparisons and conclusions difficult. Nine British studies (Ferguson, 1952; Burt, 1923; Bagot, 1941, 1944; East *et al.*, 1942; Mannheim, 1948; Carr-Saunders *et al.*, 1942; Gibbs, 1955; Mannheim and Wilkins, 1955) indicated an increase in the probability of delinquency for boys who have criminal parents or delinquent siblings, although the extent of continuity varied greatly between studies.

The most satisfactory data on parent-child continuities from these early studies were provided by Ferguson (1952). Continuities were considered in both directions. Twelve per cent of boys convicted of a juvenile offence had criminal fathers as opposed to 5 per cent of boys without convictions. It was also shown that if only the father was criminal there was little increased likelihood of the son becoming delinquent. However, the risk increased three-fold if an older or younger brother was delinquent and six-fold if several categories of relative were delinquent (63 per cent versus 10 per cent). The findings suggested that crime did run in families but continuities were not necessarily most marked between fathers and their sons. Delinquency was more strongly linked with delinquency in brothers than with crime in fathers. However, the overall number of criminal family members seemed most important.

Studies in countries other than Britain have usually produced similar results. For example, Glueck and Glueck (1950) reported that within a sample of American delinquent boys 66 per cent had criminal fathers and 45 per cent had criminal mothers, compared with 32 per cent and 15 per cent respectively for a non-delinquent control group. In Sweden, Otterström (1946) found that 21 per cent of a delinquent sample had fathers and 7 per cent had mothers convicted of 'more serious' offences: figures twice and five times the comparable general population rates. Jonsson (1967), also in Sweden, showed that 27 per cent of severely delinquent boys had criminal fathers, compared with 11 per cent in a non-delinquent control group. The difference between the delinquent and non-delinquent groups was even greater in the case of fathers who were recidivist (17 per cent versus 4.5 per cent). Hutchings and Mednick (1974) studied the crime records of adult criminals and their fathers in Denmark. Where the sons had no crime record only 10 per cent of the fathers were criminal, where the sons had committed only a minor offence the paternal criminality rate was 12 per cent but where the sons had committed a major offence the rate was 21 per cent. In their follow-up study of the sons of people referred to a psychiatric clinic in childhood, Robins and Lewis (1966) found that juvenile delinquency was more common if the father had a criminal record or had persistent social difficulties (excessive drinking, poor work record, neglect of family, etc.). But, delinquency was even more strongly associated with these features in grandfathers.

Two recent studies provide the most systematic findings on familial continuities in delinquency and crime. Robins *et al.*, (1975) examined offences in a sample of the offspring of 235 black men living in St. Louis. Delinquency in the children was associated both with delinquency in the parents when they were juveniles, and parental arrests in adult life. The association applied to boys and girls and was twice as marked when both parents had a crime record as when only one had. However, even when both parents were criminal only about half the children were delinquent. There was also an association with crime in grandparents (although, unlike the earlier clinic study finding, this was not as marked as with fathers), and with delinquency in sibs. The continuities were not explicable in terms of social class.

Broadly similar findings were found in West and Farrington's British study (West, 1969; West and Farrington, 1973; Farrington *et al.*, 1975) of 394 boys followed into early adult life. Nearly half the boys with criminal fathers acquired delinquency records compared with less than a fifth of those with non-criminal fathers; eighteen per cent of the daughters of criminal men became delinquent compared with six per cent of the daughters of men without criminal records. The risk of delinquency in the offspring was unrelated to the severity or frequency of paternal crime. Interestingly, sons who became recidivist only in adult life were more likely to have a criminal father than those who became recidivist when younger. Criminality in mothers was associated with a two fold increase in the rate of delinquency in the sons even when the father was non-criminal but delinquency rates were highest of all (63 per cent) when both parents were criminal. Maternal criminality was even more strongly associated with delinquency in the daughters (28 per cent of criminal mothers compared with 5 per cent of non-criminal mothers had at least one criminal daughter). Delinquency was also associated with delinquency in the brothers and sisters. As a result of this familial propensity towards criminality, 11 per cent of the families accounted for nearly half of all convicted individuals and, even more strikingly, 4 per cent of the families accounted for nearly half of all convictions.

As in the Robins study, the continuities were not explicable in terms of low social status, as continuities were similar at all income levels. However, there was some evidence that the continuities were explicable in part by selective prosecution of persons from families in which someone had a criminal record; boys with similar rates of self-reported delinquent acts and with similar 'troublesomeness' on teachers' reports were more likely to be convicted if a parent was criminal. On the other hand, this was not the whole explanation as self-reported delinquency and troublesomeness also both increased in frequency when the father had a criminal record. Criminal parents were particularly likely to be rated as providing 'poor supervision' of their children but the presence of a criminal parent increased the likelihood of delinquency in the sons at all grades of parental supervision.

In summary, it is evident that crime often runs in families. As the continuities are most strongly shown in the studies with the best data, the finding may be accepted as valid. However, the mechanisms underlying these continuities remain ill-understood and it should be emphasized that even when both parents are criminal about half the sons do *not* become delinquent.

Geographical Areas

It has frequently been claimed that areas can produce successive generations of delinquents and criminals. Mayhew (1862) was one of the first writers in this country to stress the influence of milieu, and since the pioneer Chicago studies by Shaw and McKay (1942) many investigations have shown that crime and delinquency tend to be concentrated in particular geographical areas. These may be city slums (Lander, 1954; Mays, 1963) or new housing estates (Mannheim, 1948; Morris, 1957; Jones, 1958; Spencer, 1954). There may be differences in delinquency rates between boroughs (Wallis and Maliphant, 1967), between wards within a borough (Power *et al.*, 1972; Edwards, 1973), between enumeration districts within a ward (Gath *et al.*, 1975) or even between streets in a small neighbourhood (Jephcott and Carter, 1954). Areas with high rates of juvenile delinquency tend to have high rates of adult crime as well and, in general, rates are higher in industrial cities than in non-industrial towns and higher in both than in rural areas (Grunhut, 1956; McClintock and Avison, 1968). On the whole, high delinquency areas tend to be poor, overcrowded and of low social status but they are not necessarily the most physically dilapidated. Offenders do not necessarily live in the area in which they commit their crimes but marked variations between areas are found regardless of whether these are examined by place of crime or by home address of offenders.

The limited available evidence suggests that these delinquency areas remain fairly stable over time. Wallis and Maliphant (1967) demonstrated that the distribution of offenders between London areas was much the same as it had been 40 years earlier (Burt, 1925). Castle and Gittus (1957) also found a distribution of social problems in Liverpool which were similar to those noted twenty years earlier (Jones, 1934). The highest rate of juveniles on probation (376 per 10,000) occurred in the same registration district as had the highest prevalence of detected immorality, crime and alcoholism (11.0 per 10,000) in the earlier survey.

The existence of very marked differences between areas in crime rate has been well demonstrated in numerous surveys. However, there continues to be uncertainty about the explanation for these differences.

Varying police practices will account for some of the findings (McClintock and Avison, 1968), but it seems unlikely that these are a major factor. In the first place, detection rates tend to be lowest in the major cities where the proportion of offenders is especially high. Secondly, the areas with high delinquency rates tend to be the same areas which have high rates of child psychiatric referral (Gath *et al.*, 1975).

An alternative explanation is that families with a predisposition towards crime drift, or are attracted into, inner city areas. This may well occur to some extent but area differences remain even when comparisons are restricted to individuals born and bred in the area (Rutter, Cox, *et al.*, 1975). Rather it seems that there is something about living in certain areas which predisposes to crime just as it seems to predispose to psychiatric disorder (see Chapter 7). Whether this influence resides in social mores and neighbourhood pressures or in personal living conditions remains uncertain. This issue is discussed in more detail later in this chapter.

Schools

Quite apart from differences according to the area in which people live, several studies have shown marked differences in delinquency rate between schools (Power *et al.*, 1967, 1972; Gath *et al.*, 1972, 1975; Cannan, 1970; Yule and Rutter, 1975; Rutter, 1975d; Clegg and Megson, 1968). Moreover, these differences were shown by Power *et al.* (1972) to remain stable over a ten year period (rank order correlation of 0.79). The differences between schools are not explicable in terms of their geographical location (Power *et al.*, 1972; Gath *et al.*, 1975). Clear differences have also been found between schools for delinquent boys in rates of absconding (Clarke and Martin, 1971).

Undoubtedly, part of the explanation for these school differences lies in selective intake. Farrington (1972) found that 38 per cent of the boys entering high delinquency secondary schools had previously been rated as 'troublesome' when in primary school, compared with only 8 per cent of the boys entering low delinquency secondary schools. Similarly, Yule and Rutter (1975) found marked variations between secondary schools in the proportion of children who had shown behavioural deviance at primary school. The range extended from a school with an intake of zero per cent deviant children to some with over 40 per cent deviant. On the other hand, selective intake was not sufficient to explain the differences in delinquency rate between secondary schools. Even after this was taken into account, marked differences between schools remained (Yule and Rutter, 1976). These were greater than in the Farrington (1972) study.

The findings suggest that the characteristics of a school play some part in determining how many children become delinquent. The size and type of school make little difference except that rates tend to be lower in schools where children are selected on the basis of high academic attainments (Power *et al.*, 1972; Gath *et al.*, 1975). Clegg and Megson (1968) noted that delinquency rates were higher in schools which made extensive use of corporal punishment. Hargreaves (1967) observed how streaming could lead to alienation among children in the lowest streams and Sugarman (1967) suggested that deep involvement in a youth culture outside the school could lead to a conflict with values in the school. Schools differ in morale, the models of behaviour set by staff, patterns of encouragement and reward, methods of discipline, inter-staff relationships, the kind of autonomy and responsibility given to pupils, the type of contacts with parents and with the community they serve, and in many other features. The role of the headmaster is clearly important in setting the tone of a school but there are few systematic findings on how this happens or on which aspects of school life matter most in influencing how children behave.

ASSOCIATIONS BETWEEN DELINQUENCY AND OTHER PROBLEMS

Psychiatric Disorder

Persistent delinquents suffer from psychiatric disorder more often than do one-time offenders. Emotional disturbance (depression and the like) is in children with non-delinquent antisocial disorders (Rutter, Graham and Yule, 1970). Furthermore, among recidivist delinquents (particularly when the delinquency is of early onset) numerous studies have shown that the delinquency is frequently preceded and accompanied by various abnormalities in behaviour including restlessness, poor concentration, aggression and attention-seeking (Glueck and Glueck, 1950; Conger and Miller, 1966; Mulligan *et al.*, 1963; West and Farrington, 1973). In the National Survey (Mulligan *et al.*, 1963) delinquents who made at least two Court appearances were nearly five times as likely as non-delinquents to be rated as aggressive by school teachers.

This association between recidivist delinquency and psychiatric disorder is confirmed by long-term follow-up studies. Antisocial* children referred to psychiatric clinics not only have high rates of adult criminality and sociopathy† but also they have high rates of psychiatric disorder of other kinds (Robins, 1966, 1972). Nevertheless, the converse does not apply. Children with emotional disorder at age 10 to 11 years only rarely become delinquent by the time they reach school-leaving age (Graham and Rutter, 1973) and follow-up studies

*Defined in terms of a variety of behaviours only some of which involve delinquent acts (see Chapter 7).

†Defined operationally as terms of severe problems in many aspects of life including work, marriage, interpersonal relationships and personal functioning.

into middle adult life show that few become criminal. The course and outcome of emotional disorders are quite different from those for disturbances of conduct (Robins, 1966, 1972).

Not surprisingly, psychiatric problems (usually in the form of personality disorder or depression) are more often found in recidivist delinquents in institutions (e.g., Gibbens, 1963; West, 1963; Cowie *et al.*, 1968) than in one time offenders in the community. It is also noteworthy that one study showed that psychiatric problems were more frequent in those who committed crimes on their own than in those who were part of a delinquent group (Gibbens, 1963). Both physical illness and mental disorder are particularly common in middle aged women who shoplift (Gibbens and Prince, 1962). Crime is only infrequently associated with psychosis or severe mental illness, although the group in which this occurs poses a problem for services (Rollin, 1969). One study reported that psychiatric ratings successfully predicted recidivism in juveniles (Hutcheson *et al.*, 1966) but the usual finding in both children (Power *et al.*, 1974) and adults (Gibbens *et al.*, 1959; Morrow and Peterson, 1966) is that the presence of psychiatric disorder is of little prognostic importance for further crime.

In short, most first offenders do not have any form of psychiatric disorder but there is a significant association between delinquency or crime and psychiatric problems. These are more marked in recidivists and most often involve abnormalities of personality and depression.

IQ and Scholastic Attainment

Very few delinquents or criminals are mentally retarded but there is a significant tendency for them to have an IQ slightly below average. Woodward (1955a and b) reviewed the literature on this point and concluded that, as a group, delinquents had a mean IQ some 5 points below that of the general population. More recent studies have produced broadly similar findings. West (West, 1969; West and Farrington, 1973) found that, on average, delinquents had lower scores than other boys on IQ tests at 8 and 11 years of age. This difference in IQ was almost entirely due to the relatively low scores of the recidivists; one-time offenders were of much the same intelligence as non-delinquent youngsters. Douglas *et al.* (1968) found that delinquents had mean test scores some 5 points below average, and recidivists scored nearly 9 points below average. Part of the poor performance may have been related to the children's poor family circumstances and low social status. However, even when these were taken into account statistically, recidivists still had mean scores some 4 points below the general population. The association between low average intelligence and delinquency is a very general finding, although it may not apply within very socially disadvantaged groups (Tonge *et al.*, 1975).

On the whole, studies have indicated that delinquent males score rather more poorly on verbal tests than on non-verbal tests (Wechsler, 1944; Prentice and Kelly, 1963; Douglas *et al.*, 1968). However, this has not always been the case (e.g., Naar, 1965; West and Farrington,

1973) and it seems doubtful whether this cognitive pattern is associated with delinquent behaviour as such. It may be, as Graham and Kamano (1958) found, that a low verbal score is characteristic of delinquents who are poor readers but not those who are good readers.

Numerous studies over the last half century have shown that delinquency and antisocial behaviour are often accompanied by reading difficulties and educational failure (see review by Rutter, Tizard and Whitmore, 1970 and Rutter and Yule, 1973). In the Isle of Wight survey of children with specific reading retardation, one-quarter showed antisocial behaviour as measured on a teacher questionnaire, a rate several times higher than in the general population. Conversely, of the children showing antisocial disorder, one-third were at least 28 months retarded in reading (after IQ was partialled out) compared with 4 per cent in the general population. Comparable results were found in London (Sturge, 1972; Varlaam, 1974). Reading difficulties were associated not only with delinquency but with socially disapproved behaviour such as lying, stealing, fighting and destructiveness which did not result in a Court appearance. However, reading difficulties have not been found in children whose antisocial problems begin during adolescence (Farrington, 1973, Rutter, Graham *et al.*, 1976), nor in individuals whose delinquency begins in adult life (Robins and Hill, 1966).

The mechanisms underlying the association between delinquent behaviour and poor educational performance are not fully understood but it is clear that there are several (Rutter and Yule, 1973). First, family influences leading to reading difficulties overlap considerably with those leading to delinquent behaviour, so that in part the association is merely a function of the underlying association between background factors. Secondly, there are temperamental features which predispose children to both sorts of problems. West and Farrington (1973) found that IQ no longer predicted delinquency when teacher ratings of children's troublesome behaviour were taken into account. Thirdly, reading failure itself may be a potent source of discouragement, loss of self-esteem, and antagonism which in some cases may contribute to the development of delinquent activities. Evidence in favour of this suggestion is available from studies in both London (Varlaam, 1974) and the Isle of Wight (Rutter *et al.*, 1970). Fourthly, it might be suggested that the labelling of a boy as delinquent could contribute to poor school attainment. However, this appears unlikely to be an important effect as delinquents are usually poor scholars long before they appear in Court, and the Court appearance has not been found to lead to any further educational deterioration (Douglas *et al.*, 1968; Fisher, 1972).

Employment

Glaser and Rice (1959), in a study of American crime rates over a twenty-five year period, found that more adults were convicted of crimes against property during periods of high unemployment, but that juvenile delinquency tended to be slightly less frequent during these times. East *et al.* (1942) found that delinquents themselves did not necessarily have particularly high rates of unemployment but offences tended to be committed at times when they were out of a job. West and his colleagues (personal communication) found that boys who became delinquent tended to have less stable employment histories than those that did not and that some delinquents had had almost twenty jobs by the age of 18 years. Maxwell (1969) showed that adult criminals were frequently unemployed when not in prison.

Robins (1966), in her study of youngsters referred to a psychiatric clinic for antisocial behaviour (see above), found that 23 per cent were not working when followed up in adult life — a rate three times that among those referred to the clinic for other problems and ten times that in controls. Those with a juvenile police record showed both poor work adjustment and downward social mobility relative to other clinic attenders and controls (Robins *et al.*, 1962). It seemed that early truancy led to leaving school before graduation, which in turn created job problems, which then encouraged theft, led to jail, and further intensified employment difficulties. Although Foster *et al.* (1972) found that few delinquent boys felt seriously handicapped by having a Police record, it is likely that being labelled as a delinquent or criminal makes it more difficult to obtain jobs (Lemert, 1967), as shown with American men by Schwartz and Skolnick (1964).

POLYGENIC FACTORS

Studies of adopted children and of twin pairs have provided the best data for an assessment of genetic influences upon crime and delinquency. The issues and findings have been previously well reviewed (Trasler, 1973; Shields, 1973, 1976) and therefore are summarized here only briefly.

All twin studies have shown that the concordance rate for juvenile delinquency within monozygotic pairs is much the same as within dizygotic pairs (Rosanoff *et al.*, 1941; Hayashi, 1967; Shields, 1976). This finding suggests that genetic influences are of only minor importance. Bohman's studies (1970, 1971, 1972) of adopted and fostered children showed that boys whose biological fathers were criminal had only slightly more school problems than other boys; in girls the difference was rather more marked. These results are in keeping with the twin findings in suggesting that behavioural disturbance in children is not strongly influenced by genetic factors.

However, the findings with respect to adult criminality are rather different. Twin studies have generally shown concordance rates within monozygotic pairs to be several times as high as those within dizygotic pairs (Lange, 1929; Rosanoff *et al.*, 1941; Hauge *et al.*, 1968; Christiansen, 1970). The findings indicate a stronger genetic component than in the case of juvenile delinquency; this is most evident with respect to severe and persistent criminal behaviour.

Studies of adoptees point to the same conclusion. Hutchings (Hutchings, 1972; Hutchings and Mednick, 1974) investigated 1,145 Danish men adopted during childhood and compared them with a non-adopted control group matched for father's occupation. The criminal records of both biological and adoptive parents were examined. The proportion of adopted sons with police records was 10 per cent if neither parent was known to the police, 11 per cent if only the adoptive father was criminal, 21 per cent if only the biological father was known to police and 36 per cent if both fathers were criminal. The higher rate of crime in the sons when the biological father was criminal than when the adoptive father was criminal indicates genetic transmission, but the further increase in rate when both fathers were criminal points to an additional environmental effect. When the 143 criminal adoptees were compared with 143 control adoptees it was found that in the criminal group there were 70 biological and 33 adoptive fathers with a criminal record compared with 40 and 14 respectively in the control group. Again, the higher rate of criminality in the biological fathers demonstrated a genetic influence, but the higher rate of criminality in the adoptive fathers of the criminal adoptees compared with the controls suggests an environmental effect. Hereditary influences seemed strongest in the case of severe and persistent criminal behaviour. Schulsinger (1972), in a similarly designed study of Danish adoptees, showed an important hereditary influence in the case of psychopathy coming to psychiatric notice. Crowe (1972, 1974), in an American study, showed that the rate of antisocial personality disorder was higher among children born to female criminals but given up for adoption than among adoptee controls not born to criminals (13 per cent versus 0 per cent). This indicates the importance of heredity, but genetic-environmental interaction was also shown by the finding that antisocial personality was more frequent in the children of criminals who had experienced adversities in childhood than in those who had not.

In summary, genetic influences are of only minor importance in most cases of juvenile delinquency but hereditary factors are much more influential in the case of severe and persistent criminality in adults, especially when this is associated with abnormalities of personality. It may be that genetic factors are also more important in the case of the small hard core of severe and persistent delinquents in childhood although evidence on this point is lacking.

CHROMOSOMAL ABNORMALITIES

There is evidence (see Hook, 1973; Trasler, 1973) that a small proportion of psychopathic offenders have an extra chromosome. The association between the chromosomal anomaly and crime is weak and indirect and the anomaly is not transmitted to the next generation. However, one study (Nielsen, 1971) has suggested that long Y chromosomes (which may be passed on from father to son) are more common in criminals attending a psychiatric clinic than in the general population. The finding needs confirmation.

PHYSICAL FACTORS

Medical aspects of delinquency and crime have been reviewed by Scott (1966) and West (1967). American studies have usually found no association between delinquency and physical ill-health (e.g., Glueck and Glueck, 1950; McCord and McCord,1959) but Eilenberg (1961) noted a high rate of minor physical disorders among delinquent boys in a remand home and Gibbens (1963) found that 38 per cent of Borstal boys had been rejected for National Service on physical grounds — a rate twice that in the general population. Stott (1966) noted that minor physical impairments were more common among delinquent boys on probation than controls and that these were especially frequent in delinquents who showed behavioural maladjustment according to teachers' ratings. He argued from these and other similar findings that some cases of delinquency arose on the basis of multiple congenital physical impairment, but this hypothesis remains largely untested. Neither the Pasamanick and Knobloch investigations (1966) nor the West and Farrington (1973) study showed any connection between perinatal complications and delinquency. On the other hand, there is evidence that low birth weight and too long or too short a period in the womb show a slight but significant association with behavioural maladjustment and poor scholastic attainment (Davie *et al.*, 1972) — features which are shown by many delinquents. Also, minor congenital physical anomalies (Quinn and Rapoport, 1974) have been found to be more common in children showing hyperactivity and distractibility, characteristics present in some delinquents.

Several studies have shown that epilepsy and neurological disorder increase the risk of psychiatric disorder (Rutter, Graham and Yule, 1970) and the prevalence of epilepsy in adult prisoners (7.2 per 1,000) has been found to be above that in the general population (Gunn and Fenton, 1969). No special relationship was discovered between particular types of crime and epilepsy (Gunn and Bonn, 1971) but epileptic prisoners were particularly prone to anxiety, depression and suicide (Gunn, 1973).

Studies of selected groups of delinquents have shown them to be of more muscular build than the general population (Gibbens, 1963; Glueck and Glueck, 1956) but it is uncertain how far this applies to delinquents as a whole. West and Farrington (1973) found no association between either height-weight ratio or strength of grip and delinquency in a prospective study of a total population of boys.

The evidence is inconclusive, but suggests that physical abnormalities show only a weak association with delinquency and crime. However, within the overall group of delinquents and criminals there may be a smaller sub-group with wider behavioural disturbances in which perinatal complications and minor physical anomalies play some part in the genesis of problems. The size of this possible sub-group, and the mechanisms by which physical factors may predispose to problem behaviour, remain largely unknown.

PHYSIOLOGICAL DIFFERENCES

Eysenck (1970) has argued that persistent delinquents and criminals differ from the rest of the population in their speed of 'conditioning' (a form of reflex learning) and their personality characteristics of extraversion and autonomic reactivity. The literature on this topic has been reviewed by Trasler (1973) who observed that the findings are inconsistent and contradictory. There is doubt as to whether 'conditionability' is a general variable (different measures of 'conditionability' often do not agree) and the associations between extraversion and delinquency are very weak (see also West and Farrington, 1973). Some of the differences between investigations may stem from variations in sampling or research procedures and it remains possible (although unestablished) that physiological features differentiate certain sub-groups of delinquents or criminals with abnormal personalities. However, physiological variables show no consistent association with delinquency or crimes as such.

SOCIAL STATUS

Many sociological theories are based on the assumption that delinquency is predominantly a working class phenomenon, and in the past both local (Mannheim *et al.*, 1957; Morris, 1957; Little and Ntsekhe, 1959) and national (Douglas *et al.*, 1966) studies have shown that delinquency is more frequent in British youngsters who are sons of manual workers than in those from professional or other middle class homes. Nevertheless, other recent investigations have found little or no association between occupational status (as assessed on the Registrar General's classification) and delinquency (Palmai *et al.*, 1967; West and Farrington, 1973).

Several explanations for these contradictory findings need to be considered. First, there are the differences that arise from varying measurements of social class. Thus, West and Farrington (1973) found no association between father's occupation and delinquency in the children,* but delinquency (particularly recidivist delinquency) was associated with low family income, poor housing and neglected accommodation. Among the boys from families with a poor income, 22 per cent became recidivist compared with 6 per cent of those from families with a good income. However, low income was also associated with poor parental supervision, separation, parental conflict and large families, so that low income usually stood for a constellation of unfavourable home features. The association between low income and delinquency was markedly reduced when these were taken into account and the association ceased to be significant when the child's intelligence was brought into the reckoning. In short, low income seems to be linked with delinquency — not so much because income is important as such, but because poor families tend to be disadvantaged in so many other ways. It may be concluded that poverty does not directly cause delinquency but it may make it more likely because it predisposes to a variety of family difficulties and troubles more directly associated with delinquency (see section on family influences below).

A further consideration is whether the higher proportion of delinquents from poor homes may stem in part from differences in the way police deal with people from varying social backgrounds (see above). In this connection it is pertinent that Farrington (1973) found no significant association between low income and delinquency as assessed from self-reports† rather than Court records. This, together with other evidence (see West and Farrington, 1973) suggests that part of the association between low income and delinquency may be an artefact of police practice.

Most self-reports and interview studies are in keeping with this conclusion. Gold (1966) in an American study, found self-reported delinquent acts to be twice as frequent among low social status boys but the social class difference did not apply to girls and even for boys was less than the two-fold difference found using official statistics. Reiss and Rhodes (1961) found delinquent acts to be more common among working class boys living in a working class area but not in those with homes in a middle class neighbourhood. Other American self-report studies have failed to find any social class trend in delinquency (Nye *et al.*, 1958; Akers, 1964; Clark and Wenninger, 1962; Dentler and Monroe, 1961) although trends have been evident in some investigations (Erickson and Empey, 1965). Belson (1968) found no social class difference in the amount of self-reported stealing among London boys, except for a slightly lower rate in the professional and managerial group (15 per cent in the top quartile for amount of stealing versus 25 per cent for unskilled manual). However, boys in the top

*However, the social class spread in their sample was quite narrow.

†Although self-reports overcome some of the disadvantages attached to official records, they are subject to a variety of other possible limitations and biases.

social group who admitted to a lot of stealing were *much* less likely to have been caught by the police (4 per cent versus 23 per cent in unskilled manual). McDonald (1969), in another British study, found no social class difference for serious theft or breaking and entering, but truancy (32 per cent in upper middle class boys versus 49 per cent in lower working class boys), the carrying of weapons (16 per cent versus 24 per cent) and various other offences showed some social class trend.

However, there are social class differences in types of offences committed. For example, Belson (1968) found that stealing milk, and stealing from a bike, from work, from a stall or barrow, and from a goods yard or the docks were much more common among working class boys. In contrast, traffic offences, embezzlement, tax frauds and other illegal financial practices are more typically middle class, for the obvious reason of greater opportunity (Wootton, 1959; Cicourel, 1968).

In short, there is some tendency for an association between social class and delinquency but to some extent this is probably an artefact of differences in the way police deal with people according to their social background. However, there are also true differences in both the extent and type of offences according to social background. Low income has little direct connection with delinquency, but it is indirectly important through its association with a host of other disadvantaged family situations which may themselves lead to crime.

FAMILY VARIABLES

Family Size

One of the most consistent associations in the literature is that between large family size and delinquency (see e.g., Wootton, 1959; Douglas *et al.*, 1968; West and Farrington, 1973). Nevertheless, to a considerable extent it seems that the association is important because of its association with other adverse factors rather than in its own right. Thus, Ferguson (1952) and West and Farrington (1973) both found that overcrowding was strongly associated with delinquency and that there was no relationship between family size and delinquency in the least overcrowded homes. Large family size in the West and Farrington (1973) study also correlated closely with poor housing, physical neglect of the children, fathers' erratic work records, and low income. When delinquent and non-delinquent groups were matched on these variables, the difference in family size between the groups was reduced.

Supervision and Discipline

The early studies by McCord and McCord (1959) and by Glueck and Glueck (1959) comparing delinquents and non-delinquents showed that poor parental supervision and lax or erratic and over-strict discipline were two of the variables which best differentiated the groups. These items were incorporated into the Gluecks' five item prediction table, and subsequent prospective studies by other workers have confirmed the predictive validity of these variables (Craig and Glick, 1965; Tait and Hodges, 1962 and 1971). Similarly, West and Farrington (1973) found that boys subject to very strict or erratic discipline were significantly more likely than other boys to become delinquent (27 per cent versus 16 per cent), and those who were poorly supervised by their parents were twice as likely to become delinquent (31 per cent versus 17 per cent). However, poor supervision was very closely associated with low income and was not itself an important precursor of delinquency independent of other background factors.

Family Conflict and Disharmony

McCord and McCord (1959) found that quarrelsome-neglecting homes were particularly likely to produce delinquent boys (70 per cent versus 30 per cent in cohesive homes) and Glueck and Glueck (1959) found the same. West and Farrington (1973) also found that boys suffering from serious parental conflict were particularly prone to delinquency (35 per cent versus 16 per cent in the remainder of the families). Most of these were also in the groups rated unfavourably on discipline or supervision, so the three ratings were combined into one global rating of 'parental behaviour'. Boys experiencing the worst parental behaviour were more than twice as likely as the remainder to become delinquent (32 per cent versus 15 per cent) and nearly five times as likely to become recidivist (20 per cent versus 4 per cent). This is in keeping with the finding from Power *et al.*'s (1974) prospective study which showed that delinquent boys from unbroken homes with serious and continuous stress were the ones most likely to reappear in Court (37 per cent had at least two further convictions in the next two years compared with 23 per cent among the boys from intact homes without serious problems). In fact, adverse family factors were the *only* variables significantly to predict reappearance in Court (school and neighbourhood variables produced non-significant differences and psychiatric ratings and type of offence did not predict at all).

In the West and Farrington (1973) study, poor parental behaviour was particularly prevalent among disadvantaged low income families. Nevertheless, delinquents and non-delinquents differed significantly in parental behaviour (rated when the boys were aged 8 years and therefore *before* they became delinquent) even after matching the groups separately on family income, family size and parental criminality. Furthermore, parental behaviour was the *only* family variable which significantly predicted delinquency after taking into account the ratings of children's 'troublesome' behaviour. It may be concluded, therefore, that poor parental behaviour — especially harsh discipline, rejecting attitudes and poor supervision — not only correlates with delinquency but probably also acts as one of the several causes of delinquency.

Broken Homes and Separations

Traditionally, broken homes and prolonged parent-child separation have been seen as important factors predisposing to delinquency and, in 1946, Bowlby claimed that prolonged separation of a child from his mother stood foremost among the causes of delinquent character formation. Numerous studies since then have shown that the rate of broken homes and separation experiences tends to be higher among delinquents than in the general population (see Bowlby, 1951; Wootton, 1959; West, 1967 and Rutter, 1972a). Nevertheless, recent work has shown that it is not the separation or break-up as such which is most important.

Firstly, several studies have shown that delinquency is particularly common in youngsters from homes broken by parental divorce or separation whereas it is not especially frequent in those from homes broken by death (Douglas *et al.*, 1968; Gibson, 1969; Gregory, 1965). Thus, in the West and Farrington (1973) study, 18 per cent of boys from unbroken homes, 21 per cent of those from homes broken by death but 38 per cent of those from homes broken by divorce or separation became delinquent. The difference with respect to recidivism was even greater (19 per cent of the separated compared with none among the bereaved). Secondly, delinquency is just as common among children from unhappy and quarrelsome but *un*broken homes as it is among those whose parents have divorced or separated (McCord and McCord, 1959; West and Farrington, 1973; Power *et al.*, 1974). Thus, McCord and McCord (1959) found that 70 per cent of boys from quarrelsome-neglecting homes were convicted of crimes compared with 51 per cent from broken homes. Furthermore, Power *et al.* (1974) showed that among delinquent boys from broken homes 27 per cent became seriously recidivist but among boys from severely stressed intact homes 37 per cent did so. Thirdly, separations of a child from his parents lasting one month or more are unrelated to delinquency or antisocial behaviour (as rated from interview data) if the separations occur because of physical illness but are related to delinquency if they occur as a result of family discord or disturbance (Rutter, 1971b; West and Farrington, 1973). However, *repeated* hospital admissions (which of course involve stresses other than those associated with separation) are accompanied by an increased rate of delinquency (Douglas, 1975).

In summary, the evidence clearly points to the conclusion that broken homes and separation experiences are associated with delinquency largely because they reflect family discord and disharmony. Separations which occur for other reasons may well lead to short-term distress and occasionally to longer lasting difficulties but they are of very minor importance in the genesis of delinquency.

Maternal employment shows no association with delinquency (Douglas *et al.*, 1968; West and Farrington, 1973). Of course, the quality of alternative care is important (Moore, 1963), just as is the quality of care provided by the child's own mother, but the fact of the mother having or not having a job is of no importance in itself with respect to delinquency.

West and Farrington (1973) found that illegitimate boys were exceptionally likely to become recidivist (40 per cent did so). However, nearly half the illegitimate boys lived with both unmarried parents in an unbroken home so that separation was not the main factor. The same applies to single short hospital admissions in early childhood but long-term sequelae are somewhat more frequent in children who experience multiple admissions.

Child-rearing Patterns and Attitudes

Gold (1963) found that delinquents and their parents shared few leisure activities, and West and Farrington (1973) similarly found that delinquency was significantly more common among boys who spent little of their leisure time at home and whose fathers rarely participated in family activities. Low maternal aspirations regarding a son's job were also related to delinquency, especially in the case of boys with above average scholastic achievements (24 per cent delinquent compared with 5 per cent among those with high aspiration mothers). Several studies have shown some association between parental authoritarianism and delinquency but West and Farrington (1973) found that the association disappeared when other aspects of family life were taken into account. As the assessment of child-rearing patterns by either questionnaire (Becker and Krug, 1965) or interview (Yarrow *et al.*, 1968) is bedevilled by serious methodological problems not much reliance can be placed on results, either negative or positive.

Parental Illness and Deviance

The extensive evidence that parental criminality is associated with delinquency in the children has already been noted. West and Farrington (1973) found that parental criminality was closely interlinked with low income and large family size, but that even after matching the groups on these variables the delinquents still had more criminal parents. However, criminal parents tended to exercise particularly poor supervision over their children and when this was taken into account the link between parental criminality and delinquency in the sons was much reduced. McCord and McCord (1959) showed that the risk of delinquency was greatest in the case of cruel and neglecting criminal fathers and that the risk was only slightly reduced if the criminal parent was loving (although the number in the latter category was too small for the finding to be reliable).

West and Farrington (1973) found that neurotic symptoms in the mother were only weakly related to delinquency in the sons and such symptoms in the father were not at all so. However, severe abnormalities of personality in the mother were strongly associated with an increase in delinquency rate (45 per cent delinquent versus 15 per cent in the remainder of the families), as was personality disorder in the father (34 per cent versus 18 per cent).

Overview of Family Factors in the Genesis of Delinquency

There is good evidence that seriously disturbed family relationships in early and middle childhood are associated with a much increased risk of delinquency in the children. This is not a function of low social status as the association remains after social class has been taken into account. Furthermore, the pattern of associations and the time sequence suggest that not only does family disharmony precede delinquency but probably it plays a part in causing it. Its action is likely to be manifest early in life as the strongest predictors from 8 years of age onwards are variables concerned with the child's behaviour. Thus, teacher and peer ratings of troublesomeness strongly predicted delinquency in the West and Farrington (1973) study even after family variables had been controlled. The converse did not apply. With the exception of the composite rating of 'parental behaviour', which still showed a just significant association with delinquency, no family variable predicted delinquency after the groups were controlled for troublesomeness. The implication is that family disturbance leads children to show troublesome behaviour which in turn leads to delinquency, but that in the absence of troublesome behaviour family variables are of much less importance. On the other hand, it would be wrong to conclude that patterns of behaviour are fixed early in life. Power *et al.* (1974) showed that even during adolescence family discord predisposed to recidivism and Rutter (1971) found that deviant behaviour was significantly less frequent in children who moved to a more harmonious family situation after early childhood. The more limited associations between family variables and delinquency in later childhood and adolescence are likely to be a function in part of the unfortunate fact that children who start in disadvantageous family circumstances usually remain in the same poor circumstances (Rutter, 1974b).

SOME SOCIO-CULTURAL THEORIES

A large variety of social theories have been put forward to explain the genesis and spread of delinquency and crime. Some of these are expressed in terms which seem to suggest they could provide a universal explanation but it is evident from the findings already discussed that no theory is likely to do so. Delinquents and criminals constitute quite heterogeneous groups and even with individual delinquents multiple influences can be seen to be operating. Furthermore, many of the theories overlap considerably with one another. In 1967, West concluded that 'an outstanding weakness of the social theories of delinquency is absence of factual evidence in support of any one in preference to the rest', and Walker (1965) has urged the need for comparative research designed to test the merits and demerits of competing hypotheses. Very little research of this kind has been undertaken but in the following section there is an attempt to draw together some of the available findings relevant to the main theoretical approaches.

Delinquency as Part of a Normal Sub-cultural Pattern of Behaviour
Mays (1954) examined patterns of delinquency in an underprivileged part of Liverpool with a high crime rate. A detailed study was made of a sample of 80 adolescent boys in regular attendance at a youth club. Although not considered to be the most delinquent in the area, two fifths had official delinquent records and over three quarters admitted to behaviours which, if they came to police notice, would have been dealt with as indictable offences. Mays (1954 and 1972) argued that, in this area, delinquency was part of an identifiable lower working class pattern of behaviour to which the majority of normal healthy, but underdisciplined, youngsters conformed. Delinquency, in his view, was not usually a matter of individual maladjustment, nor did it constitute a positive rejection of middle class culture and a reaction to status frustration.

Willmott (1969), on the basis of his interview study of adolescent boys in the East End of London, also argued that much of their petty thieving and 'lifting' from work was a normal pattern of behaviour for their social group and was regarded lightly by most local people. These boys did not feel frustrated or rejected and on the whole delinquency constituted a passing phase. However, within this broad group of minor delinquents there was a rather different, rebellious minority of more serious recidivist delinquents whose behaviour arose in a different way.

Downes (1966), too, studying boys in much the same part of London, suggested that their illegal behaviour was not due to 'alienation' or 'status frustration' but rather to a process of dissociation from middle-class dominated contexts of school, work and recreation. Most working class boys react to failure at school and at work, not by frustration and reaction-formation but by a reaffirmation of the working class ethos.

There are several observations which are in keeping with these views as an explanation for petty theft in lower working class areas in big cities. Belson's (1968) findings on the social class gradient for certain types of stealing (such as from work or from goods yards) have already been mentioned. However, the most frequently reported item with a marked social gradient (stealing from bikes or motor-bikes) was admitted to by less than half the lower working class youngsters. Furthermore, the thefts (from shops and from schools) which were admitted to by a majority of adolescents were almost as common among middle class children. On the basis of these findings it might be suggested that stealing constitutes a normal pattern of behaviour for *all* social groups but that socio-cultural variables determine which types of theft are acceptable in each culture. Also in keeping with the 'normal subculture' views are the repeated findings that for most youngsters delinquency does not continue long after adolescence. On the other hand, this applies just as much to middle class as to working class boys. The well established finding (see above) that many delinquents, especially first-time offenders, do not show any general disturbance of behaviour or emotions is also consistent with the same view. However, the same studies have shown that about half of delinquents *do* show deviant behaviour which precedes their delinquency. Furthermore, those studies which have examined the issue, both in Britain (Stott, 1960, 1966) and the United States (Conger and Miller, 1966) have found general maladjustment to be just as common in delinquents from a deprived background as in those from middle class homes. It could be argued that the measures of maladjustment are misleading in that they merely reflect middle class values and do not have the same meaning in a working class culture. There may be something in this suggestion, but the finding in a high delinquency working class area in London that delinquents tend to be *un*popular with their peers (West and Farrington, 1973) runs rather counter to the 'normal subculture' view. American follow-up studies, too, have shown that boys rejected by their peers are most likely to become delinquent (Roff *et al.*, 1972). The only exception in Roff's study was that in the very lowest socio-economic group delinquency was most rejected *and* most liked by their peers when younger — suggesting perhaps a normal subculture of delinquency in a proportion of very low status children. The findings from numerous studies (see above) that, even within high delinquency areas in big cities, family variables and measures of individual behaviour best predict delinquency, indicates that subcultural influences provide at most only a very partial explanation.

The evidence is scanty and incomplete but it may be tentatively concluded that for youngsters in all social groups there are types of petty theft which are so common and so lightly regarded that they may be considered 'normal'. The types of stealing regarded in this way vary by social class and some kinds are particularly common in working class groups but the phenomenon is found in all strata of society. However, it seems unlikely that a 'normal subculture' type of explanation accounts for more than a minority of cases of recidivist delinquency in any social group.

Area Influences

Many studies have clearly established the presence of high delinquency and high crime areas (see above), but the meaning of the finding remains a matter of controversy. To some extent the phenomenon is likely to represent the drift of socially disadvantaged criminals to underprivileged areas and to some extent it reflects deliberate housing policy (Morris, 1957). However, as already discussed, there is evidence to indicate marked area variations in crime and delinquency even when comparisons are restricted to individuals born and bred in an area by parents who were themselves born and bred in the same area (Rutter *et al.*, 1975). Differing police practices may account for some of these differences but it seems highly improbable that they account for all.

Some of the early American studies (Shaw and McKay, 1942) described large areas of high delinquency occupying much of the inner city, but the British pattern seems rather different (Mays, 1963). Many of the studies have not been concerned with metropolitan areas and have described pockets of delinquency confined to groups of streets or even groups of houses within streets (e.g. Jephcott and Carter, 1954; Gath *et al.*, 1975). Nevertheless, delinquency and crime rates tend to be particularly high in areas such as Liverpool and inner London and these require explanation. Within these areas, as in others, delinquency tends to be associated with family disharmony and disruption and probably it would be true to say that, in an immediate sense, delinquency frequently arises as a result of family problems rather than social influences. As with non-delinquent deviant behaviour in childhood (see chapter 7), it is probable that much of the difference between areas in juvenile delinquency is explicable in terms of differing rates of family disadvantage. The family variables associated with delinquency in poor areas seem much the same as those conducive to antisocial behaviour in prosperous areas.

However, this reduction of social area differences to intrafamilial psychological influences leaves two important issues unexplained. First, the difference between schools in delinquency rates cannot be accounted for. This seems to require some kind of social explanation in terms of influences acting directly on the children rather than on their families. How the social structure of a school modifies children's behaviour, and which aspects of the structure are most important, remain uncertain. However, the fact that the school does have such an effect seems highly probable. Second, the explanation of juvenile delinquency in terms of family disadvantage fails to explain why such disadvantage should be so much more common in certain areas and certain social groups. It is in this connection that social influences may well be of basic importance. The evidence is contradictory on whether personal living conditions or broader ecological influences are more important in predisposing to family disharmony, adult crime and emotional disturbance. However, the evidence does suggest that there is something about living in inner city and certain other socially disadvantaged areas which renders adults more vulnerable to a variety of troubles (see also chapter on psychiatric disorder). Research is much needed to delineate the mechanisms by which it does so.

Differential Association

Sutherland (1939) first expressed his theory of differential association in a series of propositions: criminal behaviour, like any other behaviour, is learned; learning is determined by the process of association with those who commit crimes; differential association is the specific causal process; the chances of criminality are determined roughly by the frequency and consistency of a person's contacts with patterns of criminal behaviour; individual differences are important only through their influence on differential association; and cultural conflict is the underlying cause of differential association. In his later writings, Sutherland modified these to include the notion of the nature of the association being such as to favour violations of the law rather than conformity to the law, as well as the importance of the frequency, duration, priority and intensity of differential association. These modifications are necessary to explain why most policemen do not become criminals, but as Cressey (1964) has pointed out, the major problem lies in defining what sort of associations favour violations of the law.

Several observations suggest the importance of differential association as a mechanism in the spread of delinquency and crime. Firstly, most delinquent acts are committed together with other children (West and Farrington, 1973). Secondly, delinquency is as strongly associated with delinquency in a person's brothers and sisters as with crime in his parents (see above). Thirdly, youngsters living in a high delinquency area or attending a high delinquency school are more likely to become delinquent than similar children living in other areas or attending other schools. Fourthly, boys who claim delinquents as friends are more likely to admit to delinquent behaviour than boys who say their friends are not delinquent (Voss, 1964). Fifthly, in an American study, Reiss and Rhodes (1964) showed that the probability of a boy committing a specific delinquent act was statistically dependent upon the commission of similar acts by other members of his friendship group. Sixthly, West and Farrington (1973) found that the number of delinquent acts committed by a boy's friends and acquaintances was predictive of his own future convictions.

All these findings are in keeping with the suggestion that mixing with delinquents makes it more likely that you yourself will become delinquent. However, it is difficult to rule out the possibility that at least some of the effect is due to youngsters prone to delinquency for other reasons seeking out delinquent friends (Robins and Hill, 1966) or to the group of friends all being subject to some other criminogenic influences.

The difficulties are illustrated by the interpretation of the associations with crime in parents. West and Farrington (1973) found that most of the criminal parents had ceased to commit criminal acts by the time the children were growing up and, furthermore, that parental crime predisposed to delinquency of later, rather than early, onset. This suggested that direct modelling of criminal behaviour was unlikely to be important. Furthermore, social work reports suggested that even parents who had been delinquent themselves were censorious toward delinquent behaviour in their sons. Paternal crime was linked with poor supervision and when this was taken into account there was only a slight association between paternal criminality and subsequent delinquency. It may be that the link reflects parenting standards rather than direct social learning, or it may be that parents transmit attitudes toward crime to their children (Cabral, 1969) rather than teaching them specific criminal acts.

Labelling

It has been suggested that once a person is labelled as a criminal or delinquent, his subsequent course of behaviour is shaped by public recognition of him as such (Wilkins, 1964; Lemert, 1967; Cicourel, 1968). Labelling may increase both the visibility of delinquent behaviour and also the likelihood of its recurrence. This may come about in a variety of ways. Thus, the possession of a criminal record will make it more likely that a person will come under police surveillance so that his offences come more readily to official notice. Also, however, public knowledge of his past criminal activities is likely to make it more difficult for him to obtain a job (see, for example, the study by Schwartz and Skolnick, 1964) and periods of incarceration in prison will put strains on his marriage. The ensuing employment problems and marital tensions may serve to precipitate him again into criminal activities. Thirdly, when delinquent activities are met with severe sanctions, rejection and social exclusion, the person may turn back to a delinquent group for the status and satisfaction otherwise denied him. In contrast, a tolerant response to deviance may make further deviance less likely (Wilkins, 1964). Fourthly, the experience of conviction may modify a person's self-image and attitudes in such a way that he comes to feel more aggressive and anti-authority, as suggested by the evidence on attitude changes following conviction in West and Farrington's study (1973).

How far these processes in fact lead to the perpetuation of delinquent or criminal activities is not known. Robins (1966) found that, after controlling for other factors, delinquents who had a Court appearance and a period in a penal institution were more likely to have a worse outcome in adult life than those who managed to avoid the judicial system. Gold (Gold and Williams, 1969; Gold, 1970), too, has produced findings which suggest that delinquent acts may be more likely to continue if youngsters are apprehended by the Police. Similarly, preliminary results from West's prospective study* suggest that, after controlling for initial level of delinquent activity, self-reported delinquent acts increase in frequency if the boy experiences conviction but decrease over the same period of time if he does not. De Alarcon and Noguera (1974) found that 74 per cent of young adults convicted of drug offences continued taking drugs during the next three years and many proceeded to more dangerous drugs.

*Personal communication.

Whether things would have taken the same course in the absence of conviction is not known, but Court appearance did not seem to have helped. The matter requires more systematic study but it seems that the experience of conviction may sometimes serve to perpetuate delinquent or criminal activities.

Delinquent Contracultures

American writers have tended to emphasize the development of delinquent 'contracultures'. Thus, Merton (1957) argued that if the social structure effectively blocks access to the goals desired by lower class members, the group becomes frustrated in its aspirations and some people contract out and reject both the traditional goals and means. Cloward and Ohlin (1961) similarly suggested that in a society which denies opportunities to some social groups, those who fail to achieve their goals may blame the inadequacy of the existing institutional organization and find a collective solution in delinquent gangs. Cohen (1956), too, hypothesized that working class boys develop a delinquent contraculture as a means of dealing with status frustration. Certainly, there is evidence that many adolescents are frustrated in education and employment (Fyvel, 1961). Scholastic failure is frequently associated with delinquency (see above) and it may be that this leads some youngsters to opt out and develop a contrary set of values (Rutter, Tizard and Whitmore, 1970). On the other hand, it is doubtful if many delinquents actually hold overtly oppositional views (Matza, 1964) and organized delinquent gangs are not common in Britain (Scott, 1956), although they do occur (Patrick, 1973). So far, there have been no systematic tests of the validity of this type of delinquent contraculture as an explanation for delinquency and crime in Britain. The very different social situations in this country and in the USA mean that American findings there cannot automatically be applied here.

CONCLUSIONS

Any adequate account must explain why delinquency and crime are largely found in males and are mainly restricted to the young, why rates of crime have risen so markedly during this century, why rates are so much higher in big cities, why only half of delinquents become recidivist, why delinquency and crime frequently run in families, and why delinquency and crime tend to be associated with other troubles. No biological, psychological or social theory comes anywhere near accounting for these well established findings (let alone the host of others not listed). Psychological (and to a much lesser extent biological) mechanisms go some way to explaining why X rather than Y becomes delinquent, but social explanations are required to explain why rates of crime differ so markedly both across time and place. Furthermore, the two approaches should not be seen as alternatives; to a considerable extent social forces may determine the existence of the psychological circumstances which lead to crime. However, most hypotheses about mechanisms have not been specified sufficiently precisely to allow clear evaluation and there is a lack of empirical data which might allow a choice between the various suggestions in the literature. The few studies which have been designed to test several competing views have clearly indicated that there are many causes and many mechanisms which frequently co-exist.

7 Psychiatric Disorder

It is important to consider psychiatric disorder with respect to cycles of disadvantage, both because such disorders frequently exhibit intergenerational continuities and because they commonly co-exist with various types of social deprivation and impaired social functioning. Numerous surveys have indicated an association between low social status and mental disorder (Dohrenwend and Dohrenwend, 1969); a pooling of disorders in socially disadvantaged areas of cities (Rutter *et al.*, 1975); a high rate of alcoholism and mental illness in indigent populations (Edwards *et al.*, 1968); and important links between mental disorder and family disruption and disorganization (Robins, 1966; Rutter *et al.*, 1975). However, there are many different types of psychiatric condition which vary in causation and course, and it has been necessary to make some selection in deciding which aspects of psychiatry to consider. In order to maintain comparability with other chapters we have placed the emphasis on the commoner disorders and have paid little attention to the psychoses or severe illnesses which contribute largely to mental hospital statistics but which affect only a very small proportion of the population.

As a consequence of this decision, neither schizophrenia nor manic-depressive psychosis are discussed. Although depressive disorders are very common (Rawnsley, 1968) and overlap with the psychoses (Kendall, 1968), manic-depressive psychosis in its florid form affects less than 1 per cent of the population (Rawnsley, 1968). There is no consistent association with social disadvantage (Dohrenwend and Dohrenwend, 1969) and the moderate intergenerational continuity is due in considerable part to genetic factors (Rosenthal, 1970; Shields, 1973). Schizophrenia also affects only some 1 per cent of the population (Slater and Cowie, 1971) and schizophrenic individuals are considerably less fertile than the general population (Stevens, 1969). Although the rate of schizophrenia is particularly high among the unskilled or unemployed and among those living in the deteriorated areas of cities, the findings show that this is largely due to the illness causing downward social drift rather than to the causal influence of social factors (Goldberg and Morrison, 1963). While social and psychological factors play some part in the precipitation and course of schizophrenia (Brown & Birley, 1968; Brown *et al.*, 1972), studies of adoptees, as well as of twins, leave no doubt that there is a very important genetic component to the condition (Rosenthal and Kety, 1968; Gottesman and Shields, 1972; Kety *et al.*, 1974).

With regard to child psychiatric disorders, the most important exclusion has been the hyperkinetic syndrome. This condition has a poor prognosis; disabilities frequently persist into adult life and are associated with considerable social impairment (Menkes *et al.*, 1967;

Weiss *et al.*, 1971). There is also some evidence of intergenerational continuity (Cantwell, 1972). However, the hyperkinetic syndrome has been omitted from the main body of discussion in this chapter because of continuing uncertainty over its nature, the likelihood that organic brain dysfunction plays an important role in causation, because in its extreme form it is an uncommon disorder; and because, when more loosely defined, it overlaps very considerably with the conduct disorders (Cantwell, 1976).

As a result of these exclusions, this chapter will be mainly concerned with the broad groups of emotional or neurotic conditions, disturbance of conduct and personality disorders. As many epidemiological studies have shown, these psychiatric disorders are very common problems affecting some 5 to 10 per cent of children, and a rather higher proportion of adolescents and adults (Rutter, Tizard and Whitmore, 1970; Rutter, 1973; Rutter, Graham *et al.*, 1976; Rawnsley, 1968; Rosenthal, 1970). Although constitutional factors play a role in the development of psychiatric disorders (see below), few of these conditions can be regarded as illnesses or diseases in the ordinary sense of the words (Rutter, 1975). They constitute maladaptive patterns of behaviour associated with substantial suffering and with impairment of personal and social functioning, but they differ from normality largely in degree rather than in kind.

LABELLING

It has been argued that mental illness is a consequence of a labelling process which induces people to take on a sick role (Scheff, 1966). If this were so, any study of psychiatric disorder would merely constitute an analysis of how society perceives and responds to various forms of behaviour. Certainly, there is evidence that social labels can have powerful effects. Thus, Temerlin (1968) studied the diagnoses made by American psychiatrists and psychologists on the basis of an audio-tape recording of an interview with an actor portraying a normal, healthy man. The majority of subjects diagnosed him as mentally healthy, some diagnosed neurosis of character disorder and none diagnosed psychosis. However, when the same interview was preceded by comments from a distinguished psychiatrist or psychologist indicating that he considered the man psychotic, many subjects also diagnosed psychosis and very few diagnosed the actor as mentally healthy. Similarly, Rosenhan (1973) found that healthy individuals admitted to American mental hospitals after pretending to hear voices (but no other symptoms), were retained as patients for an average of 19 days, and all were diagnosed as schizophrenic on discharge. This occurred in spite of the fact that they responded normally after admission and said that they no longer heard voices. These findings leave no doubt that psychiatric diagnoses can be influenced by labels previously attached by prestige figures. However, another study showed that a label of mental illness did not influence social rejection (Kirk, 1974). While labelling has undoubted effects (Scheff, 1974), there is little evidence to suggest that labelling processes are sufficiently powerful to constitute a major influence in producing chronic mental disorder (Mechanic, 1969; Gove, 1970). Nevertheless, it is certainly true that any study of causes in a patient sample inevitably involves both the processes leading to the development of disorder *and* the processes leading to medical referral. Because of the need to differentiate these processes, the main emphasis in this chapter is placed on general population studies, whenever possible. It should be added that labelling theorists have mainly concerned themselves with mental hospital patients, a group largely excluded from the present discussion.

INTRAGENERATIONAL CONTINUITIES

Although psychiatric disorders in children and in adults share similar symptomatology, there are important differences. Accordingly, it is necessary to begin by considering the links between child and adult psychiatric disorders in the form of intragenerational continuities and discontinuities. In doing this distinctions must be drawn between different conditions which vary in cause and course (Rutter, 1965, 1975).

In this connection there are three key problems. First, until recently there has not been a generally agreed system for classifying disorders in children so that comparability between studies is difficult. Nevertheless, valid distinctions can be made between broad groups such as conduct disorders and emotional disorders (Quay, 1972; Rutter, 1965, 1975). The second problem is that the manifestations of a disorder may change with the process of development. For example, severe *over*activity in early and middle childhood often changes to *under*activity and inertia in adolescence (Rutter, Greenfeld and Lockyer, 1967), and the childhood precursors of schizophrenia are quite different to the symptoms of psychosis in childhood (Offord and Cross, 1969). The third, and related, difficulty is that the same behaviour may have a different meaning at different ages. Thus, both bed-wetting and separation anxiety are normal at age 2 years but are not so at age 12 years. As a consequence, it would be developmentally inappropriate to expect continuity in the form of phenotypical uniformity.

Continuities have been examined in several different ways: by longitudinal studies, follow-up enquiries, retrospective investigations, and the use of pre-existing records (such as school reports) with respect to groups identified during adult life. Longitudinal studies of normal groups have shown considerable flux in temperamental features during the pre-school years (Rutter, 1970b). Continuity in broad personality attributes is more evident during middle and later childhood (Bronson, 1967; Scarr, 1969; Kagan & Moss, 1962), but even so many youngsters show substantial changes in their styles of behaviour as they mature.

However, in spite of considerable temperamental change during the early years of childhood, extreme features have been found to predict the later development of psychiatric disorder (Rutter *et al.*, 1964; Thomas *et al.*, 1968; Graham *et al.*, 1973).

The various child psychiatric disorders differ considerably in terms of chronicity (see review by Robins, 1972). Emotional disorders (i.e. those in which abnormal anxiety, fear, depression and the like constitute the main problem) often last several years, but ultimately most children recover without residual impairment. In contrast, conduct disorders (i.e. conditions characterized by socially disapproved behaviour such as bullying, destructiveness, theft and violence, which are abnormal in their socio-cultural context, and which are associated with impaired personal or social functioning) are more likely to persist, with many children showing problems which last into adult life. While these conclusions are largely based on studies of children attending psychiatric clinics, the same pattern has been evident in the follow-up of non-patient groups. As part of a total population epidemiological study of 10 to 11-year-old children, those found to have psychiatric disorder (Rutter, Tizard and Whitmore, 1970) were seen again at age 14 to 15 years (Graham and Rutter, 1973). More than half the youngsters who had shown an emotional disorder at age ten years were without disorder in adolescence, but in contrast this was so for less than a quarter of those who had shown a conduct disorder. Among those with persisting disorders, the problems were usually of the same type in adolescence as they had been in middle childhood. None of the children with an initial diagnosis of an emotional disorder developed conduct disturbance. Follow-up studies of school class groups have also indicated that it is children with poor peer relationships who are more likely to show psychiatric problems some years later (Westman *et al.*, 1967; Cowen *et al.*, 1973), just as they are also more likely to be delinquent (Conger and Miller, 1966; Roff *et al.*, 1972).

Much the same pattern according to diagnosis holds for continuities into adult life (Robins, 1972; Rutter, 1972b). Although other studies give very similar findings, the best data are available from Robins' (1966) 30 year follow-up of white American child guidance clinic patients and their matched controls. She found that only 16 per cent of the individuals classified as antisocial in childhood recovered before age 18 years and had no further psychiatric problems before 40 years. Over one quarter were diagnosed as sociopaths* in adult life, about a twelfth were alcoholics or drug addicts, one ninth were psychotic, and a sixth showed neurotic disorders. Three quarters of the men with a clinic referral in childhood for antisocial behaviour were arrested in adult life, half experienced arrest after age 31 years and 44 per cent committed a major crime. Of the children referred for other disorders,

*This was operationally defined in terms of severe problems in many aspects of life including work, marriage, interpersonal relationships, and personal functioning.

30 per cent were well at follow-up and only 4 per cent were sociopathic. Thirty per cent of males were arrested in adult life compared with 22 per cent of the male controls.

In a comparable follow-up study of Negro boys who had not attended a clinic, closely similar findings emerged despite differences in race, era, and patient/non-patient status (Robins *et al.*, 1971; Robins, 1972). Robins' findings suggest that only a minority of youths who show persistent conduct disorders will be problem-free in adult life, most will exhibit criminal behaviour in adult life and an appreciable minority will show a severe and widespread personality disorder. The picture for those with emotional disorders is quite different (Robins, 1972). Most children with emotional disorders become normal adults and only a few develop serious personality disturbance. On the other hand, if the emotional disorder in childhood does persist into adult life, or recur after maturity, it is very likely to take the form of a neurotic or depressive condition (Pritchard and Graham, 1966; Zeitlyn, 1971). Although the link applies to only a minority of neurotic disorders, adults with neurosis include more individuals who report having had phobias or anxiety states in childhood than do groups of non-neurotic adults (Abe, 1972; Tyrer and Tyrer, 1974). At the present time no reliable criteria are available to distinguish, in childhood, between disorders which prove transient and those which persist into adult life. However, it is notable that whereas emotional disorders occur with roughly the same frequency in the two sexes, these disorders in adults are very much commoner in women (Rutter, 1970b). The meaning of this sex difference and its implications for intragenerational continuities are far from clear.

Depressive disorders in adult life appear somewhat less likely than other emotional disorders to have their onset in childhood (Zeitlyn, 1971) and manic-depressive psychosis seems especially unlikely to have its roots in early life (Dahl, 1971). However, depressive disorders have so far been little studied in childhood and further evidence on this issue is needed (Rutter, 1972).

Most of the evidence on the course of child psychiatric disorder stems from British and American studies of youngsters in the middle years of childhood. Yet, much the same pattern has been found in children from other cultures (e.g., Lo, 1973; Mellsop, 1972) and in adolescents (e.g. Warren, 1965; Masterson, 1967). It may be concluded that emotional disorders in childhood usually have a good prognosis whereas conduct disorders are more likely to run a chronic course, often ending in persisting personality disturbance.

Disorders in adult life run a broadly similar course with one important exception, namely that neurosis and depression frequently occur in association with a personality disorder. The prognosis for adult neurosis or depression is generally good provided the person has not shown a persisting handicap due to personality disorder (Greer and Cawley, 1966; Rutter *et al.*, 1976). However, as the neurosis and personality disorder often co-exist, the course can be chronic (Cooper *et al.*, 1969). In the absence of such a personality disorder, the duration of symptoms is of no prognostic significance. Moreover, the prognosis is worse in the presence of persisting marital disharmony. Individuals who, at first psychiatric referral, showed abnormalities of personality going back to adolescence or early adult life were highly likely to continue to have symptoms and to remain socially impaired over the next four years in the study by Rutter *et al.* (1976). Nevertheless, it should be noted that with a change in social circumstances and/or treatment, a few people with life-long disorders of personality did recover.

Furthermore, although the prognosis for severely psychopathic men convicted of crime is particularly poor, there is a tendency for better social adjustment and diminishing aggression with age; the likelihood of further crime is no greater than for non-psychopathic offenders with similar records (Stafford-Clark *et al.*, 1951; Gibbens *et al.*, 1959).

Even in the case of disorders with a strong biological component, a marked change in social circumstances can strikingly influence prognosis. This is well illustrated by the course of heroin addiction in American servicemen in Vietnam (Robins, 1973; 1974). Heroin is known to lead to physical dependence so that withdrawal of the drug causes severe physiological disturbance. Ordinarily the prognosis is very poor with few individuals able to stop taking heroin. However, Robins' systematic study showed that on return to the United States from Vietnam, *most* regular users of heroin ceased using the drug, although many did have other problems in adjustment.

INTERGENERATIONAL CONTINUITIES

Psychiatric Disorder in the Parents of Adult Patients

Many studies have shown that adult neuroses and personality disorders tend to run in families. Thus, Brown (1942) obtained family histories from 104 psychoneurotic patients. Among parents and sibs, 16 per cent were found to have a neurosis and 17 per cent an anxious personality, compared with 1 per cent and 10 per cent among the comparable relatives of a control group. Similarly, McInnes (1937) found that 34 per cent of the parents of patients with an anxiety neurosis showed a neurotic disorder, a rate over twice that (15 per cent) in his control group. Cohen *et al.* (1951), in a study of soldiers, found that anxiety neurosis was present in 18 per cent of the fathers and 55 per cent of the mothers of those with an acute anxiety state, compared with none of the fathers and 6 per cent of the mothers in his control group of healthy or wounded soldiers.

Unfortunately, most of these studies have relied on relatively unsystematic routine clinical histories in which the diagnoses of relatives were largely based on second hand information obtained with full knowledge of whether the family involved a case or control. In view of the known unreliabilities of clinical judgement and the possibility of systematic bias, caution is needed in the interpretation of the results. Even so, more systematic studies have generally produced broadly comparable findings. For example Stenstedt (1966), in a study of patients with neurotic depression, found that 8 per cent of the mothers and sisters, and 2 per cent of the fathers and sons had had a depressive disorder, rates above those in the general population but lower than those for the relatives of patients with acute hysteria. Arkonac and Guze (1963) found a higher rate of disorder in the relatives of patients with a chronic hysterical personality disorder. Fifteen per cent of the female relatives showed a similar disorder and a third of the male relatives had alcoholism or sociopathy. The results are limited by the high proportion of relatives not interviewed but similar familial links involving hysterical personality disorders in women and alcoholism and sociopathy in men were noted in a later study of the relatives of male criminals (Guze *et al.*, 1967). Bleuler (1955) showed a 14 per cent rate of alcoholism in the parents of his chronic alcoholic patients and Amark (1951) found a 26 per cent alcoholism rate in the fathers of his alcoholic patients, compared with 3 per cent in the general population. In the same study, 15 per cent of the parents were diagnosed as showing psychopathy, a rate over 4 times that (3.4 per cent) in the general population. In a well controlled study utilizing the Danish national registers, Schulsinger (1972) found a 14 per cent rate of personality disorder in the biological parents of psychopathic patients, compared with 7 per cent in the control group parents.

In summary, the familial tendency is most marked with respect to chronic neuroses, personality disorders and alcoholism, where some 15 per cent of the parents show a similar disorder, and is least evident in the case of acute neuroses. However, even in the groups with the strongest intergenerational continuity, *dis*continuity is present in the great majority of families. In general, there is some tendency for family members to show broadly similar types of disorder but there are many exceptions.

Psychiatric Disorder in the Parents of Child Patients

A variety of early studies, reviewed in Rutter (1966), suggested that chronic neuroses, depression and personality disorders were quite common in the parents of children attending psychiatric clinics. This observation has since been confirmed by more recent systematic investigations. Rutter (1966) found that one in five children attending a psychiatric clinic had a parent who had also been under psychiatric care, a rate three times that in a matched control group of children attending dental clinics. The link with child psychiatric disorder was strongest when the parent exhibited long-standing abnormalities of personality and when the parental symptoms directly impinged on the child. There was little association between the type of disorder in the parent and that in the child. Wolff and Acton (1968) compared the parents of primary school children attending a psychiatric clinic with the parents of non-patients attending the same school classes. Half (51 per cent) of the clinic mothers and 30 per cent of the clinic fathers showed personality disorders compared with 18 per cent of the control mothers and 14 per cent of the control fathers. In an epidemiological study of 10 year old children in London and the Isle of Wight, Rutter *et al.*,(1975b) found that neuroses were much commoner in the mothers of children with psychiatric disorder than in the mothers of normal children; paternal criminality was also much more frequent in the former group. Thus, 20 per cent of the fathers of the London children with psychiatric disorder had been in prison compared with 7 per cent of the control fathers. Richman (1974b) too, in an epidemiological survey of pre-school children in London, found that emotional or behavioural problems in the children were associated with neurosis in the mothers. Among Isle of Wight 14 to 15 year olds, maternal mental disorder was associated with psychiatric problems in the adolescents whose problems began in middle childhood, but the association was much less marked in the case of disorder beginning during adolescence (Rutter, Graham *et al.*, 1976).

The findings indicate that among children with psychiatric conditions, a third to a half have a parent who shows some type of mental disorder — a rate at least double that in the general population. The link with child disorders is especially strong in the case of personality disorders and chronic neuroses or depression in mothers and criminality or sociopathy in fathers.

Psychiatric Disorder in the Children of Adult Patients

A third method of examining intergenerational continuities is to study the children of adults with psychiatric disorder. Investigations prior to 1966 were reviewed by Rutter (1966). These indicated that the children of patients with neurotic, depressive or personality disorders showed an increased rate of psychiatric problems and that the risk seemed to be especially great if the parental illness adversely influenced the parent-child relationship. On the whole, the children of psychotic parents suffered less. However, Rice *et al.*, (1971) in an American study, noted that the children of parents with severe mental illness could suffer from the disruption, turmoil and tensions associated with the illness.

The matter has been investigated further by Rutter, Quinton and Yule (1976) by means of a prospective study of a representative sample of families in which one parent had been newly referred for some type of mental disorder. The children in these families were compared with school classroom controls and both groups were followed for four years. It was found that nearly twice as many children of patients showed persisting emotional or behavioural difficulties compared with controls. Problems in the children were especially likely if the parent showed a personality disorder and if there was persisting marital discord. The clinical type or severity of the parental illness did not seem particularly important for intergenerational continuities, but the risk to the child was greater in families where the parental disorder had a marked social impact or where it was associated with irritability or hostility towards the child. In keeping with other studies, the likelihood of the child developing disorder seemed to be related more to the degree of family disturbance than to the diagnosis or symptomatology of the parental illness.

Other Approaches

Several total population epidemiological studies in Canada (Buck and Laughton, 1959) and in Britain (Kellner, 1963; Hare and Shaw, 1965b) have shown that mental ill-health in parents (especially in mothers) is associated with an increased rate of emotional or behavioural disorders in the children. However, Tonge *et al.* (1975) did not find this in a highly selected group of 'problem families' known to social service agencies. They concluded that the link between parental mental illness and child psychiatric disorder was indirect and a consequence of the associated family discord and disturbance rather than the illness *per se*.

The one study which directly investigated intergenerational continuities in child psychiatric disorder was undertaken by Robins (1966). There was a systematic and thorough follow-up into middle-life of 524 child guidance clinic patients and a matched group of 100 non-patient school children. At follow-up, the offspring of the adults who had been patients as children showed more behavioural disturbance than did the offspring of non-patients. However, the groups did not differ in terms of 'nervousness' and the difference with respect to disorders of conduct (stealing, truanting and running away) was largely confined to the small proportion of ex-patients who had gone on to show sociopathy as adults with concomitant family discord and marital strife.

In short, intergenerational continuities are strongest for conduct disorders in children and personality disorders in adult life. They are also evident with respect to adult neurosis or depression but the links are less strong. Although parental neurosis shows some association with emotional disorders in children, few of these children become neurotic adults. Intergenerational continuity in the neuroses is limited.

GENETIC INFLUENCES

Studies of adoptees and comparisons of monozygotic and dizygotic twin pairs have been the main approaches used to assess the relative contributions of genetic and non-genetic factors in the development of psychiatric disorder. The evidence has been well reviewed by Rosenthal (1970), Shields (1973, 1976), Vandenberg (1967) and Mittler (1971).

With respect to normal personality variation, a wide range of studies (mostly using questionnaires but some employing interview measures, observations or tests) have shown that concordance in monozygotic pairs is generally greater than in dizygotic pairs. The usual intrapair correlation of personality tests has been said to be about 0.46 for MZ pairs and 0.28 for DZ pairs (Lindzey *et al.*, 1971). However, the tests used vary in their reliability and sophistication, the findings are more variable than those for IQ and sometimes different heritabilities for males and females are found. In general the results suggest an important genetic component in personality variation but one less strong* than for intelligence or for a mental illness such as schizophrenia. The evidence of strong heritability is greatest in the case of extraversion or sociability but there is also evidence for a significant genetic basis to neuroticism or anxiety proneness. In addition, studies have indicated important hereditary components to infant smiling and fear responses (Freedman, 1965) and to a variety of temperamental attributes evident in early childhood (Torgersen, 1973; Torgersen and Kringlen, 1975). Because the intra-pair environmental variation is usually quite small, twin studies tend to over-estimate the importance of genetic factors to inter-family differences in the general population. Nevertheless, the few studies of monozygotic twins reared apart (Newman *et al.*, 1937; Shields, 1962) have shown a similar degree of concordance to that evident in monozygotic twins reared together. In view of this, it may be concluded that heredity plays a substantial, but by no means over-riding, part in determining personality variations.

There have been only a few twin studies of children with psychiatric disorder (summarized in Shields, 1976). The findings indicate that genetic influences are relatively minor in the case of conduct disorders and juvenile delinquency but are somewhat greater for emotional disorders. In all cases genetic factors seemed to act through their influence on temperamental features and maturity, rather than by causing the inheritance of a disorder as such. Bohman's studies of adopted and fostered children (1970, 1971) are in keeping with this conclusion, in that school adjustment problems in the adoptees were unrelated to alcohol abuse or criminality in the biological fathers, and in the fostered group the association applied only to girls and not to boys.

Many of the twin studies of neurosis and personality disorder in adults are unsatisfactory because the diagnoses of co-twins were made in the full knowledge of whether the pair was MZ or DZ and of the diagnosis of the index case. Nevertheless, these objections do not apply to the Maudsley twin study (Slater and Shields, 1969) which showed a moderately strong genetic component for anxiety states (41 per cent complete concordance in MZ pairs as contrasted with 4 per cent in DZ pairs) and personality disorders (33 per cent in MZ vs 6 per cent in DZ),

*It may be that this is partly an artefact due to the lower reliability of personality tests.

but no genetic effect in the case of other neuroses (mostly mild depressions). Shapiro (1970), in a study of 'non-endogenous depression' using the Danish twin register, also found that genetic factors operated through their influence on personality variables. Several twin studies have indicated an important genetic component in alcoholism (see reviews by Rosenthal, 1970 and Shields, 1973), and adoptee studies confirm this (see Shields, 1976).

The best genetic evidence concerning psychopathy is provided by Schulsinger's (1972) study of psychopathic and non-psychopathic adoptees identified through the Danish registers. Fourteen per cent of the first-degree biological relatives of the psychopathic adoptees had a personality disorder; this was twice the rate found in the biological relatives of the non-psychopathic adoptees and in both sets of adoptive relatives. The difference was most marked in the case of core psychopathy (i.e. the same disorder as in the index cases) in fathers, which was present in 9 per cent of the biological fathers as against less than 2 per cent in each of the other three groups. The findings provide unequivocal evidence for the operation of biological inheritance*. Nevertheless, it should be noted that the great majority of the biological parents did *not* show either psychopathy or any other type of mental disorder. This, together with the findings on twins and other considerations, suggests the importance of non-genetic factors, although the study provided no evidence as to what these might be.

In summary, it may be concluded that genetic factors are most important in the case of psychopathy, personality disorders† and chronic anxiety states; they also have a substantial effect on normal personality variations but have least influence upon mild depression in adults and conduct disorder in children. However, with all types of psychiatric disorder it is clear that non-genetic factors must also play a substantial part in causation.

OTHER BIOLOGICAL INFLUENCES

Biological determinants of psychiatric disorder have also been considered with respect to neurological disorder, EEG (brain wave) abnormalities, chronic illness, and physique. As each of these accounts

*It should be noted that a substantial genetic component does not rule out the possibility that the crucial factor in causation may be environmental. For example, the evidence suggests that a person's susceptibility to tuberculosis is genetically determined to an important extent (Carter, 1970).

†As about a quarter of children referred to psychiatric clinics because of disturbances of conduct show personality disorders when adult (Robins 1966), the implication is that the genetic component is much greater in the case of those conduct disorders which persist into adult life than in those disorders which do not last beyond childhood. However, this proposition has not been tested directly.

for just a small proportion of the intergenerational transmission of psychiatric disorder, only a very brief summary of the main research findings will be given here. There is good evidence, especially in children, that the presence of neurological abnormalities (such as cerebral palsy or epilepsy) greatly increases the likelihood of psychiatric disorder, although only rarely is this a direct causal effect (Rutter, Graham and Yule, 1970; Seidel *et al.*, 1975; Shaffer *et al.*, 1975). On the other hand, neurological abnormality is found in only a small minority of children with psychiatric conditions and, with the exception of some types of epilepsy, very few of the abnormalities are familial. In young adults there is an association between epilepsy, crime and depression, but again it accounts for only a very small proportion of cases (Gunn and Fenton, 1969; Gunn 1973). Brain injuries in adults have also been shown to increase the risk of psychiatric disorder (Lishman, 1968). EEG abnormalities are especially common in psychopathic criminals but although these may well have biological determinants, the meaning and significance of the EEG anomalies remain obscure (Fenton *et al.*, 1974). EEG abnormalities have also been said to occur more commonly in children with psychiatric disorder, but most of the studies have been poorly controlled and the results remain inconclusive (Harris, 1976). Chronic physical illness somewhat increases the risk of psychiatric disorder in children but, except occasionally, this is not a major factor (Rutter, Tizard and Whitmore, 1970). In adults, the association between physical and psychiatric disorders is rather stronger but, even here, it would be misleading to regard one as simply leading to the other (Eastwood and Trevelyan, 1972). Again, few of the physical disorders in these cases are familial. There is an extensive literature on the associations between physique, personality and psychiatric disorder (see Rees, 1973), but although some significant associations exist it seems unlikely that they are of much causal importance.

FAMILY INFLUENCES AND PATTERNS OF UPBRINGING

There is now a vast literature on the associations between a person's upbringing or family relationships and the later development of psychiatric disorder. This has been critically reviewed by Caldwell (1964), Becker (1964b), Walters and Stinnett (1971), Rutter (1972b and 1975a), Hetherington and Martin (1972), Wolff (1970 and 1973) and Granville-Grossman (1968). Waxler and Mishler (1970) have also provided a critique of experimental studies of families. A veritable legion of family factors have been associated with one or other type of psychiatric disorder and no attempt will be made to consider them all in this chapter. Rather, the emphasis will be placed on factors of major influence which might be implicated in intergenerational cycles of psychiatric troubles. For a wider discussion of family variables reference should be made to the reviews quoted above.

Family Discord

Numerous studies have shown an association between a 'broken home' in childhood and the development of antisocial problems or personality disorder (Bowlby, 1968; Rutter, 1971b and 1972a). There is also an association between broken homes and attempted suicide in adult life (Greer, 1964) but this applies particularly to those with personality disorder (Greer and Gunn, 1966). However, several independent investigations have also shown that the association is much greater in the case of parents who divorce or separate than in the case of parental death. This suggests that it may be the family discord and disharmony, rather than the break-up of the family as such, which leads to the antisocial or personality problems. This hypothesis has received support from the several studies which have shown that parental discord is strongly associated with conduct disorders in the children even when the home is unbroken (McCord and McCord, 1959; Rutter, 1971b and 1975). In short, it may be concluded that it is ongoing disturbance in family relationships which does the main damage rather than family break-up as such. With intergenerational continuities, it is relevant that marital discord is a common feature in 'problem families' and that within these families it is associated with disorder in the children (Tonge *et al.*, 1975).

Furthermore, in a study of children attending a psychiatric clinic, Wardle (1961) found that conduct disorders were associated, not only with the child coming from a broken home, but also with one or other *parent* coming from a broken home. It seemed that it was not the direct experience of disruption which mattered but rather the difficulties in interpersonal relationships in the present and succeeding generation with which disruption was associated. Data are sparse, but there is some indication that a broken home in childhood may increase the likelihood of the individual making an unhappy marriage himself and also having more difficulties in parenting (see chapter 8). If this is confirmed by further research, it would indicate that family discord played a key role in the intergenerational transmission of psychiatric disorder.

The mechanisms by which family discord leads to psychiatric disorder remain ill-understood. Although genetic factors cannot be ruled out as playing some part in the associations, it seems unlikely that they offer sufficient explanation. Marital disharmony has been found to be strongly associated with conduct disorder in children even within a sample of families in all of which a parent had a psychiatric condition (Rutter, 1971b; Rutter, Quinton and Yule, 1976). Furthermore, the association still held after controlling for personality disorder in the parents.

Marital discord may be important largely because anger and aggression are displaced onto the child, or because marital quarrels can centre around child-rearing. The child may be drawn into marital disputes (and there is some slight evidence that he is more likely to suffer if he is – Jonsson, 1967) or, in the absence of stable parenting, he may have to assume adult responsibilities before he is ready to do so. It may be that family discord is important only in so far as it is associated with erratic and deviant methods of bringing up children. Alternatively, marital discord may be operative mainly because it provides a maladaptive model of how people should behave and how they should resolve their difficulties. Finally, it has been hypothesized that a person's personality develops on the base provided by stable harmonious relationships in childhood, so that if all a child experiences is discord and distorted relationships he will suffer accordingly. The critical evidence required to differentiate between these (and other) hypotheses is lacking although there are data suggesting that the last suggestion may have some relevance. Rutter (1971b) found that a good relationship with one parent could, to a considerable extent, make up for a bad relationship with the other or for gross marital discord. Whether or not this also means that a good relationship with someone *outside* the home can exert a protective effect is not known.

The child is at a specially high risk if, in addition to marital discord, one or both parents have a personality disorder of such severity as to cause a chronic handicap (Rutter, 1971b). This means, in effect, that where the parents have shown disordered behaviour or relationships throughout their adult life, as well as not making a successful marriage, the outlook for the child is particularly poor. Although frequently persistent, the ill effects are not necessarily irreversible. Evidence (Rutter, 1971b) suggests that in cases where family relationships change for the better, risks to the children correspondingly decrease.

Separation Experiences

There is good evidence that many young children admitted to hospital or to a residential nursery show an acute distress reaction which may be followed by disturbed behaviour lasting many months (Bowlby, 1973). Bowlby has argued that the reaction is a consequence of the young child's separation from his mother. However, though this doubtless plays some part, recent evidence suggests that it is not the major factor (see review by Rutter, 1972a). In the first place, modification of the hospital environment can reduce the frequency of distress even though it does not alter the fact of separation (see studies discussed in Wolff, 1973). Secondly, the Robertsons (1971) have shown that when high quality parental care is provided during the separation experience, young children do not exhibit the same kind of disturbance as that associated with hospital or nursery admission (although obviously even in the circumstances of good care the children are not unaffected by the separation from their family). Thirdly, Hinde's experimental studies with infant rhesus monkeys (Spencer-Booth and Hinde, 1971; Hinde and Davies, 1972) have shown that much of the infant's emotional disturbance following reunion with the mother stemmed from tensions in the mother-infant relationship. Although not directly demonstrated, much the same probably applies to humans. In short, it may be concluded that acute separation experiences (from the child's *family* and familiar surroundings rather than just from his mother) may lead to acute distress reactions in young children, largely because of the frequently associated unpleasant experiences and poor quality parental care, but in part through the stress of separation itself.

In the context of this chapter, the main interest must lie in the possible long-term effects of separation experiences. Several studies have shown that children with enuresis, conduct disorders or delinquency are more likely to have suffered multiple separations in childhood (Douglas, 1970; Rutter, 1972a). However, it is uncertain how far this association is explicable in terms of the separation *per se.* Rutter (1971b) found that conduct disorders were associated only with separations due to family discord or disorder and not with those which occurred as a result of a holiday or physical illness. Several investigations have noted that children admitted into short-term care have a high risk of psychiatric disorder. But children admitted into care frequently come from (Schaffer and Schaffer, 1968) and return to (Wolkind and Rutter, 1973) disturbed families, so that the family difficulties are probably at least as important as the brief experience of going into care. Douglas (1973) found an association between a child's temporary separation from his mother and the likelihood of his being enuretic, but this applied to children who were separated *and* placed with an unfamiliar caretaker and/or placed in an unfamiliar environment. Again, the circumstances of separation seemed important. It may be concluded that, in themselves, separations play only a minor part in the causation of persistent psychiatric disorders. On the other hand, separations are important as factors in the genesis of chronic disorders by virtue of the fact that they may involve unpleasant experiences and, even more important, by the fact that they often reflect longstanding family disturbance.

Single acute stresses rarely have long-term sequelae if they are unassociated with chronic stress or disadvantage. However, the same may not apply to *repeated* or *multiple* acute stresses. In a follow-up study of the National Survey children born in 1946, Douglas (1975) found no association between single, short hospital admissions in childhood and any kind of disturbed behaviour in adolescence. However, children with several admissions, including at least one during the pre-school period, had higher rates of troublesome behaviour, delinquency and unstable employment during the teenage years. Quinton and Rutter (1976), in a general population study of 10 year old children born a generation later, have confirmed the association between repeated admissions and both disturbed behaviour and psychiatric conditions (including emotional and conduct disorders). However, children with multiple admissions more often came from disadvantaged homes and psychiatric disorder was most likely to develop in these circumstances. Repeated admission may constitute a cumulative stress resulting in disorder but this is most likely to happen where there is also chronic stress or disadvantage.

Bereavement and Loss

Permanent separation, in the form of bereavement, is also associated with the development of psychiatric disorder, although the mechanisms and effects are probably rather different. In childhood, parental death is less often associated with prolonged grief than is the case in adult life (Rutter, 1966). Nevertheless, it has been found that children bereaved during the pre-school years are more likely than other children to develop psychiatric disorders later — especially during adolescence. In these cases, the death itself is probably more influential through its family consequences rather than through the direct effects on the child of loss. Often the surviving parent becomes depressed, the family may break-up and there is social and economic privation.

In adults, loss of a loved one is commonly followed by prolonged grief (Marris, 1958). Statistical investigations have shown that bereavement of a parent or spouse is a precipitant of depressive disorder (Parkes, 1964 and 1972) and a potent factor leading to suicide (Bunch, 1972). Death of a spouse also markedly increases the likelihood of death from natural causes in the surviving married partner (Young *et al.*, 1963; Rees and Lutkins, 1967). Mental disorder following bereavement is most likely when the bereaved person lacks support from his family group. In this connection, it is of interest that, for women, moving to a new town has been found to be associated with mental disorder (Sainsbury and Collins, 1966) and in the two years following moving house there is an increased risk of suicide which seems to be associated with social isolation (Sainsbury, 1971). Moving house often involves considerable disorientation of living patterns and social contacts which may be quite stressful (Fried, 1963). It appears that loss of social ties predisposes to depression and suicide; whereas this effect is most obviously seen with bereavement it probably also applies to loss incurred in other ways.

Whether or not there are links between bereavement in childhood and adult depression or suicide remains less certain and the findings of different studies are to some extent contradictory. In 1968, Granville-Grossman concluded that the evidence was inconsistent and inconclusive. But Hill (1972), with the benefit of more recent research, argued that there was an association which was most evident in the case of severe depression and suicide in adult life following the death of a parent during adolescence. Birtchnell's conclusions (1970) were similar. His data (Birtchnell, 1972) also showed that early parental death was commoner in the lower status social groups.

Most recently, Brown and his colleagues (1975), in a general population study, found that early bereavement was not directly associated with adult depression, but that it might be important through its apparent effect in rendering the person more vulnerable to the effects of stress events (see section below). Further research is clearly indicated, but it may be tentatively concluded that bereavement in childhood or adolescence possibly increases a person's susceptibility to later stress (and hence to depression and suicide). The mechanisms involved in this process remain obscure.

Stress Events

The work of several different groups of investigators has now clearly shown that the onset of depression in adult life is frequently preceded by acute life stresses (Paykel *et al.*, 1969; Brown *et al.*, 1973 a and b, 1975; Cooper and Sylph, 1973, Jacobs *et al.*, 1974). The timing of these stresses, the much higher rate of stresses among depressed people compared to well-matched control populations, the fact that (by definition) the stresses were not brought about by the individual himself, and the confirmation of patient findings within general population samples, all indicate that the stresses are of considerable causal importance. A variety of events serve as stresses but those most strongly associated with depression seem to involve the experience of a threatened or actual major loss (e.g. separation from spouse, life-threatening illness in someone close, migration of children, notice to quit) or an actual or perceived life failure (refusal of promotion, rejection for job, rebuff by a loved one).

Stress events have also been linked with a wider variety of other mental disorders and physical illnesses (e.g. Rahe, 1968; Heisel *et al.*, 1973; Reid, 1948). Although the effect is by no means specific to any one disorder the link with depression seems strongest and most central.

It has been evident from all studies that many individuals do not succumb to even severe stresses, and Brown *et al.*, (1975) have attempted to delineate the factors associated with differences in vulnerability. They found that four factors were associated with depression in women subject to acute or chronic stress, (although the factors were not linked with depression in the absence of stress). The factors were: loss of mother in childhood, three or more children aged under 14 years living at home, lack of an intimate confiding relationship with a husband or boyfriend, and lack of full or part-time employment. The first three factors were more common in the working class and Brown and his colleagues argued that they helped to explain the social class difference in rates of depression in women. This possibility requires further investigation.

Deviance in Parents or Spouse

As noted above, there are important associations between parental mental disorders and psychiatric problems in their children. These are not a function of refusal biases or 'labelling' as the associations have been confirmed in non-patient samples (Rutter, 1973 and 1976;

Richman, 1976). A similar association has been found between parental criminality and psychiatric disorder in the children. Reasons have already been given for assuming that the links are not entirely, and probably not even mainly, attributable to genetic factors. At least part of the explanation must be sought in terms of the differences in patterns of life between families with or without a parent suffering from psychiatric disorder.

It has been shown that family discord and marital disharmony are considerably more common when one parent has a psychiatric condition (Rutter, 1975c) and that *within* a group of families in all of which one parent is a psychiatric patient, marital disharmony is strongly associated with conduct disorders in the children (Rutter, 1971b). When a parent is ill, the children are more likely to be placed in care or removed from home and this, too, has been found to be associated with the development of psychiatric problems (Wolkind and Rutter, 1973). At least so far as boys are concerned, parental mental disorder seems to lead to psychiatric problems in the children, partly because of the family discord and marital disharmony with which it is associated.

However, discord does not appear to be a major factor in the genesis of psychiatric disorder in girls and even in boys discord does not constitute a sufficient explanation. Accordingly, other explanations must be sought. The longitudinal study of patients' families undertaken by Rutter, Quinton and Yule (1976) showed that problems in the children were associated with both increased negative feelings from the parents and also with the severity of parental mood disturbance as assessed in terms of its social effects. This is in keeping with the findings from an earlier study (Rutter, 1966) which indicated that children were most at risk when the parental disorder affected them directly or when it altered the parent-child relationship. In both studies the *social* context and impact of the parents' disturbed behaviour were more important than the *clinical* type or severity of the symptoms. Weissman *et al.* (1972) have shown that depressed women are impaired in their mothering in terms of diminished emotional involvement, impaired communication, disaffection, increased hostility and resentment. This is likely to increase the psychiatric risk for the children.

Not only is the child more at risk when a parent has a mental disorder, but so is the spouse. Numerous studies of psychiatric hospital attenders (see Kreitman, 1964), of general practice patients (Pond *et al.*, 1963) and of the general population (Hagnell and Kreitman, 1974) have demonstrated that psychiatric disturbance occurs in both husband and wife more often than would be expected by chance. At one time this finding was taken as evidence of assortative mating, but the evidence from several independent studies that patient-spouse concordance in neurotic manifestations is low soon after marriage, but increases with increasing duration of marriage, is much more in keeping with a hypothesis of pathogenic interaction (Kreitman, 1964; Kreitman *et al.*,

1970; Buck and Ladd, 1965; Hare and Shaw, 1965a, Hagnell and Kreitman, 1974). This is also suggested by the finding that, during the four years after psychiatric referral, an increasing proportion of spouses show psychiatric disorder, mostly of a depressive or neurotic type (Rutter *et al.*, 1976), and that the effect is more evident in the wives of ill husbands than in the husbands of ill wives (Kreitman *et al.*, 1970, Hagnell and Kreitman, 1974). The 'contagion' of symptomatology may be related to the finding that, compared with a general population sample, patients' wives spend more time in face to face contact with their husbands, have fewer social contacts outside the family, and show poorer social integration (Nelson *et al.*, 1970). This difference is most evident in the longest married pairs which explains, perhaps, why the spouse is most likely to be affected some time after marriage. Patients' marriages are also more likely to show conflict over child-rearing and to exhibit segregation in decision making, patients' husbands show less affection, and one marriage partner is more likely to be dominant over the other (Collins *et al.*, 1971a and b). In view of the evidence linking abnormal family communication patterns with child psychiatric disorder (see Hetherington and Martin, 1972), this may also help explain why parental mental disorder is associated with psychiatric problems in the children.

As most of the above findings stem from investigations of patients, it remains uncertain how far the unusual patterns of marital interaction stem from having been labelled a patient or from the effects of hospital care, how far from personality characteristics and how far from the effects of depressive and neurotic symptomatology (Crago, 1972). The matter warrants further study. It should be added that Post (1962) found evidence of raised rates of psychiatric disorder in the friends as well as the relatives of patients. He suggested that 'contagion' might play a part in this association too, although it may have simply reflected people's choice of friends with problems similar to their own. A similar pattern of associations has also been reported for attempted suicide (Kreitman *et al.*, 1969).

Family Size

Several studies have shown that children from large families (at least 4 or 5 children) are twice as likely to develop conduct disorders (Rutter, Tizard and Whitmore, 1970; Rutter, 1975c), just as they are more liable to become delinquent (Ferguson, 1952; Trenaman, 1952; West, 1969). On the other hand, youngsters with emotional disorders are, if anything, more likely to come from small families.

The association between large family size and conduct disorder is an important one because it helps explain why disorder is more common in some communities than in others (see section below). However, the mechanisms involved remain ill-understood. One factor may be the educational retardation, which predisposes to conduct disorder, and which is a fairly common feature in children from large families (see chapter 4). Another may be the overcrowding or social disadvantage which so often follows (Land, 1969). Nutrition, too, tends to be less adequate in large families (Lambert, 1964). Discord and conflict may be more frequent in large families, although this has not been systematically studied. Also, parental discipline and supervision may be more difficult when there are a lot of children to look after. The presence of many young children seems to make mothers more vulnerable to stress and hence to depression (Brown *et al.*, 1975). Large family size may result from lack of contraceptive use and in some cases reflect a general lack of foresight and planning (Oldman *et al.*, 1971). Furthermore, some of the children may be unwanted as well as unplanned. In this connection, it is pertinent to note that Forssman and Thuwe (1966) found a high rate of problems in children born after an application for therapeutic abortion had been refused and several studies have shown emotional and behavioural problems to be particularly common in illegitimate children (Crellin *et al.*, 1971; Miller *et al.*, 1974).

Unfortunately, little is known about the ways in which family interaction and relationships are influenced by the number of children. The topic needs much further research.

Lack of Attachments in Early Childhood

The next issue to be considered with respect to patterns of upbringing concerns the variety of personality disorder characterized by lack of guilt, an inability to keep rules and an inability to form lasting relationships — a syndrome often termed 'affectionless psychopathy'. This was first noted among children brought up in institutions or subjected to frequent changes of mother-figure during the first few years of life (Bowlby, 1946). Initially, the damage was attributed to separation and the breaking of affectional bonds, but subsequent work has indicated that the syndrome is more likely to be a consequence of a failure to form bonds or attachments (Rutter, 1972b; Wolkind, 1974b). Wolkind found that indiscriminate friendliness or social disinhibition (which are thought to be the precursors of the disorder) in institutional children was almost confined to those admitted before their second birthday; and Goldfarb (1955), in a less satisfactory study, showed that the features of affectionless psychopathy were most common in those who remained in the institution until after age 3 years.

It is evident that many affectionless psychopaths do not have this background and that many institutional children do not develop the syndrome. However, the research findings do suggest that if a child is unable to make attachments during the first three years of life (because of frequently changing parent-figures or other reasons) he is probably more likely to show features of affectionless psychopathy later. Further investigations are required to confirm or refute this suggestion but its importance lies in the fact that, if true, it would pinpoint some of the factors important in a disorder which not only handicaps the individual in his own personal and social functioning but which also is likely to impair him in his role as a parent. As a result, although the facts are so far rather sparse, the issue is of special pertinence with respect to intergenerational cycles of disadvantage.

Working Mothers
Although frequently blamed for their children's troubles, it is now apparent that working mothers have children with no more problems than the children of women who remain at home (Yudkin & Holme, 1963; Etaugh, 1974; Wallston 1973). As in any other situation, of course, the attitudes of the parents and the quality of care are important, but the fact of maternal employment is not a risk factor as such.

SOCIAL CLASS

In children, the associations between social class and mental disorder are variable and inconsistent (Rutter, Tizard and Whitmore, 1970). Although there is some tendency for disorders to be more common in youngsters from low social status families, this association has not been found in many systematic studies. It seems very probable that social class as such is not very important in the genesis of child psychiatric disorders, but that in some communities (but not others), social class is correlated with other factors which are of aetiological importance.

In adults the situation is quite different. The great majority of studies have shown that the highest rates of psychiatric disorder are in the lowest social groups (Dohrenwend and Dohrenwend, 1969). However, there are three important qualifications that have to be added. The first is that the social class associations differ by diagnosis. In hospital-based studies associations with low social status are most marked for schizophrenia and least marked for neurosis and depression. The second qualification is that findings differ markedly depending on whether the figures are based on clinic or general practitioner samples or on clinical assessments of non-patients (Brown *et al.*, 1974; Mazer, 1974; Rutter, 1976). Studies in the general population have shown that depressive or neurotic disorders are commoner in working class women but probably not men — see Hagnell and Kreitman, (1974), and Rutter, (1976). However, the same investigations have also shown that working class women with psychiatric disorder are *less* likely than middle class women to seek medical help. Accordingly, hospital, clinic and general practice statistics (most of which show no social class trend for neurosis — see e.g. Langner and Michael, 1963; Shepherd *et al.*, 1966; Birtchnell, 1971) are a misleading guide to the pattern in the community at large.

The third qualification is that the meaning of associations with social class also varies by diagnosis. Thus, with respect to schizophrenia, the research findings on parental social class and disorder show that the main mechanism is an illness-determined downward social drift (Dunham, 1964; Goldberg and Morrison, 1963; Wardle, 1963). That is, schizophrenia leads to social deterioration, rather than that low social class leads to schizophrenia (although low social class does influence the course of the disorder — Cooper and Morgan, 1973). Hospital statistics provide no evidence of intergenerational social deterioration in the case of depression or neurosis (Birtchnell, 1971). However, as already noted, hospital statistics probably include only a socially biased minority of neurotics. The fact that the social class association mainly applies to women, whose social class is defined on the basis of husband's occupation, makes a drift explanation less likely but the matter has yet to be systematically studied.

In spite of a considerable body of research on the social class correlates of mental disorder, very little is known about the meaning of the association. The social class differences could be the end-product of an intergenerational accumulation of genetically vulnerable individuals or they could represent the environmental effect of social factors associated with occupational status. Unfortunately, the evidence to decide between these alternatives is unsatisfactory and inconclusive (Dohrenwend and Dohrenwend, 1969). Genetic factors probably play some part in the social correlates of psychopathy (see chapter 6) but the association between depression and low social status in women is likely to reflect environmental influences.

If an environmental effect is assumed (in the absence of any definitive findings for or against), the next question is: what is it about a working class environment which predisposes to mental disorder? Brown *et al.*, (1975) showed that working class women with young children experienced far more acute and chronic stresses than did middle class women in a similar situation. Interestingly, however, the proportion with stresses did not differ by social class in the case of childless women or those without children at home. In view of the evidence that stresses are related to depression (see above), Brown and his colleagues argue that the high rate of stresses (due to crises involving husband, children or housing) constitutes *part* of the explanation for the greater rate of depression in working class women. However, their data also show that working class women have more depression than middle class women even after the number of stresses has been taken into account. Other factors which increase vulnerability to stress seem to be operative (see above, p. 209).

Phillips (1968) too found that stress was related to psychological disturbance (as measured by questionnaire rather than by interview assessment as in the Brown study) and that stresses were more frequent in the lowest social groups. In addition, he found that disturbance was more likely if there was a lack of positive experiences (a situation more common among working class people). He suggested that it was the balance between positive and negative experience which was important.

Other studies have sometimes failed to find class differences in rates of stress factors (e.g. Langner and Michael, 1963), but Brown's findings indicate the need to take age and sex into account, as well as to provide a tight operational definition of stress. This has not been done in previous investigations.

A further factor which might be relevant is poor physical health. Although different diseases show different social class patterns, the general tendency is for lower social status persons to have poorer physical health (Susser and Watson, 1971). As already noted, there is a substantial association between physical health and mental health and it might be that the more frequent physical disabilities among the working class render them more vulnerable to depression and neurosis.

Another possibility is that the personal status of an individual matters less than the socio-cultural characteristics of the area in which he lives. This seemed to be so in the studies by Leighton and her associates (1963), as the inter-area differences were much greater than the inter-class variation. This issue is discussed further in a later section.

SEX DIFFERENCES AND MARRIAGE

Whether judged by statistics on mental hospital admissions and on psychiatric out-patient care, by general practitioner attendance, or by community surveys, the universal finding is that women suffer from neurotic and depressive disorders considerably more often than do men (see review by Gove and Tudor, 1973). As noted in our introduction to this volume, we decided that the issue of sex discrimination and the disadvantage suffered by women was too important and too large a topic to be adequately discussed as merely one aspect of inter-generational cycles of disadvantage. Nevertheless, because of the implications for the possible role of socio-cultural factors in the genesis of mental disorder, some consideration of sex differences in psychiatric disorder is required.

The first issue is whether true sex differences really do exist. It could be argued that any difference found is merely a function of sex-influenced labelling or modes of response. Men succumb to stress in terms of crime and psychopathy, whereas women react by anxiety and depression. In short, if the figures for crime are added to those for mental disorder, the sexes no longer differ appreciably in rates of deviance. There is something in this argument in that, however measured, there is no doubt that men are more delinquent than women and that delinquency and depression overlap to some extent. However, it seems unlikely that crime and depression or neurosis are merely alternative ways of responding to the same stresses, in that the background factors and psychosocial correlates of the two types of disorder differ in many respects (see elsewhere in this chapter and in chapter 7).

It could also be suggested that the sex difference in rates of mental disorder merely reflect a greater tendency of women to *complain* of emotional distress (Phillips and Segal, 1969). In this connection, it may be noted that more men than women commit suicide (Stengel, 1969) so that, if suicide is taken as an index of distress, it could be argued that more men are distressed. However, a sex-related difference in complaining appears inadequate to explain the disparity in rates of mental disorder between men and women, because attempted suicide is much commoner in women (Stengel, 1969), because the sex difference is scarcely evident with single men and women (see below) and because a higher rate of disorder in women is still found in systematic clinical studies which utilize measures of somatic impairment (loss of weight, lack of sleep etc.) as well as social handicap (inability to work or carry out household tasks etc.).

The next issue is whether the sex difference is due to biological factors. It is known that males are more vulnerable to all sorts of physical hazards than are females (Rutter 1970a). Thus, males (amongst animals as well as humans) are more vulnerable to the ill-effects of malnutrition, irradiation and infection and, of course, women live longer. That this is, indeed, a function of biological factors was neatly shown by Madigan (1957) in a study of Roman Catholic Brothers and Sisters who had entered a religious community in early adult life and who were engaged in teaching and administration. Although the men and women led closely similar lives, the women outlived the men by several years, just as they do in the general population. Could it be that there is a comparable, but opposite, biological difference which makes women more susceptible to psychological stresses than are men?

Certainly there are many biological differences between males and females (Hutt, 1972) some of which might predispose women to develop mental disorder. (It should be noted that the differenee must be one that applies only to adults, as there is no sizeable difference between pre-adolescent boys and girls in the prevalence of emotional disorder — see Rutter, 1970a.)

For example, Dalton (1969) has shown that women are more vulnerable in numerous ways during the pre-menstrual period. Also, the time after child-birth is one associated with a much increased risk of mental disorder (Seager, 1960; Paffenberger, 1964). Obviously, both these hazards apply only to women. In addition, there is some circumstantial evidence which could be interpreted as suggesting that women have a greater genetic predisposition to neurosis (Rutter, 1970a.)

However, although there may well be biological determinants which render adult females more susceptible to mental disorder, there are good grounds for supposing that a substantial proportion of the sex difference is due to social rather than physical factors. First, whereas numerous studies have shown that married women have more mental disorder than do married men, the sex difference does not apply in the same way to single men and women (Gove, 1972). Married men are much healthier (both physically and mentally) then single men, but this is not so with women. The same applies to 'happiness' (Bradburn and

Caplovitz, 1965; Gurin *et al.*, 1960). Whereas single men report themselves as unhappy much more often than do married men, there is little difference in the happiness of married women and single women. The matter requires further investigation, but it seems that whereas men may be protected by marriage; for women, child-rearing, house-keeping and the role of the passive marriage partner may sometimes constitute a stress (Rutter, 1970a). The implication is that our culture creates greater stresses for women than for men and this may partly explain why adult neurosis and depression are more common in women.

Other findings also point to the importance of socio-cultural influence. For example, studies before World War II generally showed few differences between the sexes in rates of psychiatric disorder (Dohrenwend and Dohrenwend, 1969). There are numerous methodological differences between the studies but, overall, they could be interpreted as suggesting a trend over time toward relatively higher rates of disorder in women, reflecting the altering role of women in Western society (Gove and Tudor, 1973). The community surveys of Leighton and her colleagues (1963) also point to a cultural influence on sex differences. They found, as have other investigators, that in most areas women show more psychiatric symptomatology than men. However, there were two exceptions; a disorganized rural slum area with poor employment opportunities where the overall rate of disorder was very high but slightly greater in men than in women; and a close-knit, well integrated French—Canadian community, culturally isolated from the surrounding areas.

Whereas it seems highly probable that socio-cultural factors are influential in leading to a higher rate of mental disorder in women than men, very little is known about which aspects of society are important in this connection, nor about how the factors operate. In that the difference mainly applies to married women, the answer must presumably be sought more in some aspect of family life rather than in the various education and employment discriminations which are known to operate. Brown *et al.* (1975) found that the presence of three or more children under 14 years living at home predisposed women to depression and, conversely, that employment outside the home exerted a protective effect. Although it may be true that husbands are now helping their wives in the home more than they did in the past, it is still the case that women, including those with full-time jobs, undertake far more of the household tasks than do men (Young and Willmott, 1973). Whether this acts as a stress because of the emotional and physical burdens it imposes directly, or because of its effect in cutting off women from other sources of relaxation and satisfaction, remains uncertain.

Alternatively, the stress may lie in the greater prestige and satisfaction attached to jobs outside the home compared with the status afforded to child-rearing and house-keeping. Even among professionals there are consistent tendencies to undervalue female accomplishments (Hochschild, 1973). Furthermore, in the family as well as at work, women frequently have to take second place in decision making and in other aspects of dominance and control (Susser and Watson, 1971). It also appears that the wife has to do more of the adjusting in marriage (Blood and Wolfe, 1960; Rainwater and Weinstein, 1960). As a consequence, her sources of satisfaction and self-esteem are likely to be less, and this may be important in the genesis of depression (Brown *et al.*, 1975).

As outlined in chapter 9, important changes in the family are taking place. People are marrying earlier and having children earlier, but the average number of children per family is getting smaller. Illegitimate births are increasing and divorce rates are rising. These changes may influence rates of psychiatric disorder and alter sex differentials, but there is a lack of evidence on whether this is in fact happening.

It will be appreciated that the evidence on the possible action of socio-cultural factors in leading to a higher rate of mental disorder in women is extremely meagre. Nevertheless, some kind of socio-cultural influence seems highly likely. It is an issue which would repay further research, both because of the light which could be thrown on the role of women in society and through the insights which might be gained into the genesis of depression and neurosis in both sexes.

AREA DIFFERENCES

Many studies have shown that rates of mental disorder vary greatly between different geographical areas. Thus, Sainsbury (1955) showed marked differences between London boroughs in suicide rates. He found that suicide was most frequent in areas characterized by social isolation, (as reflected in persons living alone and number of boarding houses) population mobility (daily turnover of population and number of immigrants) and social disorganization (as measured by divorce and illegitimacy), but also high social status. He argued that an environment which lacks cohesion and fails to provide stable social contacts might predispose persons to suicide. Sainsbury's data referred to the 1936–38 period; a quarter of a century later Whitlock (1973a and b) found much the same pattern and noted that the situation had been similar in 1919–23. The seven high suicide boroughs appeared in the top eight in 1919–23, 1929–33, 1946–8 and 1959–63 – a remarkable degree of continuity across the generations. This indicated that the factors influencing suicide rates in London are constant and enduring. The findings also showed that the ecological correlations in both sexes were much higher with respect to suicide in people under 65 years of age.

Similar differences in suicide rates were found between country boroughs outside London (Whitlock, 1973a and b). In men, high suicide rates were found mainly in the textile towns with a falling population and were associated with isolation and loneliness. To some extent this was also so for women but (especially in younger women) suicide rates were also high in seaside resorts and other retirement areas for the well-to-do. As these are areas with high proportions of old women, of divorced and widowed women, a paucity of men, and a high rate of extranuptial births, Whitlock suggested that the social environment might act in part through predisposing to sexual frustration.

Other investigations have tended to confirm the finding that suicide is most frequent in areas where there is a high proportion of old, widowed, and divorced individuals of good education but the findings are conflicting as to whether suicide is also higher in areas with overcrowding, poor housing and much juvenile delinquency (McCulloch *et al.*, 1967; Lester, 1970).

Several studies have found geographical differences in rates of treated mental disorder in both adults and children (see Bain, 1974; Rutter, Cox *et al.*, 1975; Gath *et al.*, 1975). In general, psychiatric referral rates have tended to be higher for persons living in high density city areas of low social status. However, this pattern is explicable in part by differences in service utilization (rather than in prevalence of disorder) and by the drift of patients into poor parts of cities. In order to examine the possible influence of community characteristics of social milieu as factors in the causation or precipitation of mental disorder, epidemiological studies of the total population are needed. As already noted, Leighton *et al.*, (1963) found that mental disorder was much commoner in rural slum areas than in socially cohesive and prosperous communities Although low status occupation and education were associated with psychiatric disorder, the lack of social integration seemed a more potent factor leading to psychological problems. The investigators suggested that lack of physical security was less important than the failure to achieve affectional ties and the lack of a sense of belonging to a social group.

Rutter and his colleagues (Rutter *et al.*, 1975a and b; Rutter, 1976) compared the rates of adult and child mental disorder in the Isle of Wight — an area of small towns and countryside — and in inner London. Emotional disorders were considerably more common in London, both in 10-year-old children and in their parents. Conduct disorders in the children and criminality in the parents were also much more frequent in London. The data in both areas were obtained by the same team of investigators using systematic standardized interviewing of representative samples of the general population. There were also a number of checks on the validity of the findings and it seemed clear that psychiatric disorder was truly twice as common in inner London as on the Isle of Wight. Furthermore, the data indicated that the difference still applied to persons born and bred in the area, so a 'drift' factor could not be invoked.

Detailed measures of family circumstances were made in both areas in order to determine why psychiatric disorder was so much more frequent in London. Both in the metropolis and on the Island, child psychiatric disorder was associated with family discord and disruption, parental illness and criminality, and social disadvantage (as indicated by large family size, overcrowding and lack of home ownership). Using these variables, an index of 'family adversity' was constructed and used to compare the two areas. It was found that such difficulties were three times as frequent in London as on the Isle of Wight. Furthermore, if the two populations were standardized for frequency of 'family adversity' the difference in rate of child psychiatric disorder almost disappeared. In short, London children showed more psychiatric disorder because they were more likely to come from overcrowded unhappy homes with ill or deviant parents. School variables also played some part (see p. 221) but to a very large extent the high rate of child psychiatric disorder in London was explicable in terms of a higher prevalence of family difficulties in the city.

It appeared that city life had little *direct* adverse effect on children, but rather that the effects were mediated through the family (Rutter and Quinton, 1976).

However, that still left open the questions of why adults in London also showed higher rates of psychiatric disorder, and why criminality and marital discord was also so much more frequent in the capital. Depression in women was more strongly linked with personal and family difficulties in the Isle of Wight and with low social status in London (Rutter and Quinton, 1976). Overcrowding and poor housing somewhat increased the risk of mental disorder and of family disharmony, but these factors were insufficient to account for the high rates in London. It may be that the study did not include measures on the appropriate aspects of family conditions, but it appeared that in addition to adverse personal circumstances, there was the additional disadvantage of living in an inner city area. Just what it is about inner city life which creates the stress was not evident from the study's findings. The answer was not to be found in the frequency of kin contact or meetings with friends, so that isolation from people did not seem to be an appropriate explanation. The type of housing as assessed in terms of high rise, low rise, house, etc., was not found to relate to mental disorder, so that these aspects of housing were not crucial, although other aspects of housing may have been. Other investigations have provided some evidence that inner city dwellers are less satisfied with life than other people but the evidence that urban life creates a sense of despair or malaise is weak (Fischer, 1973). London is characterized by a much higher rate of population turnover and by a higher proportion of immigrants than the Isle of Wight (Rutter *et al.*, 1975b; Rutter, 1976) — variables which probably influence the social cohesiveness of a neighbourhood. London is also a more anonymous area so that a person's activities there are much less likely to be observed by someone who knows him. This may lead to a diminution in social controls, although evidence on this point is lacking. Kasarda and

Janowitz (1974) using British social survey data, found that length of residence in an area was the variable most strongly associated with feelings of community attachment and sentiment. In contrast, increasing population size and density did not appear to weaken bonds of kinship or friendship. The results imply that London may be less cohesive and less neighbourly because of high population turnover rather than because of the number of people living there.

There is little doubt that the concept of a community (Suttles, 1972) or neighbourhood (Lee, 1968) is a valid one, but exactly what constitutes a community and which aspects foster or impede mental health are uncertain.

Explanations of 'deprivation' in terms of social structure are sometimes viewed as being in opposition to explanations in terms of personal or family variables. The findings on area differences in psychiatric disorder suggest that this may often be a false dichotomy. Research clearly indicates that poor social circumstances and adverse conditions of society in which people live are associated with, and probably cause, higher rates of psychiatric disorder. The implication is that improvements in society should reduce psychiatric disorder (at least in children) because they decrease the likelihood of family disharmony and tensions, poor communication and disturbed relationships in the home, and parental irritability and scape-goating of the children. In short, the direct cause of psychiatric disorder in any individual lies to a considerable extent in his personal life experiences and biological constitution, but conditions in society may sometimes constitute the basic determinants of how far his life experiences are supportive or damaging. However, the links between these variables remain largely unexplained and little is known concerning the mechanisms involved.

In view of the major differences in rates of psychiatric disorder between different areas, and in view of their considerable persistence over time (cf the findings on suicide above), research to delineate the reasons for the difference and the underlying mechanisms should provide information of crucial relevance to one aspect of intergenerational cycles of disadvantage. That research has yet to be undertaken.

SCHOOL DIFFERENCES

Finally, there is evidence that rates of behavioural problems vary according to school. Gath *etal.*, (1972 and 1975) examined psychiatric referral rates in an outer London borough and found a three fold difference between schools which was not explicable in terms of the area in which the schools were situated. The inter-school differences in that study could reflect either variations in service utilization or variations in prevalence of psychiatric disorder. However, other studies have indicated that there are marked differences between schools in how children behave — quite apart from any variation in referral practice. Thus, both Galloway (1976) and Reynolds and Murgatroyd (1974) found large variations between schools in rates of absenteeism. These remained remarkably consistent over a period of six years (Reynolds and Murgatroyd, 1974). The size of the school was of little importance for school attendance rates but absenteeism was more frequent in schools taking a high proportion of socially disadvantaged children, as assessed by the proportion eligible for free school meals (Galloway, 1976).

Of course, absenteeism occurs for many reasons and only rarely will it arise as a result of psychiatric disorder. More global measures of behavioural deviance were used in the London studies carried out by Rutter and his colleagues (Rutter, 1975; Rutter, Cox *et al.*, 1975; Rutter, 1975c; Yule and Rutter, 1976). It was found that primary schools varied markedly in the proportions of behaviourally deviant children, even after taking into account where the children lived and whether or not they came from disturbed or disadvantaged homes. Rates of disturbance were significantly higher in schools with a high rate of pupil or staff turnover, a high proportion of children from immigrant families. More schools in London than the Isle of Wight showed these disadvantaging characteristics, which suggests that less satisfactory schooling may have played some part in leading to higher rates of both behavioural deviance and psychiatric disorder in London school children.

Analyses suggested that the variations between schools reflected the influence of school life on pupils' behaviour. However, this could only be tested adequately by means of longitudinal studies in which selective factors in school intake could be taken into account. Such data are available from Yule and Rutter's (1976) follow-up of the same children into secondary school. This showed that in some schools scarcely any of the children showed emotional or behavioural difficulties, whereas in others nearly half did so. Some of this variation was attributable to differences in the children's behaviour at the time of admission from primary school, but even after this was taken into account statistically, large differences between schools remained. Considered in terms of the mean questionnaire score, there was a range of 1.2 standard deviations between schools (roughly speaking this is equivalent to an 18 point IQ difference between the most successful and the least successful schools).

The findings indicate that to an important extent children's behaviour* may be shaped by influences encountered at school, but

*None of the school studies has assessed psychiatric disorder as such, but the questionnaire used has been shown to be a reasonable screening device for psychiatric conditions (Rutter, Cox *et al.*, 1975) and it may be inferred that at least some of the school variation probably applies to overt disorder as well as to behavioural deviance.

little is known about *which* factors make for differences in a school environment and even less about *how* these operate. Schools constitute miniature societies which influence children by the values they set as much as by the personal interactions between individual staff and pupils (Shipman, 1968). Each school seems to have a distinctive atmosphere or climate which sets the tone of what is expected of staff and pupils (McDill and Rigsby, 1973). There are many suggestions concerning the factors which determine what sort of institution a school becomes and how organizational features may impinge on pupils, but so far there has been little systematic research into these matters (Biddle, 1970).

CONCLUSIONS

The term 'psychiatric disorder' encompasses a wide range of conditions from chronic illnesses with a strong biological component to acute emotional disturbance which arises as a fairly direct response to environmental stress. These various disorders have different origins, run a different course and show differing degrees of intergenerational continuity. For the most part this chapter has concentrated on the commoner disorders of a chronic type. Little attention has been paid either to the psychoses or to acute mental disturbance.

With all conditions the likelihood is that troubles will not persist into the next generation of the same family. Nevertheless, considerable continuity is evident with respect to conduct disorders in childhood and personality disorders in adult life. With the most severe of these it is quite common to find persistence of problems across several generations. Adult depression and chronic neurotic disorders also show a tendency to intergenerational continuity, although this is less marked than for personality disorders.

Many factors play a part in the transmission of psychiatric conditions; genetic factors are important in the case of psychopathy, personality disorders and chronic anxiety states and adverse family influences are crucial in a wide range of troubles. However, there is also evidence that social factors, organizational forces, circumstances of living and conditions of life generally help determine the prevalence of psychiatric disorder. Intergenerational continuities need to be viewed not only in terms of persistence within individual families but also through groups. The reasons why disorder remains at a relatively high rate among inner city dwellers are likely to be rather different from the reasons why psychiatric problems are found in succeeding generations of the Smith family but not among the Browns.

8 Parenting Behaviour

Although many crucial questions remain unanswered in the field of family studies and of parent-child relationships (Walters and Stinnett, 1971), there is now a substantial body of evidence which suggests that family influences play an important part in the development of some of the behaviour and educational problems shown by children (Hetherington and Martin, 1972; Rutter, 1972a). Many of the problems associated with family disturbance are of a kind which often persist into adult life (Robins, 1972). Other chapters in this volume have discussed how family variables might be involved in the intergenerational transmission of many types of trouble. This chapter considers the evidence on the extent to which parenting behaviours themselves show intergenerational continuities, and in so far as they do, what mediating mechanisms might be involved. In this connection it cannot be assumed that like necessarily begets like. Rather, the issue is how far an individual's personal experiences of child-rearing influence the way in which he brings up his own children a generation later.

SECULAR TRENDS IN PARENTING PATTERNS

Before considering intergenerational continuities, it is necessary to ask how far patterns of parenting in the population as a whole remain stable from one generation to the next. The answer is that they show marked shifts. One of the most striking features of secular trends is the way in which parenting patterns in the United Kingdom have undergone radical changes over the last few decades (Chester, 1971; DHSS, 1974; Illsley and Gill, 1968). Thus, during the first third of this century the proportion of teenage brides remained around 8 or 9 per cent. By 1946–50 the proportion had risen to 15.5 per cent, by 1966–70 it had risen further to 30.0 per cent and by 1971 it remained at much the same level. The proportion of boys marrying in their teens increased even more, from 2.5 per cent in 1946–50 to 10.2 per cent in 1971. This trend toward earlier marriage has been much more marked among manual workers than among non-manual and professional workers so that the difference between social classes with regard to marital patterns has considerably widened since the 1930s.

One of the likely consequences of this rise in teenage marriages is an increased rate of marital breakdown in that now, as in the past, young brides are at a greater risk of divorce than older brides at all durations of marriage. Of course it should not be assumed that the association between early marriage and marital breakdown is inevitable. Christensen (1960) showed that the consequences of premarital conception for the timing of marriage and the likelihood of marriage breakdown varied between communities according to socio-cultural mores and differing attitudes to sexual behaviour. The same could apply to age of marriage.

Nevertheless, the evidence suggests that teenage marriage remains a strong predisposing factor to marital disruption. The reasons why this should be so remain ill-understood. However, it is likely to stem in part from the fact that interests and attitudes may undergo marked changes during adult life. Individuals marrying in their teens are still developing emotionally and the husband and wife may well develop in different directions after marriage. In addition, it may be that some teenagers are not emotionally ready to cope with the responsibilities of parenting (as the birth of children frequently follows soon after early marriage: Gibson, 1974). However, probably at least as important as these individual characteristics is the fact that people marrying in their teens tend to be at an economic disadvantage compared with those marrying later, and many have difficulty finding suitable accommodation (Gibson, 1974). The problems of taut budgetting and overcrowding may well predispose to marital disharmony.

In parallel with the trend toward earlier marriage, illegitimacy ratios have also risen sharply in recent years (Hartley, 1966; Illsley and Gill, 1968; DHSS, 1974). Up to the mid-1950s the ratio (of illegitimate to legitimate births) in England and Wales had remained steady for 20 years at about 5 per cent of all live births, but by 1972 it had risen to 8.6 per cent. Compared with legitimate births, a much higher proportion of illegitimate births involve teenage mothers (Crellin *et al.*, 1971). Yet it would be incorrect to see this as largely a phenomenon associated with young unmarried girls. Many illegitimate babies are born to older women and many are born to married women or to women who subsequently marry. Nevertheless, at age seven years, about a quarter of illegitimately born children are in single parent households and another half, although in a two-parent family, are not with both their natural parents (Crellin *et al.*, 1971). In view of the poorer educational attainments and worse social adjustment of non-adopted illegitimate children as compared with legitimate, the rise in illegitimacy ratio is likely to carry with it an increase in various other forms of disadvantage.

During the earlier part of this century, death broke more marriages in the younger age groups than did divorce. A marked decline in mortality and an increase in divorce have now reversed this position. During the last 20 years the number of divorces in England has quadrupled (DHSS, 1974). Although part of the increase is due to legal and financial changes and wartime disturbances, these factors by no means account for the rise in divorce rate (Chester, 1972). Cohort analyses demonstrate that contemporary marriages are more prone to early divorce and probably are more likely to end in divorce (Chester, 1971). In view of the unknown number of marital separations not giving rise to divorce it is uncertain whether more marriages are breaking down or whether it is merely that more broken marriages end in divorce. So far as can be judged, both are occurring. Between two-thirds and three-quarters of divorced persons marry again so that only a minority of children in broken homes remain in a one-parent situation. Nevertheless, current estimates suggest that at any given time nearly one-tenth of all families with dependent children have only one parent (DHSS, 1974).

Although women are marrying earlier than they used to and although teenage births have risen markedly over the last 20 years, there has actually been a drop in birth rate and a reduction in family size during the last decade (Parkes, 1971; Registrar General, 1974; Registrar General Scotland, 1973). Thus, in Scotland the live birth rate per 1000 population halved between 1900 and 1972. In the United Kingdom as a whole, the net reproduction rate (which takes into account mortality as well as birth rate) is just adequate for the population to reproduce itself. This reduction in family size might have benefits and there is a known association between large family size and a variety of disadvantageous circumstances such as poverty, over-crowding, educational retardation and delinquency (see other chapters in this volume). However, many of the mechanisms underlying these associations are ill-understood and it does not necessarily follow that a reduction in family size *per se* will prove beneficial.

At the same time as the ultimate size of families has become smaller, the spacing between children has become closer. As a result of this, and the earlier age of child-bearing, women are likely to spend a larger part of their lives free of the care of dependent children. The social and psychological consequences of this altering pattern of family life have yet to be adequately charted.

In the USA, rather similar changes over time have been occurring (Bronfenbrenner, 1975). More mothers are going out to work, more children are being reared in single-parent families, divorce rates are rising and the illegitimacy ratio is increasing.

In summary, the last few decades have seen marked shifts toward earlier marriage and earlier child-bearing, a higher proportion of illegitimate children, more frequent divorce and smaller families. The reasons for these trends remain uncertain but are likely to reside in alterations in social mores and public attitudes rather than in the more personal factors sometimes associated with differences in parenting behaviour within a single generation. Research is needed to determine if this is indeed the case and, if it is, why it is occurring and what are the social or other forces determining it.

SOCIO—ECONOMIC CORRELATES

Some researchers (Wynn and Wynn, 1974) have seen these trends as likely to lead to an intensification of cycles of poverty, and politicians

(Joseph, 1974) have argued that the trends reflect a move towards moral and economic decline. While this could happen, the findings do not point unambiguously in that direction. In the first place, the linking together of high fertility, one parent families and poverty is misleading. One parent families actually tend to be *smaller* than average, although it is certainly true that they are frequently poor (DHSS, 1974). Teenage pregnancy and early marriage are both considerably more common in semi-skilled and unskilled manual groups (Registrar General Scotland, 1973; Bone, 1973), but the same is not true of illegitimacy. The Registrar General's figures for Scotland show that illegitimacy is most common among women with semi-skilled jobs and least common among those with either unskilled jobs or professional posts. This curious pattern almost certainly reflects the types of jobs women hold. When social class is assessed on the maternal grandfather's job in order to provide comparability with legitimate births, it turns out that illegitimacy occurs with roughly the same frequency in all social groups (Crellin *et al.*, 1971).

The assumption that the poor have more children than the rich is also rather doubtful. No data are available on whether the economic status of the mother's or father's family of origin is associated with differences in fertility. Having a large family may well lead to poverty (Ministry of Social Security, 1967; Land, 1969) but that is not at all the same thing as being reared in poverty causing one to have many children. Furthermore, fertility is only weakly associated with social class. The British census figures for 1971 (Registrar General, 1973) showed that family size (defined in terms of people in the home rather than number of children born) varied very little by social class. The Scottish figures (Registrar General Scotland, 1973) showed some tendency for unskilled manual workers to have more children (the average number of children for social classes I to V respectively was 1.83, 2.07, 2.08, 2.23 and 2.47) but the association was weak. Moreover, fertility seems to be falling more in the unskilled than in the professional groups (Registrar General, 1974), so even this social gradient may flatten out over the coming years.

The divorce rate is roughly similar in all social classes except that it is considerably higher in unskilled manual groups (Gibson, 1974). To a considerable extent, this difference may simply reflect social class variations in age at marriage. Divorce rates vary by type of job and it could be that the stresses associated with either highly competitive work or insecurity of employment predispose to marriage breakdown, but there is no clear link with social status as such (Noble, 1970). Probably much the same applies to marital discord and disharmony not leading to divorce. Although, in a general population epidemiological study, discord was found to be somewhat more frequent in semi-skilled and unskilled groups in London, this did not apply on the Isle of Wight (Rutter, 1976). Marital unhappiness may be associated with some features linked with low social class, but the very limited available evidence suggests that social status *per se* is of little direct importance.

In short, there are important socio-economic correlates of patterns in marriage and parenting but they do not lead to any clear prediction concerning intergenerational cycles. In particular, very little is known about how the social or economic circumstances in which a person is reared affect his parenting behaviour when he comes to have his own children.

INTERGENERATIONAL CONTINUITIES

Conception

Illsley and Thompson (1961), in their systematic study of nearly 3,000 Aberdeen women having their first baby, provided information on intergenerational continuities in the timing and circumstances of conception. They examined the effects of coming from a 'broken home' and found that women whose homes were 'broken' before the age of 14 years were more likely than women from 'unbroken' homes to have conceived outside marriage and to be less than 20 years of age when their first baby was born. However, the findings varied according to the reason for the breakup of the home. The women whose home had been broken by the death of a parent did not differ appreciably from those from intact homes. On the other hand, the women who had themselves been illegitimate, or whose parents had divorced or separated were twice as likely to have illegitimate children or to have a pre-nuptial conception. The age of the child at the time the parental home broke up did not affect this association. Children brought up by relatives were much less likely to have a pre-nuptial conception than those reared in institutions or by unrelated persons. The circumstances leading to the broken home, and the continuity and quality of care following the break, seemed to be more important than the parental loss itself.

More recently, in their systematic study of pregnant women in an inner London borough, Wolkind *et al.* (1976) found that childhood separations which had occurred in the context of family discord or disruption were associated with a greatly increased risk of both teenage pregnancy and unmarried motherhood. The associations did not apply when the separations had taken place in stable families.

Although providing less satisfactory data, other studies too have suggested that women coming from unhappy broken homes are more likely to marry young, to have babies young and to have illegitimate children. Crellin *et al.* (1971), in the National Child Development Study, found that mothers whose fathers had died or left the family during childhood were more likely to have illegitimate children. Illegitimacy rates were not examined separately according to whether the father died or separated from his wife. Ferguson (1966), in his Scottish follow-up study of youngsters who had been in care, found that 7 per cent of girls aged 18 to 20 years had had illegitimate children — a rate which appears high although no control group was employed. Among the 42 fostered children followed-up by Meier (1965, 1966) 7 had had illegitimate children (some more than one) by 30 years of age — a rate well above that in the general population although there was no control group. In Wright and Lunn's (1971) follow-up study of the offspring in 'problem families' (see Chapter 10), it was found that 59 per cent of the married daughters and 52 per cent of the wives of the married sons had their first child at the age of 19 years or under.

Family Size

Although there have been a number of attempts to study the relationship between family sizes in two successive generations (Pearl, 1939), there are very few adequate investigations of this kind based on appropriate sampling. Probably the best data are available from Berent (1953) who studied a representative sample of nearly 1,500 couples who had been married for at least fifteen years and in which both spouses were only once married. After controlling social class, he found that there were significant associations between the number of children born and the size of the family from which each of the parents themselves had come. This applied to both the husband's and to the wife's family size, although more so to the latter.

Roughly similar correlations were obtained within each of the social groups studied and for both those who did and who did not practise birth control. However, just as in the more selected samples of Pearson and Lee (1899) and of Huestis and Maxwell (1932), the correlations were low (that between the number of live births and number of wife's brethren was only +0.187) and explained little of the variance. Thus, when both the wife and husband came from families of at least 10 children the average number of live births was 4.37 compared with 2.05 when both came from families of only one or two children (including the subject). Interestingly, in the 20 per cent subsample for which there was information on the number of children planned at the time of marriage, there was no significant association between family size of origin and size of family desired.

A rather similar analysis (although on a less satisfactory sample) was carried out in the United States by Duncan *et al.* (1965). Again, a statistically significant relationship was found between size of family of origin and number of children born, but the association was very weak and accounted for a trivial proportion of the variance. Further, even this weak association was markedly diminished when parental education was taken into account.

Data are also available from the Aberdeen longitudinal study of women having their first child (Thompson and Illsley, 1969). The 13 women who had at least 5 children during the 10 years following the birth of the first, differed from those with smaller families in that a higher proportion were illegitimate, came from a labourer's family or were reared in a family with at least four siblings. No statistical tests were applied to the differences but in view of the small sample size it is likely that the differences were not significantly different from chance. In the same study the women were asked both at their first pregnancy and five years later how many children they wanted. Many women altered their preferences over the 5 year period so that the correlation between the two was only +0.28, but no woman stated a preference for more than 4 children either initially or later.

A later report on the Aberdeen study (Askham, 1975) describes the differences between small samples of families with just two children and those with at least four. Social class was taken into account by making comparisons within both an unskilled and a skilled manual group. The women with large families differed in wanting rather more children (an average of 3½ compared with 2½), but also a much greater proportion had had more children than they desired (55% vs 10%). This was associated with less efficient use of contraceptives and a more passive approach to family planning. Twice as many of the women with four-plus children came from large families themselves, had married in their teens, had gone out with their husbands for less than a year before marriage, and had had a premarital conception. Differences in family size were associated with only minor differences in values, aspirations and ideals, although the unskilled group with large families were more pessimistic about planning for the future. The families with four-plus children were more likely to have changed housing and changed jobs frequently for negative reasons (i.e. not for improvement) and more had experienced marital discord. A deprived background was more strongly associated with social class than with family size, but the men with at least four children had experienced more illness or disability and had been unemployed more frequently than those with two children.

Peel (1970) reports that, in the Hull survey of a random sample of 350 newly married couples, the family size intentions of couples were entirely unrelated to the size of families in which the husbands and wives originated (the actual figures are not given). As in the Aberdeen study, very few (2 per cent) wanted more than four children. However, social circumstances were felt to be a constraining factor in family planning so that the average size of the ideal family was 3.36 in spite of the average of 2.6 for the intended family size. A follow-up interview 5 years later (Peel, 1972) showed that the intended family size had constricted further to 2.23, largely for financial and health reasons.

Even in Berent's well-planned study, it was not possible to control for a number of possibly relevant variables such as age at marriage, duration of marriage, and practice of birth control in the older generation. Also the marked decline in family size over the last century (Parkes, 1971) may have somewhat attenuated intergenerational correlations, especially if the reduction mainly affected the largest families. Intergenerational comparisons are also complicated by secular changes in age at marriage (Busfield and Hawthorne, 1971). As a result it is not possible from existing data to obtain a fully accurate assessment of intergenerational continuities in family size. However, the available evidence suggests that continuity is generally low.

Quality of Marriage

A variety of studies (reviewed by Waller and Hill, 1951) have indicated that men whose parents were unhappily married are more likely themselves to show poor marital adjustment. As these studies are mostly based on highly selected samples, are retrospective in nature and sometimes utilize marriage ratings of uncertain validity, not much weight can be attached to their findings. Nevertheless, it should be noted that the quality of parental marriage is the variable most consistently associated with happiness, satisfaction and stability of a person's own marriage. More reliable, although admittedly cruder, data are obtainable from findings on parental divorce or separation. There are two major American studies with data of this kind. In the 'Midtown' study a representative sample of some 1,600 adults were systematically interviewed with respect to their mental health and to various social factors (Langner and Michael, 1963). It was found that individuals whose parents had divorced or separated were twice as likely as those from unbroken homes to have marriages which also ended in divorce or separation (24 per cent versus 14 per cent). In contrast, those whose homes were broken by parental death showed only a trivial increase in divorce rate. Again, as with illegitimacy, the child's age at the time the parental marriage broke up was of no significance.

Gurin, Veroff and Feld (1960) conducted an interview study of over 2,000 adults, using area sampling methods. As in the Midtown study, those from homes broken by divorce had much higher divorce rates than those from intact homes. Of the adults whose parents divorced, 15 per cent were currently divorced, 19 per cent were currently married but had previously divorced, and 60 per cent of those married experienced problems in their marriage. The comparable figures for those from intact homes were 5 per cent, 8 per cent and about 40 per cent. The rates for adults who had lost one or more parents by death were somewhat above those for adults from intact homes but well below those whose parents had divorced.

Meier's follow-up study of former foster children (1965, 1966) found that they, too, had relatively high rates of marriage breakdown – 14.3 per cent for the men and 11.6 per cent for the women compared with 3.8 per cent and 5.1 per cent respectively for the same age-groups in the general population.

Jonsson (1967), in a Scandinavian study, showed not only that the parents of delinquent boys were more likely to show marital discord and divorce than were controls but also that the grandparents of delinquents exhibited poorer marital harmony, worse parent-child relationships and more frequent divorce. This intergenerational continuity in family discord and disruption was closely associated with similar continuities in terms of mental illness, alcohol abuse, and criminality. It could well be that the true continuity lay in a general disturbance of personality functioning rather than in marital and parental behaviours as such. Jonsson discussed the findings in terms of social heredity, but no examination of genetically determined biological heredity was possible from his data.

In assessing intergenerational continuities in marriage breakdown, it is necessary to take into account changes over time in the number of marriages that end in divorce (see above). During the last 20 years there has been a marked rise in divorce rate which seems to be part of a general alteration in patterns of personal and social behaviour. Over the same time period illegitimate births, delinquency, drug abuse, venereal disease, and possibly attempted suicide, have also increased in frequency (Chester, 1971).

Infant Care

In spite of a widespread assumption in psychiatric circles that the way in which parents were brought up will influence how they treat their own children, there appears to be only one study relating childhood experiences to patterns of parental care in the infancy period, that by Frommer and O'Shea (1973 a, b). They studied a consecutive sample of British born women attending a London teaching hospital to have their first baby. Each woman was asked: 'were you separated from either or both of your parents before you were 11 years old?' By this means a group of 'separated' women was obtained and compared with a non-separated control group matched for age and social class. Both groups were interviewed when the baby was 2–3 months old, 6–7 months, 9–10 months, and about 13 months. Unfortunately neither the duration nor the cause of the separation was specified in defining the 'separated' group, although data on both items were obtained. There was very considerable overlap between the groups with respect to patterns of neonatal care but more of the 'separated' women propped up their 2 month old babies with a bottle so that they could feed themselves (42 per cent versus 17 per cent), more of their babies had feeding problems (58 per cent versus 23 per cent), and more became pregnant again during the 13 month follow-up period (13 per cent versus 0 per cent). The particular childhood experiences which were relevant to patterns of parental care could be inferred from a comparison (within the combined 'separated' and 'non-separated' groups) of women who did and who did not have management problems with their infants. Whereas parental death was *not* associated with problems in infant management, parental separation or disturbed family relationships *were* associated with infant problems. As with other aspects of parenting, it appears that it is the quality of family life in childhood, and not the breakup of the home as such, which is important. It is noteworthy that problems in infant management were more strongly related to *current* marital problems than to childhood experiences a generation ago.

Methods of Child-rearing
Clinical anecdotes on connections between personal childhood experiences and methods of bringing up one's own children are plentiful, but there is very little in the way of systematic information. Nevertheless, what does emerge from clinical case histories is that the apparent links between how individuals were themselves brought up and how they bring up their own children a generation later do not necessarily involve intergenerational continuities in the *same* parental patterns. This point also emerges from Stolz's study (1967) of parents' perceptions of what influenced their behaviour as parents. Some wanted to emulate their own upbringing in how they dealt with their own children, some wanted deliberately to avoid doing to their children what they had gone through when young, some did both for different aspects of parenting and in other cases the links were more indirect. Parenting may be influenced in subtle ways by attitudes, roles, personal characteristics, and emotional complexes deriving from childhood experiences. Of course, the fact that psychiatrists and parents view the links between childhood experiences and parental behaviour in this way does not make them true but it suggests the kind of links that need to be examined in systematic studies.

Unfortunately, very little research bears on this question. One of the very few investigations with relevant data is the California Guidance study, a long-term follow-up enquiry (Bronson, Katten and Livson, 1959). Their findings showed very little association between people's description of how their parents behaved and how they themselves behaved towards their own children. In short, it seemed that on the whole people did *not* follow the example of their parents. However, not much reliance can be placed on these data because information was available on only half the sample and the data on childhood experiences were entirely retrospective.

Although their published data are descriptive rather that statistical, the findings from the Newsons' (1963) longitudinal study of Nottingham families are similar. Many parents described how they were brought up differently from the way they were rearing their own children. It is noteworthy that several informants commented that the reasons for the differences lay as much in altered social conditions as in anything personal. In a small scale British study, Harrell-Bond (1969) also noted that marriage and conjugal role expectations were influenced by cultural factors in childhood upbringing.

Levy's (1943) clinical study of maternal overprotection is also relevant. He found that, compared with the control group, more overprotective mothers reported unhappy childhoods. It seemed that the overprotection arose in part through the women's attempt to compensate their children for what they themselves had lacked in childhood.

All these studies relied on retrospective information (which is notoriously open to bias and distortion — Yarrow *et al.*, 1964), only limited areas of child-rearing were considered and many of the data were impressionistic and non-qualitative. For all these reasons no firm conclusions are possible. However, what little evidence there is suggests that, within the normal range of child-rearing, there is only slight direct intergenerational continuity. More subtle and indirect links of a psychologically meaningful kind may well be present but they have yet to be demonstrated in a systematic investigation.

It might be thought that this rather negative conclusion runs counter to the extensive evidence of marked social class differences in child-rearing which are found generation after generation (c.f. Kohn, 1963; Newson and Newson, 1963, 1968). However the discrepancy is only apparent. Two points are relevant. First, the social class correlates of today are not the same as they were a generation ago (Bronfenbrenner, 1958). The magnitude of the differences is as great but the differences do not refer to the same aspects of parental care. Secondly, the social classes do not remain static (see Chapter 5). Over the course of two or three generations the same social classes come to be made up of rather different families. Thus, whereas it is true that there are marked social class differences in child-rearing, these do not necessarily imply intergenerational continuities in family patterns of child care.

Rather than any direct intergenerational transmissions of particular methods of child-rearing, it is much more likely that childhood experiences will have an indirect effect on later parenting behaviour through their influence on personality development and on the acquisition of social values and attitudes. There is evidence (see Chapter 6, and also Rutter, 1972a) that being reared in a home where there is gross family discord is conducive to the development of antisocial disorder. No direct link has been shown between this experience of child rearing and later behaviour as a parent, but longitudinal studies have demonstrated that, when adult, antisocial children are particularly likely to have marital difficulties and problems with their children (Robins, 1966, 1972). Similarly, spending the early years of childhood in an environment which does not allow the development of stable inter-personal bonds seems to increase the risk of later deficiencies in social relationships. Again it might be expected that this would have implications for parenting. The crucial data which could provide the necessary links are lacking and only hypotheses and suppositions are possible in the light of existing evidence. Nevertheless, the probability that such links might exist means that further studies would be most worthwhile.

Abnormalities in Parenting

Intergenerational continuities in abnormal parenting have largely been considered for child-battering and child abuse. In 1956, Gibbens and Walker, in a study of a consecutive sample of 32 men who had been sent to prison for cruelty to children involving violence, found that a high proportion had had very disturbed childhoods. A fifth were illegitimate and nearly a third had been separated from their fathers since birth. A fifth had been abandoned by their mothers and almost all came from large families. However, only 3 out of the 32 had been reared in institutions. More recently, Scott (1973) studied 29 men who had been charged with killing their pre-school child. Two-thirds came from punitive backgrounds and twelve remembered parental violence. Five had been reared in institutions of unknown quality. However, at least six of the 29 men seemed to have had normal homes in childhood as judged from interviews with family members or from good records.

A recent Irish study of 18 battered children (Lukianowicz, 1971) found that most of the mothers had themselves had a rather unhappy, loveless or traumatic childhood. A review of other studies (Spinetta and Rigler, 1972) produced similar conclusions. Most, but certainly not all, parents who batter their children have experienced a cold, rejecting or cruel upbringing. There are published reports such as those by Oliver and his colleagues (Oliver and Taylor, 1971; Oliver and Cox, 1973) in which actual battering runs through several generations of the same family, but the more usual story is of emotional privations and hostility rather than physical cruelty as such.

These studies lack controls but the findings are sufficiently striking for there to be little doubt that battering parents differ from the general population in the proportion who experienced seriously adverse parenting in their own childhood. It is less certain how far they differ in this respect from persons who do not injure their children but who show personality disorder or recurrent criminal behaviour. However, an association with battering as such was shown by Oliver and his colleagues (1974) in their systematic study of all cases of severe physical abuse of pre-school children occurring during a seven year period in one defined geographical area. They found that the parents who actually caused their children physical injury differed from their spouses in being more likely to have been subject to serious abuse or neglect in their own childhoods, as well as being more likely to have had an unsatisfactory or disturbed upbringing in other ways.

The relative importance of various background factors is best determined from Oliver's study and from the controlled comparisons by Smith *et al.* (1973 and 1974). As noted by others (Skinner and Castle, 1969; Helfer and Kempe, 1968), individuals who injure their children tend to come from lower social class groups, to be of low average intelligence, to have their children at an unusually young age, and to have larger families than most. However, as compared with persons from comparable social groups, they differ much more strikingly in the very high frequency of marital disharmony and marriage breakdown, the high rate of premarital conception and illegitimate births, the high proportion with mental disorder and/or criminal records, the frequency of rejecting attitudes to the children and the extent of social isolation. Over a third of the battered children in the Smith study and a quarter in the Oliver study were illegitimate.

The childhood experiences of the parents in a representative sample of 129 'problem families' obtaining help from Family Service Units were studied by Philp (1963). Sixteen per cent of the men and 12 per cent of the women had received institutional care, one in ten had been subject to parental violence, and 12 per cent of the men and 23 per cent of the women came from homes characterized by marked marital disharmony. Altogether 69 per cent of the men and 66 per cent of the women had suffered some kind of disturbing influence in childhood. No control figures are available but the rate seems high.

MEANING OF INTERGENERATIONAL CONTINUITIES

In order to arrive at some judgement on the meaning of these intergenerational continuities it is necessary to obtain answers to three main questions: how strong are the continuities? how are the continuities mediated? and how far are abnormalities in parenting behaviour permanent and irreversible?

Strength of Intergenerational Continuities

Although the strength of the association is not great, there is good evidence linking unhappily broken homes with marital disruptions, extra marital conception and, possibly, less satisfactory neonatal care a generation later. A background of a broken home is associated with an approximately two-fold increase over the general population in these outcomes, but this still accounts for only a minority of cases of marital disruption, extramarital conception and poor neonatal care. Thus, for example, in the Midtown study (Langner and Michael, 1963) the risk of divorce/separation was more than doubled for individuals whose parents had divorced or separated. Nevertheless, because intact homes are so much commoner, it was still the case that over three quarters of the divorced/separated individuals in the present generation came from intact homes in the previous generation. Conversely, over three quarters of individuals from broken homes had an intact marriage themselves. Much the same applies to other studies. In short, in spite of important and statistically significant continuities in terms of marital behaviour, intergenerational *dis*continuity is more common.

The strength of intergenerational continuities with respect to patterns of child-rearing within the normal range and to family size are even lower, as indicated by the studies reviewed above.

The studies of parents who injure their children mostly lack adequate controls but there is fairly good evidence linking an unhappy, rejecting and cruel upbringing with parental violence towards their offspring. The links seem quite strong so that at least half and probably some three quarters of battering parents come from such an adverse background. Even so, a substantial minority do not and a few seem to have had quite unexceptional childhoods. Also it should be recognized that the links are stronger looking back than they are looking forward. That is to say, although most battering parents come from unhappy affectionless and sometimes violent homes, it is likely that only a tiny minority of youngsters from such homes go on to physically abuse their children. Whether the experience of being battered commonly leads individuals to be violent to their own children later is quite unknown.

In general, it seems that intergenerational continuity is least for aspects of parenting within the normal range and greatest with seriously abnormal parenting. However, the data needed for a valid assessment of the strength of intergenerational continuities in parenting behaviour are lacking. In the first place, most studies have had to rely on crude indices such as divorce/separation rather than on more meaningful measures of the quality and characteristics of marital interactions. This is a serious deficiency as studies have indicated that with most forms of outcome the qualities of family life are more important than whether parents remain together or separate (McCord and McCord, 1959; Rutter, 1971b; Power *et al.*, 1974). Secondly, continuities have largely been examined in terms of direct transmission of identical attributes rather than in terms of how childhood experiences may influence later parental behaviour. The very limited available evidence suggests there may be links between childhood experiences and parenting without parenting behaviours being the same in succeeding generations. Further research is required to examine this possiblity, to determine what form such continuities may take, and to assess the strength of such indirect intergenerational links.

Mechanisms Underlying Intergenerational Continuities

Do continuities in parenting have anything to do with experiences in childhood or is the link due to genetic factors? This issue involves two questions — (i) can early life experiences influence parental behaviour many years later, and (ii) if they can, do such experiences in fact account for the association.

To answer the first question, it is necessary to turn to animal studies. There is evidence that, under certain circumstances, environmental influences may have effects which are 'transmitted' over several successive generations. Thus, Denenberg and Rosenberg (1967) showed that handling or stressing a pregnant rat made her more tractable and also had a similar effect on her offspring. The effects of such experiences could still be demonstrated several generations later. Direct evidence on parenting behaviour is provided by primate studies. Harlow and his colleagues (Harlow, 1958; Harlow and Harlow, 1965, 1969) have reared infant rhesus monkeys in conditions of total social isolation. Follow-up into adolescence and adult life showed that these isolated monkeys were sexually incompetent in that they failed to show normal mating behaviour (Harlow, 1965). Furthermore, those females who eventually were impregnated successfully exhibited grossly abnormal mothering behaviour (Seay *et al.*, 1964; Arling and Harlow,

1967). They generally failed to nurse their babies, had less contact with them and more often rejected them compared with non-isolated monkeys. Some of the isolated monkeys were indifferent to their offspring and some were violent and physically abusive to the extent that the infants were killed. None were adequate mothers to their first offspring. Monkeys reared with peers but without mothers also showed inadequate sexual adjustment and, possibly, inadequate mothering although the impairments were less severe than those of the isolated monkeys (Chamove *et al.*, 1973). Other workers have also found that sexual and maternal behaviour is seriously impaired in rhesus monkeys subjected to total social isolation in early life (Mason, 1960; Missakian, 1969). The effects in chimpanzees appear to be similar, although possibly less marked (Rogers and Davenport, 1969; Turner *et al.*, 1969).

The results leave no doubt that seriously adverse experiences in early life can have devastating effects on later parental behaviour. On the other hand, it is important to bear in mind that the variables affecting monkey development may not have the same importance in humans. Furthermore, the monkey experiences were of a kind and severity rarely, if ever, experienced by humans. Perhaps a closer human parallel would be the monkey offspring reared by the isolated mothers who were indifferent and brutal towards them. Studies have shown that their social behaviour is nearer normal than that of the isolated monkeys but both as infants and juveniles they were exceptionally violent (Sackett and Ruppenthal, 1973). Their behaviour as adults has yet to be studied.

The second question — whether childhood experiences in humans in fact account for intergenerational continuities in parental behaviour — is much more difficult to answer. Clearly they could account for the findings but equally (unlike the animal experiments) genetic factors could also determine intergenerational transmission. This issue might be partly resolved by a consideration of how genetic influences might operate. It seems implausible that parenting behaviour as such would be inherited. Rather, it is more likely that genetic influences would operate via personality variables or through the presence of mental disorder. There is good evidence from twin and adoptee studies that both are strongly influenced by genetic factors, although environmental influences are also important (Shields, 1973, 1976). So the question is whether the association between childhood experiences and parental behaviour is explicable in terms of personality attributes or psychiatric abnormalities.

The Midtown study (Langner and Michael, 1963) examined this point for divorce and separation. It was found that 'broken homes' were much more strongly associated with marital breakdown a generation later than with psychiatric disorder. In fact, there was no significant association between a 'broken home' and mental disorder once marital breakdown had been taken into account. Gurin *et al.*

(1960) also found no association between a broken home in childhood and adult mental disorder. Illsley and Thompson (1961) showed that the link between coming from a broken home and having an illegitimate child was not explicable in terms of the personality variable 'neuroticism'. So far as the data go, they suggest that the intergenerational continuities in these aspects of parental behaviour cannot be accounted for by either personality variables or mental disorder. Unfortunately, however, none of the studies has controlled for the type of psychiatric disorder. This is a serious omission as different types of psychiatric disorder have quite different associations with marital breakdown. Marital disharmony and disruptions are strongly associated with personality disorders and psychopathy but not to the same extent with neuroses, depression or the psychoses (Blacker, 1958; Robins, 1966; Rutter, 1966, 1971b).

With regard to neonatal care, Frommer and O'Shea (1973a) showed that the mothers who had been separated from their parents in childhood were much more likely to be depressed than were the control mothers. Unfortunately, the data were not analysed in such a way as to determine if this accounted for the association with infant problems. However, other studies (Weissman *et al.*, 1972) have shown that many depressed women have problems caring for their children.

Of all the parenting behaviours studied, child-battering shows much the strongest association with mental disorder. In their systematic study, Smith *et al.* (1973) found that some two-thirds to three-quarters of the battering parents had a personality disorder compared with only one in seven of the controls. More of the battering mothers showed neurotic disorder and more had high neuroticism scores. Also, as in the Oliver *et al.* (1974) study, many of the battering parents had criminal records. The results are in keeping with those of other studies. Regrettably none of the investigations presents data in a form which allows a decision as to whether personality disorder accounts for the associations with childhood experiences. Nevertheless, it seems reasonable to suppose that it might because, (a) battering and personality disorder are strongly associated; (b) antisocial disorder in childhood frequently leads on to psychopathy in adult life (Robins, 1966); and (c) marital discord and disharmony are strongly associated with antisocial problems in middle childhood and adolescence (Rutter, 1971b). In short, it is probable that the intergenerational continuities in many cases of child-battering are largely explicable by personality disorder whereas the continuities with respect to other parenting behaviours are less likely to be so.

So far as child-battering is concerned, assessments of the genetic component depend very much on the evidence concerning hereditary influences on personality disorder. This is discussed in Chapter 8, with the conclusion that both genetic and environmental influences play an important part. Evidence is lacking on the relative importance of nature and nurture in the genesis of the particular type of personality which gives rise to violent assault on children. Variations in parenting behaviours which are *un*associated with either mental disorder or personality characteristics are probably less influenced by genetic factors, although the matter has not been investigated directly. One study (Faust, 1974) suggested that the variance in attitudes to marriage and social advancement was not much influenced by genetic factors. However, parenting skills and capacities could be inherited as such and, in the absence of direct evidence, any conclusion must be very tentative.

Different issues arise with respect to heredity and family size. Berent (1953) approached the problem by comparing intergenerational continuities in those who did and those who did not practise birth control. He found that the continuities were similar in both. He argued that continuities in the 'non-controllors' suggested that human fertility is hereditary in the biological sense of the word. On the other hand, the similar findings for the family planners suggested that family building habits may be inherited socially. The results of his research are in keeping with this view but by no means prove it. Also, the findings still leave open the question of how psycho-social, religious or economic factors influence family size. The literature on this topic is large but inconclusive on the relative importance of different variables in determining fertility and almost totally non-contributory on how these variables might influence intergenerational continuities and discontinuities (Hawthorne, 1970; Rainwater, 1965; Busfield and Hawthorne, 1971; Glass and Grebenik, 1954; Busfield, 1972). Family size is a function of many factors including the length of the family building period, fecundity, the pattern of sexual intercourse, the use of birth control, the use of induced abortions and family size preferences. As the same variable may have differing effects on each of these factors the resulting pattern is complex. For example, high social class is associated with greater use of birth control and hence smaller families, but also with less financial restraints on family building and hence larger family size. In view of the lack of data directly relevant to intergenerational continuities little is to be gained by speculating on how the various mechanisms might operate.

In summary, no firm conclusions are possible on how far genetic factors account for the intergenerational continuities in parenting behaviour. Although heredity undoubtedly plays some part it seems clear that genetic influences do not provide a sufficient explanation. Thus, it is necessary to go on to consider how environmental factors might exert an influence.

The first issue here is which types of childhood experience are associated with parenting behaviour. With extramarital conception, marriage breakdown and problems in neonatal care, the main associations have been with parental divorce or separation during the individual's childhood. Loss of a parent through death appears to be much less important. The findings parallel those on 'broken homes' and antisocial disorders in childhood. In both cases, the crucial issue seems to be the discord and disharmony in the childhood home rather than the absence of one parent as such. Not having two parents may play a small part, but having two who fight and quarrel seems more important. The same applies to child-battering except that the childhood experiences are usually reported as much more seriously abnormal, with frank rejection and violence occurring in many cases. Again, parental death seems not to be very important. Nor is institutional rearing a common feature in the background of parents who abuse their children. It may be suggested that the damage is due more to cruel parenting than to lack of good parenting.

A variety of possible mechanisms might account for these findings. Regarding the associations between a 'broken home' in childhood and extra-marital conception or divorce and separation it could be suggested that the association merely reflects particular values. In short, those who are themselves illegitimate may regard the conception of children outside marriage as perfectly acceptable. Similarly, those individuals who saw their mother and father separate or divorce may not have any more marital difficulties than other people but may be more likely to respond to such difficulties by separation or divorce, following the model set by their parents. On the whole, the evidence is against this being the main explanation. Firstly, parental divorce or separation appears to be associated with a higher rate of marital difficulties as well as a higher rate of marriage breakdown. Secondly, the association applies not only to extra-marital conception and divorce or separation but also to teenage marriage, lack of spacing between pregnancies and problems in the care of infants.

With child-battering, it might be argued that individuals who experience violence in their own childhood have learned an inappropriate pattern of parenting. This may play a part in the genesis of child abuse but it should be noted that rejection and lack of affection are commoner than beatings and violence. Probably it is at least as much a question of *not* learning an appropriate pattern of parenting as it is of learning an inappropriate pattern.

That raises the basic question as to what are parenting skills and how are they learned. Many views are available on this topic but facts are hard to come by (see review by Blurton-Jones, 1974). Rutter (1974b) has summarized prevailing opinions in suggesting that parenting involves the existence of emotional bonds and relationships with the child; the presence of a secure base from which the child can explore and to which he may return at times of distress; the availability of models of behaviour and of attitudes; the provision of life experiences for the child; discipline and the shaping of behaviour; and the establishment of a communication network by which the child can set standards, establish norms, develop experiences and let his ideas grow. Studies of children subjected to various forms of privations and deprivations (Rutter, 1972a) suggest that a child's ability to form good deep interpersonal relationships in adulthood may be based in part on his having formed bonds with other people in the first three years of life. The nature and type of his social interactions in childhood are also affected by the quality of the personal relationships he experiences at home. Experimental evidence suggests that adult models help determine how the child behaves and the type of identifications he achieves (Bandura, 1969). Attitudes and behaviour are also shaped by influences outside the home and the effects of school in this connection can be traced into adult life (Newcomb, 1963). Furthermore, links between personal experiences and parenting must also take into account the social context. Finally, there is increasing evidence that parental behaviour is determined by an infant's own characteristics as well as by his parents' attributes and experiences (Bell, 1968, 1971, and 1973). Thus, physically abused children include an unusually high proportion of prematurely born infants (Skinner and Castle, 1969; Oliver *et al.*, 1974). Studies by Klaus, Kennell and Leiderman (Klaus *et al.*, 1972; Kennell *et al.*, 1974; Leifer *et al.*, 1972; Leiderman and Seashore, 1975) have shown that the lack of contact between mothers and their premature babies in intensive care can interfere with the development of mothering. Contact in the neonatal period is not 'critical' in that mothering usually goes on to develop normally but, depending on subsequent circumstances, events in the neonatal period may set in motion a train of events which leads to impaired family interaction.

It is evident that we have very little secure knowledge on how parenting behaviours are acquired and even less knowledge on how they are transmitted across succeeding generations. This is a topic of very considerable importance and one which greatly needs further research.

Modification of Parental Behaviour

A final issue is the question of whether parenting behaviour is modifiable. This has important implications for the feasibility of breaking intergenerational cycles of maladaptive parenting (as for example with child-battering) through direct attempts to alter how parents deal with their children. Evidence on this issue comes from three sources: (i) variations in parenting behaviour with different children in the same family; (ii) therapeutic attempts to alter parental behaviour; and (iii) animal studies.

Interview studies have indicated that parents talk and interact more with their first born, are more directive and pressuring but also are more anxious, restrictive and punitive (Lasko, 1954; Clausen, 1966). With their second child they tend to be more relaxed, more consistent, and less punitive. An experimental study has also shown that mothers are signficantly more interfering, extreme and inconsistent with their first born than with their later born (Hilton, 1967). Interestingly, it has been noted that rhesus monkey mothers also stroke and pet their first born infants more than they do later offspring (Mitchell and Schroers, 1973). Although the studies have some limitations, the results all indicate that parents can and do change their ways of bringing up children. However, it is important to note that the change in parenting with later children is apparently *not* accompanied by altered behaviour to the first child. It seems that although parenting behaviours are readily modifiable in terms of interaction with a new child, patterns already established with an existing child do not change so easily.

A variety of studies have also shown that parenting behaviours are much influenced by child variables (Bell, 1968, 1971, 1973). This has been evident from observational studies, from interviews and questionnaire measures of how parents behave towards a congenitally handicapped child and more recently by experimental studies in which children's behaviour is systematically manipulated. So far the studies are few and variable in quality, but the evidence clearly indicates that parent-child interaction is reciprocal, and that the role of the child is an important variable. It should be added that parent-child interaction is also influenced by the family situation as a whole and, in particular, by the quality and type of relationship between the child's father and mother.

There are very few therapeutic studies which have directly investigated how far different types of maladaptive parental behaviours are modifiable. Studies of case-work interventions have mainly produced negative findings (Mullen *et al.*, 1972) but the goals and methods have usually been ill-defined and poorly thought-out. The study by Reid and Shyne (1969) is an exception in terms of its careful planning, systematic methodology and demonstrated benefit. They found that brief, focussed, problem-oriented casework could be effective in improving the family functioning of individuals with marital or parent-child problems. The results of marital therapy (Gurman, 1973) and of family therapy (Wells *et al.*, 1972) remain uncertain. Although there is some indication of their effectiveness there is no evidence on whether they alter parenting behaviours as such. The systematic evaluations of family interventions using behaviour modification techniques imply that parental behaviours can be changed (Alexander and Parsons, 1973; Patterson and Reid, 1973) but the results are not presented in a form which allows any estimate of the degree of change in parenting (as distinct from changes in children's problems). Although there have been a variety of endeavours designed to help battering-parents alter their behaviour, no systematic evaluations are available as yet (Kempe and Helfer, 1972).

It is only possible to conclude that the efficacy of treatments designed to improve parenting functions remains unknown. There are indications that maladaptive parenting behaviours may be modified but no reliable evidence is available on the extent to which this is possible. Furthermore, it remains uncertain how far the improvements have been limited by inadequacies in the treatments used and how far by the immutability of parental behaviour. Animal studies are of some assistance in this connection. The profound disturbances in sexual and maternal behaviour produced by social isolation of rhesus monkeys in infancy have already been described. Several studies have now investigated the extent to which the disturbances and deficiencies are reversible. In ordinary circumstances it is evident that the behavioural abnormalities are remarkably resistant to reversal and are not appreciably influenced by social interactions with normal adult monkeys. However, it does seem that appropriate interactions with infant or juvenile monkeys may serve to modify the deviant behaviours. Some of the isolated monkeys who initially responded to their first infants by indifference or rejection seemingly became somewhat more responsive later following their infants' overtures. Moreover, those who became more maternal during the post-partum period proved to be much better mothers of their second and subsequent babies (Harlow and Suomi, 1971). If no improvement occurred during the first post-partum period, the mothers were just as abusive of their subsequent offspring. Also, the rehabilitation applied only to maternal behaviour; sexual behaviour remained just as inappropriate.

These findings led investigators to determine how far systematic attempts at rehabilitation after the isolation in infancy, but before maturity, could be successful. Suomi (1973) showed that exposure to surrogate-mothers and interactions with fellow isolates led to some improvements in behaviour but failed to lead to adequate play behaviour or social responsiveness. On the other hand, interaction with younger socially normal monkeys during the immediate post-isolation period did lead to both play and sophisticated social behaviours (Suomi and Harlow, 1972). Apparently normal social behaviour was evident on follow-up to adolescence (Suomi *et al.*, 1974; Novak and Harlow, 1975) but it is still not known whether this improvement means that later sexual and maternal behaviours will also be normal. Missakian (1972) followed the same procedure with adult male monkeys. She found that social interaction with younger monkeys improved social and sexual responses in two out of the three monkeys studied.

It is too early to be sure how far such seriously disordered parenting functions can be improved but the studies to date are encouraging. It seems that marked improvements in social behaviour are readily obtainable if corrective measures are introduced after total isolation in infancy but still during the period of early development. If corrective measures are left until maturity, changes for the better are still possible but they are brought about less readily and they are less complete.

CONCLUSIONS

Patterns of parenting are much influenced by socio-cultural factors, as indicated by the marked changes which have taken place in recent years in age of marriage, size of family, proportion of illegitimate children and frequency of divorce. However, at least with some of the abnormalities in parenting behaviour, it is apparent that how people behave towards their children is influenced by their own experiences in earlier life. Distortions of parenting which arise through disadvantages in childhood are not immutable although we do not yet know how far they can be altered in adult life or what means are required to aid better parenting.

9 Multiple Problem Families

The characteristics, frequency, correlates and continuities of various forms of disadvantage have been considered in previous chapters. In each case the focus has been on one particular type of disadvantage or problem, although the associations with other forms of disadvantage have also been discussed. Many varieties of disadvantage are interrelated (see below) and where there is multiple disadvantage the situation is more serious. In this chapter attention is specifically given to families showing multiple problems.

THE CONCEPT OF 'PROBLEM FAMILIES'

Since Booth's surveys of life in London at the end of the last century (Booth, 1902–3), there has been a widespread interest in 'problem families'. Booth, himself, was primarily concerned with what he termed the 'submerged tenth' of the population who lived in poverty amidst appalling social circumstances in the centre of industrial cities — conditions which followed in the wake of the industrial revolution. However, during the last seventy years the emphasis has tended to shift from social conditions to personal problems. Lidbetter (1933) stressed the extent to which social dependency ran in families; the Wood Committee (1929) saw the matter in terms of multiple social problems in the large families of mentally retarded parents; and Blacker (1952) laid most weight on a failure to cope with life's demands and especially on child neglect. He summarized the five commonly recognized features of 'problem families' as mental subnormality, temperamental instability, ineducability, a squalid home and the presence of numerous children (Blacker, 1952), although he was careful to point out that the factors necessarily varied according to the definitions of 'problem family' which had been employed by different writers. Since Blacker's surveys, the emphasis has continued to be placed on social inadequacy and failures in parenting. In practice, 'problem families' have usually been selected on the basis of contact with multiple social agencies. Thus, Wilson (1962) obtained her cases from families referred by local authority services to the Medical Officer of Health because of evidence of child neglect, and restricted her sample to those of families who showed 'performance-inadequacy'. Tonge *et al.* (1975) used a definition based on the number of social agencies involved with the family. Other studies (e.g. Wright, 1955; Scott, 1958; Philp, 1963; Polansky *et al.*, 1972) have followed rather similar approaches.

There have been several reviews of studies of 'problem families' defined in this way (Philp and Timms, 1957; Schlesinger, 1963). They show that the families generally show several of the following attributes: large family size; low social status; low income; poor housing conditions; criminality; occupational instability; poor physical and mental health; marital problems; child neglect; and social isolation. The implication is that social disadvantages and disturbed family relationships often go together. However, as Holman (1974b) has pointed out, the findings are to a considerable extent tautological and the concept of a distinct problem-family life style, caused by defective relationships and expressed in psychological abnormalities, is open to serious objection.

If surveys are made of mentally retarded persons (as by the Wood Committee, 1929) then, of course, the 'social problem group' will be found to be mentally retarded. If the criteria include poverty (as in Lidbetter's survey, 1933) then 'problem families' will turn out to be poor and of low social status. If child neglect forms part of the definition (as in Wilson's investigation, 1962), then it is not surprising to find that many of the children are delinquent or have other problems. If families whose difficulties stem from social circumstances beyond their control are excluded (as in Blacker's surveys, 1952), then personal inadequacies will necessarily appear more prominent. To a considerable extent, the findings of different studies (and the differences between investigations) are simply a function of how the groups have been defined, and therefore warrant little serious attention.

It is important to recognize that a trouble and the receipt of social (or other) care for the trouble are by no means synonymous. Contact with social agencies comes about not only by virtue of the existence of some 'problem' but also through a family's inability to cope with that problem. The failure to cope may stem either from additional social burdens or from personal inadequacies or from both. Thus, virtually all studies of families who have made contact with multiple social agencies show that they tend to be of low socio-economic status. But this seems not to be the case if epidemiological methods (independent of service contact) are used to select families with multiple psychiatric, educational, marital and deliquency problems (Mazer, 1972). Similarly, Langner *et al.* (1969) found that American families on welfare had more marital difficulties, and included more mothers with emotional disturbance than did families with a low income but not on welfare.

Differences will also follow from the nature of service contact used to define 'problem families'. For example, both Brown *et al.* (1975) and Rutter (1976) have shown that working class women are less likely than middle class women to contact *medical* agencies for psychiatric problems. On the other hand, within groups of families with psychiatric disorders, working class people are more likely to have contacted *social* agencies (Rutter, Quinton and Yule, 1976). Families' social circumstances may also influence the pattern of associations found. For example, in one study, depression among women living in small towns was *not* associated with low social status but *was* associated with disturbed personal relationships. In contrast, depression among women living in an inner city area *was* associated with low social status but was *not* strongly associated with relationship problems (Rutter and Quinton, 1975). When social disadvantage is uncommon, personal causes of psychiatric disorders are likely to predominate, whereas when social disadvantage and stresses are widespread these will more often play a part in the genesis of emotional disturbance.

For all these reasons, it is unjustifiable to discuss 'problem families' as if they were a homogeneous group separate from the general population. They are not. Nevertheless, there are a multitude of reasons why it is important to consider families who suffer from the combination of several disadvantages or problems. Their burdens will necessarily be more severe than those who suffer from only one trouble and it is likely that their needs for services will be correspondingly greater. It is also possible that the extent of intergenerational continuities or the mechanisms underlying such continuities may be different in families with multiple problems.

OVERLAP BETWEEN PROBLEMS

Before considering continuities, it is necessary to examine the extent to which there is overlap between various different types of problem. It is also essential to estimate the proportion of families who suffer from multiple problems, however defined. Several different issues are involved. First, there is the question of how far families with one social disadvantage also tend to suffer from others. Wedge and Prosser (1973) brought together the National Child Development Study findings on this point. Twenty three per cent of eleven-year-old children came from a one-parent or large family (five or more children); the same proportion suffered from bad housing; and fourteen per cent lived in a low income household. If there was no overlap between these social burdens some 7½ children per 1000 would be expected to have all three forms of disadvantage. In fact, 62 children per 1000 did so — an eight fold increase. In short, there was a very marked overlap between different forms of social disadvantage. Of course, this is not surprising as one type of disadvantage tends to increase the likelihood of others in very direct and predictable ways. As discussed in other chapters, single-parent families are at a serious economic disadvantage because in many cases the lone parent has to remain at home to care for the children and is therefore unable to work. The per capita income in large families is likely to be lower simply because the same number of wage earners have more people for whom to provide. The low income family is unlikely to be able to secure good housing from its own resources so that unless their disadvantage in this respect is made good through subsidized provision, the link between low income and poor housing is inevitable.

For obvious reasons, families with all three social burdens (as defined above) also tended to have more difficulties of other kinds. One in twelve of the fathers in these multiply disadvantaged families was unemployed for the whole of the previous year, compared with one in three thousand in the rest of the general population, and one in nine of the multiply disadvantaged children had been in care at some stage compared with one in a hundred of the other children. Once again this demonstrates a marked overlap between problems. But, to put the picture into perspective it is necessary to note that the same figures indicate that in spite of multiple social burdens, 90 per cent of the children had *never* been in care and two thirds of the fathers had not been unemployed at all during the past year.

These statistics all refer to social circumstances of various kinds and the same considerations must be applied to the more personal troubles of psychiatric disorder, intellectual impairment, educational backwardness and chronic physical handicap. Overlap has to be examined both in terms of the likelihood of one individual having several problems and also the likelihood of one family containing several individuals with these personal troubles. The Isle of Wight survey of nine to eleven-year-old children produced data on the first point (Rutter, Tizard and Whitmore, 1970). In this age group, 2.3 children per 1000 had all four handicapping conditions, but 161.4 per 1000 had one or other of the conditions. Of the children with handicaps, three quarters had only one handicapping condition. The overlap is greater than would be expected by chance but not so marked as with the social burdens already discussed. Thus, 78.9 per 1000 children showed educational backwardness and 53.8 per 1000 exhibited psychiatric disorder. Ten per 1000 had both troubles, a rate just over double that (4.2 per 1000) expected if there was no overlap. The findings from other studies and for other age groups (discussed elsewhere in the book for specific troubles) are generally similar. That is to say there is a significant tendency for individuals with one type of problem also to have other problems. Nevertheless, a relatively high proportion have only one isolated trouble.

The next issue is how far the individuals with these various personal troubles are the same people who suffer from disadvantageous social circumstances. Here the overlap depends to a considerable extent on the particular trouble considered. For example, Wedge and Prosser (1973) found that 58 per cent of the multiply disadvantaged children in their sample had poor reading attainment compared with 21 per cent of other children; and in the Isle of Wight study (Rutter, Tizard and Whitmore, 1970) intellectually retarded children were three times as likely to share a bed and over five times as likely to have a father out of work. West and Farrington (1973) found that just over half of the recidivists in their study came from low income homes compared with only one in six of the boys without a police record. With both educational backwardness and delinquency there is a substantial overlap with social disadvantage. However, in spite of the overlap it remains true that many educationally backward or delinquent children come from homes with an adequate income and reasonable household facilities. The overlap is very far from complete. With psychiatric disorder (see Chapter 7), it is even less. Although there is some tendency for people with psychiatric conditions to come from socially disadvantaged homes, the association with disturbed interpersonal relationships is much greater than that with low income or poor housing. Furthermore, although poverty and poor housing undoubtedly put a strain on family relationships, marital discord is common in *all* strata of society (see Chapter 8). Social disorganization is only weakly linked with poor housing (Loring, 1956) and many socially dependent families show a happy family atmosphere (Wilson, 1974).

To summarize the findings so far, there is a very marked overlap between different forms of social disadvantage; there is some association between various personal troubles but the overlap is much less than with adverse social conditions; and although social disadvantage and personal troubles go together to some extent, the connections vary with the type of trouble and are never of more than moderate strength. In spite of their material disadvantages, most poor people cope well. Furthermore, both personal problems and family disturbance are often found in financially secure homes.

The last issue with respect to overlap is how frequently several individuals with problems are found in the same families. Downes' pioneering longitudinal morbidity studies from Baltimore showed that family illness rates tended to remain stable over several years and that the illness of one child often reflected the state of health of his sibs (Downes, 1945). Families in which one member had a chronic physical or psychiatric illness showed an excess of illness in other members and this excess could not be explained in terms of social conditions (Downes, 1942; Downes and Simon, 1953). Ciocco *et al.* (1954) showed that family ill-health was associated with increased contact with social agencies; and numerous more recent studies have demonstrated increased rates of emotional and behavioural problems in the children of chronically sick parents (Buck and Laughton, 1959; Kellner, 1963; Hare and Shaw, 1965a; Rutter, 1966). Other investigations have indicated a substantial overlap between marital discord, family disruption, crime and psychiatric disorder in both parents and children (West and Farrington, 1973; Rutter, 1976). In an American study of a small town, Mazer (1972) showed that in 3.9 per cent of households at least half the members had one or more of a list of 15 specified psychiatric, educational, marital or legal problems. The figure of 3.9 per cent indicated a sizeable overlap between problems (although the data do not show how far this exceeds chance). Interestingly, only 11 per cent of the multi-problem households received public welfare assistance during the five years of the study and their social class distribution did not differ from that of the general population.

Because rates are so dependent on the definitions employed, no meaningful figure can be given for the prevalence of multi-problem households. However, some estimate of the size of the group is obtainable from the data already discussed. Wedge and Prosser (1973) found that six per cent of children suffered from multiple social disadvantage (the proportion of families with multiple disadvantage will, of course, be less than this because a child-based sample is disproportionately weighted in terms of large families). Mazer's (1972) study of an American small town showed that 4 per cent of households had multiple personal troubles. Other studies have not presented their data in a comparable form but their findings are in keeping with the conclusion that *at least one in twenty* families suffer from multiple problems. The proportion in inner city areas is certainly considerably in excess of this. Thus, multiple problem families are quite common in present day Britain.

However, these findings should not be confused with the figures on 'problem families' defined in terms of long-term social dependence. Blacker (1952) found that the rate of administratively defined 'problem families' was between 1.2 and 6.2 per 1000 – a figure which includes less than one in ten of the families with multiple problems. It should be noted that Blacker's figure excluded 'social and biological casualties'. If these are added the rate is nearly doubled but it still remains below one per cent. More recently, Tonge *et al.* (1975) found a 1.7 per 1000 frequency for 'problem families'. Several possible explanations can be suggested for the marked discrepancy between the rates of families with multiple problems and the rates of 'problem families'. First, it could be that many of the problems stem from social and environmental disadvantage, and stresses which have little to do with personal inadequacies (see, for example, the chapter on economic status). Second, many families with multiple problems may cope adequately with their difficulties without recourse to services and certainly without the need for chronic dependence on services (see, for example, Mazer, 1972). Third, it is possible that for some families the period during which they suffer multiple problems may prove temporary, particularly if their life situation improves (see Parry *et al.*, 1967). Fourth, in many cases multiple personal problems may be *un*associated with the socio-economic privations which lead to various forms of welfare assistance (see, for example, Mazer, 1972; Rutter, 1975c). No adequate data exist to determine the relative importance of these (and other) explanations but there is some evidence in favour of each of them. There appears to be little value in separating off a group of 'problem families' thought to have qualitatively different problems. Some families have a few problems and some have many. In some cases poverty is associated with family instability and in some it is not (Miller, 1964). Some families with many problems cope whereas others do not. Further study of what enables some seriously disadvantaged families to cope with life's demands would be worthwhile. The scanty evidence already available suggests that the reasons will include both social and personal factors. Even the 'hard core' group of mothers appearing before a magistrate's court for serious child neglect are often capable of change. Sheridan (1959), in a follow-up study of mothers who had received at least 4 months residential care several years earlier found that two fifths were coping satisfactorily and only a quarter failed to benefit. The best results were obtained with women who had a steady and affectionate husband. Personal inadequacies and social burdens often interact. Shaw and Wright (1960) found that mentally retarded women were often able to cope with one or two children, but that some ceased to manage when the family grew larger. Knowledge on the relative importance of social disadvantages and of personal difficulties and of the interaction between the two, is necessary if the work of Family Service Units (Goldring, 1973) and of other social agencies dealing with so-called 'problem families' is to be properly planned. It would seem that improvement in social circumstances may be as important for many families as help with their personal problems and interpersonal relationships.

INTERGENERATIONAL CONTINUITIES

Various studies have noted related families among samples of multiple problem households (Tomlinson, 1946; Wofinden, 1950) and pedigrees of 'problem families' have been constructed (Lidbetter, 1933). However, the best British data on intergenerational continuities of 'problem families' are reported by Wright and Lunn (1971). They followed up most of the children from a sample of 120 administratively defined 'problem families' studied some fourteen years earlier (Wright, 1955; Parry *et al.*, 1967) and found that many of the offspring reproduced the troubles of their parents, although in all respects the second generation were better off than the first. Twenty one per cent of the married children had had contact with agencies in connection with their children's welfare, compared with 37 per cent of their parents; 4 per cent in connection with schooling as against 31 per cent of their parents; and 10 per cent regarding 'general welfare' in contrast to 15 per cent of the parents. However, these figures underestimate agency contacts in that the rate of contacts was significantly higher among the older than the younger children (although still generally less than their parents). It is also noteworthy that 59 per cent of the daughters and 52 per cent of the wives of married sons had given birth to their first child at age 19 years or younger — a pattern which augurs ill for the future of the family (see Chapter 8).

Improvements in employment were more marked. Three quarters of the sons and 84 per cent of the daughters' husbands were working full time compared with only 45 per cent of the fathers. Only 17 per cent of the fathers were in skilled work but 28 per cent of the married sons and 43 per cent of the daughters' husbands held skilled jobs. Nevertheless, in spite of the improvements in employment in the second generation, both the unemployment rate and the proportion in unskilled or semi-skilled work was well above the Sheffield average.

On the whole, the married children born into 'problem families' had more material possessions than their parents and lived under better housing conditions, but nevertheless a high proportion were overcrowded (the average person per room ratio for married children was 1.51!).

All in all, there had been a general trend toward improved circumstances in the second generation but the rate of problems in the offspring was very high and intergenerational continuity considerable. Wright and Lunn (1971) estimated that a third were already 'problem families' or had started on a course of involvement with helping agencies which was unlikely to be reversed. A further third were coping quite adequately and were unremarkable in comparison with the general population, and a middle third were functioning only precariously. Because the original 'problem families' had so many children (seven on average) Wright and Lunn suggested that the parental 'problem family' group would produce twice as many 'problem families' in the next generation. However, these estimates must be regarded as highly provisional because not all the children had been followed up, because they were seen at varying ages, and because it is uncertain how far the difficulties found in their early married life will prove to be persistent.

One interesting, and possibly important, finding to emerge from this two generation study is the contrast between the married daughters and the married sons. In general, the daughters' families were less likely to have contacts with child welfare agencies, were more likely to have adequate household furnishings and the husbands were more likely to have stable employment records. Intergenerational continuities in family problems were more marked with the sons than with the daughters of the original sample of families.

There are three main interpretations of this observation, assuming it proves to be valid. Firstly, daughters may be more able than sons to 'marry out' of the multiple problem cycle. There is some slight evidence in favour of this suggestion in that the sons tended to marry women similar in characteristics to their sisters (e.g. the rate of teenage births was similar in the daughters and the husbands' wives), but the daughters tended to marry men with fewer problems than their brothers (e.g. 16 per cent were unemployed compared with 26 per cent of the sons; and 43 per cent held skilled jobs compared with only 28 per cent of the sons).

Alternatively, boys may be more damaged than girls by being raised in a 'problem family' household. Thus, Wolkind and Rutter (1973) found that boys who experienced periods of short-term care as a result of family discord and disruption were more likely to show psychiatric problems than were girls subjected to the same experiences. Rutter (1970a) reviewed studies on sex differences in response to stress and found evidence that, in general, boys are more likely to suffer from the effects of psycho-social disturbance. On the other hand, there are exceptions (girls seem more affected by a poor quality institutional upbringing — Wolkind, 1974a) and the findings all refer to the effects in childhood. Whether there are sex differences in terms of long-term sequelae (e.g. parenting behaviour) remains quite unknown.

Thirdly, it is possible that the characteristics of the fathers may be more influential than those of the mothers in determining 'problem-family' status. Philp (1963) believed that the wives among his 129 multiple-problem families tended to be the more effective marital partners; and Tonge *et al.* (1975) concluded that a paternal personality disorder appeared to be the most important determinant of family maladjustment. It could be that the role of men is crucial in determining family disorganization but the question has been little explored and there are no satisfactory data regarding the relative influence of men and women.

POSSIBLE MECHANISMS OF INTERGENERATIONAL TRANSMISSION

Some children in families with multiple problems develop quite normally (Lewis, 1954). If appropriate preventive or remedial action is to be taken to help members of these families it is important to understand the mechanisms by which continuities in troubles occur. It is even more necessary to identify the factors which allow children to break out of the cycles of disadvantage. Thus, in the National Child Development Study, nearly half of the children with multiple social disadvantages (see above) were well adjusted and the same proportion had satisfactory attainments in maths, although problems in both areas were more common than in the general population (Wedge and Prosser, 1973). Indeed, nine per cent of the socially disadvantaged children had above average attainments in maths and seven per cent had superior reading attainments. Although no detailed findings were presented, Wedge and Prosser reported that within the disadvantaged group much the same set of factors was associated with scholastic attainment as in the general population. Similarly, Tonge *et al.* (1975) in their study of 33 administratively defined 'problem families', found that children with psychiatric disorder differed from other children in that more had fathers with personality disorder or physical illness, more had parents with emotional disturbance, more were illegitimate, more came from low social status homes and more experienced marital disharmony. In short, within the 'problem families' child psychiatric disorder was associated with the same variables that relate to disorder in the population as a whole. So far as scholastic attainment and psychiatric disorder are concerned, the mechanisms in families with multiple problems appear just the same as in any other group of families.

However, this may not be entirely so with respect to delinquency. Tonge *et al.* (1975) found that family size was the only variable related to delinquency in their 'problem family' group and that the rate of crime was higher than in the control group only with respect to children over 18 years of age. Wilson (1974) also found that, unlike in the general population, delinquency was *un*related to the quality of family relationships. 'Happy' homes produced almost as many delinquents as 'unhappy' homes. On the other hand, the degree of parental supervision and control of the children was strongly related to delinquency. Wilson argued that middle class child-control behaviour is not operable in slum conditions, and that so far as delinquency prevention is concerned, it is strict rules strictly enforced that are needed in the milieu of poverty. More evidence is needed before this conclusion can be accepted, but it does seem that in severely disadvantaged families the factors associated with delinquency may not be quite the same as those operating in the population as a whole.

Even less is known about the factors determining long-term continuities and discontinuities. Several writers have seen disorders of personality as the main factor in intergenerational continuities, both as causes and consequences of child neglect (see, for example, Bowlby, 1951; Wofinden, 1950; Philp, 1963; Polansky *et al.*, 1972; Tonge *et al.*, 1975). Tonge *et al.* (1975) found that fathers with a personality disorder were more likely than other fathers of 'problem families' to have come from large families, to have had poor relationships with their parents and to have experienced separation. In the second generation, as already noted, paternal personality disorder was found to be associated with psychiatric disorder in the children. Certainly, in this extreme group of families with severe and prolonged multiple problems associated with social dependency, personality disorders appear to be both frequent and generative of other difficulties. However, the nature of the chain of causal factors remains ill-understood, and it is dubious whether personality disorders have quite the same importance within the broader range of families with multiple problems, many of whom are not dependent on social services.

CONCLUSIONS

'Problem families' do not constitute a group which is qualitatively different from families in the general population. Nevertheless, families with multiple social disadvantages and/or personal problems do constitute a cause for concern in terms not only of current suffering but also in terms of troubles which persist into the next generation.

Although, even in the most disadvantaged families, some children develop quite normally, the rate of educational, psychiatric, occupational and family problems in the second generation is well above the national average. There may be differences between these families and the general population in the mechanisms involved in intergenerational continuities in troubles (perhaps especially with respect to delinquency) but on the whole the factors which are important in other families are also important in those with multiple problems. Both social disadvantages, personal difficulties, biological impairment (and doubtless genetic factors too, although they have not been studied) all play a part. As with any other group, their relative importance varies both according to the type of trouble considered and according to individual family circumstances. Just as stereotypes of '*the* problem family' are to be distrusted, so are package remedies based on notions of a homogeneous group.

10 Ethnic Minorities in Britain

Britain is not culturally homogeneous. It includes people of many ethnic origins, the great majority of whom are white-skinned. Black* people form only a small proportion of the country's population although their absolute numbers are growing. A recent report (Lomas, 1973) indicated that there were 1,385,600 black people in Britain in 1971, compared with 947,120 in 1966. Much of the five-year increase is due to births occurring in Britain during this time. Approximately 60 per cent of the black population in 1971 were born abroad (first generation immigrants) and approximately 40 per cent were born in Britain to immigrant parents (second generation immigrants).

To a considerable extent the findings on issues described in other chapters are relevant for ethnic minority groups. At the same time there are differences. Moreover, immigrant populations present an opportunity to determine how various social, psychological and economic forces lead individuals into, or protect them from, disadvantage and deprivation. Some processes are related to the fact of immigration (with the upheaval and change in culture implied), some to skin colour (and the associated prejudice and discrimination) and some to circumstances shared with other groups in the population. So far as possible, these are differentiated in this chapter. Distinctions are also drawn between characteristics of the people themselves (in terms of their social background, life experiences, etc.) and the consequences of their being placed in a disadvantaged position by the majority white population. Consideration is given to the extent to which disadvantage may be continued into succeeding generations, although here many inferences have to be drawn as few facts are available.

Because of their limitations, little use can be made of official data on black people in this country. Census data give no clear indications of ethnicity and no distinction is possible between intra-racial and inter-racial unions. A further difficulty stems from unsatisfactory definitions of 'immigrant'. The Department of Education and Science, for example, defined immigrant children as those born abroad to immigrant parents together with those born in this country to foreign parents resident here for less than ten years. This meant that a child

*Throughout this chapter, the word 'black' will be used to describe people of both Afro-Caribbean and Asian descent, when their skin colour is discussed. It is recognized that the Asian communities do not refer to themselves as 'black' but the word 'coloured' has come to have offensive overtones for some minority groups and for stylistic reasons it is desirable on occasions to have one inclusive word.

born in the West Indies who came to England as an infant remained an 'immigrant' for life, whereas a child born in Britain to parents who came to this country six years earlier ceased to be an 'immigrant' by the time of school entry. This definition also prevented any comparison according to ethnic origin or between first and second generation immigrants.

This chapter focuses on the situation of persons of West Indian or Asian origin living in Britain. Some mention is made of American research, but the history and social climate surrounding black-white relations are so different in the two nations that direct parallels can seldom be drawn. The limited evidence on life styles of black families in the USA and in Great Britain suggests somewhat different patterns (Bell, 1969).

PHYSICAL HEALTH

As Rose *et al.* (1969) point out, there are two main reasons why one might expect the pattern of physical illnesses in immigrants to differ from that in the native population. First, they may bring with them illnesses from the country from which they came, although immigration policies may also prevent the admission of sick or physically handicapped persons. Second, they may be at particular risk for diseases typically prevalent in the UK Tuberculosis, which has a high prevalence in Asia and in Asian migrants (Thomas, 1968) falls into the first category, although screening and spread-prevention programmes have drastically reduced its incidence in Britain (DHSS, 1969). Venereal disease, too, has a high incidence amongst immigrants but, unlike tuberculosis, it is largely contracted after arrival in this country (Ministry of Health, 1968). Its prevalence in immigrant populations relative to the total population, is now declining (Willcox, 1966). Oppé (1964) has indicated that Jamaican women are particularly prone to rubella because of their lack of natural immunization.

Respiratory infections, which are common in West Indian children (Oppé, 1964) may be aggravated by poor living conditions and by the high humidity associated with the paraffin heaters used in many homes (Dolton, 1968). Gans (1966) noted that some children of immigrants suffer from diet deficiency disorders — such as anaemia and rickets — which are now otherwise virtually extinct in Britain. Other West Indian children presented a particular syndrome of withdrawal and non-communication, apparently associated with adversities in their upbringing (Prince, 1967). Further data on the health and development of West Indian children are available from a paediatric and social study of 101 one-year-olds in Paddington (Hood *et al.*, 1970). It was found that, relative to a control group of non-West Indian children of the same age and from the same area, the study sample were more prone to a variety of minor physical disorders (42 per cent compared with 15 per cent) and also more were admitted to hospital (15 per cent compared with 2 per cent). Pollak (1972) found more anaemia and more burns in 3-year-old West Indian children compared with indigenous English children, but the hospital admission rate in the two groups was similar. The West Indian group in the Paddington study did not suffer excessive morbidity during their first year of life, nor did they appear to have poor diets or low levels of physical care. Department of Education and Science figures (1974) suggest that the proportion of West Indian children in schools for the deaf is exceptionally high. Without epidemiological and clinical data it is not possible to rule out selection biases entirely, but it seems very likely that for some reason (at present unknown) West Indian children are more prone to deafness. Research is needed to investigate the problem.

The health surveys of both adults and children in ethnic minority groups suggest that most individuals are healthy, although lack of immunity in some immigrants and poor living conditions in others have been associated with an increased rate of certain infectious diseases and, occasionally, dietary disorders. As Stroud (1965) commented, 'Nearly all the medical problems of immigrant communities are related to environmental factors. There are many diseases and injuries to which the children of immigrant people are particularly liable, and it is essential that doctors working in immigrant areas should be aware not only of these conditions but also of their aetiologies, for one factor these diseases and injuries have in common is their preventability.' The future incidence of physical illness among ethnic minority groups will be greatly influenced by the physical conditions in which they live and bring up their children.

PARENTING AND CHILD CARE BEHAVIOUR

Family Size and Composition

Patterns of family composition may well vary by ethnic group but there is little evidence on this point. Rutter *et al.* (1975a) reported a very significant difference in family size between West Indian and indigenous groups in a study of 10-year-old children in London: 59 per cent of the West Indian and 21 per cent of the indigenous children came from families with five or more children. The Inner London Education Authority survey (Community Relations Commission, 1973) and the Pollak study (1972) also showed that West Indian children were twice as likely to come from large families. Despite the wide prevalence of fatherless families in the West Indies (Oakley, 1968), there is evidence that the situation is somewhat different for West Indians living in this country. Rutter *et al.* (1975a) found that West Indian 10-year-olds living in London were slightly more likely than indigenous children to come from one-parent families (19 per cent versus 8 per cent) but the difference fell short of statistical significance. Pollak (1972) found that less than 2 per cent of three-year-old West Indian children in her London study were being brought up by a mother living alone. Few immigrant families appear to belong to extended family networks in this country (Rutter *et al.*, 1975a) as they do frequently in the West Indies (Oakley, 1968). This is almost inevitable for the first generation immigrants, and may not be true for subsequent generations. Further study of family patterns within different ethnic minority groups would increase understanding of many aspects of behaviour.

Physical Care

The early physical care of second generation children of West Indian origin appears to be good. Hood *et al.* (1970) found that a large proportion of a sample of West Indian one-year-olds born in Paddington had been delivered in hospital and that this was not due to high risk factors. Jones and Smith (1970) also noted that, in Commonwealth immigrants, more births took place in hospital, although this could partly be explained by age differences and high multiparity. In Hood's study, West Indian children attended health services as often as white British infants up to one year of age, and seemed well cared for by their mothers, especially when availability of basic amenities was taken into account. However, there was possibly some relative deprivation in the quality of the children's diets, although the evidence was contradictory. Pollak (1972) found no height difference between West Indian and indigenous English children at age three years, and at age 10 years Yule *et al.* (1975) found that youngsters from West Indian families were taller.

The sparse available evidence suggests little difference between immigrant and indigenous families in the quality of physical care afforded to infants.

Child-rearing Patterns

Some differences in child-rearing practices have been noted between immigrant and indigenous groups. These appear to be due in large part to different cultural traditions, values and attitudes. It has been found that West Indian children in Britain are frequently discouraged from touching and playing with objects at one year (Hood *et al.*, 1970), make less excursions, have less toys and play fewer games with parents than children of native origin at 3 years (Pollak, 1972) and are more disciplined and controlled by their parents at 10 years than are their white peers (Rutter *et al.*, 1975a). Such findings do not suggest that West Indian parents are unconcerned about their children's development but they do imply some lack of understanding of the developmental importance of play, communication and parent-child interaction in the early years. On the other hand, it seems that they usually have a high regard for the value of schooling and are keen to aid their children's education (see pp. 280–1).

A lack of emphasis on parent-child experiences in the pre-school years, the desire and necessity to increase income levels, and the non-existence of extended family networks in Britain often means that immigrant mothers go out to work and have to make alternative arrangements for the care of their children. Hood *et al.* (1970) found that three times as many West Indian as native mothers were working outside the home and Jackson (1973) claimed that two-thirds of the mothers of the 120,000 West Indian children under five years in Britain go out to work. Yudkin (1965) suggested that, compared with non-immigrants, more mothers of immigrant children worked while their children were still young. Rutter *et al.* (1975a) found that 79 per cent of the mothers of a sample of 10-year-old West Indian children had a job outside the home, compared with 53 per cent of the mothers of non-immigrant children. In many cases the services of (often illegal) childminders have been employed by mothers.

Childminding need not involve harm to the child provided there is continuity of high quality care by someone the child knows well (Yudkin and Holme, 1963). On the other hand, the quality of childminding, especially under illegal conditions, is often inadequate (Yudkin, 1967; Gregory, 1969; Jackson, 1973). Large numbers of children may be cared for in an overcrowded room in squalid conditions with little toy provision or adult attention. In these circumstances the discouragement of exploratory play behaviour and the lack of linguistic opportunities are likely to put the children at a serious disadvantage with respect to their development. The lack of good quality local authority provision for pre-school children of working mothers, and the absence of grandparents who remained behind in the West Indies, have left many parents with little alternative but recourse to illegal minders. Better pre-school provision would do much to reduce the need for unsatisfactory private arrangements. Also many of the difficulties associated with childminding stem from the overcrowded conditions in which so many West Indian families live (see below). Better housing would reduce some of the risks associated with childminding. The lack of toys, too, may often stem from economic privation. In inner London, 31 per cent of West Indian children were eligible for free school meals compared with 13 per cent of indigenous children (Community Relations Commission, 1973). However, the limited available evidence suggests that children reared by minders do *not* have more developmental retardation (Pollak, 1972) and do not show more psychiatric problems (Rutter *et al.*, 1974) than other West Indian children. This does not mean that the pattern of child care provided by minders is satisfactory but rather it implies that in many respects it is similar to that provided by the child's parents. The housing difficulties and the lack of appreciation of a very young child's need for play and conversation are a feature of upbringing in many West Indian homes (Hood *et al.*, 1970; Pollak, 1972). In short, the remedies to the problems of childminding need to be found not only in better alternative provision and in improved living conditions but also in an improved understanding of the developmental needs of children.

The child-rearing findings discussed so far all apply to families of West Indian origin. Fewer data are available on other immigrant groups. However, it is known that Hindu and Muslem religious views and attitudes to women influence child-rearing patterns in a way that may mark the Asian household as different from those of white neighbours (Ferron, 1973). James (1974) described the strong family ties of Sikh families in Britain and the constraints on children which stemmed from religious or cultural duties and rituals. Arranged marriages are still common, there are restrictions on the social life of teenagers (especially of girls) and home upbringing for girls tends to be seen as largely a preparation for marriage and motherhood. Children's questioning and exploration are actively encouraged but many children have to be bilingual because Punjabi continues to be spoken at home. Families of African origin also differ in patterns of child-rearing. Holman (1973) found that West African students were much more likely than indigenous or other immigrant groups to make use of private fostering arrangements for preschool children. Although some of these arrangements provide good quality care, private foster parents were often found to be unsuitable in Holman's study.

Admission into Care

The children of black immigrants (perhaps especially West Indian), also differ from the indigenous population in the proportion admitted into care (Fitzherbert, 1967; Yudkin, 1967). Single parenthood and an absence of extended family support make it more difficult for many West Indian families to cope on their own at times of crisis. Housing problems, and economic privation too, are liable to increase recourse to local authority care. A tradition of mothering by relatives and of fostering and informal adoption without stigma may also make it easier for West Indian parents to hand over the care of their children to others. On the basis of her survey of 120 West Indian families in London, Fitzherbert (1967) suggested that, in addition, some parents believe that providing an income is a more responsible kind of motherhood than providing personal care. It remains uncertain how far this is really the case.

Again, as with childminding, the differences seem to stem both from lack of material resources and extended family support, and also from culturally determined attitudes to child care and child development.

PSYCHIATRIC DISORDER

Since Odegaard (1932) first showed high rates of mental illness in Norwegian immigrants to the USA there has been a wide interest in the psychiatric problems associated with migration. It is now well established that, at least in Western societies, adult migrants are more likely to be admitted to hospital with psychiatric disorder than are natives (Malzberg and Lee, 1956; Kiev, 1973; Taft, 1973); the disorders often take the form of schizophrenic psychoses or paranoid reactions. Investigations in this country have tended to show the same phenomenon (Murphy, 1955; Gordon, 1965; Hemsi, 1967; Bagley, 1971). However, the implications of this finding depend very much on its meaning. In this connection both methodological and conceptual considerations are relevant.

Adults

Many of the adult studies rely on mental hospital statistics, which are subject to biases due to differences between ethnic groups both in utilization of services and in the likelihood of admission to hospital. Other things being equal, a mentally ill individual without family support is more likely to be admitted to hospital simply because there is no-one to look after him. This is the situation of many recent immigrants. Moreover, it is known that the rate and type of mental illness varies markedly by age, sex and marital status, so that any valid comparison must refer to comparable groups. This control is missing from most published hospital studies. A further requirement is accurate information on the populations from which the patient sample is drawn, so that rates may be calculated. At times when there is continuing immigration this is difficult in that census figures are necessarily out of date. As most people with milder psychiatric disorders are not admitted to hospital and many do not attend psychiatric clinics, epidemiological studies of the general population are required to obtain accurate estimates of prevalence.

Kiev (1965) conducted a six-month morbidity survey in a London general practice. The findings showed that, as judged by doctor consultations, West Indian men had a higher rate of psychiatric disorder than native English men (14½ per cent versus 8½ per cent). The rate in West Indian women was also higher than in their English counterparts, but not significantly so (21 per cent versus 17 per cent). An earlier general practice study by Pinsent (1963) found that mental disorder was twice as common in West Indian women as in English women. More recently, in an interview study of a random sample of patients of 10-year-old children in London, Rutter *et al.* (1974) found no differences between West Indian and non-immigrant adults in rates of psychiatric disorder.

The studies by Pinsent (1963) and Kiev (1965) differed from that of Rutter and his colleagues in several important respects. First, the earlier studies concerned general practice consultations so that any differences in rates of disorder found might be due to differences in willingness to consult doctors rather than to differences in disorder as such. Secondly, the Pinsent and Kiev studies referred to the situation during the few years after migration whereas the adults in the Rutter study had mostly been living in England for 10 to 20 years. Thirdly, the earlier studies will have included many single people (who tend to have higher rates of disorder) whereas the later study only included adults living with their children (and usually with their spouses).

The hospital studies of migrants are not very useful for calculating prevalence rates because of the limitations noted above. However, they are of value in indicating diagnostic differences in the disorders shown by individuals receiving psychiatric treatment. Gordon (1965) found that mixed and atypical psychoses were particularly common in West Indian immigrants. Tewfik and Okasha (1965) reported much the same, whereas Hemsi (1967) found that disorders took a similar form to those in native English adults. Copeland (1968) found that mental disorders in West African students living in this country most often took the form of schizophrenic psychoses. Bagley (1971) found an excess of schizophrenia in individuals of both Caribbean and African origin who were living in London.

In summary, it seems that the rate of psychiatric disorder in adults of West Indian origin who have been in this country for at least a decade, and who are living with their families is little, if at all, different from that of non-immigrant adults. Whether the same applies to other immigrant groups is not known. On the other hand, disorders, which may often take a paranoid form, are probably much commoner in recent migrants especially when they are living apart from their families. Studies of other immigrant groups have shown that individuals who come on their own tend to adjust less well to migration than do those who migrate with their primary or family group (Kosa, 1957; Eisenstadt, 1954).

Which factors are most important in leading to a high rate of disorder in the period following migration is not known with certainty. In other groups, selective factors in migration have been thought to play a part (Odegaard, 1932; Mezey, 1960). This is unlikely to be a major factor in Caribbean migrants in this country; Hemsi (1967) found a low incidence of psychiatric disorder prior to migration and a low rate of mental illness in the families. The breaking of friendship and kinship ties following migration is probably a more important factor. Several studies have shown that major life events or changes are important factors in the causation of neurosis and depression (Brown *et al.*, 1973a and b; Cooper and Sylph, 1973). Sainsbury (1971) showed that non-immigrants in this country tended to have an increased rate of psychiatric disorder after moving house if this involved disruption of ties. In addition, many newly-arrived migrants experience severe problems of employment and accommodation, often living in overcrowded circumstances. Both these factors appeared important precipitating factors in the disorders studied by Gordon (1965). The problems associated with disruption of ties consequent upon migration and the difficulties in settling into a new country, obtaining work and a home are all ones which become less important with time. However, the problems of racial discrimination, lack of integration into the community, and poor living conditions remain for many people. They may serve to predispose to mental disorder in some cases.

Children

Several surveys using teacher questionnaires have suggested that children of immigrant parents have rates of behavioural deviance above those found in non-immigrant children. Thus, a Schools Council study (1970), using the Stott scale, found that West Indian children showed significantly more deviance on several sub-scales; Bagley (1972), using the Rutter questionnaire, also found more behavioural deviance, as did Rutter *et al.* (1974) using the same questionnaire with 10-year-old children of West Indian parents. The higher rate of deviance applied to both restlessness and poor concentration and also to socially disapproved conduct of various kinds. There was no appreciable excess in emotional difficulties (fears, misery, and the like). Bhatnagar (1970) found no differences between West Indian children and English children using his own specially constructed adjustment scale. These findings indicate that teachers perceive more problems in children of West Indian background, but high questionnaire scores cannot be regarded as the equivalent of psychiatric disorder. Questionnaires are valuable as screening devices, but they are subject to rating biases, and cannot validly be used for individual diagnoses.

Accurate estimates of psychiatric prevalence can only be obtained from epidemiological studies of the general population using personal interview methods. Only one such study has been published (Rutter *et al.*, 1974) and that refers to 10-year-old children of West Indian parents. Both the parents and the teachers of the children were interviewed. The teacher interview assessments supported the questionnaire findings in showing that the West Indian children's behaviour at school did differ from that of non-immigrant families, but the difference between the groups was much less than on the questionnaire. The West Indian children showed more socially disapproved conduct but no more emotional disorders and no more difficulties getting along with other children. The parental interview findings, in contrast, revealed no difference between West Indian and non-immigrant children in psychiatric disorder as shown at home. The results suggested that this was not a methodological artefact but rather a true reflection of the fact that West Indian children showed more problems at school but not at home. The tendency for so many disorders in West Indian children to be present only at school was particularly marked, but it is a phenomenon found in several previous studies of non-immigrant children (Rutter, Tizard and Whitmore, 1970; Mitchell and Shepherd, 1966).

There were several possible reasons for the relatively high rate of disorders at school. First, there was migration itself. This did not seem to be an important factor in that disorders were just as marked in children of West Indian parentage born in this country. However, there were very few recent migrants in the group studied by Rutter and his colleagues. The stresses of moving from one country to another may well be more important in the period immediately after migration. Also, they may well be more critical for adolescents who leave the West Indies to join their parents in this country — a group so far not systematically studied. Second, a high proportion of West Indian children are considerably retarded in their educational attainments (see pp. 270–1) and it is known that reading retardation and disorders of conduct are strongly associated (Rutter, Tizard and Whitmore, 1970). Third, children from immigrant families tended to go to schools with characteristics such as high pupil turnover (Rutter *et al.*, 1975a) which are known to be associated with high rates of problem behaviour (Rutter *et al.*, 1975b). Fourth, there is strong evidence of racial discrimination in this country (see pp. 287–9). It is likely that children's awareness of this discrimination will be greater at school and consequently more likely to lead to problems there. Other factors shown to be related to behavioural difficulties in West Indian children are a 'broken home', being admitted into care and disturbed parent-child relationships (Rutter *et al.*, 1975a). Poor housing conditions and separation from parents as such, however, do not seem to be important in this connection (Bhatnagar, 1970; Bagley, 1972; Rutter *et al.*, 1975a).

Apart from differences between children from West Indian and from non-immigrant families in the level of psychiatric disorder as shown at school, there were differences in the pattern of disorders. Unlike native English children, West Indians with conduct disorders did not show much emotional disturbance and had few major difficulties in peer relationships (Rutter *et al.*, 1974). This, together with the situation-specificity of much behaviour suggests that disorders may be more immediately reactive than is usually the case with conduct problems. On the other hand, Nicol (1971) found that the prognosis of West Indian children attending psychiatric clinics was no different from that of white children. The most striking difference between West Indian and non-immigrant children concerns the pattern of diagnosis. In non-immigrant girls, emotional disorders are much commoner than conduct disorders. However, both general population and clinic studies have shown that this is not the case in West Indian girls (Graham and Meadows, 1967; Nicol, 1971; Rutter *et al.*, 1974). As in boys, conduct disorders predominate. The reason for this diagnostic difference remains uncertain. The clinic studies suggest that the explanation may lie in the very high frequency of stressful separation experiences among West Indian girls. However, the general population studies do not support this conclusion.

Conclusions

The great majority of studies have concerned West Indian migrants and their children. The evidence suggests that adult psychiatric disorder is considerably more frequent in the years immediately following migration, probably as a result of the stresses associated with migration and accommodation to a new life, and probably especially pronounced in single migrants who come without families. However, a decade or so later, the rate of disorder seems to be much the same as in the host population, at least with respect to adults living in a family setting with children. As a group, the children of West Indian migrants do not show an appreciably increased rate of psychiatric disorder, but they do show a particularly high level of conduct problems at school. These problems seem, in part, to be reactive to difficulties in the school situation which particularly press on immigrant groups.

The very limited available evidence on other immigrant groups suggests a broadly similar pattern but the data are meagre and inadequate. In view of the very different cultural and language background of other groups some differences might be expected. Studies are needed to investigate the extent to which their needs and problems differ from those of West Indian families. Also, little is known concerning psychiatric disorder in preschool and adolescent children of immigrant parents. One clinic study (Prince, 1967) suggested that language disorders and social withdrawal might be particularly common in preschool West Indian children. This suggestion needs to be tested by means of general population studies.

CRIME AND DELINQUENCY

Some foreign studies have suggested an essential link between crime rates, migration and time (e.g. Ross, 1937, in the United States and Shoham *et al.*, 1966, in Israel). Lower levels of offending by immigrants relative to native population groups have usually been observed. First generation migrants have tended to display very low rates of criminality, second generation members rather high rates, and subsequent generations have approximated more closely to normal native patterns. In Britain there is a growing core of evidence relating country of birth to unlawful activities, but the fact that much of the black immigration has taken place within the last two decades means that only now are we beginning to be in a position where comparisons of sufficient numbers of first and second generation immigrants can be made. There is a small amount of information on this point which might prompt hypotheses but not conclusions.

However, there is some indication that, in Britain, the crime rate in white native-born adults generally exceeds that among black foreign-born. One of the most systematic studies was conducted by Lambert (1970) in Birmingham. He studied one particular sector of the city over a four month period and examined the nature of all crimes reported during that time. Although black immigrants tended to live in the areas where much crime was committed and where most criminals lived, they were not themselves responsible for most of the crimes. Only 3 per cent of thieves were born in the West Indies and less than 1 per cent (3 cases) in Pakistan. A relatively higher proportion of black immigrants, although still a small number in absolute terms, was involved in personal disputes and violence. Many of these types of crime appeared to result from the tensions between landlords and tenants or from the strains of poor housing conditions. The only types of crime in which black immigrants were over-represented were drug trafficking and motoring offences. Asians, but not West Indians, received many convictions for failing to tax, insure and license their vehicles.

In overall terms, Lambert's (1970) data showed that West Indians were involved in about 3 per cent of both indictable and non-indictable crimes. In addition, however, they were involved in 14 per cent of minor incidents to which the police were called, ten per cent intra-racial and four per cent inter-racial disputes. Most of these incidents involved only minor family conflicts. Asian groups were similarly under-represented among all categories of offenders. They were responsible for just over 1 per cent of all offences and were also involved in 19 per cent of minor incidents reported to the police, 5 per cent involving only Asians, and 14 per cent mixed nationalities.

The general conclusion to be drawn from Lambert's (1970) study is that first generation black immigrants are more law abiding than the community as a whole. This is in keeping with the evidence given to the Select Committee on Race Relations and Immigration (1972) which investigated relations between police and immigrants and is supported by Police statistics in Birmingham and London (John, 1970).

The only major findings contrary to this pattern come from McClintock's (1963) London study. He showed that the proportions of Commonwealth-born violent offenders increased from 6 per cent in 1950 through 12 per cent in 1957 to 13 per cent in 1960. If these figures are compared with the 1961 census data on population proportions it appears that the immigrants are over-represented threefold amongst offenders. However, as Bottoms (1967, 1973) suggested, certain qualifications are necessary. First, the areas studied had higher than average proportions of black immigrants. Second, the census data on immigrant groups are likely to be inaccurate. Both these factors would contribute to an overestimate of black immigrant crime rates. A further statistical adjustment must be made to allow for the age and social structure of the immigrant groups. Moreover, most of the crimes committed by Commonwealth immigrants involved domestic disputes between members of the same race. When his data were reanalysed after excluding domestic disputes, it was shown (Bottoms, 1967) that violent crimes by Commonwealth immigrants actually fell between 1957 and 1960.

Despite public views to the contrary (Chater, 1966) the evidence suggests that black immigrant adults are generally a law abiding group. Less is known about delinquency among juveniles or second generation immigrants of any age. Lambert's (1970) data from Birmingham indicated that the children of immigrants were no more likely to commit offences than were indigenous children. Both West Indian and Asians were under-represented among those in 'approved schools'. Belson's (1968) self-report study of delinquency also showed that black boys had slightly lower rates of theft than white boys. However, these figures all relate to the situation as it existed several years ago. Recent figures, although not very satisfactory, suggest that the number of West Indian youngsters in community home schools is now higher than expected on the basis of their proportion in the general population (Pearce, 1974). The majority were admitted as a result of persistent delinquent acts but some had committed only technical offences such as truancy. The unemployment rate among 16 to 20-year-old West Indian boys in the general population is twice that for the population as a whole (17 per cent compared with 8 per cent), and many of the unemployed youngsters get into problems with the police (Community Relations Commission, 1974). Some are homeless and many have broken with their parents.

There is some suggestion from these figures that although crime rates in the black population as a whole are relatively low, adolescent delinquency may be more frequent. However, reliable data are lacking. Furthermore, if the rate of delinquency is particularly high, it remains to be determined how far this represents an increase in delinquent behaviour (perhaps stemming from the rising unemployment) and how far an increase in convictions due to greater police activity. Boisterous defiant behaviour in response to police authority, in part culturally determined and in part a reaction to colour prejudice, may make West Indians more liable to arrest at times of crowd disturbance. The strained relations in some areas between the young black community and the police may cause minor difficulties to escalate in a way which precipitates police action (Banton, 1973). Some of these tensions seem to arise from misunderstanding and differences in expectations.

On the other hand, rates of juvenile and adult crime have not been particularly high among second generation migrants in areas, mainly docklands, where black settlements have been established for several generations. These include the groups studied by Little (1947), Richmond (1954), Banton (1955) and Collins (1957). Bloom (1969) followed up the minority group in South Wales where the first studies were undertaken. On the whole, the black population in these areas has tended to keep to itself. This has not been so possible for the more recent migrants coming to London and other large cities. Whether this makes settlement more or less difficult remains uncertain.

Whereas American studies (of white immigrants) have shown higher levels of crime in second (but not third) generation immigrants, and consistently high levels among black people, the social situation in Britain is not the same as in the USA. It is too early to predict the future patterns of crime and delinquency within the British black population. There is no reason to suppose that the pattern will necessarily be the same as in America; whether or not it is may depend to a considerable extent on how far black people remain disadvantaged and discriminated against (Bottoms, 1973).

ABILITY, ATTAINMENT AND EDUCATION

Measured Ability and Attainment

Numerous British studies have shown that children born to immigrant parents tend, on average, to have considerably lower scores than indigenous children on verbal and non-verbal intelligence tests as well as on a wide range of educational tests. This applies to all the main groups which have been studied — namely children whose parents came from Asia, the West Indies, or Cyprus (Little *et al.*, 1968; Payne, 1969; Bhatnagar, 1970; Halsey, 1972; Yule *et al.*, 1975). Even in children of good intelligence, reading attainments are often below age level (Bagley, 1971). In addition, it has been found that children from West Indian families here, as well as in the West Indies (Vernon, 1969), tend to score unusually poorly on Raven's Progressive Matrices in comparison with their scores on other intellectual tests (Payne, 1969; Bhatnagar, 1970). The finding suggests that a Matrices score is not as valid a predictor of educational performance in West Indian children and its meaning differs from that in a native white English group.

The only two exceptions to this general pattern are provided by Houghton (1966) and Bagley (1971), in studies of selected groups using the Terman—Merrill test. Houghton found no significant difference between English and West Indian children at the age of 5 years in a socially deprived population in which the scores of both groups were very low. Bagley also found no significant difference on the same test at 9 years of age in a very highly selected group from favourable backgrounds. In this case, both the English and West Indian children had good average scores on the test. It remains uncertain how far these two exceptions are a result of the selected samples or of the particular test used.

Studies are in general agreement that children of immigrant parents, although showing a wide range of abilities and performance, tend to have mean scores on vocabulary and reading well below those of native white children. The ILEA literacy survey (1967) found a large gap in reading performance between immigrant and non-immigrant children who were beginning their second year of primary school in inner London (ILEA, 1969). According to the definitions used 28.5 per cent of immigrant children were 'poor' readers compared with 14.8 per cent in the native group. A follow-up investigation four years later suggested that the gap in reading skills between the two groups had not narrowed substantially and that the discrepancy in mean reading age was probably at least one year (ILEA, 1973). The study has been criticized because of its reliance on group tests, but investigations in which the children have been tested individually have produced closely comparable findings (Yule *et al.*, 1975). In the study by Yule and his colleagues, West Indian 10 year-olds in London had a mean reading age over a year below indigenous children of the same age. Their mean scores on the short form of the Wechsler Intelligence Scale for children were 10 points below indigenous children on performance IQ and 14 points below on verbal IQ.

Both the ILEA study and that by Yule *et al.* showed that the groups with the lowest test scores were those of West Indian and Turkish Cypriot origin.

School Placement

There are very wide variations in streaming policies between schools, but on the whole streaming in infant schools is rare, in junior schools it is more common and in secondary schools it is most frequent (Townsend and Brittan, 1972). In the National Foundation for Educational Research (NFER) survey of the educational provision for immigrant children it was found that where streaming took place, the immigrants were especially concentrated in the lower divisions. This was most marked for children from West Indian families, followed by children of Asian background and least marked for those from other parts of the world. Asians were more likely than West Indians to be in the higher streams of schools with a high proportion of immigrant pupils.

The same disadvantages applied with respect to selection for academic schooling at the secondary stage (Townsend, 1971). Whereas one in five non-immigrant children attended (selective) grammar schools, only a tiny proportion of immigrants did so. The figures for children of Indian, Pakistani, and West Indian parentage were all below 5 per cent. Some of the differences may be due to black children living in areas with little selective schooling; but this is unlikely to constitute a sufficient explanation.

Also, children of West Indian families are much more likely than non-immigrant children to be placed in special schools for the educationally subnormal (ESN). This does not seem to apply to Asians or other immigrant groups. Thus, in 1970, the DES figures showed that some 2½ per cent of West Indian children, compared with about ½ per cent of other immigrant or native children attended ESN schools (Townsend, 1971). As a consequence, in areas such as London where there is a relatively large number of West Indian children, West Indians form a high proportion of the total population of children at ESN schools. Immigrant children do not appear to be over represented in schools for maladjusted children (Townsend, 1971).

In short, in terms of both measured ability and attainment and also school placement, children of immigrant parentage occupy a disadvantaged position within the British educational system. This disadvantage is most marked with children of West Indian or Turkish

Cypriot origin, but it is present in lesser degree (and to some extent with a different pattern) among other immigrant groups. There are a large number of possible explanations for the poor educational performance of many immigrant children, and these will be discussed in turn.

Test Artefact

There are two varieties of test artefact which might account for the low test performance of immigrant children: inappropriate choice of test and bias in the test situation.

Much heat has been engendered by the use of intelligence tests with minority groups both in Britain (Coard, 1971) and the United States and there has been a serious concern that test scores in immigrant children may be quite misleading. This concern involves several rather different issues (see reviews by Sattler, 1973 and by Tarjan *et al.*, 1972). First, there are problems in testing children who do not speak fluent English. Testing is based on the assumption that children can understand the language used by the tester. If the child does not, the score will reflect his language fluency rather than his intellectual performance. This issue obviously arises in children whose native language is not English but also it applies to some extent to children who speak English but whose use of words, pronunciation and intonation differ from those of the tester (as will be the case with many West Indian children). Second, differences in life experiences may mean that items in IQ tests have different implications. As a result, scores on certain tests may be misleading because the test requires information not likely to be available to a child from a different culture. Alternatively, answers may be correct in terms of the child's life experience but technically 'wrong' in terms of allowable answers in the test manual. Thirdly, experiences in the use of language and in the manipulation of objects may affect intellectual performance more fundamentally.

In an attempt to bypass these difficulties, attempts have been made to devise 'culture-free' or 'culture-fair' tests. Theoretically this is a dubious procedure and it has not worked in practice. Such procedures appear to have as their aim the assessment of 'innate ability'. Although in the past psychologists have claimed that this is possible (Burt, 1955b, 1970) there are many sound arguments for rejecting the claim (Vernon, 1970). As Anastasi (1968) has stated 'To criticize tests because they reveal cultural influences is to miss the essential nature of tests. Every psychological test measures a sample of behaviour. In so far as culture affects behaviour its influence will and should be reflected in the test'. An IQ score simply reflects current intellectual performance which is a result of both biological endowment and of experience; it cannot measure innate potential. Nevertheless, intelligence tests were originally designed to assess a child's likely response to education, and if IQ scores are to be used for this purpose it is necessary to ensure that they adequately serve this function in immigrant children. As Raven's Matrices do not do this satisfactorily they are an inappropriate test for West Indian children. Whether newly designed scales, such as Haynes' (1971) attempt to develop a test of children's learning ability which would be appropriate for immigrant children, will prove superior to other existing tests is not yet known. Research has shown that in most circumstances the main standardized tests predict educational attainments equally well (i.e. only moderately) for white and black subjects (Rutter, 1971a; Sattler, 1973). However, the only British study suggested that, although the differences fell short of significance, the correlations between IQ and reading attainment may be rather lower in children of West Indian parentage (Yule *et al.*, 1975). A further caveat is provided by Watson's (1973) finding that IQ scores of recently immigrant West Indian children tend to rise after a year of two in this country (more so than the changes in IQ of non-immigrant children over a comparable period in time). The last point is that there is some indication that socially disadvantaged children, more than others, tend to do less well on group tests than on individual tests (Sattler, 1973). The same phenomenon may apply to immigrant children.

These cautions all concern the use of IQ tests and do not apply to the findings on individually tested reading attainment which have consistently shown that immigrant children, on average, have a much lower level of achievement that non-immigrants.

A person's performance on IQ tests depends on motivational and situational factors (Anastasi, 1968; Wickes, 1956; Zigler and Butterfield, 1968) as well as on intellectual capacity. It appears from research both in Britain and the USA that, under certain circumstances, attitudes toward racial differences may so influence rapport that white testers have a subtle deleterious effect on black subjects' scores (Katz, 1967; Watson, 1970; Sattler, 1973). This is by no means a general effect and Shuey (1966), in her review, concluded that the effect was negligible. Studies are still too few to arrive at firm conclusions but it seems that the phenomenon occurs only in Negro (not Asian) subjects and then only in competitive situations when black subjects know that they are being directly compared with white subjects. However, there is a more general point regarding test administration. Although the evidence is incomplete it seems that early failures may be more likely to affect test scores adversely in socially disadvantaged children than other children. It is desirable in any testing to provide early success, encouragement and praise and this may be particularly so with immigrant children from disadvantaged backgrounds.

These various considerations of test artefacts are important. Nevertheless, research findings made quite clear that the effects are insufficiently marked to explain why immigrant children have lower IQ and attainment scores on average than non-immigrant children in Britain.

Effect of Migration

Many of the studies of so-called 'immigrants' in this country have failed to draw a distinction between immigrant children and native-born children of immigrant parents. This is a serious omission as several studies of children of West Indian parentage have shown that children born in this country have considerably better educational attainments and considerably higher scores on tests of intellectual performance than do children born in the West Indies who migrate during middle childhood or adolescence (McFie and Thompson, 1970; ILEA, 1973; Yule *et al.*, 1975). There are several alternative or summative explanations for this finding. First, it might be because children born in this country have better educated parents of higher social class. However, the investigation by Yule and his colleagues showed that this explanation was incorrect. Second, it could be that the stress of migration led to a depression of scores. Certainly the dislocating experience of a child finding himself in a strange school in a strange country only 48 hours after leaving 'home' is all too common (Townsend, 1971). Nevertheless, this explanation seems very unlikely to account for the main findings since children born in the West Indies have an even lower level of performance than do recent migrants to this country (Vernon, 1969; Hertzig *et al.*, 1972). Third, family adaptation to the new culture may also be important. Ashby *et al.* (1971), in a study of Asian 10 to 13 year-olds who had been in this country only a few years found significant correlations between children's scores on verbal reasoning and English attainment tests and a crude measure of parental attitude to English culture. Fourth, it could reflect more favourable living conditions or better schooling in this country. The finding that migrants have higher scores the longer they have been in this country (ILEA, 1969; Little *et al.*, 1968; Watson, 1973; Ashby, Morrison and Butcher, 1971; Yule *et al.*, 1975) is in keeping with this view. Among Asian migrants, children who have been in this country many years do not differ appreciably from native white children in level of educational performance (Ashby, Morrison and Butcher, 1971). Indeed, the immigrant children who had spent most of their lives in Glasgow were superior to native pupils on some measures, but this is not the case with children of West Indian parentage (Yule *et al.*, 1975). Although Yule and his colleagues found that 10-year-old children of West Indian origin who had been born in the UK had a WISC performance IQ 8 points higher and reading skills 10 months superior to those born abroad, both scores were still considerably below native born English white children. The indigenous children had a performance IQ 10 points higher and reading which was 8 months above UK born children of West Indian parents. It is also important to note that the ILEA data suggest that length of schooling, rather than length of residence, in this country is the relevant factor. Children born in this country had similar scores to those who arrived during the preschool years.

Streaming is also related to length of stay in Britain. Wiles (1968) conducted an investigation in a boys' comprehensive school and found that the distribution of immigrant pupils between streams was related to the years they had spent in British schools. In general the percentage of immigrants in the top streams rose and the percentage in the lower steams fell as stay increased. The DES (1972) reported, on the basis of a survey of secondary schools, that fewer pupils who had completed at least three years of junior schooling in this country were in the lowest streams. Townsend and Brittan (1972) reported the differentiating age to be lower: the headmasters in the schools they surveyed claimed that it was pupils who had come to Britain after the age of five who were concentrated within the lowest divisions; but that, otherwise, immigrants were evenly distributed across the different ability groupings.

Fethney (1972) conducted a survey of the 150 children, of whom over 70 per cent were of West Indian origin, in nine classes of an ESN school. The children were aged between 11 and 16 years and of those born in Jamaica all had arrived in the UK when they were at least 8 years old. Moreover, it was found that the sooner after arrival children had been given intelligence tests, the lower they had scored. In a longitudinal study, Watson (1973) confirmed that, at least over the course of the first 20 months in this country, recent migrants increased their scores on IQ tests. In view of these findings, it seems most undesirable to place immigrant children in ESN schools shortly after their arrival. Coard (1971) has argued that no immigrant child should be placed in a special school until he has had at least 2 years in an ordinary school (with special provision there, if necessary).

It may be concluded that rearing, and particularly schooling, in this country is associated with a markedly improved intellectual and educational performance but, at least for West Indian children, it does not eliminate the difference in mean attainment from that of native born English white children.

Language Differences

Another factor which puts a large number of immigrant children at a disadvantage is their relative unfamiliarity with the English language as used in schools. Townsend and Brittan (1972) found some indication that linguistic difficulties might be partially, but not wholly, responsible for immigrant children's lower stream placement in ordinary schools. At least a quarter of their sample of multi-racial schools placed immigrant pupils with language difficulties in classes with mentally retarded non-immigrant pupils. Coard (1971) suggested (but did not present supporting evidence) that some West Indian children are wrongly placed in ESN schools because of cultural differences between their own and their assessors' language.

In considering the importance of language skills, it is necessary to make a sharp distinction between (a) lack of knowledge of the English language; (b) a generalized linguistic deficiency; and (c) problems stemming from differences in dialect or linguistic code (Goldman, 1973). Many Asian immigrants come to this country with little or no

English. They have no impairment in linguistic skills as such in that they are fluent in their own language. It is just that they have not learned the English language. For obvious reasons their progress in English speaking schools will be severely limited until they do so. But, as already noted, it appears that once they have mastered English their scholastic attainments are as good as native English children (Ashby *et al.*, 1971), or nearly so (ILEA, 1973). What few difficulties remain may stem from the disadvantages associated with having to learn a second language.

True bilingualism, in which children learn both languages from the outset is not associated with any intellectual or scholastic deficit (Peal and Lambert, 1962). On the other hand, basically monolingual children who have to learn a second language because their first language is not the accepted tongue for the region in which they live, are at an educational disadvantage and tend to have depressed intellectual scores (Darcy, 1953; Soffieti, 1955; Alleyne, 1962). In these cases there are many factors other than bilingualism which are also operative. The second language may be learned in pidgin form and also there may be social barriers and prejudice involved in the differences between the two language cultures. Furthermore, which have to learn a second language are often socially deprived so that the disadvantage may stem from the social deprivation rather than the second language.

The second way in which language skills may be related to intellectual development and scholastic attainment is through a general impairment in linguistic competence. There is good evidence that children reared in an environment which lacks opportunities for meaningful conversation or in which the quality of verbal stimulation is poor, are likely to be delayed in their language development and to be impaired in their verbal intellectual skills and scholastic attainments (Rutter, 1972a; Rutter and Mittler, 1972; see also Chapter 4). Some socially disadvantaged immigrant families are likely to provide inadequate verbal interchange during the early years, just as some socially disadvantaged indigenous families will. Also, the lack of play and conversation with preschool children in some West Indian homes (see p. 260—2) may put them at a special disadvantage. In keeping with this suggestion is Pollak's (1972) finding that 3-year-old children in West Indian families are behind native English children in language development. How often a generalized linguistic deficiency persists and how far this is responsible for later scholastic difficulties are unknown.

However, it is likely that many of the educational difficulties of West Indian children stem from dialect differences rather than from any true linguistic impairment. It is often easier to teach standard English to immigrants who know they cannot speak it than to provide a remedial programme for those who believe their language requires little improvement (Goldman, 1973). Lederman (1969) reported that West Indian boys in English secondary schools were less intelligible to teachers than were Asian boys who originally spoke no English. In the

USA, Labov (1970) found that black boys used language just as complex as that used by white youngsters, but its structure differed from standard English. To some extent these structural differences may interfere with teacher-child communication and hence with learning. There may also be ethnic differences in the way language is used to communicate meaning and understanding, just as there are social class differences in linguistic codes (see above).

In addition, differences in dialect may reflect a clash of cultures and ideologies (Ginsberg, 1972). The language difference may be important not only because it impedes communication but because it marks out the child from an ethnic minority group as different in a way which carries derogatory overtones.

Racism in Teaching

This tendency is likely to be intensified by the racial biases and prejudices present in some teaching (Bolton and Laishley, 1972; Dummett, 1973; Glendenning, 1971; Hatch, 1962). Some of the books used to teach reading still include crude racial stereotypes and more tend to concentrate on white middle class children with the non-white and foreign appearing as subordinates or objects of sympathy. Children's story books exemplify many of the same biases. Nevertheless, readers which portray a balanced view of a multi-racial society are now available and used in some schools (Bolton and Laishley, 1972)*. School textbooks, also, all too often have presented a distorted view of history and geography in terms of out-dated facts, biased presentation of events and inaccurate and prejudiced images of black ethnic groups. The growth of the British Empire is frequently described only from the British viewpoint, with Indians and Africans described as uncivilized primitives. English literature studied in schools has also sometimes fostered ethnic biases, and religious teaching has often implied that Christianity is superior to other religions. All these tendencies (now lessening) will serve to make children from ethnic minority groups appear inferior at school. This is accentuated by the continuing prejudice against black people transmitted through the mass media (Hartmann and Husband, 1974).

School Facilities

Townsend and Brittan (1972) reported that the majority of multi-racial schools saw language teaching as a priority. However, as noted above, the language problems of immigrant children are quite varied and may well require different approaches. On the whole, more adequate provision is made for Asians whose lack of English is overt and obvious. Because their language differences are less well understood, some West Indian children may suffer through not being given the help they require.

*Novels, too, are beginning to move in this direction (Pollins, 1960).

If the right remedies are to be applied, it is necessary that there be a valid assessment of both the nature and severity of a child's linguistic difficulties. However, this type of assessment presents problems (see Stoker, 1970), and appropriate objective measures are lacking (Townsend, 1971)*.

Schools and local authorities have responded to the challenge of providing help with languages in very different ways (Townsend, 1971). Four main arrangements exist: full-time language centres; part-time language centres; full-time language classes within schools; and part-time language classes within schools. The last of the four alternatives has been the most widely adopted and the first the least. Townsend (1971) commented on the relative values of these approaches and detailed reports of individual language units in schools can be found in the literature (e.g. Burgin and Edson, 1967).

There is disagreement on the most appropriate age for concentrated language tuition. It has been suggested that the emphasis should be placed on junior and secondary school children, as younger ones readily acquire English from their classmates (Plowden, 1967). However, this may not be so if the children return home to a non English-speaking environment (Stoker, 1970), or if the problems lie in the use of language for learning rather than in language proficiency as such. Indeed, in the latter case, language tuition may not be the right approach at all.

The Department of Education and Science survey (DES, 1972) showed wide variations in school practice. In general it was found that the liaison between special class and regular class teachers was inadequate, with the consequence that many children found the transfer from special language classes and centres difficult and bewildering. The report, like that of Townsend and Brittan (1972), noted that few teachers had undergone any preparation for teaching English as a second language or for any kind of work in a multi-racial school. The Select Committee on Race Relations and Immigration (1969) recommended that this should be provided not only in colleges and institutes but also as part of in-service training and refresher courses. The training should include race relations and the problems facing immigrant children. It was also recommended that multi-racial schools should employ more teachers from the same ethnic and cultural background as the children, not just so that they should understand the children better but also to facilitate children's identification with their teachers.

Attention has also been given to the possible benefits of a more balanced social and ethnic mix in schools. In the early 1960s fears developed concerning the consequences if schools contained high

*The NFER are currently involved in the construction of a set of objective tests of linguistic proficiency. These will examine ability to listen, speak, read and write.

proportions of immigrant pupils. In 1965 a Governmnent White Paper outlined the policy of dispersal to ensure a maximum of 30 per cent immigrants per school. Local authorities have varied both in the extent to which they have practised dispersion and in the methods utilized to do so (Townsend, 1971). Arguments have been raised against dispersal policies on the grounds that undue travel was tiring for children, that attending distant schools impeded parent-school contact and that the policy interfered with parental choice.

It now appears, that, whatever its social benefits, the proportion of immigrant or black children in a school makes little difference to scholastic progress. American research suggested that true integration in schools might increase attainments to a very minor degree, but that social mix was more important than ethnic mix (Jencks *et al.*, 1973). The policy of bussing black children to white schools in the suburbs made little impact on attainments (see Chapter 4). In this country, studies in inner London (Little and Mabey, 1973; Mabey, 1974) showed that although the proportion of immigrants in a school was associated to a minor degree with the attainments of white children, there was no consistent association with the attainment of black youngsters. It may be that there are disadvantages in the segregation of immigrant children into remedial classes (Goldman and Taylor, 1966), but good education can be provided by a school in spite of a high concentration of immigrants (Burgin and Edson, 1967). The gains in scholastic attainment associated with dispersal are too slight and too variable to justify the policy on those grounds.

Quality of Schooling

Quite apart from ethnic and special language classes, attainments may be influenced by the quality of the schools attended by children from immigrant families. Yule *et al.* (1975) found that they were more likely than indigenous children to attend schools of a kind known to be associated with high rates of reading difficulties and behavioural problems. Although they were no more likely than other children to attend schools with a high turnover of teachers (a variable particularly strongly associated with behavioural deviance and low reading attainment), children from immigrant families were significantly more likely to attend schools with a high pupil turnover, a high rate of absenteeism and a high proportion of free school meals children. These variables have all been shown to be associated with poor scholastic attainments (Rutter *et al.*, 1975b) and they may contribute to the impaired performance of some immigrant children, although the ILEA findings (Barnes and Lucas, 1974) suggest that they do so only to a small degree.

Malnutrition

There is no reason to suppose that children born in this country to immigrant parents are more often malnourished than their native white contemporaries. On the other hand, malnutrition is much more common in many of the countries from which the immigrants originate and it may well be a factor which plays a part in the low levels of scholastic performance among some of the children born abroad. This is suggested by the finding that 10-year-old children of West Indian parents who were born in the West Indies were one inch shorter than those born to West Indian parents in this country (Yule *et al.*, 1975). Height is a sensitive indicator of nutritional status and it is known that severe malnutrition in early life may adversely influence intellectual development (Scrimshaw and Gordon, 1968; Birch, 1972; Hertzig *et al.*, 1972 — see also Chapter 4).

Family and Home Influences

Several studies of immigrant families have shown that their patterns of family life and child-rearing differ in some important respects from those of native white English families (see pp. 259—62), although in many ways they are similar. Some of these differences may have implications for intellectual development and educational progress.

Rutter and his colleagues (1975a) showed that three fifths of the West Indian mothers of 10-year-old youngsters had at least five children — a rate over twice that among indigenous mothers in inner London*. It is known from several studies that large family size is associated with reading difficulties and impaired verbal intelligence (e.g. Nisbet, 1953; Douglas, 1964; Rutter and Yule, 1973) and it may be concluded that this was an important factor in the poor attainments of many of the children.

Pollak (1972) found that 3-year-old children in West Indian families were much less likely than their native English conterparts to go on outings, to have toys or to play with their parents. Rutter *et al.* (1975a) found that many more children in West Indian families had experienced childminding by non-relatives during the pre-school period and more had been taken into care by the local authority. Child-minding is not always of very high quality (Yudkin, 1967) and institutional care is generally second-best. These differences in early child-care have sometimes been attributed to a lack of parental feeling for the children, but the findings of Rutter *et al.* (1975a) suggest that this is an unwarranted assumption. West Indian parents are just as warm and loving as are other parents, but it may be that they more often fail to appreciate the importance of play (Millar, 1968) and conversation (Rutter and Mittler, 1972) in children's learning and development.

*While this ratio is a valid indicator of differences in family size, it should be appreciated that the figures refer to the proportions of children in large families rather than to the proportion of large families. Because the study was based on a sample of children (rather than families), the latter proportion will necessarily be smaller (Bytheway, 1974).

Several investigations have shown that immigrant families are more likely than non-immigrant families to live in overcrowded, poor quality housing (see pp. 289—91). These adverse living conditions may make it more difficult for the children to study and read and it is known that they are correlated with low educational attainments (see Chapter 4).

It has been suggested that much of the educational disadvantage of socially deprived or black youngsters in the USA stems from poor motivation (Ginsberg, 1972). This may be true of some groups but it does not seem to be the case with most immigrant families in this country. Rutter *et al.* (1975a) found that West Indian families were just as likely as others to take their children to the library, to buy books for them and to help with homework. Townsend and Brittan (1972), in their study of 230 multi-racial schools, found that over twice as many West Indians, Indians and 'other immigrants' (and slightly fewer Pakistanis) as non-immigrants stayed on at school for fifth-year courses and also that proportionately more members of each immigrant group remained at school for sixth-year courses. Many of the immigrants were pursuing CSE and 'O' level courses into the sixth form, indicating their determination to succeed in education despite their relative under-achievement.

Genetic Factors

Lastly, a number of writers, notably Jensen (1969 and 1973) and Eysenck (1971), have argued that the balance of evidence suggests that a genetic hypothesis accounts best for the difference in intellectual test performance between Negroes and Whites. The main reasons put forward in support of this view are:–

1. It is well demonstrated that genetic factors play a major role in determining individual variations in IQ *within* racial groups (see Chapter 4).

2. While this is best demonstrated in white groups, the very limited available evidence suggests that this is also so *within* Negro groups (Jensen, 1973).

3. Family studies of 'regression to the mean' indicate that within Negro groups the regression is to a considerably lower mean IQ score than is the case with white groups (Jensen, 1973).

4. None of the environmental influences which have been studied are sufficient to account for the observed difference between Negroes and whites in IQ (Eysenck, 1971; Jensen, 1969 and 1973).

5. Although other racial groups in the USA suffer from social disadvantage and linguistic difficulties, the low IQ of Negroes stands out as different from the others (Jensen, 1969, 1973).

6. The attempts at compensatory education have generally given rise to only quite modest increases in IQ which tend not to persist into later childhood (Jensen, 1969; Bronfenbrenner, 1974).

Much of the opposition to these views has been on ethical grounds in terms of the possible misuse of the evidence in favour of racist policies.

This aspect of the controversy will not be considered here. Rather, the scientific limitations of the genetic argument will be discussed. The main points are as follows:—

(i) It is known that at least part of the Negro-white differences are due to environmental influences. The findings already discussed regarding place of birth made that clear.

(ii) The findings regarding the small effect of environmental influences have generally been based on crude and naive assessments of the environment. The results do indeed show that the lower mean IQ of Negro populations is not explicable in terms of their lower social class although black-white differences in IQ are substantially reduced if similar social groups are compared (Nichols and Anderson, 1973). However, as indicated above, the main environmental effects are not likely to come from social class as such but from family size, patterns of child-rearing, schooling and the like. In order to assess whether genetic factors account for the ethnic differences in mean IQ, it is necessary that *both* groups receive a similar upbringing. An approximation to this situation is found with children reared in institutions. Tizard (1974c) examined the IQ and language scores of white and black children brought up in good quality residential nurseries. At all ages up to 4½ years, there were no appreciable differences between the black and white children in their scores, and both groups were found to be of normal intelligence. The groups did not differ in terms of the occupational status of their fathers. The findings suggested that racial differences in intelligence could be abolished by means of similar rearing conditions and hence argued against the importance of genetic factors in accounting for differences in mean IQ between ethnic groups. The results are impressive, but inconclusive because the occupation of a third of the fathers was not known, the IQs of the parents were not measured, the sample size was small and the children were still pre-school (although already at an age when black-white differences in IQ are marked). However, Ackhurst (1975) in a study of primary and secondary school children living in a Children's Home, has also found no black-white difference in mean IQ. Again, the findings are limited by lack of data on parental IQ and occupation but both studies suggest that the IQ difference between ethnic groups may be obliterated by similar patterns of rearing.

(iii) The evidence concerning the importance of genetic factors with respect to differences in IQ *within* groups cannot validly be generalized to account for differences in IQ *between* groups. This point is accepted by most of the proponents of a genetic explanation, but they counter by arguing that the findings of a major genetic component in the first case increases the likelihood that it will also apply to the second. This may be so but it certainly does not follow automatically.

This is well illustrated by reference to height (Tizard, 1975b). This is a reliably measured characteristic, in which individual differences (within groups) are largely due to genetic factors. However, in spite of the major importance of genetic factors, the average height of London schoolchildren aged 7 to 12 years has risen 9 cm in half a century (Tizard, 1975b). This is not just a question of earlier maturation, as Marshall, Carter and Tanner (1974) in a longitudinal study of 48 London children have found that their mean adult height was 4 cm greater than that of their parents. The findings are in agreement with those of Khosla and Lowe (1968) who found a secular increase in adult male height of about 2½ cm per generation. This large between-groups difference in height could only be explained in genetic terms if there had been a marked increase in outbreeding (Tanner, 1965), which seems unlikely. It is much more probable that the increase in height is due to improved environmental conditions — probably in terms of better nutrition. In summary, with respect to height, individual differences within groups are largely due to genetic factors but in spite of this the difference between groups is almost certainly due in very large part to enviromental factors.

(iv) Although the evidence is limited, there is some suggestion that the heritability of IQ within Negro populations may be less than within white populations (Scarr-Salapatek, 1971). Jensen (1973) has pointed to the weaknesses in the published studies and although the evidence is compatible with the suggestion of slightly lower heritability within Negro groups, it is weak and by no means proves it.

(v) The genetic evidence refers to *individual* variations in IQ and it cannot be generalized to explain *group* differences in mean IQ level. The Skodak and Skeels (1949) study, within a white population, showed that it is perfectly possible for genetic factors to exert a considerable influence upon individual differences within a group, and yet for a beneficial environmental situation to account for an elevated mean IQ in the group as a whole. Similarly, it may well be that individual differences in Negro IQ are genetically determined to a large degree, but that the overall group mean is depressed by adverse environmental factors. This possibility makes the evidence on regression to the mean very weak.

(vi) Children of inter-racial marriages reared by black mothers (and white fathers) have a significantly lower IQ than those reared by white mothers (and black fathers) (Willerman *et al.*, 1970). If the mean mid-parental IQ is the same in the two instances the difference must be due to environmental factors*. Unfortunately, no data were available on the parents' intellectual level so the results are of very limited value.

(viii) While it is true that the benefits of compensatory education in terms of IQ elevation have been quite slight, the environmental modifications have also been quite minor and transitory for the most

*Provided the mother's husband was the biological father in each instance. Data suggest that this assumption may often be false — at least within a white group (Philipp, 1973).

part. The Heber project (see Chapter 4) suggests that major environmental modifications may have a major impact on intellectual development, at least in childhood.

(viii) The two groups (Cypriot and West Indian) with the lowest mean scores on intelligence and educational attainment (see above) are racially quite different, and the low performance of the Cypriot children is certainly not explicable in terms of supposed genetic differences between Negro and white races.

The only fair conclusion is that insufficient evidence is available at present to resolve the question. It is not possible to exclude the possiblity that there may be a genetic component to the difference in mean IQ between blacks and whites but equally there is no convincing evidence in favour of the proposition. What is known is that some of the difference is accountable for in terms of environmental influences. Further research to determine how far the difference can be reduced by improving the circumstances of the black population would be well worthwhile.

Conclusion

Children from immigrant families have been shown to perform less well in the British educational system and often to experience stresses associated with elements of racism in teaching. They have lower scores on tests of intelligence and scholastic attainment, they are more likely than indigenous children to be in the lower streams of ordinary schools, a higher proportion are in schools for the educationally subnormal, and as lower proportion are selected for academic schooling at the secondary stage. This pattern is most marked with respect to children from West Indian families. Other immigrant groups are also disadvantaged educationally but not to the same degree or in quite the same way. With all groups, however, children born in this country to immigrant parants have an average level of attainment considerably above similar children born abroad. Nevertheless, children of certain groups of immigrant parents, even when born here, do not have educational attainments as high as those of native white children. The reasons for their disadvantage are many and include factors such as large family size, poor living conditions, lack of play and conversation in early childhood, and less satisfactory schooling. London data suggest that children of West Indian parentage are three times as likely to suffer from multiple social disadvantage compared with indigenous children (Community Relations Commission, 1973).

These educational disadvantages may well have long term implications through limitations on employment, the attachment of stigma, and the emotional and behavioural disturbances which sometimes stem from educational failure. Both the resentments generated and the lack of scholastic skills (when present) may influence parenting in the next generation.

EMPLOYMENT

Patterns of Employment

Using census data, both Rose *et al.* (1969) and Hepple (1970) showed that black male immigrants were over-represented, compared with the indigenous population, in manufacturing, transport and communication industries and under-represented within distributive trades and service industries. Women, especially from the West Indies, were particularly likely to work in hospital or medical services and were also over-represented in professional and scientific services. The virtual exclusion of West Indian men and immigrant women from clerical work and saleswork was especially striking. London differed somewhat from the rest of the country both in the wider range of jobs held by immigrants and in the greater differences between immigrant groups. Thus, among white collar workers in London, Indians were over-represented, Pakistanis slightly under-represented and West Indians greatly under-represented.

In general, the census data showed that immigrants (and especially West Indian immigrants) were disproportionately likely to be found in the lowest status and least desirable occupations. Conversely, very few immigrants were managers, employers or professionals. In the country as a whole in 1966, 35 per cent of the population had a non-manual job, but only 10 per cent of West Indian migrants did so. The proportion of Indians with a non-manual job was similar to the general population, but the proportion of Pakistanis was rather lower (24 per cent). Local surveys have produced essentially similar findings. Richmond (1973a) found that immigrants in Bristol were less likely than native English people to be in the top social categories but considerably more likely to be in unskilled manual work. Rutter *et al.* (1975b) observed the same pattern for West Indians in London.

Both Rose *et al.* (1969) and Jones and Smith (1970), on the basis of limited evidence, suggested that patterns of employment were generally similar for immigrant and indigenous groups, although immigrants were more likely to suffer during times of rising unemployment. However, 1971 census data showed that, even in areas of high employment, the unemployment rate among young West Indian males was twice that of the general population of the same age (Community Relations Commission, 1974). The OPCS survey (1973b and 1974b) confirmed that West Indian school-leavers took longer to obtain a job and were more often unemployed during the next two years than a matched group of white school-leavers. An interview survey of unemployed young people, black and white, showed that nearly half had not registered at an employment exchange, implying that official figures underestimate the extent of unemployment (Community Relations Commission, 1974). Many were also critical of advice given by the Careers Service. Among both the white and black unemployed young people, about half reported having had problems with the police. Sometimes this involved being charged with theft or other offences, but in others it meant being stopped in the street and searched, but not charged.

Local studies have also indicated that unemployment is more widespread among black than white workers (Davison, 1964; Wright, 1968; Richmond, 1973a). To some extent this is likely to be a function of immigrants being in unskilled work and thus, as a group particularly vulnerable to unemployment. Unemployment problems will also be influenced by immigration policies.

Skills and Occupational Status

Several studies have shown that black, and particularly West Indian, immigrants tend to hold a lower status job after immigration than they did in their own country (Glass, 1960; Daniel, 1968; Richmond, 1973a and b). Glass found that half of those who had been white collar workers in the West Indies were in unskilled work in England and another two fifths were in semi-skilled manual jobs. Similarly, Richmond noted that 24 per cent of men from the West Indies were in non-manual occupations before immigration but only 6 per cent were in this country. On the other hand, Glass found that levels of unemployment were lower after coming to this country than they had been in the West Indies. Also, a few men moved up the social scale. Of those in unskilled manual jobs in the West Indies, a third obtained semi-skilled work in this country. However, although migration may well have brought other benefits, it seems that, on the whole, black people are likely to be in less skilled lower status work after coming to England.

It is difficult to judge how far this is a consequence of work skills meaning different things in the West Indies and in Britain. It is possible that non-manual work in one country is not equivalent to that in another, and Ministry of Labour estimates have suggested that only 13 per cent of West Indian workers in this country are skilled (Wright, 1968). On the other hand, where tests of skills have been given to prospective employees, immigrants have tended to show a higher level of competence than expected (Radin, 1966; Gaitskell, 1969). Furthermore, there is evidence that Careers Officers tend to underestimate the intelligence of West Indian adolescents compared with white adolescents, even when the two groups have been matched in terms of qualifications (OPCS, 1973b). Several surveys both in the USA (Blau and Duncan, 1967) and in this country (Richmond, 1973c, Rutter *et al.*, 1975a) have shown that, for a given occupational level, black workers tend to have higher educational qualifications and/or longer schooling. Of course, foreign educational qualifications should be interpreted with caution, but the findings suggest that whatever limitations there may be in work skills these are not sufficient to explain the low occupational status of so many immigrants.

Discrimination and Anti-discrimination Legislation

There is evidence of racial discrimination in employment. The PEP report (Daniel, 1968) provided unequivocal evidence of widespread discrimination by employers against black workers. The extent of this was most clearly shown by situation tests in which matched black immigrant, white immigrant, and native white English testers applied for the same job. In 27 out of 30 cases there was discrimination against the black immigrant and in 13 cases against the white immigrant. Interviews with employers confirmed discrimination practices. Many stated explicitly that they would only employ black workers in certain positions and would not allow them to have a supervisory role. The evidence showed that discrimination was most marked in the case of the most highly qualified immigrants. The PEP survey dealt with employment recruitment and not with discrimination afterwards. Yet promotion, conditions at work, training facilities and enforced redundancies may also operate to the detriment of black workers (Hepple, 1970).

The PEP evidence dealt with the situation prior to the introduction of the Race Relations Act of 1968, which made discrimination in many cases of employment unlawful. This is described in detail by Hepple (1970). In brief, the law made it illegal to deny equal opportunities in employment and trade union membership to people of different national origins. This covered inequalities in recruitment, terms and conditions of employment, the availability of training, promotion and dismissal.

Hepple (1970) noted that the Act had resulted in some employers taking on black workers for the first time, but he saw little change in internal factory rules which appeared deep-rooted. These included 'shop floor understandings about quotas of coloured labour, promotion barriers, sharing of overtime work, ethnic work-units, and the separation of toilet and canteen facilities'. Burney and Wainwright (1972) argued that 'Personnel Managers have learned to live with the 1968 Race Relations Act: where they think it necessary, they continue to discriminate with little prospect of the law intervening.' These views were substantiated by the PEP study of employers and of industrial plants (Smith, 1974). Only a few employers had taken steps to ensure that the Race Relations Act was complied with and racial discrimination occurred in over half the plants studied.

The extent of existing racial discrimination in employment since the 1968 Act has been demonstrated by a further PEP Study (McIntosh and Smith, 1974). A more sophisticated version of the situation tests used in the first survey was employed. Matched pairs of native white, black, and Greek actors were used. The black testers spoke fluent English with only a slight accent. For each job the immigrant actor made the first approach and, half an hour to an hour later, the white actor made a similar contact. Altogether, 178 effective job tests were undertaken. It was found that there was 46 per cent net discrimination against Asians and West Indians for unskilled jobs and 20 per cent for skilled jobs. The figures for Greeks were 10 per cent and 9 per cent respectively. Direct comparisons with the 1967 results are not possible, but it was concluded that in spite of some decrease, discrimination in employment still occurs on a substantial scale.

A modified version of the same procedure was used to test written or typed applications for white collar jobs. Out of 234 tests, there was 30 per cent net discrimination against Asians and West Indians and out of 71 tests there was 10 per cent net discrimination against Italians. As the method identifies discrimination only at the screening stage, this level of discrimination is very considerable. There was some suggestion that women face less discrimination than men in the more junior clerical jobs in which they have traditionally worked. Comparison with Jowell and Prescott-Clarke's (1970) study shows almost identical levels of discrimination. Detailed study of the letters of job refusal showed that employers had used imagination in framing (false) reasons for rejections and often applicants could not know discrimination had occurred.

It is all too clear that, in spite of the 1968 Act, racial discrimination in employment exists on a wide scale. Many criticisms of the Act have been made and these cover its scope, procedures, machinery to deal with complaints, and its power to dispel discrimination (Harrison, 1971; Hetherington, 1971; Hanna, 1971). During 1971 and 1972 only about one in ten complaints were upheld by the Race Relations Board. The PEP situation test findings indicate that discrimination must often occur when there is no indication of it to the job applicant. This inevitably makes the job of the Board very difficult. Even so, Hetherington (1971) suggested that there is an inequity and lack of consistency in the way complaints are dealt with. The Race Relations Board itself, in its annual reports, has urged the need for greater powers. Some improvements have been made to the Act since it came into force — particularly additional provisions for dealing with unfair dismissals and a change in exemption rules (Burney and Wainwright, 1972). Nevertheless, the situation remains far from satisfactory.

Futur prospects are difficult to assess. It has been clearly shown that first generation black immigrants are seriously disadvantaged in their employment. The next generation will have the advantage of education in this country and may well be able to obtain better work qualifications. The OPCS surveys (1973b and 1974b) have shown that, compared with a similarly educated group of white youngsters, black school leavers (of West Indian origin) are more likely to attend a course of further education and more likely to study for higher qualifications. However, the black youngsters were *less* likely to be allowed time off work to study so that they studied under more disadvantages than the white group.

It appears (Wright, 1968; Richmond, 1954) that, with time, black factory workers become better accepted by their white colleagues. Longer residence in Britain is associated with some increase in occupational status (Richmond, 1973a and b). Nevertheless, the processes involved in the industrial acceptance of black workers are slow and complex (Patterson, 1963, 1968).

All these factors indicate better prospects in the future for the offspring of black immigrants. But there are serious contrary trends. The unemployment rate among young blacks is disturbingly high and the continuing high level of racial discrimination in employment is likely to increase frustrations and resentments as black people find that they do not get the jobs they are trained to do. Much of the future of ethnic minority groups depends on the extent to which they are placed in a disadvantaged position through discriminatory practices. Although there are specific issues which arise from immigration and from difference in cultural background, to a large extent the 'colour problem' is the problem of white racism, and the 'immigrant problem' concerns the presence of socially and economically disadvantaged people who happen to come from a different country (Allen, 1972).

HOUSING

Considerable information is available on the current housing circumstances of black immigrant groups, but much remains unknown and there is uncertainty about the housing situation which will face the next generation. Possibilities depend to a large extent upon (local and central) government policies, upon the supply of accommodation, and upon racial discrimination in the allocation of housing. The personal characteristics of ethnic minority groups are much less important in this connection.

Quality of Housing

All surveys, national and local, have indicated that a higher proportion of black people, compared with the indigenous white population, live in poor quality housing. For many, overcrowding, multiple occupancy and lack of basic household amenities characterize their homes. Rose *et al.* (1969), using census data, showed that the person-room ratio (measuring overcrowding) was approximately 85 per cent greater for black immigrants than for white natives in London and the West Midlands. In Bristol, Richmond (1973a) found that 44 per cent of West Indians, but only 13 per cent of British born households were overcrowded. Furthermore, unlike the pattern in the indigenous group, overcrowding was unassociated with occupational status. Regardless of job, West Indian families tended to live in overcrowded circumstances. Rutter *et al.* (1975a), in a study of inner London, also found a high rate of overcrowding. Half of the West Indian families, compared with one in five of the indigenous group, were living at a density of at least one and a half persons per room. The high rate of overcrowding in West Indian families is likely to stem in part from the shortage of homes of sufficient size for very large families. However, that cannot be a sufficient explanation as Richmond (1973a) found that despite the larger families of black migrants they actually had significantly *fewer* rooms per family available to them.

In terms of the basic amenities of cooking facilities, bathroom, lavatory and hot running water, the 1961 and 1966 data showed that black people were disadvantaged in relation to the rest of the population. In Lambeth, only half as many black households had the sole use of a fixed bath (29 per cent versus 60 per cent), or internal WC (34 per cent versus 67 per cent) (Burney, 1967). In a different part of London, Rutter *et al.* (1975) found that only 16 per cent of West Indian families, compared with 43 per cent of indigenous white families, did not have to share any of the basic household amenities. Over two fifths of the West Indian families lived in multiple occupancy housing compared with just a fifth of the native white population. Much the same applied in Richmond's (1973a) survey in Bristol. He showed that the worse living conditions of the black families were not explicable in terms of any difference in age, sex, family type, or socio-economic status. Also, neither family size nor length of residence in Bristol seemed sufficient to account for the differences. It appeared that racial discrimination had affected housing.

Patterns of Tenure

Ethnic minority groups in this country differ somewhat from the rest of the population in their patterns of housing tenure. Both Rose *et al.* (1969) and Daniel (1968) found that, in the country as a whole, the proportion of black immigrants who owned their own homes was much the same as the rest of the population. However, these comparisons may be misleading in view of regional differences in house ownership; more valid data are provided by local surveys. In both Bristol (Richmond, 1973a) and London (Rutter *et al.*, 1975a) West Indian families were more likely than native white families to own their homes. The latter survey showed that 22 per cent of West Indian families lived in single occupancy houses that they owned compared with 6 per cent of non-immigrant families. The practice of house ownership has been found to be particularly marked in the case of large families, many of whom experience grave difficulties in renting (Richmond, 1973a). The 1961 census data showed that house ownership was slightly more common in almost all immigrant groups compared with the native English population (Davison, 1966). However, many of the houses bought by immigrants have short leases and are in a poor state of repair (Rex and Moore, 1967). Deteriorating properties have often been all that was available and as Milner-Holland (Ministry of Housing and Local Government, 1965) commented, 'It is often rubbish sold dear'. Moreover, many purchasers have been inexperienced and naive with respect to British law so that some find that they have bought a house *and* tenants. The Milner-Holland Committee (1965) reported that the great majority of abuses by black landlords arose from attempts to oust sitting tenants.

To an important extent, the practice of home ownership in immigrant groups may arise from the difficulties experienced in obtaining council housing. In 1961 only one per cent of West Indian families and 7 per cent of Asian families were in council housing compared with 24 per cent of native English families (Davison, 1966). In 1970, Rutter *et al.* (1975a) found that 30 per cent of West Indian families in an inner London borough rented from the Council but this was still far less than the 68 per cent of indigenous white families who did so. The findings in an adjacent borough a few years earlier were closely similar: 5 per cent of black housholds were council tenants compared with 20 per cent of white households (Burney, 1967).

Among families in privately rented accommodation, there is still a major difference between black and white. Most of the latter have unfurnished accommodation (which at least in the past has provided more secure tenure) whereas most of the black households are in furnished lodgings. In 1961, English tenants were nearly eight times as likely to rent an *un*furnished flat, whereas Jamaicans were five times as likely and Pakistanis three times as likely to have a furnished flat (Davison, 1966). Similar findings were shown by Rose *et al.* (1969). More recent local surveys (Rutter *et al.*, 1975a; Richmond, 1973a) suggest that the same pattern persists although the differences may be less marked.

Alternative means of obtaining accommodation are available through non-profit-making voluntary housing associations, including co-ownership societies (Waddilove, 1962; Cohen, 1971). These have the advantage of both flexibility and the possibility of local authority subsidies, so that it has been hoped that they would meet the needs of people not otherwise well catered for. However, there are difficulties in this source of provision and it remains to be seen how far they work to the advantage or disadvantage of ethnic minority groups.

DISCRIMINATION IN HOUSING

Private Sector Rented Accommodation

In 1965, Milner-Holland noted that advertisements for accommodation to let frequently made stipulations ensuring the exclusion of black people. The PEP survey in 1967 (Daniel, 1968) also found evidence of extensive discrimination in housing. In specially devised tests, West Indian, Hungarian and white English testers responded to advertisements for rented accommodation. There was discrimination against the West Indian tester in three quarters of cases in which personal application was made to landlords, and in 62 per cent of cases when telephone application was made. Discrimination against the Hungarian occurred only rarely. The pattern of racial discrimination practised by accommodation bureaux and estate agents was closely similar. In some cases the discrimination took the form of saying accommodation was unavailable and in others the West Indian was asked for a higher rent. Although discrimination was extremely common its extent was underestimated by the findings as the tests did not include accommodation in which the advertisements specially excluded black people.

These figures all apply to the situation prior to the 1968 Race Relations Act which made racial discrimination in advertisements illegal. The more recent PEP survey (McIntosh and Smith, 1974) provided evidence on the current situation. Compared with 62 per cent discrimination against West Indian testers in 1967, there was only 27 per cent in 1973 in the case of telephone applications for rented accommodation. Both this comparison and the absence of overtly discriminating advertising in 1973 indicate that discrimination in housing has decreased to a considerable extent, although it is still substantial.

Milner-Holland (Ministry of Housing and Local Government, 1965) noted that rents tended to be specially increased in the case of black immigrants. Richmond (1973a) found that the average rent paid by foreign born tenants in Bristol was 28 per cent higher than that paid by native born householders. Part of the difference was probably due to the higher proportion of immigrants in furnished accommodation. Single male immigrant workers tend to get particularly poor value for money in rented accommodation; many pay high rents for dormitory accommodation (Burney, 1967).

Public Sector Rented Accommodation

Each local authority in Britain is responsible for its own housing policy and priority listing; the systems of allocations are frequently complex, often unclear and vary considerably from area to area (Burney, 1967). As a result, accurate estimates of discrimination in council housing are very difficult to obtain. Many authorities require five years' residence in the area before council housing can be considered, thus excluding recent immigrants. While this policy also operates against white people moving from elsewhere within Britain, some authorities have required longer periods of residence from foreigners than from natives (Burney, 1967). Single men do not usually qualify for local authority accommodation, a policy which makes housing particularly difficult for the immigrant who comes to this country in advance of his family — as many have done.

There are also indications that some local authorities (Burney, 1967; Runnymede Trust, 1975), but not others (Richmond, 1973a), differentiate between black immigrants and native white families in the type of accommodation offered. Several authorities have been criticized for this policy of offering 'patched houses' (i.e. those due for demolition but 'restored') to black applicants. Some authorities have practised a deliberate policy of dispersal, others have apparently concentrated immigrant families on older housing or less desirable areas (Daniel 1968; Burney, 1967). The recent PEP survey (Smith and Whalley, 1975) suggests that local authority racial discrimination in housing is rarely deliberate. Nevertheless, the effect of various regulations has been that black people frequently receive lower quality council accommodation. Evidence from some American studies suggests that, in the right circumstances, inter-racial housing projects may promote better race relations (Jahoda and West, 1951).

Owner Occupation

The PEP survey prior to the 1968 Race Relations Act found extensive discrimination against West Indians by estate agents (Daniel, 1968). There was racial discrimination in 64 per cent of 42 situation tests involving personal application by West Indian and white testers. In some cases the West Indian was denied access to properties for sale, in some he was told that no mortgage would be available to him and in others he was offered less favourable terms. Racial discrimination was confirmed by subsequent interviews with the estate agents. Since the 1968 Act the situation has improved (McIntosh and Smith, 1974). In the 1973 PEP survey, there was 17 per cent net discrimination against black testers in the form of directing them to particular areas and an additional 12 per cent in the form of inferior treatment. However, unlike 1967, there were no cases of discrimination involving mortgage terms.

Nevertheless, Richmond's Bristol survey (1973a) showed that, on average, black immigrants are still making mortgage repayments which are double those paid by native white householders. As noted in earlier studies (Burney, 1967; Rose *et al.*, 1969) they frequently have to pay higher interest rates for loans with shorter repayment periods.

Because many black immigrants have experienced difficulty in obtaining building society mortgages, local authority financing has been particularly important. Local authorities have varied in their policies but many have regarded the granting of mortgages as a social service and in several areas immigrants have benefited out of proportion to their numbers (Burney, 1967).

Homelessness

No adequate data are available on the extent of homelessness in ethnic minority groups. The limited available evidence suggests that the overall proportion of homeless people is probably about the same as in the comparable native white population (Burney, 1967; Community Relations Commission, 1974; Brandon, 1973). However, the available figures are dependent on people's use of institutions for the homeless, so that if groups differ in their pattern of service utilization the statistics will be biased. Also, Greve's surveys in London (Greve, 1964;

Greve *et al.*, 1971) showed that a markedly rising number of Commonwealth immigrants were to be found in local authority temporary accommodation (the percentage among admissions being 1 per cent in 1959 and 30 per cent in 1969). It seemed, as noted by Burney (1967), that compared with the native white homeless, a higher proportion of black immigrants had become homeless as a direct result of housing difficulties largely outside their control and fewer had become so through unemployment or domestic problems.

Housing Areas and Ghettoes

Rex and Moore (1967) have argued that black immigrants tend to gravitate towards lodging house areas which provide the most immediate solution to their housing needs. However, their analyses were inadequately controlled for age and marital status and, when matched comparisons were undertaken by Richmond (1973a) in Bristol, black immigrants were not over-represented in the lodging house district. On the other hand, it was found that black immigrants tended to move into deteriorating neighbourhoods which were losing population and that they tended to remain disproportionately concentrated in poor housing areas. This process has been accentuated by the practice of some local authorities of placing immigrant families in old terraced houses or in less desirable parts of housing estates (Burney, 1967; Runnymede Trust, 1975).

These circumstances will tend to perpetuate both the disadvantaged housing and prejudicial stereotypes suffered by ethnic minority groups. On the other hand, it would be misleading to use the term 'ghetto' for these areas (Burney, 1967; Richmond, 1973a). The heterogeneity of the population, and the absence of separate institutional provision for the various ethnic minorities, make the areas quite different from the typical North American ghetto.

Conclusions

In some respects the housing problems of black immigrants are similar to those of all newcomers to cities, who arrive with very limited means at a time when many local authority housing lists are overfull or even closed, and in conditions where they obtain a very low priority in housing allocation. However, for black immigrants these difficulties are multiplied many times by racial discrimination in making rented accommodation and property available to them. Such discrimination has diminished following the 1968 Race Relations Act but it is still extensively practised. The inexperience of black immigrants and their acute needs has sometimes led them to ill-advised purchases of unsuitable property at high prices. In these matters they have often not received sufficient reliable professional help and advice and in a number of respects they have been shamelessly exploited. The results have frequently been overcrowding, multiple occupancy and high rents. In all these ways the situation is much the same as that existing a decade ago and described in the Milner-Holland report (Ministry of Housing and Local Government, 1965). In addition, black immigrants have become increasingly concentrated in particular parts of cities, often in low status areas with poor quality housing (Richmond, 1973a).

There are several factors which should improve the situation in the future. The longer immigrants have lived in this country, the less they will be penalized by residential requirements in the allocation of council housing. The power of local authorities to provide mortgages, and the grants available for improving housing, both provide a means of helping ethnic minority groups to buy houses and improve their property. Time may help in allowing black immigrants to become more settled and better integrated within the neighbouring population, although the extent to which this is happening is very variable (Rose *et al.*, 1969; Richmond, 1973). The pride in their houses, and the drive and initiative in buying a home for themselves shown by many black families also auger well for the future, provided appropriate guidance can be made available regarding suitable properties and provided there are safeguards against exploitation. The Race Relations Act has been beneficial in outlawing the more flagrant examples of discrimination (Burney, 1972) and this, too, should help. However, against all of this must be set the continuing practice of racial discrimination in housing. Unless this can be eliminated, black people are likely to continue to be subject to serious disadvantages in securing good housing. Traditionally, home ownership has been a way for parents to pass on advantages to their children. However, this is less likely to benefit ethnic minority groups in view of the fact that many of their houses have a low investment value and may be approaching the end of their leases. Intergenerational continuities and discrimination in the housing situation of black people in Britain will depend much more on the extent of white prejudice and discrimination than on anything the families can do for themselves.

RACE RELATIONS

Earlier sections of this chapter have indicated that black people in this country suffer from serious disadvantages in housing, employment and education and that to a considerable extent these stem from discriminatory practices by the white majority. Prejudice towards minority groups is fairly widespread (Hill, 1967; Rose *et al.*, 1969) and the PEP studies have clearly indicated that discrimination against black people continues to provide substantial barriers. It remains to consider the development of racial prejudice and the factors influencing its expression.

Ethnic Awareness and Identification

Studies in both Britain and the United States have indicated that children develop ethnic awareness at an early age (Pushkin and Veness, 1973); Clark and Clark (1947) found that most three-year-old

American black children were well able to say which doll looked black or white. Morland (1958) showed that three fifths of four-year-olds and nearly 90 per cent of five-year-olds were able to identify correctly white and black persons in pictures. In this country, too, Laishley (1971) found that, as judged by their comments, most nursery school children were aware of the differences between white and brown dolls.

In the same studies, it was found that by four or five years of age most children used skin colour to identify which doll looked most like them. However, it has generally been found that black children do so less consistently than do white children, and many identify with white dolls. Thus, Laishley (1971) found that all six non-white children in her London study said they most resembled the white doll. Why this might happen is suggested by studies of preference.

Preference as Assessed from Doll Studies

Clark and Clark (1947) found that a majority of 3- to 7-year-old black children preferred a white doll to play with or chose it as the 'nice' one. Stevenson and Stewart (1958) found the same among black children, while white children's own race choice for a playmate rose from 52 per cent to 82 per cent between 3 and 7 years. Studies by Pushkin (1967) and Milner (1970) in Britain also showed that both white and black children expressed white skin preferences. However, Laishley (1971) found that skin colour was less important in the nursery school children's choice of dolls. Marsh (1970) found little evidence of preference for own skin colour in black children fostered with white parents. Futcher (1972), in a study of a similar group found that most of the black youngsters identified with black dolls but there was still a preference for white faces. Madge (1976) showed that the expressed preferences of black West Indian and white English children aged 6 to 7 years were highly dependent upon context and upon the competing variables which could also influence choices. The findings on preference for white dolls have been linked with the evidence on awareness of identification to suggest that many black children develop a negative self-image which is associated with negative feelings about blackness (see below). However, the observations that skin colour preferences vary according to context (see above and Brand *et al.*, 1974) cast some doubt on this view.

Attitudes to Skin Colour as Assessed from Doll Studies and Questionnaires

American studies have often shown that young black children's preference for white dolls is linked with an awareness of racial discrimination and prejudice. Thus, Radke, Trager and Davis (1949) asked both white and black children, aged 5 to 8 years, to assign white and black figures to various jobs and houses. The great majority of children assigned the poor house to the Negro doll and the better house to the white doll. Children's comments have also clearly indicated that their concepts of race embody notions of social status and ethnic rejection. Much quoted is the example of the 4-year-old Negro girl who said: 'The people that are white, they can go up. The people that are brown, they have to go down' (Goodman, 1952).

Questionnaire studies have indicated that as children grow older there is an increased consistency and patterning in their attitudes to skin colour and ethnic groups (Horowitz, 1936; Blake and Dennis, 1943; Kutner, 1958; Wilson, 1963). The views of older children tend to be more crystallized and stereotyped and different measures of ethnic attitudes come to inter-correlate more highly with increasing age. The extent of racial prejudice in this country has been found to vary considerably by geographical area and by the manner of its assessment. Kawwa (1968) found that a majority of London secondary school-children expressed negative attitudes to immigrants but only a small minority of adolescents in Lowestoft did so. Moreover, even within London, hostility to blacks has been noted to be much more marked in some areas than in others (Pushkin and Veness, 1973).

Among adults in Bristol, Richmond (1973) found that a majority thought that immigrants took more out of the welfare state than they put into it, that their houses were in a bad state and that they had made the housing situation worse. Rose *et al.* (1969) found similar attitudes to be very common in other parts of Britain. A review of the evidence indicates that these views run counter to the facts and should therefore be regarded as expressions of prejudice or misinformation spread by the mass media (Chater, 1966; Jones and Smith, 1970). The same applies to views that black people are responsible for much crime (Chater, 1966; John, 1970; Select Committee on Race Relations and Immigration, 1972). Rose *et al.* (1969) showed how many people over-estimated the proportion of the British population who are black; three-quarters of those asked put the figure at least twice as high as it really was. However, it should also be noted that most of the adults in Richmond's study *dis*agreed with statements that coloured people were taking jobs away from white people and that they were inferior to white people.

The extent of racial prejudice is perhaps more realistically indicated by the frequency of discriminatory practices than by people's answers to a questionnaire. The PEP surveys (see above) have clearly indicated that discrimination in employment, and to a lesser extent in housing, remains widespread; racist tendencies in school textbooks, children's literature and the mass media also still exist (see above). The Race Relations Act has certainly diminished certain forms of discrimination but there are numerous aspects of life it does not cover and its powers seem to be severely limited.

Choice of Friends

Early American studies (Moreno, 1953; Koch, 1946), using sociometric techniques, found that skin colour played only a minor part in choice of friends by young children but became increasingly marked from age

11 years onwards. In a more recent British study, Rowley (1968) found that over 90 per cent of white children aged 7 to 15 years chose white friends to sit by, to play with and to invite home. The majority of black children also chose children of their own skin colour and there was only a slight tendency for in-group choices to increase with age. In a sociometric study of secondary schoolchildren, Robertson and Kawwa (1971) found that friends were generally chosen from those of the same colour but that exceptions to this generalization were frequent. The in-group preference (by skin colour) was more marked in the older forms and in the lower streams. Kawwa (1968) found that adolescents who chose friends of a different skin colour were just as likely to be prejudiced as those who did not, indicating that prejudicial attitudes and prejudicial behaviour do not necessarily go together.

Among adults in Bristol, Richmond (1973a) found that most people confined their social relations to people of their own skin colour. This applied both to native white people and to all immigrant groups but was most marked among the Asian immigrants. Nevertheless, 38 per cent of women from the West Indies or Asia had visited white homes and a higher proportion of men had done so. Again, as with children, white people's expressed attitudes to immigrants were only weakly related to whether or not they had spoken to a black person during the previous week.

Influences on Racial Prejudice

Parents are likely to influence their children by their expression of attitudes to skin colour and to ethnic groups. Some studies have suggested that youngsters do not recall being influenced in this way (Horowitz and Horowitz, 1938) while others have shown that most report that they do remember parental influences (Allport and Kramer, 1946). Mosher and Scodel (1960) found a significant association between the ethnic attitudes of American mothers and their twelve to thirteen-year-old children. Radke-Yarrow *et al.* (1952) found only a weak association between the ethnic attitudes of American parents and children, and another study (Bird *et al.*, 1952) found a parent-child similarity in attitudes towards Negroes but not towards Jews. Pushkin's British study (Pushkin and Veness, 1973) found that similarities between parents and children in attitudes applied only in the case of strong hostility to blacks. In summary, it appears that there is some intergenerational continuity in attitudes with respect to race but it is variable and often not very strong.

Many investigations (see review by Sanford, 1973) have shown that racial prejudice tends to be associated with a variety of 'authoritarian' attitudes (Adorno *et al.*, 1950), including rigid adherence to conventional values, a readiness to punish departures from these values, a preoccupation with toughness and dominance and a concern for the definite, unambiguous and predetermined. However, the notion that racial prejudice is closely related to patterns of child rearing has received only modest support. While some investigations have found that ethnic prejudice in children is associated with a parental emphasis on obedience, control, and submission (Gough *et al.*, 1950; Frenkel-Brunswick, 1948) others have not found a relationship with patterns of child-rearing (Mosher and Scodel, 1960; Pushkin and Veness, 1973). It seems that patterns of upbringing play some part in determining individual differences in ethnic attitude but their influence is far from decisive.

Prevailing attitudes in the school or in the general population seem more important influences. Thus, Kawwa (1968) found that racial prejudice was very much more common in London than in Lowestoft; Ward (1971) observed that prejudice (as measured by survey techniques) was less in Manchester than in the country as a whole; and Hyman and Sheatsley (1964) showed that the proportion of white Americans in favour of integrated schools doubled between 1942 and 1963. A variety of factors influence community attitudes, although little is known about their relative importance. Whether contact with other ethnic groups increases or decreases prejudice seems to depend very much on the nature and context of the contact (see review by Yinger and Simpson, 1973). Studies of areas in Britain where immigrant groups have lived for many years indicate that racial discrimination and hostility do not necessarily diminish with time and contact (Little, 1947; Rose *et al.*, 1969). Campbell (1961) found that students' anti-minority attitudes became more negative when schools in one American town became desegregated; and in Britain, Dawwa (1968) found that racial prejudice was more common among London children in contact with immigrants' families than in Lowestoft where immigrants were almost non-existent. On the other hand, Marsh (1970) found that mixed fostering seemed to aid racial harmony. Rose *et al.* (1969) found that personal contact at work with colleagues from different ethnic groups did seem to reduce prejudice; this is also suggested by Patterson (1963) and Wright (1968). American studies have also indicated that inter-racial housing is associated with prejudice in adults (Deutsch and Collins, 1951; Wilner *et al.*, 1955) and that inter-racial holiday camps may reduce prejudice in children (Yarrow *et al.*, 1958). However, much depends on the context. Yinger and Simpson (1973) have summarized the findings as follows: (a) Incidental, involuntary, tension-laden contact is likely to *increase* prejudice; (b) Pleasant equal-status contact which requires no crossing of class or educational barriers is likely to *reduce* prejudice; and (c) Contacts that bring people of minority and majority groups together in shared functionally-important activities should *reduce* prejudice, especially if the activities involve goals which can only be achieved by the active cooperation of members of all groups.

It has been found that the ethics of a school can shape political attitudes (Newcomb, 1963), and it can also modify racial prejudice. Teacher attitudes, styles of teaching and content of lessons may all play a part. Williams (1961) showed that favourable attitudes to West Africans increased when geography teaching on West Africa included details of the people and of everyday life there, but that they did not when teaching focused on regional and physical characteristics. White and Lippit's (1960) studies indicated that 'democratic' styles of teaching fostered cooperation between children better than 'autocratic' methods, and, although not studied, this might have relevance for the development of cooperation between ethnic groups. Madge (1976) showed that children's ethnic preferences in a test situation were influenced by adult approval as expressed in the stories used in the test. How far direct teaching or discussion of race relations in schools improves or worsens the situation remains to be determined. Under favourable circumstances propaganda films can reduce prejudice as measured by paper and pencil tests (Middleton, 1960), but they may actually have the reverse effect and little is known about changes in behaviour outside the test situation.

The connections between attitudes and behaviour are complex and variable. It is often assumed that we behave in the way we do because of the beliefs we hold. But sometimes the process may work in the opposite direction. For example, Lieberman (1956) found that factory workers who became foremen developed more favourable attitudes towards management and that those who became shop stewards developed more positive attitudes towards unions. It is possible that having to behave in a less discriminatory way (because of legal requirements) might also lead to a reduction in racial prejudice, although it is not known whether, or in what circumstances, this occurs. Prejudice and discrimination do not necessarily go together and little is known about the ways in which one influences the other.

Rex and Moore (1967) argued that class conflict and competition for scarce housing were of prime importance in the genesis of racial hostility*. However, Richmond (1973a and b) found no evidence that attitudes to immigrants were the outcome of any objective situation of housing competition. While it seems likely that competition for scarce resources or conflicting needs may well increase inter-group hostility (as shown by studies in other contexts: Sherif *et al.*, 1961), it remains uncertain how important a variable this is in the genesis of racial prejudice.

Conclusions

Prejudice against immigrants, and especially against black people, is fairly widespread among the white population in Britain, although it is by no means universal. Prejudicial attitudes develop early in childhood, but can be modified in adolescence or adult life, given the right circumstances. Whether a person exhibits racial prejudice is to some

*Rex (1970) has subsequently somewhat modified this view.

extent influenced by the attitudes of his parents and by his pattern of upbringing, but to a considerable extent it is shaped by the attitudes he meets at school and in the community in which he lives. The extent and nature of his contact with people from ethnic minority groups, the attitudes and teaching at school, the mass media, and legally enforced patterns of behaviour are also likely to have a major impact on how he feels about black people and how he behaves towards them.

11 Conclusions

The preceding chapters of this book have considered detailed findings on various specific aspects of disadvantage. No attempt will be made to summarize all those findings here. Instead, some of the conceptual issues which bridge these chapters will be discussed. It has been clear that there is no single problem of a cycle of transmitted deprivation. Rather there are many forms of disadvantage which arise in various ways and which show varying degrees and types of intergenerational continuity.

TO WHAT EXTENT ARE PROBLEMS OF DISADVANTAGE STILL WITH US?

The concept of a cycle of deprivation (or disadvantage, as we have preferred to call it) began with the question: 'why is it that ... deprivation and problems of maladjustment so conspicuously persist?' (Joseph, 1972). It is appropriate to begin, therefore, with a consideration of how far the assumptions behind the question are correct. As we have seen, it is indeed true that disadvantage is still very much with us. Although there have been marked improvements in the overall standards of living in this country, poverty remains. Moreover, inequalities in income and wealth are almost as great as they were at the turn of the century, and regional variations in patterns of disadvantage with respect to employment have continued with little change since the First World War. The quality of housing in Britain has steadily improved during this century but even so, one in four children is reared in a home which is overcrowded or lacking in basic amenities (Wedge and Prosser, 1973).

On the whole, educational attainments (as assessed by reading age) have shown a substantial improvement since the Second World War and the average level of intelligence may also have shown a marginal rise. Nevertheless, the level of illiteracy remains high and there are marked differences between geographical areas in reading standards. Low attainments are especially marked in inner city areas. Furthermore, the rise in reading standards after the war seems to have halted (Start and Wells, 1972).

The net amount of social mobility has probably changed little during this century but there has been a reduction in the proportion of unskilled and semiskilled workers, with a corresponding overall upward mobility. However, the gap between the social classes with respect to infantile mortality, educational progress, economic resources, working conditions, and ill-health remains almost as wide as it has ever been (Field, 1971).

Crime rates have markedly risen during the last 50 years and it seems that this reflects an increase in both the amount of crime and the number of criminals, and not simply changes in the law or police practices. No adequate data exist regarding changes over time in the rates of psychiatric disorder, but it seems unlikely that the rates have fallen appreciably. Again, there are large differences in the prevalence of crime and psychiatric disorder according to area, with inner city areas showing the highest level of troubles.

The patterns of parenting and of family life have altered considerably in recent years, with marked trends towards earlier marriage and earlier child-bearing, a higher proportion of illegitimate children, more frequent divorce and smaller families. The concept of 'problem-families' is too vague to allow any accurate estimate of changes in frequency, but what evidence there is indicates that there continues to be a substantial number of families with multiple problems, some of which involve prolonged dependency on social services.

HOW FAR DOES DISADVANTAGE SHOW INTERGENERATIONAL CONTINUITIES?

A second question is how far the continuing presence of disadvantage is due to some form of intergenerational continuity and how far it arises afresh in each succeeding generation. Undoubtedly there are continuities over time. However, only some of these involve familial continuity. Regional continuities in disadvantage, for example, are very striking. Thus, for many years Scotland and the northern parts of England have had particularly high rates of unemployment and of poorly paid workers. Since the First World War, geographical differences in suicide rates have remained remarkably stable. During a similar time period, the same parts of London have maintained the highest rates of delinquency. Over a decade at least, variations between schools in delinquency rates have been shown to be remarkably persistent. Both psychiatric disorder and reading difficulties are very much more prevalent in inner city areas. Continuities may also be evident within socio-cultural groups. During the two generations or so that black people have been in this country, they have continued to be disadvantaged in educational attainment, employment and housing. All of these patterns constitute a form of cycle of disadvantage but in no case is the continuity familial.

Nevertheless, familial continuities do occur. With respect to intelligence, educational attainment, occupational status, crime, psychiatric disorder and 'problem-family' status there are moderate continuities over two generations. Continuities for many aspects of family life are generally fairly slight although they are substantial in the case of severe abnormalities in parenting such as child-battering. Almost no information is available on their strength with regard to normal patterns of parenting, poverty or poor housing.

However, several qualifications have to be made concerning intergenerational continuities. In the first place, even with forms of disadvantage where they are strong, discontinuities are striking. At least half of the children born into a disadvantaged home do not repeat the pattern of disadvantage in the next generation. Over half of all forms of disadvantage arise anew each generation. On the one hand, even where continuity is strongest many individuals break out of the cycle and on the other many people become disadvantaged without having been reared by disadvantaged parents.* In short, familial cycles are a most important element in the perpetuation of disadvantage but they account for only a part of the overall picture.

A second qualification is that continuities are much weaker over three generations than they are over two. Reed and Reed (1965) found that a third of mentally retarded individuals had mentally retarded parents but only one in six of their children and one in twenty-five of their grandchildren was retarded. Even in cases with the strongest family histories of retardation only 16 per cent of the grandchildren were retarded. The same marked reduction in continuities over several generations has been found for all other forms of disadvantage which have been systematically studied.

Thirdly, not only does the extent of continuity vary according to *type* of disadvantage but also it varies considerably according to *level* of disadvantage. Thus, social mobility is much less marked in professional groups than it is amongst skilled manual workers. Similarly, severe mental retardation (IQ below 50) shows almost no intergenerational continuity whereas continuity is moderately strong for mild degrees of retardation or for intelligence within the normal range.

METHODS OF STUDYING INTERGENERATIONAL CONTINUITIES

As already noted, for many variables there is a lack of evidence on how far disadvantage persists over generations. Research is most needed within the areas of economic status, housing, parenting, multiple problems and prolonged reliance on social services. Several strategies may be followed. The most straightforward approach is provided by a longitudinal study. One generation is followed through its life cycle until the next generation has reached the same age. Such studies take

*This statement applies least to child-battering and to problem-family status where continuities are particularly strong. However, data on both are quite limited and even the existing studies show that continuities are not present in some third of instances.

several decades to complete, are very expensive, and suffer from attrition. As a consequence, very few have been carried through to the next generation (Wall and Williams, 1970). A further drawback is that the measures used at the beginning of a study are likely to be outdated and inadequate by the end of the study a generation later. For these reasons, it will rarely be worthwhile to plan life-time longitudinal studies for the purpose of studying intergenerational continuities. Nevertheless, where such studies exist, the opportunity should be taken to collect and utilize data for cross generational comparisons.

A modification of this method is the follow-up enquiry in which a group identified on the basis of information already collected a generation earlier is recontacted for further study. This technique has been used with great effect by Robins (1966; Robins *et al.*, 1975) who has shown the method to be both practical and informative. Its chief merit is that it can be carried out in a short period of time, cutting out the need for a generation's wait which is such a major limitation of prospective studies. As a result, of course, the follow-up study is also very much cheaper. However, like the long-term longitudinal study, it suffers from the effects of social change and secular trends and it is heavily reliant on the type of information available 30 years ago. This last point necessarily severely restricts the scope of the approach.

A third method involves data linkage from existing statistics. This technique has proved valuable in studying the transmission of such characteristics as schizophrenia and criminality, where the appropriate administrative statistics are stored in a form which makes linking possible (e.g. Rosenthal and Kety, 1968; Schulsinger, 1972; Hutchings and Mednick, 1974). Such a data store is available in only a few parts of the world, notably in Scandinavia. The method has immense practical advantages in terms of speed, cost and ease of linkage but suffers greatly from its total reliance on administrative categories, with all the limitations and distortions involved.

A fourth method uses a cross-sectional study of two generations at one point in time (e.g. Rutter, 1966; Rutter *et al.*, 1975; Farrington *et al.*, 1975; Tonge *et al.*, 1975). This approach allows a much greater depth and intensity of information gathering than any of the other strategies and for this reason provides a powerful tool. However, it inevitably means that the cross-generational comparison involves different points in the life cycle for each generation, or it requires the use of retrospective information. As a result, it is a method generally more appropriate for the investigation of mechanisms than of continuities as such.

It is important to note that all children must have *two* parents so that there is a doubling of the number of families involved for each generation studied (i.e., four grandparents, eight great-grandparents, etc.). This creates a particular problem in longitudinal studies as it is most unlikely that both marriage partners will have been followed. It should also be taken into account that parents have a varying number of children. Thus, intergenerational continuities will be influenced by family size because large families give rise to a greater proportion of the next generation. For this reason the extent of familial continuities (in population terms) requires the study of all offspring.

Furthermore, it is essential that the study of continuities should not be restricted to families. Much can be learned about the ways in which socio-cultural, political and ecological factors can increase or decrease disadvantage by studying continuities according to geographical area, type of housing, school, type of township (city, town or village) or ethnic group. Several pioneering studies of this kind have been undertaken (e.g., Faris and Dunham, 1939; Shaw and McKay, 1942) but most have been severely limited by a reliance on hospital or crime statistics which provide a very uncertain guide to true prevalence and by a lack of detailed information on the conditions of life in the groups or areas studied. However, more recent investigations have begun to take this field of study further. When all the necessary checks and corrections have been made, the results still seem to show that people born and bred in inner city areas have higher rates of several kinds of disadvantage than small town inhabitants. The findings suggest that the disadvantage stems from some aspects of living in the inner city but little is known about which features of city life are crucial. Much the same issues apply to the study of continuities with respect to schools and housing.

National or Local Studies

National longitudinal studies are sometimes assumed to be ideal because they are representative of the country as a whole. The argument is fallacious. Britain is not homogeneous and national findings no more represent the Isle of Wight, London or the Lake District than surveys in these areas represent the national scene (Rutter, Tizard and Whitmore, 1970). Planning for the country as a whole cannot be based on national figures for the very same reason. Different areas have different problems and different needs. Moreover, the idea that human development can be studied in a vacuum isolated from the social environment must be rejected. If knowledge is to accrue on how social variables influence development, longitudinal studies must include investigation of the extra-familial as well as intra-familial environment in which a person grows. This requires locally-based data of an intensive kind. That is not to say, of course, that national studies do not have their value. On the contrary, for some purposes they are to be preferred, but for other purposes more is to be gained by comparative studies of several areas, each of which is fairly homogeneous and which differs from other areas in important respects.

Life Cycle Changes and Continuities

Information on life cycle changes is required to appreciate how far different kinds of disadvantage persist throughout life and how far patterns of disadvantage at different ages are comparable. Knowledge on stability and change in attitudes and behaviour over an individual's life time is also important. It provides information about the process of development itself and also indicates the most advantageous points of intervention, including the stage beyond which intervention is too late.

Cross-sectional data are sometimes used to derive estimates of intragenerational continuities by comparing, at one point in time, individuals of one age with individuals of another age. With this method it is necessary to assume that if the rates are the same at two points in the life cycle, then there is continuity. But this argument is fallacious as there is no means of knowing if the rates represent persistence of disadvantage in the same individuals, or the loss and appearance of disadvantage in different individuals. Furthermore, the individuals at each age period come from different generations so that both life cycle changes and secular trends will influence the pattern in a way which is uninterpretable without repeated cross-sectional studies (which constitute the only acceptable measure of secular trends).

It is sometimes thought that longitudinal studies provide a clear and unambiguous measure of the continuity of individual characteristics over time. Certainly, as indicated above, they are essential for that purpose. But also they are not sufficient in themselves if there is any possibility of secular trends, because age differences must also reflect these. This drawback applies to most of the variables discussed in this review, as rates of disadvantage have changed markedly over the last generation.

These difficulties are to some extent overcome if development is studied by means of several short-term longitudinal studies of overlapping age groups (e.g. 0—5 years, 4—9 years, 8—13 years etc.) which can be followed in parallel (Bell, 1953). This strategy is appropriate for many developmental questions and ensures earlier answers than the conventional longitudinal study. However, it is limited in its power to study long-term effects of early life experiences.

One problem in assessing continuity is the difficulty of measuring any feature in the same way at different ages. This is most obvious when administrative categories of disadvantage (such as delinquency) are used. Definitions can be age specific although the underlying behaviours may not be. With other variables the problem is one of a changing pattern of manifestation. Personality variables and intelligence provide good examples; manifestations of each inevitably change during the development from infancy to maturity (Rutter, 1970b). In some cases the form of change is known but in others it has still to be established.

Another difficulty in documenting life cycles of disadvantage is that the most important types of continuity may involve links between (as distinct from within) variables. For example, if a person cannot read as a child it is probable that he will still be illiterate as an adult, but in terms of implications for quality of life this may be less important than the likelihood that reading backwardness will mean certain constraints in choice of job and hence income level. In this case, the main interest may lie in the links between educational attainments in childhood and occupational status or income level in adult life. Another difficulty stems from the fact that because behaviours 'look' the same does not mean that they are the same or have the same meaning in terms of development, course, or cause. For example, delinquency of early onset and late onset differ in their associations with both family status and school performance (Robins and Hill, 1966). The same applies to psychiatric disorder beginning before and during adolescence (Rutter, Graham *et al.*, 1976).

Finally, it has to be recognized that conclusions will be modified by how continuity is assessed. In the first place, continuities will appear misleadingly low if the measures used are weak or unreliable. Secondly, the impressions of continuity or discontinuity will be markedly shaped by the statistical techniques employed. For example, Rutter (1975c) found that when the same measure of childhood behaviour disturbance was obtained on two occasions four years apart, the intercorrelation was only 0.25. This suggests a very low continuity which accounts for only six per cent of the variance. On the other hand, the same data showed that children deviant on the first occasion were two and a half times as likely as other children to be deviant on the second. Furthermore, when data during the intervening years were taken into account it was apparent that children deviant on the first occasion were *ten* times as likely to show persisting deviance over the four year period — a very high degree of continuity. The findings all refer to the same data but the degree of continuity appeared quite different according to the method of assessment.

The same issue arises with continuities in IQ. Lockyer and Rutter (1969), in a follow-up from 6 years to 16 years of a group of children with psychiatric disorder, found that the initial IQ correlated 0.71 with the final IQ. The finding suggested that individual differences in intelligence are reasonably stable. Yet the same data on the same children also showed that, *on average*, the children made an IQ change of over 12 points from the first to the last testing. Expressed this way, the data indicate that quite large changes in IQ level are fairly common. Much the same has been found for normal children (Bradway, 1944, 1945; Bayley, 1949; Sontag *et al.*, 1958). The general issue of how the strength of associations appear rather different with different statistical techniques has been usefully discussed by Jencks *et al.* (1973).

The overall conclusions that may be drawn on intragenerational continuities are rather sparse. Severely antisocial behaviour and recidivist delinquency show considerable continuity from childhood to early adult life and when persistent there is often an association with other disabilities in adulthood. However, isolated delinquent acts or transient antisocial behaviour which are not part of this pattern of continuity are more common in the general population and criminal behaviour often begins for the first time in adult life. In middle life, criminal behaviour tends to diminish and, in particular, aggressive behaviour markedly declines.

Emotional or neurotic disorders show much less continuity over the life cycle. They more often tend to be episodic or self-limiting conditions. However, where there is continuity from childhood to adult life it is almost always similar in form — that is to say if children with emotional disorders show problems in adult life they are likely to be of an emotional kind (rather than of any other type).

Children with educational backwardness in early childhood are likely still to be backward at the time of school leaving but less is known about their adult careers. Individuals with mild retardation of general intelligence who received special education in childhood show a higher incidence of marital and occupational difficulties than do those of normal intelligence but the differences diminish with time and many individuals who show impairment in childhood are well adjusted in the community in middle life (Tizard, 1974b). Very little is known about the adult situation of mildly retarded individuals who remain in ordinary schools or about individuals of normal intelligence with specific educational retardation.

In many professional jobs occupational status tends to rise during middle life. However, illness and physical decline may sometimes lead to a reduced status toward the end of the working life of manual workers. Economic status shows marked and predictable changes during the life cycle which have remained much the same since 1900. In all social groups the periods of lowest income per head are firstly after age 65 years and secondly during the childbearing years. The most affluent period is in early adult life except in the professional managerial group when it is during the time from 50 to 64 years of age. Thus, childhood, the early years of childbearing and old age are the three main periods of relative poverty.

Causal Processes

The causes of disadvantage are many and various and it is not meaningful to attempt to identify the basic or main cause. In the first place, the causes vary according to the type of disadvantage and vary again according to which aspect of that specific disadvantage is being considered. Secondly, the process of causation usually involves a chain of circumstances no one of which can reasonably be identified as basic. Thirdly, in most cases causation involves an interaction between several different types of influence. These issues are best illustrated through examples.

Societal influences are of negligible importance for severe mental retardation but are crucial in the case of poverty. Genetic factors constitute a major influence in the determination of individual variations in intelligence but are of very little importance for variations in housing. Disordered family relationships play a substantial role in the development of certain psychiatric disorders but are insignificant in regard to variations in occupational status. These findings illustrate that different mechanisms are involved in the transmission of different types of disadvantage.

The importance of the causal question may be shown by considering jobs and unemployment. First there is the issue of *how many* people are out of work at any one time. This is determined by the national (and international) economic situation, by political decisions and by regional job opportunities. Personal factors are of little significance. The second issue is *who* is unemployed, and in this case personal factors are more important. Those who are old, who lack work skills, who have chronic physical incapacities or who show marked personality disorders are most likely to be left without jobs. On the other hand, the question of 'who' may be applied, not to individuals, but to groups, such as ethnic minority groups. Here matters of discrimination and stigma loom large and these are influenced both by population attitudes and by the law. Alternatively, the question may concern the extent of the *inequalities* which stem from different types of job or different levels of occupational status. This will be influenced by factors such as national policies regarding the spread and distribution of incomes and the passing on of wealth, by trade union activities, by housing policies, by welfare benefits and by the availability and quality of health services. There will always be teachers and dustmen, doctors and mechanics but the differences between the jobs in terms of economic and other benefits can be reduced or increased by political means. The question may also concern the ease of intergenerational mobility between different occupational levels. Data are sparse on this issue, but presumably educational and job opportunities will affect the ease of upward mobility while the retention of wealth and privilege will impede downward mobility from the top. On the other hand the question of *who shows* occupational mobility again brings in personal factors such as IQ and educational attainment. The factors mentioned for each of these different types of causal question are by no means the only influences but they serve to illustrate the multiplicity of causal questions and the futility of the seemingly simple question of 'what causes low occupational status?'

Of course, the answers to each of these questions may be similar. This is illustrated by child psychiatric disorder, an example which also shows the importance of a causal chain of processes. Although psychiatric problems in childhood constitute a heterogeneous group of disorders with differing patterns of causation, a high proportion can be attributed in large part to various family difficulties. These include such items as family disorder and disruptions, mental illness in the parents, disturbed parent-child relationships, and a large number of children in the family. Factors such as these do much to explain which children develop psychiatric disorder and also to a large extent account for the fact that disorders are generally more common in inner city areas. Family difficulties are more frequent in the metropolis and this explains why child psychiatric problems are also more common. However, although family problems constitute the immediate cause of many instances of child psychiatric disorder, the question of what causes the family problems remains open. Why is family disorder and parental illness more prevalent in the inner boroughs of London? It appears that the answer to this question lies in the effects of city life on adult behaviour. In short, at this level the answer must be sought in social and ecological influences which lie outside the family. The answer to the question of why cities are constructed in the way that they are pushes the matter back further still to political decisions.

Family influences, even in an immediate sense, do not operate in isolation. Although they explain more of the variations between children in psychiatric disorder than any other single known influence, temperamental factors and school variables also play a major role. But that only serves to emphasize the multifactorial nature of most causal processes.

Social Influences

As already discussed, there is an abundance of data showing that adverse social factors of many kinds (slum living, overcrowding, poverty, low social status, etc.) are associated with a wide range of troubles in both children and adults. To an important extent these associations probably represent causal processes which account for some kinds of continuities in disadvantage. However, there is vigorous dispute concerning the size of the effects, the setting in which the effects are mediated (home, school or community) and the mechanisms by which mediation occurs. Unfortunately, most theorists have sought only to support their own positions and have either not looked for ways of testing alternative hypotheses or have not regarded this as worthwhile activity. Nevertheless, it is important to determine the mechanisms which are operative as each carries rather different implications for social policy. This remains an area much needing further research. Both the implications and some of the types of research needed to contrast alternative views are most easily considered by noting some of the mechanisms which have been proposed.

One suggestion is that, to an important extent, continuities are a function of labelling and stigma. This may operate in several quite different ways. First, labelling may lead to purely artefactual continuities because of the way particular behaviours come to notice (Wootton, 1959; Cicourel, 1968). The children of criminal adults may be more likely to be convicted of crimes simply because the police surveillance of the family may bring to official attention behaviours which would otherwise pass unnoticed. Secondly, stigma by virtue of discriminatory practices may directly cause disadvantage (Daniel, 1968). In this way black people are denied jobs and prevented access to good housing. The same process may apply in other situations such as when people have difficulties in obtaining work because of an address which indicates they are homeless, or because of a criminal record. Thirdly, labelling may influence how other people act towards the stigmatized person. This process has been thought to operate in schools in terms of the way teachers' attitudes to children are shaped by knowledge of a child's IQ score or social background (Rosenthal and Jacobson, 1968). In fact this has proved very difficult to investigate and there is very little evidence on how important an effect it is. Fourthly, labelling may alter a person's own behaviour or attitudes. For example, there is some suggestion that the experience of conviction may modify a person's self-image in such a way that he then becomes more likely to commit delinquent acts (West and Farrington, 1973). Fifthly, the cultural climate in which a behaviour takes place may so influence peoples' attitudes towards it that it has a different significance for the future. For example, Christensen's comparison (1960) of three communities suggested that the consequences of premarital sex differed according to the community's sexual mores. In the area with strong taboos against premarital sex, premarital conception appeared more likely to lead to early marriage and to marital breakdown later.

There is good evidence that labelling exists as a phenomenon and that it can restrict individual opportunities. However, much less is known on how powerful an influence it is as a means of changing behaviour. Short-term longitudinal studies of groups with comparable characteristics but which differ in terms of labelling (by virtue of criminal convictions, psychiatric care, intellectual testing etc.) would be informative in this connection.

It has been suggested that in certain subcultures there are behaviours which are normal in that setting although not in the broader community. In this way it has been suggested that subcultural delinquency may not carry the implications of 'disordered' behaviour it sometimes does under other circumstances (Mays, 1954). A similar type of hypothesis has been proposed to account for low educational achievement in children from poor neighbourhoods of low social status (Ginsberg, 1972) and for IQ scores in the mentally retarded range among ethnic minority groups (Mercer, 1973). The suggestion is that the low scores do not carry the implications of low intelligence they would in other groups, and that normal functioning is evident in other (non-test) situations. If these views are correct, it would seem to follow that youngsters from the specified socio-cultural background who show delinquency or low IQ scores should differ from other delinquent or mentally retarded persons in three ways: (a) there should be less evidence of impairment in other areas of functioning (e.g. peer relationships, adaptive behaviour, emotions); (b) there should be less association with abnormalities in family interaction or relationships; and (c) there should be less likelihood of personality disorder or occupational problems in adult life.

As already discussed, there are indications that these suggestions do apply to some delinquency and to some low IQ scores in people from socially disadvantaged backgrounds, although as a general explanation they have proved unsatisfactory. As with other social explanations, rigorous testing is required to determine the particular circumstances in which the mechanism operates and the proportion of instances accounted for in this way.

Different forms of subcultural pattern have also been suggested in which the emphasis is on reaction to frustration rather than on normative behaviour. Thus, it has been hypothesized that the structure of society (or its institutions — e.g. schools) effectively blocks access to personal goals and public status for certain segments of the population and that delinquency or opting out of education is the result (e.g. Cohen, 1956; Merton, 1957; Hargreaves, 1967). This view of the way in which social influences work has been investigated largely by means of descriptive studies. However, as Platt (1971) has pointed out, descriptive studies are not well designed to test alternative hypotheses; these require other kinds of investigations.

These hypothesized adverse effects of social structure could lead to particular behaviours (delinquency, educational failure, etc.) independently of family and personal factors or through a lowering of the threshold for the operation of other adverse influences. Again, comparisons of the pattern of association with these behaviours in socially advantaged and socially disadvantaged groups would help in determining the extent to which these social theories are valid.

As discussed in the chapters on delinquency and education, attention has also been paid to the extent to which attitudes or behaviour are learned from the people with whom one comes in contact. For example, the debate concerning the social benefits or otherwise of comprehensive schooling is influenced by these considerations. There is evidence that this process does occur as shown by attitude change in people promoted to foremen (e.g. Lieberman, 1956), or in girls who attend a school with a particular political ethos (Newcomb, 1963). However, the matter is clearly not just a question of personal contact; the development of particular styles or behaviour is dependent on the social structure of the group as a whole, on status and role relationships and on reference groups (see Kelvin, 1969 for a useful summary of these issues). Cohort studies in which changes in attitudes or behaviour relevant to issues of disadvantage may be related to sociometric findings and social group data would help elucidate the importance of these mechanisms. Up to now, most of the systematic studies have been concerned with experimental situations which have little to do with the problems of disadvantage as discussed in this volume.

Each of the above theories has been concerned with various possible direct effects of social influence but it is necessary also to consider indirect effects. It could be that poor living conditions or a low social status neighbourhood lead to emotional disturbance, delinquency or low educational attainments — not because of status frustration, labelling, or the like, but because these social influences increase the likelihood of the types of intra-familial difficulty which predispose to those outcomes. Thus, it could be that the mechanisms underlying psychiatric disorder are just the same in the slums as in prosperous suburbia but that the conditions giving rise to the effects are more likely in the slums. Some of the findings concerning depression in working class women (e.g. Brown *et al.*, 1975) provide pointers in that direction, but so far systematic data are lacking on the extent to which particular social circumstances increase or decrease either the number of acute or chronic stresses or the likelihood of succumbing to them. Studies on these issues should be rewarding. Research is also needed on the effects of social change. Most studies of the effects of rehousing people from slum dwellings have been limited by the fact that attention has usually been confined to quite short-term effects and by the limited data available on the social consequences of housing. It is, of course, worthwhile in its own right to provide people with housing which is more spacious and better equipped with domestic amenities. But the extent to which this material improvement leads to a reduction in other forms of disadvantage may well be dependent on whether the new housing facilitates or impedes social relationships.

SOCIAL STRUCTURE AND INSTITUTIONAL FACTORS

In the previous section, social influences were considered in terms of the ways they operated on the individual. Another approach is to consider them in terms of the institutional framework provided by the social structure. This is not really an alternative so much as a complementary approach in that it focuses on how social structure leads to social disadvantage for certain groups rather than on how disadvantage leads to personal troubles.

It has already been noted that black people are subject to various forms of stigma and discrimination. This may be the result of individual attitudes and practices but it is important also to examine the ways in which society's structure leads to or perpetuates such discriminations. For example, certain local authorities have demanded a long period of residence before newcomers are placed on the housing list. The result of this policy is to exclude immigrants from council housing and force them into privately rented accommodation. When the immigrants are relatively poor and there is a period of high immigration this can lead to ghettoes of immigrants in poor quality housing. Not only does this tend to segregate immigrant families but also it leads to schools with a high proportion of immigrants and hence often schools with many children with language problems and educational retardation (because of the poorer schooling in many of the countries from which they have come).

The existing framework of society also shapes the distribution of wealth and job opportunities. For example, the possession of capital enables a person to purchase his house. This has numerous effects beyond the immediate one of home ownership. First, present tax arrangements allow borrowing of money for house purchase under particularly advantageous circumstances and this is of course not open to people unable to raise the money needed to obtain a mortgage. Second, the continually rising value of property means that this constitutes an unusually economical and profitable form of saving which is not available to tenants of rented property. Third, house ownership provides a cushioning effect against the drop of income after retirement (as neither rent nor loan payments will then be required). Fourth, it leads to the passing on of wealth (in the form of a house or the proceeds of the sale) to the next generation.

Similar issues arise with respect to borrowing money. The possession of some capital enables a person to borrow money at the more economical rates of bank overdrafts or personal loans rather than the expensive rates of hire purchase. In short, the framework of society is so organized as to lead to the perpetuation of wealth (and its growth) (Atkinson, 1972).

Wealth and property also have other effects. The ability to purchase his house allows a person to choose to live in an area with more advantageous schooling for his children (quite apart from the possibility of purchasing private schooling which stems from wealth). This in turn will influence later job opportunities. The ownership of a business also provides particular job opportunities for the children which may not be as easily available to others.

Many of these influences of social structure are most evident in the privileged sections of the population. Less is known about their impact on under privileged groups. Nevertheless, local authority housing policy may act to their disadvantage. In addition, both stigma and disruption of the family may follow poverty accompanied by loss of housing. It has been suggested that jobs may be more difficult to obtain for people with an institutional address, and policies demanding a split-up of families placed in temporary housing are creating living conditions which predispose to a variety of disorders and difficulties in children.

There are major inequalities within the United Kingdom in the geographical distribution of resources. These, too, may influence many aspects of life. Thus, medical facilities are much better in the south-east and, conversely, perinatal mortality and complications of pregnancy are generally more common in the north-west (Butler and Bonham, 1963). An unequal distribution of industry leads to pockets of high unemployment and consequent low income and low morale.

That the existing social structure does have effects of this kind which tend to perpetuate both advantage and disadvantage across generations cannot be doubted. Nevertheless, much has still to be learned about the extent and nature of these influences in leading to the intergenerational transmission of 'deprivation', and research to this end is much needed.

Institutions, too, may influence how people behave. This is illustrated by findings on schools. It is known that there are marked variations between schools in rates of delinquency, behavioural disorder and reading retardation. The evidence suggests that these variations are not entirely explicable in terms of selective intake or influences outside the school, and the question next arises as to what school-specific factors are important. Suggestions and hypotheses are available from a variety of studies but little hard evidence is available on the relative importance of different variables. Among those suggested as critical are the models provided by teachers and by peer groups, the types of labelling, the extent of child autonomy, the patterns of rewards and punishments and the nature and extent of home-school contact.

There is extensive experimental evidence that children may be influenced by the models of behaviour presented to them and some data to suggest that modelling is also important in the real life situation (Bandura, 1969). Models may be provided by the style of interaction with children outside the classroom, by the interaction between teachers and also by the disciplinary techniques used. Labelling may be important in terms of the ways in which success and failure are recognized in the school. Schools where the public recognition is oriented towards success are likely to differ from those which focus on failure. In addition, schools which emphasize competition between pupils may influence children differently from those which avoid personal comparisons or ignore rates of progress. Patterns of reward and punishment will have an effect both in terms of their efficiency and in terms of the behaviours which are discouraged or encouraged. How far there is an opportunity for children to influence school policy and practices may well help determine their commitment to school and their identification with its goals. In this connection the extent to which there is a stable 'culture' of the school is likely to be important. The nature of the school culture and the extent of a child's commitment to it are likely also to be influenced by the quality and frequency of contacts between the home and the school.

So far, these ideas remain at the stage of tentative hypotheses which have some circumstantial support but which have yet to be systematically studied. Vigorous arguments have been put forward that the school provides the answer to many of the problems shown by children (Tizard, 1973; Wall, 1973) but evidence is lacking both on how strong the school influence is and how it operates. Answers to these questions need to be obtained if appropriate action is to be taken to make schools effective agents of change.

FAMILY FACTORS

A person's experiences and relationships within his immediate family constitute one of the most important influences on his development.

The evidence discussed in previous chapters indicated that family variables are crucial in the genesis of several forms of disadvantage — but especially with respect to intelligence, educational attainment, delinquency, psychiatric disorder and parenting problems. Much of the literature in recent years on family influences has been concerned with the rather diffuse and global topic of 'maternal deprivation'. A review of this topic shows that many different influences and different effects are involved and that these need to be differentiated if the processes leading to disadvantage are to be understood (Rutter, 1972a). Most of these processes have been noted earlier in the book but it may be useful to discuss some of the research issues which arise by outlining a few of the dimensions of parenthood.

First, the family provides stable bonds or relationships which may serve as the basis for the child's growing circle of relationships outside the family (Bowlby, 1971). Much has still to be learned about the ways in which these develop (Schaffer, 1971) and we lack sound knowledge on what happens when these early bonds do not form in the normal way. Nevertheless, it appears that in some cases a serious failure in early bond formation may lead to what has been termed 'affectionless psychopathy' a condition in which the individual seems unable to sustain relationships of depth (Rutter, 1972a). This may occasionally happen as a result of rearing in a poor quality institution without caretakers with a sustained individual interest in the child, or in families in which there is a serious lack of affection and stable relationships. It should be noted, however, that there are many other causes of psychopathy which cannot be attributed to this mechanism. The evidence is meagre, but there is some suggestion that individuals who do not receive consistent early parenting may later lack the skills needed for successful parenting, even if they themselves have escaped serious disorder.

The whole subject of early attachment behaviour and its significance for personality development, for social skills and for good parenting warrants much more research. Several issues require critical examination: to what extent must the first attachments be formed during infancy and to what extent is it possible for normal bond formation to occur if the possibilities for attachments only come later in childhood? How far are the later sequelae dependent on what happens when the child is older? What are the minimal requirements for bond formation to occur? Can an early failure of bonding lead to later abnormalities of parenting (such as child abuse) even in the absence of personality disorder or mental illness? To what extent are the later problems due to what is *lacking* in childhood and to what extent to the presence of stresses and distorted relationships?

Later in childhood, after bonds develop, discordant and disturbed intrafamilial relationships may have a rather different effect in leading to disorders of conduct or to recidivist delinquency (Rutter, 1971b) and perhaps to problems in parenting. Separation experiences are often part of this process but the evidence suggests that it is not the separation *per se* which matters but rather the family disharmony which preceded and led to the separation. On the whole, the ill-effects of separation have been over-estimated in the past and most of the ills attributed to separation have turned out to be due to other adverse factors associated with, but not intrinsic to, separation (Rutter, 1972b). Nevertheless, permanent disruptions of important relationships, as by the death of family members, may be associated with later depressive disorders, perhaps especially if the loss occurs during adolescence. Several other research issues arise in connection with the problems that stem from disturbed intra-familial relationships. One is the degree to which good relationships *outside* the home can compensate for discord and hostility within it. Another is the extent to which impaired inter-personal relationships are important in their own right rather than as indications of other things going wrong in the family.

Secondly, the family provides models of behaviour for the child to follow by imitation or identification (Bandura, 1969). The child's style of coping with stress will be influenced by the strategies he sees employed by his parents (Rutter, 1975a). If they deal with difficulties by passive resignation or maladaptive aggression he is more likely to do so also. Inter-personal relationships are likely to be influenced similarly. The marital relationship between his parents is the only model of a close relationship which the child is likely to experience over a long period of time. His father's relationship with his mother will, to an important extent, serve as a model for a boy's own heterosexual relationships.

There is good evidence that in certain experimental situations children do follow adults' behaviour as shown either in real life or on film (Bandura, 1969). There is suggestive evidence that for some children under some circumstances, violence on television can lead to imitative behaviour (Surgeon General, 1972). However, much less is known about the *long term* consequences of particular models of behaviour and evidence is lacking on how far parental influences on children's behaviour occur by virtue of imitation or identification.

Thirdly, parents establish a set of attitudes which the child may follow — or rebel against. For example, children's anxiety about the separations from home involved in going to school may stem from the parents' own anxiety about separation which is communicated to the child (Eisenberg, 1958). Or, over-protective attitudes and behaviour may impede the child's development of autonomy and of relationships with his peers (Levy, 1943). There is much clinical anecdote about such processes but research evidence is distinctly sparse.

Fourthly, the family provides necessary life experiences. Thus, the linguistic environment in the home serves to develop the child's competence in language and also his verbal intelligence (Rutter and Mittler, 1972). Exactly which types of experiences have which effects remains somewhat uncertain but it appears that children reared in homes in which there is a paucity of play, little use of toys, and a failure to use language as a medium for the expression of ideas and concepts, are more likely to show intellectual and educational retardation. The quality of verbal interaction seems particularly important in this connection but the crucial elements in this are not known. Some of the problems of children in large families seem to stem from inadequate life experiences of some kind, although what aspect of interaction are responsible for this effect remains to be determined. Perhaps the topics most needing further research is this area are the importance or otherwise of toys, play and adult-child interactions in the pre-school years; the best ways in which parents can be helped to provide the necessary experiences for their children; the differences in family life and parent-child interaction which stem from the presence of a large number of children in the family; and the role of the school in compensating for privations at home.

Fifthly, parents help shape their children's behaviour by selective encouragement and discouragement of particular actions, by discipline and by the amount of freedom they allow (Becker, 1964; Hetherington and Martin, 1972). In the past the *type* of disciplinary techniques employed (corporal punishment versus withdrawal of love, etc) has been the focus of study but it now seems this is much less important than the choice of behaviours to be rewarded or punished and the efficiency with which this is done. Efficiency involves many facets but timing, consistency and selective attention to the child's behaviour are probably particularly important. However, these aspects of discipline have been little studied up to now and warrant further investigation. Obviously, living conditions will influence the ease by which efficient discipline is achieved; the interaction between social circumstances and family functioning is perhaps the area most needing further research in the field of family studies.

Sixthly, the family acts as a secure base from which the child can test out new ways of exploring and responding to the environment. The parents similarly serve as a source of comfort at times of stress and distress. The home provides a communication network by which the child can set his standards, establish his norms, develop his expectations and let his ideas grow. Disorders in the child are probably more frequent when family communication is poor or upset by conflicts or extremes of dominance and submission (Hetherington and Martin, 1972). However, although these motives constitute the basis of much family therapy in psychiatry, there is little systematic evidence on the importance or otherwise of abnormalities in family communication. This is another topic which requires study.

One of the key issues facing those who help troubled families is the question of when it is appropriate to remove a child from his home. Research into this question is greatly needed. The evidence clearly shows that children who remain in a severely disadvantaged home have a much increased risk of all sorts of problems. The same applies to children who experience periods of care in Children's Homes and foster homes. These findings stand in sharp contrast to the generally good outcome for children from a disadvantaged background who are adopted in infancy. Investigations are needed to determine how institutions for children can best facilitate normal development and what is needed to ensure high quality foster care. Comparative studies are required to delineate the circumstances in which adoption or permanent fostering in middle childhood is to be preferred to the child remaining at home with parents who are receiving the best possible social and material help.

The examples of dimensions of parenthood given above serve to illustrate the complex of varying roles served by the family during a child's development. Good evidence is available on the adverse consequences of failure to fill some of these roles adequately, but on others knowledge is quite fragmentary. It should also be evident that the family cannot be considered in isolation from its cultural setting and the institutional framework provided by society. Many of the dimensions noted above will be shaped as much by social forces and lack of material resources as by the parents' own background and experiences. Exactly how this occurs, and the relative importance of different influences, remain to be determined.

GENETIC FACTORS

Throughout most discussions in the literature on 'deprivation' and 'cycles of disadvantage', there has been an emphasis on possible environmental determinants of intergenerational continuities. However, genetic factors have also been shown to be influential. They are particularly important in the case of intelligence, some psychiatric conditions and certain disorders and attributes of personality. By implication they are also of some importance with respect to social status. They play a lesser role in the case of scholastic attainment and less still in the case of minor delinquency. In short, it may be concluded that genetic factors are responsible for an important part of some cycles of disadvantage although they are of little or no relevance for others.

Studies to determine the relative influence of heredity and environment are subject to certain limitations. The main drawback of twin studies has been the biases which may be introduced by selective sampling. Some of the earlier studies are particularly open to this objection but, with most of the main characteristics, well-controlled twin studies are now available. On the whole, these show a slightly smaller influence of heredity than had earlier investigations, but the general trends of the earlier findings have been supported. Objections have also been raised to the twin method on the grounds that monozygotic twins are more likely to be treated in the same fashion by their parents than are dizygotic twins. There is something in this argument but the meagre available evidence suggests that the overall effect is usually quite small (Mittler, 1971). In theory, the study of monozygotic pairs separated in infancy avoids this problem, although in practice most separated twins have been placed in fairly similar environments. A further criticism is that twins are different to singletons and so findings cannot be generalized to individuals who are not twins. There is one situation in which the strength of this argument has been demonstrated. On average, twins have a lower verbal intelligence than do singletons, but this is so only to a trivial extent when one member of the twin pairs dies in infancy (Record *et al.*, 1970). It appears that the lower average verbal intelligence in twins is largely due to non-genetic factors operating after birth. However, for most characteristics, twins are not much (if at all) different from singletons, so this criticism has little force.

A more important limitation to twin studies stems from the fact that the amount of variation attributable to genetic factors necessarily varies according to environmental circumstances (Bronfenbrenner, 1972; Rutter, 1974a). This poses a problem in that (with the exception of twins reared apart) the environmental variation in twin studies is merely the small variation found within a family. This is likely to be much less than the *between*-family variation in the general population. Studies of adoptees are much less subject to this distortion and for that reason are preferable for many purposes. However, children are not given out for adoption randomly (Hutchings and Mednick, 1974), which introduces a further source of bias. The extent of this bias is not known so that the degree of distortion it introduces remains uncertain. Family studies are less subject to these biases but are a much weaker tool because they often confound genetic and environmental influences with the result that each influence leads to somewhat similar hypotheses concerning familial concordance.

These (and other) limitations mean that genetic studies must be considered with some caution. It is not sensible or useful to produce a single estimate of heritability for any given characteristic because the degree of genetic influence varies with environmental circumstances. The many objections to each genetic method have led some writers to dismiss heredity as a negligible influence. However, this dismissal is quite unwarranted, as the best controlled and most stringent studies still show a strong genetic influence for many (but not all) characteristics. The weight (and variety) of evidence forces the conclusion that in all ordinary circumstances genetic factors account for a substantial proportion of the differences between people.

Nevertheless, even if that conclusion is accepted, it does not follow that environmental factors are of little importance in cycles of disadvantage. It may be useful to consider why that does not follow.

The main issues requiring explanation are why some individuals or groups of individuals have particular 'troubles' and why these 'troubles' are carried on through succeeding generations. Thus, one may ask why it is that some individuals are illiterate or poor whereas others are not; why reading difficulties and delinquency are very much commoner in London than in areas of small towns; why children with immigrant parents have, on average, lower scholastic attainments than do other children; and why the offspring in 'problem-families' so often go on, when adult, to have the same difficulties as did their parents.

Several conceptual and statistical points arise when the genetic findings are applied to these questions. The first point is that some of these questions refer to *group* levels of performance, whereas the genetic data mainly refer to *individual* differences in performance. This distinction may be illustrated by considering the Iowa study findings on intelligence for children born to parents of low intelligence (see Chapter 4). It was found that when such children were adopted and placed in reasonably favourable homes, the correlation between their IQ and that of their parents remained almost as high as that between ordinary children (who had not been adopted) and their parents. In short, the *differences* between children were still explicable in genetic terms to an important extent. But, their *level* of intelligence had risen greatly, way above that of their parents, right up to society's norms. In other words, environmental enrichment (relative to their background) had made only a slight difference to the genetic basis of individual differences, but it had succeeded in transforming a potentially impaired population into normally competent citizens.

The same phenomenon has been shown with respect to height (Tizard, 1975b). Although individual differences in height are largely a function of hereditary influences, the fact that people today are much taller than were their counterparts at the beginning of this century is almost certainly a result of environmental improvements. The same applies to the marked IQ and reading attainment differences between children of West Indian parentage born in this country and those born abroad. Although it may well be that individual differences within the West Indian group have a substantial genetic component, the superior attainments of the children born in this country seem to be a consequence of advantages in schooling and upbringing. Similarly, although doubtless genetic factors are important in determining individual differences in reading and in psychiatric disorder, they do not explain why these troubles are twice as common in London as on the Isle of Wight.

In summary, in practice as well as in theory, *intra*-group findings on heritability may not be generalized to *inter*-group differences. This issue most obviously applies to the controversy regarding the origin of racial differences in measured intelligence (Jensen, 1969). Genetic studies have clearly shown the importance of heredity in determining individual differences within a white population. Whether this applies to individual differences within a black population can only be determined by genetic studies within this group. These have yet to be done. However, even if this is found (as is quite likely), it still does not follow that genetic factors account for differences *between* 'blacks' and 'whites'. To answer that question requires a quite different strategy, involving the removal of existing barriers and privations operating to the disadvantage of black people.

Even with conditions in which the genetic component is very strong, non-genetic factors may have a critical, albeit small, effect. For example, schizophrenia has a strong hereditary component (Rosenthal and Kety, 1968). Even so, the course of the disorder has been found to be strongly influenced by both the pattern of family relationships (Brown *et al.*, 1962, 1972) and type of institutional care (Wing and Brown, 1970). Stress factors also play some part in precipitating the onset of the condition (Brown and Birley, 1968). Manipulation of these environmental variables may be critical in determining the course of the condition in individual patients in spite of the fact that genetic factors are of major importance.

Heredity is usually considered as a reason for parents and children being alike in some respect, but it is also a reason for their being different. Polygenic inheritance results in a *spread* among the children within a family with respect to the inherited characteristics. Not only does this follow from theoretical considerations but there is good evidence that it also occurs in practice. Within families there is considerable individual variation in characteristics such as height and intelligence and this variation is an important cause of intergenerational discontinuity. It is likely, for example, that genetic factors contribute to social mobility and help to explain why some children show superior talents in spite of an extremely disadvantaged upbringing.

Much of the concern regarding cycles of disadvantage centres on the transmission of 'troubles' from one generation to the next. It should not be assumed that because a condition has a strong hereditary component the intergenerational transmission is necessarily genetic. This apparent paradox may be illustrated by the findings on the children of parents with some mental illness or disorder. Many of these conditions have an important hereditary element (Shields, 1973). There is also a considerable tendency for the children to have a high rate of psychiatric problems (Rutter, 1966; Rutter, Quinton and Yule, 1976). It may be assumed that some of the transmission is genetically based, particularly where the disorders in parent and child are similar. However, in most cases the disorders in the children are *different* to those in their parents and transmission is to a considerable extent explicable in terms of factors such as marital discord and disturbed intra-familial relationships (Rutter, 1971b). In these cases, the cycle involved the transmission of 'troubles' but the troubles were not quite the same in each generation and non-genetic factors probably played an important role.

It is said that 80 per cent of the variation in human intelligence is due to genetic factors. As indicated in Chapter 4, the precise figure has little meaning but it may be accepted as a fact that the majority of the variance is due to hereditary influences. It is commonly assumed that an heritability of 80 per cent leaves little room for the operation of environmental influences. However, this is quite false. Using Burks (1928) data (which showed 93 per cent heritability), it would be expected on environmental grounds alone that the most advantaged million people in Britain would have an IQ some 24 points above the least advantaged million. This is quite a sizeable influence by any standard! It should be added that for most types of disadvantage, heritability is much less than 80 per cent so that the effects of the environment can be expected to be correspondingly greater.

Nature—Nurture Interactions

Of course, the separation of genetic and environmental influences is rather artificial as they must always both be present. It is a complete nonsense to envisage environmental forces shaping development without a biological substrate, just as it is ridiculous to consider heredity operating independently of life circumstances. Nevertheless, much remains to be learned about the ways in which nature and nurture interact.

First, there is the possibility that genetic factors have different implications for development in different environmental circumstances. This has been shown experimentally for maze-learning in rats (Cooper and Zubek, 1958). Genetic influences accounted for a large amount of individual variation in an ordinary laboratory environment but made little difference in either a very deprived or a very stimulating environment. In short, in these circumstances, genetic and environmental influences were not additive, they were interactive. It is likely that this also occurs with respect to human disadvantage but evidence on this point is lacking.

However, interaction between non-genetic biological variables and the social environment has been found. Thus, among children from a socially favoured background there is no association between low birth weight and low IQ (except in the case of overt neurological disorder). But, in the most socially disadvantaged groups there is an association between low birth weight and low IQ. It seems that mild biological impairment may render a child more vulnerable to the hazards of poor upbringing. A different sort of interaction is evident with chronic physical illness. Mild physical handicaps may have no effect on the earning power of a clerical worker but may totally prevent work in a labourer.

Interaction in a different context was studied by Rutter (1971b). Among children reared in a harmonious family the presence of a parent with personality disorder did not increase the risk of psychiatric disorder in the children. On the other hand, for children in a discordant unhappy home, parental personality disorder was strongly associated with conduct disturbances in the children. Whether this implies a nature—nurture interaction or an interaction between two environmental stresses could not be determined from the data.

It should also be appreciated that genetic factors may sometimes operate through their influence on people's experiences (see discussion in Rutter, 1975a). It has been found that temperamentally different children *elicit* different behaviours from other people. Highly active infants receive more attention from their caretakers (Campbell, 1974), an observation which may explain Schaffer's finding (1966) that more active babies are less affected by a depriving environment. Because they elicit more attention, they are actually less deprived than more passive infants. Dependent children are more likely to be controlled by their parents and congenitally handicapped children receive different parental care. Temperamentally 'difficult' children have been found to elicit more negative feelings from their parents (Graham *et al.*, 1973) and it may be that their greater vulnerability to psychiatric disorder stems in part from this temperamentally induced 'hostile' environment.

The systematic study of this type of interaction is relatively recent and data remain sparse. However, it appears a particularly rewarding field for research and further work is greatly needed.

BREAKING OUT OF CYCLES OF DISADVANTAGE

For the most part research of all kinds has focussed on the reasons why things go wrong in development. There is a considerable store of knowledge on the ill-effects which stem from various forms of privation, deprivation and stressful experience. Some of this knowledge has been reviewed in this book. It has been repeatedly emphasized that children raised in the most deplorable circumstances not infrequently develop into normal adults. It is true, of course, that many are seriously damaged by their experiences but, in our view, not enough attention has been paid to the fairly numerous exceptions. We are never likely to be in a position to remove all forms of 'bad' experience or to enable all children to have an optimal upbringing, though we should strive to that end. More frequently, those in the helping professions have to do the best they can to assist people to cope with circumstances which fall far short of the ideal. Information on the factors which enable people to overcome an unpromising start to life or to take later stresses in their stride would be of enormous practical benefit. Unfortunately very little is known on this topic and research into the factors which facilitate a breaking out from cycles of disadvantage should receive a high priority.

As already noted, children's responses to stressful situations are modified by their temperamental characteristics. Adaptable, predictable, and malleable children are less likely to develop psychiatric problems when their parents are mentally ill. Highly active children are less likely to suffer developmental impairment in an understimulating institution and children who are reflective and deliberate are less likely to suffer reading difficulties. In part, these attributes will be shaped by constitutional factors (Berger, 1973) and are important for policy only in that they indicate which children are most and which are least at risk. But the attributes may also be shaped by experiences. For example, Kagan *et al.* (1966) found that impulsive children became more reflective in response to reflective style teaching in school, and

Hertzig *et al.* (1968) found marked differences in temperamental style between middle class American and working class Puerto Rican children, differences which seemed to stem in part from patterns of upbringing.

Robins *et al.* (1975) found that black children living in broken homes of low social status were less likely to drop out of school if brought up by grandparents. In these circumstances, the extended family appeared to provide continuity and support in an otherwise unstable situation. Other studies, too, have shown that when a child is reared in an institution or when his family life is discordant and disrupted, one good relationship can have an important protective influence. Both Conway (1957) and Pringle (Pringle and Bossio, 1960; Pringle and Clifford, 1962) found that institutional children who enjoyed a stable relationship with an adult (not necessarily the parent) were better adjusted. Similarly, Wolkind (1971) found less behavioural disturbance in institutional children who had been at least two years with the same house-mother. In a study of the families of psychiatric patients, Rutter (1971b) showed that in homes characterized by severe marital discord, a good relationship with one parent served to protect children against the development of disorders of conduct. Wilson (1974) also noted that careful supervision or 'chaperonage' of children in 'problem families' was associated with a reduced risk of delinquency.

The mechanisms underlying these associations are likely to be varied. In some cases, the family ties of children living in disadvantageous circumstances are probably important because they allow early bonds to develop, in others because they provide the child with one good relationship bringing stability in the midst of instability, and in others because of the control provided. What is important, however, is that even in the worst family circumstances, a few 'good' factors can do much to balance the serious maladaptive and disruptive influences. If we knew more about these protective factors we would be in a better position to help children at risk.

It has already been noted that a complete change from a poor to a good environment, such as occurs with adoption, does much to ensure normal development. The Heber studies (see Chapter 4) also demonstrate that massive environmental change can have substantial benefits for children from a severely disadvantaged background. But little is known on what sort of environmental change, and how great a change, is needed to bring benefits. There is substantial evidence that the characteristics of a child's schooling influence his development. But we do not know how far good schooling can compensate for a poor home life. Improved housing is worthwhile for its own sake but how much difference does this make to other forms of disadvantage? Rates of various kinds of disorder are high among families living in the inner boroughs of London. How far do benefits follow from a move to one of the 'new towns' or to other parts of Britain?

As indicated by Sir Keith Joseph in the original speech on a 'cycle of transmitted deprivation', the rise in national prosperity does not seem to have made much difference to most forms of disadvantage. But perhaps it is an inequality of incomes which leads to disadvantage rather than low income as such.

At the moment it is only possible to point to isolated bits of evidence on factors which lead to discontinuities in cycles of disadvantage. These fall far short of any coherent body of knowledge, but they serve as pointers to possible variables which warrant more systematic study.

It is sometimes assumed that nothing less than a complete change of our economic and social structure could influence cycles of disadvantage. This view stems from the extensive evidence concerning inequalities in our society and the findings that poor living conditions are often associated with delinquency, educational failure and the like. We share the feelings of outrage concerning the appalling circumstances under which many families have to bring up their children and we regard both the regional maldistribution of national resources and the very large gap between the advantaged and the underprivileged sections of society as unacceptable. Of course, action is needed to remedy these problems, but we delude ourselves if we think that nothing short of massive social change can influence cycles of disadvantage. In the first place, cycles of disadvantage are to be found at all levels of society. They are by no means confined to the poor. In the second place, the associations with inadequate living conditions provide a very poor guide to levels of disadvantage in other respects. For example, the National Child Development Study makes much of the association between overcrowding and low attainment in reading. Davie *et al.* (1972) argue that this is a causal relationship and that 'the effect of overcrowding . . . is equivalent to approximately nine months' retardation in reading age'. But as both Rutter (1975b) and Burgess (1975) have pointed out, overcrowded homes are more than twice as common in Scotland as in England, yet in spite of this Scottish children are much better readers. Why? While the answer to that question is not known, the very posing of it emphasizes the existence of possibilities for action to overcome cycles of disadvantage. If research into such cycles merely reconfirms that children disadvantaged in one respect are often also disadvantaged in other respects it will have failed. What are needed are investigations to determine why this is often *not* the case and how we can bring about discontinuities in cycles of disadvantage. This is the challenge for the future.

References

ABE, K. (1972) 'Phobias and nervous symptoms in childhood and maturity: persistence and associations', *Brit. J. Psychiat.*, **120**, 275–283.

ABEL-SMITH, B. (1958) 'Whose welfare state?' in MacKenzie, N. (Ed.), *Conviction*, MacGibbon & Kee.

ABEL-SMITH, B. and TOWNSEND, P. (1965) *The Poor and the Poorest*, Occasional Papers on Social Administration No. 17., Bell.

ABRAMSON, J. H. (1966) 'Emotional disorder, status inconsistency and migration', *Milbank Mem. Fd. Quart.*, 44, 23–48.

ACHURST, B. (1975) Personal communication.

ACLAND, H. (1973) 'Social determinants of educational achievement: an evaluation and criticism of research', Ph.D. Thesis, Univ. of Oxford.

ADORNO, T. W. FRENKEL-BRUNSWIK, E., LEVINSON, D. J. and SANDFORD, R. N. (1950) *The Authoritarian Personality*, Harper.

AHERN, F. M. and JOHNSON, R. C. (1973) 'Inherited uterine inadequacy: an alternate explanation for a portion of cases of defect', *Behavior Genetics*, 3, 1–12.

AINSWORTH, M. D. (1962) 'The effects of maternal deprivation: a review of findings and controversy in the context of research strategy', in *Deprivation of Maternal Care: a reassessment of its effects*, World Health Organization, Geneva.

AKERS, R. L. (1964) 'Socio-economic status and delinquent behavior: a retest', *J. Res. Crime Delinq.*, 1, 38–46.

ÅKESSON, H. O. (1961) *Epidemiology and genetics of mental deficiency in a Southern Swedish population*, Almqvist and Wiksell.

ÅKESSON, H. O. (1962) 'Empirical risk figures in mental deficiency', *Acta Genetic et Statistica Medica*, 12, 28–32.

ALEXANDER, C. (1972) 'The city as a mechanism for sustaining human contact', in Gutman R., (Ed.), *People and Buildings*, Basic Books.

ALEXANDER, J. P. and PARSONS, S. V. (1973) 'Short-term behavioral intervention with delinquent families – impact on family process and recidivism', *J. Abn. Psychol.*, 81, 219–225.

ALLEN, J. R., McWEY, P. J. and SUOMI, S. J. (1974) 'Pathobiological and behavioural effects of lead intoxication in the infant rhesus monkey', *Environmental Health Perspectives*, May, 239–246.

ALLEN, S. (1971) *New Minorities, Old Conflicts: Asian and West Indian Migrants in Britain*, Random House.

ALLEN, S. (1972) 'Black workers in Great Britain', in Van Houte, H. and Malgert, W. (Eds.), *Foreigners in our Community*, Amsterdam, Keesing.

ALLEYNE, H. M. (1962) 'The teaching of bilingual children: intelligence and attainment of children in London, Wales and Trinidad whose mother-tongue is not English', Unpublished MA thesis, Univ. of London.

ALLPORT, G. W. and KRAMER, B. M. (1946) 'Some roots of prejudice', *J. Psychol.*, 22, 9–39.

ALTUS, W. D. (1966) 'Birth order and its sequelae', *Science*, **151**, 44–49.

AMARK, C. (1951) 'A study in alcoholism', *Acta Psychiat. Neurol. Scand. Suppl.*, 70.

AMOS, F. (1974) 'Housing — a social service of social engineering?', paper given to Royal Town Planning Institute Sessional Meeting, Glasgow.

ANASTASI, A. (1956) 'Intelligence and family size', *Psychol. Bull.*, **53**, 187–209.

ANASTASI, A. (1968) *Psychological Testing*, 3rd Edition, Macmillan.

ANDERSON, C. A. (1961) 'A skeptical note on education and mobility', in Halsey, A. H., Floud, J. and Anderson, C. A. (Eds.), *Education, Economy and Society*, Free Press.

ANDERSON, C. A., BROWN, J. C. and BOWMAN, M. S. (1952) 'Intelligence and occupational mobility', *J. Political Economy*, **40**, 218–239.

ANDERSON, V. E. (1974) 'Genetics and intelligence', in Wortis, J. (Ed.), *Mental Retardation and Developmental Disabilities, An Annual Review*, Vol. 6, New York: Bruner/Mazel.

ARKONAC, O. and GUZE, S. B. (1963) 'A family study of hysteria', *New Engl. J. Med.*, **268**, 239–242.

ARLING, S. L. and HARLOW, H. F. (1967) 'Effects of social deprivation on maternal behavior of rhesus monkeys', *J. Comp. Physiol. Psychol.*, **64**, 371–378.

ARMOR, D. J. (1973) 'The evidence on bussing', *The Public Interest*, **28**, 90–126.

ASHBY, E., MORRISON, A. and BUTCHER, H. J. (1971) 'The abilities and attainments of immigrant children', *Research in Education*, 4, 73–80.

ASHER, E. J. (1935) 'The inadequacy of current intelligence tests for testing Kentucky mountain children', *J. Genet. Psychol.*, **46**, 480–486.

ASKHAM, J. (1969) 'Delineation of the lowest social class', *J. Biosoc. Sci.*, 1, 327–335.

ASKHAM, J. (1975) *Fertility and Deprivation: A Study of Differential Fertility Amongst Working Class Families in Aberdeen*, Cambridge Papers in Sociology No. 5. Cambridge Univ. Press.

ATKINSON, A. B. (1969) *Poverty in Britain and the Reform of Social Security*, Cambridge Univ. Press.

ATKINSON, A. B. (1972) *Unequal Shares: wealth in Britain*, Allen Lane.

ATKINSON, A. B. (1973a) 'Low pay and the cycle of poverty', in Field, F. (Ed.), *Low Pay*, Arrow Books.

ATKINSON, A. B. (1973b) 'Who are the poorest', *New Society*, **23**, 466–468.

ATKINSON, A. B. (Ed.) (1973c) *Wealth, Income and Inequality*, Penguin.

ATKINSON, A. B. (1974) 'Gifts and the transmission of wealth', *New Society*, **30**, 350–351.

AUSUBEL, D. P. (1963) *The Psychology of Meaningful Verbal Learning: an introduction to school learning*, Grune.

BAGLEY, C. (1971) 'Mental illness in immigrant minorities in London', *J. Biosoc. Sci.*, **3**, 449–460.

BAGLEY, C. (1972) 'Deviant behaviour in English and West Indian schoolchildren', *Research in Educ.*, **8**, 47–55.

BAGOT, J. H. (1941) *Juvenile Delinquency*, Cape.

BAGOT, J. H. (1944) *Punitive Detention*, Cape.

BAIN, S. M. (1974) 'A geographer's approach in the epidemiology of psychiatric disorder', *J. Biosoc. Sci.*, **6**, 195–220.

BAIRD, D. (1949) 'Social factors in obstetrics', *Lancet*, i, 1079–1083.

BAIRD, D. and ILLSLEY, R. (1953) 'Environment and childbearing', *Proc. Roy. Soc. Med.*, **46**, 53–59.

BAJEMA, C. J. (1963) 'Estimation of the direction and intensity of natural selection in relation to human intelligence by means of the intrinsic rate of natural increase', *Eugen. Quart.*, **10**, 175–187.

BAKWIN, H. (1973) 'Reading disability in twins', *Develop. Med. Child Neurol.*, **15**, 184–187.

BALLER, W. R., CHARLES, D. C. and MILLER, E. L. (1966) *Mid-Life Attainment of the Mentally Retarded, a longitudinal study*, Univ. of Nebraska.

BALOGH, T. and STREETEN, P. P. (1963) 'The coefficient of ignorance', *Bull. Oxford Univ. Inst. Statistics*, **25**, 97–107.

BANDURA, A. (1969) 'Social-learning theory of identificatory processes', in Goslin, D. A. (Ed.), *Handbook of Socialisation Theory and Research*, Rand McNally.

BANKS, O. (1970) 'Social class and family life', in Craft, M. (Ed.), *Family, Class and Education: a reader*, Longman.

BANTON, M. (1955) *The Coloured Quarter*, Cape.

BANTON, M. (1973) *Police-Community Relations*, Collins.

BARKER, D. (1971) 'Negative income tax', in Bull, D. (Ed.), *Family Poverty*, Duckworth for the Child Poverty Action Group.

BARKER, D. J. P. and EDWARDS, J. H. (1967) 'Obstetric complications and school performance', *Brit. Med. J.*, **3**, 695–699.

BARNA, T. (1945) *The Redistribution of Income Through Public Finance in 1937*, Clarendon Press.

BARNES, J. H. and LUCAS, H. (1974) 'Positive discrimination in education: individuals, groups and institutions', in Leggatt, T. (Ed.), *Sociological Theory and Survey Research*, Sage.

BARTAK, L. and RUTTER, M. (1973) 'Special educational treatment of autistic children: a comparative study I. Design of study and characteristics of units', *J. Child Psychol. Psychiat.*, 14, 161–179.

BATLEY, R. and EDWARDS, J. (1974) 'The urban programme: a report on some programme funded projects', *Brit. J. Soc. Work*, 4, 305–332.

BAYLEY, N. (1949) 'Consistency and variability in the growth of intelligence from birth to 18 years', *J. Genet. Psychol.*, 75, 165–196.

BAYLEY, N. (1955) 'On the growth of intelligence', *Amer. Psychol.*, 10, 805–818.

BAYLEY, N. (1970) 'Development of mental abilities', in Mussen, P. H. (Ed.), *Carmichael's Manual of Child Psychology*,, Vol. 1, John Wiley.

BECKER, G. S. (1964) *Human Capital*, Columbia Univ. Press.

BECKER, W. C. (1964) 'Consequences of different kinds of parental discipline', in Hoffman, M. L. and Hoffman, L. W. (Eds.), *Review of Child Development Research*, Vol. 1, Russell Sage Foundation.

BECKER, W. C. and KRUG, R. S. (1965) 'The parent attitude research instrument — a research review', *Child Develop.*, 36, 329–365.

BEEZ, W. V. (1968) 'Influence of biased psychological reports on teacher behavior and pupil performance', *Proc. 76th Ann. Conf. Amer. Psychol. Assoc.*

BELL, C. R. (1968) *Middle Class Families*, Routledge & Kegan Paul.

BELL, R. Q. (1953) 'Convergence: an accelerated longitudinal approach', *Child Develop.*, 24, 145–152.

BELL, R. Q. (1968) 'A re-interpretation of the direction of effects in studies of socialization', *Psychol. Rev.*, 75, 81–95.

BELL, R. Q. (1971) 'Stimulus control of parent or caretaker behavior by offspring', *Develop. Psychol.*, 4, 63–72.

BELL, R. Q. (1973) 'Contributions of human infants to care giving and social interaction', in Lewis, M. and Rosenblum, L. A. (Eds.), *The Effect of the Child on the Caregiver*, John Wiley.

BELL, R. R. (1969) 'The lower-class Negro family in the United States and Great Britain: some comparisons', *Race*, 11, 173–181.

BELMONT, L. and BIRCH, H. G. (1966) 'The intellectual profile of retarded readers', *Percept. Mot. Skills*, 22, 787–816.

BELMONT, L. and MAROLLA, F. A. (1973) 'Birth order, family size and intelligence', *Science*, 182, 1096–1101.

BELSON, W. A. (1968) 'The extent of stealing by London boys', *Advancement of Science*, 25, 171–184.

BENJAMIN, B. (1953) 'Tuberculosis and social conditions in the Metropolitan boroughs of London', *Brit. J. Tuberc. & Dis of the Chest*, 47, 4–17.

BEREITER, C. and ENGELMANN, S. (1966) *Teaching Disadvantaged Children in the Pre-School*, Prentice-Hall.

BERENT, J. (1953) 'Relationship between family sizes of two successive generations', *Milbank Mem. Fund Quart.*, 31, 39–50.

BERENT, J. (1954) 'Social mobility and marriage: a study of trends in England and Wales', in Glass, D. V. (Ed.), *Social Mobility in Britain*, Routledge and Kegan Paul.

BERG, I. (1970) *Training and Jobs*, Praeger.

BERG, J. M. and KIRMAN, B. H. (1959) 'Some aetiological problems in mental deficiency', *Brit. Med. J.*, **2**, 848–852.

BERGER, M. (1973) 'Early experience and other environmental factors: an overview. I. Studies with humans', in Eysenck, H. (Ed.), *Handbook of Abnormal Psychology*, Pitman Medical.

BERGER, M., YULE, W. and RUTTER, M. (1975) 'Attainment and adjustment in two geographical areas. II. The prevalence of specific reading retardation', *Brit. J. Psychiat.*, **126**, 510–519.

BERLYNE, D. E. (1960) *Conflict, Arousal and Curiosity*, McGraw-Hill.

BERNSTEIN, B. (1965) 'A socio-linguistic approach to social learning', in Gould, J. (Ed.), *Penguin Survey of the Social Sciences*, Penguin.

BERNSTEIN, B. and YOUNG, D. (1967) 'Social class differences in conceptions of the use of toys', *Sociology*, **1**, 131–140.

BHATNAGAR, J. (1970) *Immigrants at School*, Cornmarket Press.

BIDDLE, B. J. (1970) 'The institutional context', in Campbell, W. J. (Ed.), *Scholars in Context: the effects of environments on learning*, John Wiley.

BIRCH, H. G. (1972) 'Issues of design and method in studying the effects of malnutrition on mental development', in *Nutrition, The Nervous System and Behavior*, Pan American Health Organization.

BIRCH, H. G. and GUSSOW, J. D. (1970) *Disadvantaged Children: health, nutrition and school failure*, Harcourt, Brace and World.

BIRCH, H. G., RICHARDSON, S. A., BAIRD, D., HOROBIN, G. and ILLSLEY, R. (1970) *Mental Subnormality in the Community: a clinical and epidemiological study*, Williams & Wilkins.

BIRD, C., MONACHESI, E. D. and BURDICK, H. (1952) 'Infiltration and the attitudes of White and Negro parents and children', *J. Abn. Soc. Psychol.*, **47**, 688–699.

BIRTCHNELL, J. (1970) 'The relationship between attempted suicide, depression and parent death', *Brit. J. Psychiat.*, **116**, 307–314.

BIRTCHNELL, J. (1971) 'Social class, parental social class, and social mobility in psychiatric patients and general population controls', *Psychol. Med.*, 1, 209–221.

BIRTCHNELL, J. (1972) 'The interrelationship between social class, early parent death, and mental illness', *Psychol. Med.*, **2**, 166–175.

BLACKER, C. P. (Ed.) (1952) *Problem Families: Five Inquiries*, Eugenics Society.

BLACKER, C. P. (1958) 'Disruption of marriage', *Lancet*, i, 578–581.

BLACKSTONE, T. (1973) *Education and Day Care for Young Children in Need: the American experience*, Bedford Square Press.

BLAKE, R. and DENNIS, W. (1943) 'The development of stereotypes concerning the Negro', *J. Abn. Soc. Psychol.*, **38**, 525–531.

BLAU, P. M. (1956) 'Social mobility and interpersonal relations', *Amer. Sociol. Rev.*, 21, 290—295.

BLAU, P. M. and DUNCAN, O. D. (1967) *The American Occupational Structure*, John Wiley.

BLAUG, M. (1965) 'The rate of return on investment in education in Great Britain', *The Manchester School*, 33, 205—251.

BLAUG, M. (1970) *An Introduction to the Economics of Education*, Allen Lane.

BLEULER, M. (1955) 'Familial and personal background of chronic alcoholics', in Diethelm, O. (Ed.), *Etiology of Chronic Alcoholism*, Charles C. Thomas.

BLOOD, R. and WOLFE, D. M. (1960) *Husbands and Wives: the dynamics of married living*, Macmillan.

BLOOM, B. S. (1964) *Stability and Change in Human Characteristics*, John Wiley.

BLOOM, L. (1969) 'Study of Butetown, Cardiff', unpublished survey material reported in Rose, E. J. B., Deakin, N., Abrams, M., Jackson, V., Peston, M., Vanags, A. H., Cohen, B., Gaitskell, J. and Ward, P. (1969). *Colour and Citizenship*, Oxford Univ. Press for the Institute of Race Relations.

BLURTON-JONES, N. G. (1974) 'Biological perspectives on parenthood', in Department of Health and Social Security, *The Family in Society: Dimensions of Parenthood*, HMSO.

BOALT, G. (1954) 'Social mobility in Stockholm: a pilot investigation', *Trans. Second World Congress Sociology II*, 67—73.

BOHMAN, M. (1970) *Adopted Children and Their Families*, Proprius.

BOHMAN M. (1971) 'A comparative study of adopted children, foster children and children in their biological environment born after undesired pregnancies', *Acta Paediat. Scand.*, Suppl. 221.

BOHMAN, M. (1972) 'A study of adopted children, their background, environment and adjustment', *Acta Paediat. Scand.*, 61, 90—97.

BOLTON, F. and LAISHLEY, J. (1972) *Education for a Multi-Racial Britain*, Fabian Research Series, No. 303.

BONE, M. (1973) *Family Planning Services in England and Wales*, HMSO.

BOOTH, C. (1902—3) *Life and Labour of the People in London 1891—1903* (18 volumes), Macmillan.

BOROW, H. (1966) 'The development of occupational motives and roles', in Hoffman, L. W. and Hoffman, M. L. (Eds.), *Review of Child Development Research, Vol. 2*, Russell Sage Foundation.

BOSANQUET, N. and DOERINGER, P. (1973) 'Is there a dual labour market in Great Britain?', *Economic Journal*, 83, 421—435.

BOSANQUET, N. and STANDING, G. (1972) 'Government and unemployment 1966—70: a study of policy and evidence', *Brit. J. Indust. Relations*, 10, 180—192.

BOSKIN, M. J. (1972) 'Unions and relative real wages', *Amer. Econ. Rev.*, 62, 466—472.

BOTTOMLEY, V. (1971) *'Families with low income in London'*, *Poverty pamphlet No. 8*, Child Poverty Action Group.

BOTTOMS, A. E. (1967) 'Delinquency amongst immigrants', *Race*, 8, 357–383.

BOTTOMS, A. (1973) 'Crime and delinquency in immigrant and minority groups', in Watson, P. (Ed.), *Psychology and Race*, Penguin.

BOWLBY, J. (1946) *Forty-four Juvenile Thieves: their characters and home-life*, Bailliere, Tindall and Cox.

BOWLBY, J. (1951) *Maternal Care and Mental Health*, World Health Organization.

BOWLBY, J. (1968) 'Effects on behaviour of disruptions of an affectual bond', in Thoday, J. D. and Parkes, A. S. (Eds.), *Genetic and Environmental Influences on Behaviour*, Oliver & Boyd.

BOWLBY, J. (1971) *Attachment and Loss. Vol. 1: Attachment*, Penguin.

BOWLBY, J. (1973) *Separation in Anxiety and Anger*, Hogarth Press.

BOWLES, S. (1972) 'Schooling and inequality from generation to generation', *J. Polit. Econ.*, **80**, S219–S251.

BOWLES, S. and NELSON, V. I. (1974) 'The "inheritance of IQ" and the intergenerational reproduction of economic poverty', *Rev. Econ. Statist.* (Harvard), Feb/March, 39–51.

BRADBURN, N. M. and CAPLOVITZ, D. (1965) *Reports on Happiness*, Aldine.

BRADLEY, R. W. (1968) 'Birth order and school related behaviour', *Psychol. Bull.*, **70**, 45–51.

BRADSHAW, J. and WAKEMAN, I. (1972) 'The poverty trap up-dated', *Polit. Quart.*, **43**, 459–469.

BRADWAY, K. P. (1944) 'IQ constancy in the revised Standford-Binet from the preschool to the junior high school level', *J. Genet. Psychol.*, **65**, 197–217.

BRADWAY, K. P. (1945) 'Predictive value of Stanford-Binet preschool items', *J. Educ. Psychol.*, **36**, 1–16.

BRADWAY, K. P. and THOMPSON, C. W. (1962) 'Intelligence at adulthood: a twenty-five year follow-up', *J. Educ. Psychol.*, 53, 1–14.

BRAND, E. S., RUIZ, R. A. and PADILLA, A. M. (1974) 'Ethnic identifications and preference: a review', *Psychol. Bull.*, 81, 860–890.

BRANDIS, B. and HENDERSON, D. (1970) *Social Class, Language and Communication*, Routledge & Kegan Paul.

BRANDON, D. (1973) *Not Proven*, Runnymede Trust.

BRANDON, M. W. G. (1957) 'The intellectual and social status of children of mental defectives', *J. Ment. Sci.*, **103**, 710–738.

BROADY, M. (1968) *Planning for People*, National Council of Social Service.

BROCK, L. G. (1934) *Report of the Departmental Committee on Sterilisation*, HMSO.

BRONFENBRENNER, U. (1958) 'Socialization and social class through time and space', in Maccoby, E., Newcomb, T. M. and Howarth, E. L. (Eds.), *Readings in Social Psychology (3rd edition)*, Henry Holt.

BRONFENBRENNER, U. (1968) 'Early deprivation in mammals: a cross-species analysis', in Newton, G. and Levine, S. (Eds.), *Early Experience and Behavior*, Charles C. Thomas.

BRONFENBRENNER, U. (1972) 'Is 80% of intelligence genetically determined?', in Bronfenbrenner, U. (Ed.), *Influences in Human Development*, Dryden Press.

BRONFENBRENNER, U. (1974) 'Is Early Intervention Effective? A report on the longitudinal evaluations of pre-school programmes', Office of Child Development, US Dept. of Health, Education and Welfare.

BRONFENBRENNER, U. (1975) 'The challenge of social change to public policy and developmental research', Paper read at the annual meeting of the Soc. Res. Child Develop., Denver, April 12, 1975.

BRONSON, W. C. (1967) 'Adult derivatives of emotional expressiveness and reactivity-control: developmental continuities from childhood to adulthood', *Child Develop.*, 38, 801–817.

BRONSON, W. C., KATTEN, E. S. and LIVSON, N. (1959) 'Patterns of authority and affection in two generations', *J. Abn. Soc. Psychol.*, 58, 143–152.

BROPHY, J. E. and GOOD, T. L. (1974) *Teacher-Student Relationships: causes and consequences*, Holt, Rinehart and Winston.

BROWN, F. W. (1942) 'Heredity in the psychoneuroses', *Proc. Roy. Soc. Med.*, 35, 785–790.

BROWN, G. W., BHROLCHAIN, M. N. and HARRIS, T. (1975), 'Social class and psychiatric disturbance among women in an urban population', *Sociology*, 9, 225–54.

BROWN, G. W. and BIRLEY, J. L. T. (1968) 'Crisis and life changes and the onset of schizophrenia', *J. Health Social Behav.*, 9, 203–214.

BROWN, G. W., BIRLEY, J. L. T. and WING, J. K. (1972) 'Influence of family life on the course of schizophrenic disorders: application', *Brit. J. Psychiat.*, 121, 241–258.

BROWN, G. W., HARRIS, T. O. and PETO, J. (1973a) 'Life events and psychiatric disorders. 2. Nature of causal link', *Psychol. Med.*, 3, 159–176.

BROWN, G. W., MONCK, E. M., CARSTAIRS, G. M. and WING, J. K. (1962) 'The influence of family life on the course of schizophrenia illness', *Brit. J. Prev. Soc. Med.*, 16, 55–68.

BROWN, G. W., SKLAIR, F., HARRIS, T. O. and BIRLEY, J. L. T. (1973b) 'Life events and psychiatric disorder. 1. Some methodological issues', *Psychol. Med.*, 3, 74–87.

BRUCE, J. M. (1970) 'Intragenerational occupational mobility and visiting with kin and friend', *Social Forces*, 49, 117–127.

BRYCE-SMITH, D. and WALDRON, H. A. (1974) 'Blood-lead levels, behaviour and intelligence', *Lancet*, i, 1166–1167.

BUCK, C. and LADD, K. (1965) 'Psychoneurosis in marital partners', *Brit. J. Psychiat.*, **111**, 587–590.

BUCK, C. and LAUGHTON, K. (1959) 'Family patterns of illness: the effect of psychoneurosis in the parent upon illness in the child', *Acta Psych. Neurol. Scand.*, **34**, 165–175.

BUNCH, J. (1972) 'Recent bereavement in relation to suicide', *J. Psychosom. Res.*, **16**, 361–366.

BURGESS, T. (1975) 'Why can't children read?', *New Society*, **32**, 10–11.

BURGIN, T. and EDSON, P. (1967) *Spring Grove: an experiment in the education of immigrant children*, Institute of Race Relations.

BURKS, B. S. (1928) 'The relative influence of nature and nurture upon mental development: A comparative study of foster parent-foster child resemblance and true parent-true child resemblance, *Yearbook of the National Society for the Study of Educ.*, **27**, 219–316.

BURNEY, E. (1967) *Housing on Trial: A Study of Immigrants and Local Government*, Oxford Univ. Press.

BURNEY, E. and WAINWRIGHT, D. (1972) *After Four Years*, Runnymede Trust.

BURT, C. (1923) 'The causal factors of juvenile crime', *Brit. J. Med. Psych.*, **3**, 1–33.

BURT, C. (1925) *The Young Delinquent*, Univ. of London Press.

BURT, C. (1937) *The Backward Child*, Univ. of London Press.

BURT, C. (1943) 'Ability and income', *Brit. J. Educ. Psychol.*, **13**, 83–93. Printed in Eysenck, H. J. (Ed.), (1973) *The Measurement of Intelligence*, Medical and Technical Publ.

BURT, C. (1955a) *The Subnormal Mind*, 3rd Edition, Oxford Univ. Press.

BURT, C. (1955b) 'The evidence for the concept of intelligence', *Brit. J. Educ. Psychol.*, **25**, 158–177.

BURT, C. (1958) 'The inheritance of mental ability', *Amer. Psychol.*, **13**, 1–15.

BURT, C. (1961) 'Intelligence and social mobility', *Brit. J. Statist. Psychol.*, **14**, 3–24.

BURT, C. (1966) 'The genetic determination of differences in intelligence: a study of monozygotic twins reared together and apart', *Brit. J. Psychol.*, **57**, 137–153.

BURT, C. (1970) 'The concept of intelligence', *Modern Concepts of Intelligence*, Assoc. Educ. Psychol. Journal and Newsletter. 16–38.

BUSFIELD, J. (1972) 'Age at marriage and family size: social causation and social selection hypotheses', *J. Biosoc. Sci.*, **4**, 117–134.

BUSFIELD, J. and HAWTHORN, G. (1971) 'Some social determinants of recent trends in British fertility', *J. Biosoc. Sci., Suppl.*, **3**, 65–77.

BUTCHER, H. J. (1970) *Human Intelligence: its nature and assessment*, Methuen.

BUTLER, N. and ALBERMAN, E. D. (Eds.) (1969) *Perinatal Problems*, Livingstone.

BUTLER, N. R. and BONHAM, D. G. (1963) *Perinatal Mortality*, Livingstone.

BUTLER, N. R. and GOLDSTEIN, H. (1973) 'Smoking in pregnancy and subsequent child development', *Brit. Med. J.*, **4**, 573–575.

BYERS, R. K. and LORD, E. E. (1943) 'Late effects of lead poisoning on mental development', *Amer. J. Dis. Childh.*, **66**, 471–494.

BYTHEWAY, B. (1974) 'A statistical trap associated with family size', *J. Biosoc. Sci.*, **6**, 67–72.

CABRAL, R. M. (1969) 'Intergenerational differences in making moral judgements', Abstract of Ph.D. dissertation in *Dissertation Abstracts International*, No. 105–81.

CALDWELL, B. M. (1964) 'The effects of infant care', in Hoffmann, M. L. and Hoffman, L. W. (Eds.), *Review of Child Development Research*, Vol. 1, Russell Sage Foundation.

CALDWELL, B. M. (1967) 'Descriptive evaluations of child development and of developmental settings', *Pediatrics*, **40**, 46–54.

CALHOUN, J. B. (1962) 'Population density and social pathology', *Scientific American*, **206**, 139–148.

CAMPBELL, E. (1961) cited by Yinger and Simpson (1973).

CAMPBELL, D. (1974) Personal communication.

CAMPBELL, E. Q. and ALEXANDER, C. N. (1965) 'Structural effects and interpersonal relationships', *Amer. J. Sociol.*, **71**, 284–289.

CANNAN, C. (1970) 'Schools for delinquency', *New Society*, **16**, 1004.

CANTER, D. (1974) 'Empirical research in environmental psychology: a brief review', *Bull. Brit. Psychol. Soc.*, **27**, 31–37.

CANTWELL, D. (1972) 'Psychiatric illness in the families of hyperactive children', *Arch. Gen. Psychiat.*, **27**, 413–417.

CANTWELL, D. (1976) 'The Hyperkinetic syndrome', in Rutter, M. and Hersov, L. (Eds.), *Child Psychiatry: modern approaches*, Blackwell Scientific.

CARLESTAM, G. (1971) 'The individual, the city and stress', in Levi, L. (Ed,), *Society, Stress and Disease, Vol. 1. The Psychosocial Environment and Psychosomatic Diseases*, Oxford Univ. Press.

CARR-SAUNDERS, A. M., MANNHEIM, H. and RHODES, E. C. (1942) *Young Offenders*, Cambridge Univ. Press.

CARTER, C. O. (1970) *Human Heredity*, Revised Edition, Penguin.

CARTER, C. O. (1974) 'The genetic basis of inequality', Royal Economic Society Conference on 'The Personal Distribution of Incomes and Property', Lancaster.

CARTTER, A. M. (1955) *The Redistribution of Income in Post-War Britain*, Yale Univ. Press.

CASLER, L. (1961) 'Maternal deprivation: a critical review of the literature, *Mon. Soc. Res. Child Develop.*, **26**, 1–64.

CASSEL, J. (1972) 'Health consequences of population density and crowding', in Gutman, R. (Ed.), *People and Buildings*, Basic Books.

CASTLE, I. M. and GITTUS, E. (1957) 'The distribution of social defects in Liverpool', *Sociol. Rev.*, **5**, 43–64.

CENTRAL ADVISORY COUNCIL FOR EDUCATION (ENGLAND) (1967) *Children and Their Primary Schools*, Vol. 2, HMSO. (Plowden Report)

CENTRAL STATISTICAL OFFICE (1973) *Economic Trends*, HMSO.

CENTRAL STATISTICAL OFFICE (1973) *Abstract of Regional Statistics*, HMSO.

CENTRAL STATISTICAL OFFICE (1973) *Social Trends*, HMSO.

CENTRAL STATISTICAL OFFICE (1973) 'The incidence of taxes and social service benefits in 1972', *Econ. Trends*, No. 241, vi–li, HMSO.

CENTRE FOR ENVIRONMENTAL STUDIES (1974) *The National Community Development Project: Inter-Project Report.*

CHAMOVE, A. S., ROSENBLUM, L. A. and HARLOW, H. F. (1973) 'Monkeys (macaca Mulatta) raised only with peers: a pilot study', *Anim. Behav.*, **21**, 316–325.

CHATER, D. (1966) *Race Relations in Britain*, Drayton Press.

CHEEK, D. B., HOLT, A. B. and MELLITS, E. D. (1972) 'Malnutrition and the nervous system', in *Nutrition, The Nervous System and Behavior*, Pan American Health Organization.

CHESTER, R. (1971) 'Contemporary trends in the stability of English marriage', *J. Biosoc. Sci.*, **3**, 389–402.

CHESTER, R. (1972) 'Current incidence and trends in marital breakdown', *Postgrad. Med. Journ.*, **48**, 529–541.

CHILMAN, C. S. (1966) *Growing Up Poor*, Welfare Administration Publication No. 13, US Department of Health, Education and Welfare.

CHINOY, E. (1955) *Automobile Workers and the American Dream*, Doubleday.

CHRISTENSEN, H. T. (1960) 'Cultural relativism and premarital sex norms', *Amer. Sociol. Rev.*, **25**, 31–39.

CHRISTIANSEN, K. O. (1970) 'Crime in a Danish twin population', *Acta Geneticae Medicae et Gemellologicae*, **19**, 323–326.

CICOUREL, A. V. (1968) *The Social Organization of Juvenile Justice*, John Wiley. (Re-issued with a new introduction, Heinemann Educational Books, 1976.)

CIOCCO, A., DENSEN, P. M. and THOMPSON, D. J. (1954) 'On the association between health and social problems in the population', *Milbank Mem. Fund Quart.*, **32**, 247–261.

CLAEYS, W. (1973) 'Primary abilities and field-independence of adopted children, *Behav. Genet.*, **3**, 323–338.

CLAIBORN, W. L. (1969) 'Expectancy effects in the classroom: a failure to replicate', *J. Educ. Psychol.*, **60**, 377–383.

CLARK, J. P. and WENNINGER, E. P. (1962) 'Socio-economic class and area as correlates of illegal behavior among juveniles', *Amer. Soc. Rev.*, 27, 826–834.

CLARK, K. B. and CLARK, M. P. (1947) 'Racial identification and preference in Negro children', in Newcomb, T. M. and Hartley, E. L. (Eds.), *Readings in Social Psychology*, Henry Holt.

CLARKE, A. D. B. (1968) 'Learning and human development – the forty-second Maudsley Lecture', *Brit. J. Psychiat.*, 114, 1061–1077.

CLARKE, A. D. B. (1972) 'A commentary on Kolochova's "severe deprivation in twins: a case study",' *J. Child Psychol. Psychiat.*, 13, 103–106.

CLARKE, A. D. B. and CLARKE, A. M. (1953) 'How constant is the IQ?' *Lancet*, ii, 877–880.

CLARKE, A. D. B. and CLARKE, A. M. (1954) 'Cognitive changes in the feeble minded', *Brit. J. Psychol.*, 45, 173–179.

CLARKE, A. D B. and CLARKE, A. M. (1972) 'Consistency and variability in the growth of human characteristics', in Wall, W. D. and Varma, V. P. (Eds.), *Advances in Educational Psychology Vol. 1*, Univ. London Press.

CLARKE, A. D. B. and CLARKE, A. M. (1974) 'Mental retardation and behavioural change', *Brit. Med. Bull.*, 30, 179–185.

CLARKE, A. D. B., CLARKE, A. M. and REIMAN, S. (1958) 'Cognitive and social changes in the feeble minded – three further studies', *Brit. J. Psychol.*, 49, 144–157.

CLARKE, A. M. and CLARKE, A. D. B. (1974) 'Genetic-environmental interactions in cognitive development', in Clarke, A. M. and Clarke, A. D. B. (Eds.), *Mental Deficiency: the changing outlook*, (3rd edition), Methuen.

CLARKE, A. M. and CLARKE, A. D. B. (1974) 'Adoption and fostering of children of the mentally subnormal', in Clarke, A. M. and Clarke, A. D. B. (Eds.), *Mental Deficiency: the changing outlook* (3rd edition), Methuen.

CLARKE, A. M. and McASKIE, M. (1975) Personal communication.

CLARKE, R. V. G. and MARTIN, D. N. (1971) *Absconding from Approved Schools*, HMSO.

CLAUSEN, J. A. (1966) 'Family structure, socialization and personality', in Hoffman, L. W. and Hoffman, M. L. (Eds.), *Review of Child Development Research*, Vol. 2, Russell Sage Foundation.

CLEGG, A. and MEGSON, B. (1968) *Children in Distress*, Penguin.

CLOWARD, R. A. and OHLIN, L. E. (1961) *Delinquency and Opportunity*, Routledge & Kegan Paul.

COARD, B. (1971) *How the West Indian Child is made Educationally Subnormal in the British School System*, New Beacon Books.

COBB, H. V. (1969) 'The predictive assessment of the adult retarded for social and vocational adjustment: a review of research', Dept. Psychol., Univ. South Dakota.

COHEN, A. K. (1956) *Delinquent Boys: the culture of the gang*, Routledge & Kegan Paul.

COHEN, K. C. (1971) *Housing Associations*, HMSO.
COHEN, M. E., BADAL, D. W., KILPATRICK, A., REED, E. W. and WHITE, P. D. (1951) 'The high familial prevalence of neurocirculatory asthenia (anxiety neurosis, effort syndrome)', *Amer. J. Human Genetics*, 3, 126–158.
COLE, M. and BRUNER, J. S. (1971) 'Cultural differences and inferences about psychological processes', *Amer. Psychol.*, **26**, 867–871.
COLEMAN, D. (1973) 'A geography of marriage', *New Society*, **23**, 634–636.
COLEMAN, J. S., CAMPBELL, E. Q., HOBSON, C. J., McPARTLAND, J., MOOD, A. M., WEINFELD, F. D. and YORK, R. L. (1966) *Equality of Educational Opportunity*, Washington D.C., Office of Education.
COLLARD, D. (1971) 'The case for universal benefits', in Bull, D. (Ed.), *Family Poverty*, Duckworth for the Child Poverty Action Group.
COLLINS, C., KREITMAN, N., NELSON, B. and TROOP, J. (1971a) 'Neurosis and marital interaction. III. Family roles and function', *Brit. J. Psychiat.*, **119**, 233-242.
COLLINS, C., KREITMAN, N., NELSON, B. and TROOP, J. (1971b) 'Neurosis and marital interaction. IV. Manifest psychological interaction', *Brit. J. Psychiat.*, **119**, 243–252.
COLLINS, J. M. and COULTER, F. (1975) 'Effects of geographic movement of the social and academic development of children of Army personnel', *Australian and New Zealand J. Sociol.*, **10**, 222–223.
COLLINS, S. (1957) *Coloured Minorities in Britain*, Lutterworth Press.
COMMUNITY RELATIONS COMMISSION (1973) 'Multiple deprivation and minority groups', CRC/73/113, Mimeographed Report.
COMMUNITY RELATIONS COMMISSION (1974) *Unemployment and Homelessness: a report*, HMSO.
CONGER, J. J and MILLER, W. C. (1966) *Personality, Social Class, and Delinquency*, John Wiley.
CONWAY, E. S. (1957) 'The institutional care of children: a case history', Unpublished Ph.D. thesis, University of London.
COOPER, B., FRY, J. and KALTON, G. (1969) 'A longitudinal study of psychiatric morbidity in a general practice population', *Brit. J. Prev. Soc. Med.*, **23**, 210–217.
COOPER, B. and MORGAN, H. G. (1973) *Epidemiological Psychiatry*, Charles C. Thomas.
COOPER, B. and SYLPH, J. (1973) 'Life events and the onset of neurotic illness: an investigation in general practice', *Psychol. Med.*, 3, 421–435.
COOPER, R. M. and ZUBEK, J. P. (1958) 'Effects of enriched and restricted early environments on the learning ability of bright and dull rats', *Canad. J. Psychol.*, **12**, 159–164.

COPELAND, J. R. M. (1968) 'Aspects of mental illness in West African students', *Soc. Psychiat.*, **3**, 7–13.

COULTHARD, M. (1969) 'A discussion of restricted and elaborated codes', *Educational Review*, **22**, 38–50.

COWEN, E. L., PEDERSON, A., BABIGIAN, H., IZZO, L. D. and TROST, M. A. (1973) 'Long-term follow-up of early detected vulnerable children', *J. Consult. Clin. Psychol.*, **41**, 438–446.

COWIE, J., COWIE, V. and SLATER, E. (1968) *Delinquency in Girls*, Heinemann Educational Books.

COWLEY, J. J. and GRIESEL, R. D. (1959) 'Some effects of a low protein diet on a first filial generation of white rats', *J. Genet. Psychol.*, **95**, 187–201.

COWLEY, J. J. and GRIESEL, R. D. (1966) 'The effect on growth and behaviour of rehabilitating first and second generation low protein rats', *Anim. Behav.*, **14**, 506–517.

COX, G. M. (1971) *Circle of Despair*, Shelter.

CRAGO, M. A. (1972) 'Psychopathology in married couples', *Psychol. Bull.*, **77**, 114–128.

CRAIG, M. M. and GLICK, S. J. (1965) *A Manual of Procedures for Application of the Glueck Prediction Table*, Univ. of London Press.

CRANDALL, V. J. (1963) 'Achievement', in Stevenson, H. W. (Ed.), *Child Psychology: the sixty second yearbook of the National Society for the Study of Education*, Part I, Univ. of Chicago Press.

CRANE, A. R. (1959) 'An historical and critical account of the accomplishment quotient idea', *Brit. J. educ. Psychol.*, **29**, 252–259.

CRAVIOTO, J. and DeLICARDIE, E. (1972) 'Environmental correlates of severe clinical malnutrition and language development in survivors from Kwashiorkor or Marasmus', in *Nutrition, The Nervous System and Behavior*, Pan American Health Organization.

CRAVIOTO, J., DeLICARDIE, E. R. and BIRCH, H. G. (1966) 'Nutrition, growth and neurointegrative development: An experimental and ecologic study', *Pediatrics*, **38**, 319–372.

CREEDY, J. (1974) *Income Changes Over the Life Cycle*, Oxford Economic Papers.

CRELLIN, E., PRINGLE, M. L. K. and WEST, P. (1971) *Born Illegitimate: social and educational implications*, NFER.

CRESSEY, D. R. (1964) *Delinquency, Crime and Differential Association*, Martinus Nijhoff.

CRIMINAL STATISTICS ENGLAND AND WALES (1973) HMSO.

CRITCHLEY, M. (1970) *The Dyslexic Child*, Heinemann Medical Books.

CROME, L. (1960) 'The brain and mental retardation', *Brit. Med. J.*, i, 897–904.

CROWE, R. R. (1972) 'The adopted offspring of women criminal offenders', *Arch. Gen. Psychiat.*, **27**, 600–603.

CROWE, R. R. (1974) 'An adoption study of antisocial personality', *Arch. Gen. Psychiat.*, 31, 785–791.

CULLINGWORTH, J. B. (1965) *English Housing Trends*, Occasional Papers on Social Administration, No. 13.
CULLINGWORTH REPORT (1969) *see* Ministry of Housing and Local Government.
DAHL, V. (1971) 'A follow-up study of a child psychiatric clientele, with special regard to manic-depressive psychosis', in *Depressive States in Childhood and Adolescence: Proc. 4th U.E.P. Congr. Stockholm*, Almqvist and Wiksell.
DALE, R. R. and GRIFFITH, S. (1965) *Down Stream: failure in the grammar school*, Routledge & Kegan Paul.
DALTON, K. (1969) *The Menstrual Cycle*, Penguin.
DANIEL, W. W. (1968) *Racial Discrimination in England*, Penguin.
DANIEL, W. W. (1974) *A National Survey of the Unemployed*, PEP.
DARCY, N. T. (1953) 'A review of the literature on the effects of bilingualism upon the measurement of intelligence', *J. Genet. Psychol.*, **82**, 21–57.
DARKE, J. and DARKE, R. (1969) '*Physical and social factors in neighbour relations*', Centre for Environmental Studies Working Paper No. 41.
DAVID, O., CLARK, J. and VOELLER, K. (1972) 'Lead and hyperactivity', *Lancet*, ii, 900–903.
DAVIE, R., BUTLER, N. and GOLDSTEIN, H. (1972) *From Birth to Seven: a report of the National Child Development Study*, Longman.
DAVIS, K. (1947) 'Final note on a case of extreme isolation', *Amer. J. Sociol.*, **52**, 432–437.
DAVISON, R. B. (1964) *Commonwealth Immigrants*, Oxford Univ. Press for the Institute of Race Relations.
DAVISON, R. B. (1966) *Black British*, Oxford Univ. Press for the Institute of Race Relations.
DAWKINS, M. J. R. (1965) 'The "small for dates" baby', in Dawkins, M. and MacGregor, W. G. (Eds.), *Gestational Age, Size and Maturity*, Clinics in Developmental Medicine No. 19, SIMP/Heinemann.
DE ALARCÓN, R. and NOGUERA, R. (1974) 'Clinical effects on drug abuse of a conviction for a drug offence', *Lancet*, ii, 147–149.
DE GROOT, A. D. (1951) 'War and the intelligence of youth', *J. Abn. Soc. Psychol.*, **46**, 596–597.
DENENBERG, V. H. and ROSENBERG, K. M. (1967) 'Nongenetic transmission of information', *Nature*, **216**, 549–550.
DENTLER, R. A. and MONROE, L. J. (1961) 'Early adolescent theft', *Amer. Soc. Rev.*, **26**, 733–743.
DEPARTMENT OF EDUCATION AND SCIENCE (1967) *Plowden Report*, *see* Central Advisory Council for Education.
DEPARTMENT OF EDUCATION AND SCIENCE (1973) *Statistics of Education, Vol. 1 Schools*, HMSO.
DEPARTMENT OF EMPLOYMENT (1969) *New Earnings Survey 1968*, HMSO.

DEPARTMENT OF EMPLOYMENT (1973a) 'Low pay and changes in earnings', *Department of Employment Gazette*, April.

DEPARTMENT OF EMPLOYMENT (1973b) *Family Expenditure Survey*, HMSO.

DEPARTMENT OF EMPLOYMENT (1974a) *New Earnings Survey*, HMSO.

DEPARTMENT OF EMPLOYMENT (1974b) *Characteristics of the unemployed: sample Survey, June 1973, Department of Employment Gazette*, March.

DEPARTMENT OF THE ENVIRONMENT (1971) *Trends in Population, Housing and Occupancy Rates 1861–1961*, HMSO.

DEPARTMENT OF THE ENVIRONMENT (1972) *The Estate Outside the Dwelling: reactions of residents to aspects of housing layout*, HMSO.

DEPARTMENT OF THE ENVIRONMENT (1973) *Housing and Construction Statistics*, HMSO.

DEPARTMENT OF THE ENVIRONMENT (1974) *Housing and Construction Statistics*, HMSO.

DEPARTMENT OF THE ENVIRONMENT (1975) *Census Indicators of Urban Deprivation*, HMSO.

DEPARTMENT OF HEALTH AND SOCIAL SECURITY (1969) *Digest of Health Statistics 1969*, HMSO.

DEPARTMENT OF HEALTH AND SOCIAL SECURITY (1971) *Two-Parent Families*, HMSO.

DEPARTMENT OF HEALTH AND SOCIAL SECURITY (1972) *Health and Personal Social Services Statistics for England and Wales*, HMSO.

DEPARTMENT OF HEALTH AND SOCIAL SECURITY (1973) *Health and Personal Social Services Statistics for England*, HMSO.

DEPARTMENT OF HEALTH AND SOCIAL SECURITY (1974) *Report of the Committee on One-Parent Families (Finer Report)*, HMSO.

DEUTSCH, M. and COLLINS, M. E. (1951) *Interracial Housing*, Univ. of Minnesota Press.

DEUTSCH, M., KATZ, I. and JENSEN, A. (Eds.) (1968) *Social Class, Race and Psychological Development*, Holt, Rinehart and Winston.

DI LORENZO, L. T. (1969) *Pre-Kindergarten Programs for Educationally Disadvantaged Children: Final Report*, Washington, DC, US Office of Education.

DOBBING, J. (1972) 'Lasting deficits and distortions of the adult brain following infantile undernutrition', in *Nutrition, the Nervous System and Behavior*, Pan American Health Organization.

DOBBING, J. and SMART, J. L. (1974) 'Vulnerability of developing brain and behaviour', *Brit. Med. Bull.*, **30**, 164–168.

DOBZHANSKY, T. (1972) 'Genetics and the diversity of behavior', *Amer. Psychol.*, **27**, 523–530.

DOEHRING, D. G. (1968) *Patterns of Impairment in Specific Reading Disability*, Indiana Univ. Press.

DOERINGER, P. B. and PIORE, M. J. (1970) *Internal Labour Markets and Manpower Analysis*, D. C. Heath.

DOHRENWEND, B. P. and DOHRENWEND, B. S. (1969) *Social Status and Psychological Disorder: a causal inquiry*, Wiley—Interscience.

DOLTON, W. D. (1968) 'Social factors and the health of immigrants', *Proc. Roy. Soc. Med.*, **61**, 19—21.

DONNISON, D. V. (1961) 'The movement of households in England', *J. Roy. Stat. Soc. (Series A)*, **124**, 60—80.

DONNISON, D. V. (1967) *The Government of Housing*, Penguin.

DOUGLAS, J. W. B. (1964) *The Home and the School*, MacGibbon and Kee.

DOUGLAS, J. W. B. (1970) 'Broken families and child behaviour', *J. Roy. Coll. Physicians Lond.*, **4**, 203—210.

DOUGLAS, J. W. B. (1973) 'Early disturbing events and later enuresis', in Kolvin, I., MacKeith, R. C. and Meadow, S. R. (Eds.), *Bladder Control and Enuresis*, Clinics in Develop. Med., Nos. 48/49, SIMP/Heinemann.

DOUGLAS, J. W. B. (1975) 'Early hospital admissions and later disturbances of behaviour and learning', *Develop. Med. Child Neurol.*, **17**, 456—480.

DOUGLAS, J. W. B., ROSS, J. M., HAMMOND, W. A. and MULLIGAN, D. G. (1966) 'Delinquency and social class', *Brit. J. Crim.*, **6**, 294—302.

DOUGLAS, J. W. B., ROSS, J. M. and SIMPSON, H. R. (1968) *All Our Future: a longitudinal study of secondary education*, Peter Davies.

DOW, T. (1965) 'Social class and reaction to physical disability', *Psychol. Rep.*, **17**, 39—62.

DOWNES, D. M. (1966) *The Delinquent Solution: A study in subcultural theory*, Routledge & Kegan Paul.

DOWNES, J. (1942) 'Illness in the chronic disease family', *Postgrad. Med. J.*, **32**, 589—600.

DOWNES, J. (1945) 'Sickness as an index of the need for health supervision of the school child', *Amer. J. Public Health*, **35**, 593—601.

DOWNES, J. and SIMON, K. (1953) 'Characteristics of psychoneurotic patients and their families as revealed in a general morbidity study', *Psychosom. Med.*, **15**, 463—476.

DRILLIEN, C. M. (1964) *Growth and Development of the Prematurely Born Infant*, Livingstone.

DRILLIEN, C. M. (1972) 'Aetiology and outcome in low-birthweight infants', *Develop. Med. Child Neurol.*, **14**, 563—574.

DUBLIN, L. J. and LOTKA, A. J. (1947) *The Money Value of a Man*, The Ronald Press Cy.

DUMMETT, A. (1973) *A Portrait of English Racism*, Penguin.

DUNCAN, O. D., FREEDMAN, R., COBLE, J. M. and SLESINGER,

D. P. (1965) 'Marital fertility and size of family of orientation', *Demography*, **2**, 508–515.

DUNCAN, O. D., HALLER, A. O. and PORTES, A. (1968) 'Peer influences on aspirations: a re-interpretation', *Amer. J. Sociol.*, **74**, 119–137.

DUNHAM, H. W. (1964) 'Social class and schizophrenia', *Amer. J. Orthopsychiat.*, **34**, 634–642.

DURKHEIM, E. (1952) *Suicide*, Routledge & Kegan Paul.

DUSEK, J. B. and O'CONNELL, E. J. (1973) 'Teacher expectancy effects on the achievement test performance of elementary school children', *J. Educ. Psychol.*, **65**, 371–377.

EAST, W. N., STOCKS, P. and YOUNG, H. T. P. (1942) *The Adolescent Criminal*, Churchill.

EASTWOOD, M. R. and TREVELYAN, M. H. (1972) 'Relationship between physical and psychiatric disorder', *Psychol. Med.*, **2**, 363–372.

ECKLAND, B. and KENT, D. P. (1968) 'Socialization and social structure', in *Perspectives on Human Deprivation: Biological, Psychological and Social*, US Dept. of Health, Education and Welfare.

ECONOMIC TRENDS (1973) *See* Central Statistical office (1973)

EDWARDS, A. (1973) 'Sex and area variations in delinquency rates in an English city', *Brit. J. Criminol.*, **13**, 121–137.

EDWARDS, G., HAWKER, A., WILLIAMSON, V. and HENSMAN, C. (1966) 'London's skid row', *Lancet*, i, 249–252.

EDWARDS, G., WILLIAMSON, V., HAWKER, A., HENSMAN, C. and POSTOYAN, S. (1968) 'Census of a reception centre', *Brit. J. Psychiat*, **114**, 1031–1039.

EELLS, K., DAVIS, A., HAVIGHURST, R. J., HERRICK, V. E. and TYLER, R. W. (1951) *Intelligence and Cultural Differences*, Chicago Univ. Press.

EILENBERG, M. D. (1961) 'Remand home boys 1930–1955', *Brit. J. Criminol.*, **2**, 111–131.

EISENBERG, L. (1958) 'School phobia: diagnosis, genesis and clinical rearrangement', *Ped. Clin. North America*, **5**, 645–666.

EISENBERG, L. (1966) 'The classification of psychotic disorders in childhood', in Eron, L. D. (Ed.), *The Classification of Behavior Disorders*, Aldine.

EISENSTADT, S. N. (1954) *The Absorption of Immigrants*, Routledge & Kegan Paul.

ELDER, G. H. (1969) 'Occupational mobility, life patterns and personality', *J. Health and Soc. Behav.*, **10**, 308–322.

ENTWISTLE, D. R. (1972) 'To dispel fantasies about fantasy-based measures of achievement motivation', *Psychol. Bull.*, **77**, 377–391.

ERICKSON, M. L. and EMPEY, L. T. (1965) 'Class position, peers and delinquency', *Sociol. and Social Res.*, **49**, 268–282.

ERLENMEYER-KIMLING, L. and JARVIK, I. F. (1963) 'Genetics and intelligence', *Science*, **142**, 1477–1479.

ETAUGH, C. (1974) 'Effects of maternal employment on children: a review of recent research', *Merrill-Palmer Quart.*, **20**, 71–98.

EYSENCK, H. J. (1967) *The Biological Basis of Personality*, Charles C. Thomas.

EYSENCK, H. J. (1970) *Crime and Personality*, Granada Press.

EYSENCK, H. J. (1971) *Race, Intelligence and Education*, Temple Smith.

EYSENCK, H. J. (Ed.) (1973a) *The Measurement of Intelligence*, Medical and Technical Publ. Co.

EYSENCK, H. J. (1973b) *The Inequality of Man*, Temple Smith.

FANNING, D. M. (1967) 'Families in flats', *Brit. Med. J.*, iv, 382–386.

FARIS, R. E. L. and DUNHAM, H. W. (1939) *Mental Disorders in Urban Areas*, Univ. of Chicago Press.

FARLEY, F. H. (1966) 'Individual differences in free response speed', *Percept. Motor Skills*, **22**, 557–558.

FARLEY, F. H. (1972) 'Correspondence', *Brit. J. Soc. Clin. Psychol.*, 11, 98–110.

FARRINGTON, D. (1972) 'Delinquency begins at home', *New Society*, 21, 495–497.

FARRINGTON, D. (1973) 'Self-reports of deviant behavior: predictive and stable?', *J. Crim. Law Criminol.*, **64**, 99–100.

FARRINGTON, D. P., GUNDRY, G. and WEST, D. J. (1975) 'The familial transmission of criminality', in *Medicine, Science and The Law*, **15**, 177–86.

FAUST, J. (1974) 'A twin study of personal preferences', *J. Biosoc. Sci.*, **6**, 75–91.

FENTON, G. W., TENRENT, T. G., FENWICK, P. B. C. and PATTRAY, N. (1974) 'The EEG in antisocial behaviour: a study of posterior temporal slow activity in Special Hospital patients', *Psychol. Med.*, 4, 181–186.

FERGUSON, T. (1952) *The Young Delinquent in his Social Setting*, Oxford Univ. Press.

FERGUSON, T. (1966) *Children in Care — and After*, Oxford Univ. Press.

FERRON, O. (1973) 'Family, marital and child-rearing patterns in different ethnic groups', in Watson, P. (Ed.), *Psychology and Race*, Penguin.

FETHNEY, V. (1972) 'ESN children: what the teachers say', *Race Today*, 4, 400–401.

FIELD, F. (1971) 'Poverty — Facts and Figures', *Journal of Child Poverty Action Group*, No. 20–21.

FIELD, F. (1974) *Unequal Britain: a report on the cycle of inequality*, Arrow Books.

FIELD, F. and PIACHAUD, D. (1971) 'The poverty trap', *New Statesman*, 82, 772–773.

FINER, M. (1974) *Finer Report, see* DHSS (1974).

FISCHER, C. S. (1973) 'Urban malaise', *Social Forces*, **52**, 221–235.

FISHER, S. (1972) 'Stigma and deviant careers in schools', *Social Problems*, **20**, 78–83.

FITZHERBERT, K. (1967) *West Indian Children in London*, Occasional Papers on Social Administration No. 19.

FLANDERS, N. A. and HAVUMAKI, S. (1963) 'Group compliance to dominative teacher influence', in Charters, W. W. and Gago, N. L. (Eds.), *Readings in the Social Psychology of Education*, Allyn and Bacon.

FLEMING, E. S. and ANTTONEN, R. G. (1971) 'Teacher expectancy as related to the academic and personal growth of primary-age children', *Mon. Soc. Res. Child Develop.*, **36**, No. 5, Serial no. 145.

FLOUD, J. and HALSEY, A. H. (1957) 'Intelligence tests, social class and selection for secondary schools', *Brit. J. Sociol.*, **8**, 33–39.

FLOUD, J. E., HALSEY, A. H. and MARTIN, F. M. (1956) *Social Class and Educational Opportunity*, Heinemann.

FOGARTY, M. P., RAPOPORT, R. and RAPOPORT, R. M. (1971) *Sex, Career and Family*, Allen & Unwin.

FORD, J. (1969) *Social Class and the Comprehensive School*, Routledge & Kegan Paul.

FORSSMAN, H. and THUWE, I. (1966) 'One hundred and twenty children born after application for therapeutic abortion refused', *Acta Psychiat. Scand.*, **42**, 71–88.

FOSTER, J. D., DINITZ, S. and RECKLESS, W. C. (1972) 'Perceptions of stigma following public intervention for delinquent behavior', *Social Problems*, **20**, 202–209.

FRANCIS REPORT (1971) *Report of the Committee on the Rent Acts*, HMSO.

FRANCIS-WILLIAMS, J. and DAVIES, P. A. (1974) 'Very low birth-weight and later intelligence', *Develop. Med. Child Neurol.*, **16**, 709–728.

FRASER, R. (1947) 'Incidence of neurosis among factory workers', *Rep. Indust. Hlth. Res. Bd.*, No. 90, HMSO.

FREEBERG, N. E. and PAYNE, D. T. (1967) 'Parental influence on cognitive development in early childhood: a review', *Child Develop.*, **38**, 65–87.

FREEDMAN, D. G. (1965) 'An ethnological approach to the genetical study of human behaviour', in Vandenberg, S. G. (Ed.), *Methods and Goals in Human Behaviour Genetics*, Academic Press.

FREEMAN, F. N., HOLZINGER, K. J. and MITCHELL, B. C. (1928) 'The influence of environment on the intelligence, school achievement and conduct of foster children', in *The Twenty-Seventh Yearbook of the Nat. Soc. Stud. Nature and Nurture. Part I. Their influence upon intelligence.*

FRENKEL-BRUNSWICK, E. (1948) 'A study of prejudice in children', *Human Relations*, **1**, 295–306.

FREW, R. and PECKHAM, C. (1972) 'Mental retardation: a natural study', *Brit. Hosp. J. and Social Service Rev.*, 82, 2070–2072.

FRIED, M. (1963) 'Grieving for a lost home', in Duhl, L. J. (Ed.), *The Urban Condition*, Basic Books.

FRIEDLANDER, B. Z. (1971) 'Listening, language and the auditory environment: automated evaluation and intervention', in Hellmuth, J. (Ed.), *The Exceptional Infant: II. Studies in abnormalities*, Brunner/Mazel.

FRIEDMAN, M. (1957) *A Theory of the Consumption Function*, National Bureau of Economic Research.

FROMMER, E. A. and O'SHEA, G. (1973a) 'Antenatal identification of women liable to have problems in managing their infants', *Brit. J. Psychiat.*, 123, 149–156.

FROMMER, E. A. and O'SHEA, G. (1973b) 'The importance of childhood experience in relation to problems of marriage and family-building', *Brit. J. Psychiat.*, 123, 157–160.

FULLER, M. M. and BONJEAN, C. M. (1972) 'Some attitudinal correlates of integration in work', *Sociol. Abstracts*, No. E8030.

FURSTENBERG, F. F. (1971) 'Mobility orientation in the family', *Social Forces*, 49, 595–602.

FURTH, H. G. (1966) *Thinking Without Language: psychological implications of deafness*, Free Press.

FUTCHER, S. (1972) 'West Indian foster children', *Social Work Today*, 29 June, pp. 4-6.

FYVEL, T. R. (1961) *The Insecure Offenders*, Chatto and Windus.

GADOUREK, I. (1965) *Absences and Well-Being of Workers*, Royal Van Gorcum Ltd.

GAHAGAN, D. M. and GAHAGAN, G. A. (1970) *Talk Reform: explorations in language for infant school children*, Routledge & Kegan Paul.

GAITSKELL, J. (1969) 'Study of employment, Croydon'. Unpublished survey material presented in Rose, E. J. B., Deakin, N., Abrams, M., Jackson, V., Peston, M., Vanags, A. H., Cohen, B., Gaitskell, J. and Ward, P. (Eds.), *Colour and Citizenship*, Oxford Univ. Press for the Institute of Race Relations.

GALLE, O. R., GOVE, W. R. and McPHERSON, J. M. (1972) 'Population density and pathology: what are the relations for man?', *Science*, 176, 23–30.

GALLOWAY, D. (1976) 'Size of school, socio-economic hardship, suspension rates and persistent unjustified absence, from school. *Brit. J. Educ. Psychol.*, 6, 40–7.

GANS, B. (1966) 'Health problems and the immigrant child', in CIBA Foundation, *Immigration, Medical and Social Aspects*, Churchill.

GARDNER, D. E. M. (1966) *Experiment and Tradition in Primary Schools*, Methuen.

GATH, D., COOPER, B. and GATTONI, F. E. G. (1972) 'Preliminary communication: child guidance and delinquency in a London borough', *Psychol. Med.*, 2, 185–191.

GATH, D., COOPER, B., GATTONI, F. and ROCKETT, D. (1975) *Child Guidance and Delinquency in a London Borough*, Oxford Univ. Press.

GAW, F. (1925) 'A study of performance tests', *Brit. J. Psychol.*, **15**, 374–392

GAY, M. and TONGE, W. L. (1967) 'The late effects of loss of parents in childhood', *Brit. J. Psychiat.*, **113**, 753–759.

GENERAL REGISTER OFFICE (1968) *Sample Census 1966 England and Wales. Housing tables*, HMSO.

GEORGE, V. and WILDING, P. (1972) *Motherless families*, Routledge & Kegan Paul.

GIBBENS, T. C. N. (1963) *Psychiatric Studies of Borstal Lads*, Maudsley Monographs no. 11, Oxford Univ. Press.

GIBBENS, T. C. N. and AHRENFELDT, R. H. (Eds.) (1966) *Cultural Factors in Delinquency*, Tavistock.

GIBBENS, T. C. N., POND, D. A. and STAFFORD-CLARK, D. (1959) 'A follow-up study of criminal psychopaths', *J. Ment. Sci.*, **105**, 108–115.

GIBBENS, T. C. N. and PRINCE, J. (1962) *Shoplifting*, Inst. Stud. Treatment Delinquency.

GIBBENS, T. C. N. and WALKER, A. (1956) *Cruel Parents: case studies of prisoners convicted of violence towards children*, Inst. Stud. Treatment Delinquency.

GIBBS, D. N. (1955) 'Some differentiating characteristics of delinquent and non-delinquent national service men in the British Army', Unpublished Ph.D Thesis, Univ. of London.

GIBSON, C. (1974) 'The association between divorce and social class in England and Wales, *Brit. J. Sociol.*, **25**, 79–93.

GIBSON, H. B. (1969) 'Early delinquency in relation to broken homes', *J. Child Psychol. Psychiat.*, **10**, 195–204.

GIBSON, J. B. (1970) 'Biological aspects of a high socio-economic group. I. IQ, education and social mobility', *J. Biosoc. Sci.*, **2**, 1–16.

GILLIS, A. R. (1974) 'Population density and social pathology: the case of building type, social allowance and juvenile delinquency', *Social Forces*, **53**, 306–314.

GINSBERG, H. (1972) *The Myth of the Deprived Child*, Prentice-Hall.

GITTUS, E. (1970) 'A study of the unemployed of Merseyside', in Lawton, R. (Ed.), *Merseyside*, Longman.

GLASER, D. and RICE, K. (1959) 'Crime, age, and employment', *Amer. Sociol. Rev.*, **24**, 679–686.

GLASS, D. V. (Ed.) (1954) *Social Mobility in Britain*, Routledge & Kegan Paul.

GLASS, D. V. and GREBENIK, E. (1954) *The Trend and Pattern of Fertility in Great Britain*, Papers of the Royal Commission on Population VI., HMSO.

GLASS, R. (1948) *The Social Background of a Plan: a study of Middlesborough*, Routledge & Kegan Paul.

GLASS, R. (1960) *Newcomers*, Allen & Unwin for the Centre for Urban Studies.

GLASSON, J. (1974) *An Introduction to Regional Planning*, Hutchinson Educational.

GLASTONBURY, B. (1971) *Homeless Near a Thousand Homes*, National Institute for Social Work Training Series No. 21, Allen & Unwin.

GLENDENNING, F. (1971) 'Racial stereotypes in history textbooks', *Race Today*, 3, 52–54.

GLUECK, S. and GLUECK, E. T. (1944) *After-Conduct of Discharged Offenders*, Macmillan.

GLUECK, S. and GLUECK, E. T. (1950) *Unravelling Juvenile Delinquency*, The Commonwealth Fund, New York.

GLUECK, S. and GLUECK, E. T. (1956) *Physique and Delinquency*, Harper.

GLUECK, S. and GLUECK, E. (1959) *Predicting Delinquency and Crime*, Harvard Univ. Press.

GOLD, M. (1963) *Status Forces in Delinquent Boys*, Univ. of Michigan Institute for Social Research.

GOLD, M. (1966) 'Undetected delinquent behavior', *J. Res. Crime. Delinq.*, 3, 27–46.

GOLD, M. (1970) *Delinquent Behavior in an American City*, Brooks/Cole.

GOLD, M. and WILLIAMS, J. R. (1969) 'National study of the aftermath of apprehension', *Prospectus*, 3, 3–12.

GOLDBERG, E. M. and MORRISON, S. L. (1963) 'Schizophrenia and social class', *Brit. J. Psychiat.*, 109, 785–802.

GOLDFARB, W. (1955) 'Emotional and intellectual consequences of psychologic deprivation in infancy: a revaluation', in Hoch, P. H. and Zubin, J. (Eds.), *Psychopathology of Childhood*, Grune & Stratton.

GOLDMAN, R. (1973) 'Education and immigrants', in Watson, P. (Ed.), *Psychology and Race*, Penguin.

GOLDMAN, R. and TAYLOR, F. M. (1966) 'Coloured immigrant children: a survey of research studies and literature on their educational problems and potential — in Britain', *Educ. Research*, 8, 163–183.

GOLDMAN, R. and TAYLOR, F. M. (1966) 'Coloured immigrant children: a survey of research studies and literature on their educational problems and potential — in the USA', *Educ. Research*, 9, 22–43.

GOLDRING, P. (1973) *Friend of The Family*, David & Charles.

GOLDSTEIN, H. (1964) 'Social and occupational adjustment', in Stevens, H. A. and Heber, R. (Eds.), *Mental Retardation: a review of research*, Univ. of Chicago Press.

GOLDTHORPE, J. H. and HOPE, K. (1974) *The Social Grading of Occupations: a new approach and scale*, Clarendon Press.

GOOCH, S. and PRINGLE, M. L. KELLMER (1966) *Four Years On: a follow-up study at school leaving age of children formerly attending a traditional and a progressive junior school*, Longman (for the National Bureau for Co-operation in Child Care).

GOODMAN, M. E. (1952) *Race Awareness in Young Children*, Addison-Wesley.

GORDON, E. B. (1965) 'Mentally ill West Indian immigrants', *Brit. J. Psychiat.*, 111, 877–887.

GORDON, H. (1923) *Mental and Scholastic Tests among Retarded Children*, Board of Education.

GOTTESMAN, I. I. and SHIELDS, J. (1972) *Schizophrenia and Genetics: a twin study vantage point*, Academic Press.

GOUGH, H. G., HARRIS, D. B., MARTIN, W. E. and EDWARDS, M. (1950) 'Children's ethnic attitudes: I. Relationship to certain personality factors', *Child Develop.*, 21, 83–91.

GOVE, W. R. (1970) 'Societal reaction as an explanation of mental illness: an evaluation', *Amer. Sociol. Rev.*, 35, 873–884.

GOVE, W. (1972) 'The relationship between sex roles, mental illness, and marital status', *Social Forces*, **51**, 34–44.

GOVE, W. R. and TUDOR, J. F. (1973) 'Adult sex roles and mental illness', in Huber, J. (Ed.), *Changing Women in a Changing Society*, Univ. of Chicago Press.

GRAHAM, E. E. and KAMANO, D. (1958) 'Reading failure as a factor in the WAIS subtest pattern of youthful offenders', *J. Clin. Psychol.*, 14, 302–305.

GRAHAM, P. J. and MEADOWS, C. E. (1967) 'Psychiatric disorder in the children of West Indian immigrants', *J. Child Psychol. Psychiat.*, 8, 105–116.

GRAHAM, P. and RUTTER, M. L. (1973) 'Psychiatric disorders in the young adolescent: a follow-up study', *Proc. Roy. Soc. Med.*, **66**, 1226–1229.

GRAHAM, P., RUTTER, M. and GEORGE, S. (1973) 'Temperamental characteristics as predictors of behaviour disorders in children', *Amer. J. Orthopsychiat.*, 43, 328–339.

GRANVILLE-GROSSMAN, K. L. (1968) 'The early environment in affective disorder', in Coppen, A. and Walk, A. (Eds.), *Recent Developments in Affective Disorders*, *Brit. J. Psychiat.*, Special Publication No. 2, Headley Bros.

GRAY, P. G. (1949) *The British Household*, The Social Survey.

GREATER LONDON COUNCIL (1973) *Housing Facts and Figures*.

GREER, H. S. and CAWLEY, R. H. (1966) *Natural History of Neurotic Illness, Austr. Med. Assoc.*, Mervyn Archdall Medical Monograph No. 3, Australasian Med. Publ. Co.

GREER, S. (1964) 'The relationship between parental loss and attempted suicide; a control study', *Brit. J. Psychiat.*, **110**, 698–705.

GREER, S. and GUNN, J. C. (1966) 'Attempted suicides from intact and broken parental homes', *Brit. Med. J.*, ii, 1355–1357.

GREGORY, E. (1969) 'Child-minding in Paddington', *Medical Officer*, **122**, 135–139.

GREGORY, I. (1965) 'Anterospective data following childhood loss of a parent', *Arch. Gen. Psychiat.*, **13**, 110–120.

GREVE, J. (1964) 'London's homeless', *Occasional Papers on Social Administration No. 10*, Codicote Press.

GREVE, J., PAGE, D. and GREVE, S. (1971) *Homelessness in London*, Scottish Academic Press.

GRILICHES, Z. and MASON, W. M. (1972) 'Education, income and ability', *J. Polit. Econ.*, **80**, S74–S103.

GRUENBERG, E. (1964) 'Epidemiology', in Stevens, H. A. and Heber, R. (Eds.), *Mental Retardation: a review of research*, Univ. of Chicago Press.

GRUENBERG, E. M. and BIRCH. H. G. (1954) 'Reading skills and school entrance age', *Milbank Mem. Fund Quart.*, **33**, 333–340.

GRUNHUT, M. (1956) *Juvenile Offenders Before the Courts*, Clarendon Press.

GUNN, J. (1973) 'Affective and suicidal symptoms in epileptic prisoners', *Psychol. Med.*, **3**, 108–114.

GUNN, J. and BONN, J. (1971) 'Criminality and violence in epileptic prisoners', *Brit. J. Psychiat.*, **118**, 337–343.

GUNN, J. and FENTON, G. (1969) 'Epilepsy in prisons: a diagnostic survey', *Brit. Med. J.*, **4**, 326–328.

GURIN, G. and GURIN, P. (1970) 'Expectancy theory in the study of poverty', *J. Social Issues*, **26**, 83–104.

GURIN, G., VEROFF, J. and FELD, S. (1960) *Americans View Their Mental Health*, Basic Books.

GURMAN, A. S. (1973) 'The effects and effectiveness of marital therapy: a review of outcome research', *Family Process*, **12**, 145–170.

GUZE, S. B., WOLFGRAM, E. D., McKINNEY, J. K. and CANTWELL, D. P. (1967) 'Psychiatric illness in the families of convicted criminals: a study of 519 first degree relatives', *Dis. Nerv. Syst.*, **28**, 651–659.

HAGNELL, O. and KREITMAN, N. (1974) 'Mental illness in married pairs in a total population', *Brit. J. Psychiat.*, **125**, 293–302.

HALL, J. R. and GLASS, D. V. (1954) 'Education and social mobility', in Glass, D. V. (Ed.), *Social Mobility in Britain*, Routledge & Kegan Paul.

HALL, J. R. and JONES, D. C. (1950) 'Social grading of occupations', *Brit. J. Sociol.*, **1**, 31–55.

HALL, P., THOMAS, R., GRACEY, H. and DREWETT, R. (1973) *The Containment of Urban England*, Allen & Unwin.

HALL, P. and TONGE, W. L. (1963) 'Longstanding continuous unemployment in male patients with psychiatric symptoms', *Brit. J. Prev. Soc. Med.*, **17**, 191–196.

HALLER, A. O. and BUTTERWORTH, C. E. (1960) 'Peer influences on levels of occupational and educational aspiration', *Social Forces*, **38**, 289–295.

HALLGREN, B. (1950) 'Specific dyslexia', *Acta Psych. Neur. Suppl.*, **65**, 1–287.

HALSEY, A. H. (Ed.) (1972) *Educational Priority No. 1: EPA Problems and Policies*, HMSO.

HAMBURG, D. A. (1971) 'Crowding, stranger contact, and aggressive behaviour', in Levi, L. (Ed.), *Society, Stress and Disease, Vol. 1. The Psychosocial Environment and Psychosomatic Diseases*, Oxford Univ. Press.

HANNA, M. (1971) 'Reforming the Race Relations Act', *Race Today*, **3**, 348–349.

HARBURY, C. D. (1962) 'Inheritance and the distribution of personal wealth in Britain', *Economic J.*, **72**, 845–868.

HARBURY, C. D. and McMAHON, P. C. (1973) 'Inheritance and the characteristics of top wealth leavers in Britain', *Economic J.*, **83**, 810–833.

HARE, E. H. (1956) 'Mental illness and social conditions in Bristol', *J. Ment. Sci.*, **102**, 349–357.

HARE, E. H., PRICE, J. S. and SLATER, E. (1972) 'Parental social class in psychiatric patients', *Brit. J. Psychiat.*, **121**, 515–524.

HARE, E. H. and SHAW, G. K. (1965a) 'The patient's spouse and concordance on neuroticism', *Brit. J. Psychiat.*, **111**, 102–103.

HARE, E. H. and SHAW, G. K. (1965b) *Mental Health on a New Housing Estate*, Maudsley Monogr. No. 12, Oxford Univ. Press.

HARGREAVES, D. N. (1967) *Social Relations in a Secondary School*, Routledge & Kegan Paul.

HARLOW, H. F. (1958) 'The nature of love', *Amer. Psychol.*, **13**, 673–685.

HARLOW, H. F. (1965) 'Sexual behaviour in the rhesus monkey', in Beach, F. A. (Ed.), *Sex and Behaviour*, John Wiley.

HARLOW, H. F. and HARLOW, M. K. (1965) 'The affectional systems', in Schrier, A. D., Harlow, H. F. and Stollnitz, F. (Eds.), *Behavior of Non-Human Primates*, Vol. 2, Academic Press.

HARLOW, H. F. and HARLOW, M. K. (1969) 'Effects of various mother-infant relationships on rhesus monkey behaviour', in Foss, B. M. (Ed.), *Determinants of Infant Behaviour*, Vol. 4, Methuen.

HARLOW, H. F. and SUOMI, S. J. (1971) 'Social recovery by isolation-reared monkeys', *Proc. Nat. Acad. Sci. USA*, **68**, 1534–1538.

HARNQVIST, K. (1968) 'Relative changes in intelligence from 13 to 18', *Scand. J. Psychol.*, 9, 50–82.

HARRELL-BOND, B. E. (1969) 'Conjugal role behaviour', *Human Relations*, **22**, 77–91.

HARRINGTON, J. A. (1962) 'Research into neurosis in industry', in Richler, D., Tanner, J. M., Lord Taylor and Zangwill, O. L. (Eds.), *Aspects of Psychiatric Research*, Oxford Univ. Press.

HARRIS, R. (1976) 'The EEG in child psychiatry', in Rutter, M. and Hersov, L. (Eds.), *Child Psychiatry: Modern Approaches*, Blackwell Scientific.

HARRISON, P. (1973) 'Making ends meet', *New Society*, **23**, 351–354.

HARRISON, R. D. (1971) 'The Race Relations Act in retrospect', *Race Today*, **3**, 331–332.

HART, P. E. (1974) 'The comparative statics and dynamics of income distributions', unpublished paper, Univ. of Reading.

HARTLEY, S. M. (1966) 'The amazing rise of illegitimacy in Great Britain', *J. Social Forces*, **44**, 533–545.

HARTMAN, C. W. (1963) 'Social values and housing orientations', *J. Soc. Issues*. **19**, 113–131.

HARTMANN, P. and HUSBAND, C. (1974) *Racism and the Mass Media*, Davis-Poynter.

HARVEY, D. (1973) *Social Justice and the City*, Edward Arnold.

HATCH, S. (1962) 'Coloured people in school textbooks', *Race*, **4**, 63–72.

HATHAWAY, S. R. and MONACHESI, E. D. (1957) 'The personalities of predelinquent boys', *J. Crim. Law. Criminol. Police Science*, **48**, 149–163.

HAUGE, M., HARVALD, B., FISCHER, M., GOTLIEB-JENSEN, K., JUEL-NIELSEN, N., RAEBILD, I., SHAPIRO, R. and VIDEBECH, T. (1968) 'The Danish twin register', *Acta Genet. Med. Gernell.*, **17** 315–332.

HAUSE, J. C. (1972) 'Earnings profile: ability and schooling', *J. Polit. Econ.*, **80**, 5108–5138.

HAVIGHURST, R. J. (1957) 'The leisure activities of the middle-aged', *Amer. J. Sociol.*, **63**, 152–162.

HAVIGHURST, R. J., BOWMAN, P. H., LIDDLE, G. P., MATTHEWS, C. V. and PIERCE, J. V. (1962) *Growing Up in River City*, John Wiley.

HAWKINS, P. R. (1969) 'Social class, the nominal group and references', *Language and Speech*, **12**, 125–135.

HAWTHORNE, G. (1970) *The Sociology of Fertility*, Collier-Macmillan.

HAYASHI, S. (1967) 'A study of juvenile delinquency in twins', in Mitsuda, H. (Ed.), *Clinical Genetics in Psychiatry*, Igaku Shoin.

HAYNES, J. M. (1971) *Educational Assessment of Immigrant Pupils*, NFER.

HAYWOOD, C. (1967) 'Experimental factors in intellectual development: the concept of dynamic intelligence', in Zubin, J. and Jervis, G. A. (Eds.), *Psychopathology of Mental Development*, Grune and Stratton.

HEBB, D. O. (1949) *The Organization of Behavior*, John Wiley.

HEBER, R. (1971) *Rehabilitation of Families at Risk for Mental Retardation: a progress report*, Madison, Wisconsin, Rehabilitation Research and Retraining Center in Mental Retardation.

HEBER, R., DEVER, R. and CONRY, J. (1968) 'The influence of environmental and genetic variables on intellectual development', in Prehm, H. J., Hamerlynck, L. A. and Crosson, J. E. (Eds.), *Behavioral Research in Mental Retardation*, Univ. of Oregon.

HEBER, R. and GARBER, H. (1974) *Progress report III.: An experiment in the prevention of cultural-familial retardation, Proc. Third Int. Congr. Int. Assoc. Scient. Stun. Mental Defic.*

HEBER, R., GARBER, H., HARRINGTON, S., HOFFMAN, C. and FALENDER, C. (1972) *Rehabilitation of Families at Risk for Mental Retardation, December Progress Report*, Univ. of Wisconsin.

HEISEL, J. S., REAM, S., RAITZ, R., RAPPOPORT, M. and CODDINGTON, R. D. (1973) 'The significance of life events as contributing factors in the diseases of children. III. A study of pediatric patients', *J. Pediatrics*, **83**, 119–123.

HELFER, R. E. and KEMPE, C. H. (Eds.) (1968) *The Battered Child*, Univ. of Chicago Press.

HEMSI, L. (1967) 'Psychiatric morbidity of West Indian immigrants', *Social Psychiat.*, **2**, 95–100.

HENDERSON-STEWART, D. (1965) 'Appendix: estimate of the rate of return to education in Great Britain', *The Manchester School*, **33**, 252–262.

HEPPLE, B. (1970) *Race, Jobs and the Law in Great Britain*, Penguin.

HERJANIC, B. M. and PENICK, E. C. (1972) 'Adult outcome of disabled child readers', *J. Spec. Educ.*, **6**, 397–410.

HERMANN, K. (1959) *Reading Disability*, Munksgaard.

HERTZIG, M. E., BIRCH, H. G., RICHARDSON, S. A. and TIZARD, J. (1972) 'Intellectual levels of school children severely malnourished during the first two years of life', *Pediatrics*, **49**, 814–824.

HERTZIG, M. E., BIRCH, H. G., THOMAS, A. and MENDEZ, O. A. (1968) 'Class and ethnic differences in the responsiveness of preschool children to cognitive demands', *Mon. Soc. Res. Child Develop.*, **33**, No. 1, Serial No. 117.

HERZOG, E. and SUDIA, C. E. (1973) 'Children in fatherless families', in Caldwell, B. M. and Ricciuti, H. N. (Eds.), *Review of Child Development Research*, Vol. 3, Univ. Chicago Press.

HESS, R. D. and SHIPMAN, V. C. (1965) 'Early experience and the socialization of cognitive modes in children', *Child Develop.*, **36**, 869–886.

HESS, R. D. and SHIPMAN, V. C. (1967) 'Cognitive elements in maternal behavior', in Hill, J. P. (Ed.), *Minnesota Symposia on Child Psychology*. Vol. 1, Univ. of Minnesota Press.

HETHERINGTON, E. M. and MARTIN, B. (1972) 'Family interactions and psychopathology in children', in Quay, H. C. and Werry, J. S. (Eds.), *Psychopathological Disorders of Childhood*, John Wiley.

HETHERINGTON, T. (1971) 'Why I left the Race Relations Board', *Race Today*, **3**, 326–327.

HEWITT, M. (1949) 'The unemployed disabled man', *Lancet*, ii, 525–526.

HILL, C. S. (1967) *How Prejudiced is Britain*?, Panther Books.

HILL, J. M. M. (1969) *The Transition from School to Work: a study of the child's changing perception of work from the age of seven*, Tavistock Institute of Human Relations.

HILL, K. T. and SARASON, S. B. (1966) 'The relation of test anxiety and defensiveness to test and school performance over the elementary schools years: a further longitudinal study', *Mon. Soc. Res. Child Develop.*, **31**, No. 2.

HILL, M. J., HARRISON, R. M., SARGEANT, A. V. and TALBOT, V. (1973) *Men Out of Work*, Cambridge Univ. Press.

HILL, O. W. (1972) 'Child bereavement and adult psychiatric disturbance', *J. Psychosom. Res.*, **16**, 357–360.

HILLIER, W. (1973) 'In defence of space', *J. Roy. Inst. Brit. Architects*, **80**, 539–544.

HILTON, I. (1967) 'Differences in the behavior of mothers toward first and later-born children', *J. Pers. Soc. Psychol.*, **7**, 282–290.

HIMES, J. S. (1964) 'Some work-related cultural deprivations of lower-class Negro youth', *J. Marr. Fam.*, **26**, 447–449.

HINDE, R. A. and DAVIES, L. (1972) 'Removing infant rhesus from mother for 13 days compared with removing mother from infant', *J. Child Psychol. Psychiat.*, **13**, 227–237.

HINDLEY, C. B. (1965) 'Stability and change in abilities up to five years: group trends', *J. Child Psychol. Psychiat.*, **6**, 85–99.

HINKLE, L. E. and PLUMMER, N. (1952) 'Life stress and industrial absenteeism', *Industr. Med.*, **21**, 363–375.

HOBBS, N. (1975a) *The Futures of Children*, Jossey-Bass.

HOBBS, N. (ed.) (1975b) *Issues in the Classification of Children: a sourcebook on categories, labels and their consequences*, Jossey-Bass.

HOCHSCHILD, A. R. (1973) 'A review of sex role research', in Huber, J. (Ed.), *Changing Women in a Changing Society*, Univ. of Chicago Press.

HODGE, R. W., SEIGEL, P. M. and ROSSI, P. H. (1964) 'Occupational prestige in the United States 1925–63, *Amer. J. Sociol.*, **70**, 286–302.

HOLE, V. (1959) 'Social effects of planned rehousing', *The Town Planning Review*, **25**, 161–173.

HOLE, W. V. and POUNTNEY, M. T. (1971) *Trends in population, housing and occupancy rates, 1861–1961*, HMSO.

HOLLINGSHEAD, A. B. and REDLICH, F. C. (1958) *Social Class and Mental Illness*, John Wiley.

HOLMAN, R. (1970) 'Combating social deprivation', in Holman, R., Lafitte, F., Spencer, K. and Wilson, H. (Eds.), *Socially Deprived Families in Britain*, Bedford Square Press.

HOLMAN, R. (1973) *Trading in Children: a study of private fostering*, Routledge & Kegan Paul.

HOLMAN, R. and HAMILTON, C. (1973) 'The British urban programme', *Policy and Politics*, **2**, 97–112.

HOLMAN, R. (1974a) 'The American Poverty Programme 1969–71', *J. Soc. Pol.*, **3**, 21–38.

HOLMAN, R. (1974b) 'Social workers and the "inadequacies" ', *New Society*, **29**, 608–610.

HOLMANS, A. E. (1970) 'A forecast of affective demand for housing in Great Britain in the 1970's', *Social Trends*, No. 1, HMSO.

HOME OFFICE (1969a) 'Community development project: a general outline', Unpublished paper.

HOME OFFICE (1969b) 'Community development project objectives and strategy', Unpublished paper.

HOOD, C., OPPÉ, T. E., PLESS, I. B. and APTE, E. (1970) *Children of West Indian Immigrants: a study of one-year-olds in Paddington*, Institute of Race Relations.

HOOD, R. G. (1962) *Sentencing in Magistrates' Courts*, Stevens.

HOOK, E. B. (1973) 'Behavioral implications of the human XYY genotype', *Science*, **179**, 139–150.

HOPE, K. (Ed.) (1972) *The Analysis of Social Mobility: Methods and Approaches*, Oxford Univ. Press.

HOPE, K. (1975) 'Trends in the openness of British society in the present century', To appear in a monograph to be published by the Clarendon Press.

HOROWITZ, E. L. (1936) 'The development of attitudes toward the Negro', *Arch. Psychol.*, 194.

HOROWITZ, E. L. and HOROWITZ, R. E. (1938) 'Development of social attitudes in children', *Sociometry*, 1, 307–338.

HOUGHTON, V. P. (1966) 'Report on individually administered tests on West Indian immigrant children and English children', *Race*, 8, 147–156.

HOUSE CONDITION SURVEY ENGLAND AND WALES 1967 (1968) *Economic Trends*, No. 175, HMSO.

HOUSE CONDITION SURVEY ENGLAND AND WALES 1971 (1972) *Housing and Construction Statistics*, HMSO.

HOUSING AND CONSTRUCTION STATISTICS (1973) and (1974) *see* Department of the Environment (1973) and (1974).

HUESTIS, P. R. and MAXWELL, A. (1932) 'Does family size run in families?', *J. Hered.*, **23**, 77–79.

HUGHES, J. (1971) 'Low pay: a case for a national minimum wage?', in Bull, D. (Ed.), *Family Poverty*, London: Duckworth for the Child Poverty Action Group.

HUNT, A., FOX, J. and MORGAN, M. (1973) *Families and their Needs*, HMSO.

HUNT, J. McV. (1961) *Intelligence and Experience*, Ronald Press.

HUNTER, L. C. and ROBERTSON, D. J. (1969) *Economics of Wages and Labour*, Macmillan.

HUNTLEY, R. M. C. (1965) 'Heritability of intelligence', in Meade, J. E. and Parkes, A. S. (Eds.), *Biological Aspects of Social Problems*, Oliver & Boyd.

HUSEN, T. (1951) 'The influence of schooling upon IQ', *Theoria*, **17**, 61–68.

HUTCHESON, B. R., BALER, L., FLOYD, W. and OTTENSTEIN, D. (1966) 'A prognostic (predictive) classification of juvenile court first offenders based on a follow-up study', *Brit. J. Criminol.*, **6**, 354–363.

HUTCHINGS, B. (1972) 'Environmental and genetic factors in psychopathology and criminality', Unpublished M. Phil. Thesis, Univ. of London.

HUTCHINGS, B. and MEDNICK, S. A. (1974) 'Registered criminality in the adoptive and biological parents of registered male criminal adoptees', in Fieve, R. R. and Zubin, D. A. (Eds.), *Genetics and Psychopathology*, Johns Hopkins Press.

HUTT, C. (1972) *Males and Females*, Penguin.

HYMAN, H. H. and SHEATSLEY, P. B. (1964) 'Attitudes towards desegregation', *Scient. Amer.*, **211**, 16–23.

ILLSLEY, R. (1955) 'Social class selection and class differences in relation to still births and infant deaths', *Brit. Med. J.*, ii, 1520–1524.

ILLSLEY, R. (1966) 'Early prediction of perinatal risk', *Proc. Roy. Soc. Med.*, **59**, 181–184.

ILLSLEY, R., FINLAYSON, A. and THOMPSON, B. (1963) 'The motivation and characteristics of internal migrants', *Milbank Mem. Fund Quart.*, **41**, 115–144.

ILLSLEY, R. and GILL, D. G. (1968) 'Changing trends in illegitimacy', *Soc. Sci. & Med.*, **2**, 415–433.

ILLSLEY, R. and THOMPSON, B. (1961) 'Women from broken homes', *Sociol. Rev.*, **9**, 27–54.

INKELES, A. and ROSSI, P. H. (1956) 'National comparisons of occupational prestige', *Amer. J. Sociol.*, **61**, 329–339.

INNER LONDON EDUCATION AUTHORITY (1969) 'Literacy Survey: summary of interim results of the study of pupils reading standards', ILEA document.

INNER LONDON EDUCATION AUTHORITY (1973) 'Literacy Survey: 1971 follow-up, preliminary report', ILEA document.

JACKSON, B. (1973) 'The childminders', *New Society*, **26**, 521–524.

JACKSON, B. and MARSDEN, D. (1962) *Education and the Working Class*, Routledge & Kegan Paul.

JACKSON, E. F. (1962) 'Status consistency and symptoms of stress', *Amer. Sociol. Rev.*, 27, 469–480.

JACOBS, J. (1961) *The Death and Life of Great American Cities*, Random House.

JACOBS, S. C., PRUSOFF, B. A. and PAYKEL, E. S. (1974) 'Recent life events in schizophrenia and depression', *Psychol. Med.*, 4, 444–453.

JAFFE, J. (1966) 'Attitudes of adolescents toward the mentally retarded', *Amer. J. Ment. Defic.*, 70, 907–912.

JAHODA, M. and WEST, P. S. (1951) 'Race relations in public housing', *J. Social Issues*, 7, 132–139.

JAMES, A. G. (1974) *Sikh Children in Britain*, Institute of Race Relations/Oxford Univ. Press.

JENCKS, C., SMITH, M., ACLAND, M., BANE, M. J., COHEN, D., GINTIS, H., HEYNS, B. and MICHELSON, S. (1973) *Inequality: a reassessment of the effect of family and schooling in America*, Allen Lane.

JENNINGS, H. (1962) *Societies in the Making*, Routledge & Kegan Paul.

JENSEN, A. R. (1966) 'Cumulative deficit in compensatory education', *J. of School Psychology*, 4, 37–47.

JENSEN, A. R. (1967) 'The culturally disadvantaged: psychological and educational aspects', *Educational Research*, 10, 4–20.

JENSEN, A. R. (1969) 'How much can we boost IQ and scholastic achievement', *Harvard Educ. Rev.*, 39, 1–123.

JENSEN, A. R. (1972) *Genetics and Education*, Harper & Row.

JENSEN, A. R. (1973) *Educability and Group Differences*, Methuen.

JENSEN, A. R. (1974) 'Kinship correlations reported by Sir Cyril Burt', *Behav. Genetics*, 4, 1–28.

JEPHCOTT, P. (1971) *Homes in High Flats: some of the human problems involved in multi-storey housing*, Oliver & Boyd.

JEPHCOTT, A. P. and CARTER, M. P. (1954) *The Social Background of Delinquency*, Univ. of Nottingham.

JESSOR, R. and RICHARDSON, S. (1968) 'Psychosocial deprivation and personality development', in *Perspectives on Human Deprivation*, US Department of Health, Education and Welfare.

JOHN, A. (1970) *Race in the Inner City: a report from Handsworth, Birmingham*, Runnymede Trust.

JONES, D. C. (Ed.) (1934) *The Social Survey of Merseyside*, Hodder & Stoughton.

JONES, H. E. (1933) 'Order of birth', in Murchison, C. A. (Ed.), *A Handbook of Child Psychology*, Clark Univ. Press.

JONES, H. E. (1954) 'The environment and mental development', in Carmichael, L. (Ed.), *Manual of Child Psychology*, John Wiley.

JONES, H. (1958) 'Approaches to an ecological study', *Brit. J. Delinq.*, 8, 277–293.

JONES, H. E. and CONRAD, H. S. (1933) 'The growth and decline of intelligence: a study of a homogeneous group', *Genet. Psychol. Monogr.*, **13**, 223–298.

JONES, K. and SMITH, A. D. (1970) *The Economic Impact of Commonwealth Immigration*, Cambridge Univ. Press.

JONES, S. (1962) 'The Wechsler Intelligence Scale for Children applied to a sample of London primary school children', *Brit. J. Educ. Psychol.*, **32**, 119–132.

JONSSON, G. (1967) 'Delinquent boys, their parents and grandparents', *Acta Psychiat. Scand.*, **43**, *Suppl.* 195.

JORDAN, B. (1974) *Poor Parents: social policy and the 'cycle of deprivation'*, Routledge & Kegan Paul.

JOSÉ, J. and CODY, J. (1971) 'Teacher-pupil interaction as it relates to attempted changes in teacher expectancy of academic ability and achievement', *Amer. Educ. Research J.*, **8**, 39–49.

JOSEPH, K. (1972) Speech to the Preschool Playgroups Association, 29 June, 1972.

JOSEPH, K. (1974) Speech, 19 October, 1974.

JOWELL, R. and PRESCOTT-CLARKE, P. (1970) 'Racial discrimination and white-collar workers in Britain', *Race*, **11**, 397–417.

JUSTMAN, J. (1965) 'Academic aptitude and reading test scores of disadvantaged children showing various degrees of mobility', *J. of Educ. Measurement*, **2**, 151–155.

KAGAN, J. and MOSS, H. A. (1962) *Birth to Maturity: a study in psychological development*, John Wiley.

KAGAN, J., PEARSON, L. and WELCH, L. (1966) 'Conceptual impulsivity and inductive reasoning', *Child Develop.*, **37**, 583–594.

KAMIN, L. J. (1974) 'Heredity, intelligence, politics and psychology', mimeographed paper.

KANGAS, J. and BRADWAY, K. (1971) 'Intelligence at middle age: a thirty-eight year follow-up', *Develop. Psychol.*, **5**, 333–337.

KANTOR, M. B. (1965) 'Some consequences of residential and social mobility for the adjustment of children', in Kantor, M. B. (Ed.), *Mobility and Mental Health*, Charles C. Thomas.

KARNES, M. B. (1969) *Research and Development Program on Preschool Disadvantaged Children: final report*, US Office of Education.

KARNES, M. B., TESKA, J. A., HODGINS, A. S. and BADGER, E. D. (1970) 'Educational intervention at home by mothers of disadvantaged children', *Child Develop.*, **41**, 925–935.

KASARDA, J. D. and JANOWITZ, M. (1974) 'Community attachment in mass society', *Amer. Sociol. Rev.*, **39**, 328–339.

KATZ, I. (1967) 'Some motivational determinants of racial differences in intellectual achievement', *Internat. J. Psychol.*, **2**, 1–12.

KATZ, I., HENCHY, T. and ALLEN, H. (1968) 'Effects of race of tester approval-disapproval and need on learning in Negro boys', *J. Person. Soc. Psychol.*, **8**, 38–42.

KAWWA, T. (1968) 'A survey of ethnic attitudes of some British secondary school pupils', *Brit. J. Soc. Clin. Psychol.*, 7, 161–168.

KELLNER, R. (1963) *Family Ill Health: an investigation in general practice*, Tavistock.

KELSALL, R. K. and KELSALL, H. M. (1971) *Social Disadvantage and Educational Opportunity*, Holt, Rinehart and Winston.

KELVIN, P. (1969) *The Bases of Social Behaviour*, Holt, Rinehart and Winston.

KEMP, L. C. D. (1955) 'Environmental and other characteristics determining attainments in primary schools', *Brit. J. Educ. Psychol.*, 25, 67–77.

KEMPE, C. H. and HELFER, R. E. (1972) *Helping the Battered Child and his Family*, Lippincott.

KENDALL, R. E. (1968) *The Classification of Depressive Illnesses*, Maudsley Monograph No. 18, Oxford Univ. Press.

KENNELL, J. H., JERAULD, R., WOLFLE, H., CHESTER, D., KREGER, N. C., McALPINE, W., STEFFA, M. and KLAUS, M. H. (1974) 'Maternal behavior one year after early and extended post-partum contact', *Develop. Med. Child Neurol.*, 16, 172–179.

KENNETT, K. F. and CROPLEY, A. J. (1970) 'Intelligence, family size and socio-economic status', *J. Biosoc. Sci.*, 2, 227–236.

KESSIN, K. (1971) 'Social and psychological consequences of intergenerational occupational mobility', *Amer. J. Sociol.*, 77, 1–18.

KETY, S., ROSENTHAL, D., WENDER, P. H., SCHULSINGER, F. and JACOBSEN, B. (1974) 'Mental illness in the biological and adoptive families of adopted individuals who have become schizophrenic: a preliminary report based upon psychiatric interviews', in Fieve, R., Brill, H. and Rosenthal, D. (Eds.), *Genetics and Psychopathology*, Johns Hopkins Press.

KHOSLA, T. and LOWE, C. R. (1968) 'Height and weight of British men', *Lancet*, i, 742–745.

KIEV, A. R. (1965) 'Psychiatric illness among West Indians in London', *Race*, 5, 48–54.

KIEV, A. R. (1973) 'Psychiatric disorders in minority groups', in Watson, P. (Ed.), *Psychology and Race*, Penguin.

KINCAID, J. C. (1973) *Poverty and Equality in Britain*, Penguin.

KING, R. D., RAYNES, N. V. and TIZARD, J. (1971) *Patterns of Residential Care: sociological studies in institutions for handicapped children*, Routledge & Kegan Paul.

KIRK, S. A. (1958) *Early Education of the Mentally Retarded: an experimental study*, Univ. of Illinois Press.

KIRK, S. A. (1974) 'The impact of labeling on rejection of the mentally ill: an experimental study', *J. Health and Social Behaviour*, 15, 108–117.

KLAUS, M. H., JERAULD, R., KREGER, N. C., McALPINE, W., STEFFA, M. and KENNELL, J. H. (1972) 'Maternal attachment:

importance of the first post-partum days', *New England J. Med.*, **286**, 460–463.

KLEINER, R. J. and PARKER, S. (1963) 'Goal striving and social status, and mental disorder: a research review', *Amer. Sociol. Rev.*, **28**, 189–203.

KLEINER, R. J. and PARKER, S. (1965) 'Goal striving and psychosomatic symptoms in a migrant and non-migrant population', in Kantor, M. B. (Ed.), *Mobility and Mental Health*, Charles C. Thomas.

KNIGHT, B. J. and WEST, D. J. (1975) 'Temporary and continuing delinquency', *Brit. J. Criminol.*, **15**, 43–50.

KNOWLES, K. G. J. C. and ROBERTSON, D. J. (1951) 'Earnings in engineering, 1926–1948', *Bull. Oxford Inst. Stats.*, **13**, 109–127.

KOCH, H. L. (1946) 'The social distance test between certain racial, nationality and skin-pigmentation groups in selected populations of American school children', *J. Genet. Psychol.*, **68**, 63–95.

KOHN, M. L. (1963) 'Social class and parent-child relationships: an interpretation', *Amer. J. Sociol.*, **68**, 471–480.

KOHN, M. L. (1969) *Class and Conformity: a study in values*, The Dorsey Press.

KOLUCHOVA, J. (1972) 'Severe deprivation in twins: a case study', *J. Child Psychol. Psychiat.*, **13**, 107–114.

KORNHAUSER, A. (1964) 'Towards an assessment of the mental health of factory workers', in Reissman, F., Cohen, J. and Pearl, A. (Eds.), *Mental Health of the Poor*, Collier–Macmillan.

KOSA, J. (1957) *Land of Choice*, Univ. of Toronto Press.

KOWITZ, G. and LEVY, L. E. (1965) 'Underachievement in deaf children', *Amer. Ann. Deaf.*, **110**, 414–419.

KREITMAN, N. (1964) 'The patient's spouse', *Brit. J. Psychiat.*, **110**, 159–173.

KREITMAN, N., SMITH, P. and TAN, E. (1969) 'Attempted suicide in social networks', *Brit. J. Prev. Soc. Med.*, **23**, 116–123.

KREITMAN, N., COLLINS, J., NELSON, B. and TROOP, J. (1970) 'Neurosis and marital interaction: I. Personality and symptoms', *Brit. J. Psychiat.*, **117**, 33–46.

KUSHLICK, A. (1968) 'Social problems of mental subnormality', in Miller, E. (Ed.), *Foundations of Child Psychiatry*, Pergamon.

KUTNER, B. (1958) 'Patterns of mental functioning associated with prejudice in children', *Psychol. Monogr.*, **72**, No. 460.

LABOV, W. (1970) 'The logical non-standard English', in Williams, F. (Ed.), *Language and Poverty*, Markham Press.

LAISHLEY, J. (1971) 'Skin colour awareness and preference in London nursery-school children', *Race*, **13**, 47–64.

LAMBERT, J. (1970) *Crime, Police and Race Relations*, Oxford Univ. Press.

LAMBERT, R. (1964) *Nutrition in Britain 1950–60*, Occasional Papers on Social Administration No. 6, Bell.

LAND, H. (1969) 'Large families in London', *Occasional Papers on Social Administration* No. 32, Bell.

LANDER, B. (1954) *Towards an Understanding of Juvenile Delinquency*, Columbia Univ. Press.

LANGE, J. (1929) *Verbrechen als Schicksal, Studien an Kriminellen Zwillingen*, Thieme.

LANGNER, T. S. and MICHAEL, S. T. (1963) *Life Stress and Mental Health*, Collier–Macmillan.

LANGNER, T. S. *et al.* (1969) 'Psychiatric impairment in welfare and non-welfare children', *Mental Health Digest*, 1, 19–22.

LANSDOWN, R. G., SHEPHERD, J., CLAYTON, B. E., DELVES, H. T., GRAHAM, P. J. and TURNER, W. C. (1974) 'Blood-lead levels, behaviour and intelligence: a population study', *Lancet*, i, 538–541.

LASKO, J. K. (1954) 'Parent behavior toward first and second children', *Genet. Psychol. Monog.*, 49, 96–137.

LAWTON, D. (1968) *Social Class, Language and Education*, Routledge & Kegan Paul.

LEACOCK, E. B. (Ed.) (1971) *The Culture of Poverty: a critique*, Simon & Schuster.

LEAHY, A. M. (1935) 'Nature-nurture and intelligence', *Genet. Psychol. Monog.*, 17, 241–305.

LEDERMAN, S. (1969) 'The social acceptance of immigrants', *Race Today*, 1, 60–61.

LEE, E. S. (1951) 'Negro intelligence and selective migration: a Philadelphia test of the Klineberg hypothesis', *Amer. Sociol. Rev.*, 16, 227–233.

LEE, T. (1968) 'Urban Neighborhood as a socio-spatial scheme', *Human Relations*, 21, 241–268.

LEEDS, A. (1971) 'The concept of the "culture of poverty": conceptual, logical, and empirical problems, with perspectives from Brazil and Peru', in Leacock, E. B. (Ed.), *The Culture of Poverty: a critique*, Simon & Schuster.

LEES, J. P. and STEWART, A. H. (1957) 'Family or sibship position and scholastic ability', *Sociolog. Review.*, 5, 85–106, 173–189.

LEES, R. (1973) 'Action-research in community development', *J. Soc. Pol.*, 2, 239–248.

LEIDERMAN, P. H. and SEASHORE, M. J. (1975) 'Parent-infant relationships', in Porter, R. and Fitzsimons, D. (Eds.), *Outcome of Severe CNS Damage*, Proceedings of CIBA Conference, Nov. 1974, *Excerpta Medica*.

LEIFER, A. D., LEIDERMAN, P. H., BARNETT, C. R. and WILLIAMS, J. A. (1972) 'Effects of mother-infant separation on maternal attachment behavior', *Child Develop.*, 43, 1203–1218.

LEIGHTON, D. C., HARDING, J. S., MACKLIN, D. B., MACMILLAN, A. M. and LEIGHTON, A. H. (1963) *The Character of Danger*, Basic Books.

LEMERT, E. M. (1967) *Human Deviance, Social Problems, and Social Control*, Prentice-Hall.

LESTER, D. (1970) 'Social disorganization and completed suicide', *Social Psychiat.*, 5, 175–176.

LEVENSTEIN, P. (1970) 'Cognitive growth in preschoolers through verbal interaction with mothers', *Amer. J. Orthopsychiat.*, **40**, 426–432.

LEVER, W. F. (1974) 'Regional multipliers and demand leakages at establishment level', *Scot. J. Pol. Econ.*, **21**, 111–122.

LEVY, D. (1943) *Maternal Overprotection*, Columbia Univ. Press.

LEWIS, A. (1935) 'Neurosis and unemployment', *Lancet*, ii, 293–297.

LEWIS, H. (1954) *Deprived Children*, Oxford Univ. Press.

LEWIS, H. G. (1963) *Unionism and Relative Wages in the United States*, Univ. of Chicago Press.

LEWIS, O. (1959) *Five Families*, Basic Books.

LEWIS, O. (1961) *The Children of Sanchez*, Random House.

LEWIS, O. (1966) *La Vida*, Random House.

LEWIS, O. (1968) 'The culture of poverty', in Moynihan, D. P. (Ed.), *On Understanding Poverty*, Basic Books.

LEWIS, O. (1969) 'Review of C. A. Valentine, "*Culture and Poverty: critique and counter proposals*" ', *Current Anthropology*, **10**, 189–192.

LIDBETTER, E. J. (1933) *Heredity and the Social Problem Group*, Edward Arnold.

LIEBERMAN, S. (1956) 'The effect of changes in role on the attitudes of role occupants', *Human Relations*, **9**, 385–402.

LINDZEY, G., LOEHLIN, J., MANOSEVITZ, M. and THIESSEN, D. (1971) 'Behavioral genetics', in Mussen, P. H. and Rosenzweig, M. R. (Eds.), *Annual Review of Psychology*,, Vol. 22, Annual Reviews Inc.

LIPSET, S. M. and BENDIX, R. (1959) *Social Mobility in Industrial Society*, Heinemann.

LISHMAN, W. A. (1968) 'Brain damage in relation to psychiatric disability after head injury', *Brit. J. Psychiat.*, **114**, 373–410.

LISTER, R. (1972) 'The administration of the Wage Stop', *Poverty pamphlet No. 11*, Child Poverty Action Group.

LISTER, R. (1974) *Take-up of Means-Tested Benefits*, Child Poverty Action Group.

LITTLE, A. and MABEY, C. (1973) 'Reading attainment and social and ethnic mix of London primary schools', in Donnison, D. and Eversley, D., (Eds.), *London: Urban Patterns, Problems and Policies* Heinemann Educational Books.

LITTLE, A., MABEY, C. and RUSSELL, J. (1971) 'Do small classes help a pupil?', *New Society*, 473, 769–771.

LITTLE, A., MABEY, C. and WHITAKER, G. (1968) 'The education of immigrant children in Inner London primary schools', *Race*, **9**, 439–452.

LITTLE, W. R. and NTSEKHE, V. R. (1959) 'Social class background of young offenders from London', *Brit. J. Delinqu.*, 10, 30–35.

LITTLE, A. and SMITH, G. (1971) *Strategies of Compensation: a review of educational projects for the disadvantaged in the United States*, OECD.

LITTLE, K. (1947) *Negroes in Britain*, Kegan Paul.

LJUNGBERG, L. (1957) 'Hysteria: a clinical, prognostic and genetic study', *Acta Psychiat. Neurol. Scand.*, Suppl. 112.

LO, W. H. (1973) 'A note on a follow-up study of childhood neurosis and behaviour disorder', *J. Child Psychol. Psychiat.*, 14, 147–150.

LOCKWOOD, D. (1958) *The Blackcoated Worker*, Allen & Unwin.

LOCKYER, L. and RUTTER, M. (1969) 'A five to fifteen-year follow-up study of infantile psychosis. III. Psychological aspects', *Brit. J. Psychiat.*, 115, 865–882.

LOMAS, G. (1973) *Census 1971: the Coloured Population of Great Britain: preliminary report*, Runnymede Trust.

LONDON BOROUGH OF HAMMERSMITH (1974) *Living in a Council Flat. A survey of attitudes on five estates.*

LONDON COUNTY COUNCIL (1962) *Report of Research Team to the Committee of Inquiry into Homelessness*, General Purposes Committee Report No. 3.

LOPREATO, J. and HAZELRIGG, L. E. (1970) 'Intragenerational versus intergenerational mobility in relation to sociopolitical attitudes', *Social Forces*, 49, 200–210.

LORGE, I. (1945) 'Schooling makes a difference', *Teachers' College Record*, 46, 483–492.

LORING, W. C. (1956) 'Housing characteristics and social disorganization', *Social Problems*, 3, 160–168.

LUKIANOWICZ, N. (1971) 'Battered children', *Psychiat. Clin.*, 4, 257–280.

LUKOFF, I. and WHITEMAN, M. (1964) 'Attitudes towards blindness', Paper presented at Amer. Fed. Cath. Wkrs. for the Blind, New York.

LUNN, J. C. B. (1970) *Streaming in the Primary School*, NFER.

LYDALL, H. (1955) 'The life cycle in income, saving, and asset ownership', *Econometrica*, 23, 131–150.

LYDALL, H. F. (1959) 'The long-term trend in the size distribution of income', *J. Roy. Statist. Society*, 122, (Series A).

LYDALL, H. F. and TIPPING, D. G. (1961) 'The distribution of personal wealth in Britain', *Bulletin of the Oxford Institute of Economics and Statistics*, 23.

LYLE, J. G. (1960) 'The effect of an institutional environment upon the verbal development of imbecile children. III. The Brooklands residential family unit', *J. Ment. Defic. Res.*, 4, 14–23.

LYNCH, G. W. and ODDY, D. J. (1967) 'Are children of the under-paid under-fed?', *The Medical Officer*, 117, 353–354.

LYNES, T. (1971) 'The failure of selectivity', in Bull, D. (Ed.), *Family Poverty*, Duckworth for the Child Poverty Action Group.

MABEY, C. (1974) 'Social and ethnic mix in schools and the relationship with attainment of children aged 8 and 11', Centre for Environmental Studies Research Paper No. 9.

McASKIE, M. and CLARKE, A. M. (1976) Parent-offspring resemblances in intelligence: theories and evidence. *Brit. J. Psychol.*, (in press).

McCALL, R. B., HOGARTY, P. S. and HURLBURT, N. (1972) 'Transition in infant sensori-motor development and the prediction of childhood IQ', *Amer. Psychol.*, **27**, 728–748.

McCLELLAND, D. C. (1958) 'The importance of early learning in the formation of motives', in Atkinson, J. W. (Ed.), *Motives in Fantasy, Action and Society*, Van Nostrand.

McCLELLAND, D. C., ATKINSON, J. W., CLARK, R. A. and LOWELL, E. L. (1953) *The Achievement Motive*, Appleton-Century-Crofts.

McCLINTOCK, F. H. (1963) *Crimes of Violence*, Macmillan.

McCLINTOCK, F. H. and AVISON, N. H. (1968) *Crime in England and Wales*, Heinemann Educational Books.

McCORD, W. and McCORD, J. (1959) *Origins of Crime: a new evaluation of the Cambridge-Somerville study*, Columbia Univ. Press.

McCULLOCH, J. W., PHILIP, A. E. and CARSTAIRS, G. M. (1967) 'The ecology of suicidal behaviour', *Brit. J. Psychiat.*, **113**, 313–319.

McDANIEL, J. W. (1969) *Physical Disability and Human Behavior*, Pergamon Press.

McDILL, E. L., MYERS, E. D. and RIGSBY, L. C. (1974) 'Institutional effects on the academic behaviour of high school students', in Marjoribancks, K. (Ed.), *Environments for learning*, NFER.

McDILL, E. L. and RIGSBY, L. C. (1973) *Structure and Process in Secondary Schools: the academic impact of educational climates*, Johns Hopkins Press.

McDONALD, A. (1967) *Children of Very Low Birth Weight*, MEIU Research Monogr. No. 1, SIMP/Heinemann.

McDONALD, L. (1969) *Social Class and Delinquency*, Faber & Faber.

McFIE, J. and THOMPSON, J. A. (1970) 'Intellectual abilities of immigrant children', *Brit. J. Educ. Psychol.*, **40**, 348–351.

McINNES, R. G. (1937) 'Observations on heredity in neurosis', *Proc. Roy. Soc. Med.*, **30**, 895–904.

McINTOSH, N. and SMITH, D. J. (1974) *The extent of racial discrimination*, London, P.E.P. Broadsheet No. 547.

McKEOWN, T. (1970) 'Prenatal and early postnatal influences on measured intelligence', *Brit. Med. J.*, iii, 63–67.

McKISSACK, I. J. (1973) 'The peak age for property crimes: further data', *Brit J. Criminol.*, **13**, 253–261.

McNEMAR, Q. (1940) 'A critical examination of the University of Iowa Studies of environmental influences upon the IQ', *Psychol. Bull.*, 37, 63–92.

MADGE, N. J. H. (1976) 'Context and the expressed ethnic preferences of infant school children', *J. Child Psychol. Psychiat.*, (in press).

MADIGAN, F. C. (1957) 'Are sex mortality differentials biologically caused?', *Milbank Mem. Fund Quart.*, 35, 202–223.

MAIZELS, J. (1961) *Two to Five in High Flats*, Housing Centre Trust.

MALZBERG, B. and LEE, E. S. (1956) *Migration and Mental Disease*, New York, Social Science Research Council.

MANNHEIM, H. (1948) *Juvenile Delinquency in an English Middletown*, Kegan Paul, Trench, Trubner.

MANNHEIM, H., SPENCER, J. and LYNCH, G. (1957) 'Magisterial policy in the London juvenile courts', *Brit. J. Del.*, 8, 13–33 and 119–138.

MANNHEIM, H. and WILKINS, L. T. (1955) *Prediction Methods in Relation to Borstal Training*, HMSO.

MARKOWE, M., TONGE, W. L. and BARBER, L. E. D. (1955) 'Psychiatric disability and employment: a survey of 222 registered disabled persons', *Brit. J. Preventive and Social Medicine*, 9, 39–45.

MARRIS, P. (1958) *Widows and Their Families*, Routledge & Kegan Paul.

MARSDEN, D. (1969) *Mothers Alone: poverty and the fatherless family*, Allen Lane.

MARSH, A. (1970) 'Awareness of racial differences in West African and British children', *Race*, 11, 289–302.

MARSHALL, W., CARTER, C. and TANNER, J. (1974) Personal Communication.

MARTIN, A. E. (1967) 'Environment, housing and health', *Urban Studies*, 4, 1–21.

MARTIN, F. M., BROTHERSTONE, J. H. F. and CHAVE, S. P. W. (1957) 'Incidence of neurosis in a new housing estate', *Brit. J. Prev. Soc. Med.*, 11, 196–202.

MASON, M. K. (1942) 'Learning to speak after six and one-half years of silence', *J. Speech Hearing Disorder*, 7, 295–304.

MASON, W. A. (1960) 'Socially mediated reduction in emotional responses of young rhesus monkeys', *J. Abn. Soc. Psychol.*, 60, 100–104.

MASTERSON, J. F. (1967) *The Psychiatric Dilemma of Adolescence*, Churchill.

MATTHEWS, P. C. (1974) *Report of the (Seebohm) Naval Welfare Committee*, Appendix 6, HMSO.

MATTINSON, J. (1970) *Marriage and Mental Handicaps*, Duckworth.

MATZA, D. (1964) *Delinquency and Drift*, John Wiley.

MAXWELL, A. E. (1972) 'The WPPSF, a marked discrepancy in the correlations of the sub tests for good and poor readers', *Brit. J. Math. Statist. Psychol.*, 25, 283–291.

MAXWELL, J. (1969) *Sixteen Years On: a follow-up of the 1947 Scottish Survey*, Univ. of London Press Ltd.

MAY, D. (1975) 'Juvenile offenders and the organisation of juvenile justice: an examination of juvenile justice in Aberdeen 1959–1967'. Ph.D. thesis, Univ. of Aberdeen.

MAYHEW, C. (1851–61) *London Labour and the London Poor*, George Woodfall & Son.

MAYHEW, C. (1862) *The Criminal Prisons of London*, Griffin Bohn.

MAYS, J. B. (1954) *Growing Up in the City*, Liverpool University Press.

MAYS, J. B. (1963) 'Delinquency areas — a re-assessment', *Brit. J. Criminal.*, 3, 216–230.

MAYS, J. B. (Ed.) (1972) *Juvenile Delinquency, The Family and The Social Group: a reader*, Longman.

MAZER, M. (1972) 'Characteristics of multi-problem households: a study in psychosocial epidemiology', *Amer. J. Orthopsychiat.*, 42, 792–802.

MAZER, M. (1974) 'People in predicament: a study in psychiatric and psychosocial epidemiology', *Social Psychiatry*, 9, 85–90.

MEADE, J. E. (1973) 'The Inheritance of inequalities', *Proceedings of British Academy*, 59.

MECHANIC, D. (1969) *Mental Health and Social Policy*, Prentice-Hall.

MEICHENBAUM, D. H., BOWERS, K. S. and ROSS, R. R. (1969) 'A behavioral analysis of teacher expectancy', *J. Pers. Soc. Psychol.*, 13, 306–316.

MEIER, E. C. (1965) 'Current circumstances of former foster children', *Child Welfare*, 44, 196–206.

MEIER, E. C. (1966) 'Adults who were foster children', *Children*, 13, 16–22.

MELLSOP, G. W. (1972) 'Psychiatric patients seen as children and adults: childhood predictors of adult illness', *J. Child Psychol. Psychiat.*, 13, 91–102.

MENKES, M. M., ROWE, J. S. and MENKES, J. H. (1967) 'A twenty-five year follow-up study on the hyperkinetic child with minimal brain dysfunction', *Pediatrics*, 39, 393–399.

MERCER, J. R. (1973) *Labelling the Mentally Retarded*, Univ. of Calif. Press.

MERTON, R. K. (1957) *Social Theory and Social Structure*, Free Press.

MEZEY, A. G. (1960) 'Personal background, emigration and mental disorders in Hungarian refugees', *J. Ment. Sci.*, 106, 618–627.

MIDDLETON, R. (1960) 'Ethnic prejudice and susceptibility to persuasion', *Amer. Sociol. Rev.*, 25, 679–686.

MILGRIM, S. (1970) 'The experience of living in cities', *Science*, 167, 1461–1468.

MILLAR, S. (1968) *The Psychology of Play*, Penguin.

MILLER, A. D., MARGOLIN, J. B. and YOLLES, S. F. (1957)

'Epidemiology of reading disabilities; some methodological considerations and early findings', *Amer. J. Public Health*, 47, 1250–1256.

MILLER, F. J. W., COURT, S. D. M., KNOX, E. G. and BRANDON, S. (1974) *The School Years in Newcastle upon Tyne 1955–62*, Oxford Univ. Press.

MILLER, S. M. (1964) 'The American lower classes: a typological approach', in Riessman, G., Cohen, J. and Pearl, A. (Eds.), *Mental Health of the Poor*, Collier-Macmillan.

MILLER, S. M. and ROBY, P. (1971) 'Strategies for social mobility – a policy framework', *Amer. Sociologist*, **6**, Suppl., 18–22.

MILLER, H. P. (1960) 'Annual and lifetime income in relation to education: 1939–59', *Amer. Econ. Rev.*, **50**, 962–986.

MILNER, D. (1970) 'Ethnic identity and preference in minority-group children', unpublished Ph.D dissertation, Univ. of Bristol.

MINISTRY OF EDUCATION (1950) *Reading Ability: some suggestions for helping the backward*, London, HMSO.

MINISTRY OF HEALTH Memorandum (1968) Reported by Deakin, N. *Colour, Citizenship and British Society* (1970), Panther.

MINISTRY OF HOUSING AND LOCAL GOVERNMENT (1961) *Homes for Today and Tomorrow*, (Parker Morris Report), HMSO.

MINISTRY OF HOUSING AND LOCAL GOVERNMENT (1963) *Living in a Slum. A study of people in a central slum clearance area in Oldham*, HMSO.

MINISTRY OF HOUSING AND LOCAL GOVERNMENT (1965) *Report on the Committee on Housing in Greater London*, (Milner Holland Report), HMSO.

MINISTRY OF HOUSING AND LOCAL GOVERNMENT (1966) *Our Older Homes: a call for action*. (Denington Report), HMSO.

MINISTRY OF HOUSING AND LOCAL GOVERNMENT (1969) *Council Housing Purposes, Procedures and Priorities*. (Cullingworth Report), HMSO.

MINISTRY OF HOUSING AND LOCAL GOVERNMENT (1970) *Families Living at High Density. A study of estates in Leeds, Liverpool and London*, HMSO.

MINISTRY OF PENSIONS AND NATIONAL INSURANCE (1966) *Financial and Other Circumstances of Retirement Pensioners*, HMSO.

MINISTRY OF SOCIAL SECURITY (1967) *Circumstances of Families*, HMSO.

MINNS, R. (1972) 'Homeless families and some organisational determinants of deviancy', *Policy and Politics*, 1, (1), 1–21.

MISSAKIAN, E. A. (1969) 'Effects of social deprivation on the development of patterns of social behaviour', *Proceedings of the 2nd International Congress of Primatology*, Vol. 2, Atlanta, Georgia, S. Karger.

MISSAKIAN, E. A. (1972) 'Effects of adult social experiences on patterns of reproductive activity of socially deprived male rhesus monkeys (macaca mulatta)', *J. Pers. Soc. Psychol.*, 21, 131–134.

MITCHELL, G. and SCHROERS, L. (1973) 'Birth order and parental experience in monkeys and man', in Reese, H. W. (Ed.), *Advances in Child Development and Behaviour*, Vol. 8, Academic Press.

MITCHELL, R. E. (1971) 'Some social implications of high density housing', *Amer. Soc. Rev.*, **36**, 18–29.

MITCHELL, S. and SHEPHERD, M. (1966) 'A comparative study of children's behaviour at home and at school', *Brit. J. Educ. Psychol.*, **36**, 248–254.

MITTLER, P. (1971) *The Study of Twins*, Penguin.

MÖNCKEBERG, F. (1972) 'Malnutrition and mental capacity' in *Nutrition, the Nervous System and Behaviour*, Pan American Health Organization.

MONCRIEFF, A. A., KOUMIDES, O. P., CLAYTON, N. A., PATRICK, A. D., RENWICK, A. G. C. and ROBERTS, O. E. (1964) 'Lead Poisoning in Children', *Arch. Di. Childh.*, **39**, 1–13.

MOOR, N. (1974) *Jobs in Jeopardy: a study of job prospects in older industrial areas*, Community Development Project Information and Intelligence Unit.

MOORE, N. C. (1974) 'Psychiatric illness and living in flats', *Brit. J. Psychiat.*, **125**, 500–507.

MOORE, R. (1973) 'Low pay and fiscal policy', in Field, F. (Ed.), *Low Pay*, Arrow Books.

MOORE, T. W. (1963) 'Effects on the children', in Yudkin, S. and Holme, A. (Eds.), *Working Mothers and their Children*, Michael Joseph.

MORENO, J. L. (1953) *Who Shall Survive*?, Beacon House.

MORGAN, J. N., DAVID, M. H. and BRAZER, H. E. (1962) *Income and Welfare in the United States*, McGraw-Hill.

MORLAND, J. K. (1958) 'Racial recognition by nursery school children in Lynchburg, Virginia, *Social Forces*, **37**, 132–137.

MORRIS, T. P. (1957) *The Criminal Area*, Routledge & Kegan Paul.

MORROW, W. R. and PETERSON, D. B. (1966) 'Follow-up of discharged psychiatric offenders in "not guilty by reason of insanity" and "criminal sexual psychopaths"', *J. Crim. Law Criminal and Police Science*, **57**, 31–34.

MORSE, N. C. and WEISS, R. S. (1955) 'The function and meaning of work and the job', *Amer. Soc. Rev.*, **20**, 191–198.

MOSHER, D. L. and SCODEL, A. (1960) 'Relationship between ethnocentrism in children and the ethnocentrism and authoritarian rearing practices of their mothers', *Child Develop.*, **31**, 369–376.

MOSTELLER, F. and MOYNIHAN, D. P. (Eds.) (1972) *On Equality of Educational Opportunity*, Random House.

MOYNIHAN, D. P. (1968) 'The professors and the poor', in Moynihan, D. P. (Ed.), *On Understanding Poverty*, Basic Books.

MUELLBAUER, J. (1974) 'Prices and Inequality: The United Kingdom experience', *Economic Journal*, **84**, 32–55.

MULLEN, E. J., DUMPSON, J. R. and Associates (1972) *Evaluation of Social Intervention*, Jossey-Bass.

MULLIGAN, G., DOUGLAS, J. W. B., HAMMOND, W. A. and TIZARD, J. (1963) 'Delinquency and symptoms of maladjustment: the findings of a longitudinal study', *Roy. Soc. Med.*, **56**, 1083–1086.

MURCHISON, N. (1974) Appendix to Finer Report. *See*, Department of Health and Social Security (1974) Report of the Committee on One-Parent Families. HMSO.

MURPHY, H. B. D. (Ed.) (1955) *Flight and Resettlement*, Unesco.

NAAR, R. (1965) 'A note on the intelligence of delinquents', *Brit. J. Criminol.*, **5**, 82–85.

NASH, R. (1971) 'Camouflage in the classroom', *New Society*, **17**, 667–669.

NATIONAL SOCIETY FOR THE PREVENTION OF CRUELTY TO CHILDREN (1972) Annual Report.

NELSON, B., COLLINS, J., KREITMAN, N. and TROOP, J. (1970) 'Neurosis and marital interaction. II. Time sharing and social activity', *Brit. J. Psychiat.*, **117**, 47–58.

NEVITT, A. A. (1966) *Housing, Taxation and Subsidies*, Nelson.

NEW EARNINGS SURVEY (1968) and (1973), *see* DEPARTMENT OF EMPLOYMENT (1969) and (1974).

NEWCOMB, T. M. (1963) 'Persistence and regression of changed attitudes: long range studies', *J. Social Issues*, **19**, 3–14.

NEWFIELD, J. G. H. (1963) 'The academic performance of British university students', *Sociol. Rev., Special Monographs*, No. 7.

NEWMAN, H. H., FREEMAN, F. N. and HOLZINGER, K. J. (1937) *Twins: a study of heredity and environment*, Univ. of Chicago Press.

NEWMAN, O. (1973) *Defensible Space*, Architectural Press.

NEWMAN, O. (1974) Unpublished paper presented to N.A.C.R.O. Conference on 'Architecture planning and urban crime'.

NEWSON, J. and NEWSON, E. (1963) *Infant Care in an Urban Community*, Allen & Unwin.

NEWSON, J. and NEWSON, E. (1968) *Four Years Old in an Urban Community*, Allen & Unwin.

NICHOLS, P. L. and ANDERSON, V. E. (1973) 'Intellectual performance, race and socio-economic status', *Social Biology*, **20**, 367–374.

NICHOLSON, R. J. (1967) 'The distribution of personal income', *Lloyds Bank Review*, No. 83.

NICOL, A. R. (1971) 'Psychiatric disorder in the children of Caribbean immigrants', *J. Child Psychol. Psychiat.*, **12**, 233–281.

NIELSEN, J. (1971) 'Prevalence and a 2½ years incidence of chromosome abnormalities among all males in a Forensic Psychiatric Clinic', *Brit. J. Psychiat.*, **119**, 503–512.

NISBET, J. D. (1953) *Family environment: a direct effect of family size on intelligence*, Occasional papers on Eugenics, No. 8, The Eugenics Society.

NISBET, J. D. (1957) 'Contribution to intelligence testing and the theory of intelligence. IV. Intelligence and age: retesting after twenty four years interval', *Brit. J. Educ. Psychol.*, **27**, 190–198.

NISBET, J. D. and ENTWISTLE, N. J. (1967) 'Intelligence and family size', *Brit. J. Educ. Psychol.*, **37**, 188–193.

NOBLE, T. (1970) 'Family breakdown and social networks', *Brit. J. Sociol.*, 21, 135–150.

NOBLE, T. (1972) 'Social mobility and class relations in Britain', *Brit. J. Sociol.*, 23, 422–436.

NOTTING HILL PEOPLES ASSOCIATION HOUSING GROUP (1972) *'Losing Out': A study on Colville and Tavistock.*

NOVAK, M. A. and HARLOW, H. F. (1975) 'Social recovery of monkeys isolated for the first year of life: 1. Rehabilitation and therapy', *Develop. Psychol.*, 11, 453–465.

NYE, F. E., SHORT, J. F. and OLSON, V. J. (1958) 'Socioeconomic status and delinquent behavior', *Amer. J. Sociol.*, **63**, 381–389.

OAKLEY, R. (1968) *New Backgrounds: the immigrant child at home and at school*, Oxford Univ. Press.

ODEGAARD, O. (1932) 'Emigration and insanity', *Acta Psychiat. Neurol. Suppl. 4.*

ODEN, M. H. (1968) 'The fulfilment of promise: 40-year follow-up of the Terman gifted group', *Genet. Psychol. Monogr.*, **77**, 3–93.

OFFICE OF POPULATION CENSUSES AND SURVEYS (1973a) *The General Household Survey: introductory report*, HMSO.

OFFICE AND POPULATION CENSUSES AND SURVEYS (1973b) *Young People's Employment Study: preliminary report No. 1*, OPCS. Social Survey Division.

OFFICE OF POPULATION CENSUSES AND SURVEYS (1974a) *Census 1971. Housing tables*, HMSO.

OFFICE OF POPULATION CENSUSES AND SURVEYS (1974b) *Young People's Employment Study: preliminary report No. 2*, OCPS. Social Survey Division.

OFFORD, D. R. and CROSS, L. A. (1969) 'Behavioural antecedents of adult schizophrenia', *Arch. Gen. Psychiat.*, 21, 267–283.

OLDMAN, D., BYTHEWAY, B. and HOROBIN, G. (1971) 'Family structure and educational achievement', *J. Biosoc. Sci.*, Suppl. 3, 81–91.

O'LEARY, V. E. (1974) 'Some attitudinal barriers to occupational aspirations in woman', *Psychol. Bull.*, 81, 809–826.

OLIVER, J. E. and COX, J. (1973) 'A family kindred with ill-used children: the burden on the community', *Brit. J. Psychiat.*, **123**, 81–90.

OLIVER, J. E., COX, J., TAYLOR, A. and BALDWIN, J. A. (1974) *Severely ill-treated young children in North-East Wiltshire*, Oxford University Unit of Clinical Epidemiology Research Report No. 4.

OLIVER, J. E. and TAYLOR, A. (1971) 'Five generations of ill-treated children in one family pedigree', *Brit. J. Psychiat.*, 119, 473–480.

OPPÉ, T. E. (1964) 'The health of West Indian children', *Proc. Roy. Soc. Med.*, **57**, 321–323.

OPPENHEIMER, V. C. (2973) 'Demographic influences on female employment and the status of women', in Huber, J. (Ed.), *Changing Women in a Changing Society*, Univ. of Chicago Press.

OTTERSTRÖM, E. (1946) 'Delinquency and children from bad homes', *Acta Paediatrica*, **33**, Suppl. 5.

OUTHIT, M. C. (1933) 'A study of the resemblance of parents and children in general intelligence', *Arch. Psychol. New York*, No. 149.

OWENS, W. A. (1953) 'Age and mental abilities: a longitudinal study', *Genet. Psychol. Monogr.*, **48**, 3–54.

PACKARD, V. (1959) *The Status Seekers*, Penguin.

PAFFENBERGER, R. S. (1964) 'Epidemiological aspects of post-partum mental illness', *Brit. J. Prev. Soc. Med.*, **18**, 189–195.

PAHL, R. (1965) 'Class and community in English commuter villages', *Sociologia Ruralis*, **5**, 5–23.

PALMAI, G., STOREY, P. B. and BRISCOE, O. (1967) 'Social class and the young offender', *Brit. J. Psychiat.*, **113**, 1073–1082.

PAN AMERICAN HEALTH ORGANIZATION (1972) *Nutrition, the Nervous System and Behavior*, Proceedings of the Seminar on Malnutrition in early life and subsequent mental development, WHO.

PARKER, R. A. (1967) 'The rents of council housing', *Occasional Papers on Social Administration, No. 22*, Bell.

PARKES, A. S. (1971) 'Environmental influences on human fertility', *J. Biosoc. Sci. Suppl.*, **3**, 13–28.

PARKES, C. M. (1964) 'Recent bereavement as a cause of mental illness', *Brit. J. Psychiat.*, **110**, 198–204.

PARKES, C. M. (1972) *Bereavement: studies of grief in adult life*, Tavistock Publ.

PARRY, W. H., WRIGHT, C. H. and LUNN, J. E. (1967) 'Sheffield problem families – a follow-up survey', *The Medical Officer*, **118**, 130–132.

PASAMANICK, B. and KNOBLOCH, H. (1960) 'Brain damage and reproductive casualty', *Amer. J. Orthopsychiat.*, **30**, 298–305.

PASAMANICK, B. and KNOBLOCH, H. (1966) 'Retrospective studies on the epidemiology of reproductive casualty: old and new', *Merrill-Palmer Quart.*, **12**, 7–26.

PASSOW, A. H., GOLDBERG, M. and TANNENBAUM, A. J. (Eds.) (1967) *Education of the Disadvantaged: a book of readings*, Holt, Rinehart and Winston.

PATRICK, J. (1973) *A Glasgow Gang Observed*, Eyre Methuen.

PATTERSON, G. R. and REID, J. B. (1973) 'Intervention for families of aggressive boys: a replication study', *Behav. Res. Ther.*, **11**, 383–394.

PATTERSON, S. (1963) *Dark Strangers*, Tavistock Publ.

PATTERSON, S. (1968) *Immigrants in Industry*, Oxford Univ. Press for the Institute of Race Relations.

PAYKEL, E. S., MYERS, J. K., DIENELT, M. N., KLERMAN, C. L. LINDENTHAL, L. J. and PEPPER, M. P. (1969) 'Life events and depression; a controlled study', *Arch. Gen. Psychiat.*, 21, 753–760.

PAYNE, J. (1969) 'A comparative study of the mental ability of 7 and 8 year old British and West Indian children in a West Midlands town', *Brit. J. Educ. Psychol.*, 39, 326–327.

PEAL, M. and LAMBERT, W. E. (1962) 'The relation of bilingualism to intelligence', *Psychol. Monogr.*, 76, No. 27, Whole No. 546.

PEARCE, K. S. (1974) 'West Indian boys in community home schools', *Community Schools Gazette*, 68, 317–339 and 376–407.

PEARL, R. (1939) *The Natural History of Populations*, Oxford Univ. Press.

PEARSON, K. and LEE, A. (1899) 'On the Inheritance of Fertility in Mankind', *Royal Soc. London Philisoph. Trans.*, Series A, Vol. 192.

PECKHAM, C. S., SHERIDAN, M. and BUTLER, N. R. (1972) 'School attainment of seven-year-old children with hearing difficulties', *Develop. Med. Child Neurol.*, 14, 592–602.

PEEL, J. (1970) 'The Hull family survey. I. The survey couples, 1966', *J. Biosoc. Sci.*, 2, 45–70.

PEEL, J. (1972) 'The Hull family survey. II. Family planning in the first 5 years of marriage', *J. Biosoc. Sci.*, 4, 333–346.

PENCAVEL, J. H. (1974) 'Relative wages and trade unions in the United Kingdom', *Economica*, 41, 194–210.

PENROSE, L. S. (1938) *A Clinical and Genetic Study of 1280 Cases of Mental Defects*, HMSO.

PETZING, J. and WEDGE, P. J. (1970) 'Homes fit for children?', *New Society*, 16, 448–450.

PHILIPP, E. E. (1973) 'Discussion', in Wolstenholme, G. E. W. and Fitzsimons, D. W. (Eds.), *Law and Ethics of A.I.D. and Embryo Transfer*. Elsevier Publ.

PHILLIPS, D. L. (1968) 'Social class and psychological disturbance: the influence of positive and negative experiences', *Social Psychiatry*, 3, 41–46.

PHILLIPS, D. and SEGAL, B. (1969) 'Sexual status and psychiatric symptoms', *Amer. Sociol. Rev.*, 34, 58–72.

PHILP, A. F. (1963) *Family Failure: a study of 129 families with multiple problems*, Faber & Faber.

PHILP, A. F. and TIMMS, N. (1957) *The Problem of the Problem Family*, Family Service Units.

PIACHAUD, D. (1971) 'Poverty and taxation', *Political Quart.*, 42, 31–44.

PIACHAUD, D. (1974) 'Do the Poor Pay More?', *Poverty Research Series 3.*, Child Poverty Action Group.

PILGRIM TRUST (1938) *Men Without Work*, Cambridge Univ. Press.

PINSENT, R. J. F. H. (1963) 'Morbidity in an immigrant population', *Lancet*, ii, 437–438.

PLANT, J. S. (1930) 'Some psychiatric aspects of crowded living conditions', *Amer. J. Psychiat.*, 86, 849–860.

PLATT, J. (1971) *Social Research in Bethnal Green*, Macmillan.

PLOWDEN REPORT (1967) *see* DES (1967).

PLUMMER, N. and HINKLE, L. E. (1953) 'Medical significance of illness and absence in an industrial population', *Ann. Intern. Med.*, 39, 103–115.

PLUMMER, N. and HINKLE, L. E. (1955) 'Sickness absenteeism', *Arch. Insutr. Hyg.*, 11, 218–230.

POLANSKY, N. A., BORGMAN, R. D. and de SAIX, C. (1972) *Roots of Futility*, Jossey-Bass.

POLANYI, G. and WOOD, J. B. (1974) *How Much Inequality? An enquiry into the 'evidence'*, Institute of Economic Affairs, Research Monograph No. 31.

POLLAK, M. (1972) *Today's Three Year Olds in London*, Heinemann/SIMP.

POLLINS, H. (1960) 'Coloured people in post war English literature', *Race*, 1, 3–13.

POND, C. (1975) *Low Pay Bulletin*, Low Pay Unit.

POND, D. A., RYLE, A. and HAMILTON, M. (1963) 'Marriage and neurosis in a working-class population', *Brit. J. Psychiat.*, 109, 592–598.

POND, M. A. (1957) 'The influence of housing on health', *Marriage and Family Living*, 19, 154–159.

POST, F. (1962) 'The social orbit of psychiatric patients', *J. Ment. Sci.*, 108, 759–771.

POWER, M. J., ALDERSON, M. R., PHILLIPSON, C. M., SCHOENBERG, E. and MORRIS, J. N. (1967) 'Delinquent Schools?', *New Society*, 10, 542–543.

POWER, M. J., ASH, P. M., SCHOENBERG, E. and SOREY, E. C. (1974) 'Delinquency and the family', *Brit. J. Social Work*, 4, 13–38.

POWER, M. J., BENN, R. T. and MORRIS, J. N. (1972) 'Neighbourhood, school and juveniles before the courts', *Brit. J. Criminol.*, 12, 111–132.

POWERS, E. and WITMER, H. (1951) *An Experiment in the Prevention of Delinquency*, Columbia Univ. Press.

PRENTICE, N. M. and KELLY, F. J. (1963) 'Intelligence and delinquency: a reconsideration', *J. Soc. Psychiat.*, 60, 327–337.

PRINCE, G. (1967) 'Mental health problems in pre-school West Indian children', *Matern. Child Care*, 3, 483–486.

PRINGLE, M. L. K. and BOSSIO, V. (1960) 'Early prolonged separations and emotional maladjustment', *J. Child Psychol. Psychiat.*, 1, 142–170.

PRINGLE, M. L. K. and CLIFFORD, L. (1962) 'Conditions associated with emotional maladjustment among children in care', *Educ. Rev.*, 14, 112–123.

PRITCHARD, M. and GRAHAM, P. (1966) 'An investigation of a group of patients who have attended both the child and adult department of the same psychiatric hospital', *Brit. J. Psychiat.*, **112**, 603–612.

PROSHANSKY, H. M., ITTELSON, W. H. and RIVLIN, L. G. (1970a) 'Freedom of choice and behavior in a physical setting', in Proshansky, H. M., Ittelson, W. H. and Rivlin, L. G. (Eds.), *Environmental Psychology: man and his physical setting*, Holt, Rinehart and Winston.

PROSHANSKY, H. M., ITTELSON, W. H. and RIVLIN, L. G. (1970b) 'The influence of the physical environment on behavior: some basic assumptions', in Proshansky, H. M., Ittelson, W. H. and Rivlin, L. G. (Eds.), *Environmental Psychology: man and his physical setting*, Holt, Rinehart and Winston.

PROSHANSKY, H. and NEWTON, P. (1968) 'The nature and meaning of Negro self-identity', in Deutsch, M., Katz, I. and Jensen, A. (Eds.), *Social Class, Race and Psychological Development*, Holt, Rinehart and Winston.

PUSHKIN, I. (1967) 'A study of ethnic choice in the play of young children in three London districts', Unpublished Ph.D dissertation, Univ. of London.

PUSHKIN, I. and VENESS, T. (1973) 'The development of racial awareness and prejudice in children', in Watson, P. (Ed.), *Psychology and Race*, Penguin.

QUAY, H. C. (1972) 'Patterns of aggression, withdrawal and immaturity', in Quay, H. C. and Werry, J. S. (Eds.), *Psychopathological Disorders of Childhood*, John Wiley.

QUERIDO, A. (1946) 'The problem family in the Netherlands', *Medical Officer*, **75**, 193–195.

QUINN, P. O. and RAPOPORT, J. L. (1974) 'Minor physical anomalies and neurologic status in hyperactive boys', *Pediatrics*, **53**, 742–747.

QUINTON, D. and RUTTER, M. (1976) 'Early hospital admissions and later disturbances of behaviour: An attempted replication of Douglas' findings'. Develop. Med. Child Neurol., (in press).

RADIN, B. (1966) 'Coloured workers and British trade unions', *Race*, 8, 157–173.

RADKE, M. J., TRAGER, H. G. and DAVIS, H. (1949) 'Social perceptions and attitudes of children', *Genet. Psychol. Mon.*, **40**, 327–447.

RADKE-YARROW, M. J., TRAGER, H. G. and MILLER, J. (1952) 'The role of parents in the development of children's ethnic attitudes', *Child Develop.*, **23**, 13–53.

RAHE, R. H. (1968) 'Life-change measurement as a predictor of illness', *Proc. Roy. Soc. Med.*, **61**, 1124–1126.

RAINWATER, L. (1965) *Family Design, Marital Sexuality, Family Size and Contraception*, Aldine.

RAINWATER, L. (1970) *Behind Ghetto Walls: black family life in a federal slum*, Aldine.

RAINWATER, L. and WEINSTEIN, K. K. (1960) *And The Poor Get Children*, Quadrangle.

RAWLINGS, G., REYNOLDS, E. D. R., STEWART, A. and STRANG, L. B. (1971) 'Changing prognosis for infants of very low birth weight', *Lancet*, i, 516–519.

RAWNSLEY, K. (1968) 'Epidemiology of affective disorders', in Coppen, A. and Walk, A. (Eds.), *Recent Developments in Affective Disorders*, Brit. J. Psychiat. Spec. Publ. No. 2.

RECORD, R. G., McKEOWN, T. and EDWARDS, J. H. (1969) 'The relation of measured intelligence to birth order and maternal age', *Ann. Hum. Genet. Lond.*, 33, 61–69.

RECORD, R., McKEOWN, T. and EDWARDS, J. H. (1970) 'An investigation of the difference in measured intelligence between twins and singletons', *Ann. Hum. Genet.*, 34, 11–20.

REED, E. W. and REED, S. C. (1965) *Mental Retardation: a family study*, W. B. Saunders.

REES, A. (1973) *The Economics of Work and Pay*, Harper and Row.

REES, L. (1973) 'Constitutional factors and abnormal behaviour', in Eysenck, H. J. (Ed.), *Handbook of Abnormal Psychology*, 2nd Edition, Pitman Medical.

REES, W. D. and LUTKINS, S. G. (1967) 'Mortality of bereavement', *Brit. Med. J.*, iv, 13–16.

REGISTRAR GENERAL (1973) *Census 1971 Great Britain Summary Tables* (1% sample), HMSO.

REGISTRAR GENERAL (1974) *Quarterly Return for England and Wales for 2nd Quarter 1974*, HMSO.

REGISTRAR GENERAL SCOTLAND (1973) *Annual Report 1972., Part 2. Population and Vital Statistics*, Edinburgh: HMSO.

REID, D. D. (1948) 'Sickness and stress in operational flying', *Brit. J. Soc. Med.*, 2, 123–131.

REID, W. J. and SHYNE, A. W. (1969) *Brief and Extended Casework*, Columbia Univ. Press.

REISS, A. J. (1961) *Occupations and Social Status*, Free Press.

REISS, A. J. and RHODES, A. L. (1961) 'The distribution of juvenile delinquency in the social class structure', *Amer. Sociol. Rev.*, 26, 730–732.

REISS, A. J. and RHODES, A. L. (1964) 'An empirical test of differential association theory', *J. Res. Crime and Delinq.*, 1, 5–18.

REX, J. (1970) *Race Relations in Sociological Theory*, Weidenfeld and Nicolson.

REX, J. and MOORE, R. (1967) *Race, Community and Conflict*, Oxford Univ. Press for the Institute of Race Relations.

REYNOLDS, D. and MURGATROYD, S. (1974) 'Being absent from school', *Brit. J. Law and Society*, 1, 78–81.

RICCIUTI, N. (1973) 'Malnutrition and psychological development', in Assoc. Res. Nerv. Ment. Dis., *Biological and Environmental Determinants of Early Development*, Williams and Wilkins.

RICE, E. P., EKDAHL, M. C. and MILLER, L. (1971) *Children of Mentally Ill Parents: problems in child care*, New York: Behavioral Publ.

RICHARDS, B. W. (1969) 'Age trends in mental deficiency institutions', *J. Ment. Defic. Res.*, 13, 171–183.

RICHARDS, B. W. and SYLVESTER, P. E. (1969) 'Mortality trends in mental deficiency institutions', *J. Ment. Defic. Res.*, **13**, 276–292.

RICHMAN, N. (1974a) 'The effects of housing on pre-school children and their mothers', *Develop. Med. Child Neurol.*, **16**, 53–58.

RICHMAN, N. (1974b) 'Behaviour problems in 3 year old children', Paper read to Association of Child Psychology and Psychiatry, London, 13 March 1974.

RICHMAN, N. (1976) 'Disorder in pre-school children', in Rutter, M. and Hersov, L. (Eds.), *Child Psychiatry: modern approaches*, Blackwell Scientific Publ.

RICHMOND, A. H. (1954) *Colour Prejudice in Britain: a study of West Indian workers in Liverpool, 1942–1951*, Routledge & Kegan Paul.

RICHMOND, A. H. (1973a) *Migration and Race Relations in an English City: a study in Bristol*, Oxford Univ. Press for the Institute of Race Relations.

RICHMOND, A. H. (1973b) 'Race relations and behaviour in reality', in Watson, P. (Ed.), *Psychology and Race*, Penguin.

ROBBINS REPORT (1963) *Report of the Committee on Higher Education*, HMSO.

ROBERTSON, J. and ROBERTSON, J. (1971) 'Young children in brief separation: a fresh look', *Psychoanal. Stud. Child*, **26**, 264–315.

ROBERTSON, T. S. and KAWWA, T. (1971) 'Ethnic relations in a girls' comprehensive school', *Educ. Res.*, **13**, 214–217.

ROBINS, L. N. (1966) *Deviant Children Grown Up*, Williams and Wilkins.

ROBINS, L. N. (1972) 'Follow-up studies of behaviour disorders in children', in Quay, H. C. and Werry, J. S. (Eds.), *Psychopathological Disorders of Childhood*, John Wiley.

ROBINS, L. N. (1973) 'A follow-up of Vietnam drug users', *Special Action Office Monograph Series A. No. 1.*, US Govt. Printing Office.

ROBINS, L. N. (1974) 'The Vietnam drug user returns', *Special Action Office Monograph Series A No. 2.*, US Govt. Printing Office.

ROBINS, L. N., GYMAN, H. and O'NEAL, P. (1962) 'The interaction of social class and deviant behavior', *Amer. Sociol. Rev.*, **27**, 480–492.

ROBINS, L. N. and HILL, S. Y. (1966) 'Assessing the contribution of family structure, class and peer groups to juvenile delinquency', *J. Crim. Law Criminol. & Pol. Sci.*, **57**, 325–334.

ROBINS, L. N., JONES, R. S. and MURPHY, G. E. (1966) 'School milieu and school problems of negro boys', *Social Problems*, 13, 428–436.

ROBINS, L. N. and LEWIS, R. G. (1966) 'The role of the antisocial family in school completion and delinquency: a three-generation study', *Sociol. Quart.*, **7**, 500–514.

ROBINS, L. N., MURPHY, C. E., WOODRUFF, R. A. and KING, L. J.

(1971) 'Adult psychiatric status of black schoolboys', *Arch. Gen. Psychiat.*, 24, 338–345.

ROBINS, L. N., WEST, P. A. and HERJANIC, B. L. (1975) 'Arrests and delinquency in two generations: a study of black urban families and their children', *J. Child Psychol. Psychiat.*, 16, 125–140.

ROBINSON, H. B., ROBINSON, N. M., WOLINS, M., BRONFENBRENNER, U. and RICHMOND, J. P. (1973) 'Early child care in the United States of America', *Early Child Dev. & Care.*, 2, 359–582.

ROBINSON, W. P. (1965) 'The elaborated code in working class language', *Language & Speech*, 8, 243–252.

ROBINSON, W. P. and RACKSTRAW, S. J. (1967) 'Variations in mothers' answers to children's questions as a function of social class, verbal intelligence test scores and sex', *Sociology*, 1, 259–276.

ROE, A. (1952) 'A psychologist examines sixty-four eminent scientists', *Scient. Amer.*, 187, 21–25.

ROFF, M., SELLS, S. B. and GOLDEN, M. M. (1972) *Social Adjustment and Personality Development in Children*, Univ. of Minnesota Press.

ROGERS, C. M. and DAVENPORT, R. K. (1969) 'Sexual behaviour of differentially-reared chimpanzees', *Recent Advances in Primatology*, 1, 173–177.

ROLLIN, H. R. (1969) *The Mentally Abnormal Offender and the Law*, Pergamon.

ROSANOFF, A. J., HANDY, L. M. and PLESSET, I. R. (1941) 'The etiology of child behavior difficulties, juvenile deliquency and adult criminality with special reference to their occurrence in twins', *Psychiat. Monogr.* (California), No. 1, Sacramento: Dept. of Institutions.

ROSE, E. J. B., DEAKIN, N., ABRAMS, M., JACKSON, V., PESTON, M., VANAGS, A. H., COHEN, B., GAITSKELL, J. and WARD, P. (1969) *Colour and Citizenship*, Oxford Univ. Press for the Institute of Race Relations.

ROSEN, B. C. (1961) 'Family structure and achievement motivation', *Amer. Soc. Rev.*, 26, 574–585.

ROSEN, B. C. and D'ANDRADE, R. (1959) 'The psychological origins of achievement motivation', *Sociometry*, 22, 185–218.

ROSENHAN, D. L. (1973) 'On being sane in insane places', *Science*, 179, 250–258.

ROSENTHAL, D. (1970) *Genetic Theory and Abnormal Behavior*, McGraw-Hill.

ROSENTHAL, D. and KETY, S. (Eds.) (1968) *The Transmission of Schizophrenia*, Pergamon.

ROSENTHAL, R. and JACOBSON, L. (1968) *Pygmalion in the Classroom*, Holt, Rinehart and Winston.

ROSS, H. (1937) 'Crime and the native born sons of European Immigrants', *J. Crimin. Law, Criminol. and Police Sci.*, 28, 202–209.

ROSSI, P. H. (1955) *Why Families Move*, Free Press.

ROSSI, P. H. and BLUM, D. (1968) 'Class status and poverty', in Moynihan, D. P. (Ed.), *On Understanding Poverty*, Basic Books.

ROUTH, G. (1965) *Occupation and Pay in Great Britain 1906–1960*, Cambridge Univ. Press.

ROWLEY, K. G. (1968) 'Social relations between British and immigrant children', *Educ. Res.*, **10**, 145–148.

ROWNTREE, B. S. (1901) *Poverty: a study of town life*, Macmillan.

ROWNTREE, B. S. (1941) *Poverty and Progress*, Longman.

ROWNTREE, B. S. and LAVERS, G. R. (1951) *Poverty and the Welfare State*, Longman.

ROYAL COMMISSION ON THE DISTRIBUTION OF INCOME AND WEALTH (1975) *Report No. 1. Initial Report on The Standing Reference*, HMSO.

RUNCIMAN, W. G. (1972) *Relative Deprivation and Social Justice*, Penguin.

RUNNYMEDE TRUST (1975) *Race and Council Housing in London*, Runnymede Trust.

RUTTER, M. L. (1964) 'Intelligence and childhood psychiatric disorder', *Brit. J. Soc. Clin. Psychol.*, **3**, 120–129.

RUTTER, M. L. (1965) 'Classification and categorization in child psychiatry', *J. Child Psychol. Psychiat.*, **6**, 71–83.

RUTTER, M. L. (1966) *Children of sick parents: an environmental and psychiatric study*, Maudsley Monograph No. 16, Oxford Univ. Press.

RUTTER, M. L. (1967) 'A children's behaviour questionnaire for completion by teachers: preliminary findings', *J. Child Psychol. Psychiat.*, **8**, 1–11.

RUTTER, M. L. (1970a) 'Sex differences in children's responses to family stress', in Anthony, E. J. and Koupernik, C. M. (Eds.), *The Child and his Family*, John Wiley.

RUTTER, M. L. (1970b) 'Psychological development — predictions from infancy', *J. Child Psychol. Psychiat.*, **11**, 49–62.

RUTTER, M. L. (1971a) 'Psychiatry', in Wortis, J. (Ed.), *Mental Retardation: an annual review III*, Grune & Stratton.

RUTTER, M. L. (1971b) 'Parent-child separation: psychological effects on the children', *J. Child Psychol. Psychiat.*, **12**, 233–260.

RUTTER, M. L. (1972a) *Maternal Deprivation Reassessed*, Penguin.

RUTTER, M. L. (1972b) 'Relationships between child and adult psychiatric disorders', *Acta Psychiat. Scand.*, **48**, 3–21.

RUTTER, M. L. (1973) 'Why are London children so disturbed?', *Proc. Roy. Soc. Med.*, **66**, 1221–1225.

RUTTER, M. L. (1974a) 'Critical notice', *J. Child Psychol. Psychiat.*, **15**, 149–151.

RUTTER, M. L. (1974b) 'Dimensions of parenthood: some myths and some suggestions', in *The Family in Society: Dimensions of Parenthood*, DHSS.

RUTTER, M. L. (1974c) 'Emotional disorder and educational under-achievement', *Arch. Dis. Childhd.*, **49**, 249–256.

RUTTER, M. L. (1975a) *Helping Troubled Children*, Penguin.

RUTTER, M. L. (1975b) 'Discussion', in Barltrop, D. (Ed.), *Paediatrics and the Environment*, Report of the Second Unigate Paediatric Workshop. Fellowship of Postgraduate Medicine.

RUTTER, M. L. (1976) 'Prospective studies to investigate behavioural change' in Strauss, J. S., Batigian, H. M. and Ross, M. (Eds.), Methods of Longitudinal Research in Psychopathology, Plenum.

RUTTER, M. L. (Ed.) (1976) *The Child, His Family and The Community*, John Wiley. In press.

RUTTER, M. L. and BARTAK, L. (1973) 'Special educational treatment of autistic children: a comparative study. II. Follow-up findings and implications for services', *J. Child Psychol. Psychiat.*, **14**, 241–270.

RUTTER, M. L., BIRCH, H. G., THOMAS, A. and CHESS, S. (1964) 'Temperamental characteristics in infancy and the later development of behavioural disorders', *Brit. J. Psychiat.*, **110**, 651–661.

RUTTER, M. L., COX, A., TUPLING, C., BERGER, M. and YULE, W. (1975) 'Attainment and adjustment in two geographical areas: I. The prevalence of psychiatric disorder, *Brit. J. Psychiat.*, **126**, 493–509.

RUTTER, M. L., GRAHAM, P., CHADWICK, C. and YULE, W. (1976) 'Adolescent turmoil: fact or fiction?', *J. Child Psychol. Psychiat.*, **17**, 35–6.

RUTTER, M. L., GRAHAM, P. and YULE, W. (1970) *A Neuropsychiatric Study in Childhood*, Clinics in Developmental Medicine Nos. 35–36. Heinemann/SIMP.

RUTTER, M. L., GREENFELD, D. and LOCKYER, L. (1967) 'A five to fifteen year follow-up study of infantile psychosis: II. Social and Behavioural Outcome', *Brit. J. Psychiat.*, **113**, 1183–1199.

RUTTER, M. L. and MITTLER, P. (1972) 'Environmental influences on language development', in Rutter, M. L. and Martin, J. A. M. (Eds.), *The Child with Delayed Speech*, Clinics in Developmental Medicine, No. 43, Heinemann/SIMP.

RUTTER, M. L. and QUINTON, D. (1975) 'Psychiatric disorder: ecological factors and concepts of causation', in McGurk, H. (Ed.) *Ecological Factors in Human Development*, North Holland, (in press).

RUTTER, M. L., QUINTON, D. and YULE, B. A. (1976) *Family Pathology and Disorder in the Children*, John Wiley. (in press)

RUTTER, M. L., TIZARD, J. and WHITMORE, K. (Eds.) (1970) *Education, Health and Behaviour*, Longman.

RUTTER, M. L. and YULE, W. (1973) 'Specific reading retardation', in Mann, L. and Sabatino, D. (Eds.), *The First Review of Special Education*, Buttonwood Farms.

RUTTER, M. L. and YULE, W. (1975) 'The ooncept of specific reading retardation', *J. Child Psychol. Psychiat.*, **16**, 181–98.

RUTTER, M. L., YULE, W., BERGER, M., YULE, B., MORTON, J. and BAGLEY, C. (1974) 'Children of West Indian immigrants. I. Rates of behavioural deviance and of psychiatric disorder', *J. Child Psychol. Psychiat.*, **15**, 241–262.

RUTTER, M. L., YULE, B., MORTON, J. and BAGLEY, C. (1975a) 'Children of West Indian immigrants' III. Home circumstances and family patterns', *J. Child Psychol. Psychiat.*, **16**, 105–124.

RUTTER, M. L., YULE, B., QUINTON, D., ROWLANDS, O., YULE, W. and BERGER, M. (1975b) 'Attainment and adjustment in two geographical areas: III. Some factors accounting for area differences', *Brit. J. Psychiat.*, **126**, 520–533.

RYAN, J. (1972) 'IQ – The illusion of objectivity', in Richardson, K. and Spears, D. (Eds.), *Race, Culture and Intelligence*, Penguin.

RYAN, T. J. (1972) *Poverty and the Child: a Canadian study*, Ryerson Press.

SACKETT, G. P. and RUPPENTHAL, G. C. (1973) 'Development of monkeys after varied experiences during infancy', in Barnett, S. A. (Ed.), *Ethology and Development*, Clinics in Developmental Medicine No. 47, Heinemann/SIMP.

SAINSBURY, P. (1955) *Suicide in London: an ecological study*, Maudsley Monograph No. 1. Oxford Univ. Press.

SAINSBURY, P. (1971) 'Moving house and psychiatric morbidity', Paper presented at Annual Conference of Society for Psychosomatic Research, London.

SAINSBURY, P. and COLLINS, J. (1966) 'Some factors relating to mental illness in a new town', *J. Psychosom. Res.*, **10**, 45–51.

ST. JOHN, N. H. (1970) 'Desegregation and minority group performance', *Rev. Educ. Res.*, **40**, 111–133.

SAMPSON, E. E. (1962) 'Birth order, need achievement and conformity', *J. Abn. Soc. Psychol.*, **32**, 251–253.

SANFORD, N. (1973) 'The roots of prejudice: emotional dynamics', in Watson, P. (Ed.), *Psychology and Race*, Penguin.

SANTROCK, J. W. (1972) 'Relation of type and onset of father absence to cognitive development', *Child Develop.*, **43**, 455–469.

SARASON, S. B., DAVIDSON, K. S., LIGHTHALL, F. F., WAITE, R. R. and RUEBUSH, B. K. (1960) *Anxiety in Elementary School Children*, John Wiley.

SATTLER, J. M. (1973) 'Intelligence testing of ethnic minority-group and culturally disadvantaged children', in Mann, L. and Sabatino, D. A. (Eds.), *The First Review of Special Education*, Buttonwood Farms.

SCALLY, B. G. (1968) 'The offspring of mental defectives', in Woolan, D. H. M. (Ed.), *Advances in Teratology*, Vol. 3, Logos Press.

SCARR, S. (1969) 'Social introversion-extraversion as a heritable response', *Child Develop.*, **40**, 823–832.

SCARR-SALAPATEK, S. (1971) 'Race, social class and IQ', *Science*, **174**, 1285–1295.

SCHACHTER, S. (1959) *The Psychology of Affiliation*, Stanford Univ. Press.

SCHACHTER, S. (1963) 'Birth order, eminence and higher education', *Amer. Soc. Rev.*, 28, 757–768.

SCHAEFER, E. S. and AARONSON, M. (1972) 'Infant education research project: implementation and implications of the home-tutoring program', in Parker, R. K. (Ed.), *The Preschool in Action*, Allyn and Bacon.

SCHAFFER, H. R. (1966) 'Activity level as a constitutional determinant of infantile reaction to deprivation', *Child Develop.*, 37, 595–602.

SCHAFFER, H. R. (1971) *The Growth of Sociability*, Penguin.

SCHAFFER, H. R. and SCHAFFER, E. B. (1968) *Child Care and the Family*, Bell.

SCHEFF, T. (1966) *Being Mentally Ill: a sociological theory*, Aldine.

SCHEFF, T. J. (1974) 'The labelling theory of mental illness', *Amer. Sociol. Rev.*, 39, 444–452.

SCHILLER, B. R. (1973) 'Empirical studies of welfare dependency: a survey', *Human Resources*, 8, 19–32.

SCHLESINGER, B. (1963) *The Multi-Problem Family*, Univ. of Toronto Press.

SCHMITT, R. C. (1963) 'Implications of density in Hong Kong, *J. Amer. Instit. Planners*, 29, 210–217.

SCHOOLER, C. (1972) 'Birth order effects: not here, not now!', *Psychol. Bull.*, 78, 161–175.

SCHOOLS COUNCIL (1970) *Teaching English to West Indian Children*, Working Paper No. 29, Evans/Methuen Educational.

SCHORR, A. L. (1964) *Slums and Social Insecurity*, Nelson.

SCHULSINGER, F. (1972) 'Psychopathy: heredity and environment', *Int. J. Ment. Health*, 1, 190–206.

SCHWARTZ, R. D. and SKOLNICK, J. H. (1964). 'Two studies of legal stigma', in Becker, H. S. (Ed.), *The Other Side Perspectives on Deviance*, Free Press.

SCOTT, E. M., ILLSLEY, R. and THOMSON, A. M. (1956) 'A psychological investigation of primigravidae. II. Maternal social class, age, physique and intelligence', *J. Obstet. Gynaecol. Brit. Empire*, 63, 338–343.

SCOTT, J. A. (1958) 'Problem Families: a London survey', *Lancet*, i, 204–208.

SCOTT, P. D. (1956) 'Gangs and delinquent groups in London', *Brit. J. Delinq.*, 7, 4–26.

SCOTT, P. D. (1966) 'Medical aspects of delinquency', *Hosp. Med.*, 1, 219–259.

SCOTT, P. D. (1973) 'Fatal battered baby cases', *Medicine, Science and The Law*, 13, 197–206.

SCOTTISH COUNCIL FOR RESEARCH IN EDUCATION (1949) *The Trend of Scottish Intelligence*, Univ. Of London Press.

SCOTTISH COUNCIL FOR RESEARCH IN EDUCATION (1967) *The Scottish Standardisation of WISC*, Univ. of London Press.

SCRIMSHAW, N. S. and GORDON, J. E. (1968) *Malnutrition, Learning and Behaviour*, MIT Press.

SEAGER, C. P. (1960) 'A controlled study of post-partum mental illness', *J. Ment. Sci.*, **106**, 214–230.

SEARLE, L. V. (1949) 'The organization of hereditary maze-brightness and maze-dullness', *Genet. Psychol. Monogr.*, **39**, 279–325.

SEAVER, W. B. (1973) 'Effects of naturally induced teacher expectancies', *J. Pers. Soc. Psychol.*, **28**, 333–342.

SEAY, B., ALEXANDER, B. K. and HARLOW, H. F. (1964) 'Maternal behavior of socially deprived monkeys', *J. Abn. Soc. Psychol.*, **69**, 345–354.

'SEEBOHM REPORT' (1968) *Report of the Committee on Local Authority and Allied Personal Social Services*, HMSO.

SEERS, D. (1951) *The Levelling of Incomes since 1938*, Blackwell.

SEGLOW, J., PRINGLE, M. L. K. and WEDGE, P. (1972) *Growing Up Adopted*, NFER.

SEIDEL, U. CHADWICK, O. F. D. and RUTTER, M. L. (1975) 'Psychological disorder in crippled children: a comparative study of children with and without brain damage'. *Develop. Med. Child Neurol.*, 17, 563–73.

SELECT COMMITTEE ON RACE RELATIONS AND IMMIGRATION SESSION 1968–69 (1969) *The Problems of Coloured School Leavers*, HMSO.

SELECT COMMITTEE ON RACE RELATIONS AND IMMIGRATION SESSION 1971–72 (1972) *Police/Immigrant Relations, 1–3*, HMSO.

SHAFFER, D., CHADWICK, O. and RUTTER, M. L. (1975) Psychiatric outcome of localized head injury in children', in Porter, R. and Fitzsimons, D. (Eds.), *Outcome of Severe Damage to the Central Nervous System.*

SHAPIRO, W. R. (1970) 'A twin study of non-endogenous depression', *Acta Jutlandica*, **42**, No. 2.

SHAW, C. H. and WRIGHT, C. H. (1960) 'The married mental defective: a follow-up study', *Lancet*, i, 273–274.

SHAW, C. R. and McKAY, H. D. (1942) *Juvenile Delinquency and Urban Areas*, Univ. of Chicago Press.

SHELTER (1968) *Notice to Quit.*

SHELTER (1969) *Face the Facts.*

SHELTER (1969) *A Home of Your Own.*

SHELTER (1972) *The Grief Report*, A Shelter report on temporary accommodation.

SHELTER (1973) *The Kids Don't Notice.*

SHEPHERD, M., COOPER, B., BROWN, A. C. and KALTON, G. W. (1966) *Psychiatric Illness in General Practice*, Oxford Univ. Press.

SHERIDAN, M. D. (1956) 'The intelligence of 100 neglectful mothers', *Brit. Med. J.*, i, 91–93.

SHERIDAN, M. D. (1959) 'Neglectful mothers', *Lancet*, i, 722–723.

SHERIF, M., HARVEY, O. J., WHITE, B. J., HOOD, W. R. and SHERIF, C. W. (1961) *Intergroup Conflict and Cooperation: The robbers' cave experiment*, Oklahoma Univ. Press.

SHIELDS, J. (1962) *Monozygotic Twins Brought up Apart and Brought up Together*, Oxford Univ. Press.

SHIELDS, J. (1973) 'Heredity and psychological abnormality', in Eysenck, H. J. (Ed.), *Handbook of Abnormal Psychology*, Pitman Medical.

SHIELDS, J. (1976) 'Polygenic influences in child psychiatry', in Rutter, M. and Hersov, L. (Eds.), *Child Psychiatry: modern approaches*, Blackwell Scientific.

SHIPMAN, M. D. (1968) *Sociology of the School*, Longman.

SHOHAM, S., SHOHAM, N. and ABD-EL-RAZEK, A. (1966) 'Immigration, ethnicity and ecology as related to juvenile delinquency in Israel', *Brit. J. Crim.*, **6**, 391–409.

SHUEY, A. M. (1966) *The Testing of Negro Intelligence*, 2nd Edition, New York, Social Science Press.

SINFIELD, A. (1968) *The Long-Term Unemployed*, OECD.

SINFIELD, A. (1970) 'Poor and out of work in Shields', in Townsend, P. (Ed.), *The Concept of Poverty*, Heinemann Educational Books.

SKEELS, H. M. (1942) 'A study of the effects of differential stimulation on mentally retarded children: follow-up report', *Amer. J. Ment. Defic.*, **46**, 340–350.

SKEELS, H. M. (1966) 'Adult status of children with contrasting early life experiences', *Mon. Soc. Res. Child Develop.*, **31**, No. 3.

SKEELS, H. M. and DYE, H. B. (1939) 'A study of the effects of differential stimulation on mentally retarded children', *Proceedings and Addresses of the American Association on Mental Deficiency*, **44**, 114–136.

SKEELS, H. M. and FILLMORE, E. A. (1937) 'The mental development of children from under-privileged homes', *J. Genet. Psychol.*, **50**, 427–439.

SKINNER, A. E. and CASTLE, R. L. (1969) *78 Battered Children: a retrospective study*, NSPCC.

SKODAK, M. and SKEELS, H. M. (1949) 'A final follow-up study of one hundred adopted children', *J. Genet. Psychol.*, **75**, 85–125.

SLATER, E. and COWIE, V. (1971) *The Genetics of Mental Disorders*, Oxford Univ. Press.

SLATER, E. and SHIELDS, J. (1969) 'Genetical aspects of anxiety', in Lader, M. H. (Ed.), *Studies of Anxiety*, Brit. J. Psychiat. Spec. Publ. No. 3, Headley.

SMITH, D. J. (1974) *Racial Disadvantage in Employment*, PEP Broadsheet No. 544.

SMITH, D. and WHALLEY, A. (1975) *Racial Minorities and Public Housing*, Research Publications Services: London.

SMITH, S. M., HANSON, R. and NOBLE, S. (1973) 'Parents of battered babies: a controlled study', *Brit. Med. J.*, iv, 388–391.

SMITH, S. M., HANSON, R. and NOBLE, S. (1974) 'Social aspects of the battered baby syndrome', *Brit. J. Psychiat.*, **125**, 568–582.

SNEDEN, L. (1970) 'An analysis of factors involved in upward social mobility from the culture of poverty', *Revue Internationale de Sociologie*, **6**, 532–541.

SNOW, R. (1969) 'Unfinished Pygmalion', *Cont. Psychol.*, 14, 197–199.

SOFFIETTI, J. P. (1955) 'Bilingualism and biculturalism', *J. Educ. Psychol.*, **46**, 222–227.

SOLIDARITY AND SOCIALIST ACTION (1967) *KCC Versus the Homeless.*

SOLTOW, L. (1965) *Toward Income Equality in Norway*, Univ. of Wisconsin Press.

SOMMER, R. (1969) *Personal Space: the behavioural basis of design*, Prentice-Hall.

SONTAG, L. W., BAKER, C. T. and NELSON, V. C. (1958) 'Mental growth and personality development: a longitudinal study', *Mon. Soc. Res. Child Develop.*, **23**, No. 2.

SPENCER, J. C. (1954) *Crime and the Services*, Routledge & Kegan Paul.

SPENCER-BOOTH, Y. and HINDE, R. A. (1971) 'Effects of brief separation from mothers during infancy on behaviour of rhesus monkeys 6–24 months later', *J. Child Psychol. Psychiat.*, **12**, 157–172.

SPINETTA, J. J. and RIGLER, D. (1972) 'The child-abusing parent: a psychological review', *Psychol. Bull.*, **77**, 296–304.

STAFFORD-CLARK, D., POND, D. A. and LOVETT-DOUST, J. W. (1951) 'The psychopath in prison', *Brit. J. Delinq.*, **2**, 117–129.

STANWORTH, P. and GIDDENS, A. (1974) 'An economic elite: a demographic profile of company chairmen', in Stanworth, P. and Giddens, A. (Eds.), *Elites and Power in British Society*, Cambridge Univ. Press.

STARR, R. H. (1971), 'Cognitive development in infancy: assessment, acceleration and actualization', *Merrill-Palmer Quart.*, **17**, 153–186.

START, K. B. and WELLS, B. K. (1972) *The Trend of Reading Standards*, National Foundation for Educational Research.

STEIN, L. (1954) 'Glasgow tuberculosis and housing', *Tubercle.*, **35**, 195–203.

STEIN, Z. A. and KASSAB, H. J. (1970) 'Malnutrition', in Wortis, J. (Ed.), *Mental Retardation: annual review. Vol. 2*, Grune & Stratton.

STEIN, Z. and SUSSER, M. W. (1960) 'Families of dull children', *J. Ment. Sci.*, **106**, 1296–1319.

STEIN, Z. and SUSSER, M. W. (1963) 'The social distribution of mental retardation', *Amer. J. Ment. Defic.*, **67**, 811–821.

STEIN, Z. and SUSSER, M. W. (1969) 'Mild mental subnormality: social and epidemiological studies', *Res. Publ. Assoc. Res. Nerv. Ment. Dis.*, 47, 62–85.

STEIN, Z. and SUSSER, M. W. (1970) 'Mutability of intelligence and epidemiology of mild mental retardation', *Review Educ. Res.*, **40**, 29–67.

STEIN, Z., SUSSER, M., SAENGER, G. and MAROLLA, F. (1972a) 'Intelligence test results of individuals exposed during gestation to the World War II famine in the Netherlands, *T. Soc. Geneesk.*, **50**, 766–774.

STEIN, Z., SUSSER, M., SAENGER, G. and MAROLLA, F. (1972b) 'Nutrition and mental performance', *Sciences*, **178**, 708–713.

STENGEL, E. (1969) *Suicide and Attempted Suicide*, Penguin.

STENSTEDT, Å (1952) 'A Study in Manic–Depressive Psychosis: clinical, social and genetic investigations', *Acta Psychiat. Neurol. Scand.*, Suppl. 79.

STENSTEDT, Å (1966) 'Genetics of neurotic depressions', *Acta Psychiat. Scand.*, 42, 392–409.

STEVENS, B. C. (1969) *Marriage and Fertility of Women Suffering from Schizophrenia or Affective Disorders*, Maudsley Monograph No. 19, Oxford Univ. Press.

STEVENSON, H. W. and STEWART, E. C. (1958) 'A developmental study of racial awareness in young children', *Child Develop.*, **29**, 399–409.

STEVENSON, O. (1975) *From the General to The Specific*, Report to DHSS.

STEWART, W. F. R. (1970) *Children in Flats: a family study*, NSPCC.

STOKER, D. (1970) *Immigrant Children in Infant Schools*, Schools Council Working Paper No. 31, Methuen.

STOLZ, L. M. (1967) *Influences on Parent Behaviour*, Tavistock Publ.

STOTT, D. H. (1960) 'The prediction of delinquency from non-delinquent behaviour', *Brit. J. Delinq.*, 10, 195–210.

STOTT, D. H. (1966) *Studies of Troublesome Children*, Tavistock Publ.

STOUFFER, S. A., SUCHMAN, E. A., DeVINNEY, L. C., STAR, S. A. and WILLIAMS, R. M. Jnr. (1949) *Studies in Social Psychology. Vol. 1, The American Soldier: adjustment during army life*, Princetown Univ. Press.

STROUD, C. E (1965) 'The new environment', *Postgrad. Med. J.*, 41, 599–602.

STURGE, C. (1972) 'Reading Retardation and Antisocial Behaviour', Unpublished M.Phil. dissertation, Univ. of London.

SUGARMAN, B. (1967) 'Involvement in youth culture', *Brit. J. Sociol.*, **18**, 151–164.

SUOMI, S. J. (1973) 'Surrogate rehabilitation of monkeys reared in total social isolation', *J. Child Psychol. Psychiat.*, **14**, 71–77.

SUOMI, S. J. and HARLOW, H. F. (1972) 'Social rehabilitation of isolate-reared monkeys', *Develop. Psychol.*, 6, 487–496.

SUOMI, S. J., HARLOW, H. F. and NOVAK, M. A. (1974) 'Reversal of social deficits produced by isolation rearing in monkeys', *J. Human Evolution*, 3, 527–534.

SURGEON GENERAL (1972) *Television and Growing Up: The Impact of Televised Violence*, United States Public Health Service.

SUSSER, M. W. and WATSON, W. (Eds.), (1971) *Sociology in Medicine*, 2nd Edition, Oxford Univ. Press.

SUTER, L. E. and MILLER, H. P. (1973) 'Income differences between men and career women', in Huber, J. (Ed.), *Changing Women in a Changing Society*, Chicago Univ. Press.

SUTHERLAND, E. H. (1939) *Principles of Criminology*, Lippincott.

SUTTLES, G. D. (1972) *The Social Construction of Communities*, Chicago Univ. Press.

SWIFT, J. W. (1964) 'Effects of early group experience: the nursery school and day nursery', in Hoffman, M. L. and Hoffman, L. W. (Eds.), *Review of Child Development Research, Vol. 1*, Russell Sage Foundation.

TAFT, R. (1973) 'Migration: problems of adjustment and assimilation in immigrants', in Watson, P. (Ed.), *Psychology and Race*. Penguin.

TAIT, C. D. and HODGES, E. F. (1962) *Delinquents, Their Families and the Community*, Charles C. Thomas.

TAIT, C. D. and HODGES, E. F. (1971) 'Follow-up study of predicted delinquents', *Crime and Delinquency*, 17, 202–213.

TANNER, J. M. (1965) 'The trend toward earlier physical maturation', in Meade, J. E. and Parkes, A. S. (Eds.), *Biological Aspects of Social Problems*, Oliver & Boyd.

TANNER, J. M. (1969) 'Relation of body size, intelligence scores, and social circumstances', in Mussen, P. H., Langer, J. and Covington, H. (Eds.), *Trends and Issues in Developmental Psychology*, Holt, Rinehart & Winston.

TARJAN, M. D., TIZARD, J., RUTTER, M., BEGAB, M., BROOKE, E. M., de la CRUZ, F., LIN, T.-Y., MONTENEGRO, H., STROTZKA, H. and SARTORIUS, N. (1972) 'Classification and mental retardation: issues arising in the fifth WHO seminar on psychiatric diagnosis, classification and statistics', *Amer. J. Psychiat.*, 128, May Suppl. 11, 34–45.

TEMERLIN, M. K. (1968) 'Suggestion effects in psychiatric diagnosis', *J. Nerv. Ment. Dis.*, 147, 349–353.

TENNANT, T. G. (1970) 'Truancy and stealing. A comparative study of Education Act cases and property offenders', *Brit. J. Psychiat.*, 116, 587–592.

TERMAN, L. M. (1921) *The Intelligence of School Children*, Harrap.

TERMAN, L. M. and ODEN, M. H. (1959) *Genetic Studies of Genius. Vol. 5, The Gifted Group at Mid-Life*, Oxford Univ. Press.

TEWFIK, G. I. and OKASHA, A. (1965) 'Psychosis and Immigration', *Postgrad. Med. J.*, 41, 603–612.

THATCHER, A. R. (1971) 'Year-to-year variations in the earnings of individuals', *J. Roy. Statist. Soc.*, 134, 374–382.

THOMAS, A., CHESS, S. and BIRCH, H. G. (1968) *Temperament and Behaviour Disorders in Children*, Univ. of London Press.

THOMAS, H. (1967) 'Some problems of studies concerned with evaluating the predictive validity of infant tests', *J. Child Psychol. Psychiat.*, 8, 197–205.

THOMAS, H. E. (1968) 'Tuberculosis in immigrants', *Proc. Roy. Soc. Med.*, 61, 21–23.

THOMSON, A. M. and BILLEWICZ, W. Z. (1963) 'Nutritional status, physique and reproductive efficiency', *Proc. Nutr. Soc.*, 22, 55–60.

THOMPSON, B. and ILLSLEY, R. (1969) 'Family growth in Aberdeen', *J. Biosoc. Sci.*, 1, 23–39.

THORNBERRY, T. P. (1973) 'Race, socio-economic status and sentencing in the juvenile justice system', *J. Crim. Law Criminol.*, 64, 90–98.

THORNDIKE, R. L. (1968) 'Review of Pygmalion in the classroom', *Amer. Educ. Res. J.*, 5, 708–711.

TITMUSS, R. M. (1962) *Income Distribution and Social Change*, Allen & Unwin.

TIZARD, B. (1974a) 'Do social relationships affect language development?', in Connolly, K. and Bruner, J. (Eds.), *The Growth of Competence*, Academic Press.

TIZARD, B. (1974b) *Pre-school Education in Great Britain*, Social Science Research Council.

TIZARD, B. (1974c) 'IQ and Race', *Nature*, 247, 316.

TIZARD, B., COOPERMAN, O., JOSEPH, A. and TIZARD, J. (1972) 'Environmental effects on language development: a study of young children in long-stay residential nurseries', *Child Develop.*, 43, 337–358.

TIZARD, B. and REES, J. (1974) 'A comparison of the effects of adoption, restoration to the natural mother and continued institutionalization on the cognitive development of four-year-old children', *Child Develop.*, 45, 92–99.

TIZARD, J. (1964) *Community Services for the Mentally Handicapped*, Oxford Univ. Press.

TIZARD, J. (1970) 'The role of social institutions in the causation, prevention and alleviation of mental retardation', in Haywood, H. C. (Ed.), *Social-Cultural Aspects of Mental Retardation*, Appleton-Century Crofts.

TIZARD, J. (1973) 'Maladjusted children and the Child Guidance Service', *London Educ. Rev.*, 2, 22–37.

TIZARD, J. (1974a) 'Early malnutrition, growth and mental development in man, *Brit. Med. Bull.*, 30, 169–174.

TIZARD, J. (1974b) 'Longitudinal studies: problems and findings', in Clarke, A. M. and Clarke, A. D. B. (Eds.), *Mental Deficiency: the changing outlook*, 3rd Edition, Methuen.

TIZARD, J. (1975) 'Race and IQ: the limits of probability', *New Behaviour*, 1, 6–9.

TIZARD, J. (1976) 'Nutrition, growth and development', *Psychol. Med.*, **6**, 1–5.

TODD, Lord (1968) *Royal Commission on Medical Education 1965–68*, HMSO.

TOMLINSON, C. G. (1946) *Families in Trouble: an inquiry into problem families in Luton*, Leagrave Press.

TONGE, W. L., JAMES, D. S. and HILLAM, S. M. (1975) 'Families without hope: a controlled study of 33 problem families', Brit. J. Psychiat. Publication No. 11.

TORGERSEN, A. M. (1973) 'Temperaments forskjeller Hos Spedbarn: Deres arsaker, belyst gjennom en tvillingundersøkelse', Ph.D. Thesis. Univ. Oslo.

TORGERSEN, A. M. and KRINGLEN, E. (1975) 'The origin of temperamental differences in infants: a study of new-born twins', *J. Child Psychol. Psychiat.* (in press).

TOWNSEND, H. E. R. (1971) *Immigrant Pupils in England*, NFER.

TOWNSEND, H. E. R. and BRITTAN, E. M. (1972) *Organization in Multiracial Schools*, NFER.

TOWNSEND, P. (1974) 'Inequality and the Health Service', *Lancet*, i, 1179–1190.

TOWNSEND, P. and WEDDERBURN, D. (1965) *The Aged in the Welfare State*, Bell.

TRASLER, G. B. (1973) 'Criminal behaviour', in Eysenck, H. J. (Ed.), *Handbook of Abnormal Psychology* (2nd edition), Pitman Medical.

TRENAMAN, J. (1952) *Out of Step — A Study of Young Delinquent Soldiers in Wartime*, Methuen.

TRINDER, C. (1974) 'Incomes policy and the low paid', in Young, M. (Ed,), *Poverty Report 1974*, Temple Smith.

TURNER, C. H., DAVENPORT, R. K. and ROGERS, C. N. (1969) 'The effect of early deprivation on the social behavior of adolescent chimpanzees', *Amer. J. Psychiat.*, **125**, 1531–1536.

TYRER, P. and TYRER, S. (1974) 'School refusal, truancy and adult mental illness', *Psychol. Med.*, 4, 416–421.

U.S. LEGISLATIVE PROGRAMME (1964) Reported by Moynihan, D. P. 'The Professors and the poor', in Moynihan, D. P. (Ed.), (1968), *On Understanding Poverty*, Basic Books.

VAIZEY, J. (1962) *The Economics of Education*, Faber & Faber.

VALENTINE, C. A (1971) 'The "culture of poverty": its scientific significance and its implications for action', in Leacock, E. B. (Ed.) *The Culture of Poverty: a critique*, Simon and Schuster.

VANDENBERG, S. G. (1967) 'Hereditary factors in normal personality traits (as measured by inventories)', in Wortis, J. (Ed.), *Recent Advances in Biological Psychiatry* Vol. 9, Plenum Press.

VARLAAM, A. (1974) 'Educational attainment and behaviour at school', *Greater London Intelligence Quarterly*, No. 29, December 1974, pp. 29–37.

VEIT WILSON, J. H. and WILSON, H. (1973) 'A study of the incomes of the focus families', in Wilson, H., *Child Development Study, Birmingham 1968–71: a study of inadequate families. Report Part 2*, Birmingham University, School of Education, Centre for Child Study.

VEREKER, C., MAYS, J. B., GITTUS, E., and BROADY, M. (1961) *Urban Redevelopment and Social Change: a study of social conditions in Central Liverpool, 1955–6*, Liverpool Univ. Press.

VERNON, M. D. (1957) *Backwardness in Reading*, Cambridge Univ. Press.

VERNON, M. D. (1971) *Reading and its Difficulties: a psychological study*, Cambridge Univ. Press.

VERNON, P. E. (1960) *Intelligence and Attainment Tests*, Univ. of London Press.

VERNON, P. E. (1965) 'Ability factors and environmental influences', *Amer. Psychol.*, 20, 723–733.

VERNON, P. E. (1969) *Intelligence and Cultural Environment*, Methuen.

VERNON, P. E. (1970) 'Intelligence', in Dockrell, W. J. (Ed.), *On Intelligence*, Methuen.

VOSS, H. L. (1964), 'Differential association and reported delinquent behaviour: a replication', *Social Problems*, 12, 78–85.

WADDILOVE, L. E. (1962) *Housing Associations PEP Broadsheet*, Vol. 28, No. 462.

WALKER, N. (1965) *Crime and Punishment in Britain*, Edinburgh Univ. Press.

WALKER, N. (1972) *Sentencing in a Rational Society*, Penguin.

WALL, W. D. (1973) 'The problem child in schools', *London Educ. Rev.*, 2, 3–21.

WALL, W. D. and WILLIAMS, H. L. (1970) *Longitudinal Studies and the Social Sciences*, Heinemann Educational Books.

WALLER, J. H. (1971) 'Achievement and social mobility: relationships among IQ score, education and occupation in two generations', *Social Biology*, 18, 252–259.

WALLER, W. W. and HILL, R. (1951) *The Family: a dynamic interpretation*, Dryden.

WALLIS, C. P. and MALIPHANT, R. (1967) 'Delinquent areas in the county of London: ecological factors', *Brit. J. Crim.*, 7, 250–284.

WALLSTON, B. (1973) 'The effects of maternal employment on children', *J. Child Psychol. Psychiat.*, 14, 81–96.

WALTERS, A. A. (1963) 'Delinquent Generations?', *Brit. J. Crim.*, 3, 391–395.

WALTERS, J. and STINNETT, N. (1971) 'Parent-child relationships: a decade review of research', *J. Marriage and the Family*, **33**, 70–111.

WARD, R. (1971) 'Coloured families in council houses: progress and prospects in Manchester', Manchester Council of Community Relations.

WARDLE, C. J. (1961) 'Two generations of broken homes in the genesis of conduct and behaviour disorders in childhood', *Brit. Med. J.*, ii, 349–354.

WARDLE, C. J. (1962) 'Social factors in the major functional psychoses', in Welford, A. T., Argyle, M., Glass, D. V. and Morris, J. N. (Eds.), *Society: problems and methods of study*, Routledge and Kegan Paul.

WARREN, W. (1965) 'A study of adolescent psychiatric in-patients at the outcome six or more years later. II. The follow-up study', *J. Child Psychol. Psychiat.*, **6**, 141–160.

WATSON, J. B. (1931) *Behaviourism*, Kegan Paul.

WATSON, P. (1970) 'How race affects IQ', *New Society*, **16**, 103–104.

WATSON, P. (1973) 'Stability of IQ of immigrant and non-immigrant slow learning pupils', *Brit. J. Educ. Psychol.*, **43**, 80–82.

WATSON, W. (1964) 'Social mobility and social class in industrial communities', in Gluckman, M. and Devons, E. (Eds.), *Closed Systems and Open Minds*, Oliver and Boyd.

WAXLER, N. E. and MISHLER, E. C. (1970) 'Experimental studies of families', in Berkovitz, L. (Ed.), *Advances in Experimental Social Psychology, Vol. 5*, Academic Press.

WEBB, A. L. and SIEVE, J. E. B. (1971) *Income redistribution and the welfare state*, Occasional Papers on Social Administration, No. 41, Bell.

WECHSLER, D. (1944) *The Measurement of Adult Intelligence*, Williams and Wilkins.

WEDDERBURN, D. (1965) *Redundancy and the railwaymen*, Univ. of Cambridge Department of Applied Economics, Occasional papers, No. 4.

WEDDERBURN, D. and CRAIG, C. (1974) 'Relative deprivation in work', in Wedderburn, D. (Ed.), *Poverty, Inequality and Class Structure*, Cambridge Univ. Press.

WEDGE, P. and PROSSER, N. (1973) *Born to Fail?*, Arrow Books.

WEDGWOOD, J. (1939) *The Economics of Inheritance*, Penguin.

WEINSTEIN, E. A. and GEISEL, P. N. (1960) 'An analysis of sex differences in adjustment', *Child Devt.*, **31**, 721–728.

WEISS, G., MINDE, K., WERRY, J. S., *et al.* (1971) 'Studies on the hyperactive child: VIII. Five year follow-up, *Arch. Gen. Psychiat*, **24**, 409–414.

WEISS, L. W. (1966) 'Concentration and labor earnings', *Amer. Econ. Rev.*, **56**, 96–117.

WEISSMAN, M. M., PAYKEL, E. S., and KLERMAN, G. L. (1972) 'The depressed woman as a mother', *Social Psychiatry*, **7**, 98–108.

WELLS, R. A., DILKES, T. C. and TRIVELLI, N. (1972) 'The results of family therapy: a critical review of the literature', *Family Process*, 11, 189–207.

WEST, D. J. (1963) *The Habitual Prisoner*, Macmillan.

WEST, D. J. (1967) *The Young Offender*, Penguin.

WEST, D. J. (1969) *Present Conduct and Future Delinquency*, Heinemann Educational Books.

WEST, D. J. and FARRINGTON, D. P. (1973) *Who Becomes Delinquent? Second report of the Cambridge study in delinquent development*, Heinemann Educational Books.

WESTERGAARD, J. and LITTLE, A. (1970) 'Educational opportunity and social selection in England and Wales: trends and policy implications', in Craft, M. (Ed.), *Family, Class and Education: a reader*, Longman.

WESTIN, A. F. (1967) *Privacy and Freedom*, Atheneum.

WESTINGHOUSE LEARNING CORPORATION (1969) *The Impact of Head Start*, Univ. of Ohio.

WESTMAN, J. C., RICE, D. L. and BERMANN, E. (1967) 'Nursery school behaviour and later school adjustment', *Amer. J. Orthopsychiat*, 37, 725–731.

WHEELER, L. R. (1942) 'A comparative study of the intelligence of East Tennessee mountain children', *J. Educ. Psychol.*, 33, 321–334.

WHITE, R. and LIPPIT, R. (1960) *Autocracy and Democracy*, Harper and Row.

WHITLOCK, F. A. (1973a) 'Suicide in England and Wales 1959–63. Part 1: The county boroughs', *Psychol. Med.*, 3, 350–365.

WHITLOCK, F. A. (1973b) 'Suicide in England and Wales 1959–63. Part 2: London', *Psychol. Med.*, 3, 411–420.

WHITWORTH, R. H., ROSENBLUM, B. F., DICKERSON, M. S., and BALOH, R. W. (1974) 'Follow-up on human lead absorption – Texas. Morbidity and mortality', *Center for Disease Control Weekly Report*, 23, 157–159, U.S. Dept. of Health, Educ. and Welfare.

WICKES, T. A. (1956) 'Examiner influence in a testing situation', *J. Consult. Psychol.*, 20, 23–26.

WILES, S. (1968) 'Children from overseas', Institute of Race Relations Newsletter, February.

WILKINS, L. (1961) *Delinquent Generations*, Home Office Research Unit Report, HMSO.

WILKINS, L. T. (1964) *Social Deviance*, Tavistock Publ.

WILLCOX, R. R. (1966) 'Immigration and venereal diseases in Great Britain', *Brit. J. Ven. Dis.*, 42, 225–237.

WILLERMAN, C., NAYLOR, A. F., and MYRIANTHOPOULOS, N. C. (1970) 'Intellectual development of children from interracial matings', *Science*, 170, 1329–1331.

WILLIAMS, H. M. (1961) 'Changes in pupils' attitudes towards West African Negroes following the use of two different teaching methods', *Brit. J. Educ. Psychol.*, 31, 292–296.

WILLMOTT, P. (1969) *Adolescent Boys of East London*, Penguin.

WILNER, D. M., WALKLEY, R. P. and COOK, S. W. (1955) *Human Relations in Interracial Housing*, Univ. of Minnesota Press.

WILNER, D. M., WALKLEY, R. P., PINKERTON, T. C. and TAYBACK, M. (1962) *The Housing Environment and Family Life: a longitudinal study of the effects of housing on morbidity and mental health*, Johns Hopkins Press.

WILNER, D. M., WALKLEY, R. P. and TAYBACK, M. (1956) 'How does the quality of housing affect health and family adjustment?', *Amer. J. Pub. Health*, 46, 736–744.

WILSON, H. (1962) *Delinquency and Child Neglect*, Allen & Unwin.

WILSON, H. (1973) *Child Development Study, Birmingham, 1968–71: a study of inadequate families. Report Part 2*, Birmingham University, School of Education, Centre for Child Study.

WILSON, H. (1974) 'Parenting in Poverty', *Brit. J. Social Work*, 4, 241–254,

WILSON, W. C. (1963) 'Development of ethnic attitudes in adolescence', *Child Develop.*, 34, 249–256.

WING, J. K. and BROWN, G. W. (1970) *Institutionalism and Schizophrenia*, Cambridge Univ. Press.

WINTERBOTTOM, M. R. (1958) 'The relation of need for achievement to learning experiences in independence and mastery', in Atkinson, J. W. (Ed.), *Motives in Fantasy, Action and Society*, Van Nostrand.

WISEMAN, S. (1964) *Education and Environment*, Manchester Univ. Press.

WOFINDEN, R. C (1950) *Problem Families in Bristol*, Occasional paper on Eugenics No. 6, Cassell.

WOLFF, S. (1970) 'Behaviour and pathology of parents of disturbed children', in Anthony, E. J. and Koupernik, C. (Eds.), *The Children in the Family, Vol. 1*, Wiley–Interscience.

WOLFF, S. (1973) *Children under Stress*, Penguin.

WOLFF, S. and ACTON, W. P. (1968) 'Characteristics of parents of disturbed children', *Brit. J. Psychiat.*, 114, 593–602.

WOLFLE, D. (1960) 'Economics and educational values', in Harris, S. E. (Ed.), *Higher Education in the United States: the economic problem*, Harvard Univ. Press.

WOLFLE, D. (1961) 'Educational opportunity, presumed intelligence and social background', in Halsoy, A. H., Floud, J. and Anderson, C. A. (Eds.), *Education Economy and Society*, Free Press of Glencoe.

WOLFLE, D. and SMITH, J. G. (1956) 'The occupational value of education for superior high school graduates', *J. Higher Educ.*, 27, 201–213.

WOLKIND, S. N. (1971) 'Children in care: a psychiatric study', M.D. thesis, Univ. of London.

WOLKIND, S. N. (1974a) 'Sex differences in the aetiology of antisocial disorders in children in long term residential care', *Brit. J. Psychiat.*, 125, 125–130.

WOLKIND, S. N. (1974b) 'The components of "affectionless psychopathy" in institutionalized children', *J. Child Psychol. Psychiat.*, 15, 215–220.

WOLKIND, S. N., KRUK, S. and CHAVES, L. (1976) 'Childhood separation experiences and psychosocial status in primiparous women: preliminary findings', *Brit. J. Psychiat.*, 128, 391–6.

WOLKIND, S. N. and RUTTER, M. (1973) 'Children who have been "in care": an epidemiological study', *J. Child Psychol. Psychiat.*, 14, 95–105.

WOOD REPORT (1929) Report of the Mental Deficiency Committee, HMSO.

WOODWARD, V. H. (1970) *Regional Social Accounts for the United Kingdom*, National Institute of Economic and Social Research regional papers No. 1, Cambridge Univ. Press.

WOODWARD, V. (1974) 'The regional dimension', in Young, M. D. (Ed.), *Poverty Report 1974*, Temple Smith.

WOODWARD, M. (1955a) *Low Intelligence and Delinquency*, ISTD.

WOODWARD, M. (1955b) 'The role of low intelligence in delinquency', *Brit. J. Delinq.*, 5 (4), 281–303.

WOOTTON, A. J. (1974) 'Talk in the homes of young children', *Sociology*, 8, 277–295.

WOOTTON, B. (1959) *Social Science and Social Pathology*, Allen & Unwin.

WOYTINSKY, W. S. (1943) 'Income cycle in the life of families and individuals', *Soc. Sec. Bull.*, 6, 8–17.

WRIGHT, C. H. (1955) 'Problem families: a review and some observations', *The Medical Officer*, 94, 381–384.

WRIGHT, C. H. and LUNN, J. E. (1971). 'Sheffield problem families, a follow-up study of their sons and daughters', *Community Medicine*, 126, 301–307, 315–321.

WRIGHT, P. L. (1968) *The Coloured Worker in British Industry*, Oxford Univ. Press.

WYNN, M. and WYNN, A. (1974) 'Can family planning do more to reduce child poverty?', *Poverty*, No. 29, pp. 17–20.

WYNN, M. (1964) *Fatherless Families*, Michael Joseph.

YARROW, M. R., CAMPBELL, J. D. and BURTON, R. V. (1964) 'Recollections of childhood: a study of the retrospective method', *Monog. Soc. Res. Child Develop.*, 35, No. 5.

YARROW, M. R., CAMPBELL, J. D. and BURTON, R. V. (1968) *Child-Rearing: an enquiry into research and methods*, Jossey-Bass.

YARROW, M. R., CAMPBELL, J. and YARROW, L. (1958) 'Acquisition of new norms: a study of racial desegregation', *J. Soc. Issues*, 14, 8–28.

YINGER, J. M. and SIMPSON, G. E (1973) 'Techniques for reducing prejudice: changing the prejudiced person', in Watson, P. (Ed.), *Psychology and Race*, Penguin.

YOUNG, M. (1952) 'Distribution of income within the family', *Brit. J. Sociology*, 3, 305–321.

YOUNG, M., BENJAMIN, B. and WALLIS, C. (1963) 'The mortality of widowers', *Lancet*, ii, 454–456.

YOUNG, M. and WILLMOTT, P. (1957) *Family and Kinship in East London*, Routledge & Kegan Paul.

YOUNG, M. and WILLMOTT, P. (1973) *The Symmetrical Family: a study of work and leisure in the London region*, Routledge & Kegan Paul.

YUDKIN, S. (1965) 'The Health and Welfare of the Immigrant Child', NCCI.

YUDKIN, S. (1967) 'O-5: a report on the care of pre-school children', National Soc. Children's Nurseries.

YUDKIN, S. and HOIME, A. (1963) *Working Mothers and their Children*, Michael Joseph.

YULE, B. and RUTTER, M. (1976) Unpublished data.

YULE, W. (1973) 'Differential prognosis of reading backwardness and specific reading retardation', *Brit. J. Educ. Psychol.*, 43, 244–248.

YULE, W., BERGER, M., RUTTER, M. and YULE, B. (1975) 'Children of West Indian immigrants: II. Intellectual performance and reading attainment', *J. Child Psychol. Psychiat.*, 16, 1–18.

YULE, W., RIGLEY, L. and RUTTER, M. 'Reading Difficulties: Prediction, Progress, and Treatment', (in preparation).

YULE, W., RUTTER, M. L., BERGER, M. and THOMPSON, J. (1974) 'Over and under-achievement in reading: distribution in the general population', *Brit. J. Educ. Psychiat.*, 44, 1–12.

ZEITLYN, N. H. (1971) 'A study of patients who attended the children's department and later the adults' department of the same psychiatric hospital', M.Phil. Thesis, Univ. of London.

ZIGLER, L. and BUTTERFIELD, E. C. (1968) 'Motivational aspects of changes in IQ test performance of culturally deprived nursery school children', *Child Develop.*, 39, 2–16.

ZIMBARDO, P. G. (1969) 'The human choice: individuation, reason and order versus deindividuation, impulse and chaos', in Arnold, W. J. and Page, M. M. (Eds.), *Nebraska Symposium on Motivation*, Lincoln Univ., Nebraska.

Author Index

**Indicates that the reference is in a footnote.*

Subject Index